THE CISTERCIAN MONASTERIES
OF IRELAND

THE CISTERCIAN MONASTERIES
OF IRELAND

*An Account of the History, Art and Architecture
of the White Monks in Ireland from 1142 to 1540*

ROGER STALLEY

YALE UNIVERSITY PRESS
LONDON & NEW HAVEN
1987

In memory of my father and mother

Published with the financial assistance of
The J.Paul Getty Trust
The Institute of Irish Studies, The Queen's University of Belfast
and Trinity College, University of Dublin

Copyright © 1987 by Yale University
Second printing 1987

The quotation from John Betjeman's poem, *Ireland with Emily*,
is reproduced by permission of John Murray (Publishers) Ltd.

Designed by Gillian Malpass
Set in Monophoto Bembo and printed in Great Britain
at the Alden Press, Oxford

Library of Congress Cataloging-in-Publication Data

Stalley, R. A.
   The Cistercian monasteries of Ireland.
   Bibliography: p.
   Includes index.
   1. Art, Cistercian—Ireland.   2. Art, Medieval—
Ireland.   3. Art, Irish.   4. Cistercians—Ireland—
History.   I. Title.
N6784.S73   1987   726'.7'09415   86-26626
ISBN 0-300-03737-6

1 (frontispiece)   Corcomroe Abbey at the end of the nineteenth century, the 'ruined abbey' described by John
Betjeman in *Ireland with Emily* (National Library of Ireland, Lawrence Collection).

Acknowledgements

MY FIRST SERIOUS encounter with Cistercian art came as a postgraduate student at the Courtauld Institute in London during the tutorials of Peter Kidson and it was his perceptive and enthusiastic teaching that focussed my interests on medieval architecture. The thought of writing a book on the Cistercian monasteries of Ireland goes back to 1976–7 when the Queen's University Belfast were kind enough to award me a fellowship in the Institute of Irish Studies. Without this opportunity it would have been difficult to embark on the project. Since that time I have received assistance and encouragement from countless friends and colleagues, both in Ireland and abroad. In particular I should like to thank George Zarnecki, Sioban Barry, Dr Terry Barry, Mme Hilda Beuer-Szlechter, John Bradley, Brian de Breffny, Mrs T. Breslin, Sister Bridget of Monasterevin, Dr Lawrence Butler, Professor John Byrne, Dr Maurice Craig, the late Tom Delaney, Catherine Fahy, Thomas Fanning, Dr Peter Fergusson of Wellesley College Massachusetts, Dr Marie Thérèse Flanagan, Dr Tessa Garton, Dr Cathal O'Háinle, Dr Ann Hamlin, Dr Peter Harbison, Richard Haworth, Michael Hayden of Graiguenamanagh, Richard Hayes, Patrick Healy, Mr T. A. Heslop, Mr Michael Hewson, Professor Christopher Holdsworth, Edward Hughes of Graiguenamanagh, John Hughes of Graiguenamanagh, Mr J. M. Lewis, Professor James Lydon, Francis Lyons, Dr Tom McNeill, Dr Edward McParland, Professor Thomas Mitchell, Dr Richard Morris, John O'Callaghan, David Park, Raghnall O'Floinn, Professor Alistair Rowan, Dr Edwin Rae of Champaign-Urbana, The Hon. Guy Strutt, David Sweetman, Dr Malcolm Thurlby, The Hon. Viscount de Vesci, the late Dudley Waterman, Dr Christopher Wilson, The Marquis of Donegall, Dr C. Nelson, Bernard Meehan, Felicity O'Mahony, Dr David Walsh of Rochester, New York, Dr Sue McNab and William O'Sullivan.

Over the years I have been a regular visitor to the National Monuments Branch of the Office of Public Works in Dublin and the staff there have been unfailingly obliging and helpful. I am especially grateful to Jim Bambury, Con Brogan, Muiris de Butlear, Robert Corrigan, David Newman Johnson, Dr Ann Lynch, Conleth Manning, Paul McMahon, John O'Brien, Aighleann O'Shaughnessy, John Scarry and Richard Stapleton. The staff of the library in Trinity College have been very persistent in tracking down obscure material on my behalf and in this regard I must particularly thank Rosemary Gleeson and Mary Higgins. Alice Tunney and her assistants in the Central Secretariat in Trinity College have coped heroically with my typescript and so too has Eithne Kavanagh in the department of the History of Art. Thanks are also due to Brendan Dempsey and Peter Butler in the Photographic Centre in Trinity College, who have processed my photographs to a very exacting standard. Much of the expenses in preparing the book, including travel costs and payments for figures and drawings, has been born by the Research Fund of the Arts and Economic and Social Studies Faculties of Trinity College. I should also mention Mary Durlacher, Gillian Malpass and John Nicoll at Yale University Press who have guided the book through the press with great skill and enthusiasm.

I must single out for special thanks Anne Crookshank, whose constant interest and encouragement has helped sustain my work for well over a decade. Finally, I owe immense gratitude to my wife, Petrina, who has endured the writing of this book with stoical patience far beyond the normal calls of marital life; also to my three children, who have lived with their father's 'ruins' for longer than they can remember.

Photographs and Drawings

The following institutions and individuals have kindly allowed me to reproduce photographs: National Library of Ireland (1, 59, 76, 113, 181); Archaeological Survey, Department of the Environment, Northern Ireland (5); Commissioners of Public Works, Ireland, photographs by Jim Bambury (7, 10, 15, 16, 19, 24, 25, 36, 38, 54, 58, 75, 82, 86, 92, 93, 95, 99, 100, 101, 104, 107, 109, 115, 124, 126, 132, 135, 142, 156, 170, 177, 199, 202, 207, 211, 213, 222, 227, 228, 231, 233, 234, 235, 255, 280); Zodiaque, La Pierre-qui-Vire, Yonne, France (40, 41, 42, 172); Professor Peter Fergusson (50); Green Studio (85); The Board of Trinity College Dublin (97, 261,273); John Kellett (128); Royal Commission on the Historical Monuments of England (217, 218, 267); Society of Antiquaries of London (265); Dr Ann Lynch (166); Pieterse-Davison International (241, 247, 250, 251); National Museum of Wales (256); Dr Tessa Garton (286); British Library (258, 259); Bodleian Library Oxford (260); National Museum of Ireland (262, 263, 264); Cambridge University Collection (copyright reserved) (17, 18, 22, 23, 29, 30); John Rylands University Library of Manchester (224); The Royal Irish Academy (3, 12, 106, 245); Bord Fáilte Eireann (26); all other photographs are by the author.

Most of the plans are based on originals kindly supplied by the Commissioners of Public Works, Ireland, though many have been altered or brought up to date. Francis Lyons made the drawings of Holycross (Fig. 37) and the chapter house of St Mary's Dublin (Fig. 52). The plan of Inch is based on a drawing supplied by the Archaeological Survey, Department of the Environment for Northern Ireland. The Dundalgan Press kindly gave permission for the publication of Harold Leask's drawing of vault centering (Fig. 40), Verlag Gebr. Mann, Berlin, for Hahn's diagram (Fig. 22) and the Bibliothèque Nationale, Paris, for Villard de Honnecourt's drawing of a Cistercian church (Fig. 23). Three drawings (Figs 36, 60, 61) are taken from publications of the Commissioners of Public Works, Ireland; the remainder were prepared by the author.

Contents

Introduction   I

1   The History of the Cistercian Order in Ireland   7

2   The Foundation and Construction of the Monasteries   31

3   The Planning and Layout of the Monasteries   51

4   The Architecture of the Churches 1142–1400   77

5   Holycross and the Fifteenth-Century Revival   113

6   Cistercian Vaulting   129

7   Cistercian Tower Building   141

8   Cloisters and Domestic Buildings   153

9   The Stone Sculpture of the Monasteries   179

10   Decoration and Furnishings   199

11   The Aftermath of the Dissolution   227

    Appendices   239
      1   Consolidated list of major Irish Cistercian Houses   239
      2   Catalogue of the major Cistercian sites in Ireland   240
      3   A note on conservation   251
      4   A selection of moulding profiles from Irish Cistercian houses   252

    Abbreviations   260

    Notes   261

    Select Bibliography   281

    Glossary   286

    Index   289

Stony seaboard, far and foreign,
   Stony hills poured over space,
Stony outcrop of the Burren,
   Stones in every fertile place . . .
Till there rose abrupt and lonely,
   A ruined abbey, chancel only,
Lichen-crusted, time befriended,
   Soared the arches splayed and splendid,
   Romanesque against the sky.

JOHN BETJEMAN

Ireland with Emily

Introduction

As THE River Boyne flows past the huge prehistoric tumuli of Newgrange and Knowth, it is joined by a tributary known as the Mattock, a stream which meanders down from the hills of County Louth. Near the confluence with the Boyne, it passes through a secluded valley, a picturesque spot where in 1142 a group of monks founded a monastery, eloquently named 'Fons Mellis' or Fount of Honey. Most of the monks had made the long journey from Burgundy, where they had been trained under the watchful guidance of its abbot, St Bernard. The founding of the new monastery, the first Cistercian house in Ireland, was an event of symbolic importance in Irish history. Cistercian monasticism played a vital part in bringing Ireland into the mainstream of western Christianity and within a few decades the buildings of the order had transformed the character of the country's architecture.

Over the course of the next 130 years, the Cistercians established thirty-three successful monasteries, a high number given the size of the country and its limited population. Throughout Ireland, from Assaroe in the north to Tintern in the south, the white monks could be seen organising their estates, constructing their monasteries and solemnly performing the ceaseless round of daily offices. At twenty-one of these sites, Cistercian buildings survive, albeit in different stages of ruin. At Abbeymahon (Cork) they amount only to meagre fragments of the church, featureless and ivy clad, but at Holycross the fifteenth-century buildings were sufficiently complete for the church to be reroofed and restored to worship a few years ago. None of the abbeys can vie with the romantic splendour of Fountains, Tintern Major or Rievaulx, but most of the ruins retain an alluring solitude, 'far from the haunts of men'.

When Robert of Molesme and his twenty-one companions founded Citeaux in 1098, there was little to indicate that this was the start of one of the most powerful religious movements in the middle ages. What began as a local search for monastic reform in Burgundy eventually extended its influence throughout the whole of Europe. Dedicating themselves to lives of poverty, hard labour, rigorous discipline and prayer, the first monks at Citeaux sought to escape from the distractions of the contemporary world. In particular they were troubled by the costly and splendid atmosphere of Benedictine monasticism and the social relationships it entailed. The early years at Citeaux were difficult, but gradually a clearer perception of a new form of monastic life began to emerge, particularly under the guidance of Stephen Harding, the Englishman who became abbot in 1109. Two important early documents, the *Exordium Parvum*, an account of the foundation of Citeaux, and the *Carta Caritatis*, which established the legislative framework of the order, are associated with his time as abbot, though both were subject to extensive revision in later years.[1] It was the *Carta Caritatis* that outlined the efficient constitution of the Cistercians which has always been extolled as a model piece of legislation, lucid and straightforward in its presentation. Here was enshrined the system of annual meetings of all the abbots at Citeaux, and the system of annual visitation of father abbots to daughter houses. The need for such a constitution became essential once Citeaux began to extend its influence with the foundation of daughter houses: La Ferté in 1113, Pontigny in 1114, and Clairvaux and Morimond in 1115. Without tight organisation, it would have been impossible to guarantee uniform observance among the affiliated communities. Under the inspired leadership of St Bernard, one of these daughter houses, Clairvaux, began to outshine Citeaux in fame and prestige, and, when Bernard died in 1153, approximately 159 monasteries belonged to its affiliation (out of a total of 340).

From the early documents of the order, it is not difficult to grasp the aims and ideals of the Cistercians as they existed by the mid-twelfth century, but it is important to appreciate that the Cistercian rule of life was the product of experience accumulated over many years and was not the result of swift or instant formulations.[2] By the time the first mission was sent to Ireland, the essential elements of Cistercian life were well established. Each monk, after completing a year as a novice, took vows of poverty, chastity and obedience. To achieve a close spiritual union with God, he pursued a life of ferocious asceticism and self-denial, based on an exacting interpretation of the Benedictine Rule. The *opus dei*, purged of ceremonial accretions added under the influence of Cluny, was characterised by a tone of dignified simplicity. Whereas a Cluniac monk spent most of his day in communal worship, the routine of a Cistercian was strictly apportioned between the *opus dei*, private prayer and reading, and domestic and manual labour. Each night the monks arose for matins (at around 1.00 to 2.00 a.m.) and there followed the regular sequence of offices: lauds, prime, terce, sext, nones, vespers and compline, as well as the daily mass. It was a life of unvarying routine and absolute discipline. Each monk performed his allotted tasks in an atmosphere of silence; meals were plain and basically vegetarian; robes were made only of coarse undyed wool. As the English monk, Ailred of Rievaulx, explained in a famous passage: 'Our food is scanty, our garments rough; our drink is from the stream and our sleep often upon our book. Under our tired limbs there is but a hard mat; when sleep is sweetest, we must rise at bell's bidding. Self will has no place; there is no moment for idleness or dissipation'.[3]

To protect themselves from the outside world, self-sufficiency was vital. Land was farmed directly, not for profit, but to serve the regular needs of the community. Assisting the choir monks in the practical tasks of running the monastery were the laybrothers or *conversi*, who worked as farm labourers, millers, smiths, tailors, carpenters, masons and cooks. The laybrothers attended church at the beginning and end of the day, following a routine that was set apart from that of the choir monks, with separate accommodation to the west of the cloister and separate stalls in the nave of the church. Solitude, self-sufficiency, the enhanced role of manual labour and the presence of laybrothers were each interlocking components of the Cistercian way of life.

Once the Cistercians began to build on a major scale, the simple purity of their rule found expression in architecture. Just as the *opus dei* was purged of inessentials, so their buildings were stripped of anything superfluous. Purity of form, clarity of proportions and good technical execution are the hallmarks of Cistercian design. Some scholars of the past have spoken of a Cistercian style, but it is better to think in terms of a Cistercian 'attitude' rather than a specific style of architecture. For the most part, the monks built in the regional styles of Europe, tempered where necessary by the demands of the order, eschewing any desire for costly or needless embellishment. The new ascetic monasticism created a new ascetic approach to architecture.

In Ireland Cistercian building had a greater importance than in most other European countries. No wealthy Benedictine abbeys existed to set imposing architectural standards, and few Irish cathedrals were affluent enough to build on a monumental scale. In the more developed areas of Europe, the restrained style of the Cistercians was usually overshadowed by the nearest cathedral, and it is ironic that a movement which began in opposition to the extravagance of the Benedictines and Cluniacs, should in an Irish context acquire a reputation for monumental architecture, a point underlined by the colloquial name of Mellifont, *An Mainistir Mhór*, the great monastery. Cistercian buildings thus have a fundamental role in the history of Irish ecclesiastical architecture. The finest Romanesque churches belonged to the order—Baltinglass, Jerpoint and Boyle—and it was the Cistercians who erected the first Gothic structures at Grey, Inch and Graiguenamanagh. Even in the fifteenth century, when the movement had lost much of its original vigour, the white monks rebuilt the pilgrimage church at Holycross, one of the most ambitious late-Gothic edifices in the country. Cistercian design also had a profound impact on churches outside the order, not least on those of the Augustinian canons.

2 Dunbrody Abbey as depicted in Grose's *Antiquities of Ireland*. The engraving was made over sixty years before the south side collapsed in 1852.

In recent years Cistercian architecture has had a bad press, acquiring a reputation for being conservative, even reactionary, and the old notion that the order was a pioneer of Gothic has largely been discredited. However, judgements based on the situation in France or England are not necessarily valid elsewhere. To the frontiers of European civilisation, to Brittany, Sweden, Poland, Wales and Ireland, the Cistercians brought the basic elements of Romanesque and Gothic design: clear principles of planning, well-proportioned, well-buttressed structures, along with excellent standards of construction. If not pioneers of Gothic, there is no doubt that the white monks were active 'missionaries' of the style.

*　　　*　　　*

Cistercian abbeys represent some of the most picturesque ruins in Ireland, and for over two hundred years they have attracted interest from artists, antiquarians and scholars. Looking back over this period it is possible to distinguish several phases of appreciation and understanding. Until the later eighteenth century, the chief concern was with the history rather than the physical remains of the monasteries. The great seventeenth century antiquarian, Sir James Ware, assembled a mass of information about Irish religious houses, which was subsequently exploited by Mervyn Archdall in his *Monasticon Hibernicum*, a comprehensive survey completed in 1786 after 'incessant toil for many years'. In the later decades of the century, artists and antiquarians began to undertake closer inspection of monastic ruins. One of the most energetic figures was Colonel William Burton Conyngham, who collected drawings and water-colours of medieval monuments and even commissioned plans. Until the 1790s, interest in antiquities was still restricted to a small circle of artists and connoisseurs, but the publication of Francis Grose's *Antiquities of Ireland* (1791–5) brought the subject to a much larger audience. Grose died (of an apoplectic fit) within a few days of arriving in Ireland and the text is almost entirely the work of Edward Ledwich, a scholar clergyman who was vicar of Aghaboe in County Kilkenny. The volumes are illustrated by 266 engravings, of which twenty-six are devoted to Cistercian ruins (Pl. 2). The illustrations are of higher quality than those in Grose's equivalent books on England and Wales, and the compositions are more specifically architectural. Although occasionally far-fetched in detail, they provide an invaluable record of the state of the monasteries two hundred years ago.

The example set by Grose was followed in the early nineteenth century by a host of topographical books, such as Cromwell's *Excursions Through Ireland* (1819), R. O'Callaghan Newenham's *Picturesque Views of the Antiquities of Ireland* (1830), S. C. Hall's *Ireland its Scenery and Character* (1842) and W. H. Bartlett's *The Scenery and Antiquities of Ireland* (1842).

The 1840s marked the advent of a more painstaking and scientific era. The reports of the Ordnance Survey investigators are full of precise observations and they frequently record local historical traditions which might otherwise have been lost. Cistercian monuments also figured among the interests of George Petrie (1790–1866), the scholar-artist who did so much to place the study of early Irish antiquities on a rational basis. As William Wakeman remarked in 1848, 'With Dr Petrie indeed, rests the honour of having removed the veil of obscurity which had so long shrouded the subject of our ecclesiastical antiquities.'[4] He was a contemporary of the Reverend Robert Willis, whose expositions of English cathedrals have much in common with Petrie's logical, well-argued approach. Another contemporary was George Wilkinson, whose *Practical Geology and Ancient Architecture of Ireland* (1845) was the first and only book to be devoted to the study of Irish building stone. Wilkinson examined almost all the Cistercian abbeys with standing remains and his comments on monastic masonry are still well worth reading.

As the nineteenth century advanced, more scrupulous architectural studies began to appear, with detailed plans and scale drawings. A pupil of Petrie's, George Du Noyer, produced a vast number of wash drawings, which included a series of architectural details from Mellifont as well as a number of attractive views of Hore and Monasteranenagh (Pl. 3). Two architectural studies of Holycross were undertaken, one by Samuel Close (1868), the other by Benjamin Woodward (1874), and a similar survey was carried out at Grey Abbey by J. J. Phillips (1874). The year 1874/5 also witnessed the formal establishment of the National Monuments Branch of the Office of Public Works and good architectural analyses began to appear as appendices to their annual reports. Large-scale clearances and excavations were undertaken at Mellifont in the 1880s, in an effort to discover more about the most celebrated of Ireland's medieval monasteries, and in the same decade more casual exploration took place at St Mary's, Dublin.

A new approach to Irish medieval architecture was signalled by Arthur Champneys, brother of the distinguished Victorian architect Basil Champneys. In a wide-ranging and perceptive book entitled *Irish Ecclesiastical Architecture* (1910), he was the first scholar to set Irish medieval buildings in a meaningful historical and European framework.

The momentum established between 1870 and 1910 did not continue far into the twentieth

3 Hore Abbey with the cathedral of Cashel in the background. A delicate wash drawing by George Du Noyer (1840).

century. The coming of independence in 1921 fostered a more introspective outlook and the Cistercians as a foreign monastic movement appeared to lack deep roots in the country's Gaelic past. The middle ages, a period associated with the domination of the Anglo-Normans, tended to be neglected by archaeologists. For many decades, one person almost alone sustained an interest in medieval architecture, and that was Harold Leask. He published his first article on the Cistercians in 1916, an excellent account of Bective Abbey and the forerunner of several further studies of the Cistercians, a subject to which he returned in volumes II and III of his *Irish Churches and Monastic Buildings* (1958–60). A man of 'gentle scholarly presence', Leask acquired during his time as Inspector of National Monuments (1923–49) an immense knowledge of Irish antiquities, and his detailed architectural descriptions provide the foundation for all modern research. To coincide with the Royal Archaeological Institute's visit to Ireland in 1931, Leask collaborated with the English scholars Hamilton Thompson and Sir Alfred Clapham in an article on the Cistercian order in Ireland, the only comprehensive study of its kind. But in the fifty years that have elapsed, excavation, fieldwork, research on monastic history and the publication of specialised studies of Cistercian architecture abroad have rendered the study obsolete.

The social and religious history of the Cistercians in Ireland has been explored by a number of scholars and particular mention must be made of Aubrey Gwynn, Father Colmcille, Gearóid MacNiocaill and Barry O'Dwyer. Foremost among them is Father Colmcille O'Conbhuidhe, a monk of the new monastery of Mellifont. In a series of books and articles he has covered almost every aspect of Cistercian history and without his labours it would have been difficult to embark on the present volume. One year after Father Colmcille's exemplary account of Mellifont Abbey, *The Story of Mellifont* (1958), came Gearóid MacNiocaill's concise study of the white monks in Ireland. Written in the Irish language, the book has regrettably had a limited readership. The 'Conspiracy of Mellifont' and the tensions that afflicted the order in the thirteenth century have subsequently been the subject of detailed enquiry by Barry O'Dwyer. There have also been developments on the archaeological front. Mellifont was the scene of further excavations in 1954–5 and excavation has also taken place at Holycross, though the results await publication. Since then more limited archaeological projects have been undertaken at Graiguenamanagh, Tintern and Boyle.

*   *   *

This book attempts to provide a comprehensive account of Cistercian art and architecture from 1142 until the dissolution of the monasteries in 1536–40. It covers not just the buildings themselves, but all the artistic activities promoted by the monks, including their patronage of stone carving, painting and metalwork. Considerable emphasis is placed on the historical context in Ireland, as questions of patronage and design were continuously affected by historical developments, particularly the racial divide that followed the Anglo-Norman invasion of 1169–70. Although the monuments have been set against a European background, I have not gone into detail about the general history and ideals of the Cistercians, the outline of which will be well known to many readers through the eloquent writings of such scholars as David Knowles, Christopher Brooke and Richard Southern. Some chapters are fairly technical, particularly those dealing with planning and vaults (chapters 3 and 6), and readers without a specialist interest in architecture might be advised to pass over them. A number of deliberate limitations in the scope of the book ought to be mentioned. The history of the Cistercians beyond 1540 is not pursued in detail, although some communities survived for many decades. Nor have I discussed the re-establishment of the order in the nineteenth century, following the foundation of Mount Melleray in 1832. I have restricted myself to the thirty-three major monasteries of the middle ages, in other words those houses founded between 1139/42 and 1272 which survived until the Reformation. With the exception of Clare Island, where the buildings are tolerably intact, I have not included those cells and minor houses which vanished from the scene long before the dawn of the sixteenth century. A number of Cistercian nunneries are known from documents (Mellifont, Inislounaght, Jerpoint, Derry and Ballymore), but none appears to have left any material remains. There is still tremendous potential for research on Cistercian granges and monastic endowment in general. Father Colmcille has reconstructed the geography of the estates belonging to Mellifont and St Mary's Dublin, and there are many other houses where this could profitably be done. As well as pinpointing the sites of granges, such studies would give a better indication of the landed wealth and agricultural resources of the individual monasteries. There are a number of ruins which may or may not be the remnants of Cistercian granges, but I have not included them here, preferring to leave them to the historical geographer and economic historian.

One difficulty in writing about Irish monastic architecture is the dearth of reliable modern monographs. There are no Irish parallels for the exhaustive accounts of Furness, Fountains and Jervaulx undertaken by William St John Hope and Harold Brakspear, nor are there any equivalents of the Department of Environment *Guides* in England. Despite these problems and the self-imposed limitations of the work, I hope the book will provide a fair impression of the contribution that the Cistercians made to the art and culture of medieval Ireland. There is a danger of studies such as this being pronounced 'definitive', thereby deterring rather than encouraging others to take an interest in the field. Many of the buildings deserve more detailed study and much remains to be discovered about such matters as the geometrical and proportional layout of the abbeys. The chronology and development of Irish Gothic between 1400 and 1650 is still very uncertain and will remain so until a detailed analysis is undertaken of such matters as moulding profiles and tracery patterns. I am conscious of the fact that some of my conclusions will have to be modified in the future. At the very least I hope the book will increase the interest in Irish monastic antiquities, both inside and outside the country. In this context it is perhaps worth recalling the plea that Archbishop John Healy made to young ordinands at Maynooth over eighty years ago:

> There are many persons who have no sympathy with monks or monasteries now, but take the greatest interest in the examination and preservation of those grand monuments of the past from the historical and artistic point of view. . . . I want you to take, at least, as deep an interest in these subjects as the non Catholic antiquarians, whom you will now find in every part of Ireland—gentlemen, too, and scholars, I assure you, of wide culture, for the study of these subjects appears to have a softening and sweetening influence on the asperities even of the rudest and most bigoted natures.[5]

Chapter 1

THE HISTORY OF THE CISTERCIAN ORDER IN IRELAND

WHEN THE CISTERCIANS sent their first colony to Ireland, the order was already established as a major force in western Christendom. By 1142, communities had ventured to some of the more distant outposts of Europe and the arrival of the white monks in Ireland was part of a general expansion to the frontiers of the Christian world. Within a year of the founding of Mellifont, a Cistercian community reached Sweden, while hundreds of miles away another group of monks was setting up the order's first monastery east of the river Elbe. The second quarter of the twelfth century was by far the most fertile period of Cistercian growth, and between 1125 and 1151 no less than 307 new monasteries were founded. The mission to Ireland was a product of a dynamic tide of Cistercian expansion.

The character of the Irish monasteries, however, was far from identical with those elsewhere. The discipline and centralisation of the Cistercian order gave a veneer of uniformity which can be misleading and it is important not to overlook the differences which existed between the monasteries at a local level. In Ireland not many years elapsed before the abbeys assumed an Irish identity, as they were absorbed into the local cultural landscape. Ireland in fact presented particular problems to the order, which even the efficient organisation of the Cistercians found difficult to overcome. Travellers from feudal Europe found the country strange and perplexing, encountering an unintelligible language, an unfamiliar culture and a very confusing political system.

Ireland in the twelfth century

Some foreign observers believed that Ireland lay beyond the frontiers of the civilised world. Needless to say, it was not a point appreciated by the Irish themselves, who were proud of their traditions and saw no reason to bow to novelties introduced from abroad. This is illustrated by an incident which took place at Bangor in 1140, when Malachy, archbishop of Armagh, began to erect a large church on continental lines. Its complex form aroused the anger of one local inhabitant, who vehemently protested: 'we are Irish not Gauls'.[1] The story was recounted by St Bernard to show the hostility and conservatism that confronted Malachy, but the story also demonstrates the firmly held belief that Irish ways of doing things were right and the rest of Europe was wrong. The incident recalls events five hundred years before, when the Celtic church had stoutly defended its religious traditions against the authority of Rome.

One of the first differences to strike twelfth-century visitors to Ireland was the appearance of the buildings. In 1142 there were few domestic dwellings built of stone and even kings were satisfied with houses of timber and wattle. So traditional was this style of building that when Henry II visited Dublin in 1171 he ordered a wattle palace to be erected for himself in order not to offend the native rulers.[2] A few years later Gerald of Wales was struck by the absence of stone castles and explained that to the Irish 'woods are their forts and swamps are their ditches'.[3] Walls of wattle, laced with mud and clay, were a fast and cheap method of building, and the excavations of Dublin have yielded whole streets of houses erected in this way. Even after the Anglo-Norman invasion, Irish kings continued to live in such buildings. Stephen of Lexington, who carried out a general visitation of the Cistercian monasteries in 1228, made no effort to

6 Iniscealtra (Clare), an early Irish monastery with scattered oratories and round tower on an island in Lough Derg. The layout of such monasteries was a contrast to the disciplined planning of the Cistercians.

7 The Romanesque doorway at Killeshin, Carlow (c1160), with a characteristic 'tangent' gable and finely etched decoration on the jambs.

4 (facing page top) The ruins of Mellifont, the first of the Irish Cistercian monasteries. The site in the gentle valley of the River Mattock was chosen by St Malachy shortly before 1142.

5 (facing page bottom) A reconstruction of Grey Abbey as it might have appeared at the end of the thirteenth century (drawing by Philip Armstrong, Crown Copyright, Historic Monuments and Buildings Branch, Department of the Environment, Northern Ireland).

conceal his contempt for them. He explained to the abbot of Clairvaux that the status of the king of Thomond should not be taken too seriously, 'for such kings have neither castles, nor halls, nor even timber houses or saddles for their horses, but huts of wattle, such as birds are accustomed to build when moulting'.[4] The stone dormitories and refectories of a Cistercian monastery may have been cold and spartan, but compared with the fragile buildings outside they aspired to luxury. Nevertheless, there were occasions when Cistercian monks themselves preferred the traditional Irish mode of living. In 1227 the Pope was informed that groups of monks had reverted to dwelling outside their monasteries in 'miserably constructed' houses of wattle.[5]

In religious architecture the contrasts between the Celtic monasteries of Ireland and the Benedictine houses of Europe were acute. The ordered sequence of stone buildings, placed around an enclosed cloister garth, was a concept virtually unknown in Ireland before the Cistercians arrived (Pl. 5). The Celtic church had refused to indulge in elaborate architecture, maintaining a policy of architectural austerity which had continued since the days of Bede. Even the monastic cities of Glendalough, Armagh and Clonmacnois had no great church as the focus of their religious life. The largest church known, the tenth-century cathedral of Glendalough, was a mere sixty-two feet (nineteen metres) in length. It had no aisles and no transepts; nor was there a clearly defined chancel. The stark interiors of these early buildings were once enlivened by wooden screens and painted panels, but in architectural terms they were of the utmost simplicity. Design remained almost untouched by European Romanesque until well into the twelfth century.[6]

The Irish view of the right form for a Christian oratory was governed by attitudes which evolved when churches were built of wood. Stone was not widely used until the tenth century and even after this it was not employed exclusively.[7] As late as the twelfth century, wooden churches could be seen in major monasteries. One survived at Clonmacnois until 1167[8] and the first church that Malachy built at Bangor was a timber structure, 'beautiful work in the Irish manner'.[9] Timber buildings subsequently left their mark on the design of stone churches. The steeply pitched roofs of Cormac's Chapel recall those found in the stave churches of Norway and the acutely pointed 'tangent' gables, fitted over Hiberno-Romanesque doorways, probably had their origin in wood (Pl. 7).[10]

The Celtic monastery, with its scattered group of oratories, stood in complete contrast to the disciplined planning of Benedictine monasticism (Pl. 6). Most noticeable was the lack of any building which approximated to a basilica, the Early Christian form which lay at the heart of medieval architecture. The Irish oratories belonged to a specifically northern tradition, almost

8 Carvings on the east window of Tuam Cathedral (Galway), c1184. Complex animal ornament of this type was repudiated by the Cistercians in Ireland.

unaffected by influences from the Mediterranean. The only link with this world was the round tower, the free-standing campanile, which came to dominate the precincts of the monastery.[11]

The architectural anomalies of Ireland were a reflection of social differences, to which most outsiders in the twelfth century reacted with contempt. The opinions of Gerald of Wales, who regarded the Irish as 'a wild and inhospitable people' are notorious, but there is no reason to suppose that his views were unique among foreigners. He went on to explain that though the Irish were 'fully endowed with natural gifts, their external characteristics of beard and dress, and cultivation of the mind, are so barbarous that they cannot be said to have any culture'.[12] Gerald not unnaturally judged the Irish by comparing them with his own society in south Wales and what was different automatically seemed inferior. A few years before, a laybrother from the English abbey of Buildwas had come to similar conclusions. While inspecting a potential monastic site, he was appalled by the 'wildness and ferocity of the barbarous inhabitants'.[13] The dress, language and social habits of the Irish were so incomprehensible that it was hard for outsiders to establish any rapport. For the Cistercians, language in particular produced enormous problems and an Irish speaking monk, who lacked a good grasp of Latin, had no ready means of contact with the rest of the order. Courses in Latin and French were the only answer, but it is clear that by the early thirteenth century many a Cistercian passed through his novitiate without mastering either language.

Although Irish customs mystified and even disgusted visitors from the French-speaking world, reactions were based on a restricted perception of what constituted civilised society. Twelfth-century Ireland had archaic features, but it was not as uncouth as some comments would have us believe. Even Gerald of Wales was forced to admire the beauty of Irish music and his sensitive description of a gospel book at Kildare (possibly a mistake for the book of Kells) reveals a keen appreciation of early Irish painting.[14] The artistic skills of the Irish goldsmith were dazzling, as the intricate beauties of the cross of Cong or the shrine of St Patrick's Bell testify.[15] But these skills were expressed in a vocabulary quite different from those of the contemporary English metalworker or the Mosan enameller. Twelfth-century Ireland was largely untouched by classical art and complex styles of animal interlace, which ultimately descended from the pre-Christian barbarian world, were alien to the mainstream of European fashion (Pl. 8, Fig. 1). To outsiders Irish culture seemed barbarous in the sense that it was unfamiliar.

The economy of Ireland also differed radically from neighbouring countries, for the vigorous agricultural expansion of Europe through deforestation had yet to make much impact. Although some arable farming was conducted, the total area under tillage remained relatively small. The chief occupations were pastoral, and cattle represented the principal source of wealth.[16] The easy-going nomadic existence which this entailed led to accusations of laziness which, in the eyes of Gerald of Wales, was another sign of Irish barbarity. Yet Gerald was impressed with the quality of the land, with crops abounding in the fields and flocks on the mountains. The opportunities that existed for agricultural development made Ireland ideal territory for the Cistercians, just as it was later to attract Anglo-Norman settlers. As today, however, large tracts of land in the north and west were impossible to farm, with rough mountain ranges and desolate expanses of bog, barren regions which the Cistercians showed little anxiety to colonise.

In contrast to the simplicity of Irish economic life, the political geography of the country in the early twelfth century was complex.[17] At a time when royal governments in England and France were becoming increasingly centralised, Ireland remained a patchwork of separate kingdoms or *tuatha*. At the beginning of the century there were still over a hundred kings and sub-kings. Some semblance of unity was provided by the high king or *ard-ri*, but this authority over the whole of Ireland was often nominal and his actual power depended on vigorous efforts to control the influence of lesser rulers. His position was frequently misunderstood by foreigners, who expected to find an all-powerful king with wide-ranging authority.

The chief benefactor of the first Cistercian monastery, at Mellifont, was Donough O'Carroll, King of Uriel, a kingdom of middling rank which stretched in a belt through the modern

Fig. 1 Tuam Cathedral, animal ornament on the jamb of the east window.

counties of Louth, Monaghan and Armagh. It formed one of the four major divisions of Ulster, along with Cenel Owen or Ailech (Tyrone and Derry), Cenel Connell (Donegal) and Ulidia (Antrim and Connor). Ulster itself was one of the five major provinces of Ireland, along with Connacht, Munster, Leinster and Meath. The relative power of individual kingdoms varied almost from year to year, with political relationships in a state of continuing flux. Political fragmentation fostered constant tensions which frequently erupted in war. The annals describe a continously shifting pattern of battles and alliances, though conditions were not as anarchic as the bare facts suggest. Warfare was usually localised and campaigns were brief, often amounting to little more than cattle raids. If Irish society was as turbulent as an initial reading of the annals implies, the architectural and cultural achievements of the twelfth century would never have been possible.

The most important addition to this catalogue of social and cultural peculiarities was the structure of the Irish church. Since the seventh century the unorthodox habits of Irish ecclesiastics had provoked unfavourable comment from foreigners and by the twelfth century many native churchmen felt the need to bring Ireland more closely into line with the rest of Europe.[18] Religious life was dominated by the monastery and there was no established episcopal government, based on defined dioceses. This was an ancient response to the Irish tribal system, with individual monasteries acquiring an identity with the local clan. It has been estimated that about two hundred monasteries existed at the end of the eleventh century, though they varied enormously in size and spiritual vitality. In many, the rigour of monastic life had long since given way to secular interests and secular control. The office of abbot or *comarb* was often held by a layman drawn from the ranks of an influential local family. Just how decadent the church was at this time is difficult to assess, for documentary evidence comes almost exclusively from the reformers, who not unnaturally blackened the picture as much as possible. There was certainly a marked indifference to pastoral care and critics lamented the absence of confession and the lack of preaching.

The Advent of the Cistercians

Before the end of the eleventh century the first ripples of the Gregorian reform began to be felt in Ireland and by the early decades of the twelfth century there were many advocates of change. Some of this group, most notably Malachy of Armagh, realised that continental monasticism could play an active role in invigorating the Irish church. Malachy was initially attracted to the Augustinian canons as his chief allies. By 1148, over forty communities of canons had been established and they proved an effective way of reviving defunct or moribund Celtic monasteries.[19] But late in his life, Malachy realised the potential of the Cistercians. He visited Clairvaux, *en route* to Rome, in 1140, at a time when its abbot, St Bernard, was nearing the peak of his spiritual influence and moral authority. The two men developed a profound respect and admiration for each other. Some years later, St Bernard was moved to write a biography of the Irish prelate. It was while he was undertaking a second continental journey in 1148 that Malachy died at Clairvaux and his tomb in the huge Burgundian abbey was held in great reverence by the Cistercian community there.[20]

Life at Clairvaux must have been an inspiring sight for Malachy. The humility of the monks, their austere dignity and the pervading atmosphere of peace and order was far removed from the secularism of the more degenerate Irish monasteries. The advantages of introducing Cistercian monks into Ireland must have been immediately obvious. The order had an efficient system of government, which would give support and prestige to the reform movement. Through its system of visitations by father abbots, the unity of Cistercian life throughout Europe was vigorously controlled and the annual meeting of all Cistercian abbots at the General Chapter was a further guarantee of uniformity within the order. As part of this international organisation, Malachy must have felt that it would be possible for Cistercian communities in Ireland to withstand the intense pressures from local interests and families. As a new and independent force, the Cistercians stood a good chance of avoiding the evils that afflicted the

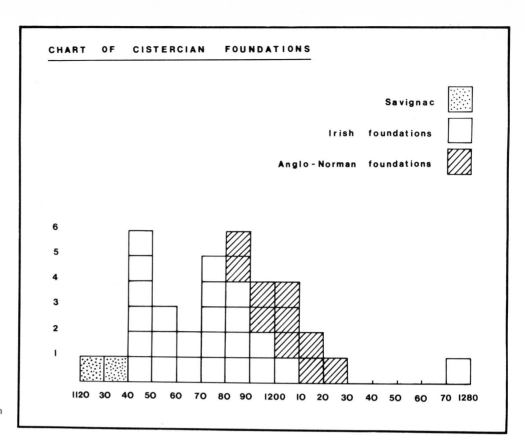

Fig. 2   Chart of Cistercian foundations in Ireland.

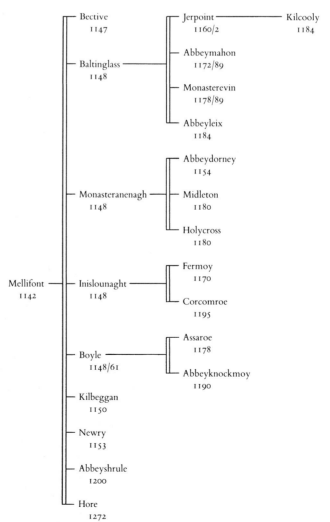

Fig. 3   The affiliation of Mellifont.

Irish church. Malachy's hopes for the order were quickly fulfilled, and within ten years of arriving in Ireland, the Cistercians of Mellifont hosted one of the sessions of the reforming 'synod of Kells'.[21]

In addition to these religious interests, there were other reasons why the Cistercians were especially suited to Ireland. Major sacrifices were not required from local rulers, since Cistercian communities were prepared to accept land that had not previously been cultivated. With its extensive tracts of waste and forest, Ireland provided plenty of scope for land clearance and new agrarian techniques. As Gerald admitted, 'give the Cistercians a wilderness or a forest, and in a few years you will find a dignified abbey in the midst of smiling plenty'.[22] Moreover, the austerity of the Cistercians, their poverty and their love of solitude had a particular appeal in an Irish context, for they awakened memories of the ascetic lives of the early Irish saints. The 'novi milites Christi', as the Cistercians described themselves, were, from an Irish point of view, well equipped to serve as an army of spiritual renewal.

It was two years after Malachy's initial visit to Clairvaux that the first Cistercian monks set foot in Ireland.[23] The group comprised both Irish and Frenchmen, Irish novices having been trained under the tutelage of St Bernard at Clairvaux. Within the first few months internal tensions threatened to break up the community, but once these early difficulties had been overcome, success followed very rapidly. Recruits flocked to Mellifont and the number of monks completing their novitiate rose at a tremendous rate. The expansion was so dramatic that within four years five daughter houses were established, at Bective (1147), Baltinglass (1148), Inislounaght (1148), Monasteranenagh (1148) and Grellachdinach (1148), the latter community eventually settling at Boyle in 1161.[24] Two more foundations followed in the early 1150s, Kilbeggan (1150), and Newry (1153). Soon after this, some of the daughter houses were in a position to send out their own communities. Abbeydorney was founded from Monasteranenagh (1154), Jerpoint from Baltinglass (probably 1160–2),[25] and Fermoy from Inislounaght (1170). By the time of the Anglo-Norman invasion, eleven Irish monasteries belonged to the affiliation of Mellifont. In addition, Mellifont had established a Scottish daughter house at Saddell, in the Mull of Kintyre, which may have been founded by Malachy himself, during his second journey to Rome in 1148. Three days after leaving Ireland, we are told that he reached a place called the Green Loch, where he had a site prepared for a monastery, an incident which may represent the origin of Saddell.[26] As well as houses founded through Mellifont, two further monasteries joined the Cistercian order in 1147, after the union with Savigny, St Mary's, Dublin, and Erenagh, so that by 1170 there were fourteen communities in Ireland altogether (Figs 2, 3).

Even by Cistercian standards the expansion of the Mellifont affiliation in the middle years of the twelfth century was spectacular. Eight (or possibly nine) new monasteries founded within eleven years was a remarkable achievement. In 1170 Mellifont alone was said to contain 100 monks and 300 laybrothers, though these figures may be exaggerated.[27] Nevertheless, even at a conservative estimate, there must have been at least 250 Cistercian monks in Ireland in 1170, and the total number was perhaps nearer 500. It is not easy to explain why the Cistercian way of life proved so popular and what brought so many Irishmen into the order. The encouragement of Malachy, a spiritual leader of immense energy and charisma, certainly gave the order a boost in the early years. There may also have been an exodus of monks from existing Celtic monasteries. At the very least the numbers joining the Cistercian order show how widespread the desire for monastic reform had become by the middle of the century.

Support for the movement had come from a wide range of kings and sub-kings and the consecration of the church at Mellifont in 1157 was something of a national event.[28] Seventeen bishops were present, along with the high king Murtagh MacLoughlin. The original benefactor of the abbey, Donough O'Carroll, was also there, as well as Devorgilla, wife of the king of Meath. At the same time the monastery received several valuable gifts, including some from MacLoughlin which show that Mellifont was regarded as far more than a local institution within the kingdom of Uriel. Indeed the growing prestige of the Cistercians is reflected in the fact that by 1170 four of the five provincial kings had become patrons of the order. Only the

O'Conor kings of Connacht showed no interest, which is surprising. Both Turlough (1106–56) and Rory O'Conor (1156–98) claimed the high kingship and must have been well informed about the new monasteries. It is difficult to explain their lack of patronage, though it is possible that the Cistercians were too closely identified with some of their enemies. Several lesser rulers had also founded monasteries, and these included the kings of Ossory (Jerpoint), Idrone (Killenny), Moylurg (Boyle) and Uriel (Mellifont).[29] The intriguing relationships between the monasteries and their patrons has never been studied in depth and it is far from clear how the Cistercians fitted into the general political and social context of Ireland. Some opposition to the order must have existed. The long-term interests of the Celtic monasteries were threatened and the Cistercians almost certainly deprived them of potential recruits and patronage. A few miles from Mellifont is the ancient monastery of Monasterboice, with its round tower and beautifully carved crosses. Its decline into obscurity coincides with the rise of Mellifont (Pl. 9).

9   The ruins of the early Irish monastery at Monasterboice, with the 'tall' cross conspicuous beside the round tower. The decline of Monasterboice into obscurity coincided with the rise of Mellifont a few miles away. (View from O'Neill's *Sculptured High Crosses*, 1857.)

In the past there has been a bland assumption on the part of historians that the Irish patrons of the order acted only from the highest religious motives. Genuine piety, combined with a desire to improve the spiritual life of the country, undoubtedly prompted many of them, especially those already converted to the aims of the church reform movement. This is invariably the impression given by the annals, written of course by ecclesiastics. Thus Donough O'Carroll's achievements were eulogised in a note inserted into the antiphonary of Armagh:

> It was this great King who founded the entire monastery both (as to) stone and wood, and gave territory and land to it, for the prosperity of his soul, in honour of Paul and Peter. By him the church throughout the land of Oirghiall was reformed, and a regular bishopric was made, and the church was placed under the jurisdiction of the bishop. In his time tithes were received, and the marriage (ceremony) was assented to, and churches were founded, and temples and bell towers were made, and monasteries of monks and canons, and nuns were re-edified, and nehmeds were made.[30]

This effusive obituary refers to several of the key elements in the reform programme and shows what an important ally Donough O'Carroll was to the reformers. The fact that he rebuilt *cloictheachs* or round towers is of particular interest, for these are to be found only in the traditional Irish monasteries. It suggests that O'Carroll's support for the Cistercians was astutely balanced by aid to some of the older houses.

It is hard to believe that the Irish kings were unaware of the political advantages which might accrue from a Cistercian monastery. Once Mellifont had established its reputation, there was prestige to be obtained from the endowment of a new house. From a royal point of view, the monastery could serve as a loyal bastion in an age of uncertainty and continual flux. Between 1170 and 1195, no less than four abbeys were founded by Donal Mór O'Brien, king of Munster, and it looks as if he at least was conscious of their political value. At the time much of his land was being overrun by Anglo-Norman settlers and three of the abbeys (Fermoy, Holycross and Kilcooly) were in areas where he was anxious to reinforce his authority. It is no coincidence that, several decades later in 1228, it was the O'Brien monastery of Monasteranenagh that led the Irish resistance to Stephen of Lexington and his Anglo-Norman allies.[31]

In addition, there were a number of personal advantages available to Irish benefactors, just as there were to their counterparts throughout Europe. Monks would pray regularly for the soul of their founder after his death, and to a prospective patron the disciplined intercession of the white monks must have seemed particularly efficacious. The monastery was also a haven to which a patron and his successors might retire in old age, as Conor MacDermot did in 1196, when he 'embraced orders in the monastery of Boyle'.[32] For an Irish king, the monastery could become a place of retirement and dignified burial, as well as a source of constant intercession for the safety of his soul. Patrons may also have been attracted by the agricultural prowess of the order, its skills at land clearance, drainage, cultivation and animal rearing. The presence of a group of intelligent, hard-working farmers in the neighbourhood could set an example to the local population and provide a focus of economic as well as religious development.

Despite the apparent success of the order in Ireland, the early years were not without their difficulties. The arguments at Mellifont which broke out only a few months after its foundation did not augur well for the future. In this case it seems that the small group of French monks found it impossible to dwell peaceably together with their Irish brethren.[33] It was not long before they decided they had had enough of Ireland and withdrew to Clairvaux. By the early thirteenth century, relationships between Irish monks and their colleagues abroad became a major source of tension and conflict. One initial difference between Ireland and most continental countries was the lack of any major Benedictine tradition.[34] Despite their criticisms of wealthy Benedictine houses in France and England, the Cistercians recruited many former Benedictine monks. To these people, the disciplined and ascetic way of life may have been a novelty, but there was still much that would have been familiar, not least the Benedictine Rule itself. The foundation of Fountains abbey (1134) is instructive in this regard. The nucleus of the community consisted of thirteen monks who had come from the Benedictine house of St Mary's, York, and they formed a talented and determined group.[35] The monks were already acquainted with the Benedictine Rule and were aware of the dangers of not following it strictly. In Ireland the Cistercians came not merely to reform, but to establish a rule of monastic life which was not widely known. The liturgy, modes of singing as well as a whole range of specific regulations, had to be learnt from scratch. It is only necessary to remember the fracas at Glastonbury in 1082, when abbot Thurstan introduced new Norman liturgical forms, to appreciate the arguments and tensions which could exist in a monastery on these occasions.[36] To judge from St Bernard's comments, this is what led to the withdrawal of the French monks: '. . . perhaps those natives of your country who are little disciplined and who found it hard to obey observances that were strange to them, may have been in some measure the occasion of their return.'[37] It seems that the stringency of Cistercian life was too harsh for some of the Irish monks.

The sheer physical remoteness of Ireland remained a permanent barrier to good communication with the rest of the order. The annual trip to the General Chapter at Citeaux was a long and unpleasant ordeal, especially for abbots in Munster and Connacht who first had to travel across the country from the west. Even the voyage to Wales, 'one short day's sailing' across the sea, was not without its perils.[38] Indeed Tintern abbey (Wexford) is said to owe its origin to a storm that threatened to drown its patron William Marshal, the monastery being founded as a thank offering for his safe deliverance.[39] After the sea voyage, there was the journey across England, and Irish abbots did not always receive a charitable Christian welcome from their English brethren. A group of tired, dishevelled Irish abbots, speaking an unintelligible language, were not regarded as ideal guests. In 1219 the abbot of Boxley (Kent) was upbraided by the General Chapter for not offering an acceptable degree of hospitality to travelling Irish abbots.[40] To make the return journey to Citeaux might take as long as three or four months for an abbot of Corcomroe or Boyle and small wonder that many of them decided not to go. Even after 1190, when the duty to attend was reduced to once every four years, complaints continued. Poor attendance at the General Chapter was symptomatic of a drift away from the mainstream of the order. Despite Stephen of Lexington's attempts at reform in 1228, the Irish record at the General Chapter was abysmal and the statutes of the order throughout the middle ages are studded with references to their non-appearance.[41]

The deterioration of links with the rest of the order was especially serious in view of local interests and pressures. The abbeys began to take on a local identity and, through their recruits, became closely associated with the neighbouring tribe and its rulers.[42] The traditional Irish relationship between monastery and tribe thus tended to re-emerge. A similar situation occurred in Wales, and David Knowles' analysis of abbeys there can be applied to Ireland with equal force:

> . . . once the fervour of the original plantation had cooled, it was possible for the whole house to take on the colour of the locality and become narrow in spirit and uncouth in manners. . .
> When the monastery concerned was of the second or third generation, and had for parent a small, provincial abbey, the stimulus provided by visitation must have been small and the safeguards given by internal observation and external public opinion of little strength.[43]

The use of the Irish language was another barrier to good communication. It was liable to cause confusion and resentment amongst French-speaking visitors and when French-speaking knights began to invade the country in 1169–70 the difference in tongues had disastrous implications.

The Anglo-Norman invasion

The Anglo-Norman conquest inaugurated a new phase in the history of the Irish Cistercians. Although initially welcomed by some churchmen, including Christian, former abbot of Mellifont, the relationship between the existing monasteries and the settlers from England soon deteriorated.[44] In many cases Irish monks saw their abbeys encircled by immigrants and watched while their relatives lost control over their lands. There were quarrels with some of the Anglo-Norman lords over the ownership of property and Mellifont, for example, was involved in disputes with Nicholas of Verdun and Walter de Lacy. For their part, the Anglo-Normans founded their own monastic houses and filled them with personnel of English origin. Between 1180 and 1222 the conquerors established ten new Cistercian monasteries, creating a rival group to the Mellifont affiliation.[45] After his rapid conquest of Ulster, John de Courcy founded the abbey of Inch in 1180/7 and his wife Affreca brought the Cistercians to Grey some years later. In 1182 Dunbrody was established on land given by Hervé de Montmorency, one of the feudal adventurers who had accompanied Strongbow in the initial invasion of Leinster (Pl. 10). Two more Cistercian houses, Tintern and Graiguenamanagh, were founded by Strongbow's successor as earl of Leinster, the illustrious William Marshal. The new abbeys were intended to make their own contribution to the settlement of newly conquered territories and subsequently they became part of the fabric of the Anglo-Norman lordship of Ireland. Meanwhile, Irish patrons continued to sponsor new houses within the affiliation of Mellifont.

Between the two groups of monasteries there were fundamental differences of outlook and in many cases a marked contrast in wealth. The Anglo-Norman houses were generally better endowed, often in areas where the soil was rich and fertile. The three great abbeys of the south-east, Dunbrody, Tintern and Graiguenamanagh, acquired lands and possessions which must have been envied by the Irish abbeys of the west, particularly those in desolate terrain, like Abbeyknockmoy or Corcomroe (Pl. 11). From the start, some of the Irish foundations were inadequately endowed. In the early-thirteenth-century Killenny, a daughter house of Jerpoint, was said to be too poor to survive, burdened with debts and unable to provide hospitality. Together with Glanawydan it was suppressed in 1227.[46] At the same time there was doubt over the survival of Holycross, which is ironic in view of the prosperity it attained in the fifteenth century, as a result of popular pilgrimage and the patronage of the earls of Ormond.[47]

In contrast to the Irish monasteries, which all belonged to the one family, the Anglo-Norman abbeys had a variety of mother houses which were, specifically, not Irish. Graiguenamanagh, for instance, was a daughter of Stanley (Wiltshire), Grey was colonised from Holm Cultram (Cumberland) and Inch was established from Furness (Lancashire). Anglo-Norman patrons had little confidence in the existing Cistercian abbeys and wished to create houses on whose loyalty they could depend. Thus the two nations in medieval Ireland managed to produce two virtually separate Cistercian orders. It was not long before the contrast was expressed in architecture, as the Anglo-Norman abbeys, constructed by English-trained masons, rose from the ground in an austere Early English style.

For Anglo-Norman lords, like John de Courcy, seeking to establish themselves in newly-acquired territory, the foundation of a Cistercian monastery was an attractive proposition. It was a way of easing the conscience if there were any lingering doubts over the moral rights to the land, and it provided a public demonstration of thanksgiving for recent success. Filled with loyal monks, it could become a valuable centre of stability and, aided by the laybrothers, a Cistercian community could be relied on to exploit the land effectively. In addition, an Anglo-Norman patron could expect all the usual personal and religious benefits, which accrued from monastic endowment.

10 Dunbrody, established in 1182 on land given to the Cistercians by the Anglo-Norman lord Hervé de Montmorency.

11 Abbeyknockmoy, founded in 1190 by the Irish king of Connacht, Cathal Crovderg O'Conor, in its bleak, windswept site.

The Conspiracy of Mellifont

Not many decades elapsed before the friction that existed between the two parts of the order degenerated into a crisis, which threatened to tear apart the whole fabric of the order in Ireland.[48] The first rumblings of trouble emerged in 1216 when the General Chapter heard disturbing reports about the conduct of some of their Irish brethren. The trouble centred on the affiliation of Mellifont and a general visitation was therefore organised. The visitors met with an unpleasant reception. When they reached Mellifont, the gates of the monastery were unceremoniously shut in their faces and at Jerpoint their appearance was greeted with a riot. It was soon apparent that there had been a massive breakdown in Cistercian discipline. Further visitations followed, abbots were deposed, but attempts at reform made little progress. In 1227, for example, a new abbot, an Anglo-Norman, was imposed on the abbey of Baltinglass, but the community drove him out, knocked him off his horse and took the monastic seal. It took an armed force to get the abbot re-installed. This was a prelude to greater violence to come. Visitors from the General Chapter were invariably greeted with hostility and hence the crisis was described as a conspiracy against the order. In a letter to the Pope the abbot of Cîteaux described the situation in Ireland, telling of 'dissipation, delapidation of property, conspiracies, rebellions and frequent machinations of death'.[49] In 1228 a new visitor, Stephen of Lexington, managed, with great courage and perseverance, to impose a modicum of order, though the underlying problems were far from settled. Many of his letters survive and they give a vivid picture of the atmosphere of violence and mistrust that he encountered. On several occasions he was faced with death, as when he was attacked by robbers in a forest near Kilcooly.[50] One of his assistants was wounded in an ambush prepared by the prior of Inislounaght and at Monasteranenagh (Pl. 12) Stephen himself was confronted with a massive array of armed force.[51] The monastery was prepared for a military siege, as Stephen himself explained:

> Moreover making the abbey, including both the cloister and the church, a fortress against God, they placed thirty dead bullocks, seasoned with salt, under the dormitory. They fortified the dormitories both of the monks and the laybrothers with stones, stakes, spades, spears and arms according to the custom of their race. Bringing together in the church grass, hay, flour and other supplies, they placed in the cloister abundant jars and receptacles sufficient for holding water. Moreover the vault over the altar they fortified like a dwelling tower with both food and arms. Finally they introduced into the cloister garth thirty living cows, feeding them with hay hidden in the church.

The main ranges around the cloister were thus being exploited like the curtain walls of a castle and it took a minor battle before Stephen of Lexington and his Anglo-Norman allies gained control.[52]

The violence provoked by the visitations is not difficult to understand, for the desire to reform lax observance became inextricably mixed up in the conflict between the Irish and Anglo-Normans. To Irish monks, French-speaking visitors, supported by Anglo-Norman lords, were another facet of encroaching Anglo-Norman power. Just as the Irish were losing their lands, now they were about to lose their monasteries. The traditional relationship between the monastery and local families made the situation worse. Monasteranenagh had been founded by the O'Brien kings of Munster and it is no coincidence that resistance to Stephen of Lexington there was led by a grandson of the reigning king, Donnchadh Cairbrech O'Brien. It is interesting to note that similar tensions occurred in the Cistercian monasteries of Wales, which were also drawn into political and racial struggles going on around them.[53] Five of the thirteen houses there were dominated by the Anglo-Normans, but the eight abbeys belonging to the affiliation of Whitland were strongly Welsh in sympathy. The position of Whitland was in many ways analogous to Mellifont, though in Wales political disputes did not become so closely enmeshed with problems of internal obedience and conduct.

'The extraordinary practices in Ireland' involved a wide range of abuses. As the abbot of Cîteaux explained, 'in the abbeys of Ireland the severity of Cistercian discipline and order is observed in scarcely anything except the habit, in that there is neither observance of choir service nor of silence in the cloister nor of the discipline of the chapter meetings nor use of the common table in the refectory nor of monastic quiet in the dormitory according to the manner of our order'.[54] A major fault was the cavalier attitude towards enclosure. Monks wandered outside the monastery looking after their own personal affairs and some actually lived outside the monastic walls. They consorted with lay friends and consequently were accused of mixing with undesirables, robbers and murderers.[55] Monastic lands, which should have been farmed directly by the community, were being alienated and leased out. Although the extent and seriousness of the problems were not exposed until 1216, observance had been sliding for several decades. The remoteness of the abbeys and the non-attendance of abbots at the General Chapter no doubt contributed to this. The system of annual visitation, which should have eliminated faults at an early stage, had failed to work and here the blame lies partly in the structure of the order in

12 Monasteranenagh, the abbey which fortified itself against Stephen of Lexington's visitation in 1228; drawing by George Du Noyer
(1840) before the collapse of the chancel.

Ireland. All the 'Irish' houses belonged to the one affiliation of Mellifont and too much depended
on the vigour and effectiveness of its father abbot. Finally there were the tensions that existed
with the Anglo-Norman houses, the foundation of which heightened the Irish identity of the
older monasteries and encouraged them to follow their own independent line.[56]

Stephen of Lexington's letter book provides much vivid detail about daily life in the Irish
monasteries and what was going wrong. After his visitation of Jerpoint he drew up a long list of
rules and regulations to be carefully followed in the future, with the clear implication that many
were being ignored.[57] There was too much idle chatter, eating and drinking had become too
lax, laybrothers were getting drunk, there was too much concern for personal belongings and
there were suspicions of theft. Contact with the outside world had become too close, so monks
were ordered not to travel outside the monastery and to remove their relatives from the
immediate locality. Nor were guests to be allowed in the inner cloister, with the sole exception
of the earl of Leinster, William Marshal. Although Stephen's criticisms were levelled at the Irish
communities, he also had a caustic word to say about Tracton, where the abbot was preoccupied
with speaking Welsh (the abbey was a daughter house of Whitland in Wales).[58] Celtic
languages were obviously a source of frustration to Stephen on his travels.

When Stephen of Lexington left in 1228, he had carried out a far-reaching programme of
reform and a measure of normality had settled over the Irish houses. The Mellifont affiliation
was broken up and new mother houses—Margam, Buildwas, Furness, Fountains and
Clairvaux—were appointed to ensure stricter control, a system which lasted until 1274.
Nobody was to be admitted as a monk unless he could first make confession in French or Latin,
an attempt to overcome the language barrier.[59] If possible, no Irish abbots were to be appointed
for three years, and regulations were drawn up to safeguard monastic property and prevent
further alienations of land. In several cases the whole character of a monastery was transformed
and this was especially noticeable at Mellifont. When Stephen first approached the monastery,

68 out of the 110 monks had fled into the hills, taking with them charters, valuables and books. Twenty-eight were allowed back, the rest were banished from the order. Stephen 'harangued the bestial people for seven days unceasingly' and supervised the election of a new abbot, Jocelyn, former prior of Beaubec in France.[60] A few years later the abbey inspired sufficient confidence among the Anglo-Norman community to receive a very substantial grant of land at Ballymascanlon from Walter de Lacy,[61] and the monastery had by now developed a strong English character. Not all the problems, however, were solved. Tension between the races was still acute and in 1230 the Anglo-Norman abbot of Fermoy was murdered, reputedly by his own monks.[62] In view of the political context, further friction was inevitable.

The cataclysm of 1216–30 came close to destroying the Cistercian way of life in Ireland and it had a major bearing on building activities. Loss of contact with the rest of the order was a major element in the disruption and a similar process can be detected in architecture. After the pioneering years of the 1150s and 1160s, when there was a strong stylistic debt to Burgundy, builders increasingly depended on more local sources of design. Some of the buildings constructed around 1200 show the same laxity of attitude which the monks were displaying in their daily lives. After 1230, specifically Irish modes of decoration and design were overwhelmed by the Early English style. Nowhere was this more apparent than at Mellifont, where the church was remodelled in a pure version of Early English, a symbol of the new regime.[63] This campaign of building reveals the extent to which the conspiracy of Mellifont marked a transition in the history of Irish Cistercian architecture.

Thirteenth-century prosperity and fourteenth-century decline

The middle of the thirteenth century was a boom period for the Anglo-Norman colony in Ireland and the Cistercian monasteries enjoyed their share of the prosperity.[64] With three-quarters of the country effectively conquered and Irish resistance limited to isolated mountain pockets, particularly in the west and north-west, more settled and peaceful conditions prevailed. Agriculture and trade flourished in the wake of the new feudal order. It is, however, difficult to assess the wealth of the Cistercians at this time, in the absence of reliable statistics of their income. The scale and quality of thirteenth-century building at monasteries like Dunbrody, Graiguenamanagh, Inch and Grey give a general hint of confidence and well-being, but even at this stage there are signs that some abbeys had over-reached themselves. In 1228, one of the Leinster houses, possibly Graiguenamanagh, was heavily in debt, occasioned perhaps by the monks' eagerness to complete their monastic buildings. Stephen of Lexington urged the whole community to strive to get the abbey out of its financial difficulties and he ruled that no houses were to be built in the granges, except barns and animals sheds, until the abbey was discharged from the bulk of its debts, 'with which it is intolerably oppressed', and until the chapter house of the monks and the kitchen of the guest house were finished.[65] The accumulation of such debts is not altogether surprising, for new communities must have been impatient to complete their church and conventual buildings.

By the middle years of the thirteenth century, many Cistercian houses in the south were beginning to appreciate the potential offered by sheep farming and joined their English and Welsh brethren in exploiting the massive demand for wool. But as in England, early success led to over-confidence. The practice of forward buying—or receiving payment in advance of production—produced colossal debts when monasteries were unable to fulfil their obligations. It has been estimated that between 1275 and 1320 most monasteries in the south of Ireland were heavily in debt to Italian merchants and bankers. In 1289 Jerpoint owed the firm of Bendinus Pannyth of Lucca 640 marks and ten years later Graiguenamanagh owed the Ricardi £466.13.4. Baltinglass, Inislounaght, Fermoy and Monasteranenagh were among other abbeys that fell heavily into debt at this time.[66]

During the course of the thirteenth century, most monasteries began to acquire feudal rights and privileges, such as tithes, altarages, mills, rights of pontage and the rights to hold fairs.

Mellifont, for example, owned the town of Collon, along with the right to hold an annual fair there[67] and Graiguenamanagh possessed similar rights for a fair outside the abbey walls.[68] The extents of Irish ecclesiastical possessions, drawn up after the dissolutions of 1540–1, reveal the scope of these feudal customs, though in many cases it is difficult to be sure how far they went back in time. An example of the rights belonging to a monastery is furnished by the 1540–1 entry for the village of Dunbrody.[69] Tenants in the village owed the abbey fifteen 'hokedays' (labour at harvest time), fifteen weeding days, fifteen hens, sixty gallons of beer and five sheep, though these payments in labour and kind had long since been commuted to cash. The abbey had additional income from the village in the form of three weirs, tithes on corn and oats, as well as revenue from a mill, called the 'Shaltmille'. Not far away on the coast at Ballyhack, income was derived from fishing. Fishermen living in houses and cottages owned by the monastery were required, each time they returned to the quayside, to give the monastery one fish out of every variety they had caught, another custom which had been commuted to cash. Such feudal rights as these had been expressly forbidden by one of the best known Cistercian statutes, which banned the possession of 'churches, altars, burials, tithes of another's labour or food, towns, villages, rents from land, income from ovens and mills, and other things similar to these, which are contrary to monastic purity'.[70] Like their English and Continental counterparts, the Irish abbeys became enmeshed in the complexities of feudal society, the very thing that the early fathers of the order had so desperately sought to avoid. As early as 1195, Irish abbots had been accused of receiving privileges which were contrary to the spirit of the order[71] and the process of leasing land became well advanced during the thirteenth century.[72] As in the majority of Cistercian abbeys throughout Europe, the monks increasingly became *rentiers* rather than active farmers, concerned with profit making rather than self-sufficiency. The financial calamities which resulted from sheep farming around 1300 gave an additional boost to the development. By no longer exploiting their land directly, the monks transferred responsibility, both agricultural and financial, to their tenants and leaseholders. The decline in the number of laybrothers accelerated this process. In earlier times it was the laybrothers who, attending services in church only twice a day, had transformed uncultivated wastes into productive farmland. But by the fourteenth century it was difficult to find recruits who would serve the monastery in this way and when the Black Death struck Ireland in 1348–9 the system had virtually died out. During the course of the thirteenth and fourteenth century, therefore, the economic structure of Cistercian monasteries was radically transformed. Instead of direct farming by the monks, most of their land was now rented out, and as a result there was little to distinguish the abbeys from the other great feudal landowners of the age.

Most of these economic developments can be paralleled in the monasteries of England and Wales. In the fourteenth century, however, the Irish houses appear to have suffered more severely from economic recession and political turmoil, to the extent that many were reduced to a state of absolute poverty. Political disorder was a major factor. Long before 1300 the fabric of the Anglo-Norman lordship began to crumble, both through internal deficiencies of government and through the increasing power of Gaelic rulers. The relative stability of c1250 was replaced by increasingly unsettled conditions. Confidence was eroded, trade disrupted and valuable farmland neglected. The invasion of Ireland by Edward Bruce between 1315 and 1318 further undermined the colony and his campaign of plunder exposed the weakness of the Dublin government. Poor harvests added to the calamities. Many manors never recovered and their lands returned to waste. The Black Death was one more catastrophe which, by reducing the labouring population, inhibited levels of agrarian output. Political instability and economic decline together brought medieval Ireland to the verge of ruin. By the dawn of the fifteenth century royal authority was restricted to the Pale, that relatively small area on the east coast around Dublin.

It is difficult to know how effectively the Cistercian monasteries survived the successive crises. There were certainly occasions when monastic lands were plundered and they could not have avoided the effects of the general economic malaise. Grey was one of several abbeys almost wrecked by the Scots and in 1374, Jerpoint complained to the bishop of Ossory that it was so

13 The Dominican friary at Kilmallock (Limerick). After 1300 the friars replaced the Cistercians as the most active ecclesiastical builders in Ireland.

impoverished by war between the Irish and English in the region that it could not fulfil its obligations of hospitality.[73] The pattern of Cistercian building also indicates that the fourteenth century was a lean period. Only Mellifont is known to have undertaken extensive architectural projects, though St Mary's Abbey, Dublin, may have been compelled to do so after a fire in 1304. This is said to have destroyed the 'beautiful and noble abbey, with church and steeple',[74] and extensive reconstruction no doubt followed. Elsewhere alterations were restricted to relatively minor tasks like the insertion of traceried windows. The architectural evidence, however, needs to be interpreted with care. By 1300 most abbeys already had a satisfactory complement of buildings and, unless some specific disaster occurred, there was no pressing need to carry out reconstruction. The building activities of the friars between 1300 and 1350 in towns like Athenry, Kilmallock, Kilkenny and Castledermot show that the economic difficulties of the time did not prevent moderately ambitious architectural projects (Pl. 13).

As well as its financial problems, the order continued to be disrupted by racial conflict. The atmosphere of distrust is well illustrated by the foundation of Hore abbey in 1272. Its patron was the Irish archbishop of Cashel, David MacCarville, and its mother house was Mellifont. Some of the local English community were deeply suspicious and in 1279 Margaret le Blunde, who detested the archbishop, complained that it was filled with rogues who killed English people and plundered the area.[75] While Hore was identified with the Irish, other monasteries had corresponding loyalties in the opposite direction. Abbeylara, founded in 1210/14 by an Anglo-Norman, Richard Tuit, not far from his castle at Granard, remained faithful to the English cause; so much so that in 1318 its monks, along with those of Inch, were accused of hunting the Irish with spears by day to be followed by vespers in the evening.[76] As the Gaelic revival gathered momentum, the local identity of the monasteries was accentuated. The Dublin government was particularly anxious about the infiltration of Irishmen into houses previously regarded as English strongholds and Mellifont itself was the cause of great concern. Apparently the abbey had ironically reversed one of Stephen of Lexington's requirements. Now nobody was admitted unless they could give an oath in Irish or at least prove that they were not related to the English. In 1321 the practice was condemned by the General Chapter, and more predictably, by Edward II.[77] Within the next few years English control of the abbey was reasserted and for the rest of the middle ages its abbots all appear to have been of English stock. The policy of rejecting Irish recruits from monasteries in loyal areas was reiterated on several occasions during the fourteenth century. In 1380, eleven houses 'inter anglicanos' were told not to accept Irish monks,[78] but as royal authority waned it was a demand that was not, and could not be, enforced.

A remarkable illustration of the racial animosities that coloured fourteenth-century monastic life, comes from a poem, entitled Land of Cokaygne, written in old English in the Franciscan friary of Kildare.[79] The poem satirises life in an Irish Cistercian monastery, depicted as a land of perfect happiness, full of delicious food and sensual pleasure.

> There is a wel fair abbei
> Of white monkes and of grei.
> Ther beth bowris and halles:
> Al of pasteiis beth the walles,
> Of fleis, of fisse, and rich met,
> The likfullist thet man mai et.
> Fluren cakes beth the schingles alle
> Of cherch, cloister, boure, and halle
>
> .   .   .   .   .
>
> There is a cloister, fair and liyt,
> Brod and lang, of sembli siyt
> The pilers of thet cloister alle
> Beth iturned of cristale,
> With her bas and capitale
> Of grene jaspe and rede corale.

The description of a cloister, with its bases and capitals of green jasper and red coral, is especially vivid, a Franciscan comment, perhaps, on the spacious cloisters of the Cistercians. A clue to the abbey which the poet had in mind comes in a passage describing a local nunnery, which provided the abbey with its sexual delights:

Anothet abbei is therbi—
Forsoth, a gret fair nunnerie,
Up a river of swet milke,
Wher is gret plente of silk

The 'river of sweet milk' (in which the nuns are subsequently found swimming naked) recalls the Irish name of Inislounaght, 'Inis Leamhnachta' or island of fresh milk, and this monastery may well be the specific target of the satirist. Written in an Anglo-Irish community, the poem combines racial antipathy with an abiding contempt for the lifestyle of the Cistercians. The depiction of gluttony and licentiousness foreshadow by over two hundred years some of the charges to be made against the Cistercian houses in the sixteenth century.

The later middle ages

Until recently it has been customary to paint a very black picture of the Irish monasteries on the eve of the dissolution. Tales of scandalous abbots or gross neglect of monastic observance are not difficult to find. There is no doubt that the life of many Cistercian monks had sunk a long way from the high ideals set by men like Stephen Harding or Bernard of Clairvaux, but whether or not this amounted to total decadence is more debatable. It is clear, however, that most monasteries were scarcely recognisable as the earnest and thriving communities which had been established in the twelfth and early thirteenth century and buildings erected three hundred years before were often ill-adapted for the handful of monks that remained. The spiritual and intellectual vigour of the monasteries appear to have declined steadily since the middle of the thirteenth century and the Cistercians were no longer capable of attracting the best minds of the age. Young men of ability were now more likely to become friars or to pursue careers in law and administration. The status and duties of the abbot had also changed and there was frequently little to distinguish him from secular landlords outside the monastery. In most abbeys the scale and character of conventual life was so different from earlier times that the traditional architectural form of the monastery ceased to be relevant.

The most obvious difference between the twelfth and sixteenth century was the actual size of the communities.[80] Although few figures are recorded, a rough guide is provided by the names of monks given pensions at the dissolution.[81] The figures are likely to be underestimates, for not every monk may have been deemed worthy or eligible for a pension. Only two abbeys had sizable contingents, St Mary's, Dublin, with eighteen and Mellifont with twenty-one. In the context of the British Isles these are impressive figures, comparable with some of the major English houses such as Rievaulx (22), Hailes (21), Byland (25) and Furness (31).[82] Cistercian communal life was still very much an active force in these two houses, but in many of the others it was on the verge of extinction. Most had only a tiny complement of monks—Jerpoint (7), Abbeylara (6), Hore (5), Inislounaght (5), Newry (3) and Kilcooly (2). These figures underline John Troy's statement of c1498 that only at Dublin and Mellifont was divine service sung according to note or the monastic habit worn.[83] Certainly these were the only two communities which were viable in the traditional Cistercian sense. The decline in numbers was dramatic. It is worth recalling that in 1170 Mellifont was reputed to contain one hundred monks and three hundred laybrothers and even in 1228 it had fifty monks and sixty laybrothers.[84] In the same year the numbers at Jerpoint (or Graiguenamanagh) were fixed at thirty-six and fifty respectively[85] and this was probably about average for one of the more prosperous houses at the time. By 1540 the laybrothers had long since vanished, to be replaced, where necessary, by hired servants. Six monks, where once there were thirty or forty, made the spacious Cistercian refectories and dormitories seem like vast, empty halls. The west range of the cloister, the laybrothers' quarters, had long been obsolete and even the standard chapter house was unnecessarily spacious. All were relics of a bygone age and, when hefty repairs were needed, it is no surprise that some buildings were allowed to decay and others altered or simplified. The shadow of former prosperity hung over the cloister and it must have been difficult for a conscientious monk to avoid a feeling of nostalgia, if not despondency.

This was very much the attitude of John Troy, who in his old age was extremely gloomy about the future of the order in Ireland.[86] As abbot of Mellifont, he was empowered to act as Reformator of the Irish houses, but in 1498 he asked to be excused on account of the 'intolerable labours' it entailed. The system of visitation had virtually collapsed and Troy explained how it was impossible to make visitations among the 'Irish of the woods' (i.e. outside the Pale). For a full hundred years none from the remote districts had visited their father abbot. He lists several causes, chief among them the ceaseless war between the two races, which made any journey outside the Pale potentially dangerous. The major monasteries of Dublin and Mellifont were isolated from the other abbeys, a lack of communication which should be borne in mind when looking at the architecture of the monasteries.

Delapidation and the alienation of monastic property was one of the most serious problems to afflict the order. As early as 1228 Stephen of Lexington had been alarmed by the disintegration of monastic lands and by the fifteenth century the evil was firmly entrenched. Endowment, which had originally maintained substantial religious communities, was being siphoned off to serve purely secular interests. As John Troy lamented, pensions and tributes were being paid by monasteries to provisors and commendatory abbots, money which could have been better employed to support spiritual activities. Particularly instructive is the despairing appeal sent by the abbot and monks of Abington to James Butler, earl of Ormond, in 1436.[87] They complained bitterly about the 'inordinate power of laymen' hostile to the king, especially Cornelius O'Mulreyan, who 'pretends that he is abbot *de facto* of this monastery; and through the aforesaid Cornelius and his son deprived and spoiled us and the monastery of all our sustenation, fruits, rents and oblations, and from day to day deprives and spoils us; so that no-one can go outside the wall of the monastery; and on this account, through the failure of our support, as if through hunger, Divine worship is neglected and given up'. The plea from Abington is a striking illustration of the disease which was gradually strangling Irish monasticism. Between 1458 and 1471 Mellifont itself was brought to the edge of bankruptcy through a policy of irresponsible and reckless leasing by abbot Waring, designed to benefit his family and friends.[88] Abbots disposed of property with little regard to the true interests of their communities, being concerned as much with personal or family profit, and the lifestyle of an abbot was not easily distinguished from that of a secular lord, as he ruled over his domain. It explains the accusations of simony, as financial inducements were made to secure valuable office. John Troy complained that many abbots were not ordained and scarcely visited their houses once a year. In these circumstances it is not surprising that communities found themselves impoverished. Even if a community did retain control of its potential resources, warfare and plunder was liable to diminish its value.

In relative terms most of the Irish monasteries remained extremely poor. The two exceptions were St Mary's, Dublin, and Mellifont. St Mary's, situated on the north bank of the River Liffey, owned sections of the city of Dublin and its surrounding villages, and in 1540–1 its total income was valued at £537.17.10. Only two English Cistercian houses, Furness (£805) and Fountains (£1,115),[89] exceeded this, and in view of its wealth the almost complete destruction of the monastery is a great disappointment. Mellifont was valued at £352.3.10, which puts it on a par with Rievaulx (£351), Hailes (£357) and Kirkstall (£329). The wealth of Mellifont and St Mary's Dublin, was altogether exceptional and it helps to explain why they alone could afford to maintain reasonably large communities up to the dissolution. There was undoubtedly a close correlation between wealth and numbers and it is worth stressing that lack of income rather than lack of vocations reduced the size of communities. Only nine other houses were worth above £50 and one of these, Tracton, on the coast of County Cork, could collect a mere fraction of its potential income in 1540–1, its lands being waste and unoccupied through war. The valuations of monastic property carried out after the dissolution are the best records available, but for various reasons they provide only a partial account. Those houses in places outside royal control, such as Abbeyknockmoy, Corcomroe or Boyle, are not included and, even when the commissioners could make detailed valuations, the figures are often incomplete. In times of peace, with their lands fully inhabited by tenants, many abbeys would have been worth far more. The figures given in the table below are, therefore, merely approximations and serve only as a general guide to relative, rather than absolute, wealth.[90]

Jerpoint	£87.17.2	
Bective	£83.18.8	
Abbeyknockmoy	£78.10.0	(inquisition 1584)
Graiguenamanagh	£76.12.5	(worth £88.5.7. in peace)
Baltinglass	£75.15.2	or £126.10.1
Tracton	£ 5. 3.4	(true value in peace £71.13.0)
Abbeylara	£69. 0.0	
Holycross	£66. 6.8	(valuations 1490, 1492)
Tintern	£96.13.4	(valuation 1543)

This group of monasteries in the middle order can be compared to English houses like Buildwas (£110), Dore (£101) and Croxden (£90). Outside this group came the bulk of Irish monasteries, whose recorded wealth in the fifteenth and sixteenth century remained exceedingly low, though some of these were worth more than the documented figures suggest. The figure for Dunbrody (£28.11.4) gives a misleading impression of its endowment, since around 1540–1 it was badly affected by local disturbances. For Abbeydorney, Monasteranenagh, Abbeyshrule, Grey, Inch, Comber, Corcomroe, Boyle and Macosquin no reliable figures survive, but none is likely to have been prosperous. Corcomroe, in its bleak outpost in County Clare, claimed to be so poor in 1417 that it could not maintain all its monks and permission was sought for one to hold a temporal benefice. In papal documents its value was cited as 30 marks in 1447 and 24 marks in 1473. The following list gives figures for those houses where statistics survive.

Abington	£44.19.4	(1553)
Inislounaght	£39.12.5	
Newry	£35.10.0	(1550)
Kilcooly	£32.18.3	(in peace potential value £46.0.4)
Dunbrody	£28.11.4	(in peace potential value £40.15.10)
Hore	£21. 4.10	
Assaroe	£21. 1.8	(1558–9 inquisition)
Monasterevan	£20.13.4	
Abbeymahon	£18. 8.4	(in peace potential value £34.11.8)
Kilbeggan	£13.19.4	
Midleton	£ 3. 5.0	(in peace potential value £23.5.0)
Abbeyleix	£ 3. 4.10	(in peace potential value £31.15.9, 1551)
Fermoy	£ 2.18.0	(in peace potential value £24.2.0)

As one might expect, there is a general relationship between recorded wealth and building projects. Complicated works of reconstruction, excluding towers and cloister arcades, were undertaken in only four monasteries, Jerpoint, Bective, Holycross and Kilcooly, three of which belong to the middle income group. The exception is Kilcooly, valued just below £50. Most Irish houses in the later middle ages had neither the energy nor the resources to embark on ambitious architectural schemes and in several cases the shrinking of the community prompted a drastic reduction in the size of the church.

Poverty, isolation and lack of monks represent only a few of the problems confronting the Cistercian order at the time. Many abbots were quite incapable of acting as a source of inspiration for their communities, a problem which affected Mellifont and St Mary's, Dublin, just as much as the other houses. In 1399 the abbot of Dublin, Stephen Ross, was absolved by

Boniface IX from every penance he had earned for impurity, unfair treatment of clerics, leaving his monastery without permission, going into convents of nuns, carrying forbidden arms, showing a lack of respect for his superiors, conspiring against them and other people, and frequenting taverns.[91] The latter must have been a particular temptation for the monks of St Mary's, situated on the edge of the city of Dublin. Troy was bitterly critical of the commendations and provisions made by the Papacy, which repeatedly led to the appointment of unsuitable abbots. To judge from the case of Richard Seymour, the worldly abbot of Abington, his criticism was not unjustified. Seymour admitted in 1452 that he had been negligent in carrying out the liturgy and administering the sacraments, and that he had carried arms into the monastery. He confessed to a charge of alienating the property of the house, also to simony and fornication: 'overcome by the frailty of the flesh, he knew carnally many women through the act of fornication and from some of them produced offspring.' After doing penance, he was confirmed in office by the Pope.[92] Lack of celibacy was an oft-repeated charge. Although in medieval Ireland it did not convey a strong social stigma, it had the unfortunate habit of producing heirs, leading to family succession in the holding of abbacies. This happened, for example, at Holycross, where Dermot O'Heffernan succeeded his father Fergal in 1448.[93]

Although the vices which affected the order were serious, there is no proof that they had extinguished all religious vitality. There were over thirty abbots in the country as a whole and not all of them can have been as infamous as Richard Seymour and Stephen Ross. A strong case has been made both by Father Colmcille and by Brendan Bradshaw to show that the picture of sordid decadence, traditionally portrayed by historians, has been much exaggerated.[94] While concubinage existed, it was not universal, nor did it amount to sexual turpitude. The basic core of Cistercian life still continued, even if obedience to the rule was frequently casual and irregular. Many of the documents of the period, which tell of scandals and corruption, should not be read at face value. Information in Papal letters concerning scurrilous abbots was often supplied by opponents or rivals to office, and character assassination was a standard weapon of the trade. Similarly, inquisitions taken prior to the dissolution were compiled by juries often intent on finding all the ammunition available. While allowing for this, however, it is important not to go to the other extreme and gloss over the very real faults that existed.

It is from Holycross that a more balanced account of monastic life in the sixteenth century survives, in the form of a report of a visitation, conducted by abbot John of Newry in 1536.[95] Although a poor monastery in its early years, Holycross acquired fame and a degree of wealth in the later middle ages through the popularity of the pilgrimage to its sacred relics of the true cross. There are indications that it displayed more devotional enthusiasm than most monasteries of the time. The abbot of Newry was nevertheless critical. He drew up a list of nine regulations to be closely followed in the future, some concerning the conduct of services, others the moral behaviour of the monks. Reading between the lines, they provide a valuable insight into the daily life of an Irish monastery on the eve of the dissolution.

1 All monks who were priests were to celebrate mass four times per week and make regular confession.
2 The abbot and prior were to ensure that the three statutory masses were celebrated each day (the mass of the Virgin, the mass of the day and the mass of the dead) as well as to ensure the correct performance of other liturgical duties. In addition, all monks were to get up at the appointed time for morning service.
3 The chanting of the divine office was to be done distinctly, solemnly and reverently and cowls were to be worn in the choir. The cellarer was to provide candles each day as required and the church was to be properly maintained, with special care taken of the sacred host.
4 Sufficient provisions were to be made available each day in order to prevent grumbling.
5 The abbot and monks were to live chaste and regular lives and women were not to be allowed in the dormitory. Nor should suspicious women be allowed within the monastic precinct or permitted to linger in the adjoining village.
6 The possession of all personal property was expressly forbidden, as stated in the Benedictine Rule.

7 Monks should not leave the monastery without permission and should sleep in the dormitory every night. All circumstances which give rise to suspicion or scandal were to be avoided.

8 Arguments between the brethren should cease, with juniors duly respecting seniors and seeking forgiveness.

9 One chapter of the Benedictine Rule was to be read out every day in chapter and, once every month for a year, this particular list of regulations.

John of Newry's list of instructions gives plenty of hints about what was wrong. The monks seem to have been all too human in character. Services were somewhat irregular, not everyone attended and they were conducted in a slovenly fashion. Some monks could not get up in the morning, there was too much quarrelling and monks were wandering off on their own without permission. The reference to women in the dormitory may refer to female servants, though in some of the regulations there is more than a hint of scandal. On the positive side, services were at least being carried out and the monks were still living together in community. The standards of obedience and discipline demanded by abbot John were relatively high and one wonders whether such standards were actually achieved in his own house of Newry.

It is doubtful whether many Irish monasteries approached this level of excellence and it is hard to forget John Troy's doleful comment of c1498 that, apart from Dublin and Mellifont, hospitality was no longer practised, divine service was neglected, and many monks lived among the nobility, throwing off the habit of religion. Troy spoke with the prejudice of the Pale, but there must be some validity in his comments. Judged by the standards of the twelfth century, monastic life was casual, relaxed, ill-disciplined and mundane, with only cursory attention paid to the rigours of the Benedictine Rule. But there were bright spots and many Cistercian monks were devout and conscientious men.

In trying to argue for the survival of a reasonable degree of monastic vitality, Brendan Bradshaw pointed to the architectural achievements of the fifteenth century. 'It is inconceivable', he wrote, 'that architectural projects on such a scale and of such quality could have originated in and been sustained by monastic communities which had sunk to the level of disorder and depravity usually attributed to Irish communities in the century preceding the Henrician dissolution campaign'.[96] In fact the architectural evidence is deceptive, as far as the Cistercians are concerned, and relatively few monasteries are known to have undertaken projects of any sophistication at this time. The most significant work was at Holycross (after c1431), Jerpoint (c1390–1450) and Kilcooly (after 1445). Even here much of the building predates the dissolution by many decades and tell us little about the communities in the sixteenth century. A number of monasteries, including Inch and Monasteranenagh, truncated their churches in a fairly crude manner, abandoning unwanted space in the nave and transepts. Elsewhere there is evidence to show that monastic buildings were crumbling into decay. In 1540–1, the church at Baltinglass was 'very ruinous' and the Extents state that the claustral buildings, unless 'quickly repaired, will entirely come to the ground'. Some years before, the church at Inislounaght was said to be 'in great part in ruins and fallen' and even the buildings at Mellifont, which had recently been occupied by twenty monks, were becoming derelict.[97] When the dissolution occurred, many monasteries were on the verge of physical, as well as spiritual, collapse.

The Dissolution

The majority of monasteries were dissolved, like those in England, during the Reformation under Henry VIII.[98] The process lasted several years and the demise of the abbeys was not the product of a swift comprehensive campaign. Over large tracts of the country, the Crown lacked the power to implement its policy and some communities lingered on for several decades. This prolonged, but did not seriously affect, the final outcome.

Five Cistercian abbeys were suppressed in an initial campaign of 1536–7 (Bective, Baltinglass, Tintern, Dunbrody and Graiguenamanagh). In the next few years a more comprehensive policy emerged and sixteen Cistercian abbeys were dissolved between 1539 and 1543. The abbot of

Mellifont, Richard Contour, surrendered his monastery on 23 July 1539 and the other great Cistercian house, St Mary's, Dublin, followed three months later on 28 October.

Outside the Crown territories, the programme of suppression was less decisive, especially where a powerful local family was protecting the abbey. In some cases the neighbourhood was considered too dangerous for the royal agents to go near the monastery. Government officials listed the property of Abbeylara while staying at Tristernagh, eleven miles away. For information they depended on the abbot and prior, explaining that it was 'not possible for us to make inquiry through others, men of the neighbourhood, because we did not venture to approach nearer for fear of the Irish'.[99] Altogether there were twelve Cistercian houses where it proved impossible to confiscate the monastic revenues and no valuation of property was attempted.[100] In some situations a compromise emerged. Three monasteries, Abington, Newry and Holycross, were changed into secular colleges, with a provost or warden at their head, but none survived for long.[101] Elsewhere an agreement was reached with the abbot. In the case of Abbeyknockmoy, Hugh O'Kelly, the lay abbot or 'perpetual commendatory', successfully defended his possessions by acknowledging the supremacy of Henry VIII and being granted the abbey and its lands for life. In return he agreed to supply troops for royal service when needed.[102] Theoretical control over the abbey thus passed to the king, though in reality the *status quo* was little affected. The monastery of Midleton was similarly retained by its former abbot.[103] In some remote areas, Cistercian houses passed into the hands of local lords with the Crown scarcely involved at all. This happened at Corcomroe, where Murrough O'Brien, earl of Thomond, was in possession of the abbey in 1544.[104] It was, incidently, the O'Briens who had founded the monastery 349 years before. Dissolution thus came in a variety of forms, but the eventual results were usually the same. The independent religious status of the abbeys was extinguished and control of monastic property passed either to the king or to a powerful local family.

The motives behind the dissolution of the monasteries were not entirely the same as those in England. The frailty of royal power in Ireland meant that the Dublin government was always searching for ways of buttressing its authority, and during the 1530s several members of the administration came to the opinion that the acquisition of monastic land could help in achieving this. In 1534 Sir Patrick Finglas proposed the suppression of several border monasteries, with the aim of repopulating the lands with 'young lords, knights and gents out of England'. The dissolution of some monasteries was thus regarded as a means of creating a pool of land which could be used to attract new English immigrants. There was also the additional point that the border monasteries had been a constant source of irritation for 'nourishing Irish rebels'.[105] The policy of suppression was thus formulated as a means of defending and preserving the colony. After the closure of the initial group of monasteries in 1536–7, the administration became more ambitious in its attitude. A policy of total dissolution became an attractive proposition as a way of enhancing the revenue of the Crown. Hence the richer monasteries of Ireland, which included Mellifont and St Mary's, Dublin, were now drawn within the net.

The suppression of the monasteries was not a revolutionary or cataclysmic event. Romantic tales of monks going heroically to slaughter are mythical and the dissolution campaign of 1536–41 was carried out without violence and without serious opposition. Many communities were so small that their departure from the neighbourhood was scarcely noticed. Nor were the spiritual consequences for the populace all that serious. Most abbeys were allowed to continue as parish churches, occasionally with one or more monks remaining as curates. Three were retained at Hore and seven of the Mellifont community stayed in the neighbourhood, receiving cures in local parishes.[106] By tradition Cistercian monasteries were supposed to be centres of charity and hospitality and there was no doubt some loss here. An attempt was made in 1539 to save Dublin and Jerpoint (as well as four non-Cistercian houses), on the grounds that they were essential 'in default of common inns' and also since they were 'the great schools of the country'.[107] But in practice the reputation of the Cistercians as teachers and philanthropists was feeble (as recently as 1498 John Troy had complained of the lack of Cistercian hospitality). At a social level, the suppression could not be seen as an unmitigated disaster.

14 The cloister garth at Holycross Abbey. Through the popularity of the pilgrimage to its sacred relics of the cross, this became one of the more active and prosperous monasteries of Ireland in the later middle ages.

In Gaelic areas where royal authority was negligible, the changes were less sudden. Although monastic land became secularised, the monks themselves were not invariably dispersed. Whereas monks living in the Crown lands were given pensions and ejected from the premises, communities in the west continued to live within the old buildings. With few resources and the future outlook bleak, morale must have been low. Assaroe survived in this twilight fashion until the end of the century and it was only after the Flight of the Earls in 1607 that the last monks are said to have been driven out.[108] An abbot of Abbeydorney was active until 1577 (when he was shot at Lixnaw Castle)[109] and in 1584 Glaisne O'Culleanain, abbot of Boyle, was executed in Dublin, after refusing to renounce his allegiance to Rome.[110] In several of the more distant abbeys the occasional monk could be glimpsed moving amidst the ancient cloisters, but the foundations of monastic life had been irrevocably undermined. The situation of Holycross, one of many abbeys acquired by the earl of Ormond, is of particular interest. While taking the endowment, the earl was ready to rent the old buildings to surviving monks. Thus in 1572 he granted John 'Monk' rooms in the abbey, with the proviso that he find 'a sufficient and lawful curate' to serve the parishioners and that the services be conducted according to the Book of Common Prayer.[111] In this case a Cistercian monk accepted, at least nominally, the new Protestant order. Holycross managed to retain some identity as a religious house, partly because its relics of the true cross had escaped the iconoclasm of the 1540s and pilgrims were still attracted there. The combination of relics, pilgrimage, a Cistercian monk and Protestant prayer books was a peculiar mixture, but no doubt a judicious and pragmatic move on the part of the earl.

A revival of the Cistercian order occurred in the early seventeenth century, led by Luke Archer, 'abbot' of Holycross, who made a determined effort to regenerate Cistercian life.[112] Much of the time he and his followers lived in Kilkenny and they opened further convents in Dublin and Drogheda. His assistant, John Cantwell, rehabilitated the ruined buildings at Holycross and subsequently the community lived there for a short time. The followers of Luke Archer were appointed as abbots to a number of dissolved Irish houses, but there is no evidence that they had communities to govern. In 1628, for example, John O'Dea, a monk of Salamanca, was appointed abbot of Corcomroe, though there is no proof of a viable monastery there.[113] The Cistercian revival was shortlived and it was obliterated during the Cromwellian wars of 1649–50. Memories of monastic life were kept alive at Holycross, Dunbrody and Kilcooly, where local priests continued to use the title of abbot for many years to come. At Mellifont the last recorded titular abbot died in 1719.[114] Meaningful links with the Cistercians of old, however, had long since been broken.

The historical sources which remain, chiefly charters, letters, and brief entries in the annals, leave us with an unbalanced view of Cistercian history. There is plenty of information about landed endowment and property, but very little about building operations or the personalities of individual monks. The lacunae are especially serious for the first hundred years. Almost nothing is known about the internal life of the monasteries before the conspiracy of Mellifont erupted. Ireland had no Walter Daniel to provide a portrait of one of the father abbots and very few Irish Cistercians emerge from the obscurity of history. Christian, the first abbot of Mellifont, who later became papal legate, was clearly a distinguished and effective leader, yet we remain ignorant of the way he conducted the affairs of his monastery. Far more is known about the abbots of the later middle ages, men like John Troy and Walter Champfleur, both of whom laboured in vain to reform the order. Champfleur was abbot of St Mary's, Dublin, and when he died in 1497, as 'an aged, prudent and learned man' he was much lamented.[115] For the most part, however, glimpses of individual characters are rare and the dearth of historical sources has transformed the 'novi milites Christi' into a largely anonymous army. To this rather bland and colourless picture, the buildings add a degree of variety and vitality. In the historical record there is not much to distinguish between, for example, Boyle and Abbeyknockmoy, but the architecture of the two abbeys is sharply differentiated, reminding us that each community had its own character and social flavour.

Chapter 2

THE FOUNDATION AND CONSTRUCTION OF THE MONASTERIES

Essential requirements

THE QUEST FOR earthly solitude was the chief motive behind the foundation of Citeaux in 1098 and the statutes of the order later insisted that 'monasteries should not be built in cities, castles or towns, but in places far removed from the conversation of men'.[1] Hidden in the quiet of the countryside, the monks could pursue without distraction their search for spiritual union with God. The advantages of rural retreat were beautifully summarised by the English abbot, Aelred, as he described the attractions of Cistercian life: 'everywhere peace, everywhere serenity and a marvellous freedom from the tumult of the world'.[2]

The relatively sparse population of Ireland and the lack of major settlements meant that seclusion was not hard to find. More critical was the requirement for potentially sound arable land, essential if the monastery was to be self-supporting. The fame of some of the more remote English houses has given the impression that the order was content to accept almost exhausted or unproductive land, but the evidence suggests that this only happened when the monks could get nothing better.[3] Although Ireland possessed vast tracts of uncultivated waste and forest, good quality soils were not available everywhere. Farming is difficult in the west and north amidst the mountains and peat bogs; the area is poorly drained and suffers from heavy rainfall. Far better, from an agricultural point of view, are the freely drained soils of the south and east, where the rainfall is less and the land is richer.[4] This was the area most heavily settled by the Anglo-Normans after 1170 and it was the area favoured by the Cistercians. Out of the thirty-three major Cistercian monasteries, twenty-seven lie in these more fertile regions. The mountainous hinterland of Ulster and Connacht, where monastic peace might have been assured, held few attractions (Fig. 4).

A good water supply was also essential and many of the Irish abbeys lie on the banks of major rivers, often where they are joined by tributaries. Bective is on the Boyne, both Holycross and Inislounaght are beside the Suir, and Graiguenamanagh is on the Barrow. These rivers were major traffic arteries and the monasteries were not therefore immune from the commercial world outside their walls. Water was required not just for drinking, but also for flushing the drains and driving the mills. A good river might additionally provide fish to sustain the diet of the monks, though the eating of fish was not officially sanctioned until the thirteenth century. At several monasteries the water source now seems inadequate, as at Kilcooly and Abbeydorney, where local streams furnish little more than a sluggish trickle. Kilcooly may have been served by a lake to the east of the abbey and at Abbeydorney the flat, exposed terrain has apparently been altered by peat cutting. Also low-lying is the monastery at Hore, which was built in what has been described as 'an alluvial meadow flat through which creeps, rather than runs an insignificant stream'.[5] More puzzling is Corcomroe, for there is no trace of a river or stream in the vicinity (Pl. 16). The limestone of the region is porous and it is possible that the monastic water supply has now gone underground. Westropp reported the existence of a 'well named Tobersheela' which 'gushes out of the crag in the enclosure to the south-east' and this or another well may have been exploited by the monks.[6] Dependence on a well was, however, cumbersome and not typical of Cistercian practice. Elsewhere, a superabundance of water provided problems and at Abbeyknockmoy and Monasteranenagh there are signs that the monks were alive to the dangers of flooding. At both abbeys the buildings were erected a little

15   The south arcade at Boyle (c1180), built with finely dressed local sandstone.

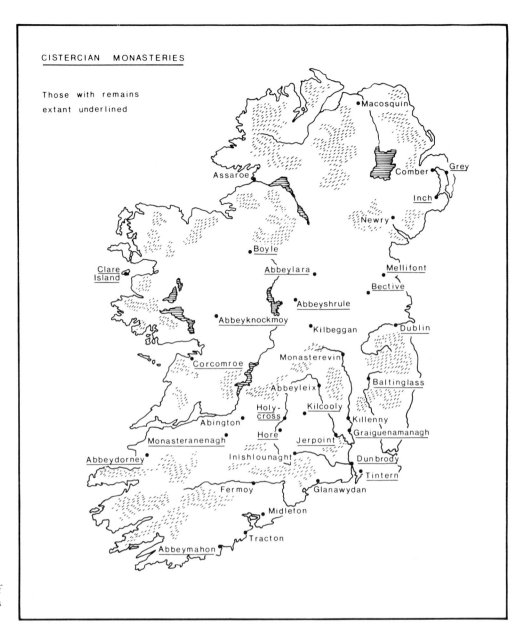

CISTERCIAN MONASTERIES

Those with remains
extant underlined

Fig. 4 Map showing the distribution of Cistercian monasteries (mountainous regions are indicated by hatching).

way from the neighbouring streams on slightly rising ground. At Boyle the swift flowing river is perilously near the south range and the monastery was only a few feet above the banks. It is no surprise to read that in 1471, following a hail storm with lightning and thunder, 'a boat could have floated over the floor of the great church of the monks'.[7] Similar difficulties existed at Graiguenamanagh. Although the church here was placed well above the broad waters of the river Barrow, some of the conventual buildings were on lower ground and in 1475 it was reported that a flood inundated the abbot's garden and the floor of the infirmary chapel.[8]

Another obvious necessity was sufficient level ground to lay out the monastic buildings. At Mellifont there were serious problems on this score, for the valley of the Mattock is relatively narrow. When the church was under construction, it proved necessary to cut away some of the rocky hillside in order to provide space for the presbytery; to the west, where the ground sloped down towards the river, a crypt was erected in order to keep the building level.[9]

When the site of a monastery was being surveyed, some thought must also have been given to the availability of building materials. The most immediate need was timber, but in the heavily-wooded landscape of twelfth-century Ireland this is unlikely to have raised problems. Equally important in the long term was the availability of stone. A major difference from England was the lack of well-established quarries, turning out good quality building stone and before the

16 Corcomroe Abbey, where there appears
to be no stream to provide water in the
immediate vicinity.

17 Monasteranenagh, with the River Mague
flowing to the north of the abbey. The outline
of the claustral buildings, largely invisible on
the ground, can be seen clearly from the air.

advent of the Cistercians, the demand for ashlar in Ireland was very limited. Apart from the stone forts of the west, secular building in stone was rare and only modest amounts were required for the round towers and small churches of the ancient Irish monasteries. In many cases the Cistercians opened up their own quarries. At Mellifont the early buildings were constructed largely of rubble, consisting of slate rock quarried in the area immediately around the monastery. Remains of quarrying are still visible near the gatehouse. For the finer dressed work a rather hard, quartzy sandstone was employed, the source of which is unknown, but it was far from ideal for it did not lend itself to precise and smooth carving. At Boyle a far better sandstone was available and this helps to account for the excellent sculpture and dressed masonry which adorns the abbey buildings (Pl. 15). When the site of the monastery was selected in 1161, it is tempting to suppose that the supply of good local stone was regarded as a major advantage. The consistent use of local stone gives each abbey its own character and nowhere is this more apparent than at Corcomroe. The grey limestone of the Burren, with its clear horizontal bedding, is easily quarried in convenient blocks nearby. The stone is hard and tough to work, but it produces exceedingly sharp details and to this day the mouldings and capitals retain their original crispness. In some cases stone was brought from further afield, and, as it was easier to transport by water, those monasteries on the banks of navigable rivers had a decided advantage. Dunbrody and Graiguenamanagh were ideally situated from this point of view and both abbeys employ substantial quantities of fine yellow limestone brought across the Irish Sea from quarries at Dundry, just outside Bristol.[10] In these instances the availability of water transport and good communications with England must have been an attraction when the site was chosen. Dundry stone was also used at Tintern, St Mary's, Dublin, Jerpoint and Mellifont. In the latter case the nearest navigable river was the Boyne, over two miles away, but in the other three cases stone could have been unloaded beside the monastery walls.

Apart from the need for a good water supply, there were other, less utilitarian, benefits to be derived from founding a monastery in a valley. This was where the most sheltered and attractive scenery was to be found and it is hard to deny that sheer beauty of the environment may have influenced the choice of some sites. Walter Daniel's description of Rievaulx, a wonderful evocation of the landscape surrounding the Yorkshire abbey, reveals how sensitive the early Cistercians were to the beauties of the natural world:

> The spot was by a powerful stream called the Rie in a broad valley stretching on either side. . . . High hills surround the valley, encircling it like a crown. These are clothed by trees of various sorts and maintain in pleasant retreats the privacy of the vale, providing for the monks a kind of second paradise of wooded delight.[11]

Isolation from society, land which could be cultivated, a good water supply, level ground for building and the availability of timber and stone, these therefore were some of the factors which influenced the selection of sites. As frequently happened elsewhere in Europe, not every community made the correct choice first time and there are at least three examples of false starts. In his studies of English abbeys, R. A. Donkin has analysed the reasons that lay behind the change of locations, showing that for the most part it was dissatisfaction with environmental conditions that prompted the moves.[12] An inadequate water supply, sites that were too exposed or too wet, land that was poorly drained, all were motives for transferring the community to a new spot. The fact that only three or four Irish communities were forced to make such transfers, in contrast to more than thirty in England and Wales, is perhaps indicative of the wider choice of site that was available in the undeveloped landscape of Ireland. The monks who eventually settled at Boyle in 1161 had tried three previous locations, but there is no evidence to show what necessitated the upheavals; interference from the lay world outside or the unsuitability of the terrain are both possibilities. The monks of Graiguenamanagh had experimented with two earlier sites before they eventually settled on the banks of the Barrow at Duiske. One of the previous locations was Annamult, only three miles from Jerpoint. As the statutes of the order expressly stated that new monasteries should not be founded within twelve Burgundian leagues of another,[13] this site was illegal and almost certain to lead to friction. The need to move must

18 The site of Aghamanister (Cork) abandoned some time before 1278 when the monks moved to the new monastery of Abbeymahon nearby.

have soon become apparent. The fact that Jerpoint was an Irish foundation and Graiguenamanagh was Anglo-Norman gave added piquancy to the dispute. After this unsatisfactory beginning, the relationship between the two monasteries continued to be strained and in 1228 the tensions developed into a long-running feud over the ownership of the dissolved abbey of Killenny.[14] The third community with a peripatetic start was Abington. This was a daughter house of the great English monastery of Furness and originally the monks established themselves at Wyresdale in Lancashire. Shortly before 1204 the community moved to Ireland, after Theobald Walter granted the island of Arklow to the Cistercians.[15] This rather exposed site on the east coast proved unsatisfactory and one year later the monks made their third move, this time across the country to Abington in County Limerick. The communities of Boyle, Graiguenamanagh and Abington all abandoned their initial sites within a few years, but almost a century elapsed before the monks of Aghamanister (later Abbeymahon) decided to move to a 'new monastery' less than two miles away[16] (Pl. 18) The new site was so close to the old that local political tensions are unlikely to have played any part in the change. It is possible that the time had come to renew the abbey buildings and the monks took the opportunity of finding a more convenient site with more space. It was about this time that the monks of Bective contemplated an even more dramatic move, from Meath to the diocese of Cashel, but the proposal in this instance came to nothing.

The choosing of sites

In one specific case it is possible to get a glimpse of the way a prospective site was surveyed. In 1171–5, a grant of land on which Dunbrody was later founded was given to the English abbot of Buildwas by Hervé de Montmorency. Subsequently, a laybrother, Alan, was sent to Ireland to take a look at the new endowment. When he arrived, he discovered 'a place of vast solitude' and he was forced to take up residence in a hollow oak tree. His impressions of the site were decidedly unpromising and when he had carried out his inspection he returned to Buildwas 'with haste'. There he reported on 'the desolation of the place, the sterility of the lands, and the wildness and ferocity of the barbarous inhabitants'. Faced with this evidence, the monastery of

19 Dunbrody, where the site, 'a place of vast solitude', was surveyed in 1171–5 by Alan, a laybrother from Buildwas, who took up residence in a hollow oak tree.

20 Tintern, founded at the head of a coastal inlet on the shores of Bannow Bay.

Buildwas showed no interest in sending a community there.[17] Alan's assessment of the land was, however, inadequate and partisan, and Dunbrody eventually became one of the more prosperous Cistercian monasteries in Ireland. His judgement was probably coloured by the hostility of the local population. The area had just been conquered by the Anglo–Normans and the native Irish were not likely to be friendly to a wandering English laybrother, whose monastery claimed to own the land. In 1182 the abbot of Buildwas relinquished the site to

St Mary's, Dublin, who sent a colony of monks there soon afterwards. By this time the conquest of Leinster was eleven years old and the local situation perhaps more stable and secure.

The sending of a suitably qualified laybrother to make an advanced inspection was probably a common procedure in the twelfth century. After 1194 the General Chapter decided to send two abbots to inspect all sites which were being offered to the Order. Thus in 1199, when William Marshal requested permission to found a monastery at Tintern, the abbots of Mellifont and St Mary's, Dublin, were asked to make diligent enquiries concerning the construction of the abbey and to report back the following year.[18] Their opinion was favourable and the new community was established in the autumn of 1200.[19] The same process can be followed for several other houses. An unusual case arose in the 1230s when Hugh de Lacy, earl of Ulster, donated lands at Ballymascanlon and petitioned the General Chapter for a monastery to be founded there. The abbots of Inch, Grey and Comber were appointed as inspectors in 1233. For some reason they failed to submit a report and so the General Chapter asked them to carry out the task again in 1234 and again in 1235. Still no report materialised. In 1236 an order was sent for the punishment of the three abbots, providing they had been duly informed of their allotted task.[20] The full circumstances of the affair remain unclear. No monastery was founded at Ballymascanlon and the grant was subsequently used to augment the landed endowment of Mellifont.[21]

In the case of the Anglo-Norman abbeys most of the donations of property were more or less spontaneous gifts from noblemen, anxious to have English Cistercian monks on their lands. In the earlier Irish houses, however, the initiative for new foundations appears to have come chiefly from within the Order itself, due to the pressure of numbers. In these instances the monks themselves must have approached lords and chieftains for suitable endowment. This was how the site at Mellifont was chosen. Malachy of Armagh apparently made the crucial decisions, following a letter he received about 1141 from St Bernard urging him to 'look for and prepare a site similar to what you have seen here, far removed from the turmoil of the world'.[22] Presumably it was Malachy who negotiated with Donough O'Carroll for the release of the land and it was the archbishop who must have approved the exact location of the monastery, prior to the arrival of the monks in 1142.

The site chosen by Malachy was almost ideal, a secluded valley, furnishing peace, shelter, fresh running water and some potentially good arable land. Not all Irish abbeys were so fortunate. Abbeyknockmoy lies in an open valley, exposed to the winds sweeping eastwards from the Connemara mountains, and much of the surrounding land is little more than heath and bog. Even more desolate is Corcomroe, founded in the bleak terrain of northern Clare (Pl. 21). The limestone hills and mountains which enclose the monastery are devoid of vegetation, and

21 Corcomroe Abbey in its bleak setting in the Burren, desolate enough to satisfy 'the cravings of an Egyptian anchorite'.

on dull, misty days, so common in that area, the walls of the abbey almost merge with the rocky surroundings. The land immediately around the precinct is greener but cultivation can never have been easy. As Canon Power commented, the desolation was sufficient to satisfy 'the cravings of an Egyptian anchorite'.[23]

Corcomroe and Abbeyknockmoy were among the few Cistercian houses to be founded on the poorer soils of the west of Ireland. The situation of the three major Anglo-Norman houses in the south-east presents an enormous contrast. Tintern lies at the head of a quiet coastal inlet on the shores of Bannow Bay and the setting of the ruins is extremely romantic, with clusters of woodland nearby and a fast flowing stream rushing down towards Bannow Bay (Pl. 20). Here is all the solitude and natural beauty beloved by the Cistercians. A few miles away is Dunbrody, where the site surveyed by Alan of Buildwas lies close to the broad estuary known as Waterford harbour. Originally the monastery was surrounded on three sides by tidal waters, but those to the south have now been reclaimed. Twenty miles upstream amidst woodlands on the Barrow is Graiguenamanagh or Duiske, one of the largest of the Irish monasteries. The setting is now obscured by the town which has grown up around the ruins but it is not difficult to appreciate the original advantages of the site. The river curves through a deep valley and in places its banks are still thickly lined with trees. The monastery was built at a point where it is joined by a tributary, the Duiske, which has given its name to the abbey. Before the days of urban development, the setting must have had all the natural beauty of Rievaulx or Fountains, though the first reports of the site were almost as discouraging as those made about Dunbrody. In a letter to the abbot of Citeaux and the General Chapter in 1204, Hugh de Rous, bishop of Kilkenny, described it as 'a place of horror and of vast solitude, a cave of robbers, and the lair of those who lie in wait for blood',[24] a lurid account, which, though coloured by anti-Irish prejudice, underlines the wildness of the terrain into which the Cistercians ventured.

The sites of the Irish houses thus vary considerably, from the mountainous environment of Corcomroe to the sylvan beauty of Tintern. The judicious choice of localities meant that many abbeys later became the focus of towns and villages, which have obliterated the original tranquillity. In towns like Newry, Comber, Kilbeggan and Fermoy, traces of the monastery have long since vanished. In most instances the towns developed into major settlements only after the dissolution, but one monastery was placed in an urban environment from the start. This was St Mary's, Dublin, founded in 1139 on the north bank of the River Liffey, immediately opposite the flourishing Hiberno-Norse trading port. The explanation for this unusual position is that the abbey belonged, in its first eight years, to the Order of Savigny and the rigorous Cistercian rules about the location of monasteries did not apply.[25] It was an unsatisfactory setting for a Cistercian house and on occasions the excitement of city life, particularly the taverns, proved irresistible to the abbot and monks.[26] The internal peace of the monastery was also, at times, shattered by political events of great moment. Shortly before the dissolution, in the year 1534, the chapter house of St Mary's provided the setting for Silken Thomas to renounce his loyalty to the Crown, the start of his ill-fated rebellion against Tudor rule in Ireland. The abbey was situated only a few hundred yards from the seat of royal administration in Dublin Castle, conveniently close in fact for government records to be stored within the monastic buildings. The eventful history of St Mary's confirmed the wisdom of Cistercian statutes regarding location and it is surprising that its situation was never questioned. In 1228, Stephen of Lexington contemplated moving the entire monastery of Mellifont to a new site,[27] but he raised no objections to St Mary's, Dublin. In the early years the political strength of the former Savigniac houses within the Order may have protected it, and after the invasion of 1170 its position was guaranteed by unswerving loyalty to the English colony.

At least five Cistercian abbeys were founded in places which already had monastic associations, though there is no evidence to suggest that older communities were still active when the monks arrived. The most remarkable example concerns the monastery at Inch. This was founded by John de Courcy, probably in 1187, and the buildings were established on an island surrounded partly by marshes and partly by the waters of the River Quoile. This physical isolation was well suited to the Cistercians but recent investigation has revealed that they were

22 Inch Abbey. The Cistercian ruins lie amidst the trees near the top of the photograph and, below, the outer bank of the old monastery of Inis Cumhscraigh can be discerned.

23 Kilcooly, showing the 'ring work' just to the east of the Cistercian ruins.

not the first monks to occupy the site.[28] An aerial photograph shows traces of an earthen bank to the north of the ruins, the remnants of an earlier monastic enclosure (Pl. 22). This was the ancient monastery of Inis Cumhscraigh, the last mention of which occurred in 1153. In 1177 the surrounding district was conquered by John de Courcy and the monastery may have been destroyed or abandoned during the military upheavals. At Boyle, the Cistercian monastery apparently occupied the site of an obscure foundation known as Ath-da-Larc.[29]

Three other abbeys founded on ancient monastic sites were Kilbeggan, Monasterevan and Comber, but at all three, the medieval buildings, both Celtic and Cistercian, have long since been demolished.[30] The introduction of the Cistercians was a way of reactivating defunct monastic communities and local acceptability was perhaps easier when the site already had a religious tradition.

Aerial photography has also provided clues to the early history of Kilcooly. A short distance to the east of the church are the unmistakable marks of a circular enclosure, perhaps the site of an early farmstead or rath[31] (Pl. 23). Beyond the enclosure lies an imposing neo-classical house, the work of those who inherited the monastic domains. Here a vast span of history is covered in a single glance, with three contrasting forms of settlement leaving their mark on the landscape.

Once a suitable tract of land had been assigned, it had to be prepared for the arrival of the monks. One of the most important early Cistercian documents, the *Carta Caritatis*, insisted that 'No abbot shall be sent to a new place without at least twelve monks and . . . without the prior construction of such places as an oratory, a refectory, a dormitory, a guest house, and a gatekeeper's cell, so that the monks may immediately serve God and live in religious discipline.'[32] In some cases it seems that an advance guard of laybrothers was sent to clear the site and erect the necessary temporary buildings. In a few instances the patron himself organised the work, as Donough O'Carroll did at Mellifont in 1141/2. The delays in preparing a site may explain the inconsistencies recorded in the foundation dates of some abbeys. At Inch seven years elapsed before the site was occupied (1180–7) and there was a four year gap at Abbeylara (1210–

14). Once the monks arrived, it is likely that a year or two passed before they began to turn their thoughts to the erection of permanent buildings in stone. The organisation of land and the cultivation of crops formed the most pressing need and it would have been unwise to embark on expensive building programmes before there was absolute confidence in the suitability of the site.

Having deliberated carefully over where to locate their monasteries, official Latin names for them were chosen with great care. The twelfth-century chronicler, Ordericus Vitalis, explained how the monks thoughtfully provided their abbeys 'with holy names, such as Maison-Dieu, Clairvaux, Bonmont, and L'Aumone and others of the like kind, so that the sweet sound of the name alone invites all who hear to hasten and discover for themselves how great the blessedness must be which is described by so rare a name'.[33] Not all the Irish titles have religious connotations and many were inspired by the local environment. Some represent the latinisation of local rivers, as at Boyle (*Buellium*), Monasteranenagh (*Magium*), Inislounaght (*Surium*), and Assaroe (*Samarium*). The latter name is particularly interesting with its similarity to biblical Samaria, though the name appears to be derived from the River Samhair, the local name for the River Erne. Jerpoint (*Jeripons*) presumably refers to a bridge over the River Eoir, which flows past the west end of the abbey and the title of Midleton—*Chorus Sancti Benedicti*—was perhaps a play on the Irish word 'cora' or weir, the local river being called the Owenacurra. Comber or *Comar* is taken from the Irish word 'comar' meaning a confluence of two streams. Newry was known as *Viride Lignum*, the green tree, after a yew said to have been planted by St Patrick. Hore was succinctly described as *Rupes*, the rock, on account of its position at the foot of the Rock of Cashel. The Latin name of Kilcooly, *Arvus Campus*, the arable plain, suitably recalls the farming expertise of the order. Monasterevan was called *Rosea Vallis*, the blooming valley, a title adapted from the old name of the place, Rosglas, meaning green copse. Tracton, on the coast of County Cork, ingeniously produced a variant of its mother house, *Alba Landa* or Whitland, by styling itself *Albus Tractus*, the white coast. This could be taken as a reference to the sandy beaches nearby, but it is more likely to be a reference to the monks themselves in their white Cistercian habits. Most eloquent of all was the name of Corcomroe, *Petra Fertilis*, the fertile rock. In a few cases a reference to the location was combined with a dedicatory formula: Abbeyshrule, *Flumen Dei*, the river of God; Fermoy, *Castrum Dei*, the camp of God; Dunbrody, *Portus S. Mariae*, the harbour of St Mary. The name of Mellifont, *Fons Mellis*, the fount of honey, alludes to the purity and sweetness of Cistercian life, a particularly beautiful use of pastoral imagery.[34] Most of the other names follow more straightforward mystical forms: Bective, *Beatitudo Dei*, the blessedness of God; Kilbeggan, *Benedictio Dei*, the blessing of God; Abbeydorney, *Kyrie Eleison*. More unusual is *Votum* or the vow, the name for Tintern, preserving memories of the oath taken by William Marshal when in peril on the Irish Sea.

Following Cistercian custom, the abbeys were dedicated to the Virgin Mary, though several had an additional dedication to St Benedict. The reference to St Benedict has caused confusion in the writings of some scholars, who have assumed erroneously that these abbeys were originally Benedictine and not Cistercian foundations.[35] (The disputed houses are Jerpoint, Killenny, Newry, Monasterevan, Kilcooly and Holycross.) At Jerpoint the Cistercian origin is confirmed by the layout and plans of the monastic buildings, which from the start contained Cistercian proportional formulae. There is only one proven example of the white monks replacing Benedictines and this took place at Cashel in 1272.[36] David MacCarville archbishop of Cashel, is said to have dreamt that the Benedictine monks who served his cathedral were plotting to cut off his head and with understandable speed he banished them from the rock. Whether his alarming nightmare was true or not, the archbishop was already deeply attached to the Cistercians several years before his new monastery was founded at Hore in 1272. In 1269 he himself had taken the Cistercian habit. The full circumstances of the affair remain unclear and, in the complex politics of thirteenth-century Ireland, there may have been much more to the story.

*　　　*　　　*

The labour force

Ordericus Vitalis has explained that the early Cistercians were accustomed to build their 'monasteries with their own hands in lonely and wooded places'.[37] The second part of his statement is largely true, but the first needs considerable qualification. The vision of monks and laybrothers toiling ceaselessly together to construct churches and monastic buildings is a romantic exaggeration, true only for the first few years of a community's existence. Manual labour was an essential ingredient of the Cistercian way of life and on occasions the choir monks must have played their part in erecting the temporary wooden structures which preceded the stone buildings. They also exercised close supervision over matters of planning and architectural form. Most of the physical effort, however, fell on the shoulders of the laybrothers, supplemented, when resources allowed, by hired labour.[38] By the middle of the thirteenth century there is plenty of evidence to show that most building was being carried out by teams of professional masons. The names of only a few Cistercian builders emerge from the sterile documentary record. By far the most interesting is the monk Robert, sent by St Bernard to Mellifont, in order to assist with 'the buildings and other things necessary for the wellbeing' of the house.[39] It has been assumed in the past that Robert was in effect the architect of Mellifont, though that is perhaps reading too much into St Bernard's statement. Clearly he advised on architectural matters and it was presumably Robert who was responsible for the many Burgundian elements in the design. This was not the only case of an architectural supremo being sent out from Clairvaux. Nine years before, in 1133, Geoffrey d'Ainai had been sent to Fountains and in 1138 Achard was despatched to the German monastery of Himmerod.[40] How long Robert stayed at Mellifont we do not know and the destruction of the church makes it difficult to assess his contribution. In a land without a tradition of monumental architecture, Robert's presence was probably very necessary.

The only other hint of direct involvement by a monk comes many decades later at Boyle. In 1230 the annals record the death of Donnsleibhe O hInmhainén, 'a holy monk and chief master of the carpenters'.[41] Whether Donnsleibhe was a skilled craftsman himself or merely a supervisor remains open to doubt. Nonetheless, it suggests the monks continued to exert responsibility for the detailed organisation of building activities, even if their own hands were rarely soiled by manual tasks. The officer most likely to be concerned with architectural projects was the cellarer, whose duties lay with finance and the general administration of the monastery. It was to the cellarer that Stephen of Lexington addressed some of his comments in 1228, when organising the building priorities of one of the Leinster abbeys. In particular the cellarer was asked to supply lead sufficient for roofing the north part of the church.[42] Elsewhere in Stephen's instructions, there is mention of a *custos operis* or keeper of the works, who was also one of the monks.[43] As in non-monastic projects, the keeper of the works was the chief organiser of building schemes. When substantial building was in progress, it was probably a common practice for one of the brethren to take over this responsibility.

Supervision should not, however, be confused with design. Apart perhaps from Robert at Mellifont, there is no evidence to suggest that monks actually carried out architectural tasks. The drawing of moulding profiles, the design of doors and windows, decisions about the height of the elevation or the thickness of walls—all were technical jobs which required the services of a professional mason. In the early years this may have necessitated a big drive to recruit skilled masons and carpenters into the monastery as laybrothers, and this could explain why carved details at Baltinglass are so close in style to those found in the nearby Romanesque churches at Glendalough and Killeshin. But it is equally possible that even at this early stage outside craftsmen were being employed by the monks. This certainly happened a few years later at Boyle. Here decisive changes of style in the church indicate the presence of different individuals, all of whom were well informed about developments in the west of England. If the monastery had produced its own masons, it is likely that the style would have been more local in flavour and more consistent throughout the church. The west bays and west facade (c1215–20) (Pl. 24) are so close to work carried out at Christ Church, Dublin, that a mason from Christ Church

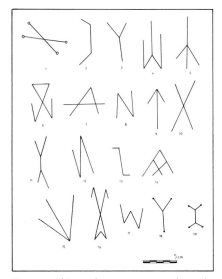

24 Boyle Abbey seen from the west. The design of this part of the church (c1215–20) includes many details akin to those in Christ Church Cathedral, Dublin.

Fig. 5 Thirteenth-century masons' marks from Mellifont.

must have made the journey to Connacht to execute it. One of the sculptors who worked on this last campaign at Boyle was also employed at the Augustinian abbey of Ballintober.[44] If he was a Cistercian laybrother, he was guilty of infringing the statute of 1157, which forbade members of Cistercian communities from working on projects outside the Order.[45] It seems more likely that he was in fact a layman.

An impressive team of professional masons was employed on the thirteenth-century reconstruction of Mellifont. Although the abbey church is completely ruined, many of the individual stones which survive are furnished with conspicuous masons' marks (Fig. 5). The exact function of masons' marks is still controversial. Obviously they were used to identify the work of a particular mason, but whether for the purposes of payment or to exercise some form of quality control is debatable.[46] On the thirteenth-century masonry at Mellifont there are eighteen masons' marks, most repeated many times, and they provide a clue to the size of the workforce. Not all the masons may have been working simultaneously, but on the other hand not all the marks may have survived. The figure of eighteen could, therefore, provide a rough indication of the number of skilled masons employed at any one time.[47] This seems a plausible figure for one of the more ambitious projects undertaken by the Cistercians. The presence of masons' marks is a reliable indication of professional workmen from outside the Order. They first appear in Ireland after the Anglo-Norman invasion and they can be found in several Cistercian buildings of the thirteenth century besides Mellifont, notably Boyle, Abbeyknockmoy, Inch, Grey, Graiguenamanagh, Hore and Bective. This wide distribution proves that manual involvement by monks in the construction of monasteries was a thing of the past, if

42

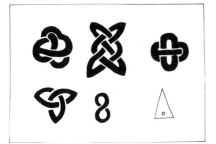

Fig. 6   Masons' marks from Hore Abbey.

25   A fifteenth-century mason's mark from Holycross, carved as a veritable piece of sculpture in contrast to marks of previous centuries.

Fig. 7   Masons' marks from Holycross Abbey. Some are merely incised lines, others are sculptured in relief.

Fig. 8.   Masons' marks from Kilcooly.

indeed it had ever existed. Unfortunately the names of individual masons are rarely recorded and when they are known it is not possible to associate them with any extant work. There was, for example, William *cementarius* who witnessed a charter of St Mary's Abbey, Dublin, around 1240–3[48] and Stephen *cementarius* who about 1280 witnessed two of the charters of Graiguenamanagh.[49] The charters of St Mary's also furnish the names of Mainard *carpentarius*, Alexander *carpentarius*, Magdan *carpentarius*, Roger *carpentarius*, Hugo de Carpinter and Richard *cementarius*.[50] There is, however, no certain proof that any of them were employed on the monastery's buildings. More explicit is a mid-thirteenth century charter which refers to a property owned by Master Walter, mason of St Mary's Abbey, next to Dublin.[51] Walter appears to have been a permanent employee of the monastery and obviously a layman.

In the later middle ages the only hint of individual personalities is again to be found in masons' marks. The fifteenth-century work at Holycross has a splendid array, many of them deeply cut designs with floral and interlace motifs. These are veritable pieces of sculpture which, unlike the earlier marks, were meant to be visible in the completed building (Pl. 25, Fig. 7). There are over twenty different motifs altogether and they clearly served more than a crude administrative function. It is hard to avoid the impression that they are emblems or personal memorials, designed to record for posterity the achievement of the masons who worked the stone. The reconstruction of Holycross was the most lavish architectural undertaking of late medieval Ireland and the evidence of the marks suggests that it was carried out by a team of approximately twenty masons. A few of the same marks reappear in Cistercian churches nearby, on the crossing tower at Hore and in the east end of Kilcooly (Figs 6, 8). Here the range of marks is more restricted and it is important to remember that the number of masons employed on most building schemes must often have dropped to single figures. The total labour force, however, would have been larger, when carpenters, labourers, tilers, glaziers and plumbers were added to the list.

The progress and sequence of building

For those monks willing and brave enough to leave the shelter of a well-established house, the foundation of a new abbey was a tough and uncomfortable ordeal. Temporary huts of timber and wattle had to suffice for the first few years and sometimes decades elapsed before the brethren slept in a stone-built dormitory or ate in a stone-built refectory. It is easy to forget that an early Cistercian monk spent much of his life in the middle of a building site. Construction was slow, often desperately slow, and only a few abbeys had the resources to accelerate the process. When the church at Boyle was consecrated in 1218 or 1220,[52] almost sixty years had passed since the first stones had been laid. The slow progress documented at Boyle is supported elsewhere by the evidence of style. At Jerpoint the details of pier forms and window mouldings at the west

end are far in advance of those in the presbytery. The church was begun soon after 1160 but clearly not finished until c1200–10.[53] There are signs that the construction of Baltinglass was not quite so leisurely, but the fastest Cistercian building on record was the church at Mellifont, consecrated in 1157, only fifteen years after the foundation of the abbey.[54] Even by European standards, this was moderately quick. The Burgundian abbey of Fontenay is said to have been erected in the eight years between 1139 and 1147, but here there was a massive injection of funds from Bishop Evrard of Norwich and other benefactors. It has been calculated that nineteen years was about the European average for a Cistercian church.[55] The evidence suggests that few Irish houses approached this figure and the exceptional speed at Mellifont was probably achieved only through the assistance of Donough O'Carroll. His obituary notice in the Antiphonary of Armagh claims that it was he who 'founded the entire monastery both [as to] stone and wood',[56] a statement which implies that he provided the materials and possibly labour too.

Several factors contributed to the slow rates of construction in Ireland, not least a scarcity of resources. As the general level of endowment was lower than that in France and England, the relative size of communities was correspondingly small. Much depended on the efforts of the laybrothers, but they had other responsibilities besides building and in the early days of a monastery there was little surplus income with which to hire masons and labourers from outside the abbey. It is significant that Mellifont, one of the few houses with wealth, was able to maintain three hundred laybrothers in 1170 and its buildings were erected with great speed. Many communities, impatient to complete their buildings, were tempted to borrow funds. While this might produce sudden spurts of progress, it was no substitute for a large regular income. The accumulation of debts was debated on several occasions at the General Chapter in the 1180s and 1190s,[57] but the statutes enacted appear to have had little effect in Ireland.

In some cases the architectural ambitions of the monks were not consistent with the resources available. Projects begun in great style ended in rudimentary fashion, as at Abbeyknockmoy and Corcomroe. In the latter case the decline in workmanship was catastrophic, a change brought about by some material crisis that hit the abbey when the church was about half built. It is likely that the disruption was associated with the famine and political unrest that seriously affected the neighbouring districts of Connacht in 1227–8, as the annals record: 'Famine in Connacht this year; and its churches and lay properties were plundered and its clerics and craftsmen driven to far foreign regions, having been exposed to cold and hunger through the war of Ruaidhri's sons at the time.'[58] Skilled masons from Corcomroe may have been among the craftsmen driven away to 'far foreign regions', wherever they were (England?). Whatever the nature of the disaster, the monastery was henceforward sunk in poverty and the distinguished architecture at the east end of the church serves as the only reminder of three decades of optimism and prosperity.

War was another potential cause of disruption. Boyle suffered particularly badly, for the monastery was raided and occupied twice in the early thirteenth century. The first attack came in 1202, when the monks were still heavily involved in building. The abbey was seized by an alliance of English and Irish troops under the command of William de Burgh and Cathal Crovderg O'Conor. The author of the annals of Loch Cé, full of ecclesiastical indignation, gave a detailed account of what happened:

> . . . and they were three days in it, so that they polluted and defiled the entire monastery; and such was the extent of the defilement that the mercenaries of the army had the women in the hospital of the monks, and in the houses of the cloister, and in every place in the entire monastery besides. No structure in the monastery was left without breaking and burning, except the roofs of the houses alone; and even of those a great portion was broken and burned. No part of the buildings of the entire monastery was allowed to the monks and brothers, excepting only the dormitory of the monks and the house of the novices. A stone wall was commenced by William Burk, round the great stone house of the guests, and two days work was devoted to its erection.[59]

While allowing for exaggeration, provoked by the annalist's sense of outrage, damage to the monastery—both moral and physical—was obviously extensive. Architectural priorities must have been altered, as the monks sought to repair their half-ruined buildings. The speed with which William de Burgh built a defensive wall around the guest house suggests that, at the time of the occupation, a convenient supply of stone was lying around waiting to be used. It is impossible to know how long it was before the monks resumed their normal programme of building, but here at least is one well-documented incident which slowed down the rate of construction in an Irish monastery. War, inadequate endowment, poor harvests, over-grandiose plans, each contributed in various ways to the desultory rate of construction, but of all the factors involved, lack of basic income was undoubtedly the most significant.

In the later middle ages several monasteries looked beyond their own resources to finance building projects. The offering of indulgences in return for contributions was a method well-tried throughout Europe and it was a scheme exploited by Abbeylara in 1411 and Jerpoint in 1442.[60] Unfortunately there is no evidence to show how successful it was as a fund-raising device. Holycross sent preachers into the countryside to beg for money[61] and no doubt other monasteries did likewise. A sizable income was acquired by Holycross in the fifteenth century, some of which was derived from gifts from the earls of Ormond and some from 'the offerings made at the wood of the holy cross', the abbey's precious relic.[62] The possession of the relic gave a considerable boost to the coffers of the monastery and it was one of the assets which enabled the monks to embark on their ambitious campaign of rebuilding.

In a number of Irish monasteries a stone church was started within a few years of the establishment of the community (Mellifont, Baltinglass, Jerpoint, Grey, Graiguenamanagh and Hore), but elsewhere two or three decades passed by before this happened (Monasteranenagh, Dunbrody, Inch, Corcomroe and Abbeyknockmoy). The design of the presbytery and transepts at Inch appears to belong to the years around 1200, ten years or so after the founding monks had arrived from Furness.[63] The Cistercians may have made temporary use of an earlier Romanesque church at the site, belonging to the defunct monastery of Inis Cumhscraigh, a possibility that has been heightened by the discovery of a piece of twelfth-century chevron ornament, which pre-dates the Cistercian buildings. At Dunbrody as much as thirty years may have elapsed before work began on the church and presumably some temporary wooden building must have sufficed during this time. At Bective and Tintern the original churches, whatever their form, were abandoned and replaced a century or more after foundation. There is scope for exciting archaeological work in this field and it is to be hoped that one day excavation will bring to light some evidence of the first transitory buildings of the order, along the lines of the remarkable discoveries at Fountains in England.[64]

In view of the delays which elapsed before the various permanent buildings were ready, the order in which they were built was an important consideration. There is plenty of evidence, both from Ireland and abroad, that shows that the eastern section of the church (the monks' choir) was usually given priority, followed by the eastern range of conventual buildings containing the chapter house and dormitory. This explains why there are often quite sharp stylistic breaks between the transepts and the nave of Cistercian churches.

Specific information about building exists amongst the comprehensive list of criticisms and instructions directed at Jerpoint and Graiguenamanagh by Stephen of Lexington in 1228. As the document is not well known, it is worth printing some of the relevant passages.[65] The orders are very specific and show how much attention Stephen paid to the detailed layout of the monastery. In view of this, it is unfortunate that the items cannot be securely related to one or other of the houses. The instructions reveal the range of buildings that existed in a large and flourishing house. Stephen made the following demands concerning art and architecture:[66]

> The house where the wine press has been erected should be separated from the infirmary courtyard by a good fence, and both the servants' entrance and the neighbouring door opposite the laybrothers' infirmary should be completely blocked up before the feast of St Denis (13).
> No building should henceforth be erected in the centre of the precinct of the abbey or of

the granges, but such buildings should be constructed along the sides in a circle on account of thieves and other dangers that might arise. Nor should any building in the abbey be covered except with a sound roof (21).

It is firmly ordered that all exits and entrances between the outer and inner courtyard should be completely blocked up except the great gate which is next to the kitchen (28).

No building should be erected in the granges except barns and animal sheds until the house is discharged from the burden of the debts, with which it is intolerably oppressed, and until the chapter house of the monks and the kitchen of the guest house are finished (36).

Before the feast of St Michael, a suitable place should be assigned for the nuns, where they can make their buildings and remain more virtuously in view of the complaints of Count Marshal (i.e. William Marshal the younger, earl of Leinster) and others. If they have not moved by then, for as long as they remain next to the abbey, we shall place the whole monastery under an interdict and we shall suspend from divine service persons belonging to the community (45).

It is strictly forbidden for any variety of paintings, or other marble objects (i.e. carvings) to be allowed in the church or other chambers, but the simplicity of the Order is to be observed. Otherwise the prior, cellarer, sacristan, and keeper of the works are to be on bread and water every Friday from the time of this presumptious behaviour until the next visitation at which time they will be punished more severely (70).

The buildings outside the gate should either be demolished or, before the feast of All Saints, put in order and blocked off with great care lest they offer an occasion for sin or a suspicion of wrong doing. Otherwise the cellarer and porter shall be on bread and water every Friday until the next visitation (78).

Diligence should be applied as circumstances demand that the stable should be enclosed within the abbey precincts according to the form of the Order on account of the innumerable expenses of the house and the grave danger to souls [i.e. of the monks?] (79).[67]

The cellarer should supply lead sufficient for roofing the north part of the church (82).

The tombs in the window of the chapter house should be placed together elsewhere according to the customary form (83).

No chapel or altar should be erected or allowed in the gatehouse and the building already begun should be finished in an honest fashion as quickly as possible. Otherwise the prior, porter, and sub-porter shall, from the time of the superfluous and useless labour, be on bread and water every Friday until the next visitation at which time they will be punished more severely (86).

The scriptorium within the enclosure of the novices should be moved and nothing else should henceforth be constructed there (92).

Instructions as detailed as these are unique in Ireland and rare elsewhere in Europe. In 1196 the French abbey of Fontfroide was reprimanded for having a carpet on the floor of the choir and for having too many lamps in the church, but these criticisms came from the General Chapter. Similarly it was the General Chapter that ordered the demolition of an inappropriate tower at Bohéries in Picardy in 1217.[68] These were negative decisions and the statutes of the order contain few positive regulations about architecture. In the absence of written rules, it has for long been unclear how the Cistercians managed to achieve so much standardisation. Stephen's visitation indicates that at a less formal level there were clearly understood conventions and practices that the monasteries were expected to follow and his report is a remarkable illustration of the way building was monitored at a local level. It is also a reminder of how much depended on the discrimination and authority of the visiting abbot.

Stephen's comments are in effect a critique of the layout of one of the Irish monasteries as it existed in 1228, embracing matters of both general policy and detail. His advice about placing outbuildings along the wall of the precinct (no. 21), in order to improve surveillance and prevent theft, is a typical example of Cistercian practicality and common sense. The reference to sound roofs reflects Cistercian stress on good quality methods of construction, as a way of

26 Jerpoint, the probable scene of Stephen of Lexington's scrupulous visitation in 1228.

guaranteeing solidity and permanence. It appears that in some of the ancillary buildings the monks had been trying to economise by using thatch or some other cheap method of roofing. Stephen's chief concern, however, was the relationship between the architecture of the abbey and the purity of Cistercian life. Thus the excessive number of entrances to the inner cloister (no. 28) was disturbing the atmosphere of tranquillity, so essential at the heart of the abbey. The criticisms of painting and sculpture are especially interesting, for they echo the statute which forbade such decoration in Cistercian churches, 'because while attention is paid to such things, the profit of godly meditation or the discipline of religious gravity is often neglected'.[69]

Although the documentary sources for Boyle are not extensive they provide some information about the order of the building. In 1202 the abbey already had a stone guest house, but the church itself was not finished for another sixteen years. Once again the completion of the nave, which housed the choir of the laybrothers, had a low priority. The eastern arm of the church was erected relatively soon after the foundation of the abbey in 1161 and the east range of the cloister appears to have followed not many years later. The switch in priorities, once the monks' choir was finished, helps to explain at least one of the stylistic breaks in the church at Boyle. This method of proceeding is not unique to Ireland and it can be paralleled, for example, at Buildwas in England, Nydala in Sweden and Lehnin in Germany.[70]

Materials

Cistercian abbeys are noted for the fine quality of their ashlar masonry and many of the more prosperous houses used it for general walling as well as for moulded features. Such expensive methods lay beyond the resources of the Irish monasteries, where the walls are invariably

27 Holycross Abbey, the north arcade of the nave before restoration. As was the case here, most Irish houses were content with walls built of rubble masonry.

28 Holycross Abbey, detail from the sedilia, constructed in the hard blue carboniferous limestone favoured by Irish masons after 1400.

constructed of rough undressed masonry, with ashlar reserved for piers, shafts, arch mouldings, etc. Despite this limitation, the standard of dressed stonework was often high. The precise jointing of the cylindrical piers in the south arcade at Boyle is worthy of the praise that William of Malmesbury lavished on Old Sarum, where the joints were almost invisible to the human eye.[71] The lavabo at Mellifont involved some extremely accomplished dressed masonry and a substantial proportion of the lower story is constructed of ashlar. The sandstone used, however, is not as tough as that at Boyle and centuries of weathering have reduced the precision of the joints. On the whole, oolitic limestone imported from Dundry was a more suitable material for complicated mouldings and this explains its popularity in the Anglo-Norman abbeys. The quality of masonry employed in the thirteenth-century presbytery at Mellifont was especially fine. But even a wealthy monastery like Mellifont could not afford to use ashlar for uncarved or unmoulded surfaces. In this respect the Irish monasteries follow a pattern found in the more remote parts of Europe, where building traditions were less sophisticated and large quarries had yet to be developed. The Swedish abbeys use rubble extensively, as do some of the monasteries of Wales and Brittany. From a visual point of view, this rather rough method of construction would not have been particularly noticeable, at least not from inside the buildings. Once plastered, whitewashed and marked out with false masonry joints, as was Cistercian custom, there would be little to show that the walls were not built of ashlar.

The best Irish building stone is the dark carboniferous limestone, found in many parts of the country. Although it was used occasionally in the twelfth and thirteenth centuries, as at Corcomroe and Abbeyknockmoy, it did not achieve widespread popularity until after 1400. It is much harder to work than normal medieval freestones, but when finely dressed the results are magnificent (Pl. 28). The smooth polished surfaces, with their sharply etched details, give a distinctive flavour to fifteenth-century architecture. Holycross, Kilcooly and Hore contain excellent examples, with stunning details as sharp today as when they left the masons' bench five hundred years ago.

In their present state of decay, it is easy to forget how much timber was required in the construction of a medieval monastery. Some was needed for scaffolding and a vast quantity was required for the roofs of the many buildings within the precinct. The charters of a monastery sometimes refer to the supply of wood. In his foundation charter of Graiguenamanagh, William Marshal allowed the monks to take from his forests whatever they needed for building and a few years later Richard de Marisco allowed them to take timber from his forests both for fuel and for constructing buildings.[72] Above the wooden frame, slates or tiles provided the normal covering. Many of the claustral buildings at Jerpoint were roofed with tiles and so too was the fifteenth-century cloister at Bective.[73] In a few select cases the church was roofed with lead, but this was a luxury available only to the wealthier monasteries. There are two documented examples of its use, at Graiguenamanagh or Jerpoint and St Mary's, Dublin.[74] In the latter instance it was paid for by Felix, archbishop of Tuam, who was buried in the monastery in 1238. Lead had been used occasionally for the pre-Romanesque churches of Ireland,[75] but the amount needed would have been small compared to the quantities required to cover the vast spaces of a Cistercian church. The source of the lead used is not known, but it was still available at various places in Leinster, including the valleys around Glendalough and the area around Clonmines (County Wexford), an ancient lead mining town.[76] Shingles and thatch, although far less permanent than lead or slates, were also found on occasions. They were probably common in the granges, and in at least two recorded instances, the same materials were employed to roof parts of the main monastery as well. In 1588–9 Assaroe was described as having 'a church and steeple, shingled and thatched'[77] and in 1620 the former monastery of Abbeyknockmoy was said to contain 'a hall of stone covered with shingles'.[78] As these latter references postdate the dissolution, it is possible that the roofs mentioned constituted repairs carried out at a relatively late stage in the monasteries' history. The use of such lightweight materials in the core of the monastery is surprising and it contradicts Stephen of Lexington's advice to ensure that all roofs were constructed in a secure fashion. The presence of thatch and shingles is perhaps another reflection of the poverty which beset so many of the Irish houses in the later middle ages.

48

Working methods

The relative simplicity of Cistercian building in Ireland would not have called for particularly sophisticated methods of design. In the twelfth century a general plan of a monastery might on occasions have been sketched at the start of work, but there is no evidence that specific details were worked out in advance. Problems were solved as they were encountered. Until the plan of a building was marked out on the ground with ropes and the line of the foundation trenches was cut on the turf, it is likely that the design remained an abstraction in the mind of the master mason. A great deal depended on his experience and foresight, qualities which, it must be reported, were not invariably present. There are many signs of what can only be described as a rather cavalier approach to construction and serious errors, particularly in setting out foundation walls, are not infrequent. At Boyle the presbytery is not accurately aligned to the rest of the church and in the first buildings at Mellifont the right angle was evidently not much admired. The east range of the cloister is misaligned by four degrees in relation to the church and the internal width of the church itself varies by over two feet.[79] The site at Mellifont, with bedrock so close to the surface, was difficult terrain for any builder and the mistakes, if not forgivable, are at least understandable. More blatant errors are visible at Corcomroe. The east crossing piers are not aligned to each other, which inevitably led to a twist in the main arch of the presbytery. A few yards away, the head of the east window is slightly cut and obscured by the line of the vault, a miscalculation which implies that the height of the vault was not accurately predicted in advance.[80]

It is ironic that these mistakes occurred at Corcomroe, for this is the only Irish abbey where some preparatory drawings survive. They are to be found incised on a surface of plaster on two walls within the church (Fig. 9). One set occurs on the north wall of the south transept chapel, the other on the north wall of the north transept. The first is little more than architectural graffiti, consisting chiefly of arcs, drawn with a large compass, the points of which are still visible on the base line.[81] Amongst the arcs are the profiles of three pointed arches. The largest is a five pointed arch, with a radius of 3 feet 5 inches (1.03 metres); the second is a three pointed arch, with a radius of 2 feet 1 inch (0.63 metres); the smallest is a two pointed arch, with a radius of 9 inches (0.24 metres).[82] The apexes of the three arches are not aligned and they do not appear to form part of an overall design. As well as the arcs, there are various architectural 'doodles', including what looks like the profile of a chamfered pier. The drawings are evidently tentative experiments, almost a series of exercises. The outer arch, however, is large enough to have served as a model for a template, from which the stones for the rere arch of a window could have been cut. Most of the other lines are too abbreviated for their purpose to be discerned.

The drawing in the north transept is different in character and forms a coherent design at full scale. It consists of an arch, 6 feet 6 inches (1.98 metres) wide, divided into two sub arches, with a circular motif inserted above. In general terms, it echoes the design of the late medieval tomb recess in the presbytery, though neither the details nor the dimensions coincide exactly. As a piece of geometrical drawing it is not very accomplished, for the lines of the sub-arches are parallel to those of the enclosing arch, producing an unsymmetrical result. If such a scheme was actually built, the visual effect would have been decidedly unattractive. The use of parallel arcs foreshadows a technique which later reappears in Irish 'switch-line' tracery.

The second drawing is situated over six feet above the present floor of the north transept and whoever executed it must have been working on a scaffold. It is likely, therefore, that it was drawn when the abbey was still under construction. The same is probably true of the exercises in the south transept chapel, and when the church was complete, both would have vanished under a fresh layer of plaster. The drawings are in parts of the church which belong to the first campaign of building and they must presumably have been carried out by the team of masons who left the abbey around 1228. The plaster drawings do not suggest a very high level of geometrical expertise and in view of this the inaccuracies found in the construction of the abbey church are not suprising. The builders of Corcomroe were excellent masons but rather poor architects.

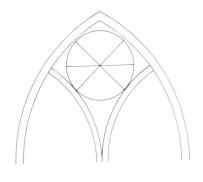

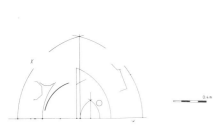

Fig. 9 Incised architectural drawings from Corcomroe.

Drawings engraved at full scale on walls and floors are not uncommon in medieval Europe, though these are the first to be discovered in Ireland. Similar methods can be found in the thirteenth-century cathedrals of Reims and Soissons and there is a late twelfth-century drawing of a pier or window on the west wall of Byland Abbey in Yorkshire.[83] The practice of using a wall, rather like a convenient blackboard, foreshadows the introduction of 'tracing floors', which are well attested in later medieval England. The surviving floors at York and Wells, with their mass of superimposed drawings, are the most famous examples.[84] The habit of making architectural drawings is generally thought to have developed during the first half of the thirteenth century, a view expounded by Robert Branner.[85] In the light of the Corcomroe drawings, it may be necessary to modify this opinion slightly. Since the abbey lies on the periphery of Europe and the engravings appear to belong to the years c1200–28, this suggests that the technique was already widespread in the major workshops of Europe by at least 1200.

Although no further Irish examples survive, engravings on plaster probably remained a standard procedure for Irish masons throughout the middle ages. Some form of preparatory drawing was essential once the Cistercians began to use ribbed vaults around 1200 and the need would have increased with the introduction of bar tracery. For a project as ambitious as the fifteenth-century reconstruction of Holycross, with its lierne vaults and complex tracery, a large plaster floor may well have been necessary and it is not impossible that a separate 'tracing house', like those mentioned in England, once existed in the abbey.

Chapter 3

THE PLANNING AND LAYOUT OF THE MONASTERIES

Introduction

THE MOST REVOLUTIONARY aspect of Cistercian planning in Ireland was the introduction of the square or rectangular cloister as the nucleus of the monastery, a scheme familiar enough in most parts of Europe, but hitherto unknown in Ireland. The absence of the claustral arrangement before 1142 was not due entirely to lack of knowledge. Celtic monks were famed for their peregrinations and many an Irish ecclesiastic, en route to Rome or perhaps to a German *Schottenkirche*, must have had the chance of visiting one of the great Benedictine houses. Irish tradition was, it seems, strong enough to resist any suggestions of change. Compared with the disciplined sequence of buildings around a central cloister garth, the plan of early Irish monasteries seems haphazard, lacking any sense of coherent pattern. At Glendalough, Clonmacnois or Iniscealtra, the various churches and oratories are scattered around the monastic enclosure, with no apparent architectural relationship between them (Pl. 29). On closer inspection, however, it is clear that early Irish planning was not without some rationale. The outer wall, usually an earthen bank with a ditch outside, gave a degree of unity as it embraced the monastic buildings in a roughly circular pattern. The largest church was often located towards the centre of the enclosure and in front there may have been some sort of courtyard, perhaps with one of the principal crosses of the monastery.[1] Some yards from the west door of the church was the round tower, providing a powerful visual focus to the whole ensemble. On occasions there are even glimpses of calculated planning, as at Devenish where the first round tower was aligned to the door of St Molaise's house. Yet however logical the layout of an early Irish monastery might have been, the general approach was essentially non-classical, an inheritance from the barbarian world of northern Europe. Classical principles of planning—the concept of axes, of well-proportioned spaces, of carefully judged relationships between buildings—were either unknown or ill appreciated. To this rather arbitrary tradition of planning, the Cistercians brought uniformity and discipline.

The enclosed cloister garth, surrounded on each side by covered walks, was one of the most attractive and enduring forms devised in European architecture (Pl. 30). As the Latin word *claustrum* implies, here was a secluded inner sanctum, a peaceful courtyard, which served as the hub of monastic life. The covered ambulatories provided an excellent circulation system, giving easy access both to the church and to the major rooms of the monastery (Pl. 31). As broad, well-lit corridors, they provided pleasant spaces for reading and meditation. The existence of four separate passages was also appropriate for those monks disposed to think in allegorical terms. The number four was redolent with Christian meaning, evoking thoughts of the evangelists, the cardinal virtues, the rivers of Paradise, the seasons of the year, etc. As one French historian has remarked, the square of the cloister was 'le carrefour d'univers'.[2] To describe the monastic cloister, medieval churchmen used a variety of images. Durandus in his 'Rationale of the Divine Offices' regarded it as 'a symbol of the heavenly paradise, a paradise where all will live together with one heart, rooted in the Love and Will of God'.[3] Whether viewed in utilitarian, aesthetic or symbolical terms, the cloister was eminently suited to monastic life.

In the context of European monasticism, there was nothing strikingly original about the general planning of a Cistercian monastery. The east range of the cloister contained the sacristy, the chapter house, the parlour, and the 'day room', with the dormitory running along the first

29 Iniscealtra, showing the scattered layout of early Irish monasteries. (Compare with Pl. 7.)

floor above.* When the church was placed on the north side, the calefactory, refectory and kitchen were fitted into the south range and the west range was given over to store rooms and accommodation for the laybrothers. In fundamentals this arrangement was three centuries old, for a similar distribution of chambers and offices had been defined on the St Gall plan of c820, and by the end of the eleventh century it was standard practice in Benedictine houses. The most obvious change brought by the Cistercians was the need to cater for a large body of laybrothers, which required a substantial building in the west range. Otherwise, the traditional cloister plan was perfectly suited to their way of life. The exact sequence of rooms around the cloister, each with its own designed purpose, suitably reflected the precise daily routine of the Cistercian monk. It was a logical and practical system which was adopted in almost all the houses of the order. This uniformity of plan coincides with the demand for uniformity of life, a theme often reiterated by the early Cistercian leaders: 'Unity of customs, of chants, of books; one charity,

30 Hore. The disciplined sequence of buildings around the square cloister garth is particularly evident in the aerial photograph.

31 The reconstructed cloister arcade at Holycross (c1450).

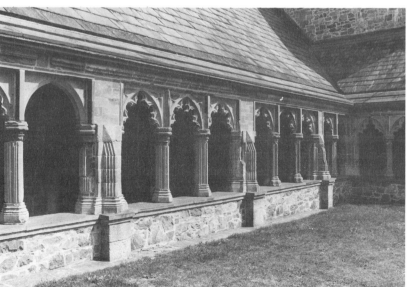

one Rule, one life'. St Bernard expounded the same ideas in his sermons and letters: 'We must be unanimous, without divisions between us all together, a single body in Christ, while being members the one of the other.'[4] Transformed into architectural terms, uniformity of observance led to uniform planning for, apart from variations in scale, the basic needs of each monastery were identical. A Cistercian monk could have found his way about blindfold in almost any monastery of the order.

Despite the stress on unity, the General Chapter did not draw up a comprehensive list of regulations to control design. The only statutes relating to architecture tended to be negative in character and took the form of bans on unwelcome developments, like the famous proscription of bell towers in 1157.[5] By the middle of the twelfth century positive instructions about the plan of a monastery were unnecessary, presumably because the layout was familiar to all. Minor deviations could be eliminated by the father abbot during his annual visitation and only when a major crisis occurred was the issue taken to the General Chapter. As a result, Cistercian documents contain few references to architectural planning. An important exception is the list of instructions drawn up by Stephen of Lexington in 1228, a good demonstration of how abberrations were controlled at a local level.

By the time the first Cistercians arrived in Ireland, the order's approach to matters of planning was well established. The Irish houses were orthodox in their arrangement and they formed a coherent and fairly stereotyped group within the order as a whole. Not until the fifteenth century did Irish monks introduce their own modifications, by which time discipline on such matters had long since been eroded. At the time of their foundation, in the twelfth and thirteenth centuries, all the abbeys were laid out in the conventional way, and they appear to have been uninfluenced by the local environment. Even the round tower, that *leit motif* of ancient Irish monasteries, which might have found its way into the new abbeys, was dutifully rejected.

Despite the relatively high total of Cistercian abbeys in Ireland, the number of cases where a complete plan can be recovered is disappointingly few. A particular loss is St Mary's, Dublin, the richest house of the order, and one which is likely to have exercised considerable influence.[6] Even where the church has survived relatively unscathed, the adjoining conventual buildings have often vanished, as at Baltinglass, Corcomroe, Tintern, Abbeydorney and Abbeyshrule. Archaeological investigation has been limited in scope and only Mellifont has been systematically excavated. It is to be hoped that more excavations will take place in the future, though such work is seriously hampered by the Irish tradition of burial. For centuries it has been customary for local families to bury their dead within the confines of a medieval abbey or friary and persistent grave-digging has often disturbed or destroyed the ancient foundations. Abbeydorney is a notorious example, for here the old cloister garth is submerged in undergrowth and encumbered with relatively modern tombs and monuments (Pl. 32). Corcomroe and Abbeyknockmoy have also suffered badly in this regard. One site where it is possible to work out the medieval plan is Graiguenamanagh, though the area is now encumbered by yards, outhouses and semi-derelict sheds (Fig. 27).[7] There is plenty of scope for clearance and excavation in these unprepossessing surroundings. The original layout can be followed with greater ease at Jerpoint, Dunbrody and Grey (Figs 10, 20, 27). Yet altogether out of a total of thirty-three major Cistercian foundations, there are only thirteen where one can speak with any confidence about the general plan.

32 Abbeydorney, where the monastic ruins are almost obliterated by relatively modern tombs and burials.

The layout of the cloisters

In eight of the monasteries the cloister forms a square, or at least approximates to it. The size varies considerably, from the diminutive cloisters of Corcomroe and Inch to the spacious courtyards of Dunbrody and Graiguenamanagh. The latter are close to 120 feet (36.5 metres) square (including the cloister walks), a dimension which is a good average for a well endowed Cistercian house (Fontenay, for example, was 117 by 123 feet and Fountains about 125 feet square).[8] The table below gives comparative dimensions in English feet:

	North Range	East Range
Graiguenamanagh	c119′	c119′
Dunbrody	119′2″	118′10″
Abbeyknockmoy	103′	106′
Boyle	100′	130′
Jerpoint	98′10″	105′1″
Monasteranenagh	98′6″	130′6″
Baltinglass	c98′	unknown
Mellifont I	88′6″	c94′
Mellifont II	88′6″	132′9″
Bective I	c80′	58′
Hore	76′	76′
Holy Cross	73′	98′10″
Kilcooly (15th-century)	71′	96′ (?)
Inch	69′	74′6″
Grey	67′	111′
Corcomroe	65′	56′6″
Bective II (15th-century)	c57′	c57′

Several interesting points emerge from the table. Only three monasteries achieved an exact square, which suggests that the size of the cloister was liable to modification as the various ranges surrounding it were constructed. It is noticeable that in six cases a dimension approximating to a hundred was employed for at least one of the sides, a notional figure which seems to have served as an obvious starting point when laying out the foundations. The hundred foot cloister was something of a European norm and it was enshrined in the Plan of St Gall (c820). In a commentary on the Rule of St Benedict written about 845, Hildemar of Corbie declared that 'it was generally held that the cloister should be a hundred feet square and no less because that would make it too small'.[9] Over the course of the next centuries Hildemar's advice was followed in many a European monastery.

There were at least five monasteries where the cloister was rectangular in plan, rather than square, and it is worth examining the reasons for this. The lopsided garth at Mellifont is the result of an enlargement about 1200 (Mellifont II in the table), and sufficient evidence remains to show that as first built the cloister formed a square (Figs 12, 13).[10] In the rebuilding the whole of the south range was apparently pushed further south. At Grey the unusual proportions are probably explained by a failure to complete the monastery according to the original plan. The aisleless nave is so simple in conception, especially when compared to the ambitious layout of the east range, that it implies that the monks were unable to complete their buildings on the scale first envisaged. It is worth noticing that if the cloister had measured a hundred feet in an east-west direction, the main axis of the refectory would have been aligned exactly in the centre, a common practice in Cistercian planning (Fig. 11). Moreover, if a south aisle was originally envisaged for the church, the east walk of the cloister would have been reduced to about a hundred feet. If this hypothesis is correct, the initial intention at Grey was to build a cloister approximately a hundred feet square. At Holycross the reason for the irregularity is somewhat different. The north gallery is only 73 feet (22.25 metres) long, but if the width of the west range is added to it, it comes to 100 feet (30.5 metres), almost exactly the same as the east side (Fig. 37). Once again the hundred-foot square lies at the basis of the layout, but in this case the west range was included within it.

A unique feature of the claustral layout at Mellifont was a narrow passage, known as the 'ruelle des convers', separating the cloister from the west range (Fig. 12). This was a common feature of twelfth-century Cistercian abbeys abroad, though it was often taken out in subsequent rebuilding. A similar passage existed at Clairvaux, which was almost certainly the model for Mellifont.[11] The purpose of the 'ruelle des convers' was to give the laybrothers free access to rooms in the west range without interrupting the peace of the monastic cloister and it gave them a direct route to their own choir at the west end of the church. It must have been a

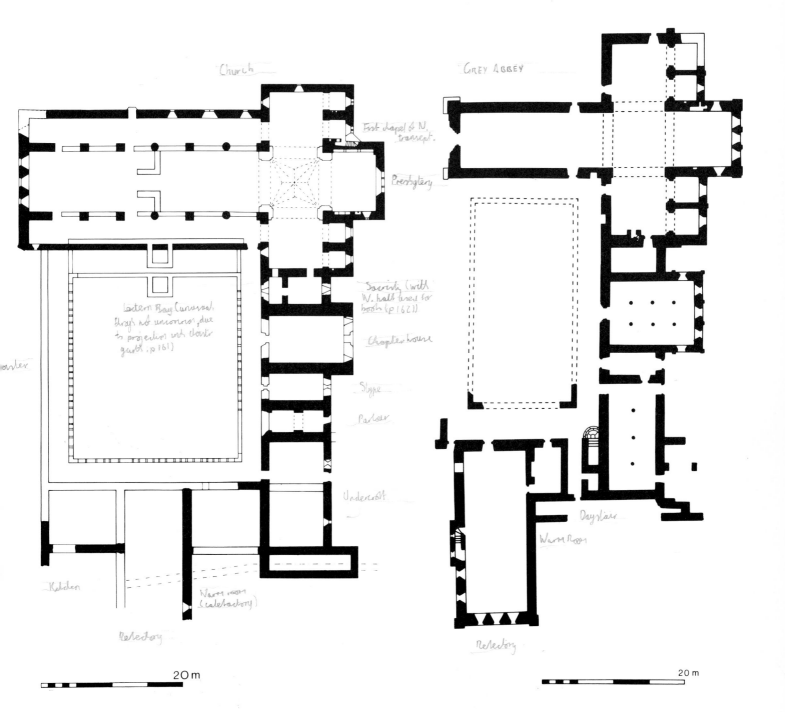

Church

GREY ABBEY

East chapel of N. transept.

Presbytery

Sacristy (with W. hall used for books (p 162))

Chapter house

Lantern Bay (unusual, stays not uncommon due to projection into cloister garth, p 161)

Slype

Parlour

Undercroft

Cloister

Dayrism

Warm Room

Kitchen

Warm room (calefactory)

Refectory

Refectory

20 m

20 m

Fig. 10   Jerpoint, plan.

Fig. 11   Grey Abbey, plan.

rather nasty functional corridor, the product of the total division of monks and laybrothers demanded by the Cistercian Rule.

In at least seven monasteries the cloisters were reconstructed during the fifteenth century and in three of them the original plan was substantially modified. The cloister at Jerpoint was enlarged slightly to the north, taking over the space formerly occupied by the south aisle of the church (Fig. 10). At Bective a drastic reduction took place. New arcades were constructed to the west and south, reducing the cloister area to a square of approximately 57 feet (17.4 metres), and they were incorporated into the main body of the ranges, a technique borrowed from friary architecture. This created a more intimate cloister garth and a greater sense of enclosure (Fig. 63). As only a handful of monks can have been living at Bective at the time, the changes were realistic and practical. The various chambers around the cloister were similarly reduced in size.

At Kilcooly some time after 1445, the cloister and conventual buildings were reorganised, but here the changes are more difficult to follow. As at Jerpoint (its mother house), the north walk of

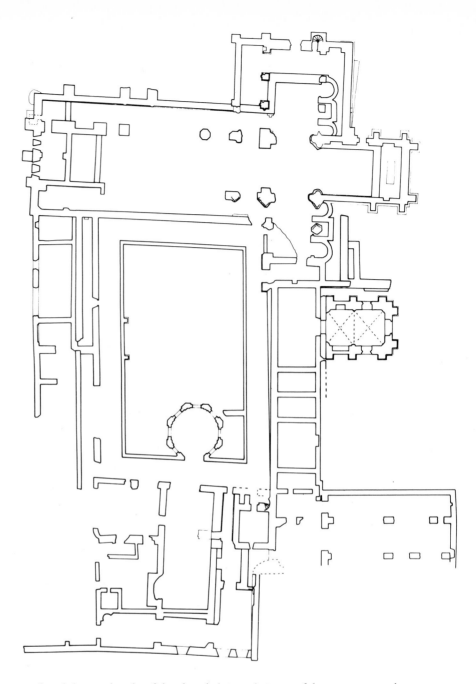

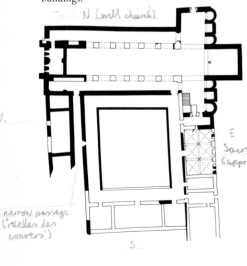

Fig. 12 Mellifont, outline plan of all the extant remains.

Fig. 13 Mellifont, plan of twelfth-century buildings.

the cloister replaced the south aisle of the church (Fig. 21). Parts of the reconstructed east range survive, as well as fragments of the south range, but the various chambers are characterless and it is impossible to be certain how they were used.

With the exception of Hore, the cloisters were located to the south of the church, the standard medieval position. This had obvious advantages, for the north walk of the cloister, where the monks did their sacred reading, was open to the sunshine and protected from northern winds by the walls of the church. In France the placing of the cloisters on the opposite side in some abbeys has been explained by difficulties with the water supply, but this does not appear to have been the case at Hore.[12]

Church plans in the Mellifont affiliation

Special interest is attached to the plan of the first church at Mellifont. As the founding monks had come directly from Clairvaux, and a French monk, Robert, was present to assist in building operations, the design of the church must have been based on ideas acquired at Clairvaux. Although the church was remodelled at various stages in the middle ages, the plan of the first building is known through excavation.[13] It consisted of an aisled nave, transepts with three

56

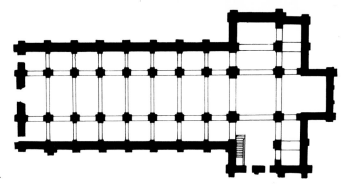

Fig. 14   Fontenay, plan of church.

33   Mellifont, showing the alternating semi-circular and square apses of the south transept, and the piers of the fourteenth-century reconstruction.

chapels opening off each arm and a presbytery, roughly square in plan (Fig. 13). The total (external) length was 188 feet (57.34 metres), not particularly large for a major monastic church. The form of the presbytery and the location of the transept chapels is typical of Cistercian practice, particularly within the affiliation of Clairvaux. There were however two unusual characteristics.

The first concerns the transept chapels, which were given alternating square and semi-circular apses, an unorthodox form (Pl. 33). The semi-circular apse was unknown in Ireland, and it must therefore be an importation from France, though it is not a feature to be expected. Between 1135 and 1153 the familiar Cistercian plan with a square presbytery and straight-ended eastern chapels was adopted universally in the Clairvaux affiliation and Mellifont is apparently the only daughter house to vary the arrangement.[14] What makes the Mellifont layout all the more puzzling is the problems it must have caused when building the roofs. If the chapels had finished in a straight east wall, they could have been covered in a continuous lean-to, but instead each chapel must have been given its own roof. Assuming the monk Robert was responsible for this design, it implies that the architectural methods he had learnt at Clairvaux were not quite as rigid as some scholars have believed. There are no exact parallels for the alternating scheme. Semi-circular apses were not uncommon in other branches of the Cistercian order, and they occur frequently in churches affiliated to Morimond. But their combination with rectangular apses is rare and the only close parallels occur in churches founded long after Mellifont was constructed.[15]

The other oddity at Mellifont is a consequence of its situation in a narrow valley. At the west end of the church, the ground sloped down to the River Mattock, and a small crypt was necessary to keep the building level. This in itself was not uncommon in medieval building, but it was unusual not to give it a stone vault. The crypt was covered by a wooden ceiling, which served as the floor of the church above, a point confirmed by the discovery of 'sizeable fragments of charred wood'.[16] There were two rather cramped chambers within the crypt but it is unlikely they were put to any liturgical use. They were probably utilised for practical purposes, as suggested by the large cupboard or safe ingeniously fitted into the west wall.

Despite the prestige of Mellifont, its plan was not a prototype for other houses. The curious alternation of apses was not copied and most abbeys in the affiliation adopted the standard 'Bernardine' or 'Fontenay' plan with two square chapels in each transept (Fig. 14). This was employed at Boyle, Jerpoint, Abbeyknockmoy, Holycross, Kilcooly, Hore and probably Bective. It is a paradox that the daughters and grand-daughters of Mellifont were closer to routine Cistercian practice than the mother house itself and this suggests that Mellifont was not the only channel through which information about Cistercian planning was reaching Ireland. The simplicity of the rectilinear plan represented the ultimate in Cistercian practicality and efficiency. It has for long been associated with St Bernard himself and there is plenty of evidence to show that the design emerged at Clairvaux around 1133–5, when plans for the rebuilding of the church were being drawn up. Some scholars have suggested that St Bernard was responsible and whether true or not, his encouragement may have guaranteed its popularity.[17] The intrinsic merits of the layout and its appropriateness for Cistercian worship ensured that it became a preferred type.

The plan conveniently provided the chapels needed for individual monks to say mass and, as

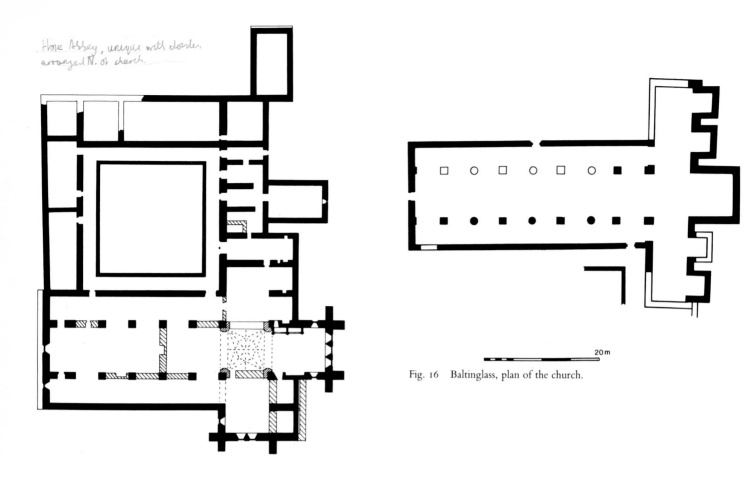

Hore Abbey, unique with cloister arranged N. of church.

Fig. 16   Baltinglass, plan of the church.

20 m

Fig. 15   Hore Abbey, plan.

the Cistercians eschewed elaborate ritual, the simple square presbytery was adequate for their needs. There has been much scholarly debate about prototypes for the short straight-ended presbytery. Some have related it to the church at Hirsau (1082–91), whereas others see the rural churches of Burgundy as the model.[18] But erudite argument seems superfluous, as a form so simple scarcely requires inspiration from other sources. It is better to regard the square presbytery as a logical expression of Cistercian requirements. It was easy to lay out, it was simple to vault and it suited the Cistercian liturgy. The avoiding of ambulatories and complex spaces underlined the white monks' desire to break away from what they regarded as the over magnificence of Cluniac churches.

The seven Irish churches which adopted the Fontenay scheme were not mirror images of each other and their plans differ considerably in scale and proportion. Hore, for example, has transepts which are 96 feet (29.25 metres) from north to south (internally), whereas the corresponding dimension at Boyle is about 80 feet (24.4 metres). The similarities in plan are further concealed by major differences in the elevation. The use of the Fontenay plan at Hore and Holycross is especially interesting. Hore was not founded until 1272 and it is surprising to find the traditional plan employed at this late date without alteration. This conservative approach is all the more remarkable since the old method had recently been abandoned in the reconstruction of Mellifont. The model for Hore must have been another member of the affiliation, perhaps the neighbouring monastery of Inislounaght. Equally surprising is the reuse of the Fontenay plan at Holycross in the fifteenth century (Fig. 37). The abbey was prospering at the time and encumbered with pilgrims, but the monks were singularly unenterprising in their choice of plan. Instead of a new design to cater for the abbey's status as a pilgrimage church, the old foundations were reused. The conservative attitudes shown by the Irish Cistercians in the later middle ages reflect their isolation from European church building and their lack of information about alternative models.

One of the merits of the Fontenay plan was that it could be conveniently adjusted to suit the size of the monastery. At Monasteranenagh three chapels were erected in each arm of the transept, but at the small monastery of Corcomroe the number was reduced to one (Figs 26, 34). Three houses in the Mellifont affiliation were planned on somewhat different lines. The most peculiar is Baltinglass, founded in 1148 as one of the first daughter houses of Mellifont. The transepts were excavated in 1955 and the foundations discovered were something of a surprise.[19] The transepts were long—about 113 feet (33.5 metres) internally from north to south—but despite the length only two chapels opened off each arm. These projected independently and they were not enclosed by a continuous east wall (Fig. 16). As a gap existed between the chapels, they must have had their own gabled roofs. Although separate roofs of this sort were used at Fountains in England, it seems likely that Baltinglass was a local adaptation of the plan of Mellifont. The result was neither neat nor economical and other monasteries in the order were not impressed. Outside the order, however, the arrangement was copied in the thirteenth century cathedral at Cashel and the parish church at St Mary's, New Ross.

More modest than other churches in the affiliation were Abbeyshrule and Abbeydorney. The ruins of both are covered in vegetation, which makes it difficult to disentangle their architectural history. Both were aisleless buildings and it is unclear whether they had transepts. Basically they were little more than long rectangular boxes, which, in their simplicity, find their closest parallels in Cistercian nunneries rather than monasteries. The church at Abbeydorney belongs to the fifteenth century, but parts of Abbeyshrule may go back to the time of its foundation in 1200 (Figs 17, 39). At a later date a solid stone screen with three vaulted compartments was inserted and this remains the chief architectural feature of the ruins.

With the exception of Baltinglass, Abbeyshrule and Abbeydorney, the plans of churches affiliated to Mellifont form a homogeneous group, adhering closely to the Fontenay type even in the fifteenth century. There is one further feature that many of them have in common. Several of the churches lack a continuous arcade between the nave and aisles, arches being replaced for short stretches by solid stone walls. At Holycross and Corcomroe the equivalent of about two bays at the east end of the nave, corresponding to the monks' choir, were treated in this way (Figs 26, 37). Presumably it was felt that as the choir stalls would partly block the arches they might as well dispense with them altogether. The effect in architectural terms was a disaster, making the central space horribly claustrophobic. At Monasteranenagh, Abbeyknockmoy and probably Kilcooly the treatment was reserved for the laybrothers' choir at the west end of the building, with equally unpleasant results (Pl. 34, Figs 18, 34). A more discreet use of the method is found at Jerpoint, Hore and the Anglo-Norman foundation at Tintern, where solid masonry takes up about a bay at the west end. It is not the only example of the Irish Cistercians sacrificing architectural effects in the interests of economy. While solid walls reduced the need for dressed stonework and speeded up building progress, it was a case of Cistercian functionalism taken to an extreme.

These economies were not restricted to Ireland, though they are found more regularly there than elsewhere. Anselme Dimier's magisterial survey of Cistercian plans includes at least fourteen additional examples, plus many more where just one arcade was blocked.[20] They are scattered across Europe from Sweden to Italy and their distribution fits no geographical pattern; nor are they related in date or affiliation. The imposing abbey of Chiaravalle in the suburbs of Milan, for example, has solid walls in the monks' choir, and both Bindon abbey in Dorset and the remote monastery of Boquen in Brittany have the same arrangement in the choir of the laybrothers, the latter pair providing close parallels for Monasteranenagh and Abbeyknockmoy. At Alvastra in Sweden blank walls at the west end of the church were used to form separate chambers in the adjoining aisles, but there is no evidence that this was done in Ireland.[21]

The use of walls instead of arcades is the consequence of a paradox inherent in medieval monastic architecture. Although the basic framework of churches was basilican, the aisles were not primarily regarded as an extension of the central space, but were treated as corridors and

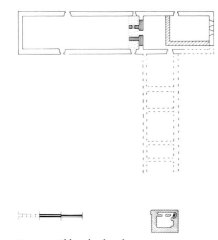

Fig. 17   Abbeyshrule, plan.

59

34 The nave of Abbeyknockmoy. Solid wall replaced arches at the west end of the church, the section corresponding to the laybrothers' choir.

20 m

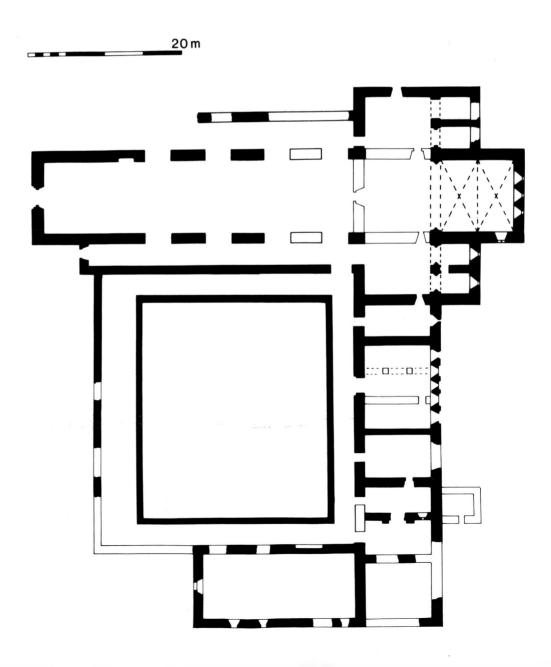

Fig. 18   Abbeyknockmoy, plan.

places for extra chapels. Hence a plethora of screens and blocking walls appeared, making a nonsense of the basilican form, with its open vistas across the building. If the building was relatively large in scale, and the arcades rose well above the stalls and screens, the visual effects were not so serious. But in smaller monastic churches, and especially those belonging to the Cistercians where two separate sets of choir stalls were ranged down the nave, the central vessel was almost completely closed off from the aisles. The next logical step was to remove the arcades, or at least part of them, and this is what many poorer houses did.

The planning of the Anglo-Norman churches

The abbeys founded and patronised by Anglo-Norman lords were laid out on the same lines as the Irish houses and all followed the so-called 'Bernardine' approach, with either two or three chapels extending east from each transept. By far the most ambitious piece of planning was the remodelling of the eastern arm of Mellifont, a project begun about 1240 but not finished until about 1320 (Fig. 19).[22] It is appropriate to include this in the Anglo-Norman group, since it was started at a time when the abbey had switched its loyalties to the Anglo-Norman regime. The new north transept was three bays long and it had aisles on both the eastern and western sides. These were divided by timber screens to form chapels and the two west piers have tiny piscinae incorporated into the masonry to serve the altars placed alongside. On account of the presence of

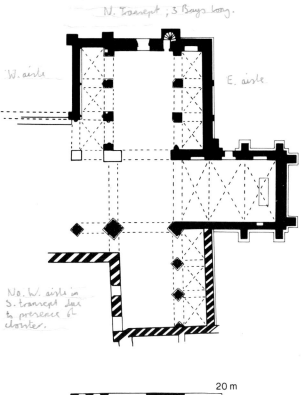

Fig. 19 Mellifont, plan of the church as remodelled in the thirteenth and fourteenth centuries.

the cloister, the plan could not be repeated in the south transept, since there was no room to build a western aisle. Consequently the overall plan ended up lopsided, like that at Cîteaux. Altogether the new design provided room for eight chapels, only two more than the twelfth century plan, and the gain was one of space and grandeur, rather than number. Transepts with two aisles could be found in several major Cistercian houses by the thirteenth century, but the inspiration for Mellifont may be Irish. St Patrick's Cathedral, Dublin, begun in 1220, has a similar plan and it is only thirty-five miles away.

As the chapels in Mellifont II were separated from each other by timber screens, there was a less enclosed feeling than hitherto, when chapels were divided by solid walls. The more open

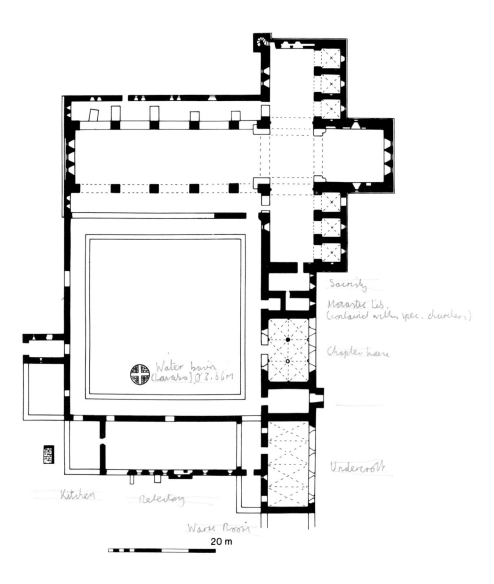

The plan includes the following handwritten annotations: Sacristy, Monastic Lib. (contained within spec. chamber), Chapter house, Undercroft, Kitchen, Refectory, Warm Room, Water basin (Lavabo) Ø 3.66m

20 m

Fig. 20   Dunbrody, plan.

spatial effects were a direct consequence of using ribbed vaults. Solid walls, needed in the past to support barrel vaults, were now superfluous. From about 1170 undivided chapels of this sort became normal in English Cistercian houses—as at Roche, Byland and Furness—and the new more Gothic approach was introduced to Ireland at Inch, probably about 1200 (Fig. 32). In addition to Inch and Mellifont II, Tintern was the only other abbey to follow the example and the practice was restricted to the Anglo-Norman houses.

Another Anglo-Norman characteristic was the extended presbytery, found at Graiguenamanagh, Mellifont II, Tintern and Inch (Figs 19, 27, 28, 32). Here the familiar square plan gave way to a rectangular space, which at Graiguenamanagh and Mellifont II was covered by three bays of ribbed vaulting. The increase in size was not dramatic (Mellifont II measured 26 feet by 44 feet 6 inches (7.92 by 13.55 metres) compared to the twelfth century 23 feet 8 inches by 25 feet (7.22 by 7.63 metres) and it could not have made a radical difference to the way the church was used. It may have allowed the choir stalls to be placed a little further east, but a more spacious sanctuary was probably the desired objective.

Included in the Anglo-Norman group are two of the largest Cistercian abbeys of Ireland, the Leinster houses of Graiguenamanagh and Dunbrody (Figs 20, 27). Both are over two hundred feet long and planned with three chapels in each arm of the transept. At Dunbrody the transepts are truly massive, stretching 139 feet 6 inches (42.5 metres) from north to south (externally), and, with the ruins well preserved, it is possible to sense the vast scale of the thirteenth-century building (Pls 64–6, Fig. 20). The size of Graiguenamanagh has for long been disguised by the church built within its walls in 1813, but this has recently been reconstructed and some of the old grandeur has returned. The full extent of the church, 203 feet 5 inches (61.7 metres) long internally, can now be grasped, but, with the nave arcades still blocked, the building lacks its former spaciousness. The other Anglo-Norman church with three chapels in each transept is Tintern, but here the building never reached the grandiose dimensions of its neighbours. It is only 162 feet (48.38 metres) long externally and the nave is equivalent to only four bays.

The two Ulster monasteries, Inch and Grey, were modest in scale, with two chapels in each transept (Figs 11, 32). Grey in particular seems conservative in flavour. Although founded as late as 1193, the chapels were left undivided and covered with pointed barrel vaults. It makes a strong contrast with Inch, not many miles away across Strangford Lough, where the chapels are open and covered by ribbed vaults. Grey, with its short aisleless nave, is in fact the smallest of the Anglo-Norman churches.

The plans of the Anglo-Norman abbeys were not, therefore, conceived in a dramatically different way from their Irish counterparts. A few modifications were introduced from England, principally the extended presbytery and the use of undivided chapels, but these are scarcely sufficient to isolate the plans as a group. It was in the design of the elevations rather than in planning that the Anglo-Norman houses can be most easily distinguished from the native foundations.

In a few instances the plan of the mother house appears to have dictated the form of its daughters and the links are relatively precise between Boyle and Abbeyknockmoy (Figs 18, 30). Both churches had the standard two-chapel arrangement, both were given relatively short transepts (north-south), both have a doorway, rather than an arch, leading from the north aisle into the north transept, and in both monasteries the north walk of the cloister was 100 feet long. Most connections between mother and daughter abbeys are too general to suggest specific influence, but when Abbeyknockmoy was founded in 1190, the plan of Boyle (still under construction) was apparently taken as the model.

Most of the mother houses of the Anglo-Norman abbeys lay in England or Wales but for various reasons it is difficult to make comparisons. Grey bears little resemblance to what is left at Holm Cultram (Cumberland)[23] and the plan of Tintern has no special connection with its famous mother house in Wales. Nor does Graiguenamanagh appear to have been closely modelled on Stanley (Wiltshire), which about 1200 had the standard 'Fontenay' plan with two chapels in each transept.[24] The only clear debt to a mother house occurs at Inch, where both the open ribbed vaulted chapels and the rectangular presbytery were foreshadowed at Furness, though in a more sophisticated and elaborate way.[25] The mother-daughter relationship was not necessarily a critical factor, therefore, in explaining the plans of the Irish Cistercian abbeys and it appears that ideas were as likely to come from a neighbouring house or another monastery in the same affiliation.

By the early thirteenth century some of the larger and more prosperous Cistercian houses of Europe had begun to improve the liturgical arrangements of their churches by the construction of chevets or aisled choirs, as at Citeaux or Clairvaux, Fountains or Abbey Dore. This was occasioned by the need for more altars, perhaps because a higher proportion of monks were now being ordained priests. These pressures were not apparently experienced in Ireland and Mellifont was the only abbey to make provision for further chapels during the thirteenth century. The Irish communities were of course relatively small and it is important to remember that additional altars could be sited in the aisles of the nave.

The location of entrances and staircases

To cater for its varied functions and its simultaneous use by choir monks and laybrothers, a Cistercian church needed five if not six doorways. The principal entrance for the monks lay at the east end of the south aisle, placed on the axis of the east walk of the cloister, providing a direct route from the claustral buildings to the choir stalls. This arrangement was employed generally in Ireland and several of these so-called 'monks' doorways' have survived. A magnificent early thirteenth-century example remains at Graiguenamanagh, ornamented with fine dog-tooth and Islamic-looking cusps (Pl. 36, Fig. 69). Two monasteries had the doorways in exceptional positions. In the aisleless church at Grey, the monks had to enter the building through a door in the west wall of the south transept and at Corcomroe the door was also placed in the south transept, this time fitted rather randomly in the south wall.

It was common practice for the laybrothers to have their own entrance to the church at the west end of the south aisle, and traces of such doorways can be seen at Mellifont, Boyle and Abbeyknockmoy. In two abbeys (Dunbrody, Graiguenamanagh) the laybrothers' quarters lay beyond the west wall of the church, so that direct access would have been impossible.

Several churches were provided with an impressive doorway in the west facade. At Boyle, for example, there is a fine doorway of c1215–20, with two orders of continuous roll mouldings (Fig. 68). Dunbrody once had a more pretentious entrance, with an abundance of dog-tooth ornament, and at Grey there still survives a splendid (though rebuilt) portal of four orders, also furnished with dog-tooth (Pl. 37, Fig. 69). These doorways provided the main entrance to the church for visitors and led directly into the laybrothers' choir. Not all abbeys, however, had a west door. At Mellifont the fall of ground towards the River Mattock prevented it, which explains why an elaborate early Gothic portal was inserted in the north transept. At Jerpoint the land falls steeply away at the west and consequently a simple doorway, later fortified with machicolis, was located in the north aisle. At Baltinglass there is no obvious reason why the church was not given a west portal, for there is level ground between the abbey and the River Slaney which flows past the façade. As at Jerpoint (its daughter house), a doorway was provided in the north aisle, and in this case it was an elaborate Romanesque portal with three orders, one of them decorated with chevron. West doorways were also omitted at Hore and Graiguenamanagh.

Many Cistercian abbeys abroad were furnished with a narthex or low porch across the west front of the church. At Pontigny (France) a beautiful Gothic porch remains and at Maulbronn

35   Boyle, the south side of the nave. The (reconstructed) doorway to the right was the principal entrance to the church for the monks.

36   Graiguenamanagh. The monks' doorway (c1220) embellished with dog-tooth and zigzag ornament.

37 The thirteenth-century west door at Grey Abbey. With its arch of four orders, decorated with dog-tooth ornament, this was one of the most elaborate Cistercian doorways in Ireland.

(Germany) there is a spacious ribbed-vaulted narthex.[26] The latter was unusually monumental and a simple lean-to porch, as at Fountains, was more common. There is no evidence for such features in Ireland. Wooden porches may have been erected in front of some portals but, if so, they have vanished without leaving traces. An unusual feature is the recently discovered north porch at Graiguenamanagh, which was approximately 20 feet (6 metres) wide.[27] Dating from the mid-thirteenth century, it had an outer doorway and was lined with stone benches on each side. It resembles the porch of a parish church and there are good parallels for it nearby at Gowran and the cathedral of Kilkenny.

Following a funeral service, the body of the deceased was taken through a special door in the north transept, the '*porte des morts*'. It opened onto a pathway leading to the monks' cemetery at the east end of the building and many, though not all, Irish Cistercian abbeys were furnished with such a portal. Normally the *porte des morts* was undecorated, as at Boyle, Abbeyknockmoy, Dunbrody and Graiguenamanagh, but at Inch it was ornamented with two orders of early Gothic mouldings. At Mellifont it may have corresponded with a simple door at the west end of the presbytery, which has no other obvious purpose.

High in the south wall of the transept was a doorway affording direct access between the dormitory and the church, for use by the monks in the night hours. It was reached by a staircase, but these have for the most part been destroyed, leaving the doorway marooned far above ground level. At Holycross an impressive flight of eighteen steps survives intact, dating from the fifteenth-century reconstruction of the abbey (Pl. 38). A thirteenth-century night stair remains at Dunbrody, but elsewhere their position is indicated only by an isolated door, as at Corcomroe, Boyle, Abbeyknockmoy, Jerpoint and Graiguenamanagh.

In order to provide access to the upper parts of the building, particularly for maintenance and repairs, an additional staircase was often included, for which there was no set position. At Boyle a straight staircase, entered from the west portal, ran up through the thickness of the west facade

38 The fifteenth-century night stair at Holycross before the recent restoration. The door to
the left leads to the sacristy.

Plan of Grey, p55

Plan of Boyle, p87

Plan of Jerpoint, p55

(Fig. 30). Commonly a newel stair was provided in the vicinity of the north transept. At Inch
and Dunbrody it lies in a buttress in the north-west angle and at Graiguenamanagh and
Mellifont II it was placed in a corresponding buttress at the north-east angle. The newel stair at
Grey is curious, for it is constructed within a buttress that projects slightly into the church in the
south wall of the south transept (Fig. 11). Although usually described as a night stair, this is
unlikely in view of its narrow spiral form, which seems unsuitable for wandering monks in the
hours of darkness. Apart from Boyle, no stairs have come to light in the early churches of the
Mellifont affiliation and there is some doubt about whether permanent access to the roof spaces
was provided. At Jerpoint in the fifteenth century a new stair was ingeniously fitted between the
presbytery and the first chapel of the north transept, leading up to chambers immediately above
the transept chapels (Fig. 10). A similar stair was included in the remodelling of Holycross,
where it was placed in the thickness of the north wall of the transept (Fig. 37).

Late medieval planning

By the fifteenth century the relaxation of the Rule, the diminishing numbers of monks and the
absence of laybrothers had so transformed Cistercian life that a completely new approach to the
planning of a monastery was called for. A relatively small chapel was all that was needed for
worship by most communities, together with a suite of private chambers to provide the
independence and privacy now demanded by the monks. With the exception of Bective,
however, few communities accepted the full architectural logic of the situation and changes
came in the form of piecemeal alterations rather than unified redesign.

Kilcooly was the only monastery to introduce major innovations into the plan of its church.

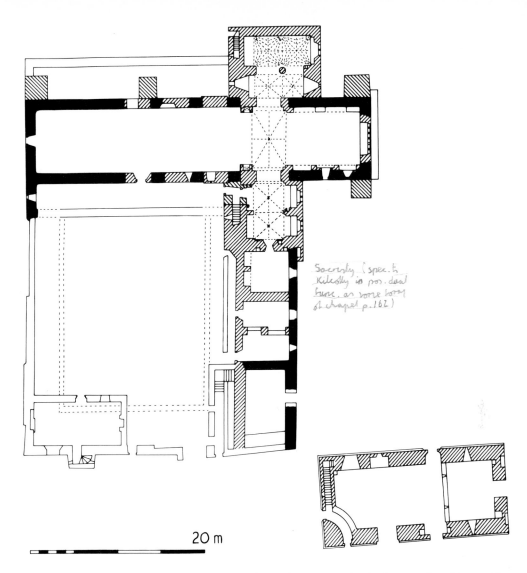

20 m

Fig. 21 Kilcooly, plan.

In 1445 a monk reported that the abbey had been almost completely destroyed and burned by 'armed men'[28] and over the next sixty or seventy years it was substantially rebuilt, using flamboyant tracery and lierne vaulting (Fig. 21). The south transept was rib vaulted in two bays at a low level and the two eastern chapels were replaced by shallow altar recesses. The north transept was also rib vaulted, this time in four irregular bays, with an octagonal pier in the centre. The narrow dimensions of the transept resulted in an awkward, oblong crossing, which had repercussions on the design of the tower above. The western walls of the transept contain staircases. That to the south was the successor to the old night stairs, but it was completely enclosed and hidden from view. The north transept stair was reached from outside the building, from a doorway in the west wall, and it led up to the vault spaces and the crossing tower. (After the armed raid of 1445, it is strange that the doorway was not more discreetly located.) In the nave, the arcades were blocked and the twelfth-century aisles demolished. The reconstructed church was smaller but more intimate that its predecessor and the crudity of the alterations in the nave were in part compensated by the attractive spatial effects of the transepts.

The decline in numbers is also reflected in the churches at Jerpoint and Bective, where south aisles were demolished and adjoining arcades blocked. At Bective the nave was further truncated by the construction of a new west facade, protected by a fortified tower. As at Kilcooly these were effective though unsightly ways of reducing over-capacious buildings.

There are several other cases where Cistercian churches were truncated after 1400, but it is not always easy to determine whether this happened before or after the dissolution. At Inch the spacious early Gothic church was reduced to a simple rectangular chapel, a frank acknowledgement of the abbey's poverty and chastened circumstances. The remodelling may have been forced on the community by the collapse of the tower and crossing arches, for the

67

39 The interior of the nave at Monasteranenagh, showing the inserted wall used to shorten the church after the dissolution.

west crossing piers were largely destroyed when the reconstruction took place. The transepts were cut off by a solid screen of masonry and a new facade was erected in the first bay of the nave. The aisleless chapel was entered through an early Gothic doorway, evidently salvaged from the redundant thirteenth-century facade (Pl. 62, Fig. 32).[29]

The most common way of reducing the size of a large Cistercian church was to insert a transverse wall across the nave, approximately where the screen dividing the monks from the laybrothers' choir had once existed. It was an obvious way of saving expense on heavy repairs to the fabric. In some cases the alterations took place after the dissolution, when many abbeys were adapted as parish churches. The inserted cross walls are usually crude in construction and hard to date. They can (or could) be found at Monasteranenagh (Pl. 39), Holycross, Graiguenamanagh, Jerpoint, Hore, Abbeyknockmoy and Corcomroe, the latter example being surmounted by a simple bell turret.[30]

Proportional methods

The similarity of so many Cistercian plans and their rectilinear design has prompted considerable speculation about the use of proportional formulae within the order. It is self evident that the layout of these churches was not a purely arbitrary process and that some method, or variety of methods, must underlie their planning. Various modular systems have been proposed, the most comprehensive study of the problem being carried out by the German scholar, Hanno Hahn, who published his conclusions in 1957.[31] These were favourably received at the time and much of what he says remains convincing.[32]

According to Hahn, Cistercian builders employed a modular system based on two squares which determined the key points of the plan. The sides of the squares had a ratio one to the other of 3:4. There were variations in the way the units were applied, depending on such questions as whether the church had two or three chapels per transept, but the basic approach did not vary. Hahn's investigations were founded on a study of the German monastery of Eberbach, a building which illustrates the proportional system well. Here the larger unit determined (a) the

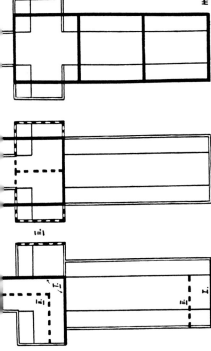

Fig. 22 Eberbach, showing Hanno Hahn's interpretation of the proportions.

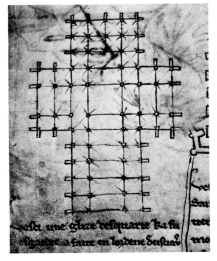

Fig. 23 Villard de Honnecourt, plan for a Cistercian church.

width of the nave and aisles, (b) the length of one transept plus the crossing and (c) the length of the crossing and presbytery; multiplied by three it gives (d) the total length of the church from the east wall of the transept to the west facade. The smaller unit defines (a) the width of the nave and one aisle and (b) the width of the transept (east-west); multiplied by two it gives (c) the total length of the transepts (north-south) and when multiplied by four (d) the length of the church from the east wall of the transept. The accompanying diagram, taken from Hahn's book, explains the method in simple visual terms (Fig. 22). The discrepancies between 'theoretical' and actual dimensions were not inconsiderable, amounting to more than one foot (0.3 metres) in some cases, but these did not undermine the validity of Hahn's propositions. He went on to show that the system was employed widely in churches of the 'Fontenay' type and he argued that it was invented in the circle of St Bernard around 1135–40. The proportions correspond to those in St Augustine's *De Arte Musica*, in which St Bernard is known to have taken a special interest. Any church laid out on the system will automatically have ratios of 1 : 1, 1 : 2 (octave), 2 : 3 (fifth), and 3 : 4 (fourth), and it is tempting to believe that whoever devised it was immersed in Neo-platonism. In an appendix to his book, Hahn listed 156 monasteries which, he believed, showed evidence of the system and, of these, thirteen were in Ireland. According to Hahn, therefore, the Cistercians brought to Ireland not just a new type of monastic architecture but also a formula for coherent proportional planning.

Before accepting Hahn's views, it is important to point out that his knowledge of Ireland was fragmentary[33] and his information was drawn from plans rather than his own surveys of the monuments. The data on which he based his conclusions was not as reliable as his own information on Eberbach and some of his opinions need modification. Although there are plenty of hints of the proportional scheme in the Irish monasteries, there are no buildings where it was used with precision. The system was apparently employed with a fair amount of 'elasticity', which suggests that it was never much more than a rough 'rule of thumb', useful at the start of operations. Its value was as a practical working formula, in effect a series of instructions for laying out an acceptable Cistercian church. There is no evidence that it was valued for aesthetic or mystical reasons, though such thoughts may have been implicit when it was first devised. If proportional relationships seriously mattered to the monks using the building, it is likely that a higher standard of accuracy would have been achieved.

One of the problems in any exercise of this sort is to establish which dimensions were critical for the original builders. It is often far from clear whether they took their measures along the centre of a wall or from its internal or external face. In theory one might expect the centre lines to be the crucial ones, since any proportional scheme must have started off as a simple linear diagram in the mind of the architect. In some of Villard de Honnecourt's drawings, as well as in the plan of St Gall, wall thicknesses appear as a single line. However, when plans were being marked out on the ground, it is easy to imagine how variations might arise. Hahn believed that the key dimensions usually lie within the thickness of the wall,[34] but in Ireland it is doubtful whether this is often the case.

Among the churches which appear to have followed the system is that at Jerpoint. Here units of 56 and 42 feet (17.07 and 12.80 metres) were apparently employed and they relate to the building as follows:[35]

Unit I	crossing and presbytery (east-west)	57′0″
	crossing and north transept (north-south)	
	(width of south transept arch excluded)	56′11″
	width of nave and aisles (internal)	55′8″
	total length of church (170′6″) divided by three	56′10″
Unit II	width of north transept (east-west)	42′5″
	width of nave and one aisle (internal)	41′3″
	length of transept (86′9″) divided by two	43′4½″
	length of church (170′6″) divided by four	42′7½″

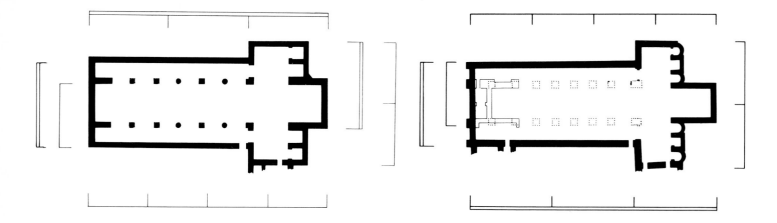

Fig. 24 Jerpoint, proportions according to Hahn's scheme.

Fig. 25 Mellifont, plan of first church showing proportions according to Hahn's scheme.

This is by no means a perfect exposition of the system. In the nave it is necessary to switch from external to internal measurements in order to make the scheme correspond with the fabric. Even more disturbing is that discrepancies occur in a building that was in other ways laid out with remarkable accuracy. The east walls of the two transepts, for example, have identical measurements and differences in the widths of the four chapels amount to less than three inches. If the masons of Jerpoint were capable of this precision, why are the same standards not found in the proportions? Despite these inconsistencies, the number of approximations to one or other of the units is telling and it is hard to deny the correlations which exist with the system defined by Hahn. It appears that, while the builders of Jerpoint were capable of a high degree of structural accuracy, precise proportional planning was not a matter of much concern.

The use of proportional formulae at Jerpoint, albeit employed in a rather cavalier fashion, has an important bearing on the history of the abbey. There is some uncertainty about whether the community belonged to the Cistercian order when building began around 1160,[36] but the nature of the plan effectively removes any cause for doubt.

At almost the same time as the foundation of Jerpoint, the monastery at Boyle was laid out in a similar manner and there is evidence that the same units of 56 and 42 feet were employed.

Unit I	crossing and presbytery (east-west) (including thickness of west wall of transept)	56′7″
	crossing and transept (north-south) including thickness of both crossing arches	55′0½″
	width of nave and aisles	56′4″
	total length of church from outer face of east wall of transepts to inner face of west facade: 170′10″ divided by three	56′11″
Unit II	width of transepts	43′6″
	width of nave and one aisle	44′0″
	length of transepts 79′4″ divided by two	39′8″
	length of church from outer face of east wall of transepts to inner face of west facade 170′10″, divided by four	42′8½″

The discrepancies between theoretical and actual dimensions are very substantial in this case and the north-south length of the transept in particular is far too short. The squeezed proportions of the transepts and their chapels has already been noticed and it is born out by this deviation from the scheme. The multiples of units I and II (unit III in Hahn's terminology) define the length of the church only as far as the east wall of the transept, a feature common to many of the buildings analysed by Hahn. The effect of this is that the nave of Boyle is somewhat longer than Jerpoint in proportion to the rest of the building. As at Jerpoint, the figures given in the table are, with one exception, external dimensions. If centre-to-centre measures are used, the proportional system will still work, with units of about 52 and 39 feet (15.85 and 11.88 metres), but the length of the nave can no longer be included within it.[37]

Both Jerpoint and Boyle belonged to the affiliation of Mellifont and it is important to establish whether the first church at Mellifont, built with the advice of Robert of Clairvaux, shows evidence of the same proportional methods. Hahn thought not, though it was a conclusion he found hard to accept. As a daughter house of Clairvaux, founded in 1142, Mellifont *ought* to have embodied the scheme, which, Hahn argued, was becoming universal by this date. To overcome this paradox, he proposed, without any historical evidence, that the ruins of the first church at Mellifont represent a pre-Cistercian building, erected before 1142.[38] In fact Hahn had no need to resort to these tortuous arguments. The proportional scheme which he defined can in fact be applied to Mellifont as the following table shows (Fig. 25). The relevant units appear to be 62 feet and $46\frac{1}{2}$ feet (18.90 and 14.17 metres).

Unit I	crossing and presbytery (east-west)	62'9"
	width of nave and aisles, varies	59'10"–62'10"
	total length of the church (188'1")	
	divided by three	62'8$\frac{1}{2}$"
Unit II	width of nave and one aisle	c47'
	centre of crossing to east wall of presbytery	47'4$\frac{1}{2}$"
	length of transepts (north-south)	
	(96'10") divided by two	48'5"

In one important respect, Mellifont deviates from the theoretical scheme. The width of the transept, which should correspond to unit II (46 feet 6 inches, 14.17 metres), is far too short (28 feet 8 inches, 8.74 metres). Perhaps the awkward site, with bedrock so close to the surface, prompted an abbreviation of the plan at the east end.

So far it has been assumed that the Irish Cistercians were using a measure based on the old English foot of twelve inches, though one cannot be certain of this. During the Middle Ages the length of a foot varied, depending on the locality, and apart from the English foot of 30.48 cm., other measures employed were the Roman foot of 29.57 cm., the Carolingian foot of 33.29 cm., and the French *pied royale* of 32.48 cm.[39] It is not easy to calculate the size of the foot employed in Ireland and, in view of Mellifont's connections with Clairvaux, the French *pied royale* is worth consideration. Ingrid Swartling has argued that this was the measure introduced by the Cistercians to Sweden, in their first house at Alvastra.[40] The major dimensions of Mellifont, however, do not make any greater sense when translated into *pieds royales*, and the fact that several Irish cloisters approximate to a hundred English feet suggests that this latter measure was the one generally employed.

It would be rash to pretend that the three Irish churches just analysed provide overwhelming proof of Hahn's proportional schema. There are many discrepancies and inaccuracies which inevitably prompt a degree of scepticism in interpreting the plans in this way. It is, however, striking that three different buildings at least approximate to the system and this is unlikely to be a coincidence. It suggests that some proportional method analagous to that defined by Hahn was used to lay out the foundations of these churches, even though the method was not followed or treated with scrupulous care.

Further evidence of proportional planning can be discerned elsewhere within the Mellifont affiliation. At Corcomroe, for example, the system was modified to suit a church with only one chapel in each transept (Fig. 26). A square of about 56 feet (17.07 metres) encloses the whole of the eastern arm and a unit of about 42 feet (12.80 metres) determines the width of the transept (east-west).[41] The late twelfth century church at Monasteranenagh also follows the scheme and there are further hints of it in the first church at Kilcooly, as well as in the late thirteenth-century church at Hore. One building which seems to defy analysis in this way is Abbeyknockmoy. The

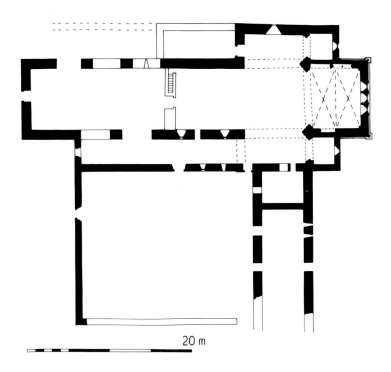

Fig. 26   Corcomroe, plan.

20 m

system can be applied only if some wall thicknesses are included and others excluded in a fairly
arbitrary way. While this might be exactly what happened, with workmen digging sometimes
one side of a rope or line, sometimes the other, it is too irregular to be convincing.

The six Anglo-Norman houses, where the plans are known, reveal the same rather spasmodic
evidence of proportional planning. Grey is a good illustration of Hahn's system, employing
units of about 62 and $46\frac{1}{2}$ feet (18.90 and 14.17 metres) (Fig. 11):

Unit I	crossing and transept (north-south)	61'8"
	crossing and presbytery (east-west)	62'4"
Unit II	width of transept (east-west)	47'2"
	length of transept (north-south) (92')	
	divided by two	46'0"

These dimensions do not relate to the short, aisleless nave, and this is further evidence to suggest
that the abbey was not completed on the scale originally planned. The transepts and eastern arm
at Inch also fit the scheme, though as Hahn noted, the extended presbytery does not coincide
with any of the proportional units.[42]

At first sight the two monasteries of Dunbrody and Graiguenamanagh appear to be planned
in an identical manner, especially as both have three chapels in each arm of the transept (Figs 20,
27). But this impression is misleading and there are many differences in the proportions of the
two buildings. The transepts at Dunbrody, for example, are more oblong in shape than those at
Graiguenamanagh and the presbytery is somewhat shorter. Moreover the width of the nave and
presbytery is greater than the transepts, which meant that the original crossing did not form a
square. Although Hahn included Dunbrody together with Graiguenamanagh in the same
category,[43] there are grave doubts whether his proportional system is relevant to either
building. The foundations of Dunbrody were laid out with considerable accuracy, but it is
remarkable how few of the major dimensions coincide with the system of proportional units.
Each transept is about 52 feet 4 inches square, a measure which in theory represents unit II. On
this basis, unit I should be approximately 70 feet, a figure which corresponds to half the length of
the transepts (69 feet 4 inches, 21.13 metres), but to very little else. Neither unit appears to define
the other major elements of the plan.

Similar difficulties are encountered at Graiguenamanagh (Fig. 27). Although some features of

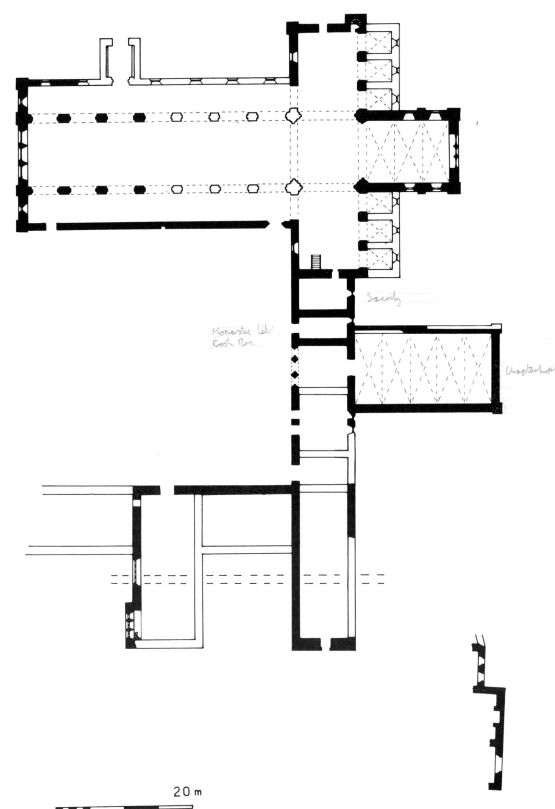

Fig. 27   Graiguenamanagh, plan of the abbey.

the plan are consistent with Hahn's system, others are not. Among several proportional oddities of the building is the fact that the aisle walls are not aligned to the dividing walls of the chapels.[44] In visual terms this meant that the inner chapels of the transepts were not in line with the axes of the aisles, a slightly arbitrary relationship, suggesting the lack of an overall proportional scheme. One careful piece of planning is, however, worth notice. The presbytery measures 29 feet 6 inches by 45 feet (8.99 × 13.72 metres), a satisfying 2:3 ratio of width to breadth.

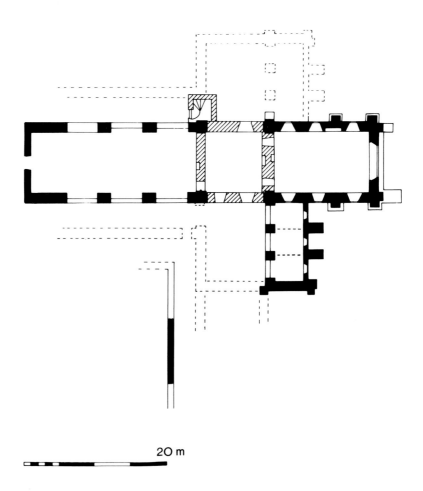

Fig. 28   Tintern, plan of the church.

20 m

Tintern is another building where there appears to be no need to invoke Hahn's theories to explain the plan (Fig. 28). The design is neatly balanced around the axis of the west wall of the transept, with the nave equal in proportion to the combined length of the presbytery and crossing. The total length of the church is 162 feet 5 inches (49.50 metres) and this divides into two elements of about 81 feet. The other major dimension of the building, the north-south length of the transepts was approximately 113 feet (34.44 metres), a measure perhaps attained by the use of the square root of 2. When the length of the eastern arm is multiplied by $\sqrt{2}$ (1.414) it produces a figure of 114 feet 6 inches, sufficiently close to 113 to suggest that this was how the transept length was generated.

The proportional system used in the rebuilding of Mellifont is easier to discern and it is clear that a serious effort was made by the thirteenth-century builders to make the design as coherent as possible (Fig. 19). The new north transept was 61 feet 4 inches wide (18.9 metres), a dimension derived from the width of the old nave (59 feet 10 inches to 62 feet 10 inches). When doubled, this measure produced the total length of the transept (124 feet, 37.8 metres), and it also defined the length of the new presbytery. The outer walls of both the transepts and the presbytery were equidistant from the centre of the crossing (62 feet, 18.9 metres). The length of the reconstructed transepts (124 feet, 37.8 metres) also corresponded to the length of the nave (125 feet 5 inches, 38.23 metres) and the remodelled building thus contained a neat series of 1:1 and 1:2 relationships. All this is consistent with Hahn's proportional theories, which Mellifont II fits as closely as Mellifont I.

Despite a number of exceptions and variants, one can conclude that the proportional methods employed in the so-called 'Bernardine' churches of Europe were also used in the design of Irish buildings. The analogies with the system as outlined by Hahn are too numerous to be dismissed as coincidence. The major weakness in his approach was that his conclusions were applied too dogmatically and too comprehensively. Using small scale plans it was easy to imagine relationships which are not born out when measured at full scale on the ground.[45] Thus several abbeys, including Dunbrody, Graiguenamanagh and Abbeyknockmoy, ought to be removed from Hahn's list. The proportional schema was clearly not a sacrosanct blueprint, incapable of alteration. At best it was a useful aid to laying out a swift plot on the ground and thereafter it was often forgotten. When the nave of Boyle was completed, for example, no attention was paid to proportional ideas worked out fifty years before by a totally different generation of monks and builders.

The system of two related squares was not necessarily the only workshop method employed in the planning of the Irish houses. The ratio of $1:\sqrt{2}$ can be found on occasions and there are also hints of the golden section. The measure of 42 feet (12.80 metres), used as a key unit in several monasteries, is a dimension generated by multiplying 100 by $\sqrt{2}$. Thus at Jerpoint, where the intention appears to have been to lay out a cloister of 100 feet square, the transept extends 42 feet further east beyond the line of the cloister. It is as if a rope placed diagonally across the cloister was swung round in order to define the adjacent transepts. A similar method may have been used at Graiguenamanagh, where the cloister of 120 feet (36.58 metres) generated a transept width of 50 feet (15.24 metres). The overall relationship (120:170) is in the ratio of 12:17, one of the favoured medieval approximations for expressing the ratio of $1:\sqrt{2}$. In several monasteries, including Mellifont, the figure of 62 feet (18.90 metres) occurs as a basic unit, a dimension derived from multiplying 100 by the golden section (1.618).[46] The presence of these ratios should not, however, obscure the fact that the Cistercian churches of Ireland were fundamentally modular in plan, the result of accumulating and combining a few square geometrical forms. At Grey, Jerpoint, and one or two other well preserved abbeys, it is possible to sense the 'square' spatial effects resulting from this approach. It is a method that is emphatically Romanesque, a point to bear in mind when deciding whether the Cistercians should be described as 'pioneers of Gothic'.

Chapter 4

THE ARCHITECTURE OF THE CHURCHES
1142–c1400

THERE WAS MORE variety in the elevations than in the planning of Irish Cistercian churches. Designs range from relatively sophisticated structures like those at Boyle and Jerpoint to the bleak austerity of buildings like Monasteranenagh and Abbeyknockmoy. During the main era of construction, from 1142 to c1250, it is possible to distinguish several architectural phases, the first of which was characterised by Burgundian influence. As the twelfth century progressed, this was gradually submerged by ideas derived from English Romanesque. After 1190 the picture became more varied as early Gothic features appeared in the new Anglo-Norman houses. With their elegant lancet windows and dog-tooth ornament, these buildings form a distinctive and easily identifiable group.

The Burgundian connection

As the first Irish houses were offshoots of Clairvaux, it is important to establish to what extent the early buildings of the order were French in character. Many years ago, the French historian, J. Vendryes, trenchantly remarked that 'Mellifont, fille de Clairvaux, marque ainsi avant l'invasion anglo-normande une pénétration en Irlande d'esprit français de style français.'[1] Although Vendryes did not produce much evidence to support his opinions, it is certainly true that one would expect the church at Mellifont to have had a strong Burgundian imprint. Constructed with the advice of a monk sent from Clairvaux, it was erected in a land where there was little experience of monumental church architecture. There were no local models to influence the design and the Cistercians were free to establish their own ideas. The loss of Mellifont I is, therefore, a great handicap and we shall never know for certain just how French its architecture was. Elsewhere in Ireland there is less room for doubt and plenty of evidence exists to show that Burgundian styles of building made a considerable impact.

Before analysing this trend, it is important to glance at Cistercian architecture in Burgundy during the middle years of the twelfth century. In the past there has been much discussion as to whether there was a specifically Cistercian style of building, a proposition which most authorities would now deny. If, however, the question is narrowed down to the Clairvaux affiliation, it is possible to be more positive. Between 1135 and c1160 definite architectural forms were favoured in this branch of the order and here it does seem possible to speak of a Cistercian style.[2] During the 1130s, under the guidance of St Bernard, there developed a distinctive, though highly reactionary, approach to the question of what a major monastic church should look like. This was prompted by the need to reconstruct the church at Clairvaux, when St Bernard, for so long a critic of Cluniac extravagence, was faced with the task of producing an alternative approach. Clairvaux was a highly influential building[3] but following its destruction in the French Revolution one depends on the neighbouring abbey of Fontenay to get an impression of the so-called 'Bernardine' style. With its bare walls and lack of ornament, Fontenay is always regarded as the very embodiment of Cistercian architectural practice (Pl. 40) The roots of its design go back to Burgundian architecture of the eleventh century, to churches like Tournus, Chapaize and St Vincent des Prés, and it is clear that the Cistercians were in effect trying to turn the clock back fifty years, to an era before church architecture had become tainted with over-sumptuous Romanesque, and specifically Cluniac, ideas.

40   The interior of the Burgundian abbey of Fontenay (c1139–47), covered throughout by pointed barrel vaults.

41 The church at Fontenay from the south-east, showing the simple angular massing of the building.

42 The interior of the nave at Bonmont (Switzerland), c1148, a plainer and more austere church than Fontenay.

This is not the place to embark on a detailed description of Fontenay, but a few of the features especially relevant to Ireland need to be mentioned.[4] Its rectilinear plan, with straight ended presbytery and square transept chapels, was copied widely throughout the order, and as we have already seen, at least seven of the Irish houses followed the same pattern (Fig. 14). The practicality and simplicity, so evident in the plan, were also a hallmark of the interior elevation. There was neither a triforium nor a clerestory and, as a result, considerable emphasis is placed on the bare wall surfaces above the main arcades. The piers of the nave are basically rectangular in shape, with applied pilasters and half columns. The church was covered throughout with pointed barrel vaults, a feature of Burgundian Romanesque. The vaults over the side aisles were constructed transversely to the main axis of the building, a system derived from the narthex at Tournus. At the springing of the vaults there is a continuous string course, one of several elements which provides a sharp sense of articulation. Pointed arches were employed in the main structural positions, with round arches restricted to doors and windows. The spatial organisation of the building is particularly noteworthy. The vaults of the presbytery and transepts were erected at a lower level than those in the nave and as a consequence the nave was very much the dominant space within the church. As no attempt was made to define a regular crossing, the nave vault runs unbroken to the presbytery arch. All this has a significant effect on the exterior form of the building, producing a simple, rather angular, arrangement of masses (Pl. 41). Seen from the east, there is a regular stepping of forms, with the roof of the nave rising well above those over the presbytery and transepts. One other detail of Fontenay is worth notice. There is no mural stair leading to the roof spaces and, in order to provide access to the roofs above the transept chapels, doorways were inserted above the chapel entrances. Isolated at a high level, these doorways could be reached only by ladders, and they appear as a rather odd utilitarian element in the design.

Although well preserved, Fontenay is not necessarily the most representative church in the 'Bernardine' group. Despite its simplicity and austerity, it seems inordinately complex when compared to a building as plain as Bonmont in Switzerland (Pl. 42). This was another daughter house of Clairvaux and the church was largely finished by 1148. As at Fontenay, there are pointed barrel vaults throughout the building, but this time they are not articulated by transverse arches. The piers are also much simpler, being reduced to a straightforward cruciform shape, devoid of half columns. There is no triforium or clerestory and, in the absence of any wall shafts or responds, the accent on plain wall surfaces is even more marked than at Fontenay. It is no surprise that François Bucher concluded his study of the building by remarking that 'in its simple austerity the church of Bonmont must be counted as the best representative of early Cistercian architecture'.[5] The severe character of the design, with its expanses of bare wall, is not without parallel in Ireland.

Despite the differences that exist between Fontenay and other churches in the so-called 'Bernardine' group, they share many common characteristics which reappear in monasteries right across Europe, from Eberbach in Germany to Alvastra in Sweden. The latter house is particularly interesting from an Irish point of view. Founded in 1143, one year after Mellifont, it was also a daughter house of Clairvaux, established with a nucleus of French trained monks.[6] In the context of local building, the church at Alvastra represented something quite novel, for Sweden was as isolated as Ireland from the mainstreams of European Romanesque. It had the typical 'Fontenay' plan, plus several features of the Fontenay elevation. It provides a further reminder that the type of architecture adopted at Clairvaux and Fontenay exercised a decisive influence in the Cistercian order, particularly within the affiliation of Clairvaux itself.

The design of buildings like Fontenay and Bonmont stems from a carefully considered theoretical approach to architecture, which was more than just a critique of Cluniac extravagance.[7] Under the leadership of St Bernard, the Cistercians were, in essence, attempting to redefine the true function of a monastic church. 'My house is a house of prayer' Christ declares in the Gospels[8] and the Cistercians took this as their axiom, seeking to eliminate everything that was not directly relevant. A monk, wrapped in meditation, should not require extra emotional stimulus from the building; in St Bernard's phrase, he should be able to transcend 'a meaningless hull of stone'.[9] Fine paintings, coloured glass and other artistic luxuries might assist the spiritual life of the general populace, but they served no purpose in a monastic church. This was a place for tough intellectual work—a 'workshop of prayer'—where the world of the senses was not to be encouraged. Above all, architecture ought not to distract the monk from his spiritual and intellectual endeavours and what was required was a neutral, passive interior. To fulfil such demands, the design could not be left to chance, for awkward proportions and irregular spaces were just as likely to disturb the tranquil atmosphere as expressive carvings or vivid paintings. The stress on carefully judged proportions, both in plan and elevation, was thus part of a consistent theoretical approach. Stripped of decorative accessories, the Cistercian church was reduced to an essential architectural framework, often dull but not devoid of intrinsic beauty. It is difficult to resist the analogies with the Miesian philosophy of architecture, which François Bucher pointed out. While too succinct for St Bernard's florid literary style, 'less is more' is a dictum worthy of the great abbot himself. It is important to remember that Ireland's first acquaintance with European Romanesque architecture came via this very purist stylistic tradition.

The most striking element derived from Burgundy was the pointed arch, used consistently in Irish monasteries for major load bearing positions. As in France, doors and windows continued to be built with round-headed arches until the advent of Gothic. Allied to the pointed arch was the pointed barrel vault, another Burgundian importation. Although generally restricted to the presbytery and transept chapels, wherever twelfth-century vaults survive, the distinctive pointed profile is visible. The best examples are at Boyle where the great pointed barrel over the presbytery is still intact (Pl. 43). The marks of a similar vault can be seen at Jerpoint and, until its collapse during a storm in the nineteenth century, another existed at Monasteranenagh. It is likely that the presbytery of Mellifont I was vaulted in the same way and that this provided the model for other Irish monasteries.

An important characteristic of the Bernardine churches was the presence of 'low' transepts, combined with a low presbytery. The arches of such a transept survive at Baltinglass, rising only a few feet higher than the adjoining nave arcade (Pl. 44). It is no longer possible to judge the height of the original presbytery, but the evidence suggests that the spatial arrangement at Baltinglass was closely related to the Bernardine group. Founded in 1148, the abbey was one of the first daughter houses of Mellifont.

Baltinglass' own daughter house at Jerpoint also had low transepts, though a certain amount of detective work is necessary to prove the point. The crossing here was totally rebuilt in the fifteenth century, but it is still possible to trace the springing points of the original transept arches (Pl. 45). They were considerably lower than their fifteenth-century successors and corresponded in height to the original presbytery. Jerpoint was a good example, therefore, of the Bernardine church, with both transepts and presbytery being roofed at a lower level than the nave. Apart from the sculptural details, the eastern arm of the church was thoroughly Burgundian in conception, an impression reinforced by the pointed arches, pointed barrel vaults and of course its 'Fontenay' type of plan (Pl. 46, Fig. 10). This work was carried out between 1160 and 1170, over twenty years after the start of Mellifont, where most of these features had probably been introduced to Ireland. Although there are no other abbeys with 'low' transepts, it is clear that almost all the churches in the Mellifont affiliation, as well as the Anglo-Norman abbey of Dunbrody, were initially designed without a regular crossing, a fact largely disguised by the subsequent erection of towers. Corcomroe is one abbey that retains the original arrangement. Here there is no western arch to the crossing and the nave continues unbroken to the chancel arch, as was often the case in France (Fig. 26).

A strong Burgundian flavour also permeates the early work at Boyle. The church here was constructed in several separate campaigns, the first of which embraced the presbytery and transepts. These were built between 1161 and c1180, making them contemporary with the corresponding parts of Jerpoint. If it were not for the carved details on the bases and capitals, it would be difficult to tell that this was an Irish building. Apart from obvious characteristics, like the pointed arches and pointed barrel vaults, there are some specific features that go back to

46 Jerpoint Abbey, the chapels of the south transept. The pointed arches and pointed barrel vaults underline the Burgundian conception of the early work at the abbey.

43 (facing page top left) The presbytery at Boyle, covered by a pointed barrel vault of Burgundian inspiration (c1170).

44 (facing page top right) The south transept at Baltinglass (c1150–60). The transept arches were low compared with the total height of the church.

45 (facing page bottom) The north-west crossing pier at Jerpoint. Traces of the capital which supported the original low transept arch can be seen in the angle.

continental prototypes. The roof spaces above the north transept chapels, for example, are reached through a doorway placed high in the wall, as at Fontenay and Noirlac (Pl. 47). A similar doorway was later constructed at Abbeyknockmoy. The springing of the barrel vault in the presbytery was defined by a string-course, another detail copied from Burgundian models. Although the thirteenth-century crossing tower has somewhat altered the original appearance of Boyle, it is here that one can measure the full extent of French influence in Ireland.

One should not assume that the masons responsible for the early campaigns at Jerpoint and Boyle had any first-hand knowledge of French architecture. The minor details of both buildings indicate that local men carried out the work. Nor is it likely that the monk in charge of building operations, probably the cellarer, had travelled to France to imbibe the principles of Cistercian design. Instead, the diffusion of Burgundian characteristics is better explained by assuming that there was a common prototype in Ireland and the obvious candidate for this is Mellifont I. If true, the design of the first church at Mellifont takes on enormous significance and so too does the achievement of the monk Robert, sent from Clairvaux in 1142 to assist with its construction. How long he stayed we do not know, but it appears that his views on architecture had a pervasive influence in Ireland for at least the next three decades.

French influence can also be detected in the form and arrangement of east windows, which were especially prominent in the straight-ended Cistercian chancels. They provided the main focus of attention inside the building and, outside, their arrangement was critical to the appearance of the eastern facade. In France it was normal to fill the wall with a triplet of windows, surmounted either by a further triplet, as at Fontenay, or a rose window, as at Noirlac. An approach closer to Fontenay was favoured by the Cistercians in Ireland, where rose windows

81

47 The north transept at Boyle (c1170), where the architecture has a strong Burgundian flavour as at Jerpoint.

48 The east facade of the presbytery at Jerpoint. Three Romanesque windows decorated with chevron were replaced by the traceried window in the fourteenth century.

did not acquire much popularity. Although the original windows were often replaced at a later date, at Boyle and Jerpoint it is possible to make out the twelfth-century arrangement.[10] Boyle had a double row of three round-headed windows, the positions of which are indicated by surviving string-courses. The excessive articulation of the wall by four separate string-courses was unusual and proved to be a source of confusion when the builders reached the transept. At Jerpoint there were three windows at a lower level, but it is unclear how many openings there were above (Pl. 48). The window arches were decorated with chevron and the string-courses were carved with Romanesque beading.

The architecture of Burgundy made less impression on the naves of Irish churches. No attempts were made to vault this part of the building and instead the Irish Cistercians followed their English brethren in opting for clerestory lighting and open wooden roofs. As no shafts or responds were needed for vaulting ribs or transverse arches, there was a complete lack of vertical accent, leaving instead wide areas of smooth wall, flowing with minimal interruption into equally plain piers. With the solitary exception of Boyle, the concept of bay division was unknown.

Pier forms contribute more than anything else to the visual impression of the buildings, but in most abbeys they were treated in starkly functional terms. Mellifont I seems to have set an example of blunt austerity which was followed by a large proportion of her affiliated houses. It is still possible to detect fragments of the twelfth-century piers at Mellifont, immured in work of later centuries, and these suggest that they were basically square or rectangular in shape.[11] The north-west crossing pier was furnished with a pilaster towards the aisle, the plinth of which remains, but it is not clear whether pilasters ornamented the faces of all the piers. The presence of a pilaster makes one think of the continent rather than England. Bonmont immediately comes

to mind. Piers of simple square form were also employed at Baltinglass and Jerpoint, though here they alternated with cylinders (Pls 51, 53). In most churches of the Mellifont affiliation far less energy was wasted on pier design and crude rectangular forms of rubble masonry were frequently considered sufficient. Examples constructed without even capitals or abaci can be found at Holycross (north arcade) (Pl. 27), Kilcooly, Corcomroe and Monasteranenagh. Later in the thirteenth century, at Bective, Hore and the Anglo-Norman abbey of Tintern, simple chamfered piers, minus capitals and abaci, continued to be employed.

Deprived of their plaster finish, the buildings now look much rougher than they once appeared. In essence this was an architecture of planes, of smooth flat areas of wall and sharp angular forms, in direct contrast to the well-modelled, sculptural shapes found in so much Romanesque architecture. Even the clerestory windows, devoid of recessions or framing colonettes, do not disrupt the even surfaces. Peter Fergusson has recently pointed to a group of early Cistercian buildings where this manner of 'stripped austerity' is very pronounced.[12] Rievaulx (Yorkshire) c1132–50, is the prime English example and a French equivalent can be found on the borders of Brittany at Clermont (Mayenne), c1152–70. This severe, desolate design could be mistaken for an Irish church, a French antecedent of Monasteranenagh or Holycross (Pl. 50). The number of resemblances is uncanny—the pointed arches devoid of mouldings, plain rectangular piers, no attached shafts, a simple clerestory and open timber ceiling. Also associated with Rievaulx and Clermont in this widely dispersed group is the nave of Margam in south Wales, an abbey which had many contacts with Ireland. While visually not very rewarding, these designs were the embodiment of the Cistercian quest for simplicity. Moreover in an Irish context they had the advantage of being cheap to erect, without the need for a large troop of expert masons.

51   The nave of Baltinglass (c1160–70) with its alternating sequence of square and round piers.

The start of English influence: Baltinglass and Jerpoint

Even before the Anglo-Norman invasion of 1169–70, English characteristics had begun to appear in Irish architecture. This is particularly noticeable at Cormac's Chapel, Cashel (1127–34), the decoration of which is closely related to buildings in the west country.[13] In Cistercian abbeys the first signs of English influence appear in sculptural details—scalloped capitals, for instance—and by c1160–70 the cylindrical pier, much favoured in English Romanesque, had

52 The nave of Buildwas (Shropshire), where the design has obvious parallels with Baltinglass and Jerpoint.

been adopted at Baltinglass (Pl. 51). The cylinders here were combined with square piers to produce an alternating system of supports in the nave. The source of these cylindrical piers was almost certainly an English Cistercian house and Buildwas in Shropshire provides obvious parallels (Pl. 52).[14] This monastery, on the banks of the Severn, became Cistercian in 1147 and the construction of its church was virtually contemporary with Baltinglass. It is worth noticing that the piers at both abbeys were surmounted by capitals and abaci of square plan, resulting in an awkward overhang at the angles. The capitals at Baltinglass consist of a series of imaginative

53　The north arcade of the nave at Jerpoint. Each of the piers shown in the photograph is different in design.

Fig. 29　Jerpoint, plan of fourth and fifth piers in the nave.

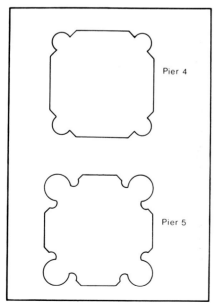

Pier 4

Pier 5

variations on the theme of the scallop and, while the variations are partly Irish, the idea of the scallop itself was derived from English practice. There is something peculiarly appropriate about these English features, for Baltinglass had as its patron the redoubtable Dermot MacMurrough, king of Leinster, the most anglophile of Irish kings.

The arcade at Baltinglass is badly disfigured by remnants of a perpyn wall, a permanent screen of masonry about five feet high, cutting off the aisle. This is bonded into the piers and it thus belongs to the orginal design. The system was copied at Jerpoint and there are parallels for it in England and Wales, at Buildwas, Fountains and Strata Florida for example. In its ruined state it now looks crude, but it is important to remember that in all Cistercian churches the lower parts of the piers were once obscured by choir stalls and wooden screens.

The design of Baltinglass was used as a prototype when work began on the nave of Jerpoint Abbey about 1170, and a similar alternating system was employed for the first three bays (Fig. 10). As building progressed, however, the design was repeatedly altered and refined (Fig. 66). Several distinct campaigns can be observed. The eastern arm of the church, including one bay of the nave, belongs to the first phase, characterised by the use of richly decorated capitals. With the second pier of the nave these were abandoned in favour of plainer scalloped ornament. Following the alternating sequence, the second pier is square and the third is circular, but at this point a further change was introduced. The circular part of the pier does not descend to the ground on the aisle side as before, but rests on a large square plinth, the height of the adjoining perpyn walls. This was a sensible alteration and it shows that the mason in charge, having accepted the inevitability of the perpyn walls, was trying to integrate them more logically into the design.[15] With the fourth and fifth piers, the elevation was altered more fundamentally. The alternating system was abandoned and octagonal piers, furnished with shafts on their diagonal faces, were introduced (Fig. 29). The purpose of this change, which disrupts the rhythm of the design, is far from obvious. The monks of Jerpoint evidently preferred variety to homogeneity in what must have been a long-drawn-out building programme. To judge from details of the west window, the final bays of the church were erected not much before 1200–10.

The clerestory windows at Jerpoint and Baltinglass were placed, somewhat eccentrically, over the piers, not the arches (Pl. 53). This became a popular device in Irish Cistercian monasteries, occurring in seven of the ten abbeys where the clerestory survives (Baltinglass, Jerpoint, Monasteranenagh, Abbeyknockmoy, Dunbrody, Graiguenamanagh and Hore). Windows situated over piers can be found sporadically throughout Europe, but the Irish Cistercian abbeys represent an unusual concentration of examples.[16] The rationale of the scheme has never been satisfactorily explained. Clerestories of this form generally occur in buildings without any great structural pretensions and Romanesque parallels outside Ireland include the church at St Briavels (Gloucestershire) and the priory church at Ewenny in South Wales.[17] No prototype has been established for the Irish examples, but the source may well have lain in Wales or the west country of England. By introducing a syncopated rhythm into the elevation, its visual effects are not unattractive. It represents the antithesis of much Romanesque design, especially in France, where the accent is placed on bay units and clearly defined spatial divisions. In unvaulted churches like those in Ireland, however, wall shafts were unnecessary and the definition of bays almost irrelevant.

The design of the nave at Boyle

Boyle is the most attractive of the Irish Cistercian churches and stylistically the most intriguing. As already explained, the eastern arm contains Burgundian characteristics, but the rest of the building is emphatically English. Like Jerpoint it was built over a long period, which gave rise to several changes of design. In the nave it is possible to distinguish three separate phases of construction, spread over the period c1175–1220 (Fig. 66).

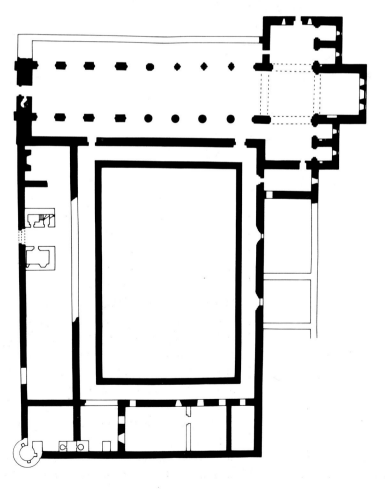

Fig. 30   Boyle, plan of the abbey.

20 m

55 Boyle Abbey, south arcade (c1180) with inserted corbel (c1215). This pier (no. 4) marks the junction of two separate campaigns, as can be seen in the change of arch design.

56 The ruined nave at Abbey Dore (Herefordshire) where the cylindrical piers and scalloped capitals recall the work at Boyle.

54 Boyle Abbey, the first two arches of the south arcade, with imposing cylindrical piers of English origin.

I.   The first four bays of the south arcade, built with impressive cylindrical piers, belong together and represent a continuation of work from the transepts. The piers are made of excellent ashlar masonry, technically the best of its kind in Ireland (Pl. 54). The arches they support consist of two orders and the introduction of a second order permitted the use of octagonal capitals and abaci. These are far more elegant than the square forms employed earlier at Baltinglass and Jerpoint. The bases (which alternate with thick and thin horizontal rolls) rest on square plinths and there are extravagant foliage spurs in the angles. Again this represents a development from Baltinglass, where the spurs are small and undecorated. In one respect the design is curiously un-Cistercian, for the arches are round not pointed, a fact which underlines how far Burgundian precedents had been abandoned in favour of English Romanesque.

In the spandrels of the arches there are a series of small corbels (Pl. 55). Although most were inserted at a later date, a few are original. No other Irish abbey has these features and their function is not immediately obvious. Those in the nave are too low to have supported a vault, nor is there any evidence of vaulting in the aisle. Probably they supported wall posts, linked to the wooden roof above and, if so, Boyle must have been one of the few Irish buildings where the division of bays was stressed by a series of vertical accents.[18] Consistent with this approach was the orthodox location of the clerestory windows over the arches, not over the piers as often happened in other Cistercian churches.

As the work at Boyle is stylistically in advance of the equivalent parts of Baltinglass and Jerpoint, it should be dated a little later, to the period 1175–80. The design is so characteristically English that one wonders whether an English master mason was in charge, perhaps a laybrother borrowed from a Cistercian monastery in the west country. The nave of Abbey Dore (Herefordshire) provides many parallels and, although now a ruin, its nave arcade corresponded

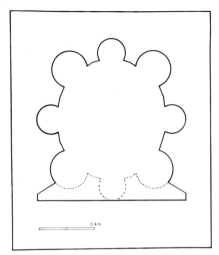

Fig. 31 Boyle, plan of piers 1–3 in north arcade.

57 Boyle Abbey, north arcade (c1200). The clustered piers and pointed arches are a complete contrast with those in the corresponding arcade to the south.

58 Boyle Abbey, view through the sixth bay of the nave (c1215–20). Note the contrast of arch forms on each side of the nave.

closely to Boyle (Pl. 56).[19] There were the same cylindrical piers, furnished with similar capitals; the bases had elaborate foliage spurs and the west face of the crossing piers, at the start of the nave arcade, was given a broad semi-circular shaft as at Boyle. Some details at Abbey Dore suggest that it was constructed marginally later, but the similarities leave no doubt about Boyle's identity with this part of England.[20] Quite how this came about is not clear, but the Irish Cistercians did have contacts with their English brethren and the abbot of Buildwas, for example, paid no less than three visits to Ireland in the 1170s.[21] It is also important to remember that St Mary's, Dublin, a daughter house of Buildwas, was anglophile in sentiment and its buildings probably served as a fountain-head of English architectural ideas.

II. The first four bays of the north arcade at Boyle were designed as if the south side did not exist and the contrast between the two halves of the church is startling.[22] Pointed arches were reintroduced and clustered piers replaced the pure cylinders opposite (Pl. 57, Fig. 31). The central shaft in each pier cuts through the abacus and rises a short distance up the nave wall. These complicated forms were abandoned fairly quickly, perhaps because they were slow and expensive to build, being replaced in the fourth bay by a simple octagonal pier.

The four northern bays are not easy to date. The capitals of the third pier have some similarities with those in the transepts of Christ Church Cathedral, Dublin (c1186–1200),[23] and the whole programme was probably carried out between 1185 and 1200. Equally difficult to assess is the origin of the eight-shafted pier, for which there are no Irish precedents. This is constructed not like an early Romanesque compound pier, with the shafts tucked inside re-entrant angles, but with shafts projecting forward from what is basically a circular core. By the end of the century piers in England were often built with detached shafts, made of dark polished stone, whereas those at Boyle are constructed with coursed masonry. This technique is associated with monastic building in the north of England and the versions at Boyle look like a clumsy attempt to copy the clustered piers at Furness or Holm Cultram, both monasteries with important Irish connections.[24] Clustered piers developed in northern France in the 1140s, in

59 Boyle Abbey, looking east down the nave at the end of the nineteenth century. The western piers in the foreground belong to the last campaign of construction (c1215–20). (National Library of Ireland, Lawrence Collection).

60 Capital at Boyle, (seventh pier from east, north side). The triple shafts, semi-octagonal abacus and the absence of a necking band are characteristic of the 'school of the west'.

such buildings as Berteaucourt-les-Dames (Somme), whence they spread into Cistercian architecture both in France and England, eventually reaching Ireland shortly before 1200.

III.   For some years the nave of Boyle terminated at the fourth bay and it was not until c1202–20 that the final phase of construction was undertaken.[25] Both north and south arcades were built together this time, though in selecting his arch forms the new master mason faced an embarassing choice. He decided to compromise by continuing with round arches on the south side and pointed arches on the north. After what had gone before, the new piers were unexciting. Square in plan, with chamfered angles, they were relieved only by a group of triple shafts on the inner faces, which support the inner order of the arch (Pl. 58). The outer order rises without any intervening capital or abacus. Facing both nave and aisle, at the level of the spandrels, are long corbels, composed of triple shafts. Further corbels, with identical abaci profiles, were inserted at the same time throughout the earlier parts of the nave. As these corbels were designed to support wall posts for the roof, it suggests that the high roof of the nave was erected in its entirety shortly before 1218/20. The west facade, with its moulded doorway and tall lancet window, ornamented with chevron, was constructed as part of this same campaign. Extensive use of grey sandstone further helps to distinguish this phase of building from earlier work.

The style of the western bays indicates that they were carried out by a master mason who was thoroughly intimate with building practice in the English west country. As his knowledge of English methods extended to small details, he must have received his training at one of the major workshops in that area. Among the features typical of the so-called 'school of the west' are:[26]

1 The continuation of a plain outer order from pier to arch, combined with an inner order having the usual capitals and bases (Pl. 58). The main arcades at Llandaff Cathedral, though more complicated, provide a good parallel for this treatment.
2 The use of triple shafts, the centre one with a pointed bowtell moulding.
3 Semi-octagonal abaci over the triple shafts (Pl. 60).
4 Capitals without necking, of which several examples occur at Boyle.
5 Wall buttresses with continuous angle shafts, as on the west facade (Pl. 24).
6 The use of mini-corbels to terminate an arch order. These are found only on the north arcade, where they support the outer keeled moulding. Diminutive corbels, such as these, are

widespread in the Severn Valley and buildings which use them include, perhaps significantly, the chapter house of the Cistercian abbey at Margam.

All of these features appear at Christ Church Cathedral, Dublin, in the crypt and eastern arm of the building. As the cathedral also provides precedents for details of the west window at Boyle (the multiple banding of shafts, the particular form of chevron in the window head and the moulding profiles), it seems likely that the master mason of the abbey first came to Ireland as part of the cathedral workshop. His roots, however, lay in England, or rather the Welsh marches. One has only to compare the corbels of Boyle with those that supported the vault in the remote Augustinian house of Llanthony, to appreciate how closely his style was based on the conventions of the west country.

In view of the location of Boyle and the historical events of the time, the Englishness of the building is paradoxical. The abbey was situated outside the area of Anglo-Norman settlement, at least until 1235, and the English characteristics of the architecture are not to be explained by the invasion. Indeed Boyle is one of the last abbeys where one would have expected English influence on this scale. The monastery was almost certainly hostile to English incursions into the area, especially after the damage it suffered in 1202. The main patron of the abbey, the local lord of Moylurg, is unlikely to have welcomed English settlers. The abbot and his community were Irish born and, to judge from their complicity in the conspiracy of Mellifont a few years later, they were equally antagonistic to Anglo-Norman influence.[27] In view of this, the community's taste for English architecture is something of a surprise. If the masons who worked on the church included Englishmen or Welshmen, as seems likely, their journey to Connacht must have taken some courage. Quite how and why they were recruited remains a mystery.

The advent of Gothic

Gothic architecture was introduced to Ireland by the Cistercians and the new style made its appearance in those abbeys founded after the Anglo-Norman invasion of 1169–70. In England at this time the Cistercians played a crucial part in spreading early Gothic forms, especially in the north, and monastic churches like Roche and Byland were among the most advanced of the time.[28] The order thus enjoyed an important role in effecting the transition to Gothic, in particular by encouraging the diffusion of forms which had originated in northern France. Once English houses began to establish dependencies in Ireland, it was to be expected that the latest architectural trends would accompany them. But just how advanced were the designs of the new Irish houses?

By the standards of Roche or Byland, a fairly muted type of Gothic made its appearance. None of the Irish houses adopted a three storey elevation and in terms of structure the churches differed little from their predecessors. Ribbed vaulting at a high level was erected in only two houses, Graiguenamanagh and Mellifont, and even here it was restricted to the presbytery. Piers retained a heavy, massive appearance and little attempt was made to dissolve their solid forms. Detached shafting, so favoured by English architects as a means of adding delicacy and colour, was rarely used and an equally restrained attitude governed the design of arch mouldings. One might, with justice, ask what was Gothic about these buildings. Gothic however they are, for the rather old fashioned reason that lancet windows can be seen almost everywhere, imparting a vertical drive to the elevations. All the early Gothic monasteries have, or had, a composition of narrow lancets in the chancel, dominating the vista up the church. The space inside the buildings also tended to be more vertical in proportion, an impression especially marked at Graiguenamanagh, where the original floor level was four to five feet lower than it is today. Thinner and more subtle mouldings are another reflection of the new style. Keeled rolls make their first appearance and there was a widespread use of fillets on both engaged shafts and arch mouldings.

There are five churches constructed between c1190 and c1250 where it is possible to study these developments. The abbey at Inch, founded in 1187, is usually regarded as the first of the

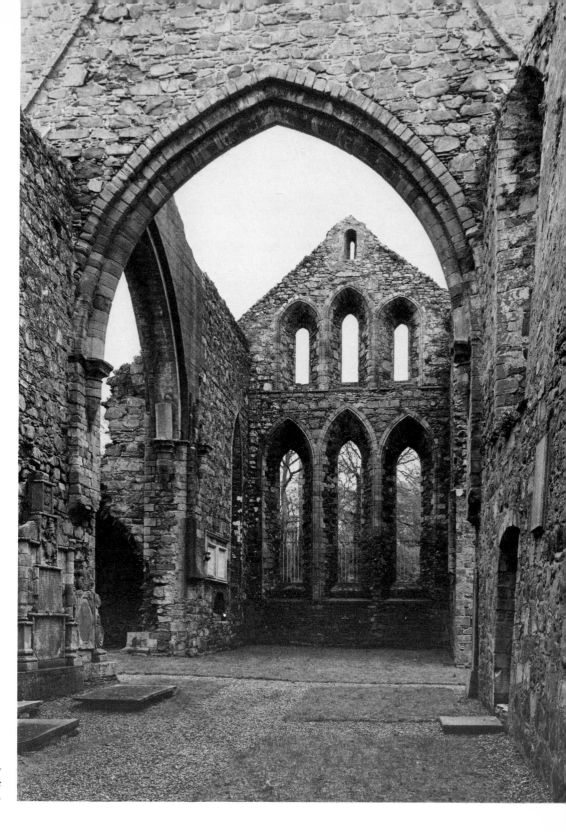

61 The interior of the church at Grey Abbey (c1193–1200), which has some claim to be considered the first Gothic building in Ireland.

group,[29] but there are reasons for thinking that the church there was not begun until c1200. Grey abbey, founded in 1193, has a good claim to be considered the first Gothic building in the country (Pl. 61). The most sophisticated was Graiguenamanagh (c1204–c1235), which was larger than the others and richer in its detailing.

Building at Grey started not long after the monks arrived from Holm Cultram in 1193 and the church has three features of considerable significance. The most noticeable aspect of the ruins is the double group of lancets in the presbytery, the rear arches of which are thinly outlined by continuous keel mouldings. When compared to the small round-headed windows used before, and still retained in the 1190s at Abbeyknockmoy, they set an acute, forceful tone to the building. Their impact is the greater since the presbytery was not designed to receive a vault, and this represents a second important development. It must have been covered only by a timber roof, as were the chancels at Dunbrody and Inch, and later in the thirteenth century, those at Tintern and Hore. The final point of interest concerns the crossing. This was defined by arches on each of its four sides and it is thus one of the first regular crossings in an Irish Cistercian abbey (Fig. 11). The arches are in three orders, the inner one supported on neat, though rather stubby corbels, typically Cistercian in character. The regular form of the crossing implies that a tower was planned from the start, following the practice in English Cistercian houses. With its central tower, its ubiquitous lancets and its unvaulted presbytery, Grey established a new type of church for the order in Ireland and set a pattern that was followed in most of the Anglo-Norman monasteries. It is however important not to overlook the conservative elements of the design— the barrel-vaulted chapels, the absence of free-standing piers in the transept and the ordering of the east windows, which despite their Gothic form, were arranged in a traditional manner.

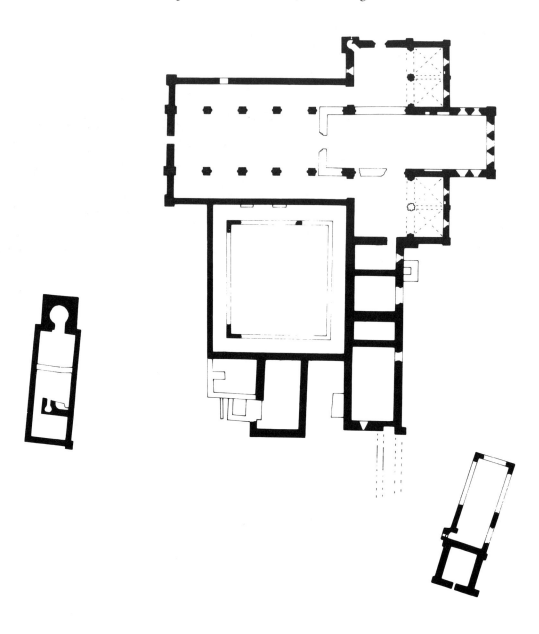

Fig. 32   Inch, plan of the abbey.

20 m

62 The ruins of the church at Inch, dominated by a striking group of Gothic lancets in the presbytery (c1200).

Fig. 33 Inch, plan of clustered pier used in transepts.

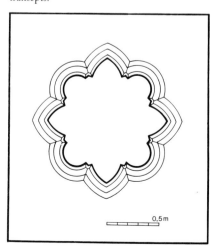

0.5 m

Although it is difficult to pinpoint the origin of the design of Grey, its background appears to lie in the north of England. Some details recall the architecture of the Augustinian abbey at Lanercost (Cumbria) in the northern Pennines, not least the double set of lancets and the stumpy corbels under the crossing arches. There are no obvious links with Holm Cultram, the mother house, though the monks there may have assisted in the recruitment of the master mason.

Inch took up the innovations of Grey and developed them in a more ambitious and stylish manner. The presbytery is again dominated by lancet windows, this time a single group reaching high into the gable. Altogether there were seven lancets grouped around the chancel, shedding light on the high altar and providing a bright focus to the church (Pl. 62). The most important developments, however, appear in the transepts. The chapels were separated by a clustered pier of far more sophisticated design than anything before in Ireland. It consists of an octofoil, with an alternating sequence of round and keeled shafts (Fig. 33). This form, ultimately French in origin, was much favoured by the Cistercians in the north of England, where it was introduced at Roche in the 1170s. A few years later it was employed at Byland, which like Inch was a daughter house of Furness.[30] In view of the fashionable nature of this pier, it is a pity that none of the superstructure survives above. Adding to the up-to-date flavour of Inch were the ribbed vaults within the chapels, a contrast to the barrel vaults at Grey with their solid dividing walls.

The ruins at Inch get progressively sparse towards the west and only the bare foundations of the nave remain. These are sufficient to show that the octofoil piers of the transept were abandoned in the rest of the building and replaced by less enterprising forms. Both nave and crossing piers are square in plan, with filleted rolls on the angles and a large triple-filleted shaft on the inner faces. It is likely that the angle rolls were continued unbroken around the nave arches.

With its octofoil piers, its ribbed-vaulted chapels, it soaring lancets and its abundance of filleted mouldings, Inch is a more progressive design than Grey. It is hard to believe it was built earlier, as foundation dates imply, and it appears that the church was not started until after 1200. Work continued on the nave until well into the century, to judge from the mouldings of the piers.[31]

Just as the two Ulster monasteries of Grey and Inch form an interesting comparative pair, so do the Leinster houses of Graiguenamanagh and Dunbrody. They were the largest Cistercian churches in Ireland and both were built at the same time. The nave elevations have much in common and, as we have already seen, the plans of the buildings are similar. But there is a noticeable contrast in tone. Whereas Graiguenamanagh is one of the more lively and ornate Early English designs in the country, the architecture of Dunbrody, particularly the eastern arm, is of the utmost severity.

The ruins of Dunbrody lie in an isolated and exposed position, sitting, as one nineteenth-century writer put it, 'in naked solitude on the edge of the whispering waves' (Pl. 63).[32] The site is dominated by a massive late medieval crossing tower, which has distorted the original appearance of the monastery. The exterior view of the church has also been affected by the Tudor house, constructed above the south transept chapels (Pl. 64). A tower did not form part of the initial design and when first constructed gabled roofs stretched unbroken from one end of the building to the other. Gaunt and barn-like, there was no avoiding the impression that this was a utilitarian building, very much a 'workshop of prayer'. The addition of the tower also altered the interior of the church. New crossing arches were inserted, more pointed than the original ones, and colossal buttress piers now disrupt the view from west to east.

The presbytery, as at Grey and Inch, was not vaulted and it is so lacking in architectural adornment that it is difficult to date with any accuracy. The three graded lancets in the east wall are exceptionally austere, devoid of mouldings on the inner jambs and arches. The transepts are equally bleak, though there is some slight relief in the chapels. Angle shafts and filleted roll mouldings once surrounded the entrance arches[33] and the vaults inside have ribs with filleted profiles. The transepts themselves form a vast, cavernous space, with wide expanses of unbroken wall surface (Pl. 65). The piers between the chapels, for example, are plain, a contrast to the attractive octofoil piers used in this position at Inch. Unlike most of the Anglo-Norman abbeys, the crossing was not defined by east and west arches. Moreover, the transept arches were low for such a huge church and they are only just pointed. The spatial impression is therefore one of width rather than height, particularly as there was originally no crossing tower. A curious feature of this austere and rather inelegant design is the use of banded masonry on some of the arches, yellow limestone alternating with darker coloured sandstone. This lively technique was favoured for a brief period, when the west wall of the transept and the crossing arches were under construction. Banded masonry, often associated with Islamic architecture, was employed sporadically by Romanesque builders, and it was used in South Wales at St David's Cathedral and in the Cistercian abbeys at Margam and Strata Florida.[34] It is a rather exotic ornament to discover in the spartan atmosphere of the Dunbrody transepts, representing perhaps a passing fad of one master mason. The technique was later adopted in the nave of Kilkenny Cathedral, though again in a random fashion.[35] It was probably difficult to ensure a continuous supply of stone from two separate quarries.

The arches that led from the transepts into the nave aisles were narrow and steeply pointed, a bizarre contrast to those in the crossing. The first arches in the nave arcade, blocked when the tower was built, also had this unusually steep form. Thereafter the nave arcades are wider and it is likely that the first pier in the nave marks a pause in operations. This raises the question of the date of the first campaign of building. The foundation date of 1182 is too early for the filleted mouldings in the chapels, which encouraged Leask to suggest that the church was built at a 'somewhat later date'.[36] Very much later was Champneys' opinion and he assigned a date of around 1250 to the work.[37] But if the seventeenth-century antiquary Sir James Ware is to be believed, a substantial amount of building was already complete by 1216. This was the year in which, according to Ware, Herlewin, bishop of Leighlin, died and he was interred in the church, 'a greater part of which he had caused to be erected'.[38] If this is correct, the eastern arm should

63 Dunbrody Abbey, sitting 'in naked soli-
tude on the edge of the whispering waves'.
View from Bartlett's *Scenery and Antiquities of
Ireland* (1842).

64 Dunbrody Abbey from the east. The chimneys belong to the Tudor house later constructed above the south transept chapels.

65 The cavernous transepts of Dunbrody.
The night stair survives intact and there is
unusual banded masonry on the crossing arches.

66 The nave of Dunbrody, with the clerestory sited in Irish fashion above the piers. The south arcade fell in 1852 (compare Pl. 2).

67 Dunbrody Abbey, the ornate clerestory window in the nave which appears to mark the division between the monks' and laybrothers' choirs.

68 Dunbrody, the second bay of the nave. Note the slight change in the arch design at this point.

be attributed to the period 1205–16. If Ware's evidence is discounted and reliance placed solely on stylistic features, a date of c1210–30 would seem more appropriate.

The ascetic qualities of the choir and transepts were relaxed a little in the nave.[39] Dog-tooth ornament makes an appearance and there is an occasional stiff-leaf capital. The south elevation collapsed in 1852, but the north wall is preserved up to the level of the roof and this gives a good impression of the design (Pl. 66). In many ways it was a characteristic piece of Irish architecture. The square piers continue into the arches without an intervening capital, recalling the treatment in the western bays at Boyle; moreover the clerestory windows are sited over the piers, as at Baltinglass and Jerpoint. Whether the English-trained builders of Dunbrody consciously copied earlier Cistercian design is a moot point. The treatment of the clerestory is curious. The internal splays of the windows stretch down into the spandrels of the arcades, creating a very disjointed impression. The location of the clerestory not only obliterates any vertical division into bays but also obscures the sense of a horizontal division between the storeys. Externally the windows were expressed as two trefoil-headed lancets, like those used nearby in the old cathedral of Waterford[40] and the parish church at Thomastown.

One window in the clerestory was treated differently from the others (Pl. 67). Here the rear arches are subdivided and decorated with dog-tooth. There are bonded shafts on the angles and a detached shaft in the centre. The engraving in Grose's *Antiquities*[41] shows the same embellishment on the south side and this extra ornament was apparently intended to stress the division between the monks' choir and that of the laybrothers. It is one of the few instances in which the liturgical arrangements of a Cistercian church were expressed in the main elevation.

The design of the piers and arches of the Dunbrody nave are a good illustration of a distinctive method that became common in thirteenth-century Ireland. In England, as Champneys observed, arches of any breadth were built in a series of recessed orders, but in Ireland the soffits were frequently designed in one plane, except for a small moulding at the corner and an isolated order in the middle.[42] Such arches are first found in the eastern arm of Christ Church Cathedral, Dublin (c1186–1200) and they reappear in the transept of St Patrick's Cathedral and in the crossing at Kildare. In a Cistercian context, something similar has already been noted at Boyle and the same treatment can be found in the domestic buildings at Neath in South Wales.[43] The method was repeated at Graiguenamanagh and probably at Inch (nave) and Mellifont II (north transept). It was an economical though ponderous technique, the simplicity of which appealed to the Cistercians. This 'simplified soffit', as it might be termed, was in effect a continuation of the undecorated square piers. To support the reduced inner order, all that was required was some species of respond, a function served by a corbel at Dunbrody and Graiguenamanagh.

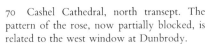

The west facade at Dunbrody was the most attractive part of the church. Its vast window, filled with a primitive form of plate tracery, was destroyed along with the southern half of the nave in 1852, and the decoration of the doorway, now blocked, is largely worn away (Pl. 69). In 1786 Mervyn Archdall reported that 'the ruins of this very extensive abbey exhibit an awful and picturesque scene. . . . The west window, of an uncommon form, is entire, and the door immediately beneath it was very magnificent, being adorned with filigree open-work (i.e. dog-tooth) cut in the stone, so raised as to allow a finger easily under it.'[44] If these features had survived, the architecture of Dunbrody would now seem less severe, but even allowing for this, it is clear that the abbey did not stray far from the austere spirit of the Cistercian Rule.

The church at Graiguenamanagh was one of the finest pieces of Early English architecture in Ireland and it is unfortunate that much of its beauty has been lost. It was badly damaged when

the tower collapsed in 1744[45] and subsequent building within the ruins has impaired its sense of space. Construction of the church began soon after the monks arrived in 1204, to judge from the style of the capitals in the presbytery and the church was probably finished about 1235–40.[46]

The design of the presbytery was a contrast to that at Dunbrody. It was well articulated, there is a strong vertical impulse and a certain amount of discreetly placed ornament (Pl. 73). Unlike the three Anglo-Norman houses so far considered, it was covered by a ribbed vault, constructed in three tall narrow bays, with steeply pointed wall arches. Only the springers of the vault remain, resting on filleted wall shafts. In two of the bays there are lancet windows, the jambs of which have engaged columns, banded at frequent intervals. Below the windows is a string-course, running continuously around the presbytery and decorated with miniature zigzag, typical of the unobtrusive ornament that characterises the whole design. Although only 5 feet 3 inches (1.6 metres) above the floor of the restored church, this string was almost 10 feet (3 metres) above the thirteenth-century floor level. Further string courses underline the clerestory windows in the nave and transepts, providing a visual emphasis that was conspicuously lacking at Dunbrody. The east windows, which are more elaborate than any hitherto seen in an Irish Cistercian church, have trefoiled inner arches, the centre one pointed. Contrary to normal practice, the jambs are not made of solid masonry, the arches resting on slender detached shafts, clumsily restored (in 1813?).

The early work at Graiguenamanagh has been compared with the chancel of Kilkenny Cathedral, particularly the design of the east windows.[47] In both churches there are lancets which have pointed arches on the interior but round heads outside, a curious and rather archaic feature. Hood mouldings which terminate in tiny foliage stops are another common characteristic. This suggests that the designs were roughly contemporary and it underlines the fact that the early Gothic architecture of the Cistercians in Leinster belonged in style with a wave of building carried out by the English settlers after the conquest.

Like most of the Anglo-Norman monasteries, Graiguenamanagh was designed with a tower from the outset. This is indicated by the staircase and mural passage which provided access from the north transept, and a tower is known to have existed in 1330, when one Richard O'Nolan was besieged inside it.[48] The crossing arches below the tower were supported on impressive

72   The interior of the transepts at Graiguenamanagh as illustrated in Robertson's *Views of Kilkenny*.

73 The presbytery at Graiguenamanagh (c1207–20) following the recent restoration.

74 Graiguenamanagh, the three surviving bays at the west end of the nave (south side). The design should be compared with that of Dunbrody (Pl. 66).

compound piers, with elaborate rolls and filleted shafts (Fig. 75). The architect of Graiguenamanagh managed to avoid the rather overwhelming and enclosed effect of the Dunbrody transepts by introducing circular windows in the clerestory. Indeed, in terms of fenestration, Graiguenamanagh has some interesting features. For the first time in Ireland, the rose window, so popular with the Cistercians on the continent, was exploited on an extensive scale, with three circular windows lighting the east wall of both transepts (Pl. 72). On the interior they have a rear arch with straight jambs and nook shafts, a treatment derived, ultimately, from mid-twelfth century France. Pontigny, Noirlac and Preuilly all provide precedents. A further oculus, this time without a rear arch, fills the north transept gable, where it was used in conjunction with two Early English lancets. The master mason also exploited the popular Early English technique of using detached columns of dark stone, in this case probably carboniferous limestone imported from south Wales or Somerset. When first installed in the clerestory of the nave and transepts, these polished shafts must have formed a bright contrast with the yellow stone from Dundry, used for the surrounding dressings.

The four eastern bays of the nave have long since been destroyed and in place of the original arcades stand the walls of the nineteenth-century church. Three bays of the thirteenth-century building survive at the west, though the arcades have been blocked (Pl. 74, Fig. 27). The elevation was in principle similar to Dunbrody. The piers were square in form (though with a wide chamfer on the angles), and the arches had the customary simplified soffits. The clerestory was sited over the piers in the Irish manner and the windows were subdivided, like those adjacent to the screen at Dunbrody. On closer inspection, however, several crucial differences are apparent. The mouldings are more sophisticated; a string-course provides a firm dividing

75 Mellifont Abbey, view looking south along the transepts. The square piers to the left belong to the mid-thirteenth century remodelling of the church.

line between arcade and clerestory and the strange disjointed effect of Dunbrody is avoided. The clerestory windows have round-headed arches, exceedingly archaic for the period 1230–40.

The mixing of round and pointed arches had been a Cistercian trait from earliest times, but to find round-headed windows at this late date is unusual, though not without parallel elsewhere in Ireland. The monks' doorway (c1220) was also round-arched, so a conservative trend was well established in the monastic workshop (Pl. 36). The final and most important distinction between Graiguenamanagh and Dunbrody concerns the proportions of the bays. Compared with the enormous bay length of 24 feet (7.3 metres) at Dunbrody, that at Graiguenamanagh was a more normal 18 feet (5.5 metres), a factor which enhances the verticality of the elevation.

Closely related to Graiguenamanagh, though slightly less enterprising, was the design of Mellifont II (c1230–40).[49] This also had a ribbed-vaulted presbytery but here the vault responds did not descend to the ground. The tight articulation of Graiguenamanagh was therefore lacking. There were the usual graded lancets in the east wall and surviving fragments show that the jambs of the windows were decorated with angle shafts, banded at regular intervals. A newel staircase was fitted into the north-east corner of the transepts, in the same position as that at Graiguenamanagh, perhaps indicating the existence of a crossing tower. The thirteenth-century

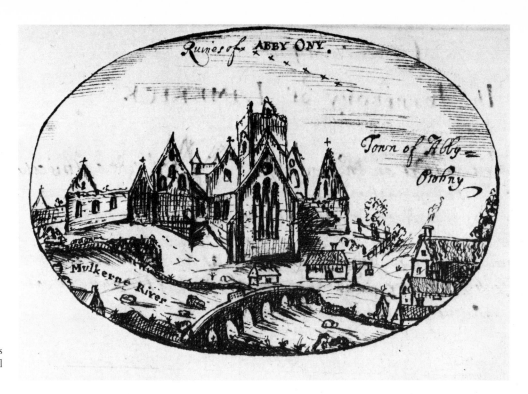

76 Abington Abbey as sketched by Thomas Dinely in 1681, when the walls were still largely intact.

work in the north transept includes piers of standard Irish form, square in plan, with filleted angle rolls and a single engaged column on the inner faces (Pl. 75, Fig. 19). From all this it is clear that the architect of Mellifont II, in contrast to his twelfth-century predecessor, was content to follow contemporary trends in Anglo-Norman Ireland, rather than introduce fresh concepts from abroad. The technical quality of the masons, however, was high. The stones are precisely cut, the mouldings crisp and fashionable.

Taken as a group, the Cistercian houses built by the Anglo-Normans were orthodox and restrained examples of the Early English style. It is unlikely that this picture would be altered if more of the 'lost' buildings had survived—Abington, Comber, Abbeylara, Macosquin and Tracton. Abington, destroyed in the eighteenth century, is known through Dinely's sketch of 1681,[50] which suggests that it followed the same pattern with graded lancets in the east windows and a tower over the crossing, two of the crucial features introduced at Grey after 1193 (Pl. 76).

There is plenty of evidence to show that Cistercian Gothic was intimately associated with local monuments, though it is not always clear which way the influence was flowing. Masons clearly moved freely between the various workshops of Anglo-Norman Ireland. The transepts of Cashel Cathedral (c1260–1310), for example, have a strong Cistercian flavour. The wall passages and the curious tracery that once existed in the north and south windows are related to Dunbrody (Pls 69, 70) and the plan of the transepts ultimately goes back to Baltinglass. The north transept arches in the Augustinian abbey of Kells have an austerity which reflects earlier Cistercian practice. As already mentioned, Waterford and Kilkenny Cathedrals had features in common with Dunbrody and Graiguenamanagh and Dr T. McNeill has recently argued that the parish church at Carrickfergus owes much to Cistercian buildings in Ulster.[51] It would be wrong to suppose that the Cistercians alone brought about the change to Gothic, for many other workshops had direct contacts with England. But the order helped to promulgate the change of fashion and its simplified Gothic style was well suited as a model for less affluent ecclesiastical patrons.

The Irish houses of the west

While English settlers were founding their new Cistercian houses, plenty of building activity was going on in the affiliation of Mellifont, especially in the west. Among the major monuments to date from this period are Monasteranenagh, Abbeyknockmoy and Corcomroe, and from them it is possible to assess the Irish response to the arrival of Gothic.

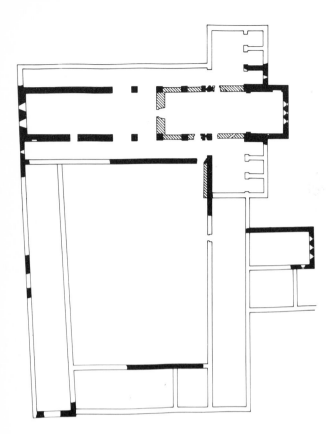

Fig. 34 Monasteranenagh, plan.

77 The presbytery at Monasteranenagh. The pointed barrel vault collapsed in 1874. (Compare Pl. 12).

78 Monasteranenagh, the north-west pier of the crossing. This was reinforced to the left soon after it was built, obscuring a fine foliage capital. The rubble walls belong to late medieval alterations.

Earliest in date is Monasteranenagh, the abbey that achieved notoriety in 1228 for its hostility to Stephen of Lexington, and the abbey which in the words of the visitor 'had drunk from the chalice of Babylon'.[52] The architecture of the church is not distinguished by the same spirit that the monks showed in this traumatic year. The ruins lack charm and romantic appeal and this perhaps explains why they have been so little studied.[53] The precise date of construction is one of several awkward archaeological and historical issues that await solution.

In many respects the design of the church follows well-established trends in the affiliation of Mellifont. A pointed barrel vault was erected over the presbytery and the responds of the chancel arch are typical of Irish Romanesque, with shallow angle rolls cut out of the corners of broad pilasters (Pl. 77). The remaining capital is decorated with weird scallops, the latter transformed into some species of plant ornament. All this work is pre-Gothic in character and should be dated between c1170 and c1190. It was the chancel roof that was made the strong point of the 1228 defences presumably because it was well fortified by the stone vault below.

The archaeological problems begin with the east window. Although a victim of the wholesale collapse of 1874, it is apparent that this had three tall lancets, the heads of which were decorated with keeled mouldings (Pl. 12). These are stylistically incompatible with the rest of the chancel and the windows must therefore be replacements. Similar lancets were inserted at Boyle some years after the church there was finished and it appears that Monasteranenagh also switched to the new Gothic fashion. Apart from these windows, there is little else that could be described as Gothic.

Further questions arise in the area of the crossing, where the western piers show signs of drastic alteration. As initially constructed, the north-west pier was only 4 feet 3 inches (1.30 metres) in length, including the engaged shafts (Pl. 78). The inadequacy of this as a support for the transept arches was quickly realised and the pier was subsequently extended a further three feet (0.9 metres) to the west. The original engaged shaft is still visible, embedded in the masonry of the pier. It is not certain how the first design would have continued down the nave, but clearly it was intended to be more elaborate than the line of simple piers that took its place.

The crossing piers contain several other unexplained features. The mouldings applied to those

79 Monasteranenagh, capital of the south-west crossing pier.

80 The dour ruins of the church at Monasteranenagh seen from the south-west. As at Abbeyknockmoy the arches of the nave do not continue to the west facade.

on the west side do not correspond to the responds opposite on the east. The transept arches were thus supported by piers of discordant character. Equally perplexing is a vertical moulding which can be seen high up in the western crossing piers. This is a continuation of the moulding lower down on the east face of the pier, but it carries on *above* the springing of the arch. Indeed the arch itself—or at least the abacus—gives the impression of having been inserted as an afterthought. In the context of Cistercian architecture, these anomalies are baffling and it is hard to deduce what the masons of Monasteranenagh were up to.

The church apparently had a tower, which is said to have fallen in 1806 or 1807.[54] One of the Ordnance Survey letters of 1840 described this as 'a noble square structure of great height' and it explained that it stood at the *west* end of the nave.[55] There is no archaeological evidence of a tower in this position and it seems the author must have made a mistake about its location. Perhaps it was at the *east* end of the nave, in the standard position over the crossing. If so it was built after the siege of 1228, for no tower existed then. It is more likely that the letter was referring to a late medieval or post-dissolution tower over the south transept. This transept was covered by a barrel vault, the springing of which in part survives. It is clear that the vault was an addition, for the walls had to be thickened to reinforce it. As barrel vaults were an inherent part of the structure of most Irish tower houses, it appears that a sixteenth-century house was constructed above the south transept and it was this that fell in 1806/7.

The architectural history of the church at Monasteranenagh is therefore confusing. Only the nave seems relatively free from problems of interpretation, but it must be admitted that it is a dull piece of design, the vista wrecked by the wall built across the nave to reduce the size of the church in the later middle ages (Pl. 39). Characterless square piers with chamfered edges support a sequence of plain pointed arches. This continues for four bays, then the line goes on as solid wall. Small round-headed windows, sited in the Irish fashion over the piers, do little to relieve the monotony. Architecture as plain as this offers few clues as to date. There are no hints of nascent Gothic, except for a pointed bowtell moulding in the twin west windows, which suggests that the church was finished around 1210.

81 Abbeyknockmoy, the east facade. The continuous mouldings around the lower windows are typical of the 'school of the west'.

Abbeyknockmoy and Corcomroe are more rewarding buildings than Monasteranenagh and they contain architectural and sculptural details of great interest. They were constructed about two decades later, in a style that has a stong regional identity. The most noticeable feature is the rejection, after fifty years, of the Burgundian pointed barrel vault in favour of ribbed vaulting. The new vaults are still profoundly Romanesque in design and like other novelties in the buildings they cannot be attributed simply to Gothic influence from the Anglo-Norman abbeys.

Both churches belong to what has been described as 'the school of the west', a regional school of building that lasted from c1200 to c1240. This was first analysed by Leask, who pointed out the common characteristics in more than a dozen buildings, situated mainly within the confines of Connacht and north Thomond.[56] There is too much variety to imply that they were carried out by a single workshop, but clearly a relatively small group of masons was involved. They worked on a variety of buildings, which included cathedrals as well as Cistercian and Augustinian abbeys, and their patrons were almost exclusively Irish. With the possible exception of Killaloe Cathedral, it was not until 1238 that there is evidence of the masons working for the Anglo-Normans.[57] The school is thus associated with a region that successfully resisted Anglo-Norman control for many years and the eventual subjugation of Connacht in

82 The Augustinian abbey of Ballintober (Mayo), the design of which has many analogies with the Cistercian houses of Abbeyknockmoy and Boyle.

83 Abbeyknockmoy, detail of east window showing grotesque heads and foliage ornament characteristic of the 'school of the west'.

1235 heralded the end of the style. Although often described as 'transitional', it is more Romanesque than Gothic in character and represents a last flowering of Romanesque in one of the more remote provinces of Europe. Much of its inspiration can be traced back to the English west country, a relationship which the Cistercians, with their contacts abroad, helped to foster. The architecture of Boyle, particularly the work carried out in the final campaign (1202–20) played a vital part in the formation of the style.

Before commenting in detail on the architecture of Abbeyknockmoy and Corcomroe, it is worth listing the more prominent characteristics of the 'school':

1 Excellent ashlar masonry, with precise jointing.
2 An abundance of foliage ornament, carved in low relief.
3 The use of trumpet scalloped capitals and their derivatives.
4 Windows completely framed by mouldings, without interruption from capitals etc. The mouldings are frequently carried across the bottom of the window.[58]
5 The retention of late forms of chevron ornament, often with the pattern undercut.
6 A preference for keeled mouldings (the one feature that can be considered authentically 'transitional'). Hollowed rolls are also common, but filleted mouldings are less usual.
7 Hood mouldings continued either side of the window, sometimes as a string-course.
8 A preference for certain specific profiles in the carving of bases.

Most of these features can be seen at Abbeyknockmoy and the group of windows in the east facade of the church furnish a beautiful example of continuous framing (Pl. 81). The chief interest of the presbytery lies in its ribbed vault, which has analogies with the vault in the Augustinian abbey of Ballintober, less than thirty miles away. The east facade of Ballintober is a more ornamental version of that at Abbeyknockmoy and the parallels between the buildings are so numerous that the same masons must have worked at both places.[59] Ballintober is securely dated to 1216–25, one of the few reliably dated monuments in the west, and from this it is clear that Abbeyknockmoy was started around 1210.

This means that Abbeyknockmoy was contemporary with Graiguenamanagh and Dunbrody and slightly later than Grey and Inch. Compared with these Anglo-Norman houses, it is hard to avoid the impression that the two halves of the Cistercian order in Ireland were building in two separate styles. In place of steep lancets, Abbeyknockmoy retains relatively low windows, most of them round-headed (Pl. 83), and the space enclosed by the presbytery lacks any verticality in its proportions. Mouldings and capitals are given greater emphasis and the

84 Abbeyknockmoy, the church from the south, showing the severe, almost rudimentary arches of the nave.

ribbed vault is much weightier than the corresponding vault at Graiguenamanagh. Yet the builders of Abbeyknockmoy were not unaware of techniques being used in the east of the country, for the crossing arches are supported on triple-filleted shafts, as at Inch and Graiguenamanagh.[60]

The nave of Abbeyknockmoy was a most extraordinary design. Indeed design is perhaps too strong a word, for it must have involved the minimum of forethought. The piers can scarcely be considered piers in the normal sense, since the arches of the nave look as if they have been punched through a continuous wall at periodic intervals (Pl. 84, Fig. 18). These elongated 'piers' were decorated with abaci and quasi capitals along their inner faces. The placing of the clerestory windows was equally arbitrary. They are sited more or less over the piers, but the relationship is not exact. In common with their brethren at Monasteranenagh and Corcomroe, the monks of Abbeyknockmoy showed no desire to waste time and money on embellishments in the nave. All the finer details were concentrated at the east end and the laybrothers were left to worship in a thoroughly bleak environment.

The contrast in quality between the two ends of the church was even more marked at Corcomroe.[61] The nave here was utterly unprepossessing and a minimal amount of dressed stone was used in its construction. The crude arcades on either side (some now blocked) are not aligned with each other and it must rank among the worst pieces of Cistercian building in Europe (Pl. 16). By the time it was built, the income of the monks seems to have fallen to a low ebb, a contrast to the atmosphere of confidence and prosperity which existed when the monastery was started. Work began around 1205 in great style and it seems that those in charge intended to produce the finest looking Cistercian church in Ireland. The exterior of the eastern arm is surrounded by an impressive double chamfered plinth and engaged shafts decorate the quoins of the presbytery. Inside, the chancel was covered by a sophisticated ribbed vault and there is an array of imaginative carving, with foliage ornament much in evidence (Pl. 85). The dressed masonry—bases, shafts, and capitals—is of the highest order, executed with precision in the local grey limestone. The eastern crossing piers are a *tour de force* in the context of the west, with a series of engaged shafts placed around the core (Fig. 75). All the shafts are round, without trace of keel or fillet. Three colonettes support the arches leading into the transept chapels, the first time that an Irish house had developed the chapel entrances in this way. The arch leading into the north chapel is furnished with two moulded orders, one carved with a peculiar ornament, proverbially known as 'orange peel' (Pl. 86).

Although there is a strong Romanesque flavour to Corcomroe, the masons in charge were trying to make the building look modern as well as sumptuous. The east windows have pointed heads and keeled mouldings and they were clearly meant to look like Gothic lancets.

The style and panache of the first building campaign was shattered by a crisis which affected the monastery in the 1220s. This was probably related to the famine of 1227–8 and the political unrest that preceded it, events which undermined the economic vitality of the abbey. When building resumed, minimum use was made of ashlar masonry or expensive carving. Standing in the crossing, it is possible to see how far work had progresssed when the crisis struck. The north transept was largely finished, but in the south transept plenty of work was yet to be done. The transept arches were erected after the crisis and their haphazard rubble makes a painful contrast with the fine dressed voussoirs of the chancel arch.

Cistercian church design from 1250 to 1400

After 1250 there was a gradual reduction in the amount of building carried out by the Cistercians and only three churches date from the second half of the thirteenth century, Bective, Tintern and Hore. As the monastery at Hore was a new foundation of 1272, one can assume that the church was erected in the course of the next two or three decades. At Bective only five much disfigured bays of the south elevation survive, dating from c1274–1300, and these represent a reconstruction of the original abbey founded in 1148.[62] There is no documentary evidence for

85 The presbytery at Corcomroe (c1210–20), with its sophisticated ribbed vault and well-modelled piers.

86 Corcomroe, arch leading into the former north transept chapel, showing the strange ornament proverbially known as 'orange peel'.

87 Bective, the south arcade of the nave (c1274–1300), much disfigured by later alterations.

88 The presbytery at Hore (c1272–80). The Gothic lancets were partially blocked in the later middle ages.

the building of the church at Tintern, but stylistic details indicate that it was erected about 1280–1310.

The naves of all three churches are remarkably uniform in design. They reproduce the familiar pattern of square piers, chamfered at the corners, continuing without interruption around equally plain arcades—an arrangement seen long before in Ireland. At Tintern the clerestory has been destroyed, but parts survive at Bective and Hore. That at Bective breaks with Irish tradition in having the windows sited in orthodox fashion over the arches (Pl. 87). In both cases the windows have a quatrefoil shape, like those at Kilkenny Cathedral and Gowran. The parallels between Bective and Hore are surprising, since the monasteries are over a hundred miles apart, though a connection can be found in the activities of David MacCarville, archbishop of Cashel, who was involved in the affairs of both houses.[63]

The architecture of Hore is extremely conservative and its chaste Early English style is more compatible with a date of 1210 than 1280. The austere chancel is reminiscent of Dunbrody, for the lancets are devoid of mouldings and, like Dunbrody, it was not vaulted (Pl. 88). The retrospective character of the design is continued in the transepts, where the chapels were covered by pointed barrel vaults, a testimony to the persistence of Burgundian tradition. The church is distinguished by a dearth of ornament and the colourless design represents Cistercian asceticism at an extreme. The numerous scaffolding holes, apparently left unfilled when building was finished, confirm the impression of a community preoccupied with function rather than beauty (Pls 49, 89).

The late thirteenth-century design of Hore reveals no knowledge of contemporary developments in England and the monks were apparently satisfied with a church that looked much like other Irish abbeys. Tintern, however, maintained contacts abroad though its mother house in Monmouthshire and one of the abbots, Henry of Lancaut, was buried at Tintern Major, where his tomb slab is still to be seen.[64] These contacts are reflected in the design of the church

89 Hore Abbey from the south-west. The monastery was founded by David MacCarville, archbishop of Cashel, whose cathedral can be seen in the background (compare Pl. 3).

(c1280–1310).[65] Although modest in scale, the inspiration for the building came from South Wales and details of the design can be compared with Tintern Major (c1270–1301) and Neath (c1280–1330).[66]

The chancel at Tintern is now reduced to a rather unsightly shell and the tracery of the windows has long since been torn away. A vast east window, perhaps employing geometrical tracery like that at Tintern Major, did not survive beyond the fifteenth century, when its expanse of glass may have made it vulnerable to the attacks made on the lands of the abbey at this time (Pl. 20) The richly moulded jamb stones were re-used, incorrectly, in the much narrower window that replaced it.[67] There is no evidence to show that the chancel was vaulted and no fragments of rib came to light in recent excavations.[68] Nevertheless the outside walls are strengthened by a sequence of shallow buttresses, linked at the top by a corbel table, carved with grotesque heads (Pl. 208). The buttresses are decorated with miniature gables, comparable with those at Tintern Major and Neath (Pl. 282). The chancel at Tintern was not a particularly distinguished piece of architecture, but in contrast to Hore it reveals a far greater awareness of contemporary techniques. The architectural divide between the Irish and the Anglo-Norman houses was thus still noticeable at the end of the thirteenth century. The destruction of the tracery at Tintern is a particular loss, since it was exactly this sort of building that provided channels for the introduction of new forms.

The church was built with a regular crossing and almost certainly a low tower was intended from the start. The arches still survive, though they are embedded in masonry added when the tower was turned into a fortified house in 1566–9.[69] Parts of the south transept also remain, in particular the eastern aisle, rib-vaulted in three bays. The aisle was originally divided into separate chapels by low screen walls, surmounted by sloping capstones, like those on the numerous screens at Tintern Major.

Following recent clearances, the nave at Tintern has now been exposed to full view (Pl. 90). It

90   The interior of the nave at Tintern, shortly after the early nineteenth-century house had been removed from within the walls.

91   Mellifont, the south-west crossing and south aisle. The clustered piers belong to a remodelling of c1325, the octagonal buttress piers to the right were added to support a late medieval crossing tower.

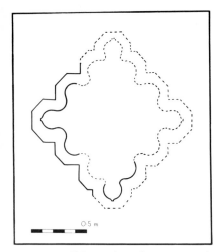

0·5 m

Fig. 35   Mellifont, plan of pier in south transept (c1325).

is such a plain piece of design that it is hard to believe that it was erected at the same time as the choir. However there are no details which contradict a date of c1300 and the plan of the church as a whole is so neatly proportioned that it must belong to one campaign (Fig. 28).[70] As noticed elsewhere, the Cistercians seem to have lost interest once building passed beyond the monastic choir. The side aisles in fact terminated before the west wall, a point demonstrated by the chamfer mouldings on the quoins of the existing west facade.[71]

The fourteenth century was a lean period for Cistercian building though the architectural picture was not as barren as the remains suggest. There must have been considerable activity at St Mary's, Dublin, following the disastrous fire there in 1304,[72] and it was about this time that fire damaged the church at Mellifont.[73] Major works were going on at Mellifont around 1320, though whether this was before or after the fire is not clear.[74] The south transept was enlarged and a start made on rebuilding the nave. An impression of this work can be gleaned from foundations *in situ* and from fragments recovered in excavations. It was an ambitious project, carried out in the Decorated style. Massive diamond-shaped piers, with a sequence of engaged shafts, supported the arcades (Pl. 91, Fig. 35). The south transept arch was decorated with double wave mouldings and similar profiles were used on the doorway into the transept (Fig. 71). It is likely that the windows were filled with curvilinear tracery, characteristic of the period. Only the south-west crossing pier and the first pier of the nave were completed in this style and the rest of the nave was subsequently rebuilt with greater simplicity, the elaborate compound piers giving way to plain octagonal forms. There is every indication that around 1320 the community at Mellifont was abreast of English fashion and it is not impossible that the monks were inspired by the great Cistercian monastery being erected by the Crown at Vale Royal (Cheshire).[75] Whether true or not, this part of Mellifont was an impressive example of Decorated architecture.

Chapter 5

HOLYCROSS AND THE FIFTEENTH-CENTURY REVIVAL

DURING THE FIFTEENTH and early sixteenth centuries a modest revival of Cistercian architecture took place. Most of the projects undertaken were limited in scope, involving such tasks as the erection of crossing towers, the renewal of cloister arcades or the refurbishing of domestic buildings. Only two houses, those at Holycross and Kilcooly, embarked on comprehensive programmes of reconstruction. Unless a monastery was afflicted by some external disaster, as happened at Kilcooly, there was no incentive to spend lavishly on architecture, particularly at a time when the number of monks was diminishing. At Inch, Monasteranenagh and several other abbeys contraction in the size of the communities led to drastic reductions in the scale of the churches. Cistercian architecture thus represents only a small proportion of the total amount of Irish building at the time, a contrast to the dominant position of the order between 1150 and 1250. Although the number of projects was restricted, the standard of craftsmanship was unusually high, and there are several Cistercian churches with fine decorative details, executed in the hard blue limestone which became popular with Irish masons after 1400. Such details are especially evident at Holycross, one of the most ambitious and impressive architectural achievements of the century.

Both Holycross and Kilcooly lay within the territory of the earls of Ormond, one of the more prosperous and stable areas of the country. James, the fourth earl of Ormond (1405–52), commonly known as the white earl, was well disposed towards the Cistercians and he gave financial help to Holycross at the time of the reconstruction.[1] For much of his life he was the most powerful of the Anglo-Irish lords, holding at various periods the offices of lord lieutenant or justiciar. A learned and intelligent man, he had travelled extensively abroad, fighting in the French wars of Henry V and making appearances at the English court. He had the opportunity of visiting some of the finest and most recent churches in England, but as a patron of Holycross he does not appear to have widened the architectural horizons of the monks, at least not as far as the design of the church was concerned. Instead of a fashionable building in the Perpendicular style, which one might have expected, the architecture drew principally on local sources. The white earl's patronage, however, did bestow on the monastery a considerable degree of prestige and legal protection, as well as boosting the revenues of the house.

The first impression of Holycross is of a compact, rugged building, lacking the finesse which one normally associates with Gothic. Modern battlemented parapets give the church a fortified air,[2] a view enhanced by over-sized buttresses and a formidable crossing tower (Pl. 92). But within this dour framework, there are individual features of interest and beauty. There is no need to quarrel with the opinion expressed by John Harden in 1797, when he described the abbey as 'an exquisite piece of antiquity' and 'a ruin the architecture of which is more than ordinarily elegant for this country and alone sufficient to reward a long ride'.[3]

Considering the importance of the abbey in the history of Irish architecture, it is remarkable how little effort has been expended on discovering when it was built. It is, therefore, worth setting out the chronological evidence in some detail. Leask assigned the church to the period c1450–75, largely on the basis of an inscription cut on a shield in the cloister arcade.[4] This shield is beautifully carved with a crosier in the centre and above it there is a sculpture of the crucifixion (Pl. 93). The inscription reads: 'Dionysius O Congail aba sce crucis me fieri fecit'. Unfortunately

92 Holycross Abbey from the opposite bank of the river Suir; the restored battlements give a fortified air to this compact, rugged building.

the dates of O'Congail's abbacy are far from clear. There is an ambiguous reference to his death in a Papal letter of 1455 and it seems possible that he was abbot sometime between 1448 and 1455.[5] But there is also mention of an abbot Dionysius in 1409[6] and it is not impossible that the Papal letter is referring to him. Despite the unsatisfactory nature of the evidence, Leask, probably correctly, accepted the later date and attributed the cloisters to c1448–55. He interpreted the cloisters as the earliest part of the reconstruction campaign, dating the church to the third quarter of the century, though there is no documentary evidence to confirm this.

The cloister arcades were decorated with at least two further shields, ornamented in this case with the arms of members of the Ormond family. One of the shields is blazoned with a chief indented, the Ormond arms, and it carries a pierced mullet on the chief (Pl. 94). This was the means of differencing the third son of a family, so that the arms are likely to be those of Thomas, the third son of the white earl. As he was not born until sometime after 1434,[7] the shield tends to confirm a date in the 1450s for the cloister.

Heraldry is also of value in working out the chronology of the church. Above the sedilia is an array of shields, the largest of which carries the royal arms of England (Pl. 235). This follows the

114

93 Heraldic shield in the cloister at Holycross, recording the name of abbot Dionysius O Congail who was responsible for building the cloister around 1450.

94 Ormond shield from the cloister at Holycross. The pierced 'mullet' at the top right is the means of differencing the third son of the family.

blazon adopted after 1405, when the number of fleurs-de-lis was reduced to three, and it thus provides a *terminus post quem* for the building. To the left of the royal arms is a shield blazoned with a Latin cross, the arms of the abbey itself. To the right are the Ormond arms, followed by those of a member of the FitzGerald family, a saltire cross against a background of ermine. The arms appear to be those of the Desmond Geraldines and in this context it is interesting to note that in 1429 the white earl's daughter, Anne, was betrothed to the son of James FitzGerald, earl of Desmond.[8]

The most reliable evidence for the date of the church comes from documentary sources, chiefly those relating to the patronage of the earls of Ormond. In 1364 the abbey was taken 'under our special protection and defence' by James, the second earl,[9] and this protection was repeated by the white earl in 1414.[10] By 1429 the earl had enriched the monastery 'with various temporal possessions', one of which was the vill of Ballycahill.[11] This was given to the abbey on condition that the abbot and monks promised to keep a candle burning in front of the high altar on behalf of the earl on certain feast days and their vigils in honour and praise of God and the Virgin Mary. Two years later the earl repeated his special protection of the monastery, extending it to include 'clerks begging for funds for the works of the aforesaid monastery'.[12] This suggests that reconstruction of the abbey had begun by 1431. Building was, however, still going on at the end of the century, as made clear by the 1484 charter of Gerald, earl of Kildare, which granted a tenement and orchard 'ad reparacionem et construccionem monasterii Sancte Crucis'.[13] Alterations to the nave may in fact have continued until well into the sixteenth century, as suggested by the rather ungainly window in the north aisle, where the tracery is designed without cusping. The great west window is likewise a late feature (the large uncusped Perpendicular panels are similar to those in a window at St Nicholas', Galway, dated by an inscription to 1583). The late Gothic church at Holycross was thus the produce of piecemeal reconstruction over a long period, with the remodelling of the eastern area probably belonging to the decades between 1460 and 1500.

The decision to remodel the church was almost certainly connected with the monastery's possession of a relic (or relics) of the true cross. Indeed the rebuilding may have been intended to stimulate popular interest in them, for both spiritual and financial reasons. The earliest reference to a pilgrimage seems to be in 1488, when a Papal letter mentions 'the oblations which are made by the faithful to the wood of the Holy Cross in the church of the same monastery and which are collected by collectors appointed for the purpose'.[14] The existence of special collectors implies that the pilgrimage was well established by this date and its popularity probably developed in the first half of the century. There appear to have been two separate shrines within the church, one of which forms an inherent part of the fabric of the building. The design of the church was, therefore, devised with the relic very much in mind.

The first of the shrines was constructed in the south transept, where it replaces the dividing wall between the two chapels (Pl. 95, Fig. 37). It is an ingenious design, turning what would otherwise have been solid wall into a miniature piece of architecture. On each side there are three arches, which rest on spirally fluted columns. These flow into the arches without a capital in a manner reminiscent of some French Flamboyant designs.[15] They stand on a low wall, ornamented with blank ogee arches and elaborate foliage pinnacles (Pl. 96). Almost hidden from sight, covering the shrine, are three bays of exquisite tierceron vaulting, carried out on a tiny scale (Pl. 126). Dividing the shrine from the plain wall above is a moulded string-course, which jumps upwards as it passes over each of the arches. The narrower side of the shrine, facing the transept, was for structural reasons built with solid piers rather than columns. It is (or was) possible to walk inside at this point, but it does not seem that this was the original intention. There are rebates on each side for a slab, which covered the shrine just below the base of the columns. With the base enclosed in this way, the lower part of the shrine resembles a tomb chest. The masonry is of supreme quality, with the carving still fresh and sharp in the cold blue limestone. The whole structure has been well thought out and executed with precision.

In the past there has been much speculation about the true purpose of the shrine. It was traditionally know as the 'monks' waking place', a curious title, which goes back to Malachy

95　Holycross, the shrine in the south transept, probably designed for the display and veneration of the relic of the true cross.

96　Holycross, detail of the side panel of the shrine. As well as the angel holding the arms of the abbey, the panel is decorated with birds, a grotesque mask and groups of dogs.

97　The shrine of St Alban as drawn by Matthew Paris in the mid-thirteenth century (Trinity College Dublin, Ms. 177, fol. 54r). The spiral columns were a common feature of medieval shrines.

Hartry, writing in 1640, who explained that it was a place for 'waking the bodies of departed monks'.[16] The tradition may have arisen from the funeral rites practised at the abbey, if, as seems possible, the body of the deceased was laid for a time in front of the relic of the cross. Hartry, however, makes no mention of the relic being kept within the shrine.[17] As he was a monk at Holycross during the brief post-Reformation revival, this might seem telling evidence against the idea that the structure was designed as a setting for the relic, but Hartry's knowledge of medieval religious practice was far from perfect. Elsewhere in his book, he reveals extraordinary ignorance by misunderstanding the purpose of the sedilia in the chancel.[18]

Some authorities have argued that the shrine was in reality a tomb, a view favoured by Arthur Champneys, who concluded: 'The whole tomb-like structure has been thought to be the Shrine of the Relic; but since this is a piece of wood only some few inches long, such an explanation appears to be quite incredible. . . . There is a slot in which the covering slab could be fixed, it is of the right size for a tomb, and it is plainly nothing else, though whether it was ever occupied, and for whom it was made, must, like so much else in the history of the monastery, remain undetermined.'[19] In support of this explanation, it is worth remembering that the patron of Holycross, the fourth earl of Ormond, must have been familiar with the splendid free-standing canopied tombs of fourteenth-century England and it would be no surprise if he had wanted something similar for himself. But there are objections to this point of view. Unless planned for a corpse of giant proportions, the interior is unnecessarily long (7 feet 10 inches). The sides of the would-be tomb chest are not furnished with weepers, apostles or saints, as might be expected in a monument of this grandeur; nor are there any arms or heraldic devices, apart from a solitary angel, holding a shield blazoned with a plain Latin cross, the arms of the abbey (Pl. 96).

The view that the shrine was intended as a setting for the relic was proposed by O'Halloran in 1772[20] and it has had many adherents since then. With its canopy, arcades and decorated base, it follows a pattern common among English medieval shrines. That of St Alban, illustrated by Matthew Paris, had an arcaded base with a canopy held up by spiral columns and many similar structures were to be seen in English churches before the Reformation (Pl. 97).[21] The use of spiral columns is particularly interesting, for they were often employed in situations of special religious importance.[22] In addition to St Albans, they were used in the shrines of Edward the Confessor at Westminster Abbey and St Swithun at Winchester Cathedral.[23] In Ireland it is

98   The second 'shrine' at Holycross, temporarily assembled in the cloister in the 1970s.

99   Detail of the second shrine at Holycross, showing a (?)fox and a pelican feeding her young.

likely that Holycross helped to popularise the spiral column and later in the fifteenth century they appeared in the cloister arcades of Dominican and Franciscan friaries.

There is no structure elsewhere in Ireland that resembles the shrine at Holycross and this in itself suggests that it was intended for an exceptional purpose. Moreover it was designed at the very outset of the rebuilding and it would be remarkable if this amount of prior planning was devoted to the construction of a tomb. The only individual who might have warranted burial in such an august setting would have been the white earl, who died in 1452, but he was buried in St Mary's, Dublin, not at Holycross.[24] If the shrine was really intended as some form of Ormond mausoleum, it is odd that there are no arms or family insignia. Finally, it is worth noticing the two carved lions which sit on the string-course at the south-west corner of the shrine. Between them stands a man with ropes or leads, holding the animals under control, and it is tempting to regard the group as guardians of the holy relic.

Any discussion of the shrine in the south transept is complicated by the existence of another shrine within the church. For many years this lay in fragmentary condition in the north transept, but it was removed from view after the recent restoration. It was briefly mentioned in 1913 in the report of the Commissioners of Public Works, which referred to 'stones belonging to a shrine or tomb which stood at the north-west angle of the north transept'.[25] During the restoration in the early 1970s the pieces were reassembled in the cloister garth (Pl. 98).[26] The design was not as delicate as the shrine in the south transept, though the general form was not dissimilar. It had a vaulted canopy and was three bays long and one bay wide. The arcades rested on piers with attached columns on their inner faces. These were carved with deep flutes which flow unbroken into the soffits of the arches. In contrast to the first shrine, the base was divided into separate bays by the buttresses, which continued the line of the piers above. The panels between the buttresses were plain. As the mouldings of the shrine are similar to those in the church, it is clearly contemporary with the general rebuilding of the abbey.

The function of the second shrine is as difficult to establish as the first. Was it a setting for a second fragment of the true cross or should it be interpreted as a tomb? Once again there is no heraldry or any other specific evidence to suggest it was a funerary monument. Holycross is thought to have had more than one fragment of the cross and it is not impossible that they were enshrined separately.[27] In the spandrels of some of the arches are small animal carvings, two of which depict a pelican feeding her young (Pl. 99). This Eucharistic symbol accords better with a shrine than a tomb.

As a place of pilgrimage, Holycross was unique among the Cistercian houses of Ireland and the rebuilding that began about 1430 must, in some measure, be explained by a desire to provide a more worthy setting for its precious relics. The builders concentrated their activities on the eastern arm of the church and much of the original nave was left intact. The early work is recognisable through its rough rubble masonry, which contrasts with the well coursed blocks used for most of the reconstruction. A late twelfth-century doorway from the cloister survives at the east end of the south aisle[28] and in the west wall there are vestiges of the lancets which preceded the sixteenth-century reticulated window. The north arcade of the nave, with crude

101 The south transept of Holycross. The central buttress contains a chimney which rises from a chamber on the first floor.

100 The interior of Holycross before restoration, where the chancel is dominated by heavy ribbed vaulting.

rubble piers and unmoulded pointed arches, also remains from the original building (Pl. 27).[29] The late Gothic builders were, therefore, content to keep the structure of the old nave, while inserting new windows and two new doorways. It is strange that no clerestory was added at this time, for even with the huge west window, the nave is relatively dark.[30]

At the east end, most of the late twelfth-century walls were dismantled, though some of the foundations may have been reused. The scale of the new work was not radically different from what went before and the height of the main vaults is only 28 feet (8.5 metres). The chief change was the introduction of rib vaulting designed with various patterns of liernes and tiercerons (Pl. 100). The ribs die back into fine tapering springers, so that there is no need for responds against the wall. The interior is thus unencumbered by wall shafts and even the inner arches of

102 The north transept at Holycross, with windows simpler than those to the south.

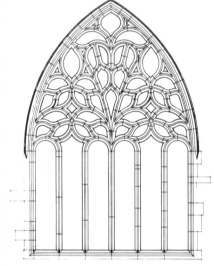

Fig. 36 Kilcooly, east window.

103 Flamboyant tracery in the north wall of the north transept at Holycross.

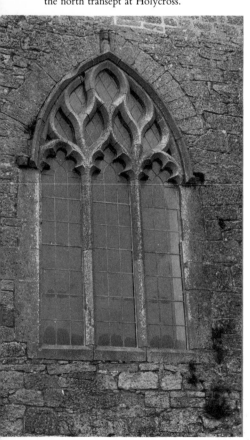

the crossing rest on corbels rather than engaged columns. Although vaults were constructed over most of the eastern arm, for some unexplained reason a high vault was never erected over the south transept,[31] one of many anomalies in the fifteenth-century building campaign.

The chancel is dominated by a reticulated window, over eleven feet (3.35 metres) wide, and impressive though it is, it must be admitted that a more daring architect would have made it large enough to fill the entire east wall. The tracery is derived from an early fourteenth-century window in the Dominican friary at Kilmallock,[32] but the Holycross example is much inferior (Pls 13, 92). It has six lights, instead of the better balanced five at Kilmallock, and the lack of cusping reduces the liveliness of the design.

The other windows at Holycross contain a heterogeneous collection of tracery patterns, the widest range in any Irish medieval building. The laudable enthusiasm for experiment, however, was rarely matched with an equivalent degree of expertise. Two of the best windows are to be found in the south transept chapels, where a more normal ration of cusps produces a pleasing, prickly effect (Pl. 101). Both windows have three lights, the side ones round-headed, the centre one ending in a curiously exotic head, made up from four separate arcs. Above the individual lights are two plump *mouchettes*, each filled with *falchions*, the arrangement of which varies in the two windows. While it is hard to find exact prototypes for these designs, their antecedents lie in the Decorated architecture of the west of England. The pattern of the south window was later used as a starting point by the architect of the east window at Kilcooly. He doubled it to form a six-light pattern and added his own filling to the gap between the two units (Fig. 36). Although the dense web of tracery bars at Kilcooly has a certain visual appeal, the curvilinear flow was wrecked by the introduction of two straight bars at the top. No cusping was used and the heavy tracery bars are lacking in delicacy.[33]

Among the less satisfactory windows at Holycross is one in a north transept chapel, where the head is filled by three pointed ovals, arranged in a radiating pattern (Pl. 102). The design has its origins in English Decorated architecture and good parallels exist at Ducklington (Oxfordshire) c1340. It is an unattractive composition—the 'petals' are too narrow—but it is not as ungainly as a window in the north aisle. This has a seemingly arbitrary pattern and the introduction of straight bars, leaning outwards, has a most unsettling effect.[34]

The best design is the flamboyant window in the north wall of the north transept, where the tracery creates a lively, flame-like impression (Pl. 103). It has three lights, the centre one with an ogee head. Then come six *falchions* and a vesica. This window succeeds where others failed because the *falchions* are pointing upwards. Even the absence of cusps does not matter since this enhances the sense of fluidity. In the years around 1500 Irish masons produced some fine

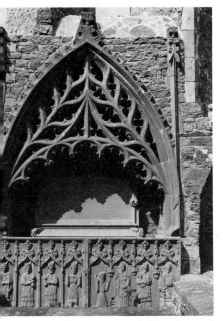

examples of flamboyant tracery—the tomb recesses at Strade and St Nicholas', Galway, come to mind—and there has been talk of a French connection (Pl. 104).[35] Similarities with France are striking but it must not be forgotten that English architecture had a flamboyant interlude in the fourteenth century. Several parallels exist for the Holycross tracery, as at Bolton Priory, Beverley Minster (reredos) and Chipping Norton, and, in the absence of any proven link with France, it seems safer to assume residual English influence.

The design of the windows at Holycross was a fairly hit-or-miss affair. There is not much sign of stylistic direction and several of the windows can only be classified as debased. Yet they underline some of the problems facing Irish masons. Cut off from major workshops, they lacked the training and geometrical expertise to produce outstanding results, especially when using complicated forms. The order in which building proceeded at Holycross is also puzzling, for there are constant alterations in design. The north transept, for example, has no buttresses on its eastern side, unlike the south transept, and its walls were given a pronounced batter (Fig. 37). This implies that work progressed in haphazard fashion and that the foundations were not laid out in a uniform campaign.[36] Indeed the church reveals an astonishing amount of stylistic variation. The windows of the four transept chapels vary in scale and, as explained, their tracery patterns are all different. Deliberate changes of tracery were characteristic of the Decorated era in England, but at Holycross the masons varied the profiles of the jambs and mullions as well.[37]

What conclusion should be drawn from these apparently arbitrary variations? The changes from complex to simple forms do not follow an even pattern, which might have occurred if money was running short. Unity or homogeneity clearly did not matter to the master mason in charge and it is as if the various parts of the building were designed one at a time, without the help of any overall schema. The taste for experiment continued even with the high vaults, where three separate rib patterns were used.

The style of Holycross reveals relatively little influence from contemporary English

104 A tomb canopy at Strade (Mayo), one of the outstanding examples of flamboyant tracery in Ireland.

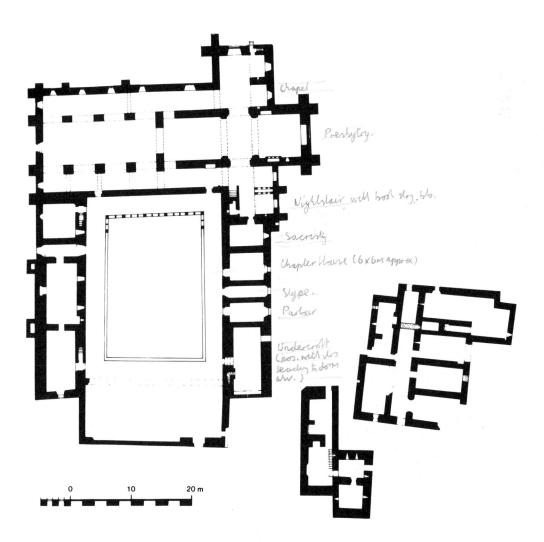

Fig. 37 Holycross, plan of the abbey.

105 One of many corbels found in the church at Holycross. The flutes on the lower taper have twelfth-century Cistercian precedents at Kirkstall (Yorkshire).

106 Corbel at Holycross, as drawn by Woodward (1874).

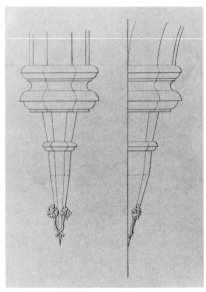

architecture. Indeed the general design is the very antithesis of English Perpendicular.[38] There is no openness or clarity of space: the transepts seem cut off from the rest of the church and the solid walls at the east end of the nave inhibit diagonal vistas. The broad grid-like windows of Perpendicular are conspicuously absent and there is an overwhelming impression of thick inert masonry. The interest and beauty of the building lies not in any unified architectural impression but rather in a series of isolated features, particularly vaulting patterns and tracery forms. The inspiration for these stems from English architecture of the Decorated era, about a hundred years earlier. Even the corbels which support the arches of the tower and transept chapels have typically Decorated profiles (Pls 105, 106, Fig. 72). In the past it has been normal for architectural historians to accept this time lapse as an inevitable consequence of the abbey's provincial location, but it is hard to believe that after 1300 or 1350 it suddenly began to take a hundred years for English ideas to filter across the Irish Sea.[39] The anachronistic style of Holycross, and of many other fifteenth-century Irish buildings, is better explained by historical factors.

Until the mid-fourteenth century, Irish architecture followed English fashions fairly closely and it was only during the Perpendicular era that it lost touch. This coincided with a decline in building activity in the second half of the fourteenth century, the consequence of economic depression, plagues and political instability. Immigration from England effectively ceased and there was no longer a flow of trained masons across the Irish Sea, as there had been in the thirteenth century. Irish craftsmen were thrown back on their own resources and their methods were largely conditioned by what they could see in their own locality. It is highly unlikely that the Decorated forms used at Holycross were copied directly from English models and most were probably adapted from early fourteenth-century buildings in Ireland, as with the reticulated east window. It is admittedly difficult to find Irish precedents for elaborate ribbed vaulting, but that does not mean they did not once exist. If the masons of Holycross had first hand knowledge of English architecture, they would have copied the latest fashions, not those which were already a hundred years old. Much hinged on the training a mason received. In the thirteenth century there were many craftsmen active in Ireland who had been apprenticed in English workshops, and this was still true in the early fourteenth century.[40] After 1350 an English trained mason, at least outside the Pale, must have been a rarity. The Decorated revival, evident at Holycross, was therefore one of the consequences of the diminishing authority of the English lordship of Ireland.

The design of Holycross was not entirely dependent on the Decorated style and there are a number of elements derived from other sources. One of the mouldings used throughout the church was a thirteenth-century form, seen previously at Dunbrody (Figs 70, 71).[41] Particularly instructive are the corbels, which illustrate in microcosm the stylistic individuality of the church (Pl. 105, Fig. 72). A considerable history lies behind their design. In the early days of the order, such corbels had been much favoured and they are one of the few features of the abbey that could be described as distinctively Cistercian. Corbels which foreshadow those at Holycross had been used in exactly the same position under the tower at Grey abbey about 1200 (Pl. 206). Several of the corbels terminate in pieces of foliage, an attractive device anticipated in the thirteenth century at Boyle, Abbeyknockmoy and Dunbrody. Others are ornamented with sharp vertical flutes cut out of the tapering base, a technique with twelfth-century precedents at Kirkstall (Pl. 105). The main body of the corbels, the part equivalent to a normal capital, has a standard Decorated form with three units of scroll mouldings. These are common in English buildings between 1300 and 1340, after which consistent use of scroll mouldings is rare.[42] The semi-octagonal shape (or plan) of the corbels, however, is characteristic of Perpendicular. The design of some doorways also shows an affinity with Perpendicular methods, for there was a marked desire to simplify the moulding by repeating the same form. Thus the door leading to the sacristy is surrounded by four filleted rolls, set monotonously in a straight diagonal line. In a thirteenth-century doorway the profiles would have been more varied. An identical moulding was used for the sacristy door at Kilcooly and it later became common, reappearing for example in the west doorway at Clontuskert (1471) (Fig. 70).[43]

The design of Holycross defies categorisation according to normal stylistic terminology. It has hints of Romanesque, Early English and Perpendicular, though the bulk of its formal repertoire belongs to the Decorated period. It is interesting that Scottish architecture shows the same belated taste for Decorated forms and curvilinear tracery. Indeed Scottish and Irish buildings in the later middle ages have many points in common, not least a resistance to English Perpendicular. Both countries developed their own version of Gothic, with distinctive regional characteristics, a reflection of the national aspirations of the time.[44] While architects in the two countries may simply have not known much about contemporary English architecture, it is hard to avoid the impression that English designs were deliberately avoided. Irish and Scottish Gothic has a conservative and introspective flavour, with the revival of older techniques like barrel vaulting, round arches and dog-tooth ornament. In Scotland influence from the Low Countries appears to have been a cogent factor, which was not the case in Ireland.[45] Nevertheless the design of Scottish collegiate churches like that at Seton (Lothian), c1470–1513, has some of the same character as Irish buildings like Holycross and Kilcooly. The similarities relate to matters of general taste and design, rather than specifics: the delight in curvilinear tracery, the preference for low vaulted spaces and the presence of powerful crossing piers and oversized exterior buttresses. It is not easy to explain the parallels, for there is no evidence of an exchange of masons between the two countries and differences of detail make this unlikely.[46] It is worth remarking, too, that sixteenth-century Ireland shared in the taste for tracery with wide uncusped loops, a form fashionable in Scotland after 1500.[47]

Above the vaults at the east end of Holycross are several chambers, some of which were designed for domestic use. The oblong space above the south transept chapels forms a particularly pleasant room, with two windows looking out to the east (Pl. 101). In the centre of the east wall is an enormous hooded fireplace, constructed with a joggled lintel, the latter supported on tapering brackets.[48] The chimney is cunningly hidden in the buttress, making it invisible from outside. A short staircase leads to further chambers over the chancel, crossing and north transept. These apartments were clearly intended for regular use and that over the south transept is traditionally known as the abbot's chamber.[49] There is no means of proving whether the monks built them as private living quarters, but after the dissolution they were certainly used in this way. In 1572 the earl of Ormond rented to James Fitzwilliam Purcell the old chapter house, 'the room or loft over the chancel' as well as 'the room over the Cross Church' with an entrance 'via the great stairs of the said church to the upper rooms', this in return for an annual rent of 16 shillings.[50] It is not difficult to see the attraction of these rooms. They were well off the ground, secure and dry, and accommodation within them was not much different from that afforded by a contemporary tower house. But how did the monks justify their construction?

The so-called abbot's chamber has narrow windows looking into the church. So too does its counterpart over the north transept chapels. They could therefore have been used as watching chambers, an important requirement with valuable relics and offerings in the church below. These rooms are not, however, peculiar to Holycross and they became something of a fashion in the fifteenth century. At Kilcooly a spacious upper room covers the whole of the south transept and it is lit by a series of twin-light windows with ogee heads. It was obviously an important chamber in the monastery, a fact underlined by the care lavished on the foliage carving above one of the windows (Pl. 164). As at Holycross, it is possible that this was the abbot's private apartment. Similar chambers were fitted over the east end of Jerpoint and a room was also constructed above the south transept chapels at Abbeyknockmoy. It is interesting that at Holycross, Kilcooly and Jerpoint separate staircases were built on the north side of the church, providing a second means of access to the upper levels (Figs 10, 21, 37). Two individuals could therefore have lived independently up above the vaults.

The amalgamation of church and living quarters, though abnormal in a Cistercian context, was not so unusual in Ireland.[51] Several of the early monasteries had buildings of this type. St Columba's house at Kells and Cormac's Chapel at Cashel both have dwelling spaces fitted above the main vault.[52] A slightly later example occurs in the extraordinary church of St Doulagh's (County Dublin).[53] During the fifteenth century it was the practice in many parish churches to

107 The fortified fifteenth-century church at Taghmon (Westmeath). The tower was designed for residence not for bells.

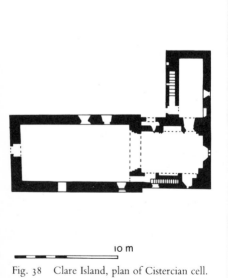

10 m

Fig. 38 Clare Island, plan of Cistercian cell.

108 The Cistercian cell on Clare Island seen from the east. A residential chamber is located above the chancel.

erect a tower house for the priest immediately beside the church and sometimes this was integrated into the fabric, as at Taghmon (County Westmeath) (Pl. 107).[54] The small Cistercian church on Clare Island off the west coast of County Mayo is an excellent illustration of the same trend.[55] This is a fifteenth-century building, which consists of a small aisleless nave and a two-storey chancel (Pl. 108, Fig. 38). Living accommodation for the monk (or monks) was provided in a room over the chancel vault, which was linked to an adjoining tower. These upper levels were reached by a mural staircase in the thickness of the chancel wall. By about 1500 almost every Irishman of any status lived in a tall stone house or 'castle' and in desiring similar accommodation well above the ground, the abbots of Holycross, Kilcooly and Jerpoint were following contemporary fashion. In view of what happened at Kilcooly in 1445, when the monastery was destroyed by armed men, it is not difficult to understand why.

The reconstruction of Kilcooly was carried out under the shadow of Holycross and it was designed in a characteristically Irish Gothic manner. Abbot Philip, under whose guidance the restoration may have begun, visited England in 1445 with two of his monks 'in search of food and clothing'.[56] During his travels, the abbot's mind must have been concentrated on physical survival, rather than the finer points of architecture, and there is little in the design of the monastery which can be attributed to a direct knowledge of contemporary English building. To judge from the tracery, much of the reconstruction was carried out long after Philip's death, after 1500 rather than 1450. The masons employed were local men, three of whom worked at Holycross. The poverty of the monastery affected the general character of the rebuilding, and in comparison with Holycross the workmanship is not as high; there is less use of ashlar and there are fewer carved details. Yet the reconstruction must have been an expensive undertaking and,

109 Kilcooly Abbey from the south-east, as rebuilt after an armed raid in 1445.

110　Kilcooly Abbey, the crossing and chancel.

111　Kilcooly Abbey, view into the low vaulted north transept. To the left is the prior's stall, fitted into the western crossing pier.

113　Abbeydorney seen from the west at the end of the nineteenth century. The facade is now engulfed in ivy (compare Pl. 32) (National Library of Ireland, Lawrence Collection).

114　Abbeydorney, the west doorway designed with a square frame and thin delicate mouldings (1500).

to judge from a number of shields carved with the Ormond arms, the monks enjoyed the patronage of the earl and his family.[57] Some years later, a branch of the Butler family, the FitzOge, chose Kilcooly as their place of burial[58] and following the dissolution it was the earl of Ormond who acquired the monastery from the Crown.

As at Holycross, the builders focussed their attention on the east end of the church. Most of the late twelfth-century transepts were dismantled, though the walls of the old presbytery were retained and thickened. A barrel vault, with a round profile, was erected over the presbytery, in contrast to the ribbed vaults used over the smaller spaces of the transepts and crossing (Pl. 110). The eccentric layout of the transepts has already been outlined[59] and they were intended more as a series of intimate chapels than major spaces within the church (Fig. 21). The south wall of the south transept was built as an ornate screen and constructed in smooth ashlar (Pl. 221). The door to the sacristy was given far more emphasis than normal in a Cistercian church, with four moulded orders and a hood mould (Fig. 70). Various carved reliefs were inserted into the wall around and the whole surmounted by a canopy, which is a blatant, though debased, copy of the canopy over the sedilia at Holycross. Beside the doorway is a large piscina, which shows that the main body of the transept was intended to serve as a chapel. As remodelled, the church was obviously designed for a mere handful of monks, for the spaces are too cramped for a community of any size. This is confirmed by the alterations to the nave, which was deprived of aisles, the arcades of the twelfth-century church being blocked up.[60] The monastery had clearly come to terms with the diminished size of its community. The most attractive feature of the building are the two stalls, designed for the abbot and prior, which are fitted into the western crossing piers at the entrance to the nave (Pl. 111). Most of the alterations in the nave belong to the sixteenth century, as indicated by the cuspless tracery of the west window, a replacement for early Gothic lancets. At this time a rood loft was inserted towards the east end of the nave, its position indicated by the location of windows in the south wall. The upper windows at this point consist of twin openings with rounded heads, a form not found much before the mid-sixteenth century.

The style of Kilcooly is closely related to Holycross and in both churches there is a similar focus on curvilinear tracery and ribbed vaulting. As already described, the spectacular, though

somewhat inept, east window at Kilcooly was composed by doubling the pattern used in one of the chapels at Holycross. The structure and patterns of the vaults are also related, and so too is the organisation of space within the church. The crossing was narrowed on its north-south axis, which resulted in an oblong tower as at Holycross (Figs 21, 37). Many other parallels can be traced between the two buildings: the incorporation of living space above the transept vaults, the design of the tower, the similarities in some of the moulding profiles (Fig. 70) and the general lack of concern for symmetry and consistency. The two designs are, however, far from identical. The labour force employed by abbot Philip and his successors, probably about twenty men to judge from masons' marks, included only three who had worked at Holycross. Their independence was expressed in numerous details. The corbels under the tower, for instance, have different moulding profiles and the forms used in the doorway from the nave to the cloister are equally distinctive (Fig. 70). The design of Kilcooly was emphatically local, with Holycross as the principal source of inspiration, and the remodelled abbey represents Irish Gothic at its most introspective.

Together Holycross and Kilcooly illustrate the changed architectural priorities of the Cistercians in the fifteenth and sixteenth centuries. What was required by both communities was a more intimate and compact church, in which the nave had far less importance than before. Vaults were desired as far as possible, not just for their aesthetic appeal, but also to reduce the risks of fire. There was a new pride in fine craftsmanship and pleasurable detail. The wide, bleak spaces of the early churches were exchanged for something more homely.

Kilcooly was a daughter house of Jerpoint, where alterations to the church took place in the fifteenth century.[61] The remodelling here was less drastic, but the objectives were similar. One of the nave aisles was removed, rooms were constructed over the transept chapels and a tower

112   Kilcooly Abbey, corbel on the north-west crossing pier.

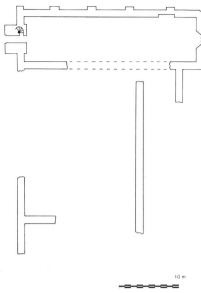

Fig. 39   Abbeydorney, plan.

erected over the crossing (Pl. 138). As at Kilcooly the presbytery was covered by a barrel rather than a ribbed vault.[62]

Another monastery to embark on an ambitious scheme of remodelling was Hore, also situated in the Ormond lands.[63] The architectural evidence here is more difficult to interpret and it is not clear how many of the changes belong to the fifteenth century. The square tower, neatly constructed over the crossing, certainly belongs to this date and there may have been an intention to vault the chancel at the same time (Pl. 136).

One Cistercian church which is entirely late medieval in date is Abbeydorney, the abbey to which Christian, first abbot of Mellifont, had retired several centuries before. Far to the west, it was remote from the architectural developments in the Ormond lands. Its simple, aisleless church, 93 feet (28.35 metres) long, tells the familiar story of a dwindling community needing less space for their acts of worship (Pl. 113). The interior lacks any architectural divisions and it was not vaulted. There were no transepts and thus no crossing tower (Fig. 39). Instead a tower-porch was erected at the west end, an arrangement more akin to a parish church than a Cistercian one. Despite the architectural simplicity, there is some well-dressed masonry, wrought in the dark limestone of the locality. A beautifully moulded doorway, with a square hood, opened into the porch and above there is an elegant window with curvilinear tracery (Pl. 114, Fig. 70). The window is slightly off-centre in the facade, a consequence of squeezing in a staircase on the north side of the tower. The chancel contains an ogee-headed tomb recess in the north wall and there is a three-light window with switch line tracery in the east facade. There is nothing about the design of Abbeydorney that identifies it as Cistercian, which suggests that by this time there was no consensus among members of the order about the right form their churches should take. Cistercian architecture had lost its distinctive identity.

Chapter 6

CISTERCIAN VAULTING

A HIGH PROPORTION of Irish medieval vaults are found in Cistercian monasteries. Most of them are modest in scale and there is nothing that can compare with the structural audacity of France or the decorative ingenuity of England. On a less ambitious level, there are a number of unusual and interesting vaults which, having been neglected in the past, deserve close examination.

As in England, vaulting in Irish Cistercian churches was restricted to the presbytery and chapels at the east end. It has been suggested that this reluctance to vault the whole building stemmed from a desire in the dull northern climes to retain clerestory lighting in the nave, a feature sacrificed in the early Cistercian churches of Burgundy.[1] But there is no evidence to suggest that the English and Irish Cistercians were desperate to fill their churches with light and, as several of the offices were held during the hours of darkness and the monks knew them by heart, a well-lit church was not essential. The high cost of vaulting and the force of local tradition were probably more cogent factors. Even in mid-twelfth century England, a completely vaulted church was rare.[2] The prime consideration was to cover the major altars with a vault to enhance their dignity and render them secure against the risks of fire.

Pointed barrel vaults were constructed over the presbyteries of at least three of the early daughter houses of Mellifont—at Boyle, Jerpoint[3] and Monasteranenagh—and it is likely that they were a standard feature elsewhere (Pl. 43). Over the transept chapels they have survived in greater numbers, most notably at Boyle, Abbeyknockmoy, Corcomroe and Jerpoint (Pls 46, 47); traces of similar vaulting exists at Hore and Monasteranenagh.[4] Although a vaulted presbytery was normal in the affiliation of Mellifont, it was not seen as a necessity in the Anglo-Norman houses. Grey, Inch, Dunbrody and Tintern were all satisfied by timber roofing and their example was followed in the Irish foundation at Hore. In all these cases, vaults were retained in the transept chapels. In the fifteenth century at Holycross and Kilcooly, vaulting was extended to the transepts, but nowhere was there any attempt to vault the nave.

The earliest vaults erected by the Cistercians are all pointed barrels, following Burgundian precedent. They were constructed on wickerwork centering, traces of which can be seen at Jerpoint, Boyle and Corcomroe.[5] In 1931 Leask argued that the pointed barrel vault was 'more probably an inheritance from native Irish traditions than an introduction from Burgundy',[6] but this is not a view that can be accepted nowadays. Irish experience at vaulting before 1142 was extremely limited and none of the spans previously covered was as wide as a Cistercian church. Barrel vaults, with semi-circular profiles, had appeared in a number of churches, in two cases helping to support corbelled roofs (St Columba's House at Kells and Kevin's Kitchen at Glendalough).[7] Dates of great antiquity have sometimes been claimed for these works and St Columba's House is popularly thought to have been built between 807 and 814.[8] If this was so, its barrel vault would be among the earliest in medieval Europe, preceding by well over a century the wider distribution of such vaults during 'le premier art roman'.[9] But these early dates are no longer feasible and it is unlikely that barrel vaulting was known in Ireland before the later eleventh century. Like the later Cistercian vaults, these early barrels were constructed of rubble and they were not articulated with transverse arches. The only sophisticated piece of barrel vaulting in Ireland that pre-dates the Cistercians is that over the nave of Cormac's Chapel, Cashel (1127–34) where transverse arches were included. Above the vault is a corbelled roof of

115 The chapter house of St Mary's Abbey, Dublin (c1200), with its four bays of ribbed vaulting supported on short corbels.

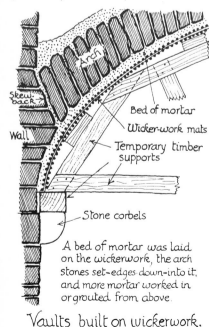

Fig. 40 Diagram of wickerwork centering (after Leask).

Arch

Skew back

Bed of mortar

Wicker-work mats

Wall

Temporary timber supports

Stone corbels

A bed of mortar was laid on the wickerwork, the arch stones set-edges-down-into it, and more mortar worked in or grouted from above.

Vaults built on wickerwork.

stone, which has an inner skin resembling a pointed barrel vault.[10] It was probably this that encouraged Leask to believe that early Cistercian vaults were part of an indigenous development.

Barrel vaulting, both pointed and semi-circular, remained popular with the Cistercians throughout the middle ages. It was obviously regarded as a simple and cheap method of covering small spaces, particularly in the conventual buildings. The sacristy adjoining the south transept was often vaulted in this way and at Jerpoint there is a sequence of barrel vaults in the east range, covering the sacristy, chapter house and parlour. In the fifteenth century barrel vaults were used on the ground floor of both the south and west ranges at Bective as well as in the east and west ranges at Holycross. These vaults are normally built of rubble, sometimes retaining traces of wickerwork centering (Fig. 40). The use of wickerwork was not common abroad and it is probably safe to conclude that this was a technique developed by Irish builders.[11] The barrel vault under the south range at Bective is unusual in being built with roughly dressed ashlar blocks.

Groin vaults (without ribs) were apparently not so popular, though the accidents of survival may give a misleading impression. It is possible that the original chapter house at Mellifont was vaulted in this way[12] and some species of cross vault was used in the north transept chapels at Monasteranenagh. Fifteenth-century groins remain in the so-called chapter house at Bective[13] and in one of the rooms of the east range at Holycross. The more complicated centering required to build them may have diminished their popularity with Irish builders. Even outside the Cistercian order they were not as common as barrel vaults and there are none which ante-date the twelfth century.

It took a long time for ribbed vaults to make an impression in Ireland. Before the arrival of the Cistercians, the only example was to be found in the chancel at Cormac's Chapel, Cashel. The span covered is tiny (13 feet 6 inches by 10 feet 10 inches; 4.16 by 3.30 metres) and in structural terms the vault is of little significance. The thick roll-moulded ribs employed suggest it was constructed by masons brought over from England.[14] The vault was not copied elsewhere in Irish Romanesque and it was not until the end of the twelfth century that ribbed vaults made another appearance, this time in a Cistercian context.

The earliest Cistercian ribs are those over the chapter house of St Mary's abbey, Dublin

116 The chapter house at Mellifont (c1210). The wall ribs are early thirteenth-century, but the diagonal ribs were replaced in the fourteenth or fifteenth century.

(c1190–1200) (Pl. 115). This has four bays of vaulting (each measuring 23 feet by 11 feet; 7.01 by 3.35 metres) and the ribs, which spring from corbels, are composed of semi-circular arcs. The system of jointing used suggests that the principle of the *tas de charge* was understood. The ribs are elaborately moulded and comparisons have been made with the profiles found in the chapter house at Buildwas, the mother house of St Mary's (Fig. 74).[15] The cells are made of rubble, coursed in the English manner and there are no *formerets* or wall arches.

Not long after this, a new chapter house was constructed at Mellifont (c1210–20).[16] Its ribbed vault of two bays was rebuilt in the fourteenth century, but the original form is clear enough (Pl. 116). Each bay measures 15 feet by 19 feet 8 inches (4.57 by 5.99 metres) and the original roll-moulded *formerets* are still in place, one of the first occasions that *formerets* were used in Ireland. The lavabo at Mellifont also employed ribs, though this time in conjunction with an annular barrel vault. This octagonal building of c1200 had a central pier, supporting a radiating pattern of thick moulded ribs. The effect must have been extremely graceful, with the ribs stretching out from the pier like the branches of a tree. Despite their date, the character of both vaults was Romanesque, rather than early Gothic. The ribs are thick for the size of the space covered and there is nothing particularly Gothic about their mouldings.

131

117 The presbytery vault at Abbeyknock-moy (c1210–20), built with thick unmoulded ribs and rubble cells.

118 Abbeyknockmoy, north side of the presbytery vault. The wall arch falls well below the true height of the vault and in the north-east corner the rib is badly distorted.

Far more intriguing are the vaults built in the west of Ireland at this time. These are found in the chancels of three abbeys, two of which were Cistercian. The technical character of the vaults is similar in all three buildings and they form an unusual regional group. They were the work of local masons and as such they carry more interest than the orthodox English-style vaults of St Mary's, Dublin. Although bold in conception, they show many signs of inexperience, which underlines the novelty of ribbed vaulting in Ireland. The vaults also form a landmark in the history of Irish Cistercian architecture, representing a belated decision to abandon the pointed barrel, a rejection of this long-established Burgundian technique.

The earliest vaults in the group are probably those of Abbeyknockmoy, erected c1210–20 (Pl. 117). The presbytery is divided by a transverse arch into two bays, each about 28 feet 6 inches by 15 feet (8.69 by 4.57 metres). The following points are of particular interest:

1 The ribs are broad and unmoulded, giving the vault a heavy cumbersome impression. Such ribs are usually associated with the earliest stages of ribbed vaulting in Lombardy and the south of France; they are also characteristic of some late twelfth-century German buildings, but they are rare in England, except in utilitarian locations.[17]

2 The ribs rest on broad pilasters which are tapered off, in Cistercian fashion, several feet above the ground.

3 Although *formerets* or wall arches appear, their purpose was misunderstood. They were built too low for a vault with level ridges and the cells meet the wall about five or six feet above the apex of the *formerets* (Pl. 118). Instead of marking the junction of wall and vault, the *formerets* are isolated and they have been reduced to meaningless arches.

4 The principle of the *tas de charge*[18] was adopted for all the springers, except those adjoining the chancel arches. Here the ribs are squeezed into the angle, almost as an afterthought. No respond was provided and a meagre corbel was inserted to give some visual support.

5 The geometry of the ribs is far from perfect. In the north-east angle this resulted in a dreadful distortion just above the springers (Pl. 118).

6 The cells are constructed of rubble, coursed in the English manner, i.e. the courses are not parallel to the axial and transverse ridges (Pl. 117).

7 Wickerwork centering was employed which has left a strong impression in the mortar on the south side of the vault.

8 No keystone was used, an unusual occurrence for the early thirteenth century.[19] Instead an ingenious piece of masonry jointing, involving seven separate stones, has taken its place, a system which has precedents in some of the early ribbed vaults in the Ile de France (the

119 The chancel at Lilleshall (Shropshire), which like Abbeyknockmoy was covered by thick ribs resting on short pilaster corbels.

Fig. 41 Keystones in the west of Ireland vaults.

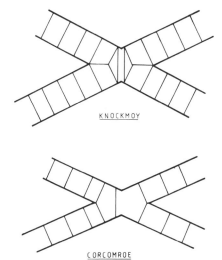

miniature ambulatory at Morienval, for example) (Fig. 41). Given the width of ribs at Abbeyknockmoy, an orthodox keystone would have been of immense size and weight.

The Abbeyknockmoy vault is difficult to classify. Its simple ribs, their semi-circular form and the lack of keystones give it an archaic flavour, but the presence of *formerets* and the *tas de charge* show that masons were not ignorant of recent technical developments. The way this understanding penetrated to Connacht is puzzling. There are no Irish prototypes for this manner of vaulting and the techniques used have diverse antecedents. It is of course possible that one of the abbeys in the east of the country furnished precedents, Mellifont or St Mary's, Dublin, perhaps, and it may be significant that among the fragments at Mellifont there is a capital decorated with minuscule dog-tooth, an exact replica of those supporting the ribs at Abbeyknockmoy. The mother house of the order in Ireland could have been the link between Abbeyknockmoy and the world outside.

The form of the vault, particularly the coursing of the cells, suggests an English rather than a continental origin and a similar vault existed in the chancel of the Augustinian abbey of Lilleshall (Shropshire), constructed c1180–1200 (Pl. 119).[20] The ribs were plain like those at Abbeyknockmoy and they rested on broad pilasters. Moreover some of the capitals have decoration which reappears on the crossing capitals at Abbeyknockmoy—scallops with slits down the centre. There is no documented connection between the two monasteries and it

121 The Lady Chapel at Glastonbury (c1184–6). As at Corcomroe the transverse rib is decorated with chevron.

120 The vault of the presbytery at Corcomroe (c1210–20). The ribs are more ornate than those at Abbeyknockmoy and the rubble cells are curved in form.

would be wrong to read too much into the similarities. However, they suggest that experience gathered in the west of England, particularly from buildings situated in the Severn Valley, contributed to the vaulting experiments in the west of Ireland. As we shall see shortly, the vault of Corcomroe also has connections with this area.

Between 1216 and 1225 a ribbed vault of similar character was erected in the chancel of Ballintober Abbey, an Augustinian church which resembles Abbeyknockmoy. The thick unmoulded ribs are repeated, so too is the ingenious masonry jointing that replaces the keystone. There can be little doubt that the same masons were responsible. More ambitious and sophisticated was the vault at Corcomroe (c1210–20), where the ribs are elaborately carved. The diagonals are embellished with a triple roll moulding and the transverse arch between the two bays is ornamented with deeply undercut herringbone chevron (Pl. 120). In contrast to Abbeyknockmoy, the purpose of the *formerets* is better understood and they correctly mask the

134

122 The presbytery at Graiguenamanagh, where the springers and wall arches of the Early English vault survive.

123 The south transept chapels at Tintern. The profile of the ribs is far simpler than the moulding of the springers and wall arches, suggesting a repair or change of design.

joints between the wall and the vaulting cells. However they are still low in relation to the height of the vault, which means that the cells curve down in order to meet them, producing a semi-domical shape. As at Abbeyknockmoy, the ribs which spring from the angle of the chancel arch are not bonded into the wall; nor are keystones deployed. Despite the greater elegance of the vault, the structural techniques were not fundamentally different. There are similar uncertainties in the construction of the ribs and the masons' grasp of the necessary geometry was far from secure. A glance at the springers on the north side is sufficient to demonstrate this, for the direction of the mouldings here is decidedly wayward.

The most striking feature of the Corcomroe vault is the presence of herringbone chevron in the transverse arch. This bears a remarkable similarity to some west of England vaults, not least that in the Lady Chapel at Glastonbury, where chevron is used in the same context (Pl. 121). This may not be a coincidence in view of the historical status of Glastonbury. Not many miles from the Bristol Channel, it was one of the richest and most illustrious of English Benedictine houses and, more relevant from an Irish point of view, it was claimed as the burial place of St Patrick. He was reputed to lie on the south side of the ancient wattle church of St Mary.[21] This was one of the buildings destroyed in the great fire of Glastonbury in 1184, a structure replaced by the new Lady Chapel of 1184–6.[22] Two centuries before, during the lifetime of St Dunstan, 'pilgrims of Irish race' frequented Glastonbury and there is no reason to believe that things were different around 1200. It is not too fanciful to suggest that the master mason of Corcomroe was attempting to reproduce the vault which covered the relics of Ireland's most revered and honoured saint.

By the second quarter of the thirteenth century, a considerable amount of competent Early English vaulting was being carried out in the Anglo-Norman territories, among which were the vaults over the presbytery at Graiguenamanagh (Pl. 122). The vault itself has long since vanished, but the springers and *formerets* survive. There were three bays of vaulting, presumably quadripartite in form. The *formerets* are brought to a steep point, which demonstrates that, unlike Corcomroe, the transverse ridges of the vault must have been approximately level. A similar vault in three bays was apparently erected at Mellifont between 1230 and 1250.[23] Although rib vaults are not found in the chancels of other Anglo-Norman abbeys, they were employed in the transept chapels at Inch, Dunbrody and Tintern. The chapels in the south transept at Tintern, which were vaulted as a continuous aisle, are of interest since the design was evidently altered during construction (Pl. 123). The springers were intended for roll-moulded ribs, but plain chamfered ones took their place. A variety of circumstances could explain the change—a loss of skilled masons, impatience to complete the work or perhaps a later reconstruction of the vault. The ribs spring from corbels and foliage bosses ornament two of the three keystones.

A huge gap separates the quadripartite vaults of the thirteenth century from the more elaborate lierne and tierceron vaults of the fifteenth. After Tintern there are no surviving vaults in Cistercian abbeys until Holycross, a hundred and fifty years later. Indeed, in Ireland as a whole there is an almost total dearth of vaulting in this period. It is unlikely that any continuity of method or training was maintained within the building workshops, which implies that the art of vaulting had to be relearnt.

At Holycross, the four transept chapels, the presbytery, the crossing and the north transept are covered by ribbed vaults. Five different designs were used and as work progressed it seems that the builders gained in confidence (Figs 42, 43). The two oblong bays of the presbytery, each measuring 22 feet by 11 feet (6.70 by 3.30 metres), have straightforward tierceron vaults, with four ribs (excluding the *formerets*) springing from each corner (Pl. 100). In the crossing the number of ribs was increased to six and liernes appear for the first time, forming an irregular octagon in the centre of the vault (Pl. 124). In the north transept cusping was introduced, a feature which enormously improves the appearance of the design (Pl. 125). The cusps help to focus attention on the octagonal and triangular motifs in the centre and they break up the harsh linearity of the ribs. Regrettably, the use of cusps was not copied elsewhere. No doubt they were time-consuming and expensive to carve, a luxury which other churches could not afford.

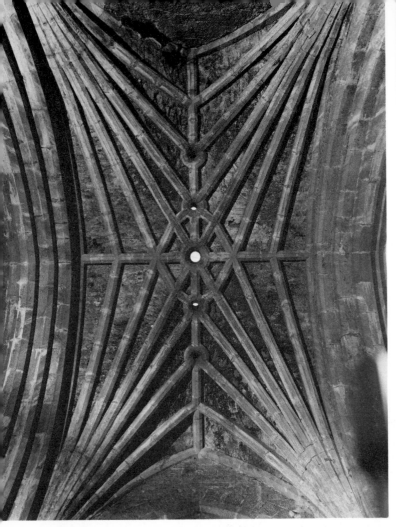

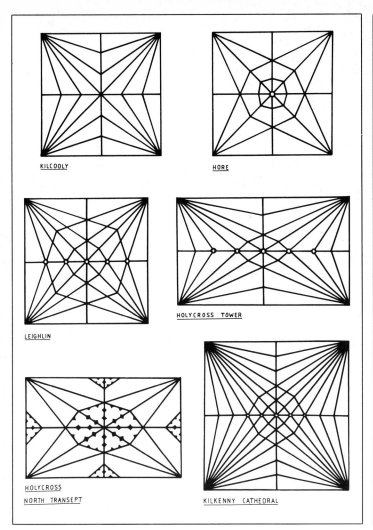

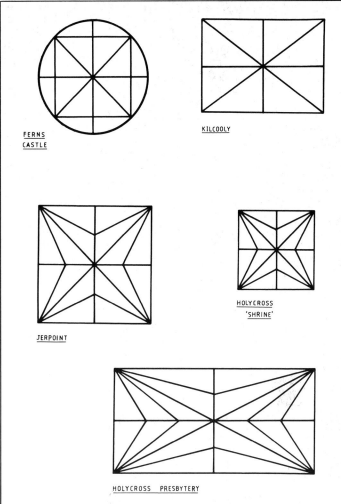

Fig. 42   Fifteenth-century rib vault plans (not to scale).

Fig. 43   Fifteenth-century rib vault plans (not to scale).

127   Vault over one of the bays of the north transept at Kilcooly. The absence of bosses at the intersection of the ribs was a feature of Irish vaults.

124 (facing page top left)   The tierceron vault under the crossing tower at Holycross.

125 (facing page top right)   The north transept vault at Holycross, where cusping improves the appearance of the design. The rubble cells have been plastered since this photograph was taken.

126 (facing page bottom)   The miniature vault which covers the shrine in the south transept at Holycross.

As might be expected in a building so lacking in homogeneity, the design of the vaults in the transept chapels do not correspond with each other. Those to the north are quadripartite with ridge ribs, whereas those to the south, adjacent to the shrine, have tiercerons and liernes. None of these smaller vaults have cusps. The miniature vaults, neatly constructed inside the shrine and sedilia, echo the pattern of the high vaults above, both having tiercerons like those in the presbytery (Pl. 126).

Holycross has by far the most ambitious display of medieval vaulting in Ireland and it is interesting to watch the gradual elaboration of the patterns, first with the introduction of liernes, then with the addition of cusps. A few years later, the builders of Kilcooly had the desire, but not the resources or expertise, to emulate them. The ribbed vaults erected here over the crossing and transepts were not as involved as those at Holycross. Except for the two outer bays of the north transept, where tiercerons are found, they are all quadripartite vaults with ridge ribs, akin to those in the north chapels at Holycross (Pl. 127, Figs 42, 43). This simple scheme had precedents in Ireland and the same pattern was used for the vault cleverly fitted into one of the thirteenth-century towers at Ferns Castle (Wexford).[24]

By English standards, the Irish vaults seem heavy-handed and provincial. Even the most ornate of them, the north transept vault at Holycross, is archaic in form, having its origin over a hundred years earlier in the Decorated era. In the early fourteenth century, cusps had been used to emphasise geometrical motifs in the vaults at St Augustine's, Bristol, and the octagonal pattern at the centre of some of the Holycross vaults also goes back to this period.[25] It was a motif that remained popular in English architecture throughout the later middle ages.[26]

There are, however, a number of specific features, which were not so routine in England.

1   The pitch of the Holycross vaults is low and the diagonals are composed of semi-circular arcs.

128 The vault under the crossing tower at Kilkenny Cathedral (c1460–78), where eleven ribs taper together at the angle.

129 The ribbed vault under the fifteenth-century tower at Jerpoint.

This gives the vaults, especially those in the chancel, a heavy, rounded profile (Pl. 100). They have neither the steep accents of early Gothic vaults nor the flat pitch of later English vaults, when four centred arches were fashionable.

2 There was a general reluctance, both at Holycross and elsewhere, to soften the line of the ribs by using mouldings. Most Irish ribs have a chisel or wedge-shaped profile, formed by cutting a steep chamfer along the edge of a rectangular block. Ribs of this type are not uncommon in England—they can be found in the fourteenth-century ambulatory at Tewkesbury, for example—but they were not usually employed in positions of prominence. At Holycross, only the diagonals in the presbytery are moulded, in this case with a series of parallel hollows.[27] These mouldings, rather than stressing the most important ribs, do the reverse, making them appear thinner and more linear. A few of the ribs at Kilcooly are decorated with filleted rolls, but this was not common in the fifteenth century.

3 Another peculiarity of later Irish vaulting is the omission of carved bosses at the intersection of ribs. Bosses are such a feature of English vaulting at this time that their absence is surprising. At Jerpoint there is a fine fifteenth-century keystone, decorated with a female figure (possibly St Margaret of Antioch), but this did not belong to the fabric of the abbey.[28] None of the Cistercian vaults extant are furnished with sculptured bosses.

4 The most skilful characteristic of Irish vaulting is the way the ribs are handled as they descend to the wall. They normally merge together, tapering to a fine point without the presence of a capital or corbel. A beautiful instance of this occurs on the north wall of the presbytery at Holycross, where the cluster of ribs is treated with great finesse. On a tiny scale the same treatment is accorded to the ribs inside the sedilia, where the delicate taper is ornamented with two carved leaves (Pl. 236). The absence of responds and the termination of ribs *en fuseau* was almost universal in Ireland. It is a feature that the Cistercians popularised and the technique can be traced back to the late twelfth-century vaults of Burgundy.[29] Where and how it reached Ireland is uncertain, but it was almost certainly in a Cistercian context. Outside the order, a spectacular example of ribs ending *en fuseau* can be seen under Bishop Hacket's tower (c1460–78) at Kilkenny Cathedral.[30] With the *formerets* included, no less than eleven ribs flow down to a slender point in the angles of the vault (Pl. 128).

These characteristics are not specific enough to speak of an 'Irish style' of vaulting, but they do provide a distinctive regional flavour. The simplicity of the vaults, especially the absence of mouldings and bosses, is to be attributed to a lack of money rather than a lack of skill, for the craftsmanship at Holycross is of high quality. It would be interesting to know how the masons learnt, or relearnt, the art of vaulting. The geometrical problems encountered in carving ribs were normally overcome through the use of well-tried practical formulae, but it is unclear how this body of 'know-how' reached Ireland.[31] The vaults appear to have been carried out by local men and, in contrast to the thirteenth century, there are none which seem to be the work of immigrants. The fact that the masons adhered to relatively straightforward patterns suggests that they were in part self taught. No doubt English vaulting provided the general inspiration, but in the actual task of construction, the masons relied heavily on their own skill and local experience.

Ribbed vaults were also built in the fifteenth-century towers at Hore and Jerpoint. Hore has a well balanced pattern of ribs, with a double octagon motif in the centre. The inner octagon is highly irregular, being flattened almost to a square, and this produces cells of peculiar shape. The overall effect, however, is symmetrical and not unattractive. A more complex version of this design was used at Leighlin Cathedral (Carlow)[32] and it was elaborated even further in Hacket's tower at Kilkenny Cathedral (Fig. 42). Twenty ribs meet in the octagonal nucleus of this vault, creating a dense web of intersecting lines. The Kilkenny vault forms an impressive climax to a development which may have began earlier at Holycross, a development particularly associated with the territories of Ormond.[33]

The Jerpoint vault is plainer than those elsewhere but it has some similarities with that at Hore. It has the same number of ribs rising from the corners (five including *formerets*), but no liernes and consequently no geometrical motif in the centre (Pl. 129, Fig. 43). The design is more open and, unlike the other vaults considered, the tapering of the ribs is not so skilfully handled. As we shall see, the tower at Jerpoint does not belong to the same stylistic group as Holycross, Kilcooly and Hore, and this is confirmed by the character of the vaulting.[34]

Although the crossing at Jerpoint was provided with a tierceron vault, the presbytery was rebuilt with a barrel vault. This curiously archaic procedure was followed at Kilcooly, a daughter house of Jerpoint (Pl. 110). As the most sacred part of the church, one would have expected the presbytery to receive the most attention. In both cases the barrels have a round profile and this 'Romanesque revival' is not easy to explain. It is true that quasi-barrel vaults had been employed in fourteenth-century England, as in the choir of Wells Cathedral, but here the ribs were still retained. A similar revival of barrel vaulting took place at the same time in Scotland, where it was a standard feature in the collegiate churches. The technique of barrel vaulting also formed an inherent part of the design of contemporary tower houses, a means of improving their structural stability and a safeguard against the risks of fire. In a Cistercian context a hint of how they might be treated can be found at the Cistercian cell on Clare Island, where ribs were painted onto the surface of a vault. At Jerpoint and Kilcooly the plaster has vanished but it is not impossible that they too were once bedecked with coloured ribs. The painted barrel vault was a cheap alternative to full scale Gothic ribbed vaulting.

Chapter 7

CISTERCIAN TOWER BUILDING

ONE OF THE most notorious Cistercian statutes was the decree passed in 1157 which forbade the construction of stone bell towers.[1] The statute was generally obeyed in France, where wooden bell turrets were often built over the crossing instead. Even these tended to become over elaborate and in 1240 'wooden towers of immoderate height' were also circumscribed.[2] In Ireland the statutes were gradually ignored and by the end of the middle ages very few Cistercian churches lacked a substantial stone tower over the crossing. The first Irish house which is known to have broken the rule was Grey, where the tower formed an inherent part of the 1193 design (Pl. 130).[3] As Grey was an English foundation, it is clear that the practice was copied from English Cistercian houses, where such towers were a standard feature. Monasteries in the affiliation of Mellifont at first scrupulously followed the letter of the rule and it was not until well into the thirteenth century that one of the Irish foundations succumbed to the imported English fashion.

The apparent contravention of the statutes by the English Cistercian houses has provoked considerable discussion. The words of the 1157 decree seem explicit enough—'Turres lapideae ad campanas non fiant'—and if taken literally it is difficult to understand why the directive was so flagrantly ignored. In 1217 the General Chapter compelled one French monastery, Bohéries, to demolish a newly constructed tower[4] but there is no evidence that the English abbeys received any rebuke for their activities. Twelfth-century towers still survive at Buildwas and Kirkstall (later heightened) and there is evidence that similar towers existed at Fountains, Roche and Dore (Pl. 131).

The most recent attempt to explain these contradictions has been made by Peter Fergusson,[5] who suggests that the 1157 statute did not represent 'an across-the board prohibition of all towers' and that the low crossing towers erected in England were permissible. He points out that the construction of towers was intimately associated with changes in the crossing below. The English abbeys after Rievaulx abandoned the Burgundian or 'Bernardine' approach, in which the nave roof or vault extended without interruption up to the presbytery, in favour of the more normal regular crossing. Fergusson argues that the 1157 discussion at the General Chapter clarified Cistercian attitudes to tower building and indirectly encouraged English monasteries to build them. He suggests that the towers at Fountains, Kirkstall, Buildwas and Roche were afterthoughts, introduced after the General Chapter of 1157. He thus reverses the apparent meaning of the statute, arguing that it prohibited only the more ambitious projects.

Fergusson is no doubt right to assume that what really worried the General Chapter were extravagant towers with multiple storeys. The low English towers scarcely came within the definition. It is unlikely that they were conceived primarily as bell towers and it is perhaps better to regard them as structural expedients, a convenient abutment for the roofs of the chancel, transepts and nave. A tower allowed the building to be roofed in separate stages and it may have had some value in unvaulted churches as a fire-break. At Buildwas and Kirkstall the towers were modest in height, barely rising above the apex of the surrounding roofs, and it is difficult to see how the communities could be accused of architectural extravagence, especially when they are compared to such pagoda-like structures as that at Chiaravalle Milanese in Lombardy.[6] English-style towers were erected in at least two French abbeys, Savigny (Manche) and Loc-Dieu

130 The crossing at Grey Abbey, where a tower formed an inherent part of the original design. The ruins of the chapter house can be seen in the foreground.

131 The church at Buildwas (Shropshire), where the crossing was covered by a low tower as in several English Cistercian houses.

(Aveyron), and elsewhere in France low stone platforms were sometimes used as a support for wooden towers and spires.[7] The debate at the General Chapter in 1157 was very likely prompted by the introduction of the regular crossing, which had brought with it the temptation to erect an imposing tower above. The General Chapter may have tolerated the English towers as an established local technique, which was not worthy of castigation, providing they remained low and simple in form. But Fergusson's suggestion that the 1157 statute actually permitted them goes beyond the available evidence, and the fact remains that most French monasteries interpreted the words of the decree quite literally. Moreover, the view that there was a 'sudden switch to low stone towers on the part of the English abbeys' is archaeologically suspect.[8]

The introduction of the Cistercian crossing tower to Ireland was a direct consequence of the Anglo-Norman invasion. With one exception, all the early towers were built in monasteries founded from English mother houses or with English affiliations at the time. At Grey only short stretches of the north and west walls of the tower survive and many features of its design are not clear.[9] The height of the tower is uncertain and so too is the means of access to chambers within it. Although there are no remains of a tower at Inch, the western crossing piers are substantial enough (5 feet by 6 feet 5 inches; 1.5 by 1.93 metres) to support one, and there is a spiral staircase conveniently near in the north transept (Fig. 32).[10] Towers existed at Graiguenamanagh (1204–

132 The tower at Boyle, added to the church in the thirteenth century.

133 Boyle, corbel inserted into the north-west crossing pier. 'Tapering corbels' were a favourite characteristic of Cistercian design. Note the three centering holes at the springing of the arch.

40), St Mary's, Dublin (before 1235) and Tintern (c1300) and one may have been envisaged at Mellifont during the mid-thirteenth century remodelling.[11]

The most impressive of the thirteenth century towers is that at Boyle, the one tower outside the Anglo-Norman group. It remains intact to a height of over sixty feet and dominates the ruins of the abbey (Pl. 132). It fits comfortably over the piers of the crossing and Leask regarded it as an integral part of the post-1161 church.[12] The tower was, however, an addition of the thirteenth century, as can be proved by a study of the crossing arches and their supports. The western arch of the crossing rests on corbels, which have nailhead ornament and round abaci. These are thirteenth-century in style and contrast with the scalloped capitals and square abaci on the other three arches (Pl. 133). Disturbed masonry either side of the corbels shows that they have been inserted, together presumably with the western crossing arch. The church at Boyle, therefore, was not designed with a regular crossing and a tower was not part of the original conception of the building. Of all the Irish houses, Boyle was the one which most rapidly assimilated English architectural forms and the decision to add a tower was consistent with this approach. The room in the tower was reached by a spiral staircase in the east wall, entered from the vault over the presbytery. A wooden floor separated the chamber from the crossing below and simple pointed doorways opened into the roofs of the nave and transepts. There are remnants of a string course at the north-west corner, but apart from this the tower lacks embellishment. Its design could not be considered a major contravention of the simplicity of the order.

By the middle of the fifteenth century, the Irish Cistercians regarded a crossing tower as an essential component of their churches. In at least six cases new towers were raised from ground level, elsewhere earlier towers were remodelled or heightened.[13] Lack of documents and firm stylistic evidence make it difficult to follow the sequence of building and there is no means of proving which abbey started the trend. Among possible candidates is Mellifont, where a massive enlargement of the crossing piers, designed to support a tower, took place at some unknown date between c1350 and c1500.[14] Most of the other towers can be attributed to the middle or later years of the fifteenth century. That at Holycross belongs to the rebuilding begun c1431, though the tower was probably not erected until c1460–1500. It is stylistically related to the neighbouring towers at Kilcooly and Hore, which can be ascribed to c1450–1500 (Pls 100, 109, 136). The erection of the tower at Jerpoint probably followed the indulgence granted in 1442 for repairs to the abbey.[15] The heightening of the tower at Tintern belongs to the same period, for in 1447 it was recorded that the abbot had rebuilt his house 'at his own particular cost and charge' (Pl. 140),[16] and it is reasonable to suppose that the remodelling of the tower was part of the expenses he incurred. Altogether seventeen Cistercian monasteries are known to have had towers or 'belfries' associated with their churches as the following table shows:

Towers extant

Grey, Boyle, Tintern, Dunbrody, Abbeylara, Jerpoint, Holycross, Kilcooly, Hore and Abbeydorney

Towers known from documentary or archaeological evidence[17]

Graiguenamanagh, Abington, Mellifont, St Mary's, Dublin, Assaroe, Inislounaght and Bective

Only at Corcomroe is there clear evidence that a tower was never built. In the remaining sixteen major abbeys, the buildings have either been destroyed or there is insufficient evidence. At St Mary's, Dublin, and Inislounaght the location of the towers is not known, though there is every probability that they were erected over the crossing. At Abbeydorney the tower was constructed above the western porch (Pl. 113).

The motives behind the upsurge of tower building, especially marked in the years 1440–1500 have never been satisfactorily explained. The towers have a stark, functional appearance, which has led to suggestions that defence was a prime consideration. As the mid-fifteenth century was a turbulent period in the history of the monasteries, there is plenty of evidence to support this. The rebuilding of Kilcooly after 1445 was necessitated by violence and in 1447 the abbot of Tintern complained that his monastic estates 'were very much wasted' by raiders.[18] Indeed, Tintern and Dunbrody were continually exposed to attacks from the Kavanaghs, who made regular forays into south Wexford. The abbot of Dunbrody, as a lord of Parliament, was a key figure of authority in the area and in 1375 he had been appointed 'one of the guardians of the public peace in the county of Wexford with power to protect true subjects, destroy rebels, restrain the giving of victuals, horses or alms to the Irish, who might waver in their allegiance, and seize at sea any small vessel employed in the conveyance of such'.[19] An imposing tower, rising above the monastic buildings, was one way an abbot might assert his authority over the surrounding district. There are many examples of abbots complaining about incursions on to their property. In 1467 the abbot of Fermoy explained that he had insufficient money 'for the repair of the cloister and other places of the monastery which, by reasons of wars and other misfortunes in times past, are in great part threatened with ruin'.[20] There is one documented occasion of a crossing tower being used for military combat, though it occurred in circumstances which would not have been welcomed by the General Chapter. Abbot Troy's description of the Cistercian monasteries of Ireland in 1498 recounts that, when making a visit to some of his daughter houses, the provisors and commendatories who occupied the abbeys, supported by

134 Abbeylara, where the ruins of the crossing tower are the principal remnant of the medieval abbey.

armed men, retired to the battlements of the churches and belfries. From here they repulsed the abbot with showers of javelins, stones and arrows.[21] We have already seen that as early as 1228 the monks of Monasteranenagh had assailed their visitor, Stephen of Lexington, from the roofs of the church. A well-fortified tower was thus a useful way of defending the independence of the monastery against outside interference, both secular and ecclesiastical. The defensive value of the crossing tower was underlined at the dissolution, when many of them were taken over by laymen and used as tower houses. In a few (non-Cistercian) cases this function was envisaged by the commissioners responsible for surveying monastic property in 1540–1. When referring to the Augustinian abbey of Great Connell (Kildare), for example, they stated that 'the belfry is very necessary for the farmer, for constructing a castle or fortilage for the defence of the town and vicinity'.[22] The crossing towers at Abbeylara, Hore, Dunbrody, Tintern and Kilcooly all appear to have been taken over for use in this way.

Convenient though a tower might be in times of crisis, the Cistercian crossing towers were not designed in terms of defence. Arrow loops are missing and their position over the crossing made it impossible to resist attack with traditional military devices like machicolis.[23] Nor were the towers limited to the more remote and exposed areas. By the end of the fifteenth century they had become an accepted feature in many non-Cistercian churches and these included buildings in relatively safe urban locations, like the Dominican friary in Kilkenny. The idea that the Cistercian towers were intended solely for military purposes must therefore be discounted, though many an abbot might have felt a little more secure for having one.

The crossing was an awkward place in which to erect a tower, so this location clearly mattered to the monks. The use of the choir must have been badly disrupted while building was going on and the undertaking was on occasions not without structural repercussions on the fabric below.[24] At Dunbrody it was necessary to block some of the arches at the east end of the nave in order to guarantee the stability of the tower and there are signs of similar difficulties at Mellifont. Here additional buttressing had to be placed behind the first (south) pier of the nave in order to prevent lateral movement. It would have been easier to construct the towers outside the lines of existing buildings, as happened at Furness and Fountains. But a tower over the crossing certainly looked more impressive, as it provided a solid visual focus to the exterior massing of the church. It was the traditional site for the tower of a monastic church and it was perhaps thought appropriate for the bells to be hung in the centre of the building.

In contemporary documents the towers are invariably described as belfries and there is no reason to doubt that this was their main function. That they held bells is not in doubt. In 1541, for example, there is a reference to 'a bell still hanging in the belfry of the church' at Graiguenamanagh.[25] The Cistercian statutes rigorously controlled the number of bells permitted in monasteries of the order. One could be hung above the refectory, another in a bell-cote above the south transept gable, and two were allowed in the church itself.[26] The south transept bell immediately above the cloister garth was used for sounding the regular hours, but no turrets survive in this position in Ireland. At the time of the dissolution, bells were listed among the chattels of the monasteries, and the royal commissioners recorded those that remained unsold at the time of their visits.[27] Although the lists are an incomplete guide, they provide a general indication of the numbers involved. Two bells were found at Dunbrody in 1541 and three at Tintern. In the monastery of St Mary's, Dublin, two bells were still unsold, 'one of greater and the other of less weight'. Two bells discovered by the commissioners at Bective weighed 180 lbs and were estimated to be worth 35 shillings. On the basis of these figures, it seems unlikely that any of the monasteries hung more than two bells in the crossing tower, despite some suggestions to the contrary.[28]

There are some hints that the towers were intended to provide domestic accomodation, either for the abbot or for his monks. At Holycross and Jerpoint, there is easy access to the towers from the domestic chambers fitted over the south transept chapels and it is tempting to believe that the rooms in the tower were an extension of this space. At Jerpoint the lower chamber was entered through a doorway decorated with dog-tooth ornament and the upper chamber has a seat in the north window, providing a pleasant spot from which to survey the countryside around. In 1572 the room 'over the Cross church of the Holy Church' at Holycross was rented out to James Fitzwilliam Purcell,[29] presumably as a dwelling place, which shows that after the Reformation the room in the tower was thought to be habitable. By the middle of the fifteenth century many Irish lords had built tower houses for themselves and at first sight the Cistercian crossing towers seem to be an ecclesiastical equivalent. Abbots frequently belonged to local families and in many cases their relations would have been living in fortified houses in the vicinity. It would be no surprise to learn that Cistercian abbots regarded a substantial stone tower as appropriate to their status and an indication of the importance of their monasteries.

Prestige was in fact a more likely motive for the construction of towers than any utilitarian function. There is no proof that they were used as living quarters before the dissolution and none of them have fireplaces. A fair proportion of the space in the upper chamber would have been occupied by the bells and their supporting frame (a cumbersome and noisy impediment in the living room). Many domestic towers were built by the Cistercians elsewhere in the precincts, but they should not be confused with those erected over the crossing of the churches.

Utilitarian motives do not, therefore, provide a complete explanation for the building of crossing towers. They were not well adapted for defence, nor were they fitted out as comfortable dwelling spaces.[30] Their nominal purpose was for hanging bells, but as monastic life had continued satisfactorily in many abbeys without belfries for over two centuries, why

135 The tower house at Burnchurch (Kilkenny), the standard form of residence for gentry in late medieval Ireland.

136 Hore Abbey from the north-east. The low stunted tower barely rose above the level of the surrounding roofs.

137 Corbel on the north-west crossing pier at Hore. A fine mason's mark is visible above the centering holes. The 'hanging' shield is charged with the arms of the Earl of Ormond.

were they deemed a necessity by the mid-fifteenth century? It appears that the towers were a means of asserting the prestige and authority of the monastery, a symbol of its importance in an age of political flux. While an abbot might claim they were an essential response to the turbulence of contemporary society, architectural fashion and human pride were equally cogent factors.

Cistercian towers have several distinctive characteristics. Except for those at Holycross and Kilcooly,[31] they are approximately square in plan, with Dunbrody attaining the greatest dimensions, 37 feet by 36 feet (11.3 by 11.0 metres). They were designed with two floors, from the lower of which doors opened into the adjacent roof spaces. The chamber above, the belfry proper, was normally lit by ogee headed windows, a pair on each wall.[32] Given their width, the total height of the towers was relatively low, a point which has occasioned much adverse comment. Thus one nineteenth-century antiquary remarked that the tower at Hore abbey 'does not look at all graceful, being too low for its length and breadth and for the great arch on which it rests' (Pl. 136).[33] Hore at 55 feet 4 inches (16.86 metres) is not in fact the lowest of the towers. To the bottom of the parapet, Kilcooly is a mere 47 feet 6 inches (14.47 metres). In this latter case the apex of the chancel roof overlapped the upper storey of the tower, which meant that the single ogee-headed window on the east wall had to be pushed to one side.[34] The tallest towers are those at Jerpoint (69 feet 6 inches; 21.18 metres) and Dunbrody (73 feet 6 inches; 22.40 metres). On account of its greater slenderness Jerpoint is the more elegant of the two (Pl. 138). Its upper storey is slightly taller than normal (approximately 16 feet; 4.87 metres) and, combined with exaggerated corner turrets and parapets, this gives it a stronger vertical *élan*. To the top of the turrets, the total height is 86 feet (26.21 metres). The tower has a slight batter, a feature which is more marked at Tintern and Dunbrody.

The walls of all the towers are constructed of rubblework and, unlike the Perpendicular towers of medieval England, they are devoid of ornament and buttresses. The base of the parapet is marked either by a string-course or a small overhang, which adds a valuable accent to an otherwise bare design. At Jerpoint the string-course jumps up at the corners around the turrets, a feature repeated not far away at the Black Abbey in Kilkenny (c1500). It is also found occasionally on fifteenth-century tower houses, as at Burnchurch (Kilkenny) and Kilclief (Down) (Pl. 135).[35] Parapets survive more or less intact at Kilcooly, Tintern and Jerpoint and in all three places these take the common Irish form with 'crow stepped' battlements.

In those churches where towers had not formed part of the original design, it proved necessary to construct new piers and arches from ground level. At Holycross, Kilcooly, Hore and Jerpoint the new arches consisted of two or three chamfered orders, the inner one supported on a corbel, the others descending to the ground as broad chamfered pilasters. At Mellifont the new piers were given an octagonal form to correspond with the piers in the reconstructed nave (Pl. 91). In every case the modifications resulted in a narrowing of the crossing area and a restriction of the vista eastwards. At Dunbrody, where the new piers are plain and characterless, the projection is especially noticeable and the builders here took no chances over the stability of their tower (Pl. 139). The original arches into the transepts were retained and more pointed ones added alongside, producing a combined arch width of 9 feet (2.74 metres). The bulk of the tower rests on the fifteenth-century insertions. The new transept arches also provided a support for the barrel vault which covers the crossing. This form of vault was a curious choice at a time when some type of ribbed vault would have been both structurally and aesthetically more satisfying. Barrel vaulting was no doubt simpler to erect, but the ribbed vaults constructed over the crossings at Holycross, Kilcooly, Hore, Jerpoint (and probably Mellifont) were far more attractive. The towers at Tintern and Boyle were never provided with vaults.

The means of reaching the upper rooms varies considerably from tower to tower. At Jerpoint there is a straight staircase in the north wall, reached from the vault over the presbytery. At Dunbrody both the east and west walls of the tower have straight flights of steps which lead from the transept wall walks up to the first floor chamber. A further stair in the north wall continues up to the belfry and battlements. At Holycross the lower chamber was entered directly from the presbytery vault and a spiral staircase in the north-east angle leads up to the belfry. When the towers at Tintern and Abbeylara were converted to secular use after the

138 The tower at Jerpoint, the tallest and most elegant of the Irish Cistercian towers.

139 The fifteenth-century tower at Dunbrody, supported on inserted piers which reduced the width of the crossing.

140 The crossing tower at Tintern, built shortly before 1447. After the dissolution, it was turned into a fortified residence.

141 Bective Abbey, residential tower at the south-west angle of the cloister. The corbelled projections contain chimneys.

dissolution, separate stair turrets were erected, at Tintern intruding into the space of the north transept and, at Abbeylara, blocking what was once the south aisle (Pl. 134). The variety of arrangements even before the Reformation shows that, however similar the towers might appear from a distance, there was no uniformity in their planning.

When considered in detail, it is possible to distinguish at least two local groups. The towers at Holycross, Kilcooly and Hore, situated within twenty miles of each other, are identified by their sharp limestone dressings, the structure of the supporting piers and the use of lierne and tierceron vaults. The towers of the two Wexford abbeys, Tintern and Dunbrody, are related by their pronounced batter and the absence of hood mouldings over the windows (Pls 139, 140). While the fashion for towers was universal across the country, this evidence suggests that the monasteries employed local masons, who did not travel far outside their own neighbourhood.

In addition to crossing towers, the Cistercians frequently erected other towers and turrets with a more obvious defensive purpose. Thus the 1540 extent of Mellifont explains that 'the church and divers houses and mansions on the site with certain towers and fortilices are built of stone and surrounded with stone walls'.[36] The account goes on to add that 'the mansion is very necessary for the protection of the inhabitants in time of insurrection and attack by the Irish attempting to prey on that country'.

The most heavily fortified Cistercian monastery was that at Bective, where two substantial towers were erected as part of the remodelling of the abbey in the fifteenth century. One was constructed at the west end of the church, the other is a massive structure at the south-west

142 The Augustinian abbey of Kells (Kilkenny) with its fortified *enceinte*. Several Cistercian abbeys are known to have been defended by strong walls and towers.

corner of the cloister, dominating the ruins of the abbey (Pl. 141, Fig. 63). It consists of three storeys above a barrel-vaulted basement and it was well equipped with chimneys and latrines. It was clearly designed as a well-defended habitation, presumably for the abbot. On the south face two projecting turrets reinforce the robust appearance of the building, which echoes in its general form the great fortress of the Plunketts at Dunsoghly, twenty miles away.[37] There is no doubt that the tower belongs to the monastic phase of Bective. Relieving arches in the east wall intelligently reduce the stress on the barrel vaults of the cloister and south range below and the building itself is neatly aligned to the reconstructed cloister walks. The imposing strength of the tower conveys, better than any document, the sense of fear which dominated the lives of small monastic communities in the later middle ages. The monks were in no position to resist an army, but they could at least withstand harassment from casual raiders. Not far away the Augustinians at Fore strengthened their monastery in a similar manner and by 1541 most Cistercian abbeys seem to have had 'castles' in the precincts. The impressive array of walls and towers which surround the Augustinian abbey of Kells (Kilkenny)[38] may in fact be more typical than is often imagined (Pl. 142). More vulnerable than the monastery itself were outlying granges and the extent of the depredations on monastic estates is made clear by the comments of the royal commissioners in 1541, when the term 'waste' is used repeatedly. It is no surprise that communities tried to defend their lands with towers and 'curtilages' and thus Baltinglass is reported to have owned castles at Graungeforth, Knocwyrc, Mochegraunge, Graungerosnalvan Grangecon, Littlegraunge, etc.[39] Neither the cattle, produce nor equipment of tenants was safe without some degree of fortification.

Chapter 8

CLOISTERS AND DOMESTIC BUILDINGS

The survival rate of claustral buildings in Ireland is disappointing. With one exception the cloister arcades were demolished after the dissolution (though at several abbeys parts have been reassembled) and in most places the one-time intimacy of the cloister garth has given way to the windswept bareness of an open courtyard. The conventual buildings have fared little better. The eastern ranges, with the chapter house and parlour, tend to be best preserved, but nowhere in Ireland does a dormitory, reredorter, calefactory or kitchen remain intact. The most impressive survivors are the chapter houses at Mellifont and Dublin, the refectory at Grey, the late medieval west range at Holycross and the octagonal lavabo at Mellifont. Nevertheless the destruction of most domestic architecture has left a major void in our picture of Cistercian design.

Despite the losses, there have been rapid developments in our understanding of cloister design within the last few years, achieved through excavation, fieldwork, and one sensational chance discovery. Altogether there is information, some of it admittedly fragmentary, about thirteen cloisters, roughly a third of the total, and they form a varied and interesting group. The accompanying table gives a synopsis of the evidence.

Evidence For Cloister Arcades

	MONASTERY	EVIDENCE	DATE
1	Mellifont	5 reconstructed Romanesque arches	c1150–1200
2	Graiguenamanagh	Fragments of an Early English arcade described 1892[1]	13th century
3	Baltinglass	One reconstructed trefoiled arch	c1300
4	Jerpoint	38 rebuilt piers, many with sculpture	c1390–1400
5	Dunbrody	Fragments in store	c1400–50
6	(?) Dublin, St Mary's	196 fragments discovered 1975	c1440(?)
7	Holycross	(a) 17 reconstructed Perpendicular arches	c1448
		(b) 6 rebuilt round headed arches	16th century (?)
8	Inch	Fragments in store	15th century
9	Hore	(a) Fragments	c1300
		(b) One reconstructed arch	15th century
10	Bective	Two ranges extant	c1450–1540
11	Kilcooly	Fragments in two styles	c1450–1540
12	Abbeyknockmoy	Fragments excavated 1983	c1475–1540
13	Abbeydorney	Fragments in graveyard	c1450–1540

With one exception, Irish cloisters were built in the conventional manner as simple pentices with lean-to roofs, the latter supported on arcaded walls. The earliest schemes followed the standard continental arrangement, with paired colonettes supporting a sequence of round arches. This was the design introduced at Mellifont in the twelfth century, parts of which were reconstructed after the excavations of 1954–5 (Pl. 143).[2] With its coupled shafts and scalloped capitals, this repeats the pattern of many a Cistercian monastery in England, Rievaulx providing a good comparison.[3] It is likely that the Mellifont cloister became the norm in Ireland, but evidence from other sites is scarce.[4]

By the thirteenth century more advanced forms appeared, in accord with early Gothic taste.

143　Mellifont, the octagonal lavabo (c1200) and reconstructed section of cloister arcade.

144　Baltinglass, reconstructed cloister arcade (probably c1300).

The cloister in the great Anglo-Norman monastery at Graiguenamanagh seems to have been particularly impressive. Although the site is now derelict and overgrown, vital details came to light in 1892 when Robert Cochrane reported that 'the cloister arcade appears to have been formed with small double columns of blue limestone, carrying ornamental double capitals in one stone, with semi-circular arched heads and trefoil cusping'.[5] This sounds like a characteristic piece of Early English design, making full use of the colour contrasts so loved by thirteenth-century architects, and it is the type of arrangement to be expected in a wealthy English house. It is interesting to note that the frame of the collation seat in the north walk has a trefoil head, echoing the form of the erstwhile cloisters. Another arcade with trefoiled arches, this time of pointed form, was erected about 1300 at Baltinglass.[6] One arch has been reconstructed, but the unmoulded arches and excessively thick shafts give a clumsy, inelegant impression (Pl. 144). The trefoiled arch was a standard decorative motif in Gothic architecture, but apart from the recently discovered arcade at Haughmond (Shropshire),[7] there is little evidence of its use in English cloisters. The Irish examples suggest that it was once a common form.

By 1300 several Cistercian abbeys in Europe had begun to adopt the contemporary Gothic fashion for wide traceried screens instead of simple arches. The cloister at Noirlac, with its elaborate geometrical tracery, is a spectacular example,[8] but the fashion never found favour in Ireland. Instead Irish masons hit upon an ingenious way of improving traditional cloister design, preserving the elegance of thin coupled shafts, while adding greater strength. This was the so-

145 The decorated cloister at Jerpoint (c1390–1400), the earliest known example of the 'dumb-bell' pier.

called 'dumb-bell' scheme, in which the twin shafts were cut out of a single block of stone and linked together by a thin plate or web. The appearance of colonettes was retained, though in fact they had been replaced by a sturdy pier. Where and when this development occurred is impossible to say, but the scarcity of foreign parallels suggests an Irish invention.[9] The new form improved the stability of the arcades, and it may have been prompted by structural problems with older designs. The earliest known example was constructed c1390–1400 at Jerpoint,[10] a cloister famous for its carving (Pl. 145). The architecture here is curiously archaic. Round arches recall Romanesque practice and the mouldings of capitals and bases would not be out of place around 1300. This is often taken as an illustration of the retrospective flavour of later medieval culture in Ireland, an indication too of the Gaelic revival. But to any discerning monk or visitor from afar, the antiquated character of the design must have been self-evident and it is difficult to believe that a community situated close to the power base of the earls of Ormond could be so backward looking. It is possible that construction of the cloister began in piecemeal fashion and the monks attempted to harmonise it with older work. Alternatively an earlier cloister in some neighbouring monastery may have been taken as a model.

The 'dumb-bell' pier subsequently became a standard feature of Irish cloister design. The Cistercians used it in at least eight other abbeys and outside the order it was exploited to great

146 The cloister of the Franciscan friary at Askeaton (Limerick), the best preserved of the fifteenth-century Irish cloisters.

147 Holycross, one of the cloister arches.

148 Fragments of the cloister arcade at Abbeyknockmoy (c1475–1540).

effect by the friars as in the magnificent Franciscan cloister at Askeaton (Pl. 146).[11] Although all are similar in structural terms, three types of dumb-bell pier can be distinguished (Fig. 44). First, there is the basic type (A), where the pseudo-colonettes are round (Jerpoint, Inch, Dunbrody), following Romanesque traditions. Then there are examples with polygonal colonettes (B), a form that was quicker and cheaper to cut (Abbeydorney, Kilcooly, Abbeyknockmoy). Finally, there is a more elaborate version (C), in which triple shafts take the place of single colonettes (Inch, Hore, Holycross, Bective). Recent clearances at Abbeyknockmoy have brought to light many pieces from an impressive arcade of type (B) (Pl. 148).[12] Piers, capitals and bases, all moulded with precision out of the hard local limestone, appear to date from c1475 to 1540. Pseudo-octagonal shafts were popular at this time in the west, particularly among the friars, and the style of the Abbeyknockmoy capitals can be compared with those in the Franciscan cloister at Adare (c1464–1500).[13] The design relates to local practice, rather than to any specifically Cistercian tradition. Fragments of a similar cloister, now submerged in undergrowth, can be found at Abbeydorney. This also has links with the Franciscans, on this occasion with the friary at Muckross.

Other monasteries, however, were more cosmopolitan in approach. What remains of the fifteenth-century cloister at Holycross has recently been reconstructed (for the second time this century)[14] and it presents an enormous contrast with Abbeyknockmoy and Abbeydorney. It is more authentically 'Perpendicular' than anything in Ireland outside the Pale (Pls 147, 149). The pointed arches, made up of two blocks of stone, are grouped in triplets and decorated with an elaborate array of sub-cusps. The spandrels are decorated with tracery and each arch is set firmly within a Perpendicular frame. There is a considerable amount of variation in the design, and two different types of pier were employed, one of which has delicate foliage ornament on its inner face (Fig. 45).[15] Despite the appearance of homogeneity, the details at Holycross also vary considerably, with four different types of capital and three different bases. The corner piers were decorated with coats of arms, three of which remain (abbot O'Congail, and two Ormond shields), and it is possible that the intermediate piers once had further escutcheons (Pls 93, 94).

149 The north range of the cloister at Holy-cross (c1450) following the recent reconstruction. The design has a stronger 'Perpendicular' flavour than most Irish architecture of the time.

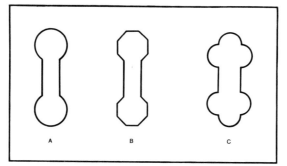
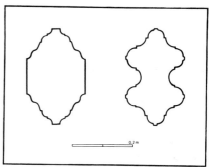

Fig. 44 Types of 'dumb-bell' cloister piers.

Fig. 45 (far right) Plan of the piers in the cloister at Holycross.

Fig. 46 The cloister arcade at Hore.

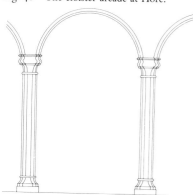

Such ostentatious displays of heraldry were a feature of late Gothic architecture in England and this, together with the general style of work, made the cloister a suave and fashionable piece of architecture.

Until recently the Holycross cloister was an isolated design in an Irish context, that is until a remarkable discovery in one of the streets of Dublin. During demolition work near the old city wall in Cook Street in September 1975, sixty-eight blocks of dressed sandstone came to light, all of them reused as rough building material in the sixteenth or seventeenth century. When the blocks, together with a further 128 fragments, were assembled together, it became apparent that they belonged to a fifteenth-century cloister arcade and one that had affinities with Holycross—the rectangular frame (Figs 47, 48), the multi-cusped arches and the traceried spandrels all reappeared. As with Holycross, the arcades were moulded on both their inner and outer faces. Parts of one of the corner piers survived and at springing level this was decorated with a small ogee-headed niche, where the coats of arms had been at Holycross.[16] It is by no means clear where the cloister came from, for, like all major cities of the medieval world, Dublin had a wide variety of religious houses. Chevron ornament and a piece of bowtell moulding, found amongst the debris, suggested one of the older monasteries in the city. The Augustinian house of Christ

150 The west range of the cloister at Bective, where the arches are supported on attractively moulded piers.

151 The cloister garth at Bective looking west, the most intimate and secluded of the Irish Cistercian cloisters.

152 Reconstructed arches of the cloister of Fore (Westmeath). Although not a Cistercian house, there are obvious similarities with the cloisters at Bective.

153 The cloister of the Austin friars at Adare (Limerick). The compact design bears resemblance to the cloisters at Bective.

Church and St Thomas are both possible candidates, but the leading contender must be the Cistercian abbey of St Mary's. During the seventeenth century this was used as a quarry by Dublin builders (in 1674 stones from the abbey were used to reconstruct Essex Bridge)[17] and the abbey was only 530 metres from the find spot.[18] A Cistercian context would explain the link with Holycross as well as the sophistication of the design, one that was appropriate for the richest monastery in the country. However, excavation will be needed before the issue can be settled.

The multi-cusped arch set within a rectangular frame was such a standard component of English Perpendicular architecture that it provides no clues about the origin of the design. There are dozens of fifteenth-century examples of the motif, from the north transept window of Merton College Chapel, Oxford (1416–24)[19] to the blind arcading on the west tower of the parish church at Cirencester. But the newly discovered cloister does illustrate the way that Dublin acted as a channel for the importation of Perpendicular features and it seems almost certain that the Holycross arcade was inspired by it. The two cloisters differ in details so the same masons were not responsible (Fig. 73). The Dublin mouldings have a sharper, more Perpendicular flavour, and a date of c1440, some years before Holycross, seems likely.

The most intimate and secluded of the Cistercian cloisters was that at Bective. Here the fifteenth-century arcades were constructed around a small court, only 33 feet (10 metres) square, and the design was particularly well conceived (Pl. 151).[20] Each range was divided by thick buttresses into three bays, each of these comprising three cinquefoiled arches, a neat and logical play of triplets. The two surviving ambulatories (west and south) were roughly vaulted in stone

1 m

Fig. 47 Reconstructed cloister arcade from Dublin, possibly from St Mary's Abbey.

Fig. 48 Reconstructed cloister arcade from Dublin, inner elevation.

and integrated into the adjoining buildings, so that the upper floors extended across them. As the arcades had more to support, they were reinforced by thick embracing arches on the outer side. The other ranges had conventional lean-to roofs. The surviving piers are an attractive development of the 'dumb-bell' type (type C) giving the impression that the arcade was supported by sets of clustered colonettes (Pl. 150). At least two of the piers were decorated with figures and there is some unobtrusive ornament on a few of the arches (interlace and foliage) (Pls 216, 220).[21]

Bective is the best preserved of the Irish Cistercian cloisters and it is ironic that it is not typical of the order. The tiny garth was heavily shaded, in contrast with the wide open spaces of the normal cloister and the integration of two of the ranges is also exceptional, though a parallel for this can be found in abbot Dovell's work at Cleeve in Somerset (c1534).[22] Compact cloisters and integrated arcades are characteristic of the friars, rather than the white monks, and the well-preserved cloister in the Austin friary at Adare makes a particularly telling comparison (Pl. 153).[23] Like Bective this has cinquefoiled arcades as well as embracing arches and flat vaulting in the ambulatories. Each range was also divided into three bays. It is clear that in architectural terms the monks of Bective, forsaking the traditions of their order, had fallen under the inspiration of the friars, the most energetic religious builders in fifteenth-century Ireland.

The arcades at Bective also have a connection with those at Fore, a Benedictine abbey twenty-two miles to the west. Piers and arches are remarkably similar and Leask suggested that the same masons were responsible (Pl. 152).[24] Differences of detail, however, leave this open to doubt (Fig. 73).

The chronology of these cloisters presents serious difficulties. In the absence of documentary evidence, style usually provides the only hints, but even here mouldings vary in such an arbitrary way that dating is hazardous. The cloisters at Kilcooly can perhaps be assigned to the decade 1460–70, since the capitals are similar to those at Muckross (c1468).[25] Similarly one can suggest dates of 1460–1500 for Bective on the basis of comparisons with the Franciscan cloister at Adare (started c1464–86).[26]

An acute illustration of the difficulties is provided by the remnants of the cloister at Inch.[27] On the basis of style this could be placed almost anywhere between 1350 and 1500. The arches were cinquefoiled, but with ogee heads, giving an exotic flavour to the design (Fig. 49). A variety of supports has come to light—pairs of free-standing octagonal shafts, and 'dumb-bell' piers of type A and C, but how these were employed is not known. The best parallels for the capitals are to be found in the Dominican cloister at Sligo, dated by Leask to 1470 or later,[28] so the work at Inch probably comes from the second half of the fifteenth century. It is a pity that none of this exceptional cloister remains *in situ*. With its sequence of ogee arches, it must have been as lively as any in Ireland.

Out of thirteen cloisters, it is remarkable that ten belong to the later middle ages, a time when the communities were in decline. Only at Bective, and possibly Kilcooly, was the rebuilding prompted by the need to adapt to smaller numbers. Why did long-established houses like Jerpoint and Abbeyknockmoy embark on such extensive reconstruction? The obvious answer is that the original cloisters were falling apart after two to three hundred years' existence. In 1467 the abbey of Fermoy claimed that it had no money 'for the repair of the cloister and other places of the monastery which, by reason of wars and other misfortunes in times past, are in great part threatened with ruin'.[29] Violence, natural decay and inadequate maintenance made some rebuilding inevitable, but it is odd that so little trace remains of earlier arcades. There is no sign of debris from previous work reused as building material. This makes one wonder how many monasteries had stone cloisters from the start. At the birth of most communities temporary cloisters of wood were erected,[30] and even in the relatively prosperous Yorkshire monastery of Meaux a stone cloister was not begun until fifty years after its foundation. It is possible that in some of the poorer houses of Ireland temporary expedients became semi-permanent and the resurgence of cloister construction in the fifteenth century may be explained by the replacement of ancient timber galleries.[31]

The Irish cloisters represent an attractive and almost unknown aspect of European architecture. Although there are many gaps, it is possible to trace the general evolution over a period of 350 years. For much of this time, English methods were paramount, but with the introduction of the 'dumb-bell' pier local characteristics began to emerge, giving the Irish designs an identity of their own. Most distinctive of all was the cloister at Jerpoint, with its array of figure carving, a cloister unique among the Cistercian houses of northern Europe.

The north alley of a Cistercian cloister was used each evening by the community for a short reading known as the Collation, a ceremony which took its name from the *Collationes* of St John Cassian, one of the recommended books.[32] In 1228 Stephen of Lexington suggested a more basic text to the Irish monks, urging them to read the Cistercian *Liber Usuum* every two years so

Fig. 49 Reconstructed cloister arcade from Inch.

*abbot pro. also
charged with expenses
of giving news
to lay congregation*

that nobody was ignorant of Cistercian rules and customs.[33] The monks listened to the reading before going into church for Compline, the last service of the day. It was also a moment when they were allowed a drink. Normally the community sat together on benches against the wall of the church, with the abbot presiding in the centre. The reader stood opposite, beside the cloister arcades. In some abbeys a special bay was constructed to accommodate the lectern, consisting of a small pavilion projecting into the cloister garth, an arrangement which provided more space for the reader.[34] The foundations of such a bay, square in outline, can be seen at Jerpoint, midway along the north range. In fact there is a double set of foundations and it is clear that the original reader's bay was rebuilt a few feet further north when the cloister was remodelled

154 Graiguenamanagh, architectural frame of the abbot's seat in the north walk of the cloister, used each evening during reading of the Collation.

155 Cleeve Abbey (Somerset), the collation seat.

Fig. 50 (facing page bottom centre)   Graiguenamanagh, reconstruction of door to chapter-house vestibule.

Fig. 51 (facing page bottom right)   Graiguenamanagh, plan of pier in door to chapter-house vestibule.

c1390–1400 (Fig. 10). It was about this time (1373) that a *pulpitum collationis* was specified in a contract for the reconstruction of the cloister in the English abbey of Boxley (Kent).[35] Jerpoint provides the only Irish evidence for the feature, but in two houses there are remains of the abbot's seat. At Graiguenamanagh this takes the form of a trefoil-headed niche (frequently mistaken for a blocked doorway) which acted as a frame for a wooden seat, a design strikingly similar to the collation seat at Cleeve in Somerset (Pls 154, 155). At Grey abbey, the seat was fitted inside a pointed arch and flanked by detached colonettes.[36] The rarity of these stone seats suggests that in other monasteries the abbot's throne may not have been constructed with so much dignity as a permanent feature in masonry.

The east walk of the cloister was more important as a thoroughfare, with the principal entrance to the church at its north end. Near the 'processional door' was the book cupboard, sometimes a recess set into the wall of the south transept, sometimes a small chamber, with its own doorway from the cloister. In Ireland no wall cupboards or *armaria* survive, and in most abbeys the western half of the sacristy was used for books, as at Jerpoint, where there is a dividing wall. The use of the sacristy in this way is suggested by the presence of doorways, giving access from the cloister.[37] At Dunbrody and Graiguenamanagh special chambers for the monastic library were devised between the sacristy and chapter house and in later years at Mellifont the book cupboard may have been situated under the night stairs, a space reached through a door in the adjoining transept wall.[38]

Unlike some of the medieval orders, the Cistercians were not great bibliophiles and the stock of books in most Irish houses was probably small. The collection would include psalters, lectionaries, Bibles and gospel books, as well as liturgical books like graduals, missals and antiphonaries. There would be commentaries by the early Christian fathers, devotional treatises and no doubt the letters, sermons and other writings of St Bernard, plus Cistercian monastic documents and copies of the Benedictine Rule.[39]

The sacristy, the first chamber in the east range beyond the church, was a small barrel-vaulted space, lit by a single window to the east. They were gloomy, utilitarian rooms, with no architectural pretensions. The doorway communicating with the south transept was usually simple in form, but the fifteenth-century examples at Holycross and Kilcooly were transformed into ornate entrances. In the latter case, the sacristy may have served as some form of chapel, and this seems to have been the case at Hore where there is an attractive piscina of c1300, neatly framed by a trefoiled arch.[40] The main purpose of the sacristy, however, was to house the vestments, chalices and other items required for services in the church. As such it contained some of the most precious objects a monastery might possess, which explains why the sacristy at Boyle was raided in 1235 when soldiers 'took away its valuables, chalices and vestments'.[41]

Beyond the sacristy lay the chapter house, the most important room in the monastery after the church. Here the monks gathered after morning mass, seated on benches around the wall, with the abbot presiding. After prayers, a passage from the Rule was read out (hence *domus capituli* or chapter house) and there followed comments and spiritual advice from the abbot. Then came prayers for the dead and the ceremony terminated with public confession, each monk in turn speaking openly in front of his brethren.[42] The chapter house was the conference room of the monastery and as such merited dignified architectural treatment. The entrance was normally an impressive doorway and it is sad to report that only at Holycross does an example survive intact, the latter a curious fifteenth-century affair with an ogee head (Pl. 156). Elsewhere, footings and base mouldings remain which give some hints of the splendour that has been lost. At Grey six orders of detached shafts flanked the door and at Boyle there were five orders of shallow roll mouldings (Fig. 68). The most impressive entrance, however, was at Graiguenamanagh, where the chapter house was reached through a vestibule. This opened on to the cloister through a sequence of three moulded arches, which rested on quatrefoil piers, the latter ornamented with marble colonettes. Parts of this attractive Early English work remain, embedded in later masonry (Pl. 157, Figs 50, 51). The triple arcades reflect a scheme that was common in English Cistercian design, and comparisons can be made with Furness, Fountains, Tintern and Calder. The doorway to the thirteenth-century chapter house at Mellifont is known

162

from an engraving of 1748.[43] It had four orders and the arches were elaborately decorated, one with openwork foliage ornament (Pl. 158). A carved angel was placed on the keystones. This doorway was unusual since the decoration faced inwards, making it visible to the community as they attended their meetings.[44] Alongside the doorway there were frequently two open arches or windows, a rather draughty arrangement which is supposedly explained by the occasional

156 Holycross, the chapter house doorway, furnished with an exotic display of billet ornament.

158 (right) Mellifont, the chapter house doorway (c1220) as depicted in Wright's *Louthiana* (1748). It was removed in the second half of the eighteenth century.

157 Graiguenamanagh, the remnants of the fine arcaded doorway that led into the chapter house vestibule.

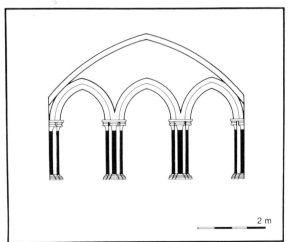

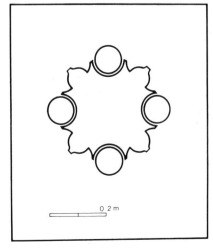

159 The well preserved chapter house at Cleeve (Somerset). As at Jerpoint and Dublin, this was vaulted in a single span.

attendance of laybrothers, who could follow proceedings from the adjoining cloister walk. Traces of these windows can be seen at Boyle, and their general disposition can be judged from English abbeys such as Cleeve, where the chapter house is well preserved (Pl. 159).[45] The facade of the chapter house of the Augustinian abbey at Cong, which has similar windows, may have been inspired by the work at Boyle.

The Irish chapter houses varied considerably in design. Those at Corcomroe, Inch and Holycross were exceptionally small, measuring less than twenty feet (six metres) along each side (Figs 26, 32, 37). The first to be erected was presumably that at Mellifont, where the original building of c1150 was a rectangular chamber 41 feet 4 inches by 26 feet 7 inches (12.6 by 8.1 metres), with proportions of approximately 3:2 (Fig. 13). It was lit by small Romanesque windows in the east wall, two of which remain. The room was probably vaulted in six bays, a 3 × 2 arrangement which would have required a pair of intermediate piers. This was a standard Cistercian scheme, and perfect examples can be seen in France at Noirlac and Le Thoronet.[46] A similar design was adopted by the Anglo-Normans at Dunbrody, where the six bays of ribbed vaulting rested on octofoil piers (Fig. 20). The chapter house of c1220 at Abbeyknockmoy was analogous in proportion, but its original appearance was ruined by a drastic modelling in the fifteenth century.[47] It was once a fine room, with five lancets, emphatically decorated with herringbone chevron (Fig. 18).

The chapter house at Grey was approximately the same size (35 feet by 28 feet 4 inches; 10.67 × 8.64 metres) but here the main axis was east-west so that it projected beyond the line of the east range. Slender octagonal piers supported twelve bays of vaulting, in a 3 × 4 arrangement (Pl. 130, Fig. 11). It was an impressive piece of architecture, a point underlined by the substantial

160 Mellifont, the chapter house (c1220). This replaced a Romanesque chapter house which was converted into a vestibule.

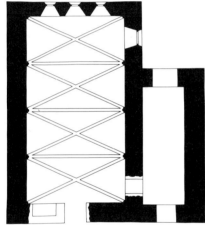

Fig. 52 Dublin, St Mary's Abbey, plan of chapter house.

Fig. 53 Mellifont, plan of second chapter house.

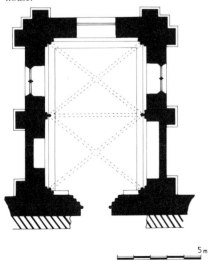

outer plinth and the elaborate doorway.[48] The subdivision of all these chapter houses by intermediate piers or columns gave them an intimacy which, in their ruined state, is difficult to appreciate without looking at comparative examples abroad.

A completely different approach was adopted at Jerpoint and Dublin. Here the chapter houses were long undivided rooms, vaulted in a single span. In both cases they projected beyond the east range. Jerpoint was covered by a plain barrel vault, and devoid of its original dressed masonry, it is a dark, sombre room. Far more imposing is the chapter house of St Mary's, Dublin, the only architectural relic of that great Cistercian monastery (Pl. 115, Fig. 52). Surrounded by sheds and warehouses in a run down quarter of the city, its environment is uninspiring. The present floor is 6 feet 9 inches (2.07 metres) below the modern street level, giving it the appearance of an underground cavern. Measuring 47 feet by 23 feet 3 inches (14.32 by 7.09 metres), it is covered by four bays of ribbed vaulting, supported on corbels of typically Cistercian character. Three lancet windows occupy the east wall, and there was a further window in the south wall, where it projected forward of the east range. These windows are now bricked up and disfigured, but ancient photographs show them ornamented with a sumptuous array of continuous roll mouldings.[49] These, together with keeled profiles on the ribs and triple shafts on the corbels, give the design an unmistakable west of England pedigree.[50] The dressed stone was also imported, from the quarries at Dundry in Somerset.[51] Chapter houses vaulted in a single span, like those at Jerpoint and Dublin, are more common among the Benedictines than the Cistercians, but there is a good Cistercian parallel at Cleeve (Pl. 159).

The chief problem confronting the architect of a chapter house was the presence of the dormitory on the floor above. Vaults had to be kept low, which prevented the development of a taller, more open interior. One standard solution was to build the chapter house beyond the east range, with access via a low vestibule under the dormitory. This was how the polygonal chapter houses of England were organised and it was a solution adopted in four of the Cistercian abbeys of Ireland. The first was erected at Mellifont around 1220 and the original chapter house of c1150 was converted into a vestibule (Fig. 53). The new room was smaller than its predecessor, and it is difficult to understand what prompted the work. The rich ornamentation of the doorway and capitals made the new chapter house an attractive design and there was probably some gain in lighting. The room was covered by two bays of ribbed vaults, which rested on bold clusters of shafts (Pl. 160). A modern concrete bench runs around the interior wall, evoking the

161 The early Gothic chapter house at Monasteranenagh, looking east.

162 Jerpoint, the door of the slype which gave access to buildings on the east side of the monastery.

163 Jerpoint, the surviving windows of the dormitory.

medieval seating arrangements. During the fourteenth or fifteenth century, some remodelling took place, when traceried windows were inserted and new ribs were installed in the vault.[52]

A far more spacious early Gothic chapter house was erected at Monasteranenagh (22 feet 3 inches by 62 feet; 6.78 by 18.9 metres) (Fig. 34). The building had a strong east-west axis and it terminated with three great lancets in the eastern gable (Pl. 161). There is no indication that it was ever vaulted. The grandest of all was built at Graiguenamanagh, the dimensions of which (66 feet by 33 feet 6 inches; 20.12 by 10.21 metres externally) merit comparison with those at Stanley, Fountains and Furness (Fig. 27).[53] It is ruined almost to foundation level and the site has never been excavated. There are some signs that it was vaulted, possibly in four or five bays, and its lengthy walls were no doubt filled with lancets, like those in the church alongside. Access to this magnificent room was achieved through a vaulted vestibule. This had a central pier with marble colonettes, the famous 'marble tree' of Graiguenamanagh, which, it is reported, was stolen 'in the night' at the beginning of the nineteenth century and 'removed to Carlow by a man named Cheevers'.[54] The last of these almost free-standing chapter houses was built at Hore around 1280, but, apart from a lancet in the east wall, few details remain. From this brief survey it is apparent that the Irish chapter houses were surprisingly varied in design and it is hard to detect any underlying pattern. Nor was there any sharp distinction between the Irish and Anglo-Norman foundations, though Early English detail is more noticeable in the latter. The two finest were probably those at Grey and Graiguenamanagh, both Early Gothic in design, yet a contrast to each other in form.

The remaining chambers in the east range were the parlour, the slype and the so-called 'dorter undercroft'. The parlour served as an office for the prior and, as its name implies, it was a place where essential conversation was allowed. In Ireland it was normally a narrow barrel-vaulted space, as at Jerpoint. In several cases there was a doorway at both ends, which can make it difficult to distinguish from the adjoining passage or slype. The parlour at Graiguenamanagh was an unusually large room, 25 feet (7.62 metres) long, and rib-vaulted in four bays (Fig. 27). Beyond the parlour came the slype, a corridor which linked the privacy of the cloister with the open area to the east, where the infirmary was usually situated. At Hore and Dunbrody the slype was aligned to the south alley of the cloister, which may have been the case at other monasteries too (Figs 15, 20). The final chamber in the east range was the so-called dorter undercroft. In plenty of monasteries outside Ireland these were spacious, vaulted rooms, with a line of columns down the centre. There is a magnificent thirteenth-century example at Neath in Wales.[55] The size of the undercroft was determined by the length of the dormitory above, so the larger the community the longer the undercroft. In most Irish houses they were understandably quite short. The standard Cistercian design can still be detected at Grey where the chamber was divided by a line of three octagonal columns, forming eight vault compartments, and, although less survives, the undercroft at Dunbrody was similar (Figs 11, 20). The well-preserved fifteenth-century undercroft at Holycross is less sophisticated, being covered by a barrel vault in a single span. The way the undercroft was used has never been satisfactorily determined. Some scholars have interpreted it as a place for the instruction of novices, others as the day room where the monks might carry out practical tasks, particularly during inclement weather. The magnificent architectural treatment that they were sometimes accorded suggests a central role in the life of the monastery. The Cistercian customs refer to the 'auditorium iuxta capitulum', and although this is thought to apply to the parlour, there are times when it seems more applicable to the dorter undercroft.[56]

The only Irish abbey in which the lower storey of the east range survives intact is Holycross, and here it is possible to appreciate the full sequence of rooms—sacristy, chapter house, slype, parlour and undercroft (Fig. 37). Unfortunately the diminutive scale and the consistent use of barrel vaults gives the architecture a primitive appearance which belies its fifteenth-century date and it is no guide to the grandeur that once existed at Grey or Graiguenamanagh. As far as can be discerned, stone vaults rather than timber ceilings were de rigueur in the east range of Irish houses. These provided good structural support for the floor of the dormitory and, should fire break out, the monks were less likely to be engulfed in their beds.

The dormitory was a long, single room stretching from the wall of the transept to the end of the east range. Apart from occasional windows (at Jerpoint, Graiguenamanagh, Dunbrody and Boyle), few architectural details remain. In the early years beds were ranged against the outer walls but by the later middle ages, monks demanded greater personal privacy, and the dormitory was divided into smaller chambers by wooden partitions. This process is well attested in England and France,[57] and there is little doubt that Irish monks followed suit. In the early years the abbot often had his own bedroom at the north end of the dormitory but, as their social status developed, they moved to more spacious apartments elsewhere. At Boyle there was a separate room above the sacristy, fitted with a fireplace, and at Mellifont a fine private apartment was constructed in the fifteenth century (?) above the chapter house, complete with a fireplace and arched cupboard. Further apartments were sometimes found above the south transept chapels, reached by a doorway in the north-east corner of the dormitory, as at Jerpoint and Abbeyknockmoy.[58] The equivalent apartment at Holycross was fitted with a magnificent fireplace (with a fine joggled lintel) and tiny windows looked down into the church below. Such a chamber must have been occupied by one of the senior officials of the monastery. At Kilcooly the entire space above the south transept was given over to a bedroom or dormitory, after the remodelling of the abbey between 1450 and 1520 (Pl. 164). Again this was a room of some pretensions, for its twin-light windows were embellished with sculpture, it had its own

164   Kilcooly, the south transept seen from the cloister garth. The whole of the upper floor was used as a private dwelling-chamber.

165 The remains of the thirteenth-century day stairs at Grey, the last three steps attractively curved as they reach the floor of the cloister.

garderobe, and a staircase gave direct access to the church. In all likelihood it was the private chamber of the abbot or prior.

The night stairs, or their doorways, remain in nine of the abbeys, but evidence for the day stairs at the other end of the dormitory is surprisingly scarce. They were normally situated in the angle of the east and south ranges, but only at Grey do parts survive, the final steps attractively curved as they descend to the floor of the cloister (Pl. 165, Fig. 11). Despite the lack of remains elsewhere, there is every reason to suppose that this was the usual location, at least in the twelfth and thirteenth centuries. Just as the slype often lay on the axis of the south walk of the cloister, so the main staircase lay on the axis of the east walk in line with the door to the church. In the mid-fifteenth century at Holycross, however, such refinements were ignored. Here the dormitory is reached by a steep and awkward stair, fitted into the walls of the undercroft (Fig. 37). For some reason the late Gothic architects of Ireland had a penchant for tight winding staircases, as testified in innumerable tower houses throughout the country. It comes as no surprise to read of the fate of Turlough, prior of Lough Derg and rector of Derryvullen, who died after falling down a stone staircase in a house at Athboy in 1504.[59]

To the south or east of the dormitory lay the latrines, otherwise known as the rere-dorter or *domus necessarii*. They were situated at the same level as the dormitory so that there was easy communication between them. The foundations of a sizeable rere-dorter exist at Hore but elsewhere remains are scant. All too often their existence is implied only by an arch or doorway in the dormitory which at Abbeyknockmoy and Bective now open into a void. The Cistercians are renowned for their expert drainage systems, and stone-lined sewers were normally constructed directly under the rere-dorter.[60] At Jerpoint and Grey one can follow the course of such a sewer as it passes under the rere-dorter, then under the floor of the refectory, past the kitchens and away to the nearby river or lough.[61] In 1983 a deep, stone-lined drain was

166 Tintern Abbey looking north. Excavations in 1983 at the end of the south range revealed a substantial drain or sewer.

167 The refectory at Dunbrody, looking east. The reader's pulpit was located on the wall to the right.

168 The ruins of the early Gothic refectory at Grey, one of the longest refectories in Ireland.

excavated at the south end of the dormitory range at Tintern, in the vicinity of the erstwhile latrines (Pl. 166).[62]

The first chamber in the south range, beside the day stairs, was the warming house or calefactory, the only room in the monastery (outside the kitchen and bakehouse) where a fire was maintained in the winter months. Reading and meditation were allowed here on exceptionally cold days and it was the place where shoes were greased, heat being necessary to allow the grease to penetrate leather. Scribes prepared their ink and parchment in the warm atmosphere and it was the room where blood-letting was carried out, a privilege granted to each monk four times a year.[63] This was supposedly a health-inducing exercise, though this was not the effect it had on abbot O'Maelbhrenauin of Boyle, who died from the process in 1225.[64] The foundations of several calefactories can be identified, and at Grey there are remains of the fireplace, built as was often the case into the wall of the adjoining refectory (Fig. 11). Given the dangers of fire, the calefactories were usually vaulted in stone, rather than covered with timber ceilings.

After the church, the tallest and most imposing room in a Cistercian monastery was likely to be the refectory. The plans of ten are known and they fall into two groups. In five cases (Boyle, Abbeyknockmoy, Monasteranenagh, Dunbrody and Hore), the refectory was parallel to the cloister walk, a standard Benedictine scheme, derived ultimately from the plan of St Gall (c820). As this layout was widespread in Ireland, it may have been adopted in the first refectory at Mellifont. Dunbrody has a well preserved refectory of this type, and it is surprising to find an Anglo-Norman house following this scheme in the thirteenth century (Pl. 167). Early English lancets fill the south wall and it was entered by an attractive Gothic doorway at the south-west angle of the cloister. Like most of the Irish refectories, this was a ground floor hall.

In the refectories of the second group (Mellifont II, Jerpoint, Grey, Graiguenamanagh and Inch) the axis was changed so that the building lay at right angles to the cloister, the scheme which became the Cistercian norm after 1200.[65] In several English houses the original refectories were demolished to make way for the new layout, a change that seems to have occurred at Mellifont around 1200.[66] The new alignment had several advantages. The length could be adjusted to suit the size of the community and space was left each side for the calefactory and kitchen. As the building was not so tightly wedged into the south range, a better balance of windows was possible. The plan was also more logical and striking in architectural terms. The entrance could be placed in the centre of the cloister walk, from which a splendid vista opened to the windows in the south wall, sixty or seventy feet away. A hint of these effects can still be obtained at Grey, where much of the refectory, although roofless, survives to its full height (Pl. 168, Fig. 11). At 71 feet (21.64 metres), it was one of the longest refectories in Ireland. The south gable is pierced by three lancets, and with further windows in the side walls, the interior must have been flooded with light. The refectory was a relatively tall room and there is no sign that any of the Irish houses followed French models like Noirlac or Longpont and vaulted them in stone. Most were probably covered in a single span by an open timber roof.

Within the refectory, meals were conducted with great solemnity, as the monks sat in silence, listening to an appropriate reading from the scriptures. In summer two meals were permitted, in winter just one.[67] Cheese, fish and milk, which had originally been banned, gradually found their way on to the menu. Meat, at first restricted to the sick and infirm, was also increasingly tolerated, though in Ireland there is no evidence for 'misericordiae', the special buildings for meat eating, found in a number of English houses. An interesting feature of the refectory was the reader's pulpit, which projected from the wall at least six feet above the floor. When the refectory was parallel to the cloister as at Dunbrody, it was located on the south side, but when aligned at right angles it was situated towards the end of the west wall. The pulpit was reached by a short mural staircase and the wall of the refectory was widened at this point to accommodate it (Pl. 169, Fig. 20). Even when the refectory has been reduced to foundation level, as at Mellifont, the site of the pulpit can be identified by the thickening of the wall. Although devoid of their dressed masonry the stair passages survive at Grey and Dunbrody. There are further remnants at Graiguenamanagh, now overgrown and obscured by derelict sheds. The stairway here was beautifully conceived, with an elaborate five-light window and a miniature ribbed vault.

Before entering the refectory, the monks washed themselves in a lavabo or water basin,

169 Jerpoint Abbey, as depicted in Grose's *Antiquities* (1791–5). At this time the refectory (extreme right) was intact, and the gabled projection of the reader's pulpit is clearly visible.

170 The lavabo at Mellifont (c1210). The emphatic mouldings are crisply cut in yellowy-brown sandstone.

171 Mellifont, capital of the lavabo.

172 The Cistercian monastery of Poblet (Spain), where an octagonal lavabo is especially well preserved.

usually built into the wall beside the door. Traces of the arch which surmounted the basin can still be seen at Abbeyknockmoy. Far more sumptuous was the lavabo at Mellifont, which was designed as a separate pavilion projecting into the cloister garth (Pl. 170). Over half this building survives and it is the most attractive piece of Cistercian architecture in the country. Octagonal in plan, each side is pierced by a deep arch of three orders. The mouldings are crisply cut in yellowy-brown sandstone and there is an abundance of keels and bowtells, typical of the period 1200–1210 (Fig. 71). The exterior is strongly articulated, with an emphatic plinth, sharp mouldings and a bold string-course. There is a clarity and subtlety about the building which repays patient scrutiny. The interior was vaulted and the ribs radiated out from a central column like the branches of a tree. Capitals were attractively sculptured, some with leaf motifs and another with birds (Pl. 171). Judging from parallels abroad, around the central column was a wide circular or octagonal basin, and above this a smaller basin with a series of spouts, into which the water was fed by pipes from the nearby river Mattock. A description of the late Gothic lavabo at Durham helps us to envisage the Mellifont lavabo when it was in full working order:

> Within the Cloyster Garth, over against the Frater House door, was a fair Lover or Connditt, for the Mouncks to washe ther hands and faces at, being made in form round, covered with lead, and all of marble, saving the verie uttermost walls. Within the which walls you may walke round about the laver of marble, having many little cunditts or spouts of brasse, with xxiiij cockes of brasse, round about yt, having in it vij faire wyndows of stone woorke . . .[68]

Centrally planned lavabos can be found in a number of Cistercian houses abroad and octagonal examples were constructed at Poblet (Spain), Maulbronn (Germany), and Citeaux (France) (Pl. 172),[69] The central column was rare, though one was used to support the vault in the square lavabo at Fontenay. The source of the Mellifont design almost certainly lay in England. Similar structures are known to have existed in the Cistercian houses at Fountains, Melrose and Louth Park and in the later years of the twelfth century there was a spate of lavabo construction in the English Cluniac houses (Battle, Exeter St Nicholas, Lewes and Much Wenlock).[70] The fine detail of the Mellifont structure is more in accord with Cluniac than Cistercian taste and it may therefore owe something to these Cluniac examples. To judge from the mouldings, the immediate inspiration came from the west of England.

The vaulting system is a miniature version of that employed in the circular chapter house at Worcester, c1130, and it is worth noting that one of the Cluniac lavabos stood in the cloister at Wenlock (Shropshire).[71] Here the stone basin was enriched with Romanesque figure-carving

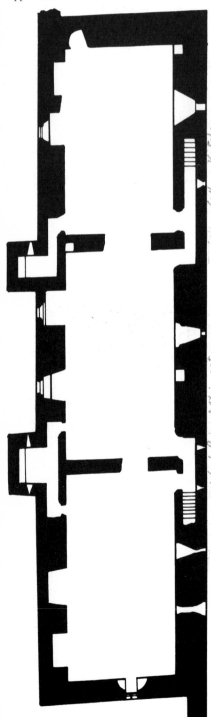

Fig. 54 Holycross, plan of the west range, upper floor.

and sculptured fragments suggest this may have been the case at Mellifont too.[72] The concept of a large circular basin or fountain is a classical idea which had precedents in Roman architecture. An octagonal fountain existed at Lincoln, and Bede describes how St Cuthbert was impressed with the Roman fountain he saw at Carlisle.[73] Where and when they passed into the vocabulary of monastic architecture is yet to be established.

A lavabo as attractive as that at Mellifont was scarcely an essential building and it is hard to avoid the impression that it was intended to enhance the abbey's status within the order. Although fundamentally a utilitarian structure, Georges Duby has suggested that it had a symbolic function. The sound of running water echoing across the cloister garth was a permanent reminder of baptism and of 'the pure river of the water life'.[74] In the later middle ages the Carthusians at Champmol, near Dijon, developed this symbolism by erecting a huge sculptured crucifix above the well in the centre of their cloister. Whether the Cistercians had formulated such ideas two hundred years before is unclear.

The Mellifont lavabo was not copied elsewhere in Ireland, except at Dunbrody, where a circular foundation was discovered opposite the refectory doorway during clearances in the nineteenth century.[75] It was only 12 feet (3.66 metres) in diameter, half the size of the lavabo at Mellifont.

At the south-west corner of the cloister lay the kitchen, conveniently situated so that it could serve both the monks' refectory and the laybrothers' refectory in the west range. It was a standard practice in Cistercian monasteries for the latter range to be devoted to the accommodation of the laybrothers, often with cellars on the ground floor. In Ireland one searches in vain for the great vaulted basements that exist at Fountains or Neath, and in many abbeys there is no evidence of the west range whatsoever. Bare foundations survive at Mellifont and Hore (Figs 12, 15), but it is doubtful whether some Irish abbeys completed the laybrothers' quarters in stone. At Corcomroe and Abbeyknockmoy there are neither foundations nor masonry junctions on the walls of the adjoining church. If these abbeys ever had a west range, it was likely to have been built of wood. By the time the poorer houses had acquired sufficient funds to build more permanent structures, laybrothers were a thing of the past. This is apparently what happened at Cymmer, a relatively poor house in the mountains of Wales.[76]

The west range was the site of the main entrance to the cloister and in 1228 there is mention of 'the great gate' at Jerpoint (or Graiguenamanagh) 'next to the kitchen'.[77] At Boyle the impressive gateway with an arched passage and porter's chambers either side (Fig. 30) is not in fact monastic, having been built after the dissolution of the abbey, when the monastic ruins were adapted as a barracks. At Dunbrody the position of the thirteenth-century gate through the west wall of the cloister is visible and here an outer porch or barbican was added, similar to that at Neath (Pls 173, 174).

It is to Holycross that one must turn for the only complete west range, built as part of the remodelling of the abbey in the fifteenth century. It is a dour building in roughly coursed limestone, with relatively few windows. The ground floor was equipped with a barrel-vaulted passage, cutting through the range and serving as the main entrance to the cloister. Three barrel-vaulted cellars provided space for storage.[78] All this is entirely characteristic of Cistercian practice, but the layout of the upper floor was less typical. It was planned as three private apartments and represents one of the most fascinating pieces of domestic architecture in the country (Fig. 54). Two straight mural staircases led up from the cloister and each chamber was furnished with its own garderobe, the latter neatly incorporated into a pair of turrets. Looking south was an attractive window with curved splays for window seats. Complete with fireplaces, these were spacious and comfortable rooms. The basic concept of a hall or chamber with a vaulted basement underneath had been a standard formula in domestic architecture since the twelfth century, but a suite of such rooms is far less common.[79] It would be intriguing to know for whom the rooms were designed—whether as private flats for three of the brethren or for the more illustrious visitors to the shrine of the true cross?

Beyond the cloister lay a host of other buildings, which have largely vanished from the landscape—the infirmary, the guest house, the abbot's lodgings, as well as stables, barns, mills

173 Dunbrody from the south-west (Grose, *Antiquities of Ireland*, 1791–5). The entrance to the cloister is visible near the tree.

174 Neath Abbey (West Glamorgan). The well preserved west range has a porch similar to that at Dunbrody.

and workshops. Documents give us an occasional glimpse of these structures, though they tell us nothing of their architectural form. The letters and instructions of Stephen Lexington give an indication of the complexity of these outbuildings at an Irish abbey in the thirteenth century. As well as stables, barns and animal sheds, Stephen referred to the shoemaker's workshop, which he decided should be moved to a grange, and 'a house where the wine press has been erected'. (The consumption of wine was originally banned by the order, but like the eating of fish and meat, it gradually became acceptable.) There is mention of a kitchen for the guesthouse, a scriptorium, and a series of separate infirmaries—for monks, for laybrothers and for the poor.[80] The guesthouse was a surprising priority, a reminder of how important a monastery might be for the medieval traveller. In 1202 Boyle already possessed a 'great stone house' for guests, and this was nearly twenty years before the church was finished.[81] By 1540 most abbots had their own private houses, which were soon commandeered for secular use after the dissolution. The abbot's lodging at Newry still existed in 1795, 'converted into a common dwelling house',[82] and that at St Mary's, Dublin, survived at least until 1674.[83] This must have been an imposing residence. In 1541 it was described as 'a mansion in the precincts called the Abbotts lodgynge', with sundry buildings attached, including the abbot's stable, 'together with the Abbott's Garden'. Shortly before the dissolution, it was leased to the Lord Deputy of Ireland, Leonard Grey, a testimony to its grandeur.[84]

At Baltinglass one of the late medieval abbots apparently built himself a tower house, described as a 'Castle' in the *Extents* of 1541.[85] After the dissolution of the abbey, this became the home of the FitzEustace family, but it was broken down, along with parts of the monastery, when James FitzEustace rebelled in 1580. A 'small habitacion' was subsequently erected by Sir Henry Harington in 1587, possibly a rebuilding of the former tower house. Although damaged some years later, this appears to have survived until 1882, when it was demolished by the local rector to supply materials for building the glebe house and the new church.[86] It seems to have been a typical sixteenth-century tower house, with three storeys and battlements, 'an irregular and not very extensive structure, evidently built at different periods' (Fig. 55).[87] It was set within a bawn, defended by corner turrets. How much of the edifice went back to the monastic period is impossible to say, but the fact that the last abbot, John Galboly, lived in a 'castle' suggests that there was little to distinguish his style of living from the secular lords of the district.

Among other buildings mentioned regularly in the documents was the monastic prison. These were permitted by the General Chapter of 1206 and in 1229 a further statute positively encouraged their construction, insisting that they should be solid and strong.[88] A tiny chamber in the crypt at Mellifont has sometimes been interpreted as a prison, but in truth it was a safe or cupboard. There is no doubt that monastic prisons were put to regular use in Ireland. In 1390, David Esmond, a commissioner of Richard II, who had been appointed to investigate extortion in the county of Wexford, found himself captured by the abbot and monks of Dunbrody. Having taken 'by force and arms David himself and imprisoned him, and fastened him in chains of iron to a pillar', they destroyed his Royal letters patent and other writs, 'detaining the said David in the prison of the said Abbey for 16 days until he would consent to swear upon the Holy Evangelist that he would not prosecute any of them for these proceedings'.[89] A more orthodox use of the prison was for incarcerating thieves, incendiaries, forgers, murderers and other local criminals who had fallen into the abbot's jurisdiction, along with the occasional renegade monk. Such was William Kedenor, a monk of St Mary's, Dublin, who lost his sanity in 1320. Having

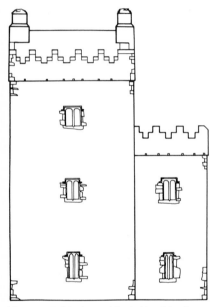

Fig. 55 Baltinglass, Abbot's 'Castle', after a nineteenth-century drawing.

175 Holycross, the abbot's lodging, first floor chamber. The curved embrasure of the window is equipped with two seats. The door to the right leads to the garderobe.

secreted himself in the retro-choir during vespers, he suddenly dashed into the monks' choir, flung off his clothes, and stabbed to death two of his brethren, including the sacristan Thomas. The rest of his days were spent in chains in the monastic gaol.[90] This was not the first such scandal at St Mary's, for in 1227 a laybrother and seven accomplices had been consigned to the same fate after murdering a certain John Comyn near the abbey's grange at Portmarnock.[91] The monastic prison, it appears, was a much inhabited room but like so many other structures in the monastery our knowledge of its location and design is almost non-existent.

Even where foundations and ruins of outbuildings survive, they are difficult to match with the literary references. At Holycross, however, more certainty is possible with a building situated to the south-east of the cloister. This two-storey dwelling of fifteenth-century date has traditionally been identified as the abbot's lodging. One of the upper rooms retains many of its ancient features—a discreet garderobe, a fireplace (with a well cut joggled lintel) and two fine window seats, set in curved embrasures like those in the west range of the abbey (Pl. 175). It is a rare piece of domestic architecture, which deserves more attention than it currently receives.[92]

Among utilitarian structures within the precincts was a 'columbarium' or dovecot. Mellifont once had four[93] and a stone example survives in relatively good condition at Kilcooly, a circular, domed building, with an oculus in the centre. It stands like a mini-Pantheon, isolated some distance from the rest of the abbey buildings (Pl. 176).

The purpose of another outbuilding at Kilcooly is less explicit. This is an austere, rectangular structure, with massive battered walls, over six feet thick (Pl. 177, Fig. 21). The ground floor, although subsequently divided into two, was designed as one vast barrel-vaulted cellar (60 feet by 22 feet; 18.29 by 6.71 metres) illuminated only by narrow slit windows. A mural staircase in the west wall led up to what must have been a fine first floor hall. Apart from one window with a drip sill, few architectural features now remain. The building has been misleadingly described as an infirmary, but there are better parallels with the great hall of Askeaton Castle than with any monastic hospital (Pl. 178).[94] It was either a powerful lodging built for the abbot shortly before the Reformation or a residence erected by one of the post-dissolution occupants of the abbey.

Enclosing the various buildings, gardens and orchards in the outer precincts was a substantial wall of stone. As well as its value in deterring felons, miscreants and, at Holycross, 'suspicious women', it was there to keep the monks inside, a barrier between the spiritual world of the monastery and the secular world beyond. The temptation to roam abroad was ever present and it was one of the transgressions most criticised by Stephen of Lexington in 1228. In the later middle ages the precinct wall came to be valued by local inhabitants as a means of defence. Thus at Baltinglass in 1540, we hear of 'a curtilage with stone-walls, in which the beasts belonging to the people of the neighbourhood are kept at night'.[95] A powerful enceinte, fortified with towers, exists at the Augustinian abbey of Kells (Kilkenny),[96] but nothing comparable is left at any of the Cistercian sites (Pl. 142). Mellifont was once protected by 'certain towers and fortilices' and the line of its boundary wall is marked today by a deep ditch and bank to the east

176 The domed columbarium at Kilcooly, a common feature of medieval monasteries.

177 Kilcooly Abbey, the enigmatic 'hall' at the south-east corner of the monastery.

178 The great hall of Askeaton Castle (Limerick), built by the earls of Desmond in the fifteenth century.

Precinct Wall

180 The gatehouse at Mellifont. The turret to the right contains a spiral staircase.

of the abbey.[97] Similar banks define the precinct at Inch where the Cistercians reused part of an Early Christian boundary.[98] Speed's map of Dublin (1610) shows a complete circuit of walls around the site of St Mary's abbey, walls which are regularly mentioned in documents (Pl. 179). Remote granges were more vulnerable than the monastery itself, and many were likewise defended by castles or towers. The grange of Carrickbrenan (Monkstown) belonging to St Mary's, Dublin, was described in 1540 as a 'capital messuage with three towers, surrounded by stonewalls, necessary for the defence of the inhabitants'.[99] Two of the towers, along with a section of bawn wall, still remain amidst the suburban sprawl of south Dublin. Not far away an impressive fifteenth-century castle overlooks the abbey's former port at Bullock harbour, built no doubt as an insurance against the pilfering of goods at the quayside. Baltinglass possessed at least seven castles protecting its various estates, as well as a further castle at the abbey.[100]

The main approach to the monastery was through the gatehouse, which at Mellifont took the form of a formidable stone tower (Pl. 180). There was a wide barrel vaulted entrance at ground level and a spiral stair led to three storeys above. The ruins of another gate can still be seen at Corcomroe, the upper parts of which collapsed soon after 1839.[101] The medieval gatehouse was manned by a porter, whose attitude to visitors was not necessarily as warmhearted as it should have been. In 1228 the porter at Jerpoint (or possibly Graiguenamanagh) was rebuked for his lack of mercy and humanity towards the poor.[102] Unwelcome visitors, however, were as likely to be royal officials or emissaries from the General Chapter of the order, as in the celebrated scandal of 1217, when the gates of Mellifont were slammed shut in the face of a visitation from Clairvaux.[103] Eleven years later Stephen of Lexington was to encounter many a locked and bolted gate.

Not far from the main gate was a chapel for the use of local layfolk, the 'capella ante portas'. Those at Kirkstead and Furness in England were fine early Gothic churches, and there is nothing comparable in Ireland. Occasionally the site of the chapel is marked by a graveyard and at Kilcooly the nineteenth-century Protestant church, a few hundred yards from the abbey, is known to have replaced an ancient chapel.[104] At Dunbrody there is a small graveyard south-west of the abbey, beside the fragmentary ruins of the monastic gatehouse. The sixteenth-century chapel on the rock above Mellifont might well mark the position of an early 'capella

176

181 Mellifont from the south about 1890. The gatehouse is visible in the distance. Above the chapter house (on the right) is the sixteenth- or seventeenth-century chapel, which may mark the site of a *capella extra portas*. (National Library of Ireland, Lawrence Collection.)

ante portas' (Pl. 181). The best preserved chapel is at Tintern, a single cell building several hundred yards south-east of the abbey. The simple window tracery may belong to the fourteenth century, though the north door is far later. The building contains a monument with an interesting inscription about Anthony Colclough, who acquired the abbey in the 1550s and it was one of the few chapels that survived after the Reformation. In most cases the 'capellae ante portas' seem to have fallen out of use long before the dissolution. They are not mentioned in the *Extents* of 1540–1 and at many places the royal commissioner remarked that the abbey church had 'from time immemorial' served as the local parish church.[105] The formal barrier between the enclosed world of the monks and the local population outside had long since disintegrated.

182 Jerpoint Abbey, carving of a knight
(c1390–1400), one of a series of figures that
watched over the cloister of the monastery.

Chapter 9

THE STONE SCULPTURE OF THE MONASTERIES

Introduction

IN VIEW OF the uncompromising austerity of the early Cistercians, it is a surprise to discover how much sculpture exists in the Irish abbeys of the order. At Fontenay or Pontigny there is scarcely a capital decorated with anything but the most cursory leaf motifs, whereas the churches at Baltinglass, Jerpoint, Boyle and Corcomroe contain a rich array of carvings, including some with animals and human figures. Even more extravagant is the late medieval cloister at Jerpoint, where a series of sculptured figures—saints, abbots, knights and aristocratic ladies—watch over the inner courtyard of the monastery. Some of Ireland's most important medieval sculpture in fact comes from a Cistercian context.

Of the rules that the Cistercians made about art and architecture, none is more notorious than the prohibition of painting and sculpture. First expressed in 1119 and subsequently codified in 1151,[1] the statute forbade both sculpture and pictures in the churches and other offices of Cistercian monasteries, because 'whilst attention is paid to such things, the profit of godly meditation or the discipline of religious gravity is often neglected'. It was this declaration that established the purism of Cistercian architecture and guaranteed the general austerity of their churches. Although the rule lost its force in the later middle ages, it was quoted by Stephen of Lexington in 1228 as part of his criticism of Irish abbeys.[2] It is customary to see the persuasive force of St Bernard behind the formulation of the statute, since it coincides with the views expressed in his famous *Apologia* to William of St Thierry of c1123–5.[3]

This rhetorical outburst has given St Bernard a reputation for iconoclasm and he has come to be regarded as an enemy of art. As he proclaimed in the *Apologia*, monks ought to renounce 'anything precious or attractive for the sake of Christ' and 'account as filth everything of shining beauty'. Much has been made of the fact that St Bernard could not remember how many windows existed in the chapel where he worshipped as a novice, a sign, it is argued, of his visual insensitivity.[4] But St Bernard's reputation as an artistic 'philistine' is much exaggerated. There is abundant evidence to show that he was a man of aesthetic sensibility and it was precisely because he was aware of the appeal of works of art that he sought to exclude them from his monasteries. Indeed, it is ironic that his stringent views on art were put forward in an elaborate prose style, full of metaphors and literary mannerisms. It is important to appreciate that Bernard's strictures were aimed primarily at monks. Sensory images, as well as being an expensive luxury contrary to the poverty and simplicity of the Order, were a barrier to mystical union with God, the goal of monastic life. In one of his sermons on the Song of Songs, he remarked: 'but you have not flown far, unless, by the purity of your mind, you are able to rise above the images of sensible objects, which are constantly rushing in upon you from every side'.[5] Painting and sculpture was a meaningless distraction, which had no place in the Cistercian 'workshop of prayer'.

It should not be forgotten that the Cistercian colony in Ireland was founded under the watchful guidance of St Bernard and the expansion of the order in the 1140s came at a time when his opinions dominated Cistercian thought. Those first Irish monks, who had been trained at Clairvaux, could have been left in no doubt about the irrelevance of elaborate Romanesque carving. Copies of St Bernard's writings were circulated throughout the order and it is not unlikely that the library at Mellifont included texts of his sermons as well as the *Apologia*. Moreover the presence of the monk Robert, sent from Clairvaux, was a further guarantee that the statutory purism of the order would not be ignored. The three or four early capitals recovered from Mellifont are unadorned cushion or scalloped capitals and there is every reason to believe that the first church was designed according to the rigours of the statute.

In the Ireland of 1142, however, the presence or absence of painting and carving was not a pertinent issue. Irish Romanesque sculpture was still in its infancy and compared with most Irish churches of the time, Mellifont would not have seemed unusually austere. The first genuine Romanesque building in Ireland, Cormac's Chapel at Cashel, had been consecrated only eight years before. It is true that its rich display of animal and grotesque carving, as well as its painted interior, was the antithesis of Cistercian design, but at the time of the foundation of Mellifont these new Romanesque fashions were yet to make a widespread impact.[6] If there was any artistic tension in the early houses, it was probably in the area of metalwork and manuscript illumination. During the first half of the twelfth century, Irish workshops had produced a magnificent range of shrines and crosses, but such artefacts were clearly proscribed by the Cistercian statutes. Cistercian crosses were to be made of wood and candlesticks of iron. Gold and silver were forbidden, though an exception was made for chalices.

Decorative carving from 1142 to 1200

Between 1142 and c1200, the Irish Cistercians made a serious effort to obey the spirit of the rule in artistic matters. While some embellishment of capitals was tolerated, this usually took the form of foliage or abstract designs. The subjects denounced by St Bernard in his *Apologia*, the 'ridiculous monstrosities in the cloister' and the 'lascivious apes, fierce lions and monstrous centaurs', were dutifully avoided. Exceptions are minor and discreet. At Baltinglass a base at the entrance to the presbytery has a plinth decorated with a small lion (Pl. 183). With its head turned backwards, the lion fills the left half of a semi-circular surface, the remaining space being taken up with a foliage scroll.[7] There are similar carvings in the old monastery at Glendalough[8] and the carved base can also be related, in its shape and structure, to those on the portal at Killeshin (Carlow), one of the most delicately carved Romanesque doorways in Ireland (Pls 7, 184).[9] The connections with Glendalough and Killeshin show that while the monks of Baltinglass depended on local masons they exercised a degree of control over the designs employed. Animals, beasts and human masks form important ingredients of the decoration at Glendalough and Killeshin, but such themes are largely absent from the Cistercian church.

The same contrast with Hiberno-Romanesque is evident in the early work at Boyle, but, as at Baltinglass, there were momentary lapses from the rigours of Cistercian purism. Not many years after the foundation of the abbey in 1161, a stunning beast head was carved on the jamb of the sedilia (Pl. 185). Cut with a strong diagonal accent and with its features sharply incised, it illustrates Hiberno-Romanesque at its best. It is in fact an Irish version of the 'column swallowers' which were popular in western France and England. Further down the river Shannon, cousins of this monster can be seen biting the jambs of the portal and chancel arch of the Nuns' church at Clonmacnois (1167) and a similar beast appears on a Romanesque portal at Kilmore (Cavan).[10] It may have been the same sculptor at Boyle who carved the face, that leers out from some leaves on a capital in the north transept, a grotesque ancestor of the 'green man' common in Gothic art. Cut in the low relief technique, characteristic of Hiberno-Romanesque, it foreshadows the sculpture that appeared some years later in the chancel of Tuam Cathedral (c1184).[11] These two details at Boyle go unnoticed by most visitors and nobody could pretend that they compromise the austerity of the eastern limb of the church. On the whole the Cistercians successfully resisted the explosion of Romanesque ornament that characterised Irish architecture in the second half of the twelfth century.

In fact at Baltinglass and Jerpoint, the monks worked out their own distinctively Cistercian brand of ornament. The design of both churches necessitated large square capitals, approximately 4 feet (1.2 metres) wide and 9 inches (23 cm) high.[12] The surfaces of these capitals were treated as a continuous ornamental frieze, with the designs etched on the stone like chip carving. A dozen different themes are used at Baltinglass, fourteen at Jerpoint, and the majority

183 Baltinglass, north-east crossing pier. The base is decorated with a 'lion' and foliage ornament.

184 Killeshin (Carlow). The bulbous bases of the Romanesque doorway (c1160) are similar in type to those at Baltinglass.

185 Boyle Abbey, a stylised beast head carved on the sedilia (c1165–70).

186 Baltinglass, first pier of the south arcade, one of the early designs of the so-called 'Baltinglass Master'.

187 Jerpoint, south-west crossing pier. Beaded strapwork and foliate infills were favourite motifs of the carvers.

188 Jerpoint, north-west crossing pier, capital with beaded zigzags and floral motifs.

have the scalloped motif running along the bottom (Fig. 56, Pls 186, 187, 188).[13] The general structure of the capitals is derived from Mellifont, where there are three fragments of straight scalloped capitals, coming from pilasters or square piers. The masons at Baltinglass took this as their starting point and proceeded to weave intricate patterns in the space above the cones. Beaded strapwork and guilloche designs abound, often with floral or foliate infills. There are also weird geometrical motifs, some vaguely reminiscent of Greek key. At Baltinglass the designs got increasingly bizarre as construction proceeded towards the west facade. From the fifth pier onwards, the cones of the scallops were embellished with a rim, which recall the 'claw' settings used for fixing jewels on medieval metalwork. The workshop responsible for these carvings subsequently turned its attentions to Jerpoint, where the eastern chapels and first bay of the nave have a similar repertoire of ornament.[14] As at Baltinglass, repetition of the same design was scrupulously avoided, though it is hard to avoid the impression that the masons gradually ran short of ideas. It is likely that all the capitals were painted, which would have enhanced their rich, carpet-like texture.

The men who carried out these decorative schemes must have worked between 1160 and 1180 and it is not impossible that they moved back and forth between the two monasteries. It is perhaps appropriate to describe the head of the workshop as the Baltinglass Master. Many of the patterns he devised were unique and, although the technique of carving is typically Irish, his artistic vocabulary was not. The interwoven beaded ribbons are alien to the tradition of Irish interlace (they are in fact closer to the strapwork found on capitals at Hereford Cathedral). The sculptors of the high crosses had shown an interest in angular patterns, particularly fretwork, but there are no exact prototypes in Ireland for the majority of the motifs used at Baltinglass and Jerpoint.[15] There are some hints that the sculptors were familiar with carving in Wales and the

Fig. 56 Baltinglass, designs of Romanesque capitals (after Leask).

189 Strata Florida (Cardiganshire), capital from the south transept. As in Ireland, Welsh masons developed the decorative potential of scalloped capitals.

west of England. At Hereford Cathedral there are scalloped capitals in which the top of the cone is filled with geometrical ornament. Moreover, a fragment from Baltinglass, decorated with interlocking rings, can be paralleled on the west doorway of Leominster Priory (Hereford-shire).[16] The artistic background of the Baltinglass Master is far from clear, but it appears to include an English or Welsh element. One of the Baltinglass designs later turns up in the Welsh Cistercian abbey of Strata Florida (Cardigan)[17] and it is not impossible that ideas moved both ways across the Irish Sea (Fig. 56, Pl. 189).

In view of the efforts made to carve the capitals at Baltinglass and Jerpoint, it is important to notice how studiously animal or figural motifs were avoided. The monks obviously realised that purely abstract ornament—beaded scrolls, scallops, floral and geometrical motifs—came within the terms of the rule. One could almost believe that the monasteries had made their own study of St Bernard's *Apologia*, working out what was and what was not acceptable. It is important to remember that neither St Bernard nor the Cistercian statutes demanded the exclusion of all ornament. Cistercian grisaille glass, as at Pontigny and Obazine, shows that patterns of interlace and foliage were an acceptable way of breaking up the monotony of plain windows and the capitals of Baltinglass and Jerpoint are a sculptural equivalent.[18]

The most surprising aspect of Cistercian decoration in the twelfth century is the lack of interest in the more traditional Irish themes. In fact a high proportion of the ornamental features were ultimately of English derivation, even though they may have reached the Cistercians through Hiberno-Romanesque workshops. The scalloped capital, chevron decoration and even some of the foliate patterns can be traced back to English sources. The scalloped capital was ideally suited to Cistercian requirements—sufficient to provide an accent at the top of a pier or shaft, without being too intricate or expensive. The first examples appeared in the middle of the

190 Boyle Abbey, south-east crossing pier. The scallops on the capitals have been transformed into plants.

191 Boyle Abbey, north chapel of the north transept. The centre capital with broad pointed leaves was a Burgundian type that became widespread in the Cistercian monasteries of England.

192 Boyle, north-west crossing pier (c1170). Foliate designs with leaves tucked under long juicy stems were a common Romanesque pattern.

century at Mellifont and, as it was not common in Burgundy, it suggests the Irish Cistercians already had the services of masons who were familiar with English techniques.[19] Plain scallops were employed at Mellifont and Jerpoint, and, over the course of the next fifty years, variations and embellishments appeared in other abbeys. A particularly attractive one can be found in the crossing at Boyle, where the scallops are transformed into a plant. The cones are split down the centre, as if to suggest the opening of a flower and the head of the capital is filled with leaves or petals (Pl. 190). Less sophisticated versions occur in the crossing at Abbeyknockmoy. Outside Ireland, parallels for this type exist in the English monasteries of Buildwas and Lilleshall (Shropshire).

The scalloped capital was gradually replaced in popularity by capitals decorated with plant and leaf designs, of which there is a magnificent array at Boyle. Some of the earliest were carved for the north chapel of the north transept. The main capitals here have a pair of broad, pointed leaves filling most of the available surface, a Burgundian form that became widespread in the Cistercian monasteries of Yorkshire (Pl. 191).[20] It was also used at Buildwas (north-west crossing pier) in the west of England, whence it probably reached Ireland. At Boyle the space between the leaves is covered by smaller foliate motifs, the stems of which curl around the corners of the capital, just above the tip of the main leaf. The design is neat and well conceived. The curl is reminiscent of the classical volute and the composition is closely related to the waterleaf capitals so beloved by the English Cistercians.[21] Curiously the waterleaf capital itself never found favour in Ireland, and instead there was a preference for more detailed foliage patterns, particularly palmette and acanthus. At the start of the nave of Boyle (east reponds of the arcade) there are some interesting examples. Those to the south are covered with simplified acanthus, growing up the face of the capital with naturalistic vigour. To the north there is a capital with long juicy stems, terminating in narrow pointed leaves, one of which is tucked beneath the stem itself (Pl. 192). This distinctive arrangement can be paralleled in both English and Irish manuscript illumination and it reappears on Hiberno-Romanesque portals.[22]

Chevron ornament, the most popular decorative motif of English Romanesque, spread to Ireland in the second quarter of the twelfth century and it was taken up with great gusto by local sculptors and masons. It was not long before it spread to the Cistercian monasteries. In its simplest form, as a running zigzag, it can be found on one of the nave capitals at Baltinglass (c1150–60). A more developed type, with tiny pieces of foliage filling the angles of the zigzag, was chosen for the north doorway of the same abbey, and about the same time a similar version was used on the east windows of its daughter house at Jerpoint (c1160) (Pl. 48). To judge from fragments discovered at Mellifont and Boyle, more elaborate chevron arches with nailhead and beading were in use by the end of the century.[23] The pieces from Mellifont probably belonged to a portal in the cloister and they suggest that a note of luxury was creeping into this previously austere environment. A late form of chevron, with the zigzags undercut ('herringbone') was employed early in the thirteenth century at Abbeyknockmoy and Corcomroe (Pl. 120).[24] This type of chevron was common in the English west country at the end of the twelfth century and it can be found in the Benedictine abbeys of Glastonbury (Lady Chapel, 1184–6) and Gloucester (west gate) (Pl. 121). It is one of a number of intriguing links between this area and the monasteries of Connacht. Although chevron might seem an inappropriate ornament for a Cistercian monastery, the evidence suggests that it was employed in a relatively restrained manner, especially when compared with its uninhibited exploitation outside the order in such late Romanesque portals as Clonfert and Killaloe.

The level of restraint shown by the Cistercian houses in their attitude to decoration is all the more impressive when one considers the pressures and temptations to indulge in elaborate sculpture. Donations of gold and other valuables, the general increase in affluence and the employment of lay craftsmen—all provided opportunities for enriching the monastic buildings. On the day that the church of Mellifont was consecrated (1157), the abbey was presented with three score ounces of gold and a golden chalice,[25] the latter contrary to the letter of the rule. Not many years before, St Bernard had warned of these very dangers: 'You cannot, O wretched servants of Mammon, at once glory in the Cross of our Lord Jesus Christ, and hope in the treasures of many; go after gold, and prove how sweet is the Lord'.[26] When the Cistercians arrived in Ireland in 1142, the art of Romanesque sculpture was still in its infancy, but by 1200 there were many professional masons with experience of ornamental carving. When such masons were present in a monastic workshop, as at Boyle around 1215–20, it must have been difficult to ignore their skills and suppress their ideas. By this time the Cistercians were no doubt conscious of the contrast between their own large, austere churches and the exuberantly decorated oratories of the early Irish monasteries. After 1200 infringements of the statute relating to sculpture thus began to multiply. This trend coincides with the general weakening of discipline within the order, later to culminate in the conspiracy of Mellifont.

Late Romanesque carving west of the Shannon

The two greatest 'offenders' against the rule were the monasteries of Boyle and Corcomroe. When the nave of Boyle was being completed between 1215 and 1220, approximately forty new capitals were required, both for the newly constructed piers and for the corbels that were inserted along the length of the building. The majority are decorated with an attractive range of foliage patterns. In most cases a single broad capital has been fitted above a group of three shafts and the sculpture is spread across it in a continuous freize. Some have long stringy intertwined stems, occasionally transformed into ropes; others have berries and fruits tucked under the leaves and everywhere there is an abundance of palmette foliage, carved in gentle relief (Pl. 197). Displaying plenty of ingenuity, the masons covered the entire surface of the capitals with ornament and the resulting compositions are lively and varied. A few of the leaf patterns were foreshadowed in earlier carving at Boyle, which suggests an element of continuity in the workshop there.

Seven of the capitals were ornamented with animals and human figures. At least five were carved by a mason who also worked at the Augustinian monastery at Ballintober and he has therefore been described as the Ballintober Master.[27] The finest of his carvings depicts a confrontation of two dogs and a pair of cockerels fighting over some tiny creature (south pier 5,

193 Boyle Abbey, capital with dogs and cocks tussling over prey (c1215–20), the work of the 'Ballintober Master'.

194 Boyle Abbey, corbel with entwined birds or beasts (c1215–20).

195 Boyle Abbey, corbel with men fighting beasts (c1215–20).

196 Boyle Abbey, capital with four tunic-clad figures standing between trees (c1215–20).

197 Boyle Abbey, capital with foliate designs (c1215–20).

198 Boyle Abbey, foliate capital with fourteen tiny figures holding stems, their faces peering out between the leaves (c1215–20).

west face) (Pl. 193). Below them is a snake rolled into a coil. The composition skilfully makes use of the available surface and a potential void in the centre was filled by giving the dogs long twisting tails, which burst into foliage. The animals are cut in relatively deep relief and the quality of the carving can be judged by comparing it to the facing capital (south pier 6, east face). The latter shows a line of dogs, two of them tussling over prey. The relief is thinner, the composition lacks energy and the space is not filled so effectively. It may be the work of a less gifted assistant.

Nearby are more capitals by the Ballintober Master. One is carved with a row of six birds, their elongated necks intertwined (south pier 6, north corbel) (Pl. 194). The wings were carefully delineated and the long tails tied in a loop. On the next pier is a corbel with two naked men struggling with lions (south pier 5, north corbel) (Pl. 195). One wields a sword, the other forces open the jaws of a lion with his bare hands, a composition analogous to David wrestling with the lion in the Romanesque sculpture at Kilteel (Kildare). More figures appear on a capital on which four individuals are shown standing solemnly between trees (south pier 6, east face) (Pl. 196). They are dressed in short tunics, held up by belts with neatly carved buckles. The two central figures, adopting a traditional *orans* pose, reach up to grasp adjoining branches. In this case the composition is rather lifeless, suggesting that the sculptor's limitations were exposed when he abandoned his favourite leaf and animal motifs (it is unlikely to be by an assistant, since the faces correspond to those on other capitals by the Ballintober Master).

The same sculptural style is conspicuous in the chancel at Ballintober, where the capitals retain some of their original sharpness, having been protected by a vault. Birds with interlocking

199 Ballintober Abbey, capital in the chancel by the master who also worked at Boyle (c1216–25).

200 Dublin, Christ Church Cathedral, capital with griffons and human busts (c1200). Some of the subjects found in Dublin foreshadow those at Boyle and Ballintober.

201 Crowle (Worcestershire), stone pulpit (c1190–1200). These foliage patterns, with berries tucked under the leaves, subsequently became popular in the west of Ireland.

necks, dragons and beasts in confrontation, plus the usual range of foliage motifs, represent the main themes (Pl. 199). The sculpture is noticeably deeper and bolder than at Boyle, and the beasts are more rounded and ferocious. Jaws are longer and more sharply defined. Snakes with tightly coiled bodies are also prominent, and on one capital they twist around the necks of the two confronted beasts.

The sculpture at Ballintober was executed between 1216 and 1225[28] and the development of the Master's style shows that he came here after working at Boyle. As the church at Boyle was consecrated in 1218 or 1220,[29] this accords well with the documentary evidence. The vigour of the Ballintober Master's compositions and their incisive execution leaves us in no doubt that he was one of Ireland's foremost Romanesque artists. His style is not however entirely typical of Hiberno-Romanesque, since many of his designs were cut in comparatively deep relief. Nor do the animals come from the usual Irish repertoire. The master may in fact have had some knowledge of English sculpture, a knowledge that could have been acquired in Dublin, from the capitals in Christ Church Cathedral. Some of the subjects here foreshadow those in the west— bloated looking birds, violently twisting animals and battles between man and beast. There are also dragons with knotted tails and human figures with belted tunics (Pl. 200).[30] Two of the capitals in the choir of Christ Church have the same structure as those at Boyle, with a single capital placed over a group of three shafts. Some of the foliage patterns of the Ballintober Master also seem to have an English background. Those with small palmette leaves and long stringy intertwined stems can be paralleled at St Frideswide's, Oxford,[31] and others, with berries and fruit tucked under the leaves, recall the ornament on the stone lectern at Crowle (Worcestershire) (Pl. 201).[32]

While absorbing a number of compositional ideas from English art the Ballintober Master retained many distinctively Irish traits. He took delight in the Celtic triskele, which was sometimes fitted into the tails of his animals. At Ballintober he carved grotesque masks like those at Tuam and he followed the precedent of Annaghdown (Galway), c1190, by transforming roll mouldings into sinuous snakes (Pl. 202). The sharp spiralling cuts seen on the neck of the great snake at Annaghdown were copied in many of the animals at Ballintober.[33] His human faces, with their ovoid eyes and tightly clenched lips, are typically Irish, as a glance at metalwork or the high cross at Tuam will quickly reveal.[34] One capital at Boyle, not previously mentioned, has a veritable gallery of such faces (north pier 7, west face). Fourteen disembodied heads peer out between a mass of leaves; in each case tiny hands emerge from the background to grasp the stems of foliage. These miniature faces could have been copied straight from the pages of the Psalter of Cormac, a late twelfth-century manuscript that belonged to one of the Cistercian monasteries (Pl. 258).[35] The style of the Ballintober Master was therefore embedded in local practice, but his willingness to learn from foreign sources added a new force and drama to his sculpture.

The identity and early career of the Ballintober Master remains a puzzle. As the foliage carving at Boyle seems to evolve from earlier sculpture in the abbey, it is tempting to believe that he was trained in the locality.[36] But if he was a professional mason from Connacht, how did he acquire his knowledge of English art? It may be that he acquired some of his sculptural ideas from the master mason at Boyle, who was certainly trained in an English workshop. The sculptor's subsequent career is easier to plot. After working at Boyle and Ballintober, he was employed at the Augustinian abbey of Cong. Although there are no animal or figural carvings, the three late Romanesque portals have capitals with the distinctive vegetation first seen at Boyle.[37] This foliage style was rapidly diffused in territories west of the Shannon during the 1220s and it is clear that the Cistercians played an important role in developing and encouraging the fashion. The style was not entirely restricted to abbeys in the west of the country. At Mellifont, both the lavabo and the chapter house contain capitals with foliate ornament and among many loose fragments there is one with a particularly attractive design of palmette and berries.[38] But in general the capitals lack the flair and quality of those at Boyle.

The sculpture in the church at Corcomroe is more unorthodox and eccentric than that at Boyle. It is restricted to the eastern limb of the building, erected before the catastrophe that affected the abbey in the 1220s. On the external angles of the presbytery two dragons can be seen crawling down the quoinstones. Their ferocious jaws bite the string course and their bodies extend up the building as an attached shaft (Pl. 203). This deliberate confusion of architectural and zoomorphic features is not uncommon in Irish Romanesque and its effect is to make the building come alive with creeping beasts. Similar dragons enliven the portal at Killaloe.[39] Inside the church at Corcomroe, two well-rounded heads appear on capitals in the south transept, one of which has the large protruding eyes and tense lips typical of Irish figural carving (Pl. 204). The imagination that characterises the decoration of Corcomroe also led to the creation of new floral motifs. Some of the capitals are based on plants that could be found in a monastic herb garden, as Dr Nelson has recently pointed out. The masons also produced their own idiosyncratic moulding for the north transept chapel, furnished with a design that has been described, not very accurately, as orange peel.[40]

The carving of large single heads on capitals was an established feature of Hiberno-

202 Ballintober Abbey, carving between the east windows (c1216–24). The bodies of the snakes form the architectural moulding around the window.

203 Corcomroe Abbey, north-east corner of the presbytery. The dragon bites the string course and its body forms the angle moulding (c1210–20).

204 Corcomroe Abbey, capitals at the entrance to the south transept chapel (c1210–20).

205 Abbeyknockmoy, miniature carving of a (?)dog on one of the nave piers (c1220–30).

206 Grey Abbey, 'hollow bell' capitals on the corbels in the crossing, a form well-suited to Cistercian austerity.

Romanesque and the tradition reappeared at Abbeyknockmoy, where there is a fine royal head on one of the nave piers. Sadly the nose and chin are smashed, but the carefully defined eyes, elaborate crown and long curly hair are still intact. Abbeyknockmoy was founded by a king of Connacht, Cathal Crovderg O'Conor, and this was perhaps a tribute to his benefactions. The head must have been carved about the time of the king's death in 1224. There are further carvings on the chamfered angles of the piers at Abbeyknockmoy, a barking dog and two creatures with conjoined heads (Pl. 205).

Although the abbeys which retain animal or figural sculpture are concentrated west of the Shannon, this was not always so. Carving of this type was used in buildings erected at Mellifont in the years around 1200–20. Among several fine fragments recovered in the excavations is a base carved with a grotesque animal head, the details of which are still exquisitely sharp.[41] One of the capitals in the lavabo was ornamented with birds, but sadly this was destroyed by vandals in the last century, as William Wilde related (traces of its wings and claws are still visible).[42] Among other fragments from Mellifont are carved figures that belonged to a large circular plinth or base, which may have formed part of the central column of the lavabo.[43]

The years around 1200 marked a turning point in the Cistercian attitude to sculptural decoration. The architectural austerity, which had been maintained for over half a century, finally gave way to local taste, as extensive programmes of Romanesque carving were undertaken at Boyle, Corcomroe and Mellifont. In content, these sculptures were a direct contradiction both of St Bernard's *Apologia* and the statute of 1151, a relaxation of discipline characteristic of the order as a whole. In 1196, for example, the abbot of Fontfroide had been reprimanded for laying a carpet in the choir of his church[44] and about the same time grotesque carving appeared in the cloister at Chiaravalle della Columba. The most surprising aspect of the Irish carvings is the lack of interest shown in some of the popular Hiberno-Romanesque themes. The occasional triskele and spiral appear, but interlaced knots and ribbon shaped animals are totally absent. Nor is there any sign of the contemporary vogue for Urnes ornament. The twelfth-century crosses at Tuam and Dysert O'Dea are covered by dense patterns of interlace and coiling snakes and the same themes occur with regularity on portals and chancel arches (Pl. 8). It is hard to avoid the impression that this ornament was specifically censored by the Cistercians, perhaps because it was too closely associated with the older Irish monasteries, in particular with their expensive shrines and metalwork. Cistercian sculpture is thus less 'ethnic' in flavour and the masons employed by the order seem to have been more receptive to English influence. Even before the Anglo-Norman settlement began to take effect, there were obviously contacts and lines of communication across the Irish Sea. There is one other characteristic of the sculpture which should not go unnoticed—the complete absence of anything French. Although Burgundian forms provided a basis for the general design, Burgundian influence did not extend to carved details. The French monks who arrived at Mellifont in 1142 were obviously not accompanied by French masons.

When Stephen of Lexington conducted his visitation of the Irish monasteries in 1228, he must have been struck by the differences that existed in the decoration of the native and the Anglo-Norman houses. Built in the Early English style, the new foundations eschewed all but the simplest carved details. Stiff-leaf or roll-moulded capitals were neutral enough, when compared to the Romanesque carvings of Boyle and Corcomroe. The English houses also used one of the simplest of all capitals, the 'hollow bell', which, as Bilson explained, was a kind of Corinthianesque capital, minus the leaves.[45] It is characteristic of the early Cistercian abbeys of France—Fontenay and Pontigny, for example. Although the type was adopted in England, it was never universal in Ireland. Apart from isolated examples at Boyle, they were used extensively only in the early thirteenth century, when they appear at Dunbrody, Grey and Inch. Those under the tower of Grey are rather stumpy in proportion (Pl. 206), but one in the crossing at Dunbrody (south-east pier) is unusually elegant. By eliminating ornament, the capital was reduced to its basic architectonic form and as such represents Cistercian austerity at its extreme. The most attractive Early English capitals, with well proportioned stiff-leaf foliage, can be found at Graiguenamanagh (Pl. 207). They were carved at the same time as the late Romanesque

207 Graiguenamanagh, monks' doorway, a fine example of an Early English capital with stiff-leaf foliage.

208 (above right) The corbel table on the north side of the presbytery at Tintern (c1300). The vigorous modelling of the faces has few parallels elsewhere in Ireland.

209 Jerpoint cloister (c1390–1400), an abbot or bishop arrayed in vestments, at his feet a disembodied face.

capitals at Boyle and the contrast between the two branches of the Cistercian order could not be more explicit. There is no trace of animal or figure sculpture at Graiguenamanagh or at Dunbrody, Inch and Grey. This was not entirely the result of conscientious observation of the rule, for such carvings were not fashionable in the Early English style.

Jerpoint cloister and the late Gothic revival

After the flurry of activity in the period 1200–30, the art of sculpture was almost ignored by the Cistercians for the next century and a half. The few carvings that did appear were generally innocuous. Hore abbey (1272–c1300) is as dour as most medieval castles, with only an occasional stiff-leaf capital to enliven the otherwise bleak design. At Jerpoint, however, the masons of the fourteenth-century east window produced one unexpected vignette, an angel at the base of the south jamb. The carving is peremptory enough, but there is a genuine tenderness about the way the angel holds a tiny soul in his hands—an isolated piece of Last Judgement iconography. More secular in spirit are the carved corbels on the exterior of the choir of Tintern abbey (c1300). Corbel tables are rare in Ireland but the Cistercians can boast two of them. There are twenty-four heads at Tintern, some human, some monstrous, plus a fair smattering of hybrids in between. They are carved with fleshy cheeks and wide nostrils and there is a satisfying 'roundness' in the modelling (Pl. 208). Except for one corbel at Mellifont, there is nothing like them elsewhere in Ireland at this date and it is possible that the masons responsible were recruited through the mother house of Tintern Major. The other Cistercian corbel table can be found at Grey, where the corbels are inferior in quality but more varied in subject. They were inserted when the roof of the presbytery was raised, probably early in the fifteenth century. Sculptured examples are restricted to the north side. There are eight of them altogether: one is carved with oak leaves, another has a lady with a reticulated hair style and there are several with human and animal heads. Anthony Weir has also identified an anal 'exhibitionist', equipped with a large scrotum, though weathering has obscured much of the detail.[46]

None of these minor carvings prepare us for the Cistercian *tour de force* of the later middle ages, the cloister at Jerpoint (Pls 145, 209). As it stands at present, the cloister is a reconstruction of 1953, a reassembly of the numerous fragments found lying about at the site. Many sculptures had found their way to neighbouring graveyards and gardens and not all of them have been returned.[47] But even in its partially reconstituted state, what remains is impressive. Not since the Romanesque era had there been such a rich ensemble of architectural sculpture. According to Edwin Rae, who carried out a meticulous examination in the 1960's, there are over fifty carvings from the colonettes alone, plus a varied display of *Kleinkunst* that spills over the surrounding architectural framework. There is no Cistercian parallel for such a spectacle, which represents a complete repudiation of St Bernard's *Apologia*. Even the fifteenth-century cloister at Cadouin (Dordogne), with its carvings of angels, prophets, apostles, monks and biblical subjects, scarcely compares with the exuberance of Jerpoint.[48] The form, iconography, and tone of the Irish cloister is completely different, a rare and spectacular rejection of Cistercian austerity.

210 Jerpoint cloister, figure relaxing between the bases of the colonettes.

211 Jerpoint cloister, grotesque hybrid.

212 Jerpoint, sculptured bracket on one of the cloister piers.

The cloister arcade rests on twin 'pseudo' colonettes or 'dumb-bell' shafts. The web of masonry that links the colonettes provides the main field of sculpture. It is a narrow, vertical surface and in many cases the carving expands on to the adjoining shafts. Capitals and bases are similarly paired and many of them are ornamented with marginalia or drolleries—human faces, animals, hybrids, grotesques and flowers (Pls 210, 211). There are dragons, monkeys and a squirrel eating a nut, plus the heads of a pig and a fox. All of these are executed with humour and *joie de vivre*, described appropriately by Dr Rae as 'witticisms of the chisel'.

Although Edwin Rae's scrupulous study solved most of the iconographic difficulties, there are still questions to be answered. Why is the architecture of the cloister so archaic in style and why did the masons choose to erect round arches rather than pointed Gothic forms? What was the motivation behind such an array of sculpture and was the programme designed to have an overall meaning? Where did the monks recruit their masons and how much did they know about sculpture beyond the confines of Leinster? Even the date of the cloister is controversial, with opinion oscillating from c1400–25 (Leask) to c1500 (Rae) and back to c1400 (Hunt).[49]

The subjects portrayed on the piers can be divided into several different categories—saints, ecclesiastics, religious images, civilians, grotesque beasts.[50] At least four of the apostles can be identified—St Peter, St James the Greater, St Bartholomew and St John the Evangelist—and as there are further fragments, it is likely that all twelve were originally present. The saints include three of the most popular intercessors of late Gothic Christianity—St Catherine, St Christopher and St Margaret (Pl. 213). As the patron saint of childbirth, St Margaret was not perhaps to be expected in a Cistercian cloister. A second relief of St Christopher, this one over five feet high, was also carved by the same workshop (Pl. 214). It is obviously too large for the cloister arcades, but it may have been fixed to one of the piers at the corners.[51] Among the other subjects which fall within the familiar repertoire of late Gothic art are images of the Trinity and a shield with the symbols of the Passion. Two of the best preserved figures depict churchmen. One is an abbot, portrayed with his monastic cowl, a crosier, and a weighty set of rosary beads (Pl. 145).[52] On the reverse is a bishop or another abbot, arrayed in liturgical vestments (Pl. 209). A further ecclesiastic, with his hands open, as if conducting the Mass, is more fragmentary. Moving to the secular sphere, there were at least seven knights in armour, two of whom carried shields with the arms of local families (Ormond and Walsh).[53] There are three noble ladies to complement the knights, plus a girl and two civilians with shoulder capes (Pls 182, 215). Finally there are a few piers with grotesques only—a long-tailed dragon, a human-headed quadruped and a double-bodied beast with a single face.[54] The programme as a whole forms a chaotic mixture of the sacred and the profane and it is not easy to discern any unified or coherent theme. Although the original order of the sculptures is now lost, it is clear that the arrangement was not entirely arbitrary. Many of the carvings were conceived as pairs, placed back to back on either side of the piers. Thus two of the ecclesiastics complement each other (abbot and bishop?), the Ormond knight is backed by a lady, presumably his wife, St Peter and St James are linked together, and St Catherine is combined with another (unidentified) saint. It is possible that the various categories were arranged separately in different walks of the cloister, but this is unproven.

Only Edwin Rae has given serious thought to the purpose of this ambitious programme. He believes that the knights represented local benefactors of the abbey, with the cloister thus assuming 'the aspect of an extensive memorial'. 'Revered ancestors and relations, perhaps some of them still alive, mingle with the apostles who will assist at the Day of Judgement and with saints'.[55] Attractive though it sounds, it is not easy to accept this as a complete explanation. Even if some of the figures were commemorative, laity and churchmen occupy only half of the programme, and Jerpoint cannot be regarded as another Naumburg, with the founders watching over the religious community they helped to establish. Yet it is difficult to suggest an alternative theme which encompasses all the figures. Most can be explained individually or in groups, but not as a totality. The apostles, for example, are appropriate in a cloister, since the *vita apostolica* was fundamental to the monastic ideal. Their presence underlines the fact that the monks of Jerpoint were, at least in theory, the spiritual heirs of Christ's disciples. Such an analogy had been suggested as early as c1100 in the cloister at Moissac (Tarn et Garonne),[56]

213 Jerpoint cloister, fragmentary figure of
St Catherine.

214 Jerpoint cloister, carved relief of St
Christopher, the largest of the cloister sculptures.

where individual reliefs were carved on the piers, and later in the twelfth century the apostles
reappeared as column figures in the cloister of Notre Dame en Vaux at Chalons-sur-Marne
(Marne).[57] At Moissac, significantly, the apostles were accompanied by a portrait of one of the
abbots. In view of St Bernard's scathing comments about Cluniac cloisters, there is a certain
irony in finding such precedents.

A secular atmosphere pervades the whole ensemble and it is difficult to believe that the cloister
carvings were intended for the eyes of the monks alone. The sculptures in fact offer a cross-
section of the upper echelons of society, both in this world and the next, with knights, ladies and
high ranking churchmen balanced by the disciples and the saints. Medieval visitors to Jerpoint
must have been impressed by this vista of society, with its display of secular and religious
auctoritas. While the programme may have been designed to commemorate local families and to
affirm the monastic vocation (hollow claim, perhaps, in the fifteenth century), it must indirectly
have contributed to the status and prestige of the monastery as a social institution.

For those with eyes attuned to the sophisticated statuary of Gothic Europe, the style of
Jerpoint seems provincial and debased. The carvings are usually regarded as local products,
which have few affinities with any of the major schools of European sculpture. The figures are
stiff and frontal and, apart from a naive smile, the faces lack expression and individuality. Necks
are too thick and chins too prominent. The anatomy of the bodies is frequently unconvincing.
There is a suspicion that the Ormond knight has 'knock knees' and the legs of the larger
St Christopher, even allowing for his giant reputation, seem excessively massive (Pl. 214). But
despite these observations, the style is not as rustic as it first appears. The simplicity and clarity of
the forms is instantly appealing and the drapery is arranged with a keen awareness of pattern.
Although carved in relatively thin relief, the figures have a sense of volume and substance. And
there are some delightfully expressive details—the gigantic fingers of the blessing ecclesiastic,
the lady with her hands thrust deep into her pockets, the outstretched hand of Jesus in the arms of
St Christopher, not to mention the amusing character fast asleep between two of the bases
(Pls 209, 210, 215). Almost all the sculptures betray a zest and vitality which bring the whole
programme to life. In its simplicity and expressiveness the sculpture has a 'neo-Romanesque'
flavour, a contrast to the elegant piety usually associated with Gothic.

Many observers have realised that the style is not like other sculpture in Ireland, but none have
appreciated its links with English art of the fourteenth century. The stiffening of the figure style,
the sharp delineation of drapery and 'attitudes of impassive calm' are established characteristics
of sculpture in the reign of Richard II.[58] The dress of the civilians also corresponds with this
period. After a detailed analysis of the armour, John Hunt suggested a date of c1400 for the
Ormond knight.[59] This armour consists of a cuirass, over which there is a tight-fitting jupon or
surcoat, a common feature of fourteenth-century effigies (Pl. 182). The head is protected by a
barbut with a T-shaped opening, almost identical to one found at Lough Henney (Down). The
legs are covered by greaves and the knees are protected by poleyns decorated with rosettes. The
knight carries a small heater-shaped shield and a dagger is slung from the belt. A lance is carved
against the adjoining colonette. The lady behind the knight is also dressed in late fourteenth-
century costume. She wears a long gown, which falls in regular corrugated pleats below the
waist (Pl. 215). It has long slits or fitchets at the sides, into which she puts her hands, and there are
lengthy lappets which, attached at the elbow, float out over the neighbouring colonettes. A
fragment from the cloister, now at Newtown Jerpoint, depicts a similar figure, but this time
with a line of buttons stretching from the neck to the waist. Parallels for both the style and the
dress of these figures can be observed on English tombs. None is more illustrious than the tomb
of Edward III (d. 1377) in Westminster Abbey, where one of the female weepers (Joan de la
Tour) has the same stiff pose and reticulated hair style (Pl. 217). She too has sharply bent elbows
and her hands pushed deep inside the fitchets. Another female weeper (Mary, Duchess of
Brittany) has a prominently buttoned bodice (Pl. 218).[60] This Court style was widespread in
England and related figures can be found in the small parish church at Clifton Reynes
(Buckinghamshire).[61] The weepers on the tomb of Sir Thomas Reynes (c1375–80) include in
their company knights with pointed greaves, cuirasses and tight fitting jupons, and the dress of

215 (right) Jerpoint cloister, an aristocratic lady with a mitred bishop above her head.

217 (facing page top left) Westminster Abbey, tomb of Edward III. The female 'weeper', Joan de la Tour, has the same stiff pose and reticulated hair style of some of the Jerpoint ladies.

218 (facing page centre) Westminster Abbey, tomb of Edward III, Mary of Brittany. The broad flat drapery folds foreshadow those on the figures at Jerpoint.

219 (facing page right) Clifton Reynes (Buckinghamshire), weepers on the tomb of Sir Thomas Reynes. The stiff poses were characteristic of late fourteenth-century sculpture.

216 Bective, kneeling abbot on one of the cloister piers (c1450–1500).

one of the women is remarkably close to that on the fragment at Newtown Jerpoint (Pl. 219). It is not just the costumes that are similar, but the style as well. At Westminster one of the weepers (Mary, Duchess of Brittany) has drapery arranged in broad flat strips, a technique repeated on the robes of some of the apostles at Jerpoint, most notably St James and St John. The style of the cloister should not therefore be dismissed as a provincial aberration, for it reflects the best English fashions of the last quarter of the fourteenth century.

Although the sculptors at Jerpoint were not as skilful as those at Westminster or Clifton Reynes, their repertoire of images belonged to the common stock of motifs used by Gothic

220 Johnstown (Meath), pier decorated with a bishop, from the cloister arcades at Bective.

craftsmen throughout the British Isles. There are no local or specifically Irish elements, not even the odd triskele or triquetra knot. Some of the minor carvings recall the world of misericords. The squirrel nibbling nuts, for example, is found on the choir stalls at Lincoln Cathedral and the man with three faces, 'triune man', appears on the stalls at Whalley (Lancashire) as well as in manuscript illumination.[62] The long-tailed dragon, which wriggles up one of the piers, is equally common, and it reappears on two fourteenth-century Irish shrines, the Domnach Airgid and the shrine of St Patrick's tooth.[63]

These analogies suggest that the Jerpoint sculptors were experienced at making tombs and church furnishings. The range of saints and religious images are those one finds on many a Gothic font as at Crickstown (Meath), for example, where the highly accomplished font is decorated with apostles, saints (St Margaret, St Catherine and St Michael), plus an archbishop, an abbot and an abbess.[64] Similarly six of the eight subjects carved on the late fourteenth-century font at Clifton Reynes (Buckinghamshire) reappear at Jerpoint (St Catherine, St Margaret, St Michael, the Trinity, St Peter and one other apostle). The scale of the Jerpoint figures and the relief technique employed suggests the same background.

Although the artistic milieu of the sculptors is now clearer, the date of their work at Jerpoint is liable to remain controversial. Both the style and dress of the figures point unmistakably to the decades 1380–1400, but this contradicts the only available piece of documentary evidence. In 1442 a Papal indulgence mentions that the cloisters were in bad repair.[65] It is difficult to accept that a cloister arcade could become delapidated within fifty years of its construction, so many have assumed that the rebuilding was not carried out until c1442–50. If so, the sculptures were curiously, and consistently, old fashioned. The words of the indulgence, however, should not be taken too literally, as the phraseology of fund raising appeals are all too frequently exaggerated. The artistic evidence clearly suggests that the project was commissioned shortly before 1400.[66]

Decorative schemes of the fifteenth century

In its pristine state, with the carvings highlighted by colour, the cloister at Jerpoint must have been a memorable sight, yet it did not set a fashion in Ireland. When other Cistercian monasteries came to rebuild their cloisters, they did so in a more sober and orthodox manner. Only the Augustinians at Inistioge, four miles away down the river Nore, made a serious attempt to emulate the design, but this was not until a century later.[67] A fine but isolated piece

221 Kilcooly, the decorated screen wall which surrounds the door to the sacristy.

222 Kilcooly, mermaid with comb and mirror, carved in hard, semi polished limestone.

of sculpture remains in the south range of the fifteenth-century cloister at Bective. It depicts an abbot kneeling under an ogee arch, with a coat of arms prominent above the head (Pl. 216). This is almost certainly the abbot responsible for building the cloister and it is frustrating that he cannot be identified.[68] The face is smashed, but other details are still quite sharp. The abbot kneels on an elaborate plinth or footstool and he holds a large floriated crosier. His robes are cut in regular tubular folds and over his shoulders there is a plain hood. What makes the carving unusual is the pose. The bend of the head is sensitively balanced by the curve of the robes, and the sculptor has achieved a delicate suggestion of movement and humility.[69] The Bective cloister contained at least one further carving of an ecclesiastic, now built into the tower of a modern church at Johnstown (County Meath). In this case the figure, probably a bishop, stands frontally, but otherwise it displays the same stylistic details as the abbot at Bective (Pl. 220).

After Jerpoint the most ambitious display of figure sculpture was carried out at Kilcooly, where again the architectural context was unorthodox. As part of the reconstruction of the abbey c1450–1520, a splendid doorway with five moulded orders was erected between the transept and sacristy. The surrounding wall was treated as a decorated screen and embellished with a series of carved panels, scattered about in a random fashion (Pl. 221). At first sight the

carvings appear to be insertions, but this cannot be so as the stones have all been carefully cut to suit their present positions.[70] High above the doorway is a pseudo canopy, a debased copy of that over the sedilia at Holycross. Even here a general casualness is apparent, for two of the tracery panels are smaller than the others. Although the cutting of the masonry in the wall is very exact, there is an extraordinarily *ad hoc* character to the design, which makes it self evident that preparatory drawings were not employed. To the right of the door is an oblong panel showing a mermaid with a comb and a mirror, accompanied by two corpulent and cheerful fishes (Pl. 222). This was a favourite subject in Gothic art—there are over three dozen examples on English misericords—and it was popular in Ireland.[71] The mermaid is equivalent to the classical siren that lured sailors to their fate with sweet melodies, and, as the medieval Bestiary explained, that was 'the way in which ignorant and incautious human beings get tricked by pretty voices when they are charmed by indelicacies, ostentations and pleasures'. In particular they were associated with sexual enticement.[72] On three occasions (558, 887 and 1118) mermaids were said to have been captured off the Irish coast![73]

Above the mermaid is a carving of an abbot, set in a frame under a floriated ogee arch, but, as is to be expected at Kilcooly, figure and arch are not aligned (Pl. 223). With its 'bull neck' and extraordinary ears, the sculpture is decidedly uncouth, although the face has sufficient humanity to suggest a smile. The abbot is arrayed in liturgical vestments, complete with maniple, and he holds a book in one hand and a crosier in the other. It is a frontal, formal image and as such is the antithesis to the lively abbot at Bective. There are no arms or identifying inscription, but there is a good chance that the abbot is meant to be Philip O'Molwanayn, who rebuilt the monastery after the disaster of 1445. His tomb slab, executed by a far more proficient craftsman, is still preserved in the chancel (Pl. 241). Above the abbot and immediately below the enframing arch is a striding angel wielding a very substantial censor. The wings of the angel are symmetrically arranged under the arch and, with its arresting combination of pattern and movement, it evokes memories of Romanesque art rather than Gothic. The arch is crowned by a short pinnacle, to the right of which is a small carving of a pelican feeding her young, another favourite Gothic motif.[74] There are at least fourteen examples of this subject in Ireland, but in one respect the Kilcooly pelican is unusual. Here the nest takes the form of a chalice, underlining the eucharistic significance of the blood that the pelican shed to revive its young.[75]

As popular as the pelican in Gothic religious imagery was St Christopher, who occupies a square panel above the doorway at Kilcooly (Pl. 225). His role as a protector of travellers is well known, a meaning underlined by the inscription under a painting at Wood Eaton (Oxfordshire): 'KI CEST IMAGE VERRA LE JUR DE MALE MORT NE MURRA'—'he that sees this image

223 Kilcooly, sculptured panel to the right of the sacristy door. Above the arch is a pelican feeding her young in a nest that takes the form of a chalice.

224 German woodcut of St Christopher (1423). The narrative flavour of the iconography was the type followed by the sculptor at Kilcooly.

225 Kilcooly, carved reliefs above the sacristy door. The bold stepping figure of St Christopher is a contrast to the statuesque interpretation of the subject at Jerpoint (Pl. 214).

will not die an ill death this day'.[76] More than just a patron of travellers, he was also regarded as a patron of Man on his journey through life. As the middle ages progressed, St Christopher became an increasing favourite and E. W. Tristram counted over four hundred illustrations of him in fifteenth-century English wall painting. The Kilcooly panel shows the saint in profile, taking a giant stride to the right. He pulls himself forward with his flowering staff, which is held in both hands, leaving the Christ child unsupported, virtually 'floating' above his shoulder. Christ raises one hand in blessing and uses the other to clutch St Christopher's head. The water is not indicated, except indirectly by two fishes and an eel. The narrative flavour of the iconography is a contrast to the two Jerpoint carvings, where St Christopher was erect and statuesque (Pl. 214). In those cases the Christ child was held firmly in the saint's left arm. The Kilcooly composition follows a type common in fifteenth-century Europe and it shares many details with the famous Buxheim St Christopher of 1423, one of the earliest German woodcuts (Pl. 224).[77] Despite the robust vigour of the carving, the figure style is clumsy and ill proportioned.

Alongside St Christopher is a square panel depicting the crucifixion (Pl. 225). This is the centrepiece of the screen wall, but disconcertingly it is not aligned with the doorway below. The cumbersome figure style is again in evidence and Christ in particular has an undersized torso and oversized limbs. More attractive are the robes of the Virgin and St John, where the regular vertical stripes of the undergarments make a pleasing contrast with the broad curving folds of the cloaks. A characteristic of both the upper panels is the flat 'plate' like drapery consistently employed for the figures. It is unlikely that the man responsible was a specialist sculptor and it is difficult to trace his activities elsewhere. The decoration of the sacristy wall is completed by two shields, charged with the Ormond arms, below which is a large aumbry, surmounted by an emphatically floriated ogee gable.

The best parallels for the sacristy facade at Kilcooly are the portals at Clonmacnois (1450–9) and Clontuskert (c1471), where sculptured panels are also arranged around a doorway. At Kilcooly, however, the organisation is more arbitrary and irrational. Why the entrance to the sacristy was selected for such grandiose treatment is hard to discern, for this splendid doorway led into a gloomy chamber only fifteen feet (4.57 metres) square. Was it perhaps a private chapel or mausoleum belonging to the Ormond family, whose arms are so prominently displayed? The subjects selected by the craftsmen do not belong to a specifically Cistercian repertoire of images, nor were they particularly monastic in flavour. Instead they are among the most popular themes in medieval art, which could be expected in almost any parish church, demonstrating, as at Jerpoint, the extent to which the Irish Cistercians had lost any sense of religious exclusiveness. The style of the masons can only be described as rudimentary and the tenuous links with the mainstream of Gothic fashion which existed at Jerpoint around 1400 had now been severed.

The reconstruction of Holycross after 1431 produced a wealth of decorative carving, which forms one of the delights of late Gothic art in Ireland, justifying eighteenth-century descriptions of the abbey as 'an exquisite piece of antiquity'.[78] There is little figural sculpture, but animals and foliage patterns abound. The shrine and the sedilia as well as corbels and string courses are enlivened by sprays of ivy leaves, crisp and varied in design. The leaves are stylised rather than naturalistic and follow conventions established throughout the British Isles over a century before. The south wall of the shrine has a particularly attractive display, with five large leaves symmetrically clustered around the centre pinnacle in each bay. The shrine repays minute investigation, for hidden within the tracery and foliage is an abundance of small creatures—pairs of dogs' heads, affronted birds (including two owls), and three dogs running down a pinnacle (Pl. 226). There is also a feline mask, akin to that found on fourteenth-century tiles,[79] as well as an angel holding a shield charged with the arms of the Holy Cross (Pl. 96).[80] All these details are boldly modelled in the hard limestone, with a good sense of volume and plastic vigour. The same qualities are apparent in the two guardian lions, now defaced, that occupy the string course immediately above the shrine (Pl. 95). The miniature animal heads and the varied foliage that characterise the shrine are reminiscent of carving in the Decorated era in England, a retrospective flavour which has already been noticed in the architecture of Holycross.

226 Holycross Abbey, side panel of the shrine, with birds, dogs' heads and foliage patterns sharply modelled in the hard local limestone.

227 Holycross, sculptured corbel on the south-east pier of the crossing.

228 Holycross, the famous owl which flutters against the north-west crossing pier.

The decoration of the sedilia in the chancel is equally stunning and on the whole less worn than the ornament on the shrine. Here the blue-grey limestone is seen at its best, with the sharply cut leaves standing out against the smooth polished masonry (Pls 235, 237). Carved on one of the fluted piers is a diminutive kneeling angel. Although there are differences between the shrine and the sedilia, particularly in the mouldings and the general design, the similarity of the ornament and sculptural technique make it clear that the same workshop was responsible.

Further carvings can be found decorating the architecture of the church. A corbel head on the south-east crossing pier is flanked by two kneeling angels, both wearing crowns (Pl. 227). The features are coarsely executed, and the figures are much inferior to the chubby smiling angels on the shrine and sedilia. The most famous of all the abbey's sculptures is the owl, wings outstretched, that flutters below a corbel on the north-west pier. It has no enclosing frame and seems about to fly off across the church (Pl. 228). While it represents a superb piece of decoration, the choice of an owl against a *northern* pier was not entirely arbitrary. Associated with the hours of darkness the owl signified blindness in matters of faith and hatred of the light of truth.[81] It was a bird of ill omen that, in Chaucer's words, 'of deth the bode bryngeth'.[82] The

229 Tintern Abbey, fifteenth-century ecclesiastic, redeployed by the Colcloughs when they turned the chancel into a private house.

owl thus watched over the pilgrims to Holycross, just as it ominously watched the dishevelled and indecisive traveller in Hieronymous Bosch's famous painting of the Wayfarer.[83]

On the exterior of Holycross there are two short stretches of highly decorated string-course where the concave surface is filled with a variety of motifs, chiefly leaves and rosettes. At the north-west corner of the transept, animals appear—a lion and two unicorns with interlocking necks. Both are well-modelled in full rounded relief. The entwined neck is an age-old device (it appeared in the thirteenth century at Boyle) and Peter Harbison has drawn attention to the remarkable similarity between the Holycross unicorns and those on the misericords at Limerick Cathedral.[84] Another misericord at Limerick depicts an angel standing on clouds, comparable with the small angels on the sedilia and shrine in the Cistercian abbey. These comparisons demonstrate the extent to which in fifteenth-century Ireland, wood-carvers, stone masons, painters and metalworkers were all drawing on the same common stock of motifs.

Ecclesiastics seem to have been among the most popular subjects in Cistercian art, as if the abbots had a predilection for their own image, as a way of underlining their status. Those at Jerpoint, Bective and Kilcooly have already been mentioned and at Tintern there are three such carvings, all small in scale. The best preserved shows a portly churchman with a large rounded head and his robes cut in strong tubular folds, similar to the style of the Ormond 'school' in the sixteenth century (Pl. 229).[85] None of the figures is in its original location. Two were reused by the Colclough's after the dissolution as interior decoration for one of the rooms they built into the old Cistercian chancel.[86]

Apart from the ecclesiastics, Cistercian abbeys showed little consistency in their choice of subjects, nor was there any uniformity in the application of sculpture. At Jerpoint, Kilcooly and Holycross, carving was exploited in quite different ways and there was no identifiably Cistercian approach. The decoration of the three abbeys represents the most extensive range of architectural sculpture anywhere in the country and they clearly made a considerable impact. Sculptors from Jerpoint can be traced at Cashel Cathedral (two corbels in the nave) and Kilkenny (a figure from the Dominican Friary)[87] and the canons at Inistioge had the Jerpoint cloister in mind when they came to rebuild their own cloister around 1510. The ornament at Holycross, however, was probably the most influential. As Dr Hourihane has shown, Holycross craftsmen and their favourite themes can be traced at Kilconnell, Ennis and Fethard,[88] and the famous shrine in the south transept may have had some effect on the design of tomb chests at Fertagh and Cashel.[89] If anything, the Cistercians were more disposed to architectural sculpture than other orders, an ironic reversal of the twelfth-century situation. Most of the imagery employed was conventional enough and the extent to which English and European themes dominated at the expense of local ones is remarkable. The Gaelic Revival had a negligible impact and, apart from the odd piece of interlace or triquetra knot,[90] there are no motifs of local origin. In style and execution the local flavour is more explicit, for the tough native limestone gives Irish Gothic sculpture a polish and hardness lacking in most contemporary English work.

Chapter 10

DECORATION AND FURNISHINGS

230 Hore Abbey, piscina and aumbry (c1275). The rebate around the aumbry suggests it had a wooden door.

231 Holycross, piscina in the north transept.

The Furnishing of the Church

CONFRONTED BY desolate ruins, it can be difficult to imagine Cistercian abbeys in their original state, complete with furnishings and decoration. With the masonry plastered in white, coloured tiles on the floor, patterned or even stained glass in the windows, and the stalls of the monks stretching down into the nave, these were once places of beauty and intimacy. Stone furnishings like sedilia and piscinae occasionally survive, but such timber fitments as screens and choir stalls have without exception been destroyed.

Vanished in most cases, too, are the steps which established a series of ascending levels at the east end. The whole presbytery was usually raised one or two steps above the monks' choir and further east two more steps led up to the high altar (at Hore there is evidence of this on the adjoining walls, where the position of the steps is marked by jumps in the string-course). The side chapels were also elevated two steps above the general floor level and at Hore some of the steps remain *in situ*. Medieval stone altars, found in a number of abbeys, were relatively plain affairs, undecorated apart from mouldings on their edges and corners.[1] The fifteenth-century example on Clare Island is the most elaborate and the best preserved. A Cistercian altar would normally be covered by a plain linen cloth (multi-coloured altar frontals were proscribed by statute) and upon it there was a simple wooden cross with the crucified figure of Christ.[2] This at least was the official situation. It is clear, however, that coloured altar cloths and vestments were gradually tolerated and by the sixteenth century, if not long before, crosses of wood had given way to crosses of gilded silver.

The piscina, required for washing the chalice after the celebration of mass, was located in a wall to the south of the appropriate altar, following standard medieval practice. Their design ranged from the rudimentary to the ornate. In the chancel at Inch (c1200) it consists of an undecorated niche with a curved head, whereas at Hore (c1272–80) it formed part of an attractive and well considered Early English design. In this case the piscina had twin compartments, each framed by colonettes and trefoiled arches; alongside there was an aumbry of similar form which, to judge from the presence of a rebate, once had a wooden door (Pl. 230). A common feature of later piscina niches was a 'credence' shelf for storing the cruets of wine and water. An unusually elaborate series of piscina niches can be seen in the church at Holycross. Carved in dark limestone, with broad decorative mouldings, they are characteristic products of later Irish Gothic, without any hint of Cistercian reticence. One in the north transept, with a multi-cusped ogee arch, is especially striking (Pl. 231).

Alongside the piscina lay the sedilia, the seats for the officiating priest, deacon and subdeacon. They were usually designed as arches recessed into the wall and they were frequently the excuse for a decorative outburst. At Jerpoint the sedilia (c1160–70) consisted of three round-headed niches, each highlighted by a strip of chevron (Pl. 232). The sedilia at Baltinglass, inserted in the thirteenth century, are similar, but the seats are not so deep and the arches are trefoil-headed. Rows of nail-head ornament replace the chevron used at Jerpoint. At Boyle the sedilia (c1161–70) consisted of a single arched recess, covering a stone bench below, but this was an unusually straightforward arrangement.[3] Far more exotic is the design of the early thirteenth-century example at Corcomroe, carved in the distinctive fashion of the school of the west. It is basically a development of the Boyle type—a single arched recess with an undivided seat (now missing)

232　Jerpoint, the sedilia (c1160–70), designed as three separate arched recesses.

233　The ornate sedilia at Corcomroe (c1210–20), where a bench was enclosed under a single arch.

234　Detail of the sedilia at Corcomroe.

235　The elaborate sedilia in the chancel at Holycross, with the piscina to the left.

(Pls 233, 234). The pointed arch is decorated with a late form of chevron and it rests on robust shafts with foliate capitals. The rear wall is embellished with two blind arches, each supported on capitals, which in turn rest on tapering corbels, that *leitmotiv* of Cistercian architecture. A delightful touch is a piece of knotted foliage, arranged like tassels, that serves as a foil between the arches. Few Cistercian sedilia survive as well as these and in many abbeys all that is left are scars on the wall, as at Abbeyknockmoy, Inch and Hore.[4]

The most sumptuous of all Cistercian fittings, indeed the finest piece of church furnishing in medieval Ireland, are the sedilia in the chancel at Holycross (Pls 235, 236, 237). Over 17 feet (5.2 metres) high, they were designed with three elegant ogee arches, which support an ornate attic and canopy. The bench is fronted by a panel of leaf carving, arranged in units of four, like tiles on a medieval pavement. Between the ogee arches are five shields, three of them charged with the arms of England, Ormond and Fitzgerald respectively.[5] Above are displays of blind tracery and foliate finials, symmetrically organised but with much variation of detail. The recessed space of the sedilia is covered by a miniature tierceron vault and similar vaults decorate the underside of the canopy. Surmounting the whole structure is a hipped roof, immaculately constructed in punched dressed limestone. The destruction of the cusping on the main arches has deprived the structure of some of its delicacy, but nevertheless by Cistercian standards it is a decorative *tour de force*, elegant in proportion and clinical in its sculptural finish. Many of the details are repeated on the shrine in the south transept and the sedilia are clearly a product of the same workshop. The design appears to have been much admired, for one can trace its influence in neighbouring abbeys. The canopy was copied, albeit out of context, in the south transept at Kilcooly and not dissimilar sedilia were constructed by the Augustinians at Callan, just over twenty miles away.[6] The vocabulary of forms used at Holycross—ogee arches, cusping, canopies with pseudo vaults,[7] floriated pinnacles and blind tracery—were standard features of ecclesiastical furnishing throughout the British Isles in the later Gothic era. The general design, with ogee arches to the fore, is reminiscent of the fourteenth-century sedilia in the cathedrals of Rochester and Southwark, though the Holycross version is considerably more exuberant.[8] Such florid designs are rare in Cistercian churches, though an exception can be found at Furness where the Tudor sedilia excel even Holycross in their richness. What makes the Holycross example unique is the solidity of the general structure, plus the clarity and flatness of the ornament (an English mason would have been tempted to add more projecting canopies and detached arches). Above all, however, it is the smooth polish of the dark grey limestone which makes the Irish flavour unmistakeable. It would be interesting to know more about the background of the master mason who designed it. Similar fittings possibly existed in the more affluent monasteries of Dublin, knowledge of which could have filtered south into Ormond. The type of ornament

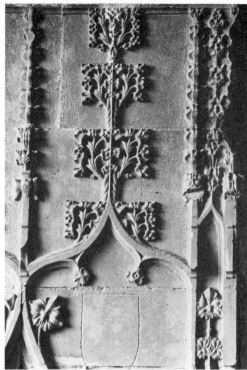

236 The miniature vault constructed within the sedilia at Holycross.

237 One of the floriated pinnacles on the sedilia at Holycross.

used at Holycross was ubiquitous on timber screens and choir stalls, and the sedilia give us a hint of the lost woodwork of medieval Ireland.

It was standard practice in Cistercian abbeys for the monks' stalls to occupy the crossing and the first bays of the nave. The brethren faced each other across the central space of the choir, with the novices seated on benches at the front.[9] Even in Cistercian churches the stalls could be lavish pieces of carpentry. About 1440 the monks of Melrose in Scotland commissioned a set of carved oak stalls from a master carpenter in Bruges,[10] and likewise one must imagine the choirs of Mellifont, St Mary's, Dublin, or Holycross filled with resplendent woodwork. In the centre of the choir, at the entrance to the presbytery, was a lectern and the stone base of one was discovered in this position at Mellifont.[11]

Separating the monks' choir from that of the laybrothers was a substantial timber screen. In fact, this often consisted of two parallel screens, the space between forming a small retrochoir, where elderly and infirm monks could attend services inconspicuously. It was in this secluded spot that the deranged monk of St Mary's, William Kedenor, hid himself, before dashing out with a dagger to assault his fellow monks in the choir.[12] At Dunbrody the location of the original screen was marked by a double window in the clerestory, which cast its light equally into the two adjacent choirs. The stalls of the monks thus stretched for two bays down the nave and the back of the stalls was approximately 7 feet 6 inches (2.30 metres) high, a point marked by the start of a decorative chamfer on the piers behind (Pl. 68).[13] A similar chamfer at Corcomroe suggests that the stalls there were a little lower in height. There are also clues about the location of the screens at Boyle. A stone projection on the fourth pier of the nave (north side only) probably marks the position of the transverse screen, and flanges on the three eastern piers helped to ensure a smooth fitting for the choir stalls. The monks were thus snugly enclosed on three sides by timber partitions (in some cases masonry walls). While these guaranteed privacy during the daily offices, they had the added bonus of cutting out draughts in what must often have been a very cold environment.[14]

At Kilcooly stalls of solid stone were erected for the abbot and prior. They were neatly fashioned out of the western piers of the crossing and covered by miniature vaults. Each was equipped with a hinged wooden seat or misericord, as indicated by grooves in the stone (Pl. 238). These robust and handsome stalls may have been modelled on equivalent stalls at Mellifont, only fragments of which remain. They are an unusual feature in Cistercian churches.

Kilcooly was one of the many abbeys which was retained as a local parish church after the

238 The abbot's stall at Kilcooly, with two Ormond shields carved above the arch. The curved groove for the wooden seat or misericord can be seen inside.

239 Sixteenth-century font at Kilcooly, ornamented with rib-vault patterns.

dissolution. About this time a rood loft and screen was installed, as in some parish churches of the Pale,[15] and from this time too comes a simple square font, decorated with vaulting and tracery patterns (Pl. 239).[16] Fonts were not generally required in Cistercian churches for infant baptism was a duty of the local parish priest rather than the local monks.[17]

A final item of furnishing that deserves a mention is the organ. Organs had been installed in the larger parish churches of England by the thirteenth century and there is no doubt that some of the Cistercian houses in Ireland acquired them too. 'A pair of organs' (the usual medieval way of referring to organs with several pipes) was listed amongst the chattels of Graiguenamanagh in 1541.[18] This implies a degree of musical elaboration contrary to the early dictates of the order. St Bernard denounced fancy singing just as he denigrated extravagant art:

Let the chant be full of gravity; let it be neither worldly, nor too rude and poor . . . let it be sweet, yet without levity, and, while it pleases the ear let it move the heart. It should alleviate sadness and calm the angry spirit. It should not contradict the sense of the words, but rather enhance it. For it is no slight loss of spiritual grace to be distracted from profit of the sense by the beauty of the chant, and to have our attention drawn to a mere vocal display, when we ought to be thinking of what is sung.[19]

By 1228 the chanting of some Irish monks seems to have been getting out of hand. Stephen of Lexington in one of the injunctions of 1228 instructed them to follow the form of the order 'according to the writings of the blessed Bernard' and he forbade them to sing with 'duplicate voices' ('vocibus duplicis').[20] Evidently the monks were embarking on some tentative polyphony. Unfortunately we know even less about the music of the Irish monasteries than about their art and architecture.[21] The location of the organs is far from clear, but they must have been close to the choir, possibly above the screen separating it from the laybrothers.

Burials and tomb monuments

There is a certain irony in the fact that burials, which now so disfigure the monastic ruins of Ireland, were originally banned from the interior of Cistercian churches.[22] In the early years burial within the monastic precinct, let alone within the church, was something of a privilege.[23] Each community had its own cemetery, usually to the north or east of the monastery and only kings and queens, bishops and archbishops had the honour of burial inside the abbey. As for the use of the cemetery by laymen, this was not officially allowed until 1217, though the rule had been circumvented for decades. During the 1180s abbot Leonard of St Mary's, Dublin, angered local clergy by proclaiming the spiritual advantages that would accrue if one chose to die in the Cistercian habit and was buried in a Cistercian graveyard.[24] It was a cunning way of attracting patronage and, so long as the deceased had joined the Cistercian community before death, it was not contrary to the statutes. Just how successful abbot Leonard was is difficult to say, but in the west of Ireland many Gaelic lords followed his advice, retiring to die in their local Cistercian abbey.[25] When the General Chapter eventually changed the rule in 1217 and allowed monasteries to bury laymen, they added the proviso that local parish priests should acquiesce. In fact there were objections from Irish priests, for what was at stake was both status and the delicate matter of fees.[26] Where laymen were concerned, money was often linked to the question of burial. In the early thirteenth century a certain Alan Beg granted property to Graiguenamanagh and, after describing the land involved, the charter goes on to specify his place of interment.[27] It was as if Alan was purchasing his grave plot from the order.

240 Early thirteenth-century grave slab of an abbot at Boyle. The design with an arm and crosier was a standard Cistercian form.

Communities were particularly keen to acquire the bodies of their founders or other distinguished benefactors. In 1168 Donough O'Carroll, king of Uriel, was buried at Mellifont, the monastery he had founded twenty-six years before. Cathal Crovderg O'Conor, king of Connacht, 'a meek, devout pillar of faith and Christianity', was likewise laid to rest at Abbeyknockmoy,[28] a monastery which became a necropolis for the O'Conor family, just as Boyle did for the MacDermotts of Moylurg. Not every monastery could obtain the body of their founder, particularly if he had been responsible for establishing several houses, like Donal Mor O'Brien, king of Limerick. Dermot MacMurrough was buried at Ferns rather than Baltinglass and William Marshal, founder of Tintern and Graiguenamanagh, was interred in the Temple church in London. After 1195 a macabre dispute took place between the Cistercian monastery of Bective and the Augustinian abbey of St Thomas', Dublin, over which of them had the right to the body of the Anglo-Norman lord, Hugh de Lacy, who had been murdered at Durrow nine years earlier. In truth the feuding monks were more concerned about lands conferred to Bective along with his corpse, rather than the mortal remains of Hugh himself.[29] Once again, endowment and burial were closely entwined.

Many of the graves in a Cistercian chancel were those of bishops and archbishops, as permitted by statute. Thus in 1235 Felix O'Ruadan, archbishop of Tuam, was interred at the foot of the altar of St Mary's, Dublin, a place of honour he attained both as an archbishop and as a benefactor, having paid for the lead roofing of the church and the belfry.[30] Excavations near the altar at Mellifont uncovered the remains of an ecclesiastic holding a silver chalice, almost certainly a bishop.[31] According to Cistercian custom, abbots were buried in the chapter house, a practice known to have been followed in Ireland during the twelfth and thirteenth centuries.[32] This was probably the original location of the abbot's slab from Boyle. Decorated with an arm and crosier, it is a unique survivor in Ireland, although a standard design elsewhere (Pl. 240).[33] It

241 Kilcooly Abbey, memorial slab of abbot Philip O'Molwanayn who died in 1463 after performing 'many good works both spiritual and temporal'.

242 Jerpoint, effigy traditionally attributed to Bishop Felix O'Dullany, who died in 1202, though the carving appears to be somewhat later.

243 Jerpoint, effigy traditionally attributed to Bishop William of Cork who died in 1266/7. The style of the carving has similarities with the cloister sculptures (c1390–1400).

244 Mellifont Abbey, fragments from an ornate thirteenth-century tomb canopy.

belonged to a thirteenth-century abbot, but there is no inscription to identify him. At Jerpoint there is a fourteenth-century incised effigy of an abbot, but the drawing is coarse and the tomb is a poor specimen.[34] The finest memorial to an abbot belongs to Philip O'Molwanayn of Kilcooly, who died in 1463 (Pl. 241). Philip restored religious life in his monastery after its devastation in 1445 and his tomb is a worthy testimony of his achievement.[35] A simple stylised effigy of the abbot is carved in false relief, the main elements of the composition reduced to a few bold forms. It is a striking image, almost Romanesque in its abstract simplicity. The abbot is dressed in his liturgical vestments, and he holds a book and crosier, the latter with an enormous floriated crook. The upper third of the slab is filled by a shield, displaying the instruments of Christ's Passion, and around the periphery is a magnificently cut inscription in Gothic black lettering, which reads:

HIC JACET PHILIPP O MOLWANAYN QUONDAM ABBAS HUJUS LOCI CUM SUIS PARENTIBUS QUI PLURA OPERA BONA SPIRITUALIA (E)T TEMPORALIA FECERUNT QUORUM ANIMABUS PPICIETUR DEUS ANNO DOMINI MCCCCLXIII.

Here lies Philip O Molwanayn, formerly abbot of this house, together with his parents, who performed many good works both spiritual and temporal; on whose souls God have mercy A.D. 1463.

Episcopal tombs tend to be more impressive than those of the abbots. At Jerpoint there are two ecclesiastical effigies in full relief, one of which is traditionally said to be Felix O'Dullany, the first abbot of the house, who later went on to become bishop of Ossory.[36] The vestments are delicately carved, complete with attractive details like the fringes of the maniple and stole (Pl. 242). The attribution to Felix, however, is very dubious. He died in 1202, but the fine curves of the chasuble and the thin foliage along the edge of the slab are more in tune with a date of c1230–50. The other effigy is ascribed to Bishop William of Cork, who died in 1266/7.[37] Before his elevation to the see of Cork, he had been a monk at Jerpoint. Once again, however, there is doubt about the attribution. The figure is curiously broad in proportion and the drapery is carved in a few plain folds (Pl. 243). The flat sculptural technique and the broad formalised folds have a resemblance to the figures on the nearby cloister arcade of c1390–1400. As the head is tonsured and there is no mitre, we may be dealing with an abbot rather than a bishop.

From the thirteenth century the monks began to construct specially prepared tomb recesses in the north wall of the chancel for the burial of honoured benefactors.[38] At Grey and Inch the recesses are plain (and much rebuilt), but those installed in the presbyteries at Mellifont and Jerpoint were embellished with early Gothic ornament (Pl. 244).[39] In several abbeys the tombs have been removed, leaving only outlines on the wall.[40] A fifteenth-century tomb canopy at Abbeydorney, which has disintegrated in recent times, was covered by a sweeping ogee arch,

245 (top left)   Abbeydorney, ogee-headed tomb canopy in the chancel, now collapsed (drawing by Benjamin Woodward, 1874).

246 (top right)   Clare Island, fifteenth-century tomb canopy with traceried screen.

247 (centre)   Corcomroe, effigy of king Conor O'Brien, who died in 1268. His grandfather had founded the monastery seventy-four years earlier.

248 (right)   Abbeyknockmoy, tomb of Malachy O'Kelly (d. 1401), 'a truly hospitable and human man'. The design is a strange conglomeration of Romanesque and Gothic elements (Ledwich, *Antiquities of Ireland*, 1790).

249 (facing page top)   Abbeyknockmoy, St John's head on a plate at the apex of Malachy O'Kelly's tomb.

250 (facing page bottom)   Graiguenamanagh, sword-seizing effigy of c1300. Carved in heavy relief with great attention to detail, this is one of the finest medieval effigies in Ireland.

flanked by decorated pinnacles (Pl. 245). It was related to a group of such tombs in the Kerry and Limerick area. The most ambitious tomb canopy to be found in a Cistercian church is that on Clare Island, where a traceried screen was fitted beneath an ogee arch (Pl. 246). It is a simplified version of other tombs in the west, notably those at Strade (County Mayo) and in the church of St Nicholas, Galway (Pl. 104). The tracery patterns have been compared with French designs and described as 'Flamboyant', but whether they were really inspired by late Gothic tracery in France is open to doubt. Curvilinear designs were popular on English church furniture: a pattern similar to that at Strade was used on the fourteenth-century choir stalls at Lancaster.[41]

It is normally difficult to establish who was buried in these ornate tombs, but in a couple of instances there is some certainty. In 1268 Conor O'Brien, King of Thomond, was killed by his cousin at the battle of Siudaine and it is recorded that 'his body was honourably interred in the Monastery of East Burren [Corcomroe] by monks of that convent, who also raised a grand marble figure to his memory'. Conor had ruled over Thomond for twenty-six years, though in the later part of his reign 'he was filled with despondency and no longer cared to play the king'. The monastery of Corcomroe was founded by Conor's grandfather, seventy-four years earlier. An effigy of a king, attired in a shin length tunic, still remains in a gabled recess at the abbey (Pl. 247). The tomb fits the space perfectly and there is no reason to doubt that it is the monument of Conor O'Brien. It is a confident but gauche piece of carving by a mason who had little experience of figure sculpture. The king held a sceptre (now broken) in one hand and with the other he tugs at the cord of his mantle, a stylistic device used with finesse by thirteenth-century sculptors in France. As John Hunt observed, the effigy is copied from that of Felim O'Conor (d. 1265) at Roscommon, though the latter has considerably more fluency and poise.[42]

By the end of the thirteenth century, the isolation and provincialism of the monasteries of the west was already very marked. The abbots of Corcomroe were notorious for their non-attendance at the General Chapter and their knowledge of contemporary architecture and sculpture must have been slight. This artistic introspection is illustrated by a remarkable, but sadly delapidated, tomb in the north wall of the chancel at Abbeyknockmoy. Fortunately an engraving in Ledwich's *Antiquities of Ireland* (1790) shows the tomb still intact, revealing it to have been a strange conglomeration of Romanesque and Gothic elements (Pl. 248).[43] The main arch of the recess was decorated with Romanesque looking zigzags and the hood mould terminates in a Romanesque-style animal head. However, there are Gothic cusps on the inside of the arch and thick Gothic pinnacles either side. Finishing off this unusual design was a carving of St John's head, complete with the dish on which it was presented to Salome, a favourite devotional image of the late middle ages and one much favoured by English alabaster carvers (Pl. 249).[44] Above St John is a cross, made up of four equal arcs, looking like a piece of abandoned tracery.[45] The master mason responsible for the tomb made very little attempt to unite all the disparate features into anything approaching a uniform ensemble. Originally there was an inscribed stone at the base of the arch, which was taken out in 1853 for display at the Dublin Exhibition, an injudicious move which led to the collapse of the arch soon afterwards. The inscription, which is in Irish, indicates that the monument was erected for Malachy O'Kelly, king of Uí Maine, and Finnuola his wife. Malachy, 'a truly hospitable and human man', died in 1401, his wife two years later. Also mentioned in the inscription is Matthew O'Anly, the craftsman responsible for making this bizarre but well documented memorial.[46] An interest in the Celtic past is reflected in another tomb at Abbeyknockmoy, a magnificent fifteenth-century cross slab, decorated with interlace. A Gothic inscription records the name of Maurice O'Concannon. These memorials at Abbeyknockmoy provide a rare illustration of the Gaelic revival's effect on monumental sculpture.

There are many other secular tombs and grave slabs in the Irish abbeys which can only be mentioned briefly. Outstanding are two 'sword seizing' effigies of knights with crossed legs dating from c1300, one at Graiguenamanagh, the other at Grey (Pl. 250). Although both were carved in Ireland, using local stone, the lively and arresting images reflect a profound knowledge of contemporary English fashion.[47] Also at Grey is an effigy of a woman, carved in high relief, a stiff, solemn figure, attired in thickly cut robes. Tradition relates that this is Affreca, founder of the abbey, but the style suggests that the effigy belongs to the early fourteenth century, a hundred years after her death.[48] The burial of women in Cistercian abbeys was not uncommon. Devorgilla, wife of Tiernan O'Rourke, king of Breffny, died at Mellifont in 1193, and the daughter of Hugh de Lacy II was buried at Boyle in 1253.[49]

An impressive collection of medieval tombs is to be found at Jerpoint, where the monuments span a period of nearly three hundred years.[50] In addition to the ecclesiastical effigies already mentioned, there is a beautiful thirteenth-century slab, engraved with a pair of knights, the so-called 'Brothers' (Pl. 251). It is one of the finest pieces of drawing from medieval Ireland, a composition full of sensitive movement and subtle contrasts. Not far away there is a less sophisticated slab of a layman named Thomas, depicted in civilian dress, with a long coat and (?)trousers. Several elaborate tombs date from shortly before the Reformation, showing that the abbey was then still a focal point of religious life. Two funerary chests, only partially complete, are decorated with apostles, characteristic work of the O'Tunney atelier (Pl. 252). This prolific sixteenth-century workshop also carved the famous effigy of a harper and his wife, presumably a musician of some renown to warrant such an expensive memorial. Another work of the O'Tunneys is to be found at Kilcooly, in the form of a huge mensa tomb, commemorating Piers Fitzjames Oge Butler, who died in 1526. The effigy, clad in a typical Irish mixture of mail and plate armour, is one of the masterpieces of Irish funerary sculpture (Pl. 253). William Cantwell, lord of Ballintogher and Clogharily, who died two years after Piers Fitzjames, was also buried in the chancel at Kilcooly. The elaborate funerary monuments, favoured by the sixteenth-century nobility of Ormond, are thus well represented in the Cistercian abbeys. In fact the only relic of Abbeyleix, which has otherwise vanished from the landscape, is another characteristic Ormond effigy. Made in 1502, it commemorates Malachy O'More, lord of Leix.[51]

Out of all these monuments, the abbot's slab from Boyle remains the only one with a specifically Cistercian character. Otherwise the tombs reflect the general fashions prevailing in

251 Jerpoint Abbey, engraved slab of the so-called 'Brothers'. The difference in head defences is one of many contrasts in this delicate and subtle drawing.

252 Jerpoint Abbey, figures of Saints Matthias and Thaddeus from an early sixteenth-century tomb chest by the O'Tunney workshop.
253 (above right) Kilcooly, the hugh mensa tomb of Piers Fitzjames Oge Butler (d. 1526), surrounded by apostles, a product of the O'Tunney workshop.

medieval Ireland. The fact that layfolk of both middle and upper ranks opted for Cistercian burial may reflect the lowly status of parish churches which, outside the south and east of the country, never attracted the endowment and support they did in England. Even the strict Cistercian rules about the location of burials collapsed in the thirteenth century and imposing monuments came to be scattered about the presbytery and transepts, as in any other church of the time. The temptation to bury the rich proved irresistible.[52]

Floor tiles

Decorated pavements were among the most attractive innovations in thirteenth-century architecture. Compared with floors made of beaten earth, rough mortar or stone flags,[53] glazed tiles added a note of luxury and colour, which ecclesiastical patrons found hard to resist. The Cistercians eventually became enthusiastic clients of the new fashion. A medieval tiled floor, with its infinite variations of colour and texture, can be extraordinarily beautiful, quite unlike its monotonous Victorian counterpart. Differences in the content of the clay, impurities in the glazes, variations in the heat of the kiln and the length of firing, all helped to provide tiny modulations which made the medieval tile so different from the machine-made products of more modern times.

The early history of tiled flooring is still far from clear. It is assumed that the technique spread to England and Ireland from the continent and tiles were certainly being employed in French Cistercian houses before the close of the twelfth century.[54] At first, the attitude of the Cistercian authorities to the new technique was ambivalent. The smooth, tidy appearance of a tiled floor was a distinct improvement but there were dangers of extravagance and frivolity. Decorated pavements had been scathingly denounced by St Bernard in his *Apologia*: 'Should we not at least reverence the images of saints, with which the very paving that is trodden underfoot abounds? Often the face of an angel is spat upon or the visage of some saint is scuffed by the feet of passers-by.'[55] St Bernard probably had mosaic floors in mind, but his warning was clear enough. In 1205 the argument surfaced at the General Chapter, when the abbot of Pontigny was ordered to remove or alter a pavement which had recently been laid. Five years later a monk of Beaubec was accused of making floors which exhibited 'too much levity and curiosity' and his abbot was required to do three days' penance for allowing the transgression.[56]

Even in the more prosperous houses of Europe, tiles were not usually employed throughout the monastery. The church was the main priority, particularly the presbytery and adjoining chapels. At Graiguenamanagh the whole church was evidently paved with tiles, an extravagance restricted to the wealthier abbeys. Occasionally, claustral buildings were tiled and the chapter house at Dunbrody is known to have had them. In England one of the finest thirteenth-century pavements comes from the refectory at Cleeve and it is possible that some of the Irish refectories were similarly treated, though excavation is needed to confirm this.

Tiles of various types were being manufactured in England and Wales by the 1230s and they have been recovered from fifty-three of the seventy-eight Cistercian monasteries there.[57] Mosaic tiles were used extensively in the northern abbeys of Rievaulx, Byland and Meaux and it is recorded that Fountains had a 'pictim pavimentum' before 1247.[58] In the south and west the most popular tile was the two-coloured form, in which a thin slip of white clay was inlaid into the red base to form a contrasting pattern. This type was introduced to Ireland, probably in the 1230s, and it was used extensively in cathedrals, monasteries and parish churches. Other techniques followed, most significant being the line impressed tile, whereby a design was stamped on the surface of the clay.[59] The pattern was deeply incised and tended to survive better than those inlaid. By altering the glazes, a variety of different colours was produced. The line impressed tiles at Mellifont were manufactured in particularly telling shades, various greens and yellows, a rich orange and a deep chocolate brown. This type of tile was used in Ireland during the first half of the fourteenth century and it achieved its greatest popularity in the fifteenth.

The beauty of a tiled pavement rests on three factors: the colour of the tile, its pattern, and the overall layout. The latter was crucial, for by skilful juxtaposition of different coloured tiles, medieval paviours could produce striking patterns across the floor of a church. In the north transept at Graiguenamanagh, for example, alternating rows of black and white (or two-coloured) tiles were laid in bold zigzags (Pl. 254).[60] Much of the skill of the paviour was reflected in his choice of overall pattern and it is disappointing that so few are known. Here antiquarians and early archaeologists are much to blame. Until recent times, medieval pavements were not regarded seriously and even when found *in situ*, it was customary to gather up the tiles without noting the complete design.[61] The floors at Mellifont and St Mary's,

254 Graiguenamanagh, excavations in the north transept in 1977 uncovered part of the thirteenth-century tiled floor. Note the zigzag pattern created by alternating dark tiles with inlaid or two coloured ones.

Fig. 57   Mellifont: inlaid tiles.

Fig. 58   (above right)   Mellifont: line impressed tiles.

Fig. 59   Mellifont: line impressed tiles.

Dublin, were both vandalised in this way during the 1880s. Apart from Graiguenamanagh only one other Irish pavement has been recorded intact, the fourteenth-century example in the archbishop of Dublin's residence at Swords Castle.[62]

The tiles excavated at Graiguenamanagh were among the earliest in Ireland and it is likely that they were laid around 1250, soon after the completion of the building.[63] Inlaid tiles with simple foliate and geometrical designs were used along with plain coloured tiles. Only two animal patterns (a lion and a pair of affronted birds) were found and the general sobriety of the floor was well in accord with the dictates of the order. As a daughter house of Stanley (Wiltshire), Graiguenamanagh was no doubt quick to hear of the tiled floors of Wessex, a region noted for its prolific tile making in the thirteenth century.

Two-coloured tiles were also used at Mellifont, probably in conjunction with the mid-thirteenth century remodelling of the presbytery and north transept.[64] Six patterns have been recovered, four with characteristic foliage and floral motifs, the other two with animals (Fig. 57). One of the animal tiles portraying a griffon within a circle is outstanding, and the forceful way the feet and wings burst through the circular frame is especially dramatic. This is one of the finest tiles to be discovered in Ireland and the other animal tile, depicting a lion, is feeble in comparison. Animal roundels were a favourite motif of English west country paviours and the lion and griffon both appear on the floors of Henry III's palace at Clarendon.[65]

Most of the tiles found at Mellifont were line-impressed, suggesting that new floors were laid in the church, perhaps as early as the mid-fourteenth century. Thirteen different designs were used, some of which formed part of nine tile units; others could be combined to make continuous circular patterns (Figs 58, 59). There is nothing intrinsically Irish about these designs and three of them (including one depicting a lion rampant) reappear at Norton Priory (Cheshire), giving rise to suggestions of a Cheshire/Irish 'school'.[66]

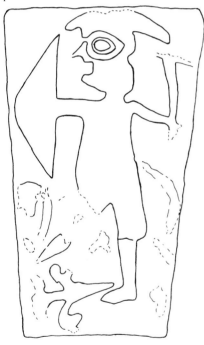

Fig. 60 Baltinglass, tile from a large circular pattern.

Tiles have so far been recovered from eight Irish houses,[67] and these include a number of interesting examples from Baltinglass. Here, some of the tiles were shaped like voussoirs so as to fit together in radial patterns, a technique used in the magnificent floor of the King's Chapel at Clarendon (c1244). One of the designs, depicting a warrior thrusting forward with a circular shield (Fig. 60), is curiously reminiscent of an armed figure on the shrine of the Stowe Missal (1045–52), which might imply some awareness of earlier Irish art on the part of the tile-maker. However, not dissimilar figures appear at Halesowen Abbey (Worcestershire), so it may have been a stock motif.[68] Great roundels were a feature of the tiled pavement at Christ Church Cathedral, Dublin, where one of the circles was made up of a sequence of foxes disguised as pilgrims.

As the Beaubec incident reveals, there were occasions when Cistercian monks manufactured and laid tiles themselves. The monk of Beaubec also worked for clients outside the order and clearly he was something of a professional paviour. It has been suggested that laybrothers made tiles in England, but there is no evidence of such activity in Ireland.[69] There is nothing specifically Cistercian about the tiles, nor is there all that much repetition of design amongst the Cistercian abbeys. This indicates that the floors were not laid by monastic craftsmen moving from one house to another and were the work of secular craftsmen, recruited specially for the task. The team employed at Graiguenamanagh were almost certainly professionals, probably from Dublin.[70]

To minimise the cost of transport, the tiles were either baked on site or as near the clay beds as possible. There is plenty of evidence from English abbeys to show that the tiles were made beside the monastery,[71] but no kiln has yet come to light in Ireland. As Elizabeth Eames has pointed out, the medieval tiler was a mobile craftsman moving from site to site, taking his stamps and patterns with him.[72] Local clay deposits were exploited and kilns were constructed where the tiles were needed. It is possible that some tiles were exported from Bristol or Chester, but there is no documentary confirmation of such a trade.[73]

The cost of laying tiles was considerable and their popularity in Anglo-Norman Ireland is a measure of the prosperity of the colony between 1250 and 1320. Depending on the quality, the price of tiles varied from six to ten shillings per thousand. The sacrist rolls of Ely, for example, record the purchase at Lynn of 10,000 tiles in 1345–6 at a price of seven shillings per thousand, and this gives some idea of the quantity of tiles required for a medieval church.[74] Approximately 83,000 would have been needed to cover the floor at Mellifont and, on the basis of the rate charged at Lynn, the cost would have amounted to £29.[75] If the tiles were made on site, there might be an additional charge for digging and transporting the clay.[76] There was also the cost of actually laying the tiles, assessed at the rate of two to three shillings per thousand.[77] Tiles were therefore a luxury and it is no surprise that many Irish houses could not afford them. Thomas Fanning has shown that their use was confined to the monasteries of Leinster and their distribution is closely associated with the pattern of Anglo-Norman settlement.[78] None has been found west of the Shannon, not even in the monastery at Boyle. More than any other architectural feature, they were a sharp indication of economic status and English artistic affiliations.

Mural painting

The interior walls of Cistercian churches were normally coated in white plaster and it was customary to mark out false masonry joints, sometimes in red paint, to give the impression of ashlar stonework.[79] To modern eyes this seems horrendously *kitsch*, destroying the simple purity of the white surfaces. The practice is well-attested in France and England and there is no reason to suppose that it was not widespread in Ireland (traces have been found at Grey and Graiguenamanagh).[80] From an early date, some abbeys began to accentuate architectural features in colour. Westropp noticed deep crimson and blue in the chapter house at Mellifont, and red can still be seen on the stones of the lavabo.[81] Similar colours can be detected on the east windows at Corcomroe and Westropp remarked that 'there were traces of fresco painting in the groining (of the chancel) red, black, drab, and perhaps green' when he first saw the abbey in 1878.[82] Although the statutes forbade painting and sculpture, such ornamental work did not constitute an infringement of the rules.

As the monks were drawn closer into local society and the severity of the rules relaxed, paint was used more frequently to brighten up the architecture. Four large coats of arms in red and yellow were painted on the north wall of the presbytery at Jerpoint in the fifteenth century, no doubt to commemorate benefactors of the abbey. More elaborate mural painting survives at Holycross, Abbeyknockmoy and Clare Island.

A hunting scene is depicted along two walls of the north transept at Holycross.[83] It begins on the west wall with a group of hunters, two of them wielding bows and arrows, a third blowing a horn and restraining a hound (Pl. 255, Fig. 61). The hornblower is dressed in a hooded cape and wears a pleated skirt, like one of the corbel figures in the Jerpoint cloister. Their prey is shown around the corner on the north wall—a stag crouching behind a stereotyped oak tree. The layout of the scene is disconcertingly arbitrary. There is no surrounding frame and the paintings straggle along the walls for almost fifteen feet. By European standards the drawing is naive, but there is a certain narrative vitality in the way one archer prepares to shoot and the dog strains at the leash. Gay colours once compensated for the lack of sophistication in the drawing, but the paintings are now no more than faded outlines. The rustic verve of the figures recalls the dancers on a sixteenth-century whalebone plaque from Donabate (County Dublin) in the National Museum of Ireland and the Holycross paintings likewise may belong to the period after 1500. A

Fig. 61   Holycross, drawing of the paintings on the west wall of the north transept.

255 Holycross, the much decayed hunting scene on the west wall of the north transept.

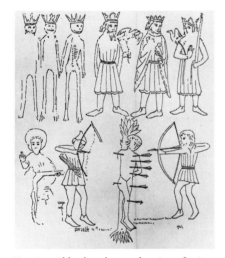

Fig. 62 Abbeyknockmoy, drawing of paintings on the north wall of presbytery.

large and prominent hunting episode seems out of place on the walls of a Cistercian church. It might be interpreted as the conversion of St Eustace, but if so the cross which Placidus saw in the antlers of the stag has vanished completely. It is better to treat it at face value as a piece of secular painting. Hunting was a favourite medieval subject, which occurred elsewhere in a Cistercian context. The nave of Hailes Abbey (Gloucestershire) was embellished with a similar scene and a spectacular stag hunt was depicted on a group of inlaid tiles from the Welsh abbey of Neath (Pl. 256).[84] Donatus O'Kelly, a monk from Monasterevin, also had hunting on his mind when he added a drawing of a stag assailed by arrows to one of the margins of the ordinal he was transcribing for his abbey in 1501.[85] Hunting and shooting were not as far removed from the cloister as one might think. In 1291, the abbot of St Mary's, Dublin, was accused of hunting illegally in the royal forest of Glencree, and in 1460 a monk of Graiguenamanagh suffered the embarrassment of accidently killing a boy, when practising archery in the precincts of the monastery.[86]

The paintings on the north wall of the chancel at Abbeyknockmoy were more characteristic of Gothic religious art.[87] They are now so utterly decayed that they can only be interpreted with the aid of eighteenth- and nineteenth-century drawings (Fig. 62). Within the arch which covers the tomb of Malachy O'Kelly, lord of Uí Maine (d. 1401), and his wife Fionnuola (d. 1403), was a crucifixion with four attendant figures. In England this was a common way of decorating such recesses and a well-preserved example remains in the parish church at Turvey (Bedfordshire). The wall to the east of the O'Kelly tomb was divided into two registers. The upper one contained a *memento mori*, the encounter of the three living with the three skeletons of

256 Inlaid tiles from Neath Abbey (West Glamorgan), showing the popularity of hunting scenes in Cistercian decorative art.

the dead. The living were dressed as kings, arranged in fine robes, each with a hawk. Below the three spectres was a characteristic inscription in Gothic black lettering: 'FUIMUS UT ESTIS VOS ERITIS UT SUMUS NOS. (We have been as you are, you shall be as we are)'. In the register below was an image of the Trinity and beside it the martyrdom of St Sebastian.[88] Following standard iconographical procedure, Sebastian is bound to a tree and pierced with arrows, while alongside two archers draw their bows. The subjects chosen by the monks of Abbeyknockmoy were amongst the most popular in late Gothic painting: the three living and three dead, a macabre reminder of impending judgement, and Sebastian, a saint frequently invoked against the plague. It is impossible to make any assessment of the paintings in terms of style and quality. The colour had largely disappeared by the eighteenth century, though in 1917 Crawford discerned traces of green, brown and yellow. The question of date is equally elusive. The crucifixion may belong with the tomb, c1403, but a date of c1500 has recently been suggested for the other paintings.[89] In a country where so few medieval churches are preserved intact, the decoration at Abbeyknockmoy provides the best illustration of what must have been a fairly typical scheme of late Gothic mural painting.

The chancel of the small daughter house of Abbeyknockmoy, situated on Clare Island, was once covered with paintwork, substantial patches of which remain on the surfaces of the vault.[90] The colours are still bright and visible—slate blue, crimson red, chocolate brown and golden yellow. Unfortunately, the plaster on which the paint is laid is gradually disintegrating and falling away. The painters attempted a remarkable piece of *trompe d'oeil*. Although built with a simple semi-circular barrel vault, the observer was tricked into believing that the chancel was covered with four bays of quadripartite rib vaulting. The artists added false mortar joints between the stones and painted corbels on the walls to support the pseudo ribbing. The form of the ribs was copied almost exactly from the genuine examples at Abbeyknockmoy (Pl. 117). Even the slate colour repeats the blue tones of the local carboniferous limestone. Illusionist tricks were of course a feature of Italian painting of the time, but one does not expect to encounter them in a remote outpost of County Mayo. Adding ribs in paint was far cheaper than carving them in stone and it is tempting to believe that other Irish barrel vaults, at Jerpoint and Kilcooly, were painted in similar fashion.

The space between the ribs at Clare Island was filled with a menagerie of man and beast; dragons and monsters spitting fire, greyhounds, mounted riders, a herdsman with cattle and goats, a harper in long yellow robes, a stag with a wolf savaging its throat, a cockerell, birds and rabbits (Pl. 257). The only items of explicit Christian significance are an angel with the scales of the Last Judgement and possibly a pelican. The animals and figures are consistently aligned each side of the central axis, but otherwise there is little co-ordination or logic in the composition. Each element appears to have been added one by one, regardless of the context. Some of the vignettes are vigorously drawn, with sweeping curves and strong rhythms, but this does not disguise the rustic flavour of the whole. The choice of subjects confirms this provincial Gaelic identity: the harper, the stag and the mounted rider are all themes which had appeared long before in Irish art. Whereas the painters of Abbeyknockmoy reproduced standard Gothic imagery, those at Clare Island drew on a range of local motifs. Beneath parts of the plaster, Westropp detected an earlier scheme of decoration, which suggested that the existing work belonged to a late stage in the church's history. The paintings in this bleak and lonely setting are unlikely to predate the sixteenth century.[91]

257 Clare Island, detail of paintings on the vault. The figure carries a spear and (?)cross-bow.

Manuscript illumination

The rapid expansion of the Cistercian order in the twelfth century called for the production of books on a prodigious scale.[92] Just as each new monastery required a number of basic buildings, so it needed a group of basic texts—a missal, gradual, antiphonary, psalter, hymnale, lectionary, as well as copies of the *liber usuum* and the Benedictine Rule. Scribes must have been hard at work throughout the second half of the twelfth century to meet the demands and many members of each community must have been qualified at the task. Unfortunately we cannot be

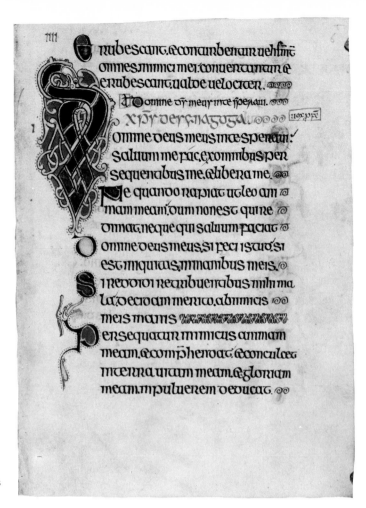

258 Cormac's Psalter, decorated initials (British Library, Add. Ms. 36.929).

sure where in the monastery the scribes worked. It is known that the cloister was sometimes used and there is a vivid tale from Fountains of a monk laying out freshly inscribed parchment in the cloister walk to dry. A separate scriptorium existed in at least one Irish house by 1228,[93] but in small monasteries it is likely that the calefactory or the dorter undercroft was put to use as a writing room during cold and windy weather. Another matter which is hard to resolve is the question of whether the Cistercians acquired the traditional Irish calligraphic skills and decorative flair. It would be interesting to know how many scribes, trained in the old school, joined the new communities. Unfortunately illuminated manuscripts from Cistercian houses are so rare that it is difficult to judge the extent of the continuity.

There is however one attractive Cistercian book, decorated in a characteristic Irish manner. It is a small psalter, now in the British Library (Additional Ms. 36.929), written by Cormac the scribe.[94] Folio 59r carries a colophon with an earnest request from the artist for prayers: 'Cormacus scripsit hoc psalterium ora pro eo. Qui legis hec ora pro sese quelibet hora.' Cormac was an outstanding craftsman, with an excellent Irish majuscule. The text is alive with richly coloured ornament and each psalm begins with an elaborate zoomorphic initial (Pls 258, 259). These normally consist of a large twisting beast, enveloped in tendrils, and the whole design is set against a scarlet background. Those that introduce the three fifties are especially magnificent, with a mesh of coils, ending in beast heads, foliage and tiny human faces. The first letter of every verse is also decorated, either by a simple coloured background or by being transformed into a springy, elongated beast. Outlines are stressed by red dots, a device which adds sparkle to the letters and one that had been used by Irish artists almost continuously for five hundred years. Stylised animals appear at the foot of the page or at the end of the psalm and, like all the ornaments, they are executed in vivid colours—mauve, red, green, yellow and sky blue. The decoration was not finished, for at the start of each of the fifties are elaborate frames designed for miniatures. Prayers were subsequently inserted into the first of the vacant spaces. The style of the

259 Cormac's Psalter, introductory page to the first fifty psalms. Note the tiny faces hidden in the scrolls, akin to those on a capital at Boyle, Pl. 196. (British Library, Add. Ms. 36.929.)

decoration is related to two books of hymns of c1100, but the late Mlle Henry and Genevieve Marsh-Micheli have shown that Cormac's Psalter is at least half a century later.

The joyful colour and vitality of Cormac's Psalter seems at odds with the austere atmosphere of a Cistercian monastery. It contradicts an oft-quoted Cistercian statute that insisted that initials should be of one colour,[95] and it displays all the *levitas* that St Bernard so roundly condemned in his *Apologia*. It is possible that the Psalter was made outside the order and subsequently presented to a Cistercian house, particularly as the clearest mark of its Cistercian origin, a sacramental absolution headed 'absolutio bernarddi' (*sic*), was added to the unfilled frame on folio 1v. However, this point is not conclusive. The colophon of Cormac is neatly fitted into lines of musical notation, which have Cistercian affiliations. Moreover, textual experts have pointed out a number of French ingredients in the Psalter, which are best explained by a Cistercian provenance. Extravagant painting was not exceptional within the order. The rule against multi-coloured initials is now known to be later than once thought, 1145–51 rather than 1134, and it was not very effective in its impact.[96] During the twelfth century sumptuous manuscripts emerged from the scriptoria at both Cîteaux and Clairvaux and, although Cormac's psalter postdated the rule about initials, its exuberant decoration was far from unique.[97] It appears, therefore, that Cormac was a Cistercian scribe, trained in the finest tradition of Irish illumination, representing at least one case of continuity between Celtic and Cistercian monasticism.[98]

The Psalter implies that indigenous art had more impact on manuscript painting than it did on the carved decoration of the abbeys. The designs concerned are not found in Cistercian sculpture, except in an isolated instance at Boyle. Here the capital of c1215–20, embellished with tiny faces peering out between leaves, is not unlike initials in the manuscript (Pl. 198). In any attempt to pinpoint the monastery where Cormac worked, Boyle must be included among the candidates.

During the thirteenth century there is evidence of the employment of professional scribes. Such was Diarmid O'Culechain, who wrote a missal for Abbeyknockmoy, and Donnchadh Mor O'Dalaigh, who was buried at Boyle in 1244.[99] But we have to wait three centuries for another extant Cistercian manuscript with decoration. This is an Ordinal, written in 1501 by Donatus O'Kelly, a monk from Monasterevin (Oxford, Bodleian Library, Rawlinson Ms C32).[100] A colophon on folio 65v explains that it was made on the instructions of Abbot Thomas MacCostelloe, and that it was written in the monastery at Mellifont. Donatus presumably went to Mellifont to make use of an exemplar in the library there. The Ordinal shows that some religious energy was still left at Monasterevin and that relations between the Irish abbeys was not quite as desperate as John Troy of Mellifont had argued in his morbid letter to Citeaux three years before.

Donatus O'Kelly decorated his Ordinal with amusing marginalia—faces, pointing fingers, a bag piper, two horn blowers, a four legged sea monster swallowing a fish, a kneeling abbot and warrior wearing a fine crested helm (Pl 260a,b). There is plenty of *joie de vivre*, but not much artistic skill. His colours are straightforward—browny-yellow, pink and green. Although some faces have a traditional Kells-style profile, the general idiom is Gothic rather than Gaelic. There is no sign of the brightly coloured initials and zoomorphic interlace that characterise Gaelic revival manuscripts, such as the Book of Ballymote or the Leabhar Breac. As a scribe and craftsman, Donatus was far inferior to his twelfth-century predecessor Cormac. Like the wall paintings at Holycross and Clare Island, his anecdotal style reveals a loss of direction. There is nothing Cistercian about them nor anything particularly Christian for that matter.

One remarkable book that found its way into a Cistercian monastery was the Bective Hours, a mid-fourteenth-century manuscript of the so-called East Anglian school.[101] As well as calendar scenes, there are thirteen miniatures and a rich display of decorated initials and ornamental borders. The illuminations include an elaborate Annunciation and several fine

260 The Monasterevin Ordinal, marginalia by Donatus O'Kelly (Bodleian Library, Ms. Rawlinson C32): (a) an Irish piper; (b) an abbot and a (?)queen.

261 The Bective Hours, fol. 84r, showing the Entombment of Christ (Trinity College, Dublin, Ms. 94).

paintings devoted to the Passion. As William O'Sullivan has pointed out, the manuscript is an odd thing to find in a Cistercian monastery. Books of Hours were usually produced for the private devotions of lay people, so presumably this was the private property of one of the monks. How it got to Bective is not known, but it does indicate one of the ways in which English religious images and decorative motifs came to the attention of Irish artists.

Metalwork, wood carving and monastic seals

The Cistercians are not usually associated with the production of fine metalwork. The regulations which proscribed the use of gold and silver meant that in the early years the order had little use for the arts of the goldsmith.[102] It is no surprise that, in contrast to the early Irish monasteries, the Cistercians did not develop their own ateliers, and, as argued above, their lack of interest in costly ornament helped to destroy the ancient traditions of Irish metalworking. In their early years many communities struggled to survive, so the rigours of the statutes were reinforced by the strains of poverty. But as the monasteries grew in affluence, the lure of gold and silver became irresistible and by the Reformation most abbeys had built up a range of fine chattels, which were eagerly seized by royal officials in 1540–1. The chalices, crosses, censers and statues found in the average Cistercian church were probably not much different from those in other religious houses. Most items were acquired through gifts or purchase, and there was nothing particularly Cistercian about them.

262   Silver chalice, only 80 mm high, found in a grave at Mellifont.

As early as 1157 Mellifont received pieces of gold as well as a golden chalice from its benefactors.[103] In 1524 the abbot of Graiguenamanagh gave his monastery 'a silver cross, gilded and decorated with gems' and other abbeys are known to have had similar crosses.[104] In 1413 the abbot of Tintern in Wales, fearing that Tintern (Wexford) 'might be laid waste and destroyed by rebels' sent a servant there to bring back for safe keeping a silver-gilt cross.[105] To warrant such a journey, this was obviously an object of some value. Under the year 1312, the annals describe the setting up of 'a holy cross' in the abbey of Boyle, though what exactly this was is not made clear.[106] In the panic that preceded the dissolution, the abbot of St Mary's, Dublin, sent Thomas Cromwell a great pyx worth £20, a fruitless bribe intended to save the monastery from its impending demise.[107] Some houses must have amassed extensive relics, not least Mellifont, which had been founded on the initiative of St Malachy, a figure much revered in the order as a whole. Other abbeys had relics of Malachy and it is known that Mellifont had its own collection of venerated items.

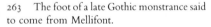

263   The foot of a late Gothic monstrance said to come from Mellifont.

A vivid picture of the precious belongings of a Cistercian house is provided by an inventory drawn up in 1396 by the Yorkshire abbey of Meaux.[108] The revenues of Meaux (£298 in 1539) were less than those of Mellifont and St Mary's Dublin, and the items listed indicate the type of objects to be expected in the wealthier Irish houses. In the sacristy there was a large gilded silver cross, an ivory carving of the Virgin Mary with two attendant angels, a crystal urn with diverse relics, and a variety of other reliquaries, including a green velvet purse containing the belt of St Malachy. There were two silver crosiers, two silver thuribles, a large gold chalice and a further eighteen chalices for the various altars. In the church itself, there were painted panels and statues at the high altar, four iron candelabra and a 'candelabrum electrinum' hanging in the middle of the choir. There was a large organ at the west end of the church, a small organ in the choir, and a clock that rang out the hours of the day. The abbey also possessed a magnificent range of vestments and altar cloths. Equally splendid was the domestic silverware in the abbot's lodgings. Three gilded silver cups (all given by benefactors of the abbey), silver jars and water jugs, a set of six silver goblets, a silver 'spyceplate', a silver salt-cellar and even a silver chain for the seal of the abbot. Compared with the valuables of a great Benedictine house, like Christ Church Canterbury or St Etheldreda's Ely, the collection at Meaux was modest, but the inventory reminds us that Cistercian churches were not as bare as one is sometimes led to believe. By 1235 the treasures and vestments at Boyle were extensive enough to attract an armed robbery and by 1228 at least one Irish house already had a fine collection of silver goblets.[109]

When the Irish monasteries were dissolved between 1536 and 1541, their goods and chattels

264 The Sheephouse cross, one of a number of liturgical objects discovered in 1899, which may have come from Mellifont, two miles away.

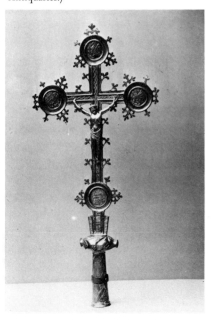

265 Processional cross of similar type to that found at Sheephouse. (London, Society of Antiquaries.)

were sold off by the royal commissioners. The documents speak of diverse pieces of silver and gold, jewels, pictures, images, relics, bells, furniture, ornaments and drinking vessels.[110] In an emotional passage Malachy Hartry described the losses at Holycross: 'Why should I speak of the fifteen silver-gilt chalices, of the precious and varied ornaments of the church, made of gold, silver and silk stuffs, and other things of the same kind? The spoilers' hands profaned these and scattered them not among the poor but among the rich. . . .'[111] The sale at St Mary's, Dublin, yielded the prodigious sum of £192.1.2½, Mellifont produced £141.7.3, and Bective £108.3.0, but in most other houses the profits were in the range of £10–£20.[112] In many cases the monks must have hidden or sold their possessions before the commissioners arrived, and at Bective we hear of 'certain goods and chattels carried off by the late abbot', worth *in toto* £35.11.0. The sale of two silver crosses, one from Kilcooly and the other from Inislounaght, fetched £3.7.6. Apart from reusable things such as eating and drinking utensils, most objects were probably sold for melting down. Bells were a problem and the market response was poor. Many were left without buyers, including two from St Mary's, Dublin, 'one of greater, the other of less weight'. Bells did not readily lend themselves to alternative uses and they were awkward objects to melt down or transport.

The efficiency of the royal agents in 1540–1 was such that we are left with only a few dismal remnants of Cistercian metalwork. Even in the Gaelic west, where the monasteries were outside royal control, no items of any quality have survived. What remains probably gives a very misleading impression. From Baltinglass comes a bronze crucifix figure in the Romanesque style.[113] Although the angular pose has some expressive force, the workmanship is poor and, if it belonged to the abbey, it is hard to believe it occupied a place of any significance. There are several better quality objects associated with Mellifont. In the 1880s an attractive Gothic ring was found in a grave in the chancel and this is now a treasured possession of the monks of new Mellifont.[114] During the 1953–4 excavations a further grave in the choir yielded a tiny silver chalice and paten, the plain but well modelled chalice being a mere 80 mm high (Pl. 262).[115] It can be compared with a number of English thirteenth-century chalices and may be an import. A similar chalice was found in the tomb of Richard de Carew, bishop of St Davids in Wales, who died in 1280. Also from Mellifont is the foot of a late Gothic monstrance, made of bronze (Pl. 263). The hexagonal base has compartments alternately engraved with the monograms IHC and XPC in Gothic black lettering. The main stem is decorated with pieces of twisted wire, detached from the background like miniature columns. There are two knops, the upper one typically late Gothic, with six lozenge shaped settings occupied by foliage motifs. Judged by European standards, the quality is no better than average.

In 1899, a small hoard of liturgical objects was discovered in a quarry at Sheephouse, two miles from Mellifont.[116] The hoard consisted of a late Gothic processional cross, a pricket candlestick and a tiny bell. It is tempting to believe that the objects once belonged to the abbey and were concealed at the time of the dissolution to avoid confiscation. Alternatively, they may have been taken from the monastery some years before. In 1495, the monks complained to the archbishop of Armagh about lay encroachment, speaking of local lords who 'retain and conceal the books, the jewels [ornaments] and other goods and property of the said monastery of Mellifont which had been lent them, for their use or given to them to hold as a pledge. . . .'[117] All the items were made of gilded bronze. The floriated cross, which is 65 cm high, is a standard type, mass-produced in the fifteenth century (Pl. 264). The arms terminate in circular medallions, filled with symbols of the evangelists. The cross itself is decorated with an ornamental band of lozenges, and the base is engraved with interlacing ribbons. The figure of Christ, wearing the crown of thorns, is well modelled, though it lacks the expressive power of the figure from Lislaughtin, Ireland's finest Gothic cross. At the base of the shaft are two empty sockets, designed to take figures of the Virgin Mary and St John. It is difficult to decide where the Sheephouse cross was made. It belongs to a group of almost identical crosses, found in both Ireland and England, which were routine products of a large workshop c1450–1500 (Pl. 265).[118]

Now restored to the church of Holycross is the shrine of the relic of the True Cross.[119] This

consists of a silver case (19.5 × 8.2 cm) enclosing a double armed cross of wood. The relic itself, a thin wooden slip, was attached to the double armed cross, but it vanished from the shrine sometime between 1807 and 1888. The late medieval silver case is embossed with a figure of Christ enthroned as judge, the four evangelist symbols, a crucifixion and an image of the Madonna and child. The style is rudimentary and much inferior to the quality of stone sculpture at the abbey. If this was the major shrine, it is difficult to understand why more attention was not lavished on it.

The design of a reliquary was a unique operation, in contrast to the manufacture of more routine liturgical objects. In general the Cistercians acquired their metalwork on the open market, which helps to explain the lack of Irish features. Many items were imported from abroad and this is probably true of the only wooden sculpture to survive, the life-size oak Madonna from St Mary's, Dublin, now preserved in the Carmelite Church in Whitefriar Street (Pl. 266). It has been venerated by the faithful for centuries but almost ignored by art historians.[120] As so little wooden imagery survived the iconoclastic onslaughts of 1547–53, this is a remarkable carving. It is a work of considerable beauty, with a well-expressed contrast between the thoughtful dignity of the Virgin and the playful activity of the Christ child stretched out across her waist. The face of the Madonna is cut incisively, her eyes narrow and refined. The pose of the child, with a knee bent prominently and the sole of one foot held in his mother's hand, was much favoured by German sculptors like Michael Erhart in the years between 1480 and 1500.[121] The young Christ holds a pomegranate, one of the conventional symbols of the Resurrection. The modelling of the Virgin's face, its ovoid shape and the long wavy hair parted in the centre, are characteristic of pre-Reformation carving; so too are the thick folds of drapery. These details can be paralleled on carvings from the lower Rhineland, which is a likely provenance for the Dublin figure. We have, however, lost so much English sculpture of the period that the possibility of an English origin should not be excluded. Indeed, the arrangement of the robes, with a series of angular 'box' folds in the centre, can be matched on a number of late medieval sculptures in England. There are parallels with the figure of St Edmund in Henry VII's Chapel at Westminster (1503–19) (Pl. 267),[122] as well as with figures on the west facade of Exeter Cathedral (upper tier of image screen c1500).[123] All this suggests that the Dublin statue was carved about 1500–20 and whether by an English or continental workshop, it has a thoroughly cosmopolitan flavour, which shows that the art of the Pale was not isolated from the mainstreams of European art. Incidently, 1520 was the year in which the churchwardens of the parish church of St Werburgh's Dublin paid for an image of St Martin. It cost a total of twenty-four shillings, ten shillings for the carving itself and fourteen for the pedestal to support it.[124] The Madonna from St Mary's is large and is likely to have cost considerably more.[125] It was originally painted, with much blue and gold, but all trace of the polychrome vanished when the statue was cleaned and scraped in 1914.[126] A large image of the Madonna, the patron saint of the Cistercian order, became a standard feature of every abbey from the fourteenth century onwards.[127]

One of the most precious possessions of any convent was the monastic seal, essential for validating letters and legal transactions. As such it was the key to a monastery's wealth and a symbol of conventual authority. During the fraught circumstances of the conspiracy of Mellifont, the seal sometimes figured in the arguments and disputes. When the newly appointed French abbot of Baltinglass arrived at his abbey in 1227, his seal was violently snatched from his belt, as he was set upon by his monks and laybrothers, and Stephen of Lexington was horrified to discover that the abbot of another monastery had pawned a seal in a beer tavern for eighteen pence.[128] Among the richer orders of medieval Europe, seals became veritable status symbols and many Benedictine houses commissioned seal matrices that were exquisite works of art. Cistercian seals were usually more restrained, as befitted the order, and until the fourteenth century they tended to follow a few established conventions.[129] Before 1350 it is not too difficult to recognise a seal as Cistercian but in the later middle ages one encounters more local variety. Uniformity of practice gradually declined, just as it had in architectural design.

The survival of Irish Cistercian seals is uneven.[130] Thanks to the preservation of the vast

267 Westminster Abbey, Henry VII's chapel, figure of St Edmund. The angular 'box' folds were a feature of English carving at this time.

266 Life sized Madonna, carved in oak, from St Mary's Abbey, Dublin (c1500–20), one of the few wooden images that survived the iconoclasm of 1547–53.

268 The seal of Jerpoint Abbey. The standing figure of an abbot, holding a crosier, was a standard form in the thirteenth century (National Library of Ireland, Ms. D.359, 1288).

269 The seal of Hore Abbey, made about 1272 (National Library of Ireland, Mss. D.360/ 1, 1289).

270 The second seal of Hore Abbey, a poor example which shows the abbot kneeling below the Virgin and child. Circular seals replaced the ovoid forms in the fourteenth century (National Library of Ireland, Ms. D. 2250, 1533).

271 The fourteenth-century seal of Boyle Abbey, with the Madonna shown standing in an elaborate Gothic frame (from a cast in the Society of Antiquaries, London).

Ormond archives, there are some good impressions from monasteries within the Butler lordship (Graiguenamanagh, Jerpoint, Hore, Holycross), but seals from monasteries in the west are scarce. Only a small proportion of Cistercian documents retain their seals and, when they do, they are often broken or damaged. The only surviving matrix is a fourteenth-century example from Kilbeggan.[131] The commissioning of a new seal was a rare event, and most Irish houses changed them only two or three times during their history.

The first official reference to seal design comes in 1200, when the General Chapter, alarmed by growing discrepancies within the order, insisted that monasteries follow one or two approved patterns.[132] The simplest consisted of a hand and crosier, the latter acting as a succinct reminder of the authority of the abbot. This was precisely the same composition used for some early Cistercian grave slabs, a fine example of which can be seen at Boyle. However, no Irish seals survive with the device, except for a late specimen from Tracton.[133] This is the private seal of the sixteenth-century abbot John Barry, and represents a revival of the earlier form. The other design permitted by the General Chapter was the 'effigial' type, showing the standing figure of an abbot holding his crosier. All the early Cistercian seals from Ireland follow this pattern, which also became universal in thirteenth-century England. They are ovoid in shape, and good impressions survive from Tintern, Graiguenamanagh, Jerpoint and Hore (Pls 268, 269).[134] The figure is usually set within a delicately beaded frame and the ecclesiastical robes are modelled with considerable detail. With one hand clasping a staff, the other is either raised in blessing or shown holding a book. It is likely that the matrices were all made in the middle years of the thirteenth century, and that belonging to Hore was no doubt commissioned in 1272, the year of the abbey's foundation. The matrices were apparently ordered from local goldsmiths, and as such they demonstrate the accomplished levels of craftsmanship available in Anglo-Norman Ireland.[135] The uniform acceptance of a common design to some extent nullified the point of a seal as a mark of identification. The inscription was thus crucial, but as a further aid against confusion small emblems—stars, crosses, fleurs-de-lis etc. were sometimes added.[136] The seal of Graiguenamanagh has a star on both sides of the abbot's effigy and Jerpoint has a single star to the right.

The fourteenth century brought major changes both in the way seals were used and in their design. The abbot was hitherto the sole guardian of the seal, but the statute of Carlisle (1307) insisted that it be kept in the custody of the prior and four of 'the worthier and more discreet members' of the community. The statute prevented the abbot acting independently of his brethren, and as such served as a check to his authority. In 1335 Pope Benedict XII's reform of the Cistercian constitution extended this principle of conventual involvement to all the Cistercian houses of Europe. At the same time, the General Chapter ordered that seals were to be circular discs of copper and they should carry an image of the Virgin Mary, the patron saint of the order.[137] The effigy of the abbot was thus deposed as the visual symbol of the monastery. Furthermore, after 1335, if not after 1307, the inscription usually included a specific reference to the convent or community. Whereas the thirteenth-century seal of Jerpoint carries the legend 'SIGILL ABBATIS DE IERIPONTE', the fourteenth-century seal of Boyle reads 's. CONVENTUS MONASTERII DE BUELLIO'. In Ireland as elsewhere, circular seals henceforth became the norm.

There are seven seals which appear to have been prompted by the reforms of 1335 (from Jerpoint, Graiguenamanagh, Inch, Hore, Tintern, Boyle and Kilbeggan). All depict the Madonna and child as stipulated by the General Chapter and the use of Lombard lettering suggests a date before 1400.[138] They vary in both size and quality. A poor example is the second seal of Hore, which shows the abbot kneeling under a trefoil canopy below the Virgin Mary (Pl. 270).[139] The composition is weak and the figure style crude. It is tempting to believe that the matrix was made by a goldsmith in the neighbouring town of Cashel, and if so it says little for his expertise. In comparison the equivalent seal from Inch is far more attractive.[140] Here the Madonna is placed within a quatrefoil frame and her drapery is organised in a lively, fluttering manner. The second Jerpoint seal survives on a number of documents ranging in date from 1362 to 1536, but in all of them the image of the seated Madonna is unclear and the inscription indistinct.[141] The most interesting seal in the group is that from Boyle, which shows the Virgin

272 The large fifteenth-century seal of Holycross. It is no coincidence that the monastery with the finest late Gothic architecture also commissioned the most ornate Gothic seal.

273 Detail of the shrine of the Book of Dimma (c1400). The crucifixion is remarkably similar to that on the Holycross seal and appears to be by the same artist.

274 Personal seal of abbot John de Barry (1542). The design with an arm and crosier is a revival of an earlier Cistercian form (from a cast in the Society of Antiquaries, London).

Mary standing in an attractive Gothic frame (Pl. 271).[142] This is equipped with folding wings, decorated with geometrical tracery, and the whole composition gives the impression of being copied from a contemporary ivory, perhaps one belonging to the monastery at Boyle. The second seal of Graiguenamanagh also depicts a standing Madonna, this time holding a lily as well as the Christ-child.[143] Beside her is a standing figure, difficult to decipher, who may be John the Baptist. The figures are set under twin canopies and the central composition is flanked by traceried wings. Another fine fourteenth-century seal is that from Tintern, which portrays a half-length Madonna and child, placed within a trefoiled niche.[144] Below is a representation of a kneeling abbot, holding his crosier and lifting his hands in prayer. The diapered background is decorated with tiny dog-tooth ornament and there is further dog-tooth embellishing the sexfoil frame which surrounds the whole composition. The delicacy of the designs from Tintern, Inch and Graiguenamanagh demonstrates that in the mid-fourteenth century competent metal-workers were to be found in a number of Irish towns.

Most of these seals were still in use at the Reformation, and Holycross was exceptional in deciding to commission a new one in the later middle ages. This is the most splendid of all the Irish Cistercian seals, a testimony to the artistic pretensions of the abbey just as it was embarking on the wholesale reconstruction of its buildings (Pl. 272). The seal was in use by 1429 and it was still being employed in 1534.[145] It has a fine inscription in Gothic black lettering, s. COMMUNE MONASTERII SANCTE CRUCIS', and the main design is neatly organised. Set beneath an intricate Gothic canopy is the crucified Christ, flanked by the Virgin Mary and St John. The poses are all very lively and the drapery is modelled in vigorous folds. Below the crucifixion, under a tiny trefoil arch, is the figure of the abbot, set between shields charged with the arms of Ormond and the English Crown. Delicate pieces of tracery fill the gap between the main design and the surrounding inscription. The seal is exceptional in many ways. It is ovoid in shape, rather than round, and it is unusually large (46 × 70 mm). Although the choice of image was highly appropriate, it represented a break with Cistercian convention. It can be no coincidence that the monastery with the finest late Gothic architecture also produced the finest late Gothic seal. The goldsmith responsible can be identified with the craftsman who added a crucifixion to the shrine of the Book of Dimma around 1400 (Pl. 273).[146] He was presumably a local man, as the shrine came from Roscrea, only twenty three-miles away.

Once the abbot no longer had complete control over the convent's seal, private ones became more common and there are a number of Irish examples, all ovoid in shape. None reveals much imagination and most reuse earlier designs. The abbots of Graiguenamanagh (1530) and Monasteranenagh (1499) adopted the effigial type and John Barry of Tracton revived that ancient Cistercian image, the arm and crosier.[147] In the latter case the design was modified slightly with the addition of a kneeling abbot, clasping the base of the pastoral staff (Pl. 274). William, abbot of Holycross (1450), employed a crucifix on his seal, with his name(?) inscribed below, the whole a rather crude reflection of the splendid communal seal.[148] One other seal that deserves to be mentioned is a counterseal from Dunbrody. The matrix was found at Kilkile Castle, not far from the abbey, and it is now at Dunbrody Park. It is circular in shape (43 mm in diameter) and shows an abbot seated with his crosier in a niche under a Gothic canopy. The legend reads 'CONTRASIGILLUM DOMUS SCE MARE DE PORTU'.[149]

Seals furnish a valuable record of the art of the medieval goldsmith, providing a census of the skills available at different times and places. The thirteenth-century Irish seals indicate a broad level of professional quality, but after 1300 standards became more variable, ranging from the rudimentary (at Hore) to the outstanding (at Holycross). There was, no doubt, a direct correlation between the quality of the design and the price. The production of a matrix represented many days work and could be an expensive undertaking. In 1232/3 Canterbury Cathedral paid Nigel the goldsmith £7.6.8 for a new seal,[150] though admittedly this was far more complex in form than any of the Irish Cistercian seals. Nigel appears to have spent six to eight weeks on the task and even a relatively simple seal might represent many days' labour. Seals were miniature works of art and the skill, experience and patience needed to execute the finer details, especially the inscriptions, should not be underestimated.

Chapter 11

THE AFTERMATH OF THE DISSOLUTION

ONCE THE MONKS had been expelled from the monasteries, anything of value was quickly stripped away. There was no sentimentality on the part of the Crown or the new lay tenants, who regarded the monastic buildings as assets to be exploited for maximum profit. In a few cases this meant immediate demolition, for there were lucrative building materials to be salvaged—floor pavings, ashlar masonry, timber and lead. The church at Bective was an early victim and already by 1540 the roof had been 'thrown down and the timber so detached' used 'for the repairs of the King's mills at Tryme'. In recommending the demolition of the cloister buildings at Jerpoint, the royal commissioners themselves put a sale value of £10 on the timber, stone and tiles.[1]

Several monasteries were subsequently destroyed during military operations in the Elizabethan era. In 1572, Brian O'Neill burnt Grey Abbey in order to stop it being used as a refuge for English colonists trying to settle in the Ards Peninsula. Comber was burnt the following year during the Ulster campaigns of the earl of Essex, and Monasteranenagh was the scene of a major battle during the Geraldine rebellion of 1579–80. After this battle the defeated Irish sought protection in the abbey, one of the few where monastic life still continued, and Sir Nicholas Malby consequently turned his guns on the buildings with devastating effect.[2]

In many instances the abbey church—or part of it—survived for a time as the local parish church. The scale of such buildings, however, was ill adapted for small rural congregations and they were far too expensive to keep in repair. Although some were reduced in size by the insertion of cross walls, over the course of the next hundred years most Cistercian churches gradually disintegrated. In the eighteenth century only four remained as places of worship: Baltinglass, Grey, Holycross and Graiguenamanagh. At Baltinglass the old Cistercian presbytery was adapted as a Protestant church and a solid tower was erected in the area of the crossing. In this form it was depicted in Grose's *Antiquities of Ireland* (1795) and so it remained until 1883. Grey received a new roof over the nave in 1626 or 1685, which lasted throughout the following century, and at Holycross the solid rib vaults at the east end of the church facilitated its survival (Pls 275, 276). Long after the Reformation, pilgrims still resorted to Holycross in large numbers and the earls of Ormond allowed the church to continue in use. In the 1570s a priest, John Monk, was granted the altarages of the abbey for £10 per annum and this brought with it the duty 'to repair and uphold the chancel or choir of the said abbey'.[3] During the Cistercian revival in the seventeenth century, the monk John Cantwell rehabilitated the church. It is recorded that after 1637 he 'took care to cover in the whole church which through the inclemency of the seasons and the cruelty of the heretics had remained without a roof'.[4] The medieval timbers over the nave had probably collapsed in the previous century. There must be some doubt about whether Cantwell reroofed the entire building and it is more likely that his efforts extended only as far as the cross wall, half-way up the nave. He may indeed have been responsible for constructing this wall. For many years the abbey was a national monument but it has recently been restored to serve as a local Catholic church.[5] The ruins of Graiguenamanagh have similarly been converted to modern worship. In 1754 the west end of the nave was fitted up as a Protestant church,[6] but by 1813 the local Catholic community had taken over the abbey, which now forms the parish church of the town.

275 Holycross Abbey looking west from the chancel. The church remained in use until the mid-seventeenth century (Grose, *Antiquities of Ireland*, 1791–5).

276 Grey Abbey, where the nave was re-roofed and fitted up for worship in the seventeenth century (Grose, *Antiquities of Ireland*, 1791–5).

The most valuable and sought after monastery was St Mary's, Dublin, strategically located across the river from the castle, the seat of government. By 1541 the church had been taken over by John Travers, master of the King's ordnance, 'being a place very proper and mete to lay in ordnance and artillery'.[7] The great church of St Mary's was thus transformed into an arsenal for the royal army. Within weeks of the dissolution, the abbot's lodging and garden was occupied by the lord deputy, Leonard Grey, as a convenient dwelling close to the city. One of Grey's enemies, numerous by this time, sourly remarked that he had managed to acquire 'all the good lodgings' in the abbey.[8] He did not enjoy them for long. Found guilty of treason, he was executed in June 1541. Two and a half years later a substantial part of the abbey was leased to James, earl of Desmond, and the grant included the abbot's lodgings, the abbot's chambers and the infirmary.[9] The monastic buildings survived for more than a century and as late as 1673 there are references to the abbot's house, the dormitory and the cloister.[10] These vanished in the 1680s, when this part of the city was redeveloped by Sir Humphrey Jervis and Sir Richard Reynell. Only the chapter house escaped.

Many an English mansion was built from the spoils of the Reformation and in Ireland, too, a number of Tudor houses emerged from the relics of the middle ages.[11] They were built by the 'new English', a group of civil servants and professional soldiers who came to prominence after the failure of the Kildare rebellion in 1534. Thomas Agard was a typical example. He arrived in Ireland as a protegé of Thomas Cromwell in the 1530s and eventually became vice-treasurer of the Mint, being known as 'Agard of the Mint'. In December 1537 he took a lease on the monastery of Bective, a particularly valuable property since it was situated in the Pale, within easy reach of Dublin.[12] Agard was something of an industrial entrepreneur and within three months he was boasting of a cloth weaving project that he had established at Bective which, he claimed, would employ over a hundred people.[13] No more is heard of this project, but some time between 1538 and 1557 he adapted the old monastery into a distinguished fortified mansion (Pl. 277).[14] Another English official, William Brabazon, the vice treasurer, took possession of Mellifont in 1540.[15] Brabazon was one of the senior figures in the Dublin government and it is no coincidence that the two richest Cistercian prizes went to the lord deputy and the vice-treasurer respectively. Some years later further Englishmen took over the more exposed Cistercian monasteries in Wexford. In 1545 Dunbrody was granted to an English soldier, Sir Osborne Etchingham, who had been marshal of the royal army for the past four years, a man

277 Bective Abbey, converted into a Tudor mansion after 1537. The broad staircase is one of the post-monastic additions.

well qualified, in the words of the lord deputy, to 'reduce that corner to much quyet and civilitie'.[16] This was a characteristic example of monastic land being used as bait to encourage English gentry to settle in Ireland and so reinforce the authority of the Crown. When the suppression of the monasteries was proposed by Sir Patrick Finglas eleven years before, it was precisely for this purpose, to entice 'young Lords, Knights and Gents out of England which shall dwell upon the same'. Unfortunately for the government, Sir Osborne was 'somewhat grown in years' and he was dead by 1546. Whether it was he or his son Edward who began the 'manor house of Dunbrody' is not known. It was the mid 1550s before a permanent tenant was found for the neighbouring house of Tintern. This was Anthony Colclough who, like Thomas Agard before him, was an English civil servant employed by the Dublin government and he was married to Agard's daughter.[17] His descendants lived in the old church at Tintern until a few years ago.[18]

Agard, Etchingham and Colclough erected remarkable houses for themselves amidst the monastic ruins. There was no agreed formula as to how one went about converting a medieval monastery, and some of the results were bizarre. At Tintern the Colcloughs moved into the Cistercian chancel and at Dunbrody the Etchinghams perched their manor house on top of the south transept chapels. In each case new floors, windows, fireplaces and chimney stacks were inserted into the old walls. By far the most ambitious of the conversions was that at Bective, which is worth describing in some detail. Thomas Agard designed his residence around the sides of the old cloister court, and the great fifteenth-century tower acted as a pivot for two wings (Fig. 63). The main approach to the building was beside the tower and a broad flight of steps led up to a pointed entrance on the first floor (Pl. 277). This opened into the main hall (the old refectory), which was brightly lit by five sixteenth-century mullioned windows. A fireplace was installed in the north wall. From the hall a wooden stair led up to a doorway high in the south-west corner, giving access to the second storey of the tower, which thus functioned as a 'solar', or private chamber. At the opposite end of the hall a door led into the east wing (the old

278 Bective Abbey, the dormitory in the east range, where Thomas Agard added an extra floor.

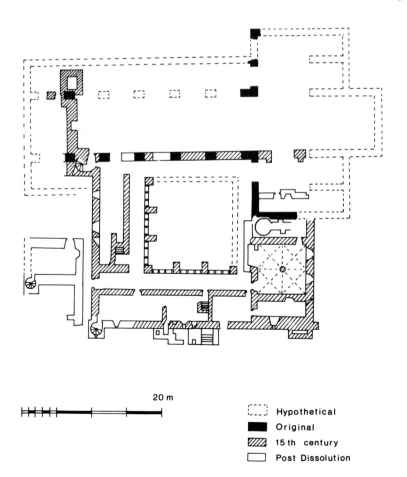

20 m

‿ ‿ ‿ ‿ ‿ ‿ Hypothetical

▬ Original

▨▨▨ 15th century

◻ Post Dissolution

Fig. 63 Bective, plan of the abbey.

279 Bective Abbey from the south: a sprawling Tudor manor house, dominated by the great tower erected by the monks.

280 The manor house at Carrick-on-Suir, built by the earl of Ormond (c1565). Incorporating older towers at the rear, it had many similarities with Bective.

dormitory). Here Thomas Agard added an extra floor to the medieval range, and this new attic level was probably lit by dormer or gabled windows (Pl. 278). Such garrets were a feature of Tudor architecture, often used for accommodating the servants. At the same time this wing was extended northwards to a new gable wall on the site of the south transept. There are sixteenth-century fireplaces at both floor levels. The west side of the house is not so well preserved, but Agard clearly incorporated the west range of the monastery as well as the tower at the west end of the former church. A further wing, consisting of a single storey over a barrel-vaulted basement, projected near the north-west corner of the great tower.[19]

The result of these adaptations was a sprawling mansion offering plenty of space, but not much architectural coherence (Pl. 279). The main living accommodation was on the first floor, which could be described as a *piano nobile*, and below each wing there were vaulted basements dating from the monastic era. These were used as cellars and for other utilitarian purposes. A groin-vaulted chamber (sometimes known as the chapter house) under the dormitory may have been used as a kitchen, and in the same range there was a large baking oven. It was probably

Agard who inserted the stone stair leading from the cloister up to the hall, which would thus have formed the route from the kitchen. The layout of the house was far from ideal and the elevations were decidedly irregular, but a degree of visual unity was provided by the repetitive Tudor mullioned windows.

Although it contained two medieval towers, Thomas Agard's house was not designed for sustained defence (determined raiders could have gained entry through the first floor windows with relative ease). With its lack of symmetry, its irregular gables, its towers and turrets, it provided just the sort of picturesque silhouette dear to the hearts of nineteenth-century romantics, the Gothic atmosphere being reinforced by the preservation of the medieval cloister. It was, however, a Tudor manor house and in this respect it is worthy of comparison with 'Black Tom' Ormond's mansion at Carrick-on-Suir (c1565) (Pl. 280). It, too, has a U-shaped plan, conceived around a courtyard. As it also incorporated older towers, its appearance was not dissimilar to that of Bective in the later sixteenth century.[20]

At Dunbrody it was probably Edward Etchingham who converted the abbey into a residence around 1546–50. The nucleus of the house was a three-storey block constructed above the chapels of the south transept (Pl. 281). This might seem an odd place to erect a dwelling, but it had a number of attractions. The rib vaults of the chapels provided a strong foundation and the wall-walks of the house gave direct access to the crossing tower, a valuable defence in times of crisis. To the south the house was linked to the old dormitory and it is likely that this became

281 Dunbrody Abbey, where a Tudor house was perched above the south transept chapels.

some sort of hall. The new building thus acted as a bridge between the tower and dormitory. The large cloister served as a convenient bawn, reached through the slype which was converted into a fortified gateway. The main entrance to the house was apparently via the old transept and up the night stairs, a somewhat circuituous and inelegant route. There are three enormous chimney stacks, one of which forms the focal point of the east facade, corbelled out immediately above an Early English lancet. At the south-east corner the builders amusingly reused monastic masonry, alternating square quoin stones with pieces of thirteenth-century roll moulding. The house is narrow, and, with its low ceilings and large fireplaces, it was snug but scarcely commodious. Present impressions, however, may be misleading, for it is hard to know how much use was made of the old claustral buildings. Nevertheless, it must have been a peculiar place in which to live, especially if the semi-derelict church was still roofed.[21] The Etchinghams tolerated the architectural eccentricities for less than a century and in the 1630s John Etchingham began 'a good large house of lime and stone' a few hundred yards away, which due to the Great Rebellion of 1641 was never completed.[22]

Anthony Colclough's possession of Tintern was confirmed in 1566 by Elizabeth I, when he agreed to build within three years 'a sufficient fortress on the site of the Abbey, and to maintain three English horsemen and four archers or arquebusiers'.[23] Colclough concentrated his building activities on the crossing tower which was converted into a five-storey tower house (Pl. 140). Arches were blocked, floors and fireplaces inserted, and a stair turret added at the north-west corner. There were few windows and the rooms must have been gloomy. It was an unattractive dwelling, to judge from the comments of Gabriel Beranger and John Barralet, who stayed there in 1780. They slept in the tower, and described how the rain came into their room, which was 'full of various vessels placed to catch the drops'. Nor were they enamoured by the 'parcels of rats and mice' that warmed themselves before the fire.[24] The old chancel may have furnished more attractive accommodation. Colclough (or one of his successors) blocked the Gothic windows and, between the buttresses of c1300, inserted Tudor mullions, the design of which correspond to those at Carrick-on-Suir (c1565) (Pls 280, 282). Turrets were erected above the eastern corners and three fifteenth-century sculptures were reused as part of the internal decor. With the floors and internal fittings destroyed, it is no longer possible to work out how Sir Anthony's house functioned in domestic terms. It is worth stressing, however, that the medieval tower was a focal point of the design, as it had been at Bective and Dunbrody, a reflection of the insecure atmosphere in which these English tenants lived.

At the end of the eighteenth century, Tintern was given a new lease of life under Sir Vesey Colclough, who readily entered into the spirit of the Gothic revival. In 1794 it was reported that he had 'surrounded the Abbey with walls and battlements in the ancient style, and so well executed that a few years will give them the appearance of being part of the original building'.[25] Two elegant circular turrets from this scheme remain to the south of the abbey, their ancient appearance ready to deceive the unsuspecting visitor.[26] In the ensuing years under Sir Caesar Colclough, the ruins of the nave and part of the south transept were transformed into a Georgian Gothic house, the windows filled with thin wooden tracery (Pl. 283). Much of this survived until a few years ago, and it is a matter of local debate whether the Office of Public Works should have destroyed it in their desire to reinstate the medieval ruins. In its nineteenth-century form, Tintern bore a remarkable resemblance to Buckland (Devon), an English Cistercian abbey, similarly converted into a 'Gothic' country house.[27] Not everyone approved of the changes, however, and about 1830 John Windele described Tintern as 'a vile tasteless wretched mansion', . . . 'never was there so woeful a display . . . so barbarous a refitting'.[28]

Among the other monasteries converted into private residences were Mellifont, Kilcooly and Hore. At Mellifont the old refectory seems to have formed the nucleus of a 'castellated house', probably erected by Edward Moore after 1566.[29] It has been suggested that the lavabo was retained as a porch, and it is certain that a tower, with a barrel-vaulted cellar and spiral stair, was constructed on the site of the calefactory. The cloister was turned into a cobbled courtyard. The Moore family sold the estate in 1727 and the house, already 'much decayed' in 1690,[30] evidently collapsed soon after their departure. Following the suppression of the community at Kilcooly,

282 The chancel at Tintern Abbey, converted into a private dwelling by the Colcloughs in the later sixteenth century. The Gothic lancets were blocked and replaced by mullioned windows.

283　Tintern Abbey, shortly before 1900. The arches of the nave were skilfully used to stress the rhythm of the neo-Gothic windows.

there were several centuries of habitation. A sixteenth-century hall exists just to the east of the abbey, but exactly when it was built and by whom is not known. The east range bears much evidence of post-monastic alterations, including a brick vaulted passage. John Stevens in 1690 noted that the ruined walls were 'divided into two or three little tenements',[31] and one of these, above the south transept, was still occupied in the first half of this century. At Hore the old buildings seem to have taken on the appearance of a mini-village. The chapter house was converted into a two-storey dwelling, and the presence of corbels and joist holes show that further houses were carved out of the south transept and the western part of the nave. These domestic changes explain what is otherwise a puzzling feature of the nave—a pair of window seats set in one of the clerestory windows high above the ground. In the midst of these private dwellings, the chancel and crossing continued to function as the local parish church. Hore and Kilcooly belong to a substantial group of religious houses that were granted to the earl of Ormond, but there is no evidence that he exploited the buildings for his own use. This was left to sub-tenants, men like Edward Heffernan, 'a clerk', who occupied the lands of Hore in 1545.[32]

The history of the Cistercian monasteries after 1540 is a neglected episode in Irish architecture and the adaptation of the old buildings in a new religious and political climate provides an unexpected glimpse of Tudor social history. The abbeys converted by the 'new English' lay in the eastern half of the country, with a concentration in the Pale. The authorities not surprisingly found it difficult to attract tenants to the more remote sites in the hinterland, amongst the 'wild Irish'. It is unclear how the local populace reacted to the desecration of the monasteries, but there must have been some hostility, as the old buildings were exploited by tough, ambitious owners, insensitive to the past. As has often been pointed out, there are similarities between the fate of medieval abbeys in the sixteenth century and the fate of many historic country houses in the twentieth.

Conclusion

In terms of quality and scale, nobody could pretend that the Irish monasteries should be numbered among the more distinguished examples of Cistercian architecture in Europe. They are very basic in their structural form and there are few glimpses of the artistic sophistication encountered at monasteries like Royaumont or Longpont, Fountains or Furness. But in contrast to these illustrious houses, the Irish abbeys are in many ways more typical of the order as a whole. They offer insights into the thinking of the early Cistercian leaders, which are of interest since they relate to communities that were far removed from the heart of the movement.

The strength of the architectural concepts that emerged from Clairvaux in the 1130s and 1140s is especially apparent in the Irish abbeys. Mellifont, Baltinglass, Jerpoint, Boyle and Monasteranenagh each contained significant ingredients of the so-called 'Bernardine' style, both in regard to plan type and structural components. The lack of a strong native tradition of Romanesque building highlighted the imported techniques and, until English architecture began to exert an influence in the 1170s, the major stimulus came from Burgundy: pointed arches, pointed barrel vaults, 'low' transepts and presbyteries, the 'Fontenay' plan and the use of distinctive proportional formulae. Despite the subsequent impact of English art, it is remarkable how long these Burgundian features endured. The monks at Hore in 1272–90 were still building chapels with pointed barrel vaults, and in the fifteenth century the monks at Holycross were content to follow a plan type established in France three hundred years before. There is a certain irony in the fact that features of the 'Bernardine' church survived far longer in Ireland than they did in Burgundy itself, where the start of the new chevet at Clairvaux in 1153/4, designed with an ambulatory and ribbed vaults, signalled the end of the earlier tradition. Once the 'Bernardine' forms had been introduced to Ireland in the 1140s, their continued use was perpetuated by Irish prototypes. The builders of the first Irish monasteries, led by Robert of Clairvaux, were thus responsible for introducing a body of 'know how' which helped to dictate the course of Irish architecture for over a century. It is important, however, to make a distinction between theory and practice. There is no evidence that French masons worked in Ireland, and stylistic details invariably have an Irish or English flavour. The monks determined the principles of the design, but execution was left to professionals, usually recruited from outside the monastery. Even the most skilled local mason was not allowed a free hand and at Baltinglass and Jerpoint one gets the impression that it was dutiful adherence to the spirit of the rule that produced the distinctive capitals of the Baltinglass Master, with their unique range of abstract designs.

The documents associated with Stephen of Lexington provide some fascinating hints about the 'unwritten rules' that governed the appearance of Cistercian architecture. It has long been acknowledged that decisions of the General Chapter tend to be negative, banning undesirable developments, rather than outlining positive architectural forms. A set of basic assumptions existed and it was only the aberrations that were documented. The strictures of Stephen of Lexington provide a unique insight into the way these unwritten rules were applied and it is particularly interesting to find him insisting on well-made roofs, for high quality workmanship has always been recognised as a feature of Cistercian building.

There are a number of features that can be specifically associated with Ireland. The abbeys are constructed of rubble masonry, rather than ashlar, a consequence of poverty and the scarcity of easily worked freestone. The ubiquitous native carboniferous limestone was time-consuming to quarry and carve, though when it was employed, as at Corcomroe or Holycross, the results were stunning. Another consequence of poverty was the tendency to eliminate some of the arches in the nave, closing off part of the aisles with solid walls, a technique found in eight of the churches. It had a functional and economic logic, but little aesthetic appeal. The need for economy also encouraged the simplification of pier design, through the elimination of responds and decorative shafts. Only at Graiguenamanagh (presbytery) and Boyle (nave) was there any attempt to introduce a sense of bay division. The absence of well-defined bays helps to explain a further curiosity of the Irish abbeys, the unorthodox location of clerestory windows over the piers rather than over the arches. In rubble buildings it may have been thought that this had some structural advantage and it certainly imparted an unusual rhythm to the designs. The fact that the technique was employed in at least seven abbeys, both Irish and Anglo-Norman in origin, suggests that cogent arguments were being voiced in its favour. By the end of the middle ages almost every monastery was equipped with a central crossing tower, in apparent defiance of the ruling of 1157. None were unusually tall or ornate and all were apparently designed to hold bells. More specifically Irish were the types of vault employed, once Burgundian barrel vaults had been abandoned, and two regional styles are well illustrated in the Cistercian abbeys: the western vaults of the period 1210–30 and the Ormond vaults of the fifteenth century. As so often with the Cistercians, however, it is the sculptural details which most readily betray the hand of local masons, whether in the discreet Hiberno-Romanesque carvings at Baltinglass or in the incisive Gothic decoration at Holycross.

Outside the church, the most remarkable feature of Cistercian building was the cloister arcades, particularly the fact that so many were rebuilt in the later middle ages. It appears that wooden galleries sufficed in many an abbey for over two hundred years. The 'dumb-bell' pier, widespread after 1390, is another distinctively Irish phenomenon, a simple and economical form well-suited to the Cistercian ethos. The sculptured cloisters at Jerpoint are altogether more exceptional, not only among the Cistercian houses of Ireland, but throughout the rest of Europe.

Attempts to summarise the 'Irishness' of Irish Cistercian art are bound to be misleading, for the complexities of Irish society, both religious and secular, produced an overall picture that was far from uniform. It was inevitable that cultural and racial tensions within the monastic body would assume visual expression in architecture. The robust late Romanesque or Transitional style, employed at Abbeyknockmoy and Corcomroe around 1210–20, makes a telling contrast with the suave Early English forms of Graiguenamanagh or Inch. Sharp though the divide was between the Irish and the Anglo-Norman communities in these years, it was not always straightforward or consistent. Boyle, the most Irish of monasteries in social structure, was an avowed follower of English fashion when it came to building. Similarly, some distinctively Irish features, like the unorthodox location of clerestory windows, could be found in a complete cross section of abbeys, regardless of their allegiance. Nevertheless, contrasts of taste and cultural outlook were often acute and remained so until the end of the middle ages. The coloured floor tile was employed only in the more anglophile monasteries and none has been found west of the Shannon. Whereas two monasteries erected cloisters in the English 'Perpendicular' manner, most were content with simple arcades of native design. At Holycross, fashionable and outdated forms existed alongside in a heterogeneous mixture which makes nonsense of normal stylistic concepts. The same anomalies are apparent in metalwork and sculpture. The rustic Gothic of the carvings at Kilcooly has little in common with the cosmopolitan Gothic of the Dublin Madonna. It is clear that by the fifteenth century there were enormous differences in artistic outlook between the affluent houses of the Pale and the remote monasteries of the west, but the loss of Mellifont and St Mary's, Dublin, makes it difficult to chart these contrasts with any precision.

The first hundred years were unquestionably the most decisive period of Cistercian art in Ireland, a time when the order was still a dynamic religious force. It forged a crucial link with the outside world, breaking down the artistic isolation of the country. It was through Cistercian design that Irish patrons became better acquainted with European Romanesque, and it was through the Cistercians that integrated monastic planning was established. Later it was the Cistercians who gave the Irish their first taste of the Gothic style, which they helped to spread across the country. Communication with houses abroad, stuttering and inadequate though it was by the standards of the order, nevertheless provided artistic channels which helped to keep Ireland in touch with the rest of Europe. Without the Cistercians, Irish art and architecture might have been even more introspective than in fact it was.

284 Limerick Cathedral, looking from the nave to the north aisle. The blunt ponderous arcades are a striking testimony of the power of Cistercian influence.

There were however negative aspects to the Cistercian contribution. The insistence on visual simplicity conflicted with the traditional Irish delight in subtle and colourful metalwork and it cannot be a coincidence that the Cross of Cong, made just a decade or so before the founding of Mellifont, is the last outstanding piece of early Irish metalwork. The Anglo-Normans are usually blamed for the demise of native art, but thirty years before they arrived, the Cistercians had already begun to redirect the artistic tastes of the country. It is particularly noticeable that the Cistercians avoided the complex animal patterns found so frequently on the crosses and Romanesque portals of the time. Moreover, the bleak and spacious churches of the order set a standard of austerity which tended to colour the whole of Irish Gothic architecture. A few cathedrals, mostly notably those in Dublin and Waterford, were built with grandeur and finesse, but Cistercian buildings were more widely scattered and influential. The blunt, ponderous arcades of Limerick Cathedral (as well as elements in its plan) are a striking testimony to the power of Cistercian example (Pl. 284). Gothic, for the Cistercians in Ireland, was neither a complex structural system nor an intricate interplay of aesthetic forms. Purged of its inessentials, it was reduced to a few basic components, dependent for their visual appeal on proportions and simple shapes. A church like that at Hore, rational in form but utterly devoid of ornament, is the epitome of Cistercian architectural purism.

Long before 1540, the loss of economic and religious direction, which is so apparent from the documentary records, was taking its toll of monastic buildings. Abbots complained of repairs they could not afford and several houses were on the verge of structural collapse when the royal commissioners arrived at the gates. One point to emerge from the story of the dissolution is how many abbeys had served, and continued to serve, as parish churches. This helps to explain the number of lay burials at places like Kilcooly and Jerpoint and it may also explain the occasional appearance of a font. After the dissolution, many an abbey remained in use, often with former monks as parish priests. Patched and disfigured, the nave shortened, the transepts cut off, many survived for over two hundred years until the crumbling fabric was replaced by a smart Protestant church, as at Midleton, Tracton, Kilbeggan, Macosquin, Inislounaght, Comber and Abbeyleix.

The continuous use of Cistercian sites, combined with the Irish tradition of burial amidst ancient ruins, are factors which will seriously circumscribe archaeological investigation in the future. Nevertheless, there are several abbeys where excavation might be fruitful, notably Bective (church), Monasteranenagh, Abbeylara, Dunbody and Graiguenamanagh (cloister and conventual buildings). But by far the most important potential site is St Mary's, Dublin, the richest of all the Irish houses, where opportunities are now available which will soon be lost for ever. The excavations at Bordesley (Worcestershire) have set new archaeological standards and have demonstrated just how much can be discovered about the history of a medieval monastery by scrupulous scientific investigation—the diet of the community as indicated by remains in sewers and refuse pits or the routes taken by the monks in their processions as shown by the wear on the floor tiles. The need for a meticulous investigation of an Irish Cistercian abbey is long overdue, an investigation which should encompass the *whole* precinct. Almost nothing is known about the ancillary buildings outside the cloister area. The lines of precinct walls have not been established, nor the location of mills and fishponds. No evidence has been brought to light about the wooden structures that preceded the permanent stone buildings and this is especially relevant for the early cloister arcades. Despite the popularity of glazed floor tiles in the east of the country, no kilns have been uncovered near the monasteries, as in England. Even within the church the liturgical arrangements have not been investigated thoroughly—the location of wooden screens, choir stalls and steps. The achievements at Bordesley offer a challenge to future generations of Irish archaeologists. Recent excavations by the Office of Public Works have been dictated by the needs of conservation or public display, a piecemeal approach which is inevitably limited in its results.

These pressures are understandable, however, for Cistercian ruins are among the most attractive and oft-visited antiquities in the country. Ireland possessed neither a Wordsworth nor a John Sell Cotman to extol the beauty of her ancient monuments, but there was no lack of

285 Jerpoint Abbey from the west (Robertson's *Views of Kilkenny*).

nostalgic sentiment for them in the early years of the nineteenth century. The abbey of Dunbrody prompted a number of laments—'its glories, its anthem, and the strain of its hooded choir, "mingling with the cadence of the waters", have died away in the stream of time'. Jerpoint also stimulated nostalgic enthusiasm and formed the subject of a lengthy poem, 'Lines Written at Jerpoint Abbey', published in 1823. The emotion is heartfelt but the literary quality a trifle indifferent. The following is one of the better passages:

> Ne'er from its chancel soars the midnight prayer,
>   Its stillness broken by no earthly thing,
> Save when the night-bird wakes the echoes there,
>   Or the bat flutters its unfeather'd wing . . .
> Who that had seen the Abbot in his power,
>   Lord of a palace and a rich domain,
> Had thought that time would bring a blighting hour,
> And prove that all his honours bloom'd in vain

The outbursts of the nineteenth century poet were far removed from the cool, disciplined minds of the first Cistercian monks and it should not be forgotten that many of the buildings now admired for their romantic decay were constructed as unemotional 'workshops of prayer'.

CONSOLIDATED LIST OF MAJOR IRISH CISTERCIAN HOUSES

Parts of the original fabric remain at those sites italicised.

		Latin Name	Foundation Date	Mother House
1	*Mellifont*	Fons Mellis	1142	Clairvaux
2	*Bective*	Beatitudo	1147	Mellifont
3	*St Mary's, Dublin*	S. Maria iuxta Dublin	1147 (1139)	Savigny
4	*Baltinglass*	Vallis Salutis	1148	Mellifont
5	*Boyle*	Buellium	1161 (1148)	Mellifont
6	*Monasteranenagh*	Magium	1148	Mellifont
7	Inislounaght	Surium	1148	Mellifont
8	Kilbeggan	Benedictio Dei	1150	Mellifont
9	Newry	Viride Lignum	1153	Mellifont
10	Abbeydorney	Kyrie Eleison	1154	Monasteranenagh
11	*Jerpoint*	Jeripons	1160–2	Baltinglass
12	Fermoy	Castrum Dei	1170	Inislounaght
13	*Abbeymahon*	Fons Vivus	1172/89	Baltinglass
14	Monasterevin	Rosea Vallis	1178/89	Baltinglass
15	Assaroe	Samarium	1178	Boyle
16	Midleton	Chorus Sancti Benedicti	1180	Monasteranenagh
17	*Holycross*	Sancta Crux	1180	Monasteranenagh
18	*Dunbrody*	Portus Sanctae Mariae	1182	St Mary's, Dublin
19	Abbeyleix	Lex Dei	1184	Baltinglass
20	*Kilcooly*	Arvus Campus	1184	Jerpoint
21	*Inch*	Insula Curcii	1187	Furness
22	*Abbeyknockmoy*	Collis Victoriae	1190	Boyle
23	*Grey*	Iugum Dei	1193	Holm Cultram
24	*Corcomroe*	Petra Fertilis	1195	Inislounaght
25	Comber	Comerarium	1199	Whitland
26	*Tintern*	Votum	1200	Tintern
27	*Abbeyshrule*	Flumen Dei	1200	Mellifont
28	*Graiguenamanagh* (Duiske)	Vallis Sancti Salvatoris	1204/07	Stanley
29	Abington	Woneyum	1205	Furness
30	*Abbeylara*	Lerha	1214	St Mary's, Dublin
31	Macosquin	Clarus Fons	1218	Morimond
32	Tracton	Albus Tractus	1224	Whitland
33	*Hore*	Rupes	1272	Mellifont

Houses suppressed before 1536–41

		Latin name	Foundation Date	Suppression Date	Mother House
34	Erenagh		1127	1177	Savigny
35	Killenny	Vallis Dei	1162–5	1227	Jerpoint
36	Glanawydan	Vallis Caritatis	1171/1200	1228	Inislounaght

Appendix 2

CATALOGUE OF THE MAJOR CISTERCIAN SITES IN IRELAND

Abbeydorney Kerry (Pls 32, 113–14, 245; Fig. 39)

The ruins of the monastery lie in open fields about half a mile north of the village of Abbeydorney and six miles north of Tralee.

Founded in 1154 as a daughter house of Monasteranenagh, it was known as Mainistir OdTorná (i.e. the monastery of the O'Torneys, now Dorneys). Christian O'Conarchy, first abbot of Mellifont, retired to the abbey late in life and was subsequently buried here in 1186.

The site is still in use as a local graveyard and the monastic ruins are badly obscured by burials. The chief remnant of the middle ages is a long, aisleless and ivy clad church, 94 by 23 feet (28.6 by 7.0 metres), with a projecting western tower, all apparently of fifteenth-century date. There are a number of fine details executed in hard grey limestone, including an elaborately moulded west door with a square hood. This leads into a vaulted passage under the tower. A chamber on the first floor is lit by a two-light window with curvilinear tracery. There is an ogee headed tomb recess (now largely collapsed) on the north wall of the chancel and a three-light switchline window in the east gable. Parts of the east and west walls of the cloister remain, the former extending south for approximately 85 feet (26 metres). In 1841 the gable of a building in the south range still survived. Fragments of a stone cloister arcade remain at the site, including 'dumb-bell' piers of type B.

Bibliography: *Ordnance Survey Letters, Kerry*, (1841), 18–19; Power, 'Cistercian Abbeys of Munster', *JCHAS*, XXXIV (1929), 91–4; Leask, *Irish Churches*, III, 177; Gwynn and Hadcock, *Medieval Religious Houses*, (1970), 123.

Abbeyknockmoy Galway (Pls 11, 34, 81, 83–4, 117–18, 148, 205, 248–9; Figs 18, 62)

This is one of the most impressive Cistercian monuments in Ireland and a substantial portion of both the church and claustral buildings remain. It lies in bleak countryside seven miles south-east of Tuam and the buildings were placed about a hundred yards north of the Abbert River. Founded by Cathal Crovderg O'Conor, king of Connacht, in 1190, the abbey became a mausoleum for several generations of

the O'Conor family. Cathal Crovderg O'Conor was buried here in 1224, as was his wife seven years before. The monks came from Boyle and there are a number of architectural links with the mother house (see chapter 3). In the later middle ages the abbey fell under the control of the O'Kelly family, kings of Uí Maine, and there is an elaborate canopied tomb in the chancel commemorating Malachy O'Kelly (d. 1401) and his wife Finnuola (d. 1403). At the time of the dissolution Hugh O'Kelly was commendatory abbot and, renouncing the supremacy of Rome in 1542, he was granted the abbey and its lands for life.

The church and the east range were erected c1210–30, in a style which in many respects is more Romanesque than Gothic. The church is of standard Cistercian plan, with two barrel-vaulted chapels opening off each arm of the transept.

The presbytery is covered by two bays of heavy ribbed vaulting, the design of which is analogous to that at Ballintober (1216–25). On the north wall are the remnants of late Gothic painting—a crucifixion, a Trinity, St Sebastian and the three living and the three dead. There was a regular crossing, though the transept arches were subsequently blocked, probably when a late medieval or post-Reformation church was fashioned out of the eastern arm. The nave is a rudimentary piece of architecture, with blunt pointed arches, alleviated only by some attractive sculptural details on the abaci of the piers. The fine thirteenth-century chapter house, lit by five decorated lancets, was disfigured in the later middle ages by the insertion of additional piers, walls and vaults. The refectory was still intact in 1620, when it was described as a 'hall of stone, covered with shingles', with 'a cellar under the hall'. Much of this, together with most of the east range, still survive, albeit in a ruined state. Fragments of the cloister arcade of c1500 have been recovered, which show that it had 'dumb-bell' piers of type B.

The architecture of Abbeyknockmoy is a typical product of the 'school of the west', characterised by fine ashlar dressings, distinctive sculptural details and mouldings carried continuously around the windows.

Bibliography: Archdall, *Monasticon Hibernicum*, 266; Blake, 'Knockmoy Abbey' (1900–1), 65–

84; Glynn, 'Knockmoy Abbey' (1904), 239–42; Cochrane, 'Notes on the Building and Frescoes' (1904), 244–53; Cochrane, 'The frescoes, Abbey Knockmoy' (1905), 419–20; Brenan, 'A note on Abbey Knockmoy' (1905), 420–1; Crawford, 'Mural Paintings and Inscriptions at Knockmoy Abbey' (1919), 25–34; Hamilton Thompson, Clapham and Leask, 'Cistercian Order in Ireland' (1931), 25, 17; Leask, *Irish Churches*, II, 37–9; Gwynn and Hadcock, *Medieval Religious Houses* (1970), 124.

Abbeylara Longford (Pl. 134; Fig. 64)

The gaunt ruins of the crossing tower at Abbeylara form a conspicuous landmark on the south-east edge of the village. Founded by the Anglo-Norman lord, Richard de Tuit, shortly before his death in 1210/11, the monastery was colonised from St Mary's, Dublin, in 1214. Richard's huge motte castle lies only two and a half miles away at Granard. About a hundred yards to the west of the abbey is a stream, the monastery's water supply, which probably determined the choice of this particular site. Although anglophile in origin, long before the dissolution of 1539–40 the abbey had lost its English affiliations and fallen under the control of the O'Farrells, the dominant local family.

All that remains of the abbey is the central tower and adjacent walls. The church had a regular crossing from the start and the creasing of the steeply pitched roofs which covered the nave, chancel and transepts is still to be seen. Doorways led from the first floor of the tower into the interior of the roofs. The presbytery was evidently square ended, following routine Cistercian practice, and it was flanked by one or

Fig. 64   Abbeylara, plan of remains.

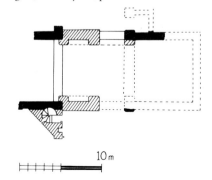

10 m

240

more barrel-vaulted chapels. In the nave there are no remnants of arcades or aisles, but roof marks on the outer side of the north wall suggest the existence of a pentice, as at Grey (Down).

The tower was remodelled in the fifteenth or sixteenth century. The transept arches were blocked by inserted walls north and south, and a barrel vault, now collapsed, was erected over them. Seven sockets for floor joists are visible at the base of the vault. A new stair turret was added at this time on the site of the south aisle. Although most of the church was demolished in 1539–40, the tower was preserved and probably adapted as a fortified dwelling.

The conventual buildings, now completely vanished, lay in the field to the south, as indicated by numerous bumps and hollows.

Bibliography: Archdall, *Monasticon Hibernicum*, 422–3; Hamilton Thompson, Clapham and Leask, 'Cistercian Order in Ireland' (1931), 19, 31; Gwynn and Hadcock, *Medieval Religious Houses* (1970), 124; *Extents*, 280–2.

Abbeyleix Laois

This was a daughter house of Baltinglass, founded in 1184 on the banks of the River Nore, over thirty miles upstream from Jerpoint. It was surrendered to the Crown in 1552 and the estates were acquired by the earl of Ormond eleven years later. The name Abbeyleix was derived from the Latin name of the monastery 'Lex Dei'. The site of the abbey lies within the demesne of viscount de Vesci, probably in the vicinity of the nineteenth-century Protestant church, but even in 1786 Archdall reported that 'No trace of the abbey can now be found'. When the old village was demolished and replaced by the planned village of the de Vesci's in the eighteenth century, 'many stones of antique and curious workmanship' were found. The major relic of the abbey is the effigial tomb of Malachy O'More (1502), preserved in a walled garden within the demesne. In style and design this is closely associated with products of the O'Tunney workshop. There is also a grave slab (1531) in memory of William O'Kelly, carved by William O'Tunney and decorated with a foliated cross. There is no architectural certainty that the ancient stone bridge over the Nore, the so-called 'Monks' bridge' was in fact built by the Cistercians, as commonly supposed.

Bibliography: Archdall, *Monasticon Hibernicum*, 586–8; *Ordnance Survey Letters, Queen's County* (1838–9), 88–94; Gwynn and Hadcock, *Medieval Religious Houses* (1970), 124–5; Rae, 'Irish Sepulchral Monuments—II' (1971), 2, 29, 31; Hunt, *Irish Medieval Figure Sculpture* (1974), I, 198–9.

Abbeymahon Cork (Fig. 65)

The monastery was founded as a daughter house of Baltinglass in 1172/89 by Dermot MacCormac MacCarthy, king of Desmond. The site is unusual for a Cistercian abbey, lying on the picturesque shore of the estuary of

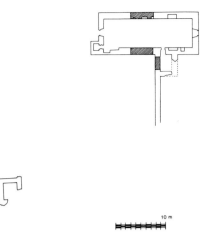

Fig. 65   Abbeymahon, plan of remains.

Argideen River, just over a mile east south-east of Timoleague on the road to Courtmacsherry. The monastery was originally sited at Aghamanister, two miles away to the south-west, but the community had moved by 1278 when a burial took place in the 'new monastery'. Both Smith in 1750 and O'Sullivan in 1944 tried to prove that the abbey was situated at Carrigiliky near Glandore, sixteen miles away, but their arguments can be refuted on both historical and architectural grounds.

The beauty of the site is unfortunately not matched by the beauty of the remains. Devoid of attractive details, they consist largely of the east end of the church, which had a square ended presbytery of standard Cistercian form. There were transepts to north and south, but both transept arches have been blocked. (Parts of the original arch moulding are visible on the south side.)

To the south of the chancel was a roughly square chapel 10 by 9 feet (3.0 × 2.7 metres) and portions of its barrel vault and entry arch remain. This shows that Abbeymahon was planned along standard Cistercian lines, with a square-ended chancel, flanked by one or more transept chapels. At some stage in the later middle ages the church was drastically reduced in size by the insertion of a cross wall in the nave and by the blocking of the transepts. A turret was incorporated into the new facade as part of the remodelling. At the south-west corner of what was once the cloister are the remnants of a tower.

Bibliography: C. Smith, *The County and City of Cork* (1750), I, 263; J. M. Burke, 'The Abbey of Sancta Mauro', *JCHAS*, X (1904), 251–3; Power, 'Cistercian Abbeys of Munster', *JCHAS*, XXXIV (1929), 22–9; O'Sullivan, 'Cistercian Abbey of Fonte Vivo', *JCHAS*, XLIX (1944), 1–9; Gwynn and Hadcock, *Medieval Religious Houses* (1970), 125; *Extents*, 151–2.

Abbeyshrule Longford (Fig. 17)

The monastery lies beside the River Inny (much altered now by recent drainage schemes), four and a half miles east north-east of Ballymahon

on the borders of Longford and Westmeath. A large graveyard has developed immediately to the north of the abbey and there are many burials in and around the medieval buildings. The history of the monastery is poorly documented and the ruins have been much neglected.

The abbey was colonised from Mellifont in 1200 and the founders were the O'Ferralls, the Irish chieftains of the district. By the later middle ages it was completely under the influence of the O'Ferralls, many of whom acted as commendatory abbots, and in 1540/1 it was reported that 'long before the dissolution' the goods of the monastery 'were carried off and consumed by certain Irish called O'Feralleys'. It is unlikely that monastic life, if it survived until 1540, continued beyond this date. In 1476 it was recorded that the abbey had been burnt by English forces.

The interior of the church is filled with impenetrable brambles and the standing remains, overwhelmed by ivy, do little to elucidate the history of the site. Parts of the early thirteenth-century presbytery, with two round-headed lancet windows, survive and there is some evidence of a wide arch leading into the south transept. What was probably the western crossing arch was blocked at a later period, when three low barrel-vaulted chambers were erected, the latter apparently acting as the base of a (?)rood screen. A bellcote was constructed on the wall above. The remnants of an aisleless nave stretch out to the west, giving the building a total length of approximately 135 feet (41 metres). At a very late date, possibly in the seventeenth or early eighteenth century, a chapel was built within the original presbytery, reusing two of its walls. Some formless masonry and mounds represent the site of the east range. About a hundred feet south of the church is a tower, built above a vaulted basement, evidently a post-Reformation 'tower house'. The discovery of bones and skulls outside the east wall of the church (the site of the monastic cemetery) has led to mythical tales of monks being slaughtered there *en masse*. Without clearance and excavation, this disappointing and frustrating monument will remain difficult to interpret, but there is no indication that its architecture was ever particularly impressive.

Bibliography: Langan, 'Abbeyshrule, Co. Longford' (1884), 652–6; Hamilton Thompson, Clapham and Leask, 'Cistercian Order in Ireland' (1931), 13, 27–8; Gwynn and Hadcock, *Medieval Religious Houses* (1970), 125–6; *Extents*, 284.

Abington Limerick (Pl. 76)

Variously known as Mainistir Uaithne, Woney or Owney, the monastery at Abington, nine miles east of Limerick, lay on the banks of the River Mulkear, a tributary of the Shannon. The monastic buildings were located near the existing graveyard, but their exact position is unclear. There is no certainty that the two ruined structures outside the graveyard wall formed part of the medieval fabric, as is commonly supposed, and there is a surprising lack of medieval dressed stonework in neighbouring walls. The obliteration of the monastery is disappointing, since it was one of the major Anglo-Norman houses of Ireland. The abbey was colonised from Furness in Lancashire and after brief sojourns at Wyresdale (Lancashire) and Arklow (Wicklow), the monks settled at Abington in 1205. Their patron was Theobald Walter, brother of Hubert Walter, archbishop of Canterbury, and founder of the Butler fortunes in Ireland. Theobald was buried in the abbey in 1206, though it is unlikely that any of the stone buildings had been completed by then. In the later middle ages, the community succumbed to the excessive attentions of the local O'Mulryan family and at the time of the Reformation in 1540 John O'Mulryan was abbot of the house. He managed to escape the dissolution by getting Abington established as a secular college with himself as provost, a status which was abandoned by 1552. Four years before, the abbey is said to have been attacked and burnt by O'Carroll and the medieval buildings sustained further damage when they were burnt during the Cromwellian wars in 1647.

An illustration of the monastery by Thomas Dinely, made thirty years after this second attack, shows the extensive buildings roofless but otherwise intact. Dinely's perspective is erratic, but it cannot conceal the 'Early English' character of the church, most marked in the steep lancets of the east gable. The presbytery had an additional buttress (or buttresses) at the angle, which might suggest a vault, and there is a prominent tower over the crossing. Shortly after Dinely's visit the ruins were apparently swept away by Joseph Stepney, who built a manor house on the site. Like the monastery before it, this too has perished. As a daughter house of Furness, the architecture of Abington may have played an important role in introducing the Early English style to the west of Ireland and the east gable, as drawn by Dinely, is reminiscent of the corresponding parts of St Brendan's Cathedral, Ardfert (Kerry).

Bibliography: Archdall, *Monasticon Hibernicum*, 411–13; *Ordnance Survey Letters, Limerick* II, 120–7; Seymour, 'Abbey Owney' (1907), 165–80, 360–73; Power, 'Cistercian Abbeys of Munster' (1929), 91–7; Gwynn and Hadcock, *Medieval Religious Houses* (1970), 126.

Assaroe Donegal

The monastery at Assaroe occupied an unusual site on a hillside overlooking the estuary of the River Erne, about three-quarters of a mile north-west of Ballyshannon. The buildings were placed near the confluence of the Abbey river and a small tributary, on ground which was unusually steep for the Cistercians. The site is now jointly occupied by a graveyard and a farmyard. The monastery was founded in 1178 as a daughter house of Boyle, evidently under the patronage of the kings of Tirconaill. A fire in 1377 may have necessitated substantial

rebuilding in the later fourteenth century. Following the Reformation a Cistercian community appears to have survived until about 1607, although the estates had been granted out to English lords many years earlier. An inquisition of 1588–9 mentions a church and steeple, shingled and thatched, a ruined dormitory and three other stone buildings. The abbey was depicted with a tall crossing tower on a map of the battle of Ballyshannon (1593), though the drawing may be a cartographer's convention. In 1795 substantial parts of the abbey still remained and Seward recounted that 'this piece of antiquity is worth attention; some of the gilding in the vault of the cloister is still visible'.

The only part of the abbey to survive is what appears to be the west end of an aisleless church, 27 feet 6 inches (8.39 metres) wide. This includes a section of the south wall and part of the west gable, heavily ivy clad. Several moulded stones lying in the graveyard have profiles of c1200, which can be related to work in the mother house at Boyle. Further fragments, including capitals and a piece of tracery, are built into the graveyard wall. There appears to be no sign of the tomb of 'abbot O'Quin', mentioned by O'Donovan in 1835 (*Ordnance Survey Letters, Donegal*, 151–2).

Bibliography: Archdall, *Monasticon Hibernicum*, 93–5; Seward, *Topographia Hibernica* (1795); Gwynn and Hadcock, *Medieval Religious Houses* (1970), 127; B. Lacy, *Archaeological Survey of County Donegal* (Lifford, 1983), 327–8.

Baltinglass Wicklow (Pls 44, 51, 144, 183, 186; Figs 16, 55, 56, 60)

Founded by Dermot McMurrough, king of Leinster, in 1148, this was the second daughter house of Mellifont. The site lies beside the River Slaney to the west of the Wicklow mountains. After the Anglo-Norman conquest of Leinster, the abbey maintained a strong Irish identity and it was deeply implicated in the conspiracy of Mellifont. In 1227 abbot Malachy, described by Stephen of Lexington as 'that perverse and deceitful fox', was deposed and sent to Fountains Abbey for two years, though he soon absconded to fight his case at Citeaux and Rome. The monastery was dissolved in 1536, one of the first Cistercian victims of the Reformation, and the estate passed to Sir Thomas FitzEustace, later Viscount Baltinglass. The old Cistercian chancel was adapted as a Protestant church and remained in use until 1883. The 'abbot's castle' to the south-east was demolished in 1882 by the rector to provide materials for the construction of a new parish church and glebe house.

Although none of the conventual buildings survive, the ruins of the monastic church (c1148–80) are of great interest, with an imposing nave arcade and a variety of sculptural details. The square-ended presbytery (probably covered by a barrel vault) and the relatively low arches leading into the transepts reflect the influence of early Cistercian churches in Burgundy. Contrary to Cistercian norms,

however, is the way the two transept chapels project separately, a feature discovered during excavations in 1955. Unobtrusive carvings at the east end of the church are the work of local Romanesque craftsmen. The nave arches are supported on alternating square and cylindrical piers, the capitals of which are decorated with a range of unusual designs by the so-called Baltinglass Master, who is subsequently found working at Jerpoint. The clerestory windows (only the lower splays survive) are sited over the piers, not over the arches, the first example of an arrangement which was to become popular in Ireland. Other features of interest are the bases of two Romanesque doorways in the nave aisles and well-preserved sedilia in the presbytery.

In the later middle ages a substantial tower was erected in the old crossing, the supporting walls of which remain. This was replaced in 1815 (at a cost of £500) by a more slender neo-Gothic tower, which still occupies part of the nave.

Bibliography: Archdall, *Monasticon Hibernicum*, 761–4; FitzGerald, 'Baltinglass Abbey' (1906–8), 379–414; Hamilton Thompson, Clapham and Leask, 'Cistercian Order in Ireland' (1931), 13, 21–3; Leask, *Irish Churches*, II, 26–8; Gwynn and Hadcock, *Medieval Religious Houses* (1970), 127–8; Beuer-Szlechter, 'Débuts de l'Art Cistercien en Irlande' (1970), 201–18; *Extents*, 126.

Bective Meath (Pls 87, 141, 150–1, 216, 277–9; Fig. 63)

This was the first daughter house of Mellifont, founded early in 1147 by Murchad O'Melaghlin, king of Meath. It is situated about fifteen miles south-west of Mellifont on the banks of the River Boyne. This was an area of heavy settlement following the Anglo-Norman invasion of Ireland and in 1228 the abbey was said to lie 'in a strongly fortified place', a reference perhaps to the great castle of Trim, just over four miles away. In 1274 the archbishop of Cashel considered moving the community to a new site, but nothing came of this. In the later middle ages Bective lay within the Pale and it was one of the few abbeys to remain in touch with Mellifont, its mother house. The monastery was dissolved in 1536 and by 1540 the roof of the church had been dismantled. The site was taken over by Thomas Agard, a successful Tudor bureaucrat, and it subsequently passed through the hands of a variety of secular owners.

The ruins of the abbey are outwardly formidable in appearance, more military than religious in flavour. Nothing survives of the original twelfth-century monastery and the earliest work is the south arcade (later blocked) of the church, rebuilt after 1274. With its plain piers and clerestory windows of quatrefoil shape, this design is closely related to the church at Hore. The five surviving bays were exactly laid out with individual widths of 16 feet 6 inches (the medieval perch). The plan of the east end is not known, but it is likely to have followed the standard Cistercian scheme, with two chapels in each arm of the transept. The cloister and conventual buildings were totally reconstructed in the later middle ages and the two surviving cloister walks are particularly attractive. One of the piers is decorated with a carving of a kneeling abbot. The surrounding ranges were built over vaulted basements and two massive towers were erected about the same time, turning the monastery into a veritable fortress. A further tower appears to have been erected over the crossing of the church, to judge from the reinforcement of the south transept arch. Following the dissolution, the abbey was remodelled as a sprawling Tudor mansion, with the insertion of new fireplaces, chimneys and large mullioned windows (see chapter 11).

Bibliography: Leask, 'Bective Abbey' (1916), 46–57; Hamilton Thompson, Clapham and Leask, 'Cistercian Order in Ireland' (1931), 11, 29; Leask, *Irish Churches*, III, 27–8, 145–7; Gwynn and Hadcock, *Medieval Religious Houses* (1970), 128; *Extents*, 267–70.

Boyle Roscommon (Pls 15, 24, 35, 43, 47, 54–5, 57–60, 132–3, 185, 190–8, 240, 271; Figs 30, 31)

A community which set out from Mellifont in 1148 eventually settled at Boyle in 1161, after experimenting with three previous sites. The buildings were erected on the banks of the River Boyle, about a mile from the point at which it enters Lough Key. An earlier monastery, known as Ath-da-Larc, previously existed here, but no remnants of it survive and it had probably died out before the Cistercians arrived. The patrons and probable founders were the MacDermots of Moylurg, many of whom were buried in the abbey. The history of the monastery is relatively well documented by the local annals, one set of which was written at Boyle (the so-called Cottonian Annals, British Library, Cotton Ms. Titus A XXV). During the struggle for control of Connacht, the monastery was twice attacked by English forces, in 1202 and in 1235, and several further violations of the abbey are recorded. By 1231 the church had become a centre of local pilgrimage. It is not clear exactly when the monastery was dissolved, but in 1569 its lands were granted to Patrick Cusack of Gerardstown (County Meath). From 1592 the monastic buildings were used as a barracks, known as 'Boyle Castle', and for this reason the abbey was besieged in 1645 during the Cromwellian wars.

The well-preserved church at Boyle is the most attractive and rewarding Cistercian monument in Ireland. Built over a long period from 1161 to 1220, it illustrates several distinct phases of architectural design. The eastern limb is planned according to the standard Cistercian scheme, with two chapels in each transept, and together with the barrel-vaulted presbytery this work carries a strong Burgundian imprint. The sources of the nave arcade, with its heterogeneous collection of pier forms, lie in the

Romanesque and Transitional architecture of the west of England: the cylindrical piers of the south arcade are remarkably similar to those at Abbey Dore (Herefordshire). The crossing tower was a thirteenth-century addition, and so too were the three Gothic lancets in the presbytery. The chief delight of the building is an array of sculptured capitals and corbels, several of which are decorated with animals and human figures, the work of the so-called Ballintober Master. The conventual buildings were much altered and disfigured during the military period. One wall of the east range survives, with remnants of elaborate doorways to the chapter house and (?)parlour. The recently restored gatehouse is largely seventeenth-century and so too is much of the south range, where there are fine Jacobean chimneys and a defensive turret, the latter often mistaken for an early Irish round tower. Excavations in the cloister garth in 1983 uncovered a large drain, but failed to produce any trace of the medieval cloister arcade.

Bibliography: Archdall, *Monasticon Hibernicum*, 601–6; Champneys, *Irish Ecclesiastical Architecture* (1910), 147–51; Hamilton Thompson, Clapham and Leask, 'Cistercian Order in Ireland' (1931), 12, 24; Leask, *Irish Churches*, II, 32–5, 61–3; Gwynn and Hadcock, *Medieval Religious Houses* (1970), 128–9; Stalley, *Architecture and Sculpture* (1971), 100–10; Stalley, 'A Romanesque Sculptor in Connaught' (1973), 1826–30.

Clare Island Mayo (Pls 108, 246, 257; Fig. 38)

A community of monks living on Clare Island is said to have been driven off by pirates in 1224, following which the church became a cell of Abbeyknockmoy. It certainly belonged to Abbeyknockmoy in 1584, when it was listed among its possessions. The settlement was small and it is unlikely that more than two or three monks ever lived there. The community survived until the early years of the seventeenth century and Ware reported that about 1650 'there were people living who remembered they had seen Monks in this Abbey and that it was then standing, well built and full of pictures'. The site lies one and a half miles west of the harbour on the slopes beneath Knockmore, a spectacular position with views across Clew Bay to the Connemara mountains. It was exceedingly remote and even today rough seas often prevent any crossing to the island.

The ruins of the cell date from the late middle ages, and there may be some truth in Luckombe's assertion that the abbey was founded (or rebuilt) in 1460. There is a short aisleless nave, and an arch, with four plain orders, leads into a simple square chancel. This is barrel-vaulted and, with only two slender ogee-headed lights, it must always have been very dark. A straight staircase in the south wall leads to a domestic chamber above the vault. To the north of the chancel is an annexe, an addition to the main structure. This has a sacristy on the ground floor and another

domestic chamber above, the latter reached by a mural stair and furnished with a garderobe. The chief interest of the building are the fragmentary paintings on the vault of the chancel—a heterogeneous collection of figures and animals set within a framework of painted ribs—all of which must have been virtually invisible in the gloomy interior. The design of the pseudo-ribs appears to be modelled on the real ribs at Abbeyknockmoy. There is also a fine traceried tomb canopy in the church and a water stoop carved with animals.

The ruins at Clare Island provide an excellent illustration of the tight combination of church and living accommodation found frequently in late medieval Ireland.

Bibliography: Alemand, *Monasticon Hibernicum* (1722), 195–6; Luckombe, *Tour Through Ireland* (1780), 216; Westropp, 'Cliara Abbey' (1911–15), 29–37; Leask, *Irish Churches*, III, 175, 179; Hadcock, *Medieval Religious Houses* (1970), 129.

Comber Down

The monastery at Comber vanished completely during the Tudor and Stuart period. It was founded in 1199/1200 as a daughter house of Whitland in Wales. The site of the abbey and subsequent town lies at the north-west end of Strangford Lough, at the mouth of the river Enler. An early Irish monastery, founded by St Patrick, existed here, but this was probably defunct when the Cistercians arrived (it had been attacked in 1031, when its oratory was burnt and four of its clerics killed). The monastery was surrendered by the last abbot in 1543 and the property eventually passed in 1607 to Sir James Hamilton, viscount Clandeboye. The buildings were burnt in 1573 during the earl of Essex's campaigns in Ulster. The ruins were exploited as a quarry by Scottish settlers and materials from the abbey were also used in the construction of Mount Alexander, home of the Hamilton family (now destroyed). The monastery was on the site of St Mary's Protestant church and there is a moulded stone in the graveyard wall (north side). A building to the south of the church reuses a dressed stone with a mason's mark. A fragment of a thirteenth-century tomb slab has recently been identified, set upside down as a grave marker (information from Ann Hamlin).

Bibliography: Archdall, *Monasticon Hibernicum*, 112–13; Reeves, *Ecclesiastical Antiquities* (1847), 198; O'Laverty, *Down and Connor*, II (1880), 136–40; *Triumphalia*, xxxviii; *ASNI*, 289–90; Gwynn and Hadcock, *Medieval Religious Houses* (1970), 130.

Corcomroe Clare (Pls 1, 16, 21, 85–6, 120, 203–4, 233–4, 247; Figs 9, 26)

Situated in an unforgettable position amidst the stony mountains of the Burren, Corcomroe lies five miles west of Kinvara, on the south side of Galway Bay. Cultivation of the soil can never have been easy, but the spot was not as desolate as it first appears, a point appropriately made by the latin name of the abbey, Petra Fertilis. As there is no stream beside the monastery, its water supply probably came from local springs or a well. The site was colonised from Inislounaght in 1194/5 and the founder was either Donal Mór O'Brien, king of Thomond, or his son Donough Cairbreach. The community was always small and in the later middle ages extremely poor. Although a titular abbot is named in 1628, the house had long ceased to exist as a monastic entity. In 1554 the abbey was granted to Murrough O'Brien, earl of Thomond, the site thus reverting to the same family who gave the original endowment over three hundred years before.

The church dates from 1210 to 1225, and was planned as a reduced version of the normal Cistercian scheme, with only one chapel opening off each transept. There is an aisled nave, though the roughly built arches are not arranged symmetrically north and south and there is some doubt about whether a north aisle was ever built. The east end of the building is distinguished by the high quality of its stonework—carved capitals, decorated bases, chevron and other ornament—much of it characteristic of the 'school of the west'. The presbytery is rib-vaulted in two bays. Before work progressed beyond the transepts a serious deterioration in quality occurred, perhaps due to the famines of 1227–8. In the later middle ages the church was shortened by an inserted wall, surmounted by a bell turret, and at the same time the roofs and upper walls were extensively remodelled. Fragmentary buildings survive in the east range and there are a number of featureless ruins in the outer precincts, including the remains of a gatehouse. Inside the church is a magnificent sedile, together with the effigy of King Conor na Suidane O'Brien (d. 1267), grandson of the founder. There are also some incised architectural drawings on the walls.

Bibliography: Power, 'Cistercian Abbeys of Munster' (1928), 78–81; Hamilton Thompson, Clapham and Leask, 'Cistercian Order in Ireland' (1931), 17, 25–7; Leask, *Irish Churches*, II, 58–9; Gwynn and Hadcock, *Medieval Religious Houses* (1970), 130; Stalley, *Architecture and Sculpture* (1971), 118–19; Stalley, 'Corcomroe Abbey' (1975), 23–46.

Dublin St Mary's (Pls 115, 179; Fig. 52)

The early history of St Mary's, Dublin, is obscure but it appears that it was founded as a daughter house of Savigny in 1139. After the order of Savigny was united with the Cistercians in 1147, it was made subject to Combermere (Cheshire) and then in 1156 to Buildwas (Shropshire). Since it was founded three years before Mellifont, this led to controversies between the two houses over seniority, the General Chapter recognising the claims of St Mary's in 1313. With its two daughter houses at Dunbrody (1182) and Abbeylara (1214), it was the head of a clearly marked group within the order, strongly anglophile in sentiment. It was the richest Cistercian monastery in Ireland

(valued at £537.17.10 in 1540) maintaining twelve and possibly eighteen monks at the time of the dissolution in 1539. Many of the buildings remained intact until the late seventeenth century, when the site was re-developed by Sir Humphrey Jervis and Sir Richard Reynell. At this time, the abbey was being used as a quarry and in 1676 stones from St Mary's were used in the construction of Essex Bridge.

The monastery was located on the north bank of the River Liffey, opposite the old city of Dublin, a most inappropriate site for a Cistercian house. The community was frequently involved in the affairs of city and state. The buildings lay between Capel Street and Arran Street East, with Meetinghouse Lane following the line of the east walk of the cloister. All that is left today is the chapter house of c1200, rib-vaulted in four bays, and an adjoining passage or slype. Excavations in the mid-1880s produced numerous tiles and uncovered some walls and piers, but no authoritative record was made of the discoveries and published plans of the abbey are speculative. A wooden carving of the Madonna, reputedly from St Mary's, is now in the Carmelite church, in Whitefriar Street, and fragments of a Perpendicular cloister arcade, discovered in 1975 in Cook Street, may have belonged to the monastery.

There is little doubt that St Mary's Abbey had some of the finest medieval buildings in Ireland and, located beside the port of Dublin, it was open to strong architectural influence from England. Of all Cistercian monuments in Ireland this is the one most in need of excavation. In 1983 planning permission was given for the construction of a shopping precinct and offices on a major section of the site.

Bibliography: CMA; *Extents*, 1–25; Archdall, *Monasticon Hibernicum*, 132–47; *Remains of St Mary's Abbey, Dublin* (1886); Hamilton Thompson, Clapham and Leask, 'Cistercian Order in Ireland', 11–12; 'Proceedings', *Archaeological Journal* (1931), 348; Gwynn, 'Origins of St Mary's Abbey' (1949), 110–25; Leask, *Irish Churches*, II, 47; MacNiocaill, *Na Manaigh Liatha* (1959), 191–5; Gwynn and Hadcock, *Medieval Religious Houses* (1970), 130–1.

Dunbrody Wexford (Pls 2, 10, 19, 63–9, 139, 167, 173, 281; Fig. 20)

Situated on the east shore of Waterford harbour, 'beside the whispering waves', the austere ruins of Dunbrody form one of the most imposing Cistercian monuments in the country. The neighbouring estuary was an important transport artery in the middle ages and the abbey lies about eleven miles downstream from the Anglo-Norman town of New Ross. The site was given to the abbey of Buildwas in 1171–5 by Hervé de Montmorency, the seneschal and uncle of Strongbow. After the English abbey received an unfavourable report from one of its laybrothers, the land was transferred to St Mary's, Dublin, who sent

a community to the site in 1182. During the turmoils that affected the Cistercian order in the 1220s, Dunbrody, as an Anglo-Norman house, gave support to Stephen Lexington during his visitation. In the later middle ages, it suffered badly from the depredations of the Kavanaghs and many of its estates were waste when the monastery was dissolved in 1536. The propery was granted to Sir Osborne Etchingham in 1545 and soon after part of the south transept was converted into a Tudor manor house.

The ruins are dominated by the spacious early Gothic church (c1210–40), which has large cavernous transepts, and three rib-vaulted chapels in each arm. The five-bay nave lost its south arcade in 1852, but the north elevation is well-preserved. The arches are unusually wide and the clerestory windows are placed, as so often in Ireland, over the piers. A massive central tower was erected in the fifteenth century, supported on additional arches and buttress piers inserted into the crossing. Still partially intact in the east range are the sacristy, chapter house, slype or parlour and dorter undercroft, and in the south range the walls of the refectory are standing almost to full height. The vast cloister (almost 120 feet square) included what may have been a small circular lavabo and there are fragments of a fifteenth-century cloister arcade. Across the fields to the south are the remnants of a gatehouse and (?) chapel.

Bibliography: CMA, I, 354–5; *Extents*, 353–7; Archdall, *Monasticon Hibernicum*, 736–40; Power, 'Dunbrody Abbey' (1895), 67–82; Hore, *Wexford*, I, 36–46, II, 116–92; *Reports of Commissioners of Public Works* (1896), (1904), (1910); Hamilton Thompson, Clapham and Leask, 'Cistercian Order in Ireland' (1931), 15, 29; Leask, *Irish Churches*, II, 83–4; Gwynn and Hadcock, *Medieval Religious Houses* (1970), 131–2; Stalley, *Architecture and Sculpture* (1971), 120–4; Beuer-Szlechter, 'L'Abbaye de Dunbrody' (1977), 208–23.

Fermoy Cork

This daughter house of Inislounaght was situated in the picturesque valley of the Blackwater, but all trace of the monastery has long since vanished beneath the modern town. It lay on the south side of the river where its memory is kept alive by the name 'Abbey Street'. The site was colonised in 1170 and the founder was Donal Mór O'Brien, king of Thomond. Like other O'Brien foundations, the abbey was opposed to English influence in the neighbourhood and in the 1220s the community was heavily involved in the conspiracy of Mellifont. A non-Irish abbot imposed on the monastery in 1227 was murdered three years later, reputedly by his own monks. In the later middle ages several pleas of poverty are recorded, most notably in 1467 when the abbey claimed it was impoverished 'by reason of wars and other misfortunes in times past' and had no resources to repair its buildings. The house was evidently dissolved in 1539–41, when most of its landed possessions were said to be waste. Archdall claimed that 'the church of the abbey, now the parish church, was a mean Gothic building', but this together with other remnants of the abbey perished after the foundation of the town by the Scottish merchant John Anderson in 1791.

Bibliography: *Extents*, 144–5; *Monasticon Hibernicum*, 69–70; Power, 'Cistercian Abbeys of Munster' (1929), 23–4; O'Sullivan, 'Cistercian Abbey of St Mary de Castro Dei' (1946), 170–81; Gwynn and Hadcock, *Medieval Religious Houses* (1970), 132–3.

Graiguenamanagh (also known as Duiske) Kilkenny (Pls 36, 71–4, 122, 154, 157, 207, 250, 254; Figs 27, 50, 51)

The early Gothic church at Graiguenamanagh was the largest Cistercian building in Ireland and the monastery's vast cloister garth (120 feet square) was equalled only by Dunbrody. It was founded in 1204 as a daughter house of Stanley (Wiltshire) and its founding patron was William Marshal, earl of Leinster. The fact that his charter was not issued until 1207 has led to the mistaken belief that this was the year of the monastery's foundation. The community had brief sojourns at two places nearby, before settling permanently in the valley of the River Barrow on a site between the main river and its fast-flowing tributary, the Duiske. It was a wild and picturesque spot in the shadow of Brandon Hill, ideally suited to the Cistercians.

At the end of the century the monastery was heavily in debt on account of forward selling on the wool market, and in 1299 it owed 700 marks to the Ricardi of Lucca. The last abbot, Charles Kavanagh, who made a pilgrimage to Santiago in 1530, presented his monastery with precious vestments and a silver-gilt cross in 1524. The house was dissolved in 1536 and two years later the property passed to the earl of Ormond. In 1813 the ruins of the chancel, transepts and parts of the nave were reroofed and restored 'in a poverty stricken, untutored manner', to use the words of the *Shell Guide*. The floor was laid over countless burials and accumulated debris 4 feet 9 inches (1.45 metres) above the original. The west end of the church was restored and partly rebuilt in 1886. A major restoration of the church began in 1974, but it has not proved possible to reinstate the original floor level. Excavations in the north transept in 1977 brought to light large sections of the thirteenth-century tiled pavement.

The church had a rib-vaulted presbytery (only the springers remain), transepts with three chapels in each arm, an octagonal crossing tower (which fell in 1744), and a seven-bay nave. The four eastern bays of the medieval nave, together with almost all the aisles, have been destroyed, but it is still possible to get a good impression of the thirteenth-century design. The building is an outstanding example of the Early English style and is noted for much fine detail—stiff-leaf capitals, dog-tooth ornament, banded shafts, etc. Considerable remnants of the claustral buildings survive amidst sheds, backyards and neighbouring gardens.

These include a fine triple archway which led into the chapter house vestibule and fragments of the refectory pulpit. Inside the church there is a high quality effigy of a knight in sword-seizing pose (c1300).

Bibliography: 'Charters of Duiske'; *Extents*, 193–8; Archdall, *Monasticon Hibernicum*, 351–5; O'Leary, 'Notes' (1892), 237–43; Cochrane, 'Notes' (1892), 243–7; O'Leary, *Graiguenamanagh Abbey* (1924), Hamilton Thompson, Clapham and Leask, 'Cistercian Order in Ireland' (1931), 19, 28–9; Leask, *Irish Churches*, II, 86–9; Carville, *Norman Splendour* (1979); Bradley and Manning, 'Excavations at Duiske Abbey' (1981), 397–426.

Grey Abbey Down (Pls 5, 37, 61, 130, 165, 168, 206, 276; Fig. 11)

Founded in 1193 by Affreca, wife of John de Courcy, Grey was colonised from the English monastery of Holm Cultram (Cumberland) with which it maintained close ties in the early years. In 1222 and again in 1237 abbots of Grey went on to become abbots of Holm Cultram. These northern English connections are reflected in architecture, the buildings of Grey being among the first examples of Gothic in Ireland. The monastery is located in the Ards Peninsula, seven miles from Newtownards, at a point where a small river rushes into Strangford Lough. Two other houses lay in close proximity: Inch sixteen miles across the Lough to the south and Comber (founded six years later) only eight miles to the west. Little is known about the history of the abbey, though it is clear that it suffered badly during the invasion of Edward Bruce (1315–18). It was dissolved by 1541, when some of its lands were granted to Gerald, earl of Kildare. In 1572 the buildings were burnt by Sir Brian O'Neill to prevent them being used as a refuge by English colonists in the Ards. The nave was reroofed in 1626 or 1685 and served as a parish church until 1778.

There are impressive remains of both the church and some of the conventual buildings, dating from c1193 to c1250. The east end of the church was laid out in conventional manner, with two barrel-vaulted chapels in each transept. The double set of pointed lancets in the presbytery provide an unmistakable Gothic stamp. A crossing tower, now partially fallen, was erected as part of the original design. The most surprising feature of the church is the plain, aisleless nave, the only embellishment of which is an attractive Early English doorway in the west facade. This was rebuilt in 1842 and it may have been moved from another part of the abbey in 1626/85. In the fifteenth century the roof of the presbytery was remodelled and a sculptured corbel table was added at eaves level. Possibly at the same time, tracery was added to two of the windows. The conventual buildings were laid out with some grandeur, a point evident in the well-built foundations of the chapter house, slype and dorter undercroft. The most memorable building, however, is the refectory, with three lancet windows in the south gable. The contrast between the well-proportioned claustral buildings and the simple nave suggests that the original architectural intentions of the monks were not fulfilled.

Bibliography: Archdall, *Monasticon Hibernicum*, 120–1; Phillips, *Grey Abbey* (1874); O'Laverty, *Down and Connor*, I, 433–40; *Reports of Commissioners of Public Works* (1908); Hamilton Thompson, Clapham and Leask, 'Cistercian Order in Ireland' (1931), 17, 27; Leask, *Irish Churches*, II, 49–51; *ASNI*, 275–9; Gwynn and Hadcock, *Medieval Religious Houses* (1970), 134.

Holycross Tipperary (Pls 14, 25, 27, 28, 31, 38, 92–6, 98–103, 105–6, 124–6, 147, 149, 156, 175, 226–8, 231, 235–7, 255, 272, 275; Figs 7, 37, 45, 54, 61)

An unusually ornate church and a remarkable array of monastic buildings make Holycross the most distinguished monument of fifteenth-century Ireland. It lies on the banks of the River Suir, nine miles north of the Rock of Cashel. Although it struggled to survive in the thirteenth century, the combination of Ormond patronage and the popularity of its relics transformed the fortunes of the house in the later middle ages. It was colonised from Monasteranenagh in 1180, though its foundation charter from Donal Mór O'Brien, king of Thomond, dates from 1185/6. Arguments for the existence of an earlier monastery at the site are not conclusive. Although it lay in an area of heavy Anglo-Norman settlement, the abbey remained Irish in attitude and personnel. There was doubt about the abbey's ability to survive, but in 1228 Stephen of Lexington confirmed that it had sufficient resources for an independent existence. The monastery escaped dissolution in 1539–40 by transforming itself into a secular college, with Philip Purcell, the last abbot, installed as Provost. This status was extinguished by 1561 when the abbey and its property was granted to Thomas Butler, earl of Ormond. The abbey continued to function as a parish church and its famous relic remained an object of veneration. In the early years of the seventeenth century, the monastery was the focus of a modest revival of the Cistercian order, subsequently extinguished during the Cromwellian wars.

Of the original late twelfth/early thirteenth-century buildings, there remain only the north arcade of the nave, parts of the south aisle, the monks' doorway to the cloister and traces of early Gothic lancets in the west gable. Otherwise the architecture belongs to the later middle ages, representing a process of reconstruction that began around 1431. The rebuilt church followed a conventional layout, with a square presbytery and two chapels in each transept. There are lierne vaults over the presbytery, crossing and north transept, and the windows contain a varied range of curvilinear tracery. The building is decorated with an array of minor carvings and masons' marks, executed in the blue-grey limestone of the locality. In addition to the magnificent sedilia, there is a beautiful stone shrine in the south transept. The walls of the north transept contain the faded remnants of a painted hunting scene.

The ground floor of the east range survives, including a barrel-vaulted sacristy and diminutive chapter house. Even better preserved is the west range, which contains three linked dwelling chambers above vaulted basements. A section of 'Perpendicular' cloister arcade has recently been re-erected along the north walk beside the church. To the east of the cloister are two further groups of buildings, generally described as the infirmary, the abbot's lodgings or the guest house.

In 1971–5 the abbey was restored as the local parish church, and since then many alterations have taken place in the claustral buildings. Some of the more recent work is of an unacceptably low standard for what is one of Ireland's outstanding national monuments.

Bibliography: *Triumphalia*; Long, 'Old Cistercian Abbeys' (1896), 250–6; *Reports of the Commissioners of Public Works* (1881–2), (1906), (1913); Champneys, *Irish Ecclesiastical Architecture* (1910), 172–7; Hamilton Thompson, Clapham and Leask, 'Cistercian Order in Ireland' (1931), 15, 30–1; Power, 'Cistercian Abbeys of Munster' (1938), 1–6; Leask, *Irish Churches*, III, 59–69, 142–3; Carville, *Heritage of Holycross* (1973); Beuer-Szlechter, 'Eglise de l'Abbaye de Holycross' (1982), 423–46; Stalley, 'Irish Gothic and English Fashion' (1984), 80–4.

Hore Tipperary   (Pls 3, 30, 49, 88–9, 136–7, 230, 269–70; Figs 6, 15, 46)

Hore was the last Cistercian foundation in Ireland, being colonised from Mellifont in 1272 at the instigation of David McCarville, archbishop of Cashel. The site, approved by the abbots of Graiguenamanagh and Monasteranenagh in the previous year, was unusual, for it lay only half a mile west of the town of Cashel, within sound of the cathedral's bells. The water supply came from a small stream rising from a spring at the foot of the rock a few hundred yards away. The monastery was dissolved in 1540, though three monks stayed on as priests to serve the local parish, and the east end of the church remained in use as the parish church. The lands eventually passed to James Butler, earl of Ormond, and various parts of the monastery (the nave, south transept and chapter house) were converted into private houses.

The church and sections of the east range survive and they provide a good indication of Cistercian attitudes to design in the later thirteenth century. There is little decorative embellishment and the buildings are distinguished by their austere dignity. The church follows the usual Cistercian plan in Ireland, with two chapels in each transept, those to north still partly intact. The presbytery was not vaulted and was lit by three graded lancets in the east wall. The nave was exceptionally plain, with clerestory windows of quatrefoil form (cf. Bective) sited over the piers. The original design did not include a tower, so the roof must have run unbroken from east to west. The existing tower is a mid-fifteenth century addition and, with its fine limestone dressings and lierne vault, it is a typical example of Ormond architecture of the time. Many of the windows in the church were remodelled following the dissolution. The cloister lay to the north, the only Cistercian example of this in Ireland, and some fragments of cloister arcade remain. The walls of the church are characterised by a regular sequence of unfilled scaffolding holes. The overall design of Hore is a remarkable testimony to the conservative approach of the Cistercians, containing as it does several features of twelfth-century Burgundian origin.

Bibliography: Hamilton Thompson, Clapham and Leask, 'Cistercian Order in Ireland' (1931), 19, 30; O'Conbhuidhe, 'Abbey of the Rock of Cashel' (1961), 307–20; Leask, *Irish Churches*, II, 115–16; III, 45–6; Gwynn and Hadcock, *Medieval Religious Houses*, (1970), 129.

Inch Down   (Pls 22, 62; Figs 32, 33, 49)

The monastery at Inch was founded as a daughter house of Furness (Lancashire) by John de Courcy, soon after his conquest of Ulster. The foundation was made in recompense for the destruction in 1177 of Erenagh, a former Savigniac house, three miles away. The effective result was the replacement of an Irish community with a predominantly English one. Although Furness apparently received the grant in 1180, the new monastery was not established until 1187, allowing for the erection of essential buildings. The picturesque site, originally an island in the marshes beside the River Quoile, was not all that remote by Cistercian standards, being only three-quarters of a mile away from Downpatrick across the water. The island had been the site of a previous monastery known as Inis Cumhscraigh, which became defunct after 1153, and the enclosure of this earlier foundation has recently been detected in aerial photographs. Little is known about the history of the Cistercians at Inch and the community never appears to have been all that prosperous. It was suppressed before 1541, when the property was granted to Gerald, earl of Kildare.

The east end of the thirteenth-century church is well preserved, but otherwise the buildings have been reduced to foundation level. The seven tall lancet windows, which light the square-ended presbytery, form a striking early Gothic composition. In each transept, there were two rib-vaulted chapels, designed as an open aisle rather than separate spaces. The octofoil piers, which divide the chapels, reflect the abbey's links with the Cistercian monasteries of the north of England. The nave may have been constructed somewhat later in the century, to judge from the mouldings on the angle of the piers which can be paralleled on the late thirteenth-century chancel of Downpatrick Cathedral. In the later middle ages the church was reduced to a simple aisleless chapel, with an early Gothic doorway salvaged from part of the redundant building. The drastic remodelling of the church may have been forced on the community after the collapse of the crossing tower. The cloister was relatively small and in the fifteenth century it was rebuilt with delightful ogee arches and 'dumb-bell' piers of type A and C. The walls of buildings in the east and south range survive, though largely destitute of dressed masonry. There is no trace of the west range and it may never have been constructed in stone. There are a number of outlying foundations, including the remnants of a bakehouse. In the 1870s 'a considerable quantity of stained glass, exhibiting foliage and animals' was found inside the chancel.

Bibliography: Archdall, *Monasticon Hibernicum*, 122; O'Laverty, *Down and Connor*, I (pt. 4), 4–7; *ASNI*, 279–81; Leask, *Irish Churches*, II, 47–9; Gwynn and Hadcock, *Medieval Religious Houses* (1970), 135; Hamlin, 'A Recently Discovered Enclosure at Inch' (1977), 85–8.

Inislounaght Tipperary   (Pl. 286)

Founded as a daughter house of Mellifont in 1148, the affiliation of Inislounaght was transferred to Monasteranenagh three years later. The chief benefactor is said to have been Malachy O'Phelan, but it seems that the monastery was re-endowed by Donal Mór O'Brien, king of Limerick, in 1187. The monastery was situated in the modern village of Marlfield, two miles west of Clonmel. It was an attractive site, about three-hundred yards from the River Suir, and the beauty of the place is reflected in its Irish name, Inis Leamhnachta (Island of the fresh milk). The monastery had daughter houses at Fermoy (1170), Corcomroe (1195) and Glanawydan (suppressed 1228). The community was deeply implicated in the conspiracy of Mellifont (1227–8) and in a notorious episode the prior laid an ambush for one of Lexington's assistants, hiding armed supporters behind a hedge in the house of the nuns. In 1467 the monastic buildings were said to be in need of repair. The abbey was dissolved in 1540 and some of its lands subsequently passed to Sir Thomas Butler. Although the royal commissioners stated in 1541 that the abbey church could be 'thrown down', the walls were standing in 1654 and ruins were still visible in 1746. No trace of the old walls can be

286 Inislounaght, Romanesque doorway (with fifteenth-century hood) rebuilt in the Protestant Church at Marlfield.

seen today, but the Protestant church at Marlfield incorporates some interesting fragments. The east window—a debased Perpendicular affair with five lights—may have been taken from the abbey and inside there is a Romanesque doorway (c1180–1200) with two keeled rolls and scalloped capitals. The outer order and hood moulding are fifteenth-century additions. Built into the churchyard wall is a tomb slab with an elaborate cross and an inscription.

Bibliography: Extents, 337–9; Archdall, *Monasticon Hibernicum*, 661–3; *Ordnance Survey Letters, Kilkenny*, I, (1840), pp. 40–50; Bagwell, 'Innislonagh Abbey' (1909), 267–8; Power, 'Cistercian Abbeys of Munster' (1938), 8–11; O'-Conbhuidhe, 'Cistercian Abbey of Inislounaght' (1955–6), 3–52; Gwynn and Hadcock, *Medieval Religious Houses* (1970), 135–6.

Jerpoint Kilkenny (Pls 26, 45–6, 48, 53, 129, 138, 145, 162–3, 169, 182, 187–8, 209–215, 232, 242–3, 251–2, 268, 285; Figs 10, 24, 29)

Familiar to railway travellers *en route* to Waterford, Jerpoint is the best known and best loved of Irish Cistercian monasteries, its ruins containing architecture and sculpture of high quality. It is situated beside the River Eoir or Arrigle, about half a mile from its confluence with the Nore, just over a mile south-west of Thomastown. It was a daughter house of Baltinglass, founded either about 1160 or in 1180 (see Chapter 1, note 25). The architectural evidence strongly favours the earlier date, in which case the founder was Donal MacGillapatrick I, king of Ossory. It had two daughter houses, Killenny (1162–5) and Kilcooly (1184). When Killenny was suppressed and united with Graiguenamanagh in 1228, it unleashed a dispute which lasted over sixty years. In 1227 the first inklings of the trouble that erupted in the conspiracy of Mellifont occurred at Jerpoint when visitors, sent on behalf of the General Chapter, were greeted with a riot. In 1442 the monastery was granted an indulgence to help pay for repairs to the cloister, dormitory, bell tower and other offices. The community was dissolved in 1540 and the property granted to James Butler, earl of Ormond.

The church (c1160–1200) is well preserved and laid out in a conventional way with a square presbytery and two chapels in each transept. The austere Burgundian forms of the east end are tempered by an attractive array of capitals, the work of the Baltinglass Master. A substantial crossing tower was constructed in the fifteenth century, an imposing addition to the monastery. The six-bay nave has piers of alternating square and circular form (a sequence abandoned in the final two bays). Heavy screen walls of masonry divide the nave from the aisles. The east range of the conventual buildings has been much altered, but the vaulted sacristy, chapter house and parlour remain, together with a number of dormitory windows. The south and west ranges are more fragmentary. The chief delight of the abbey is

the sculptured cloister arcade (c1390–1400), reinstated in 1953. In addition, the church contains a variety of interesting tombs and grave slabs, including two fine effigies of ecclesiastics. About two hundred yards to the north are the ruins of a rectangular structure, perhaps the remains of a 'capella ante portas'.

Bibliography: Extents, 181–4; Archdall, *Monasticon Hibernicum*, 355–9; Carrigan, *History and Antiquities* (1905), IV, 278–98; Langrishe, 'Notes on Jerpoint Abbey' (1906), 179–87; Champneys, *Irish Ecclesiastical Architecture* (1910), 132–5, 232–4; Hamilton Thompson, Clapham and Leask, 'Cistercian Order in Ireland' (1930), 15, 23; Leask, *Irish Churches*, II, 28–32, III, 45, 136–7; O'Conbhuidhe, 'Origins of Jerpoint Abbey' (1963), 293–306; Rae, 'Sculpture of the Cloister at Jerpoint Abbey' (1966), 59–91; Gwynn and Hadcock, *Medieval Religious Houses* (1970), 136–7.

Kilbeggan Westmeath

This was an early daughter house of Mellifont, founded in 1150, probably by the MacCoghlans, the chief family of the district. It was the site of an early Irish monastery, founded by St Beccan in the fifth or sixth century and probably long since defunct by the time the Cistercians arrived. The monastery was dissolved in 1539 and in 1570 the site is said to have contained 'a church, hall, dormitory, three chambers and a cloister'.

The abbey was situated beside the River Brosna on a site occupied by the Protestant parish church, itself now a ruin. There are no architectural remains, nor apparently any recorded mention of them. Even in 1837 the remains of the monastery were described as 'very inconsiderable' (Lewis, *Topographical Dictionary*).

Bibliography: Archdall, *Monasticon Hibernicum*, 717–20; Gwynn and Hadcock, *Medieval Religious Houses* (1970), 137.

Kilcooly Tipperary (Pls 23, 109–12, 127, 164, 176–7, 221–4, 238–9, 241, 253; Figs 8, 21, 36)

The ruins of the monastery lie three miles south of Urlingford within the wooded demesne of an eighteenth-century house, also known as Kilcooly Abbey. The ancient name of the monastery (Arvus Campus—the arable plain) suitably reflects the flat terrain immediately around the buildings, which surprisingly were not situated close to a river or major stream. A 'ring work' just to the east of the abbey shows that the site had been inhabited before the Cistercians arrived. The community was a daughter house of Jerpoint, founded in 1184 by Donal Mór O'Brien, king of Thomond. The monastery was burnt in 1418 and then almost destroyed in 1445 when it was burnt again, this time by armed men. The abbey was dissolved in 1540 and the property passed to James Butler, earl of Ormond. The buildings continued to be inhabited until relatively recently, and it is possible that Cistercian monks returned

to the abbey for a short time in the 1640s, when one named John Stapleton is said to have served his novitiate there. About 1790 a large winged house was built east of the medieval buildings by Sir William Barker, whose family had previously resided in the old abbey. He erected 'a study or summer house' in the ruins, and when his own house was burnt in 1840, the family again lived in the medieval abbey for a short while.

Little remains of the earliest phase of the monastery's existence. The church apparently had an orthodox Cistercian plan, with two chapels in each transept, and an aisled nave, with plain piers and arches. The arcades were blocked in the fifteenth or sixteenth century as part of a wholesale reconstruction of the monastery. The barrel-vaulted presbytery has a large window with uncusped curvilinear tracery and the low, narrow transepts have an interesting range of ribbed vaults. The arches of the crossing tower are supported on a series of well-cut corbels. Built into the piers of the tower at the entrance to the nave are two elaborate stone sedilia for the abbot and prior. The wall which divides the south transept from the sacristy is decorated with several sculptured panels, executed in hard polished limestone. The night stair is built within the wall of the transept and gives access to a pleasant domestic chamber immediately above. The cloister buildings have been so much altered since 1540 that it is hard to disentangle their medieval form. The cloister garth was clearly used as a bawn, reached through a gateway in the south range. Some fragments are left of a late medieval cloister arcade. To the south-east is a large semi-fortified hall, built over a vaulted basement, and to the north-east is a well preserved columbarium. The Protestant church to the north-east was built on the site of an old chapel, which may have served as a 'capella ante portas'. Within the church is a fine group of tombs, including the sculptured slab of abbot Philip O'Molwanayn (d. 1463) and the magnificent effigy of Piers Fitz Oge Butler (d. 1526), carved by Rory O'Tunney.

Bibliography: Extents, 322–4; *Triumphalia*, 75, 115; Healy, 'Cistercian Abbey of Kilcooly' (1890), 216–27; Hamilton Thompson, Clapham and Leask, 'Cistercian Order in Ireland' (1931), 16, 31; Power, 'Cistercian Abbeys of Munster' (1938), 96–9; Moloney, 'Kilcooly: Foundation and Restoration' (1944), 219–23; Leask, *Irish Churches*, III, 69–72; Gwynn and Hadcock, *Medieval Religious Houses* (1970), 137–8; Bence-Jones, *Burke's Guide to Country Houses* (1978), 165.

Macosquin Londonderry

The remains of the abbey at Macosquin are extremely sparse and the history of the Cistercian community there is poorly documented. It was founded in 1218, apparently as a daughter house of the French monastery of Morimond. The exact date of its suppression is unknown. Early in the seventeenth century the site was given to the Merchant Taylors as part of the plantation of Derry. It lies three miles south-west of Coleraine, beside a tributary of the River Bann.

The nineteenth-century parish church of St Mary's, Camus Iuxta Bann, is built on the site of the abbey church. To the east of the chancel there are the foundations of a rectangular structure, possibly the old Cistercian presbytery, and a lancet window of thirteenth-century type has been reused in the north wall, known locally as the 'leper window'. Recent excavations to the south-west of the church did not uncover any of the medieval walls, though the excavated area probably lay beyond the boundaries of the cloister buildings. In the 1840s it was reported that 'the last of the ruins of the Abbey was a tall gable with a chimney which was put to the purpose of keeping beehives in'—evidently a part of the south range. This was demolished in about 1770, when the Glebe House (now a lounge bar) was erected. The Ordnance Survey investigators encountered an old man who 'seems to remember other buildings round about the Abbey as well as the old gable end'; his age however was 'too great for him to express himself with sufficient distinctness'.

Bibliography: Ordnance Survey Manuscripts (Box 43, Londonderry XV, RIA); Gwynn and Hadcock, *Medieval Religious Houses* (1970), 139; Brannon, 'Rescue Excavations in Macosquin' (1983), 93–9.

Mellifont Louth   (Pls 4, 33, 75, 91, 116, 143, 158, 160, 170–1, 180–1, 244; Figs 5, 12, 13, 19, 25, 35, 53, 57–9)

The ruins of Mellifont are more fragmentary than many other Irish houses, but they are of enormous historical and architectural interest. As the first Cistercian monastery in Ireland, it was the head of an affiliation that eventually numbered over twenty. It was founded in 1142 at the instigation of Malachy, archbishop of Armagh, after a visit to Clairvaux, on land which was granted by Donough O'Carroll, king of Uriel. The site lies in the valley of the River Mattock, about two miles from its confluence with the Boyne and five miles north-west of Drogheda. The initial community, a mixture of French and Irish monks, had been trained at Clairvaux and a French monk, Robert, was sent to advise on the buildings. The first church was consecrated in 1157 and by 1170 the abbey was said to contain a hundred monks and three hundred laybrothers. In the early thirteenth century it was the focus of a major breakdown in monastic discipline, a crisis known as the 'conspiracy of Mellifont', during which it resisted visitations from the General Chapter and interference from the new Anglo-Norman Cistercian houses. After the resolution of the crisis by Stephen of Lexington in 1228, the number of monks was fixed at fifty, with allowance for sixty laybrothers. It remained one of the more prosperous Irish monasteries and when it was dissolved in 1539 it was valued at £352.3.10, making it the second most wealthy Cistercian house. At this time there

were approximately twenty-one monks, an unusually high number compared with other abbeys. Following the dissolution, the property eventually passed to Sir Edward Moore, who established a fortified house within the ruins in the 1560s. His descendants continued to live at Mellifont until 1727, when the house, like the monastery before it, rapidly fell into decay.

The only parts of the abbey still standing are the lavabo (c1200), the chapter house (c1220) and the late medieval gatehouse, but a series of excavations (1880s, 1902 and 1954–5) have uncovered the foundations of the church and conventual buildings. The church was remodelled on several occasions and the excavations revealed at least four separate stylistic phases. The first church (1142–57) was a cruciform building, with an unusual arrangement of chapels in the transept and a crypt at the west end. In the mid-thirteenth century the presbytery was enlarged in the Early English style and the north transept rebuilt with east and west aisles. The remodelling of the south transept (c1320) belongs to the Decorated era and involved the use of huge diamond-shaped piers with multiple shafts. Later work included the reconstruction of the nave and the addition of a substantial central tower.

At the south end of the cloister garth is the octagonal lavabo, which, with its fine mouldings and decorated capitals, is one of the most delicate medieval buildings in Ireland. Alongside is a section of the Romanesque cloister arcade, re-erected in 1955.

A huge cache of 1,600 carved and moulded stones has been recovered from the site, together with many thousand pieces of floortiles. Although the remains of Mellifont are fragmentary, they are sufficient to show the seminal importance of the abbey in the history of Irish architecture—a major point of contact with the rest of Europe and a major source of influence for building elsewhere in Ireland.

Bibliography: Extents, 212–22; Archdall, *Monasticon Hibernicum*, 479–89; *Reports of the Commissioners of Public Works* (1882–7, 1903); Hamilton Thompson, Clapham and Leask, 'Cistercian Order in Ireland' (1931), 21, 28; Leask, 'Mellifont Abbey' (1945), 29–33; O'Conbhuide, *Story of Mellifont* (1958); Leask, *Irish Churches*, II, 6, 8, 40–3; de Paor, 'Excavations at Mellifont Abbey' (1969), 109–64; Gwynn and Hadcock, *Medieval Religious Houses* (1970), 139–40; Stalley, 'Mellifont Abbey' (1980), 263–354.

Midleton Cork

The monastery at Midleton, thirteen miles east of Cork, was founded in 1180 beside the River Owenacurra, just before it enters the waters of Cork harbour. It was an excellent site lying in fertile countryside, screened by hills to the north. It was a daughter house of Monasteranenagh, and in view of the native character of the mother abbey, the founders were almost certainly Irish and not Anglo-Normans as has been suggested. This point is confirmed by Midleton's involvement in the conspiracy of Melli-

font in 1227–8. At the time of the dissolution of the monasteries in 1539–41, the property was surveyed by royal commissioners but the last abbot, Philip FitzDavid Barry, managed to obtain a lease for twenty-one years. Some form of religious life may thus have survived for a while, but by 1573 the abbey had been granted to John FitzEdmond FitzGerald. The modern town was founded by the Brodericks, later earls of Midleton, about 1670.

The monastic buildings lay on the site of the Protestant parish church (1825), but there are no standing remains. A number of moulded stones are scattered about the graveyard, including a late medieval door head and a piece of circular shafting.

Bibliography: Extents, 150–1; Power, 'Cistercian Abbeys of Munster' (1929), 22–3; O'Sullivan, 'Some Medieval Religious Houses' (1945), 104–11; Gwynn and Hadcock, *Medieval Religious Houses* (1970), 140–1.

Monasteranenagh Limerick   (Pls 12, 17, 39, 77–80, 161; Fig. 34)

The rather dour ruins of Monasteranenagh lie in flat countryside beside the River Camoge, two and a half miles east of Croom and ten and a half miles south of Limerick. The monastery was founded in 1148 by Turlough O'Brien, king of Thomond, as a daughter house of Mellifont. It subsequently established three daughter houses of its own in Munster (Abbeydorney 1154, Midleton 1180 and Holycross 1180). With its O'Brien patrons, the monastery was the focus of resistance to Anglo-Norman influence and it played a major role in the conspiracy of Mellifont, having 'drunk from the chalice of Babylon' in the words of Stephen of Lexington. In 1228 the community attempted to thwart Stephen's visitation by turning the abbey buildings into a minor fortress. Later in the century the monastery fell heavily into debt, owing £209.6.8 to the Ricardi of Lucca in 1302. It was suppressed in 1539–40, but some form of religious life may have survived until 1580, when the abbey was the scene of a battle during the Desmond rebellion. The tale of forty monks being massacred after the battle by the victorious soldiers of Sir Nicholas Malby is not supported by reliable evidence.

The ruins consist principally of the church (c1170–1220) and early Gothic chapter house. The church was planned on a grand scale with three chapels opening off each transept, but these have been almost completely destroyed. Fragments of one chapel in the north transept show it to have had groin or rib vaults, as well as fancy arch mouldings. The square presbytery, lit by three inserted Gothic lancets, was covered by a pointed barrel vault which fell in 1874. The aisled nave has four plain arches on each side, then a long section of blank wall. The general austerity of the church is alleviated by a number of crisp foliage capitals. The building was subject to at least one major change of design, involving the enlargement of the western crossing piers, and its precise chronology is difficult to determine. At a late date it was drastically reduced in size, the transept arches blocked and a new west wall inserted after the second bay of the nave. In the later middle ages, possibly after the dissolution, a barrel vault was erected over the south transept, as part of a fortified tower. Either this or a crossing tower fell in 1807, soon after which the outbuildings were demolished by a Mr White of Manister, who used the materials for stables and yards. The layout of the cloister and conventual buildings are clearly visible in aerial photographs. West of the church lie the remains of a rectangular structure, the nature of which is unknown. The site of the monastery is one that would repay major archaeological investigation.

Bibliography: *Ordnance Survey Letters, Limerick*, I (1840), 114–21 (RIA); Westropp, 'History of the Abbey of Monasteranenagh' (1889), 232–8; Power, 'Cistercian Abbeys of Munster' (1930), 43–6; Hamilton Thompson, Clapham and Leask, 'Cistercian Order in Ireland' (1931), 12–13, 24–5; Leask, *Irish Churches*, II, 35–8; Gwynn and Hadcock, *Medieval Religious Houses* (1970), 141.

Monasterevin Kildare

Monasterevin was the site of an early Irish monastery founded by St Evin (or Emin) in the seventh century. This had almost certainly died out when the Cistercians were brought from Baltinglass by Dermot O'Dempsey, king of Offaly. His foundation charter dates from c1178, but the Cistercian tabula gave 1189 as the date of foundation. The site of the monastery lies on the banks of the River Barrow, six and a half miles west of Kildare. The abbey was apparently dissolved in 1539–40 and the property was granted to George, Lord Audley, who assigned it to Adam Loftus, Viscount Ely. It was subsequently acquired by the Moore family (earls of Drogheda) of Mellifont, who moved their main residence here in 1727. A Jacobean house, erected on the site in 1607, was replaced in 1767 by a neo-Gothic mansion known as Moore Abbey. This now serves as a hospital run by the Sisters of Charity of Jesus.

In 1837 some walls of the old abbey were said to survive at the rear of the house, but these are no longer visible. Preparations for a sunken garden in 1846 produced a mass of skeletons on what was presumably the site of the monastic cemetery. Earlier in the century a skeleton was found with a wooden chalice laid on the chest. It is popularly supposed that carvings around a window on the east side of the house belonged to the medieval abbey, but their style is seventeenth century. Nor are the vaulted basements medieval, as Comerford supposed. An attractive circular font, decorated with carved angels, has a medieval appearance, but the presence of cherub heads indicates a date nearer 1600.

Bibliography: *Ordnance Survey Letters, Kildare*, II (1837), 39–46 (R.I.A.); Comerford, Monasterevin—Abbey and Parish (1874–9), 115–30;

Gwynn and Hadcock, *Medieval Religious Houses* (1970), 142.

Newry Down

The monastery was founded by Maurice MacLoughlin in 1153 and colonised from Mellifont, thirty miles away. Before the growth of the existing town, the site must have been spectacular: a rich green valley at the edge of the mountains of Mourne, only six miles from the head of Carlingford Lough. The name is derived from a yew tree (An Iubhar), reputedly planted by St Patrick himself. Despite this tradition, there is no evidence of the existence of a monastery before the arrival of the Cistercians. In 1162 the monastery, together with its library and sacred yew tree, was burnt in a fire. The community temporarily staved off the threat of dissolution in 1538 by becoming a collegiate college, with the abbot as warden. However this proved ephemeral and the former abbot voluntarily surrendered the house to the Crown in 1550. Two years later it was granted to Sir Nicholas Bagenal, marshal of the royal army in Ireland and founder of the modern town of Newry.

The monastic buildings have vanished completely though their memory lives on in street names like 'Abbey Yard'. A stone carved with a cross in low relief is built into the walls of McCann's Bakery, which lies on part of the site. A 'chapel' survived until shortly before 1744 and Luckombe (1780) explained that 'the abbot's house yet remains and is converted into a common dwelling house'. It is reported that about 1788 'the remaining ruins of the abbey, which had, for a long time, afforded shelter only to vagrants, were levelled and enclosed, for the purpose of building'.

Bibliography: Archdall, *Monasticon Hibernicum*, 126–7; Luckombe, *Tour Through Ireland* (1780), 300 ; Harris, *State of County of Down* (1744), 90; Reeves, *Ecclesiastical Antiquities* (1847), 116–19; *ASNI*, 290; Gwynn and Hadcock, *Medieval Religious Houses* (1970), 142.

Tintern Wexford (Pls 20, 90, 123, 140, 166, 208, 229, 282–3; Fig. 28)

Tintern was founded by William Marshal, earl of Pembroke and earl of Leinster, following his escape from shipwreck during a storm on the Irish Sea, and it was colonised from Tintern Major (Monmouthshire) in 1200. The site lies in a picturesque wooded demesne at the head of a creek in Bannow Bay, where the monks were well served by a swift flowing stream. It is approximately twelve miles south of New Ross and only five miles west of the Cistercian abbey of Dunbrody. The ruins of the church, the only part of the monastery to survive, appear to date from c1300. In 1447 the abbot was said to have 'rebuilt the house at his own particular cost and charge' and part of the crossing tower may relate to these operations. The abbey was dissolved in 1536 and the property passed to Sir Anthony Colclough in the 1550s. His descendants lived in the abbey until 1963. Sir Anthony

converted the crossing into a fortified tower (1566–9) and subsequently he or one of his immediate successors occupied the old chancel as well. In the early years of the eighteenth century the nave was transformed into a neo-Gothic house, with interior fittings that have been described as 'churchwarden Gothic'.

Of the medieval church, the presbytery, crossing tower, nave and parts of the south transept survive. The three-bay rectangular presbytery was lit by lancets in the side walls (replaced by Tudor mullioned windows), and there is a well-preserved exterior corbel table. The south transept has a rib vaulted eastern aisle originally divided by screens into three separate chapels. The crossing tower was probably heightened in 1447 and further remodelled in 1566–9, the likely date for the addition of the north-west stair turret. The nave, which has lost its aisles, has three bays of very plain arches. None of the conventual buildings are standing and stones from them are said to have been used for building the nearby bridge.

The ruins of what appear to be a 'capella ante portas' survive near the bridge to the south-east of the abbey.

Extensive excavations took place in 1982–3 under the direction of Dr Ann Lynch on behalf of the Office of Public Works. The floor of the nave was cut back to its original level, exposing the bases of the piers, and a set of massive foundations was uncovered below the south transept aisle. Curiously, no trace was found of the north aisle or the north transept. The east wall of the cloister arcade was also revealed, as well as a deep drain at the south end of the east range.

Bibliography: *Extents*, 358–63; Archdall, *Monasticon Hibernicum*, 752–5; Hore, *Wexford*, III (1901); Bernard, 'Foundation of Tintern Abbey' (1916–17), 527–9; Leask, *Irish Churches*, II, 121; Gwynn and Hadcock, *Medieval Religious Houses* (1970), 142–3; Bence-Jones, *Burke's Guide to Country Houses* (1978), 273.

Tracton Cork (Pl. 274)

Tracton is situated ten miles south of Cork and seven miles north-east of Kinsale, beside a small river which flows into Ringabella Bay. It was founded by Odo de Barry in 1224 and was colonised from the Welsh abbey of Whitland (Carmarthen). The community was criticised by Stephen of Lexington in 1228 on account of its enthusiasm for the Welsh language, though the abbot was praised as 'vir strenuus et religiosus'. For most of its history the abbey was staunchly English in outlook, and from 1483 onwards the office of abbot was exclusively held by members of the Barry family, descendants of the original founder. A seal of the last abbot, John de Barry, is preserved on a deed of 1542. By this time the monastery was in the process of dissolution and most of its lands were said to be waste due to wars and rebellions. In 1568 the property was granted by Elizabeth I to Henry Gylford and by the early seventeenth century it had been acquired by

Thomas Daunt of Gloucestershire, who apparently lived in the old abbey. The Daunts built a new house in the middle of the century, when most of the medieval buildings were probably destroyed.

The Protestant parish church (1817) occupies the site of the abbey church. There are no medieval remains apart from a variety of carved and moulded stones scattered about the neighbourhood or built into nearby houses. In the 1920s these were gathered together by Mr Coveney in his garden and Power described 'quantities of carved stones, chamfered and moulded arch heads, sections of columns and broken window mullions'. There was a tomb slab decorated with a floriated cross, as well as two arches which Mr Coveney had reconstructed. The base of a clustered column was also uncovered at this time. Much of this material appears to have been dispersed, but a stiff-leaf capital is still to be seen in a neighbouring farmyard, along with other fragments.

Bibliography: Extents, 143–4; Archdall, *Monasticon Hibernicum*, 79; Power, 'Cistercian Abbeys of Munster' (1929), 27–9; O'Sullivan, 'Cistercian Abbey of Tracton' (1939), 1–15; O'Riordain, 'Sculptured Stone at Tracton Abbey' (1944), 56–7; Gwynn and Hadcock, *Medieval Religious Houses* (1970), 143; Bolster, *Diocese of Cork* (1972), 140–50.

Appendix 3

A NOTE ON CONSERVATION

While antiquarian interest in Cistercian monuments increased steadily after 1790, very little was done to arrest their disintegration and decay. Collapses of walls and towers were occurring at regular intervals. During the first half of the nineteenth century one person to take an active interest in preservation was Dr Charles Wall, a Senior Fellow of Trinity College, Dublin, who purchased the ruins of Holycross in 1833. He has been described as a 'genuine scholar, whose five volumes on Hebrew orthography brought him some reputation in his day'.[1] He also deserves to be remembered for his enlightened moves at Holycross, where he repaired the east window and restored parts of the nave. The arcades on the south side were reinforced and arches were erected over the adjacent aisle, alterations which admittedly were more classical than Gothic in spirit.

Nevertheless, he received belated acclaim for his work from the Kilkenny Archaeological Society in 1852. At the time this body was much concerned with the 'disgraceful state of neglect and ruin' at Jerpoint, where scarcely a month elapsed 'without some new act of barbarism'.[2] In 1852–3 the society spent over £100 on repairs, preventing the abbey becoming, in their own words, 'a heap of shapeless rubbish'.[3] But they were too late to do anything about the massive collapse which took place at Dunbrody on Christmas eve 1852. As long as the abbeys remained in private hands, conservation depended on the goodwill and resources of the owners. In the case of Dunbrody, the agent of the owner (Lord Templemore) horrified the Kilkenny Archaeological Society by offering 'the astounding opinion that the abbey was *improved* by the fall of the arcade—the ruin being rendered more picturesque thereby', a not uncommon attitude at the time. When Lord Templemore was eventually persuaded to undertake repairs it was said that his operations 'were calculated highly to deface the beauty of what remained of the structure, whilst doing but little for the judicious preservation of the building'.[4]

About 1874, the vaults of the chancel of Monasteranenagh fell, the last major catastrophe on a Cistercian site before the formal establishment in 1874–5 of the National Monuments Branch of the Office of Public Works.[5] By 1900 the Commissioners of Public Works were responsible for twelve Cistercian abbeys and today only four out of the twenty-one Cistercian ruins are not listed as national monuments, either in the north or south of the country (Abbeydorney, Abbeylara Abbeymahon and Abbeyshrule). In their early years the Commissioners carried out a number of vital rescue operations, such as the construction of 'flying' buttresses at Grey Abbey in 1908, which saved the nave from collapse.[6] But not all their achievements at this time were without blemish. Many sites were cleared of 'rubbish' in a fashion that makes the modern archaeologist wince and Mellifont was excavated in the 1880s without serious recording of what was found. Conservation methods also left much to be desired. At Grey Abbey, repairs were executed with a lavish display of concrete, the crudity of which is still obvious today. The 1909 report of the Commissioners explained with bland optimism that 'the newness in the appearance of the concrete and cement pointing is wearing off and the new work will soon be of the same colour as the old'.[7] Since 1922, however, Cistercian ruins have for the most part been scrupulously maintained by the ancient monuments departments, both north and south.

Appendix 4

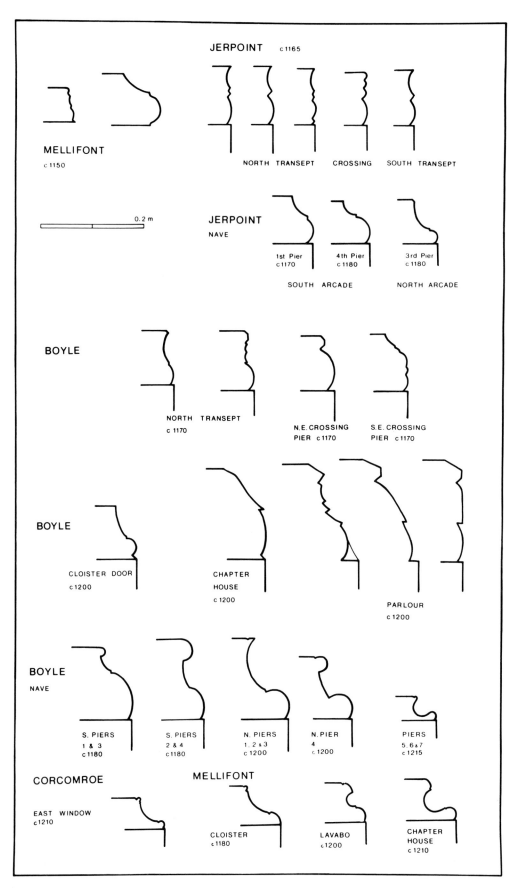

Fig. 66 Base mouldings.

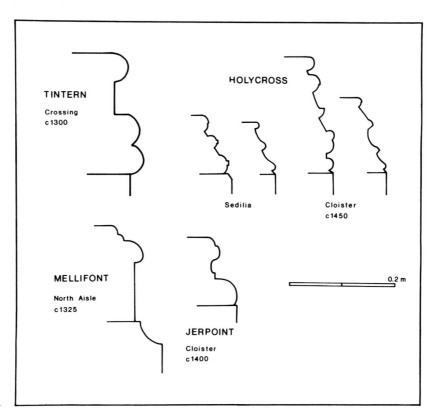

Fig. 67 Base mouldings.

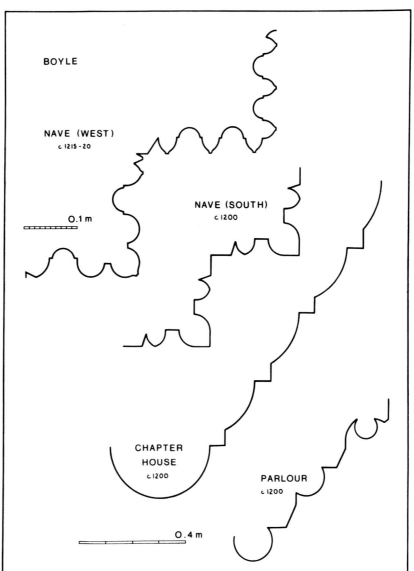

Fig. 68 Mouldings of doorways.

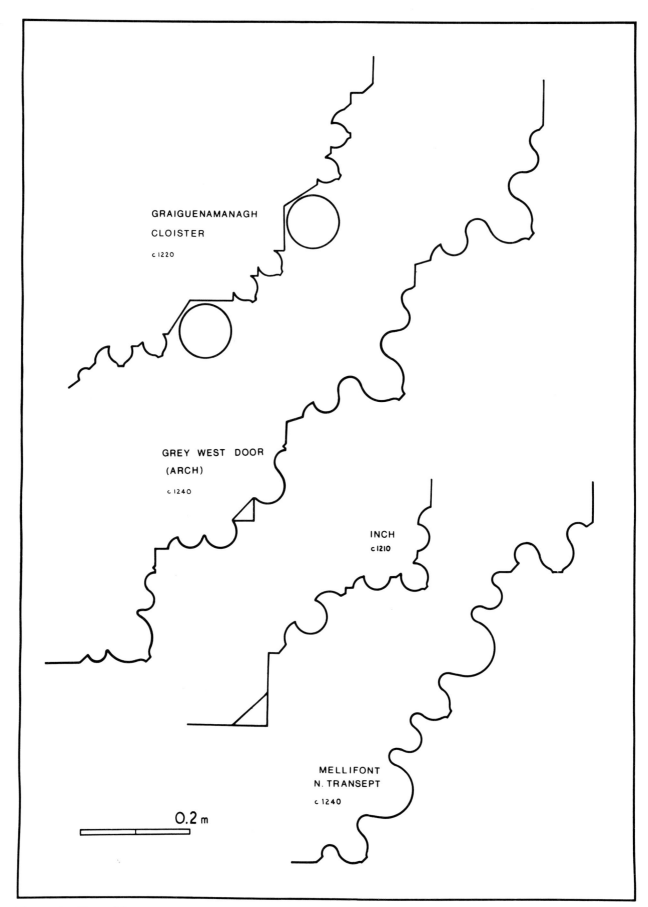

GRAIGUENAMANAGH
CLOISTER

c 1220

GREY WEST DOOR
(ARCH)

c 1240

INCH
c 1210

MELLIFONT
N. TRANSEPT

c 1240

0.2 m

Fig. 69   Mouldings of doorways.

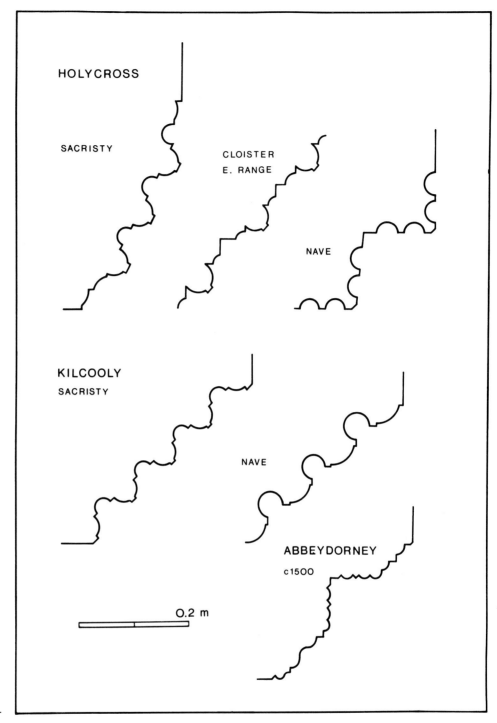

HOLYCROSS

SACRISTY

CLOISTER
E. RANGE

NAVE

KILCOOLY

SACRISTY

NAVE

ABBEYDORNEY

c1500

0.2 m

Fig. 70   Mouldings of doorways.

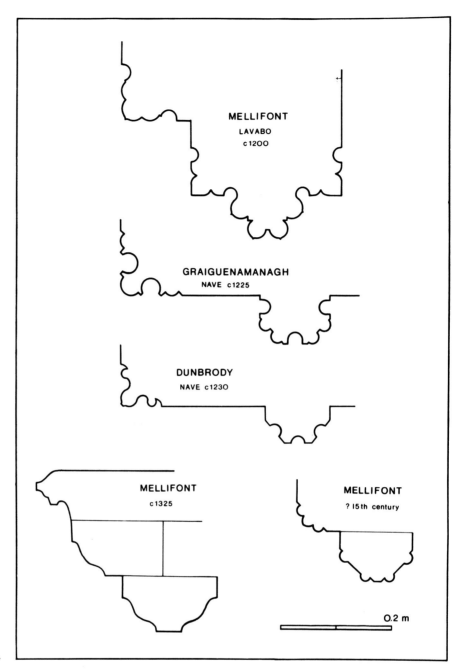

MELLIFONT
LAVABO
c1200

GRAIGUENAMANAGH
NAVE c1225

DUNBRODY
NAVE c1230

MELLIFONT
c1325

MELLIFONT
? 15th century

0.2 m

Fig. 71   Miscellaneous arch mouldings.

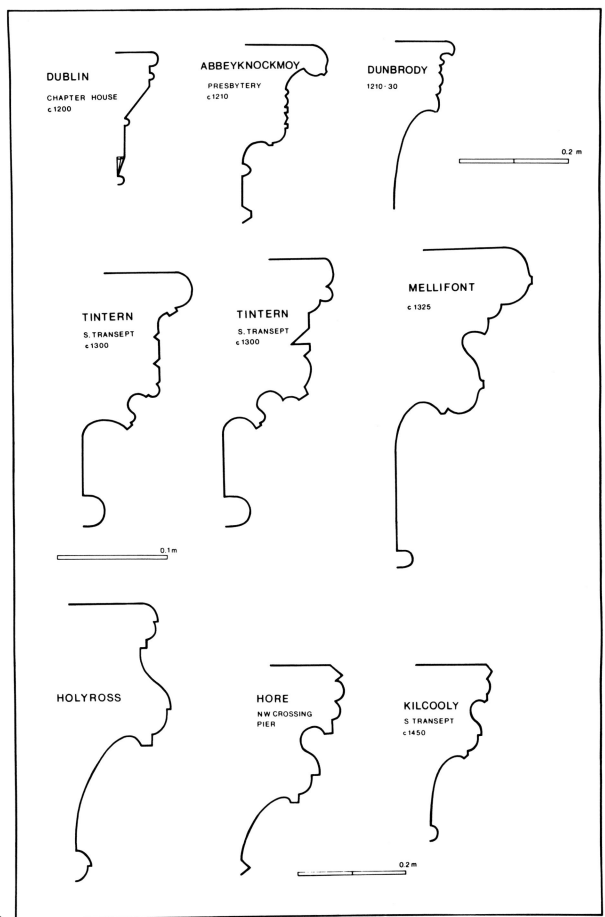

DUBLIN
CHAPTER HOUSE
c 1200

ABBEYKNOCKMOY
PRESBYTERY
c 1210

DUNBRODY
1210·30

0.2 m

TINTERN
S. TRANSEPT
c 1300

TINTERN
S. TRANSEPT
c 1300

MELLIFONT
c 1325

0.1 m

HOLYROSS

HORE
N W CROSSING
PIER

KILCOOLY
S TRANSEPT
c 1450

0.2 m

Fig. 72   Capitals and corbels.

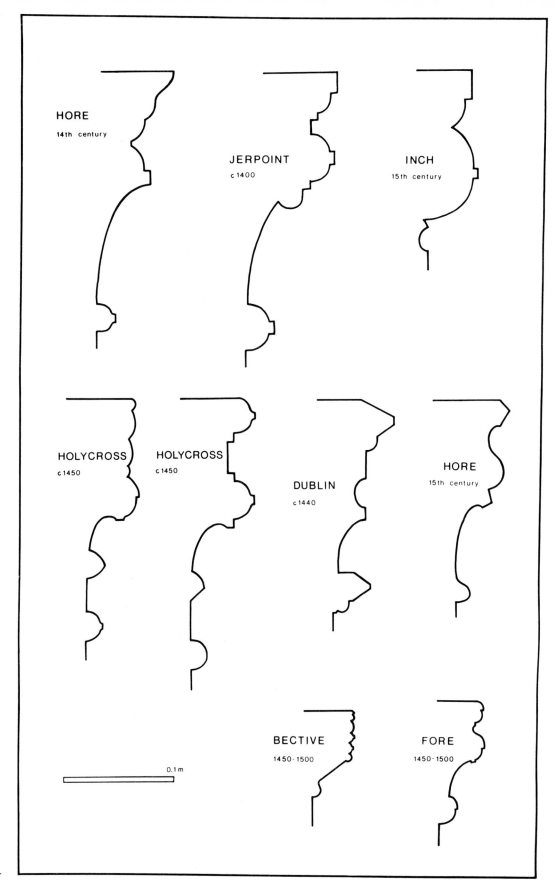

HORE
14th century

JERPOINT
c 1400

INCH
15th century

HOLYCROSS
c 1450

HOLYCROSS
c 1450

DUBLIN
c 1440

HORE
15th century

BECTIVE
1450-1500

FORE
1450-1500

0.1 m

Fig. 73   Capitals of cloister arcades.

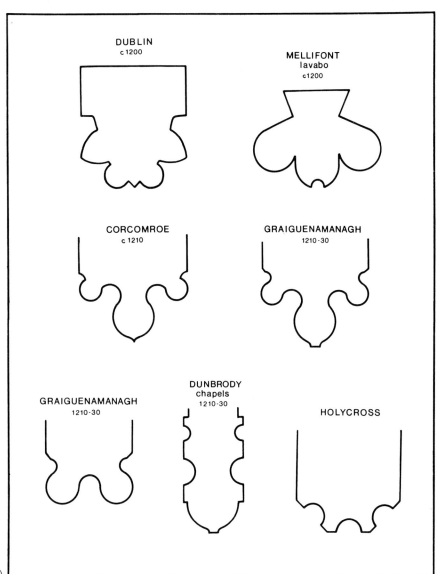

Fig. 74 Mouldings of vault ribs (not to scale).

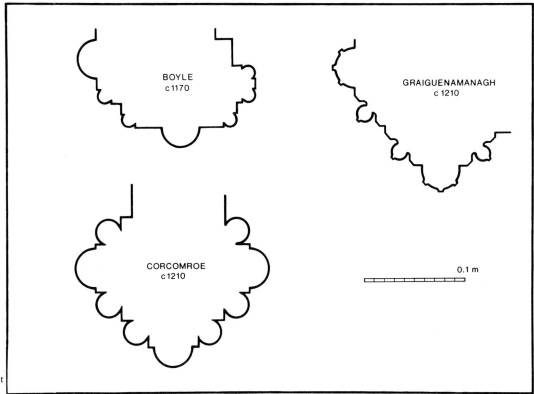

Fig. 75 Comparative plans of south-east crossing piers.

Abbreviations

AC	*Annals of Connacht*, ed. A. Martin Freeman (Dublin, 1944).
AFM	*Annals of the Kingdom of Ireland by the Four Masters*, ed. J. O'Donovan (Dublin, 1848–51).
ALC	*Annals of Loch Cé*, ed. W. M. Hennessy (London, 1871, Rolls Series).
ASNI	*Archaeological Survey of Northern Ireland, County Down* (Belfast, 1966).
AU	*Annals of Ulster*, ed. W. M. Hennessy and B. MacCarthy (Dublin, 1887–1901).
CCC	*Citeaux, Commentarii Cistercienses.*
CMA	*Chartularies of St Mary's Abbey, Dublin*, ed. J. T. Gilbert, 2 volumes, (London, 1884, Rolls Series).
CPL	*Calendar of Papal Letters*, ed. W. H. Bliss, J. A. Twemlow and C. Johnson (London, 1893–).
CPR	*Calendar of the Patent Rolls* (England).
JBAA	*Journal of the British Archaeological Association.*
JCHAS	*Journal of the Cork Historical and Archaeological Society.*
JRSAI	*Journal of the Royal Society of Antiquaries of Ireland.*
PRIA	*Proceedings of the Royal Irish Academy.*
RCHM	*Royal Commission on Historical Monuments.*
UJA	*Ulster Journal of Archaeology.*

Notes

The full titles of works cited more than once are given in the Select Bibliography

Introduction

1 Knowles, 'Primitive Cistercian Documents' (1962), 199–222; J. de la Croix Bouton and J.-B. Van Damme, *Les Plus Anciens Textes de Citeaux* (Achel, 1974).

2 This point has been underlined by modern research on early legislation, led by Monsignor Turk and Jean Lefèvre, which has drastically altered the old rather simplified picture. There is now far less certainty about when and how individual rules were devised and the codified set of statutes, once confidently assigned to 1134, is now thought to belong to 1152. The chronology given by Canivez in volume I of *Statuta* is thus largely obsolete, F. Kovacs, 'A Propos de la Date de la Redaction des "Instituta Generalis Capituli Apud Cistercium"', *Analecta Sacri Ordinis Cisterciensis*, VII (1951), 85–90. For a recent review of the problems see Holdsworth, 'Chronology and Character of Early Cistercian Legislation' (1986).

3 Ailred of Rievaulx in *Speculum Caritatis* as quoted by Knowles, *Monastic Order* (1940), 220.

4 William Wakeman, *Archaeologia Hibernica, A Handbook of Irish Antiquities* (Dublin, 1848), 56.

5 Healy, 'Cistercians in Ireland' (1901), 481, 497.

Chapter 1

1 *Life of St Malachy*, 109–10.

2 *Gesta Regis Henrici Secundi*, ed. W. Stubbs (London, 1867, Rolls Series), I, 28–9; *Chronica Magistri Rogeri de Hovedene*, ed. W. Stubbs (London, 1869, Rolls Series), II, 32.

3 *Topographia Hiberniae*, 103.

4 *Lexington*, 112.

5 *Lexington*, 14.

6 The most detailed account of early churches in Ireland is furnished by Leask, *Irish Churches*, I (1955); see also Hughes and Hamlin, *Modern Traveller to the Early Irish Church* (1977), 54–79, Ralegh Radford, 'The Earliest Irish Churches', (1977), 1–11; Hamlin, 'The study of early Irish churches' (1984), 117–26.

7 The date of the general transition from timber to stone building is contentious. The first clearly dated reference in the annals to a stone church relates to an oratory at Armagh in 789, and the first reference to a round tower is at Slane in 948. Mention of stone structures is rare before the tenth century and this seems the likely period of transition. For a recent contribution to the debate see P. Harbison, 'How old is Gallarus Oratory?', *Medieval Archaeology*, XIV (1970), 34–59.

8 *AFM*, 1167.

9 *Life of St Malachy*, 32.

10 Compare the steeply gabled porches of some wooden churches in Norway, e.g. the church at Gol, illustrated in J. Strygowski, *Early Church Art in Northern Europe* (London, 1923), pl. XLVI.

11 This view is denied by Barrow, *Round Towers of Ireland* (1979), 32–46, but his arguments relating to date and provenance are not acceptable. For more orthodox opinions see M. and L. de Paor, *Early Christian Ireland* (London, 1958), 151–3, Henry, *Irish Art During the Viking Invasions* (1967), 49–56. The relationship with Carolingian architecture is briefly discussed by Horn and Born, *The Plan of St Gall*, I, 129, 206–8.

12 *Topographia Hiberniae*, 84. Medieval ecclesiastics were prone to criticise local inhabitants. Lanfranc complained of the local Anglo-Saxons and the Augustinians of Wigmore found the local population 'vulgar and coarse', Platt, *Abbeys and Priories* (1984), 12, 28.

13 *CMA*, I, 354–5.

14 *Topographia Hiberniae*, 67, 87.

15 Henry, *Irish Art in the Romanesque Period* (1970), chapter 4; *Treasures of Early Irish Art*, ed. G. F. Mitchell (New York, 1977), 187–220.

16 For the economic life of twelfth-century Ireland see *Topographia Hiberniae*; a good modern survey is provided by D. ÓCorráin, *Ireland Before the Normans* (Dublin, 1972), 48–74.

17 Curtis, *Medieval Ireland* (1938), 1–44; ÓCorráin, *Ireland Before the Normans*, 142–74.

18 Watt, *Church in Medieval Ireland* (1972), chapter 1.

19 *Ibid.*, 45–6, Gwynn and Hadcock, *Medieval Religious Houses* (1970), 146–200.

20 *Life of Malachy*, 122–5. For the cult of Malachy at Clairvaux, see Scott, *Malachy* (1976), 21–2, 93–8 and Chabeuf, 'Voyage d'un Délégue', 299–304, 316.

21 Watt, *Church in Medieval Ireland* (1972), 24.

22 *Opera Giraldi Cambrensis*, ed. J. F. Dimock (London, 1886, Rolls Series), VI, 45.

23 O'Conbhuidhe, *Story of Mellifont*, 6–16, provides a detailed account of the foundation.

24 MacNiocaill, *Na Manaigh Liatha*, 1–19; Gwynn and Hadcock, *Medieval Religious Houses*, 114–44: There is some uncertainty over the foundation of Inislounaght, in particular whether it was a daughter of Mellifont or Monasteranenagh.

25 The foundation date of Jerpoint is controversial. In 1905 Carrigan argued that it was founded about 1158 or shortly after, since its daughter house of Killenny is known to have been in existence by 1162–5. Carrigan's interpretation has been rejected by O'Conbhuidhe, who believes that Jerpoint did not become a Cistercian house until 1180, the date given in the Cistercian tabulae. He argues that although a monastery known as 'the abbey of Ossory' had been established by 1162–5, this was a Benedictine community, which did not join the Cistercian order for almost twenty years. O'Conbhuidhe points out that the tabulae evidence for 1180 is the best available and it would be odd for a community to tolerate a loss of almost two decades seniority in the hierarchy of the order, if it had in fact been Cistercian in 1162. But against O'Conbhuidhe's arguments must be set the architectural evidence, which definitely favours the earlier foundation date. The proportional system used in planning the abbey church is specifically Cistercian and the architectural details of the eastern arm would be outmoded for the 1180s. The links with Baltinglass,

founded in 1148, are close and it is unlikely that more than fifteen years separates the construction of the two churches. For further details of the documentary aspects of the controversy see: Carrigan, *History and Antiquities of the Diocese of Ossory* (1905), IV, 278–98, and O'Conbhuidhe, 'Origins of Jerpoint Abbey' (1963), 293–306.

26 *Life of St Malachy*, 120; A. L. Brown, 'The Cistercian Abbey of Saddell, Kintyre', *Innes Review*, 20 (1969), 130–7; *Royal Commission on Ancient and Historical Monuments of Scotland, Argyll, I, Kintyre* (London, 1971), 140–5; a reference to Saddell also comes in *Triumphalia* (1640), 209, where it is described as 'Sandale in Scotland'. Saddell seems a more likely location for Malachy's monastery at the Green Loch than Soulseat, suggested by Scott, *Malachy* (1976), 64, n. 14.

27 Trinity College, Dublin, Ms. 77, fol. 48v, translated by Petrie, *Ecclesiastical Architecture of Ireland* (1845), 394.

28 *AFM*, 1157.

29 The names of founders are given by Gwynn and Hadcock, *Medieval Religious Houses*, 123–43, and MacNiocaill, *Na Manaigh Liatha*, 8–19.

30 See note 27.

31 Lexington, 16, 18–20; O'Dwyer, *Conspiracy of Mellifont* (1970), 24, 31–2.

32 *ALC*, I, 200–3; *AFM*, III, 104–5.

33 *Letters of St Bernard*, 454.

34 There were some Benedictine houses in Ireland, but only Cashel appears to have had Benedictine monks before the foundation of Mellifont in 1142 (Gwynn and Hadcock, 104–5). Bishops like Malchus of Lismore, who had been trained as a monk at Winchester, would have been familiar with the Benedictine Rule.

35 Gilyard-Beer, *Fountains Abbey* (1970), 4–5.

36 Knowles, *Monastic Order in England* (1940), 114–15.

37 *Letters of St Bernard*, 454.

38 *Topographia Hiberniae*, 13.

39 *CMA*, II, 307; Bernard, 'Foundation of Tintern' (1917), 527–9.

40 *Statuta*, 1219.48.

41 Non-attendance at the General Chapter is discussed by MacNiocaill, *Na Manaigh Liatha*, 77–82. A typical example of poor attendance is the record of the abbot of Kilcooly, who in 1228 had not attended the General Chapter for seven years, Lexington, 79.

42 O'Dwyer, 'Gaelic Monasticism', *IER* (1967), 19–28; O'Dwyer, 'Impact of Native Irish' (1967), 287–301.

43 Knowles, *Monastic Order* (1940), 655.

44 MacNiocaill, *Na Manaigh Liatha*, 26–7; O'Conbhuidhe, *Story of Mellifont*, 53–4.

45 For details of the new foundations, Gwynn and Hadcock, *Medieval Religious Houses*, 123–44.

46 Charters of Duiske, 44–6, 48–9, 56–7; Lexington, 38, 42; MacNiocaill, *Na Manaigh Liatha*, 91–2.

47 Statuta, 1227.36; Lexington, 24, 31; MacNiocaill, *Na Manaigh Liatha*, 91.

48 O'Dwyer, *Conspiracy of Mellifont*; see also O'Conbhuidhe, *Story of Mellifont*, 55–70; MacNiocaill, *Na Manaigh Liatha*, 84–92.

49 Lexington, 12–13.

50 *Ibid.*, 36.

51 *Ibid.*, 14–16.

52 *Ibid.*, 16–18. The practice of storing food and valuables inside a church or monastery in times of crisis was an ancient custom in Ireland, A. T. Lucas, 'The Plundering and Burning of Churches in Ireland, 7th to 16th Century', *Munster Studies*, Essays in commemoration of Monsignor Michael Moloney, ed. E. Rynne (Limerick, 1967), 196–205.

53 Cowley, *Monastic Order in South Wales* (1977), 24–6, 47, 126.

54 Lexington, 14.

55 *Ibid.*, 34–7, 93–4.

56 An interesting aspect of this assertion of Irish identity within the Mellifont affiliation was the cult of Irish saints like St Brendan and St Evin, MacNiocaill, *Na Manaigh Liatha*, 33.

57 Lexington, 96–106. The document is a list of injunctions imposed by the visitor in 1228. While most appear to refer to Jerpoint, items relating to Graiguenamanagh and Mellifont (and possibly other abbeys) are also included. As it stands the document appears to be a conflation of instructions sent by Stephen of Lexington to several monasteries. Items 1, 11 and 32 definitely relate to Graiguenamanagh. Item 1 refers to 'Ethelmolt', or Annamult, a grange of the abbey and it also mentions 'Master P' who is known from the Charters of Duiske (p. 58) to have held several chapels belonging to the abbey. Item 11 contains a further mention of Master P, as well as William Marshal junior, whose father had founded the monastery. Item 32 refers to 'Grange Castri', a grange belonging to Graiguenamanagh. Many items, however, are aimed at an Irish house, as for example number 40 which insists that the Rule should be expounded in French and that nobody should be received as a monk unless he could confess his faults in French or Latin. Moreover in many cases the tone of the injunctions suggest that Stephen was criticising one (or more) houses deeply involved in the conspiracy of Mellifont (e.g. items 3, 5, 7, 25, 57, 67, 69). An exhaustive study of the document which might clarify the issues is long overdue. At present it remains unclear whether the architectural matters listed amongst Stephen's injunctions refer to Jerpoint or to Graiguenamanagh.
   MacNiocaill, *Na Manaigh Liatha* (1959) identified the visitation with Graiguenamanagh, but since then other scholars have argued that it related to Jerpoint: Gwynn and Hadcock, *Medieval Religious Houses* (1970) 136; Watt, *Church in Medieval Ireland* (1972), 59; O'Dwyer, Stephen of Lexington, *Letters from Ireland* (1982), 10, 14 (fn. 34), 170 (fn. 8).

58 Lexington, 91.

59 *Ibid.*, 93–4.

60 *Ibid.*, 45–8.

61 O'Conbhuidhe, *Story of Mellifont*, 52, 76–9.

62 O'Dwyer, *Conspiracy of Mellifont*, 21.

63 Stalley, 'Mellifont Abbey' (1980), 350.

64 The economic activities of the Cistercians are discussed by MacNiocaill, *Na Manaigh Liatha*, 45–75.

65 Lexington, 102, cf. footnote 57.

66 MacNiocaill, *Na Manaigh Liatha*, 52–4.

67 *Ibid.*, 65; O'Conbhuidhe, *Story of Mellifont*, 131–3.

68 Carville, *Duiske Abbey* (1979), 60.

69 *Extents*, 354–5.

70 *Statuta*, 1134.IX: 'Ecclesias, altaria, sepulturas, decimas alieni laboris vel nutimenti, villas, villanos, terrarum census, furnorum et molendinorum redditus, et cetera his similia monasticae puritati, adversantia, nostri et nominis et ordinis excludit institutio'.

71 *Statuta*, 1195.95.

72 MacNiocaill, *Na Manaigh Liatha*, 45–8.

73 *CPR*, 1317–21, p. 388, Ormond Deeds, II, 137.

74 Archdall, *Monasticon Hibernicum*, 138.

75 O'Conbhuidhe, *Story of Mellifont*, 83; MacNiocaill, *Na Manaigh Liatha*, 34.

76 *Irish Historical Documents*, 1172–1922, ed. E. Curtis and R. B. McDowell (London, 1943), 43.

77 O'Conbhuidhe, *Story of Mellifont*, 102–3; MacNiocaill, *Na Manaigh Liatha*, 34.

78 MacNiocaill, *Na Manaigh Liatha*, 35.

79 P. L. Henry, 'The Land of Cokaygne, Cultures in Contact in Medieval Ireland', *Studia Hibernica*, XII (1972), 120–41. I am grateful to Professor Lydon for bringing this article to my attention.

80 The size of communities is discussed by O'Conbhuidhe, 'Suppression of Irish Cistercian Abbeys' (1959), 108–10 and by the same author in *Story of Mellifont*, 169. Some monks received pensions, others annuities. It has been suggested that those in receipt of annuities may not have been monks, in which case the size of communities would have been even smaller, O'Conbhuidhe (1959), 206.

81 *Extents*, passim.

82 Figures are taken from Knowles and Hadcock, *Medieval Religious Houses, England and Wales* (1953), 112–32.

83 O'Conbhuidhe, *Story of Mellifont*, 155–6.

84 Lexington, 103. See also note 27.

85 *Ibid.*, 100. The figures may refer to Graiguenamanagh (see note 57).

86 O'Conbhuidhe, *Story of Mellifont*, 155–8.

87 Seymour, 'Abbey Owney' (1907), 174.
88 O'Conbhuidhe, *Story of Mellifont*, 130–6.
89 Irish figures are taken from *Extents*, English figures from Knowles and Hadcock, *Medieval Religious Houses, England and Wales* (1953).
90 Figures are again taken from *Extents*, supplemented by information from Gwynn and Hadcock, *Medieval Religious Houses*, 123–43, from MacNiocaill, *Na Manaigh Liatha*, 159–62 and from O'Conbhuidhe, 'Suppression of Irish Cistercian Abbeys' (1959), 115–17.

Two separate valuations are given in the *Extents* for Baltinglass, £75.15.2 and £126.10.1. In his publication of figures from the *Extents*, it is important to note that MacNiocaill has made some minor adjustments to the totals to allow for sums apparently overlooked by the commissioners when they made their additions. For a general analysis of Cistercian income in the later middle ages see MacNiocaill, *Na Manaigh Liatha*, 57–75. The valuations of Tintern are discussed by Hore, *Wexford*, III, 85–8.
91 *CPL*, V, 192–3.
92 *CPL*, X, 678–9.
93 *CPL*, X, 389; see also Nichols, *Gaelic Ireland* (1972), 108.
94 Bradshaw, *Dissolution of the Religious Orders* (1974), 17–35; O'Conbhuidhe, 'Suppression of Irish Cistercian Abbeys' (1959), 44–8.
95 *Irish Monastic and Episcopal Deeds*, 81–3. The visitation is discussed by Bradshaw, *Dissolution* (1974), 20–1.
96 Bradshaw, *Dissolution* (1974), 26.
97 *Extents*, 126, 213; *CPR*, XIII, 531.
98 Detailed accounts of the suppression are furnished by O'Conbhuidhe, 'Suppression of Irish Cistercian Abbeys' (1959) and Bradshaw, *Dissolution* (1974).
99 *Extents*, 280.
100 The twelve were Assaroe, Abbeydorney, Boyle, Comber, Corcomroe, Grey, Holycross, Inch, Abbeyknockmoy, Macosquin, Newry and Abington.
101 MacNiocaill, *Na Manaigh Liatha*, 128–9.
102 Glynn, 'Knockmoy Abbey' (1904), 241; Archdall, *Monasticon Hibernicum*, 268.
103 MacNiocaill, *Na Manaigh Liatha*, 125.
104 Gwynn and Hadcock, *Medieval Religious Houses*, 130; Archdall, *Monasticon Hibernicum*, 786.
105 Bradshaw, *Dissolution* (1974), 39–45.
106 *Extents*, 219, 327.
107 *Letters and Papers, Foreign and Domestic*, 14(I), p. 465.
108 *Triumphalia*, 257.
109 O'Conbhuidhe, 'Irish Cistercians under the Tudors' (1965), 6.
110 *Ibid.*, 6–10.
111 *Ormond Deeds*, V, 220–1, 271, 311.
112 The chief source of information about the revival is Malachy Hartry's *Triumphalia* (1640). See also O'Conbhuidhe,

'Irish Cistercians Under the Stuarts' (1965–7).
113 *Triumphalia*, 99–105.
114 O'Conbhuidhe, *Story of Mellifont*, 195.
115 Archdall, *Monasticon Hibernicum*, 143.

Chapter 2

1 *Statuta*, 1134. I.
2 Ailred in *Speculum Caritatis* as quoted by Knowles, *Monastic Order* (1940), 220.
3 Hill, *English Cistercian Monasteries* (1968), chapter 2.
4 G. F. Mitchell, *The Irish Landscape* (London, 1976), 183–8. The comment by Carville 'Cistercian Settlement' (1973), 23, that Cistercian houses were founded 'all over Ireland', is misleading.
5 Power, 'Cistercian Abbeys of Munster' (1938), 6.
6 Westropp, 'Corcomroe Abbey' (1900), 302.
7 *AC*, 554–5. Recent excavation in the cloister at Boyle by Dr Ann Lynch has uncovered a variety of drainage expedients designed to cope with flooding.
8 Carville, *Duiske Abbey* (1979), 91.
9 Stalley, 'Mellifont Abbey' (1980), 335.
10 Waterman, 'Somersetshire and Other Foreign Building Stone' (1970), 63–75.
11 *The Life of Ailred of Rievaulx by Walter Daniel*, translated by F. M. Powicke (London, 1950), 12–13.
12 Donkin, *The Cistercians* (1978), 31–6. Similar motives were suggested for transfers in France, Aubert *Architecture Cistercienne* (1947), 80.
13 *Statuta*, 1135.6; 1152.1.
14 Charters of Duiske, passim.
15 *Irish Monastic and Episcopal Deeds*, 99–101; MacNiocaill, *Na Manaigh Liatha*, 14; Gwynn and Hadcock, *Medieval Religious Houses* (1970), 126.
16 Gwynn and Hadcock, *Medieval Religious Houses* (1970), 125; *Annals of Inisfallen* (ed. S. Mac Airt, Dublin, 1951), 1231, 1278.
17 *CMA*, I, 354–5. The exact date of the grant to Buildwas is uncertain, see Orpen, *Ireland Under the Normans*, I, 323–4, where c1172–3 is suggested. Hore, *Wexford*, II, 40, gives c1175. MacNiocaill, *Na Manaigh Liatha*, 11–12, opts for a date before 1173. The issue is also discussed by Gwynn, 'Origins of St Mary's Abbey' (1949), 124.
18 *Statuta*, 1199. 43.
19 Hore, *Wexford*, III, 16–24; MacNiocaill, *Na Manaigh Liatha*, 13; Archdall, *Monasticon Hibernicum*, 752.
20 *Statuta*, 1233.25, 1234.23, 1235.34, 1236.26; MacNiocaill, *Na Manaigh Liatha*, 18.
21 O'Conbhuidhe, *Story of Mellifont*, 76–9.
22 *Letters of St Bernard*, 453.
23 Power, 'Cistercian Abbeys of Munster' (1928), 78.
24 Charters of Duiske, 23.

25 Gwynn, 'Origins of St Mary's Abbey' (1949), 110–25.
26 See for example *CPL*, V, 192–3.
27 Lexington, 42.
28 Hamlin, 'Enclosure at Inch Abbey' (1977).
29 Gwynn and Hadcock, *Medieval Religious Houses* (1970), 30; Lennox Barrow, *Round Towers* (1979), 177–8, argues that there are remains of a round tower at Boyle, but the remains he had in mind are more likely to belong to a post-dissolution turret.
30 Gwynn and Hadcock, *Medieval Religious Houses* (1970), 33, 388, 398; Carville, 'Cistercian Settlement' (1973), 28 and *Occupation of Celtic Sites* (1982), 118, has made further claims for the reuse of Celtic monastic sites without providing the necessary supporting evidence.
31 E. R. Norman and J. K. St Joseph, *The Early Development of Irish Society* (Cambridge, 1969), 108. The authors relate the ring work to the early monastery of Daire Mór—'unquestionably the site of the first monastery'—but there is no positive evidence for this nor have any Early Christian ecclesiastical remains come to light at Kilcooly. The opinions of Norman and St Joseph have been repeated almost verbatim by Carville, *Occupation of Celtic Sites* (1982), 87.
32 As cited by Fergusson, *Architecture of Solitude* (1984), 23, where the author examines the problems raised by the first temporary buildings in wood.
33 *Ecclesiastical History of Orderic Vitalis*, IV (1973), 326–7. The names of French Abbeys are discussed by Aubert, *Architecture Cistercienne* (1947), I, 91–3. The Latin names of Irish abbeys are listed by MacNiocaill, *Na Manaigh Liatha*, 6.
34 The 'Mell' in Mellifont may be derived from a local place name, C. Manning, 'St Buite, Mellifont and Toberboice', *Peritia*, III (1985).
35 This view has been given wide credence by Gwynn and Hadcock, *Medieval Religious Houses* (1970), 102, 104, 117, but the evidence that these houses were Benedictine before joining the Cistercians is slight. There is nothing surprising about a joint dedication to St Mary and St Benedict: indeed Midleton was named 'Chorus Benedicti'.
36 Gwynn and Hadcock, *Medieval Religious Houses* (1970), 129; O'Conbhuidhe, *Story of Mellifont*, 83; O'Conbhuidhe, 'Abbey of the Rock of Cashel' (1961).
37 *Ecclesiastical History of Orderic Vitalis*, IV (1973), 326–7.
38 Aubert, *Architecture Cistercienne* (1947), I, 95–100; Fergusson, *Architecture of Solitude* (1984), 165–172, discusses the identity of the builders of English abbeys.
39 *Letters of St Bernard*, 455.
40 Aubert, *Architecture Cistercienne* (1947), I, 97.

41 *ALC*, I, 304–5. Raghnall O'Floinn has pointed out that the English translation of the passage describing Donnsleibhe as a carpenter may be misleading. The word used is 'saor', which can be interpreted more widely as a craftsman.

42 Lexington, 105. For the problems concerned with this evidence see chapter 1, note 57.

43 *Ibid.*, 104.

44 See chapters 4 and 9.

45 *Statuta*, 1157.47.

46 R. H. C. Davis, 'A Catalogue of masons' marks as an aid to architectural history', *JBAA*, 3rd ser., 17 (1954), 43–4; Salzman, *Building in England* (1967), 127.

47 Stalley, 'Mellifont Abbey' (1980), 329–31.

48 *CMA*, I, 439.

49 Charters of Duiske, 105–6.

50 *CMA*, I, 71, 227–8, 234, 459, 520.

51 *Ibid.*, 514.

52 *ALC*, I, 261; *AFM*, III, 194–5.

53 For the foundation of Jerpoint see note 25, chapter 1.

54 *AFM*, II, 1124–5.

55 Bucher, Bonmont (1957), 55, 179, 183; Bégule, *Fontenay* (1928), 6. Some of Bucher's interpretations of recorded dates are perhaps too dogmatic and the real average is probably in excess of nineteen years. Ingrid Swartling, *Alvastra Abbey* (1969), 83, suggested forty years as a normal building period 'for abbeys in general'.

56 Petrie, *Ecclesiastical Architecture* (1845), 394.

57 *Statuta*, 1182.9, 1188.10, 1191.1, 1192.4. When Aaron the Jew died in 1186, nine English Cistercian abbeys were in his debt to the tune of 6,400 marks, Knowles, *Monastic Order* (1950), 353.

58 Stalley, 'Corcomroe Abbey' (1975), 30–2; *AC*, 341.

59 *ALC*, I, 225.

60 *CPL*, IX, 248; Gwynn and Hadcock, *Medieval Religious Houses* (1970), 124.

61 *Irish Monastic and Episcopal Deeds*, 23.

62 *CPL*, XIV, 225, 256.

63 Some uncertainty surrounds the exact foundation date of Inch. *The Coucher Book of Furness Abbey* (ed. Atkinson, 1886–8), vol. I, 12, gives June 1180 but the Cistercian tabulae give 1187, Mac-Niocaill, *Na Manaigh Liatha*, 5, 12. The seven year gap may represent the time which elapsed between the grant to Furness and the arrival of a community at the site.

64 Excavations in the church at Fountains, recently conducted by the Department of the Environment under the direction of Glynn Coppack, revealed evidence of a wooden building and an earlier stone church. A full report is yet to be published.

65 Lexington, 100–6. It is unfortunate that it cannot be established which architectural items apply to Graiguenamanagh and which to Jerpoint (see note 57, chapter 1). Item 45 relating to the nunnery almost certainly belongs to Jerpoint, whereas items 36 and 82 are more likely to relate to Graiguenamanagh. It is hard to believe that item 82 about the roofing of the northern part of the church (north aisle or north transept?) could refer to Jerpoint since the church had been begun at least fifty years earlier and the fabric is Romanesque in style. The year 1228 is about the time that the north transept of Graiguenamanagh (founded in 1204) might have been nearing completion. Similarly it is hard to believe that the chapter house of Jerpoint mentioned in item 36 was still unfinished in 1228, whereas this could well have been the case at Graiguenamanagh.

66 The Latin texts of the relevant passages are printed below (Greisser's edition, 1946). My translations, which were undertaken with advice from Dr T. N. Mitchell, Professor of Latin in Trinity College, do not always agree with those of O'Dwyer, *Stephen of Lexington, Letters from Ireland* (1982). The original manuscript is in the Biblioteca Nazionale in Turin, Ms. D.VI.25.

Item domus, ubi torcular erectum est, diuidatur per bonam sepem et altam a curia infirmorum et tam postica famulorum quam porta proxima uersus infirmitorium conuersorum omnino obstruatur infra festum sancti Dionisii (13).

Item nulla domus de cetero erigatur in medio curie abbatie uel grangiarum, sed edificetur per latera in circuitu propter fures et alia fortuita pericula. Nec in abbatia de cetero cooperiatur aliqua nisi saluo coopertorio (21).

Item firmiter precipitur, ut omnes exitus et introitus inter curiam exteriorem et interiorem omnino obstruantur excepta magna porta, que est prope coquinam (28).

Item nulla domus edificetur in grangiis nisi orrea et tecta animalium, donec domus a magnitudine debitorum, qua intolerabiliter opprimitur, exhoneretur et donec capitulum monachorum et coquina hospicii consummentur (36).

Item infra festum sancti Michaelis locus conpetens monialibus assignetur, ubi sua faciant edificia et de cetero honestius maneant propter querelam comitis Marescalli et aliorum. Alioquin ex tunc, quamdiu iuxta abbatiam manserint, abbatiam totam supponimus interdicto et personas inibi constitutas suspendimus a diuinis (45).

Item districte precipitur, ne de cetero fiat in ecclesia uel aliis officinis aliqua uarietas picturarum marmorea uel alia, sed simplicitas ordinis obseruetur. Alioquin prior, cellerarius, sacrista et custos operis a tempore huius presumptionis omni feria VI. sint in pane et aqua ad sequentem uisitationem in eadem gravius puniendi (70).

Item edificia extra portam aut cadant aut infra festum omnium Sanctorum tanta cautela ordinentur et obstruantur, ne occasionem peccandi pariant uel suspicionem infamie. Alioquin cellerarius et portarius omni VI. feria sint in pane et aqua usque ad sequentem uisitationem (78).

Item diligentia pro tempore apponatur, ut stabulum secundum formam ordinis propter domus dispendia innumera et graue periculum animarum claudatur infra septa abbatie (79).

Item cellerarius ministret plumbum sufficienter ad cooperiendum partum ecclesie aquilonarem (82).

Item tumbe in fenestra capituli alibi secundum formam usuum collocentur (83).

Item nulla capella uel altare erigatur aut habeatur in porta et fabrica iam incepta, quam cito fieri poterit cum honestate terminetur. Alioquin prior, portarius, subportarius a tempore superflui et inutilis laboris omni VI. feria sint in pane et aqua usque ad sequentem visitationem in eadem grauius puniendi (86).

Item scriptorium infra clausum nouitiorum amoueatur nec ibi de cetero aliud construatur (92).

67 The Latin in this passage is obscure and I am grateful to Professor Mitchell for help in clarifying it. Some of the phraseology used by Stephen (e.g. 'periculum animarum') is taken from Cistercian statutes (*Statuta*, 1134.21).

68 *Statuta*, 1217.27.

69 *Statuta*, 1134.20.

70 Swartling, *Nydala Abbey* (1967), 68–77; Eydoux, *Églises Cisterciennes d'Allemagne* (1952), 135.

71 William of Malmesbury, *De Gestis Regum Anglorum*, ed. W. Stubbs (London, 1887–9, Rolls Series), II, 484.

72 Charters of Duiske, 19, 39–40.

73 *Extents*, 181, 267.

74 Lexington, 105 (see footnote 62); Archdall, *Monasticon Hibernicum*, 137.

75 For example at Armagh, 1008: *AU*.

76 J. B. Whittow, *Geology and Scenery in Ireland* (Harmondsworth, 1974), 258, 261.

77 Gwynn and Hadcock, *Medieval Religious Houses* (1970), 127; Archdall, *Monasticon Hibernicum*, 789.

78 Archdall, *Monasticon Hibernicum*, 268.

79 Stalley, 'Mellifont Abbey' (1980), 346–8.

80 Stalley, 'Corcomroe Abbey' (1975), 29–30.

81 I am grateful to Dr Peter Fergusson of Wellesley College, who first pointed out the interest of the engravings in the south transept chapel.

82 In describing the arches, I am following the terminology established by R. Branner, 'Villard de Honnecourt, Archimedes, and Chartres', *Journal of the Society of Architectural Historians* [of USA], 19, 1960, 91–3. Incised drawings can also be found in Scotland on the interior walls of the refectory at Dunfermline and in the crypt at Roslin Chapel.

83 C. F. Barnes, 'The Gothic Architectural Engravings in the Cathedral of Soissons', *Speculum*, 47 (1972), 60–4; Branner, 'Origin of Gothic Architectural Drawing' (1963), 129–46; Fergusson, 'Notes on Two Cistercian Engraved Designs' (1979), 1–17.

84 J. H. Harvey, *The Medieval Architect* (London, 1972), 98, 102, 114–16, and L. S. Colchester and J. H. Harvey, 'Wells Cathedral', *Archaeological Journal*, 131 (1974), 214.

85 Branner, 'Origin of Gothic Architectural Drawing' (1963), 129–46.

Chapter 3

1 Herity, 'The Buildings and Layout of Early Irish Monasteries' (1983), 247–284, and Herity, 'The layout of Irish early Christian monasteries' (1984), 105–16. The problems involved in early monastic planning are manifold. The bulk of the buildings, constructed in wood, have vanished, usually without trace, and it is difficult to prove that the few surviving stone buildings, often with differing dates, were erected as part of a coherent scheme.

2 Duby, *St Bernard, L'Art Cistercien* (1976), 149. Various allegorical interpretations of the cloister are outlined by P. Meyvaert, 'The Medieval Monastic Claustrum', *Gesta*, XII (1973), 57–8.

3 *Rationale divinorum officiorum* by William Durand as translated by J. M. Neale and B. Webb, *The Symbolism of Churches and Church Ornaments* (Leeds, 1843), 35.

4 Duby, *St Bernard, L'Art Cistercien* (1976), 15, quoting St Bernard's sermon for the feast of St Michael.

5 *Statuta*, 1157.16.

6 The plan of St Mary's published in *Remains of St Mary's Abbey* (1886) is largely speculative.

7 A speculative plan of Graiguenamanagh was drawn by Robert Cochrane in 1892, which, despite its inaccuracies, has often been reproduced. A more thorough survey of the claustral area was carried out in 1975 by David Newman Johnson and Robert Corrigan and this was published in Bradley and Manning, 'Excavations at Duiske Abbey' (1981), 425.

8 Dimensions from Bégule, *L'Abbaye de Fontenay* (1928), 32 and Gilyard Beer, *Fountains Abbey* (1970), 41.

9 Cited by Horn and Born, *Plan of St Gall* (1980), I, 184.

10 Stalley, 'Mellifont Abbey' (1980), 309–10.

11 Aubert, *Architecture Cistercienne* (1947), I, 53; II, 123.

12 *Ibid.*, I, 112–16.

13 The plan of Mellifont is discussed at length in Stalley, 'Mellifont Abbey' (1980).

14 Esser, 'Über den Kirchenbau' (1953), 202.

15 For example at Valbuena and Fontfroide.

16 de Paor, 'Excavations at Mellifont Abbey' (1969), 131.

17 Esser, 'Über den Kirchenbau' (1953), 193–204, where the case is made for a specifically 'Bernardine' approach to the planning of churches. Esser's excessive views were criticised by Swartling, 'Cistercian Abbey Churches in Sweden' (1967), 193–7.

18 Esser, 'Les Fouilles à Himmerod' (1953), 315; Esser, 'Über den Kirchenbau' (1953), 208; Hahn, *Die Frühe Kirchenbaukunst* (1957), 101–2.

19 No excavation report was published, but the discoveries were briefly described by Leask, *Irish Churches*, II, 26.

20 Dimier, *Recueil de Plans* (1949/1967).

21 Swartling, *Alvastra Abbey* (1969), 55–63.

22 Stalley, 'Mellifont Abbey' (1980), 271, 283–92, 350–1.

23 For Holm Cultram see N. Pevsner, *Cumberland and Westmoreland* (Buildings of England, Harmondsworth, 1967), 57; Martindale, 'Holm Cultrum' (1913), 244–50; Ferguson, 'Holm Cultram, Remains lately brought to light' (1867), 269–73.

24 Brakspear, 'Stanley Abbey' (1908), 541–81.

25 St John Hope, *Abbey of St Mary in Furness* (1902), Dickinson, 'Furness Abbey—an archaeological reconsideration' (1967), 51–80.

26 For Maulbronn see Eydoux, *Architecture des Églises Cisterciennes d'Allemagne* (1952), 120–1; for Pontigny see Aubert, *Architecture Cistercienne* (1947), I, 364–5; for Fountains see Gilyard Beer, *Fountains Abbey* (1970), 26.

27 These foundations were discovered in 1981 when preparations were being made for the construction of a new porch. No proper archaeological investigation was conducted.

28 *CPL*, IX, 458.

29 The crossing arches had fallen by the time the church was remodelled since the new masonry overlays the stub of the thirteenth-century south-west crossing pier. The mouldings of the re-used doorway are almost identical to those in the north transept doorway, implying a similar date. As the nave was completed long after the transept, there is no absolute certainty that the door came from the thirteenth-century facade. The contraction of monastic churches in Ireland and Scotland is discussed by Colin

Platt, 'Relaxation of the Rule', *History Today* (July 1985), 21–6, an article brought to my attention by Ann Hamlin.

30 The foundations across the nave at Jerpoint have been wrongly interpreted as the base of a screen. They are too massive for this and in the early nineteenth century a stone wall in this position reached almost to the full height of the building, cf. drawing by R. Gibbs (1805–10) and the illustration in Hall, *Ireland, Its Scenery and Character* (1842), II, 4. The blocking wall at Graiguenamanagh (which may have dated from the early nineteenth century) has recently been demolished.

31 Hahn, *Die Frühe Kirchenbaukunst* (1957), 66–81, 314–39; see also Bucher, *Bonmont* (1957), 88.

32 For example Bucher's review in *Art Bulletin*, XL (1958), 274–7; Schmoll gen Eisenwerth, 'Zisterzienser Romanik' (1959), 153–80. While accepting Hahn's ideas as a useful rule of thumb, Eisenwerth expressed doubts about the universality of the system in view of the number of local exceptions. Hahn's theories have also been discussed at length by D. A. Walsh in regard to Bordesley Abbey (Hirst, Walsh and Wright, *Bordesley Abbey* (1983), 208–29). With some reservations, Walsh accepts the value of Hahn's interpretations.

33 In the few pages devoted to Ireland, Hahn made over a dozen errors. He made use of a largely hypothetical plan of the church at Bective and he misdated the churches at Tintern and Holycross. He stated that Mellifont was a seventh-century foundation and that the first Cistercian church (1142–57) was not finished when the second was begun—views for which there is no supporting evidence.

34 Hahn, *Die Frühe Kirchenbaukunst* (1957), 315–16.

35 Unless otherwise stated, the dimensions are external. If centre to centre dimensions are taken, discrepancies with Hahn's proportional system become more marked.

36 See chapter 1, note 25.

37 As there are two changes of design in the nave of Boyle and the church was not finished until nearly sixty years after its start, it is not surprising that the original proportions of the plan were abandoned by later builders.

38 Hahn, *Die Frühe Kirchenbaukunst* (1957), 126, 210–12.

39 For a recent discussion of medieval metrology, see Fernie, 'Historical Metrology' (1978), 383–99. Walsh has shown that the Roman foot of 29.57 cm was employed at Bordesley and a number of other English abbeys, see Hirst, Walsh and Wright, *Bordesley Abbey* (1983), 224–5.

40 Swartling, 'A new unit of measurement' (1966), 25–30.

41 Stalley, 'Corcomroe Abbey' (1975), 28–30.

42 Hahn, *Die Frühe Kirchenbaukunst* (1957), 322.

43 *Ibid.*, 326.

44 This also occurs at Tintern.

45 Ingrid Swartling reached a similar conclusion in her study of Alvastra Abbey. Although Hahn believed the proportions of the building fitted his system (*Die Frühe Kirchenbaukunst*, 214–15, 326), this was not confirmed by detailed measurement, Swartling, *Alvastra Abbey* (1969), 77–9, 87.

46 The golden section, traditionally regarded as one of the most satisfying proportional relationships, is expressed in numerical terms as the ratio of $1:1.618$ (or approximately $5:8$), in arithmetical terms as $\frac{1}{2}(\sqrt{5}\pm1)$, and in geometrical terms as the ratio of one side of a regular pentagon to a line drawn between two of its angles. For a summary of its history since Euclid see *The Oxford Companion to Art*, ed. H. Osborne (Oxford, 1970), 488–9.

Chapter 4

1 Vendryes, 'Mellifont Fille de Clairvaux' (1927), 281.

2 The best analysis of this period of Cistercian architecture is by Hahn, *Die Frühe Kirchenbaukunst* (1957), 84–128. There are also some pertinent comments in Schmoll gen. Eisenwerth, 'Zisterzienser—Romanik' (1959), 153–80.

3 The design of Clairvaux is discussed by Aubert, *Architecture Cistercienne* (1947), I, passim; Hahn, *Die Frühe Kirchenbaukunst* (1957), 119–22; Bucher, *Bonmont* (1957), 123–4; for a description of the abbey before destruction see Chabeuf, Voyage d'un Délégue (1883–4), 290–318; the initiative for the rebuilding came from Prior Godefroid, Fergusson, *Architecture of Solitude* (1984), 166.

4 The design of Fontenay is analysed by Aubert, *Architecture Cistercienne* (1947), I, passim; Hahn, *Die Frühe Kirchenbaukunst* (1957), 97–104; Bucher, *Bonmont* (1957), 179–81; also Bégule, *L'abbaye de Fontenay* (1928); Gilbert, 'Un chef-d'œuvre d'art cistercien' (1970), 1–3, 20–45.

5 Bucher, *Bonmont* (1957), 278.

6 Swartling, *Alvastra Abbey* (1969).

7 The Cistercian theory of art has been discussed by Esser, 'Über den Kirchenbau' (1953), 204–11; Bucher, *Bonmont* (1957), 26–7; Bucher, 'Cistercian Architectural Purism' (1960–1), 85–105 and Melczer and Soldwedel, 'Monastic Goals in the Aesthetics of St Bernard' (1982), 31–44.

8 Matthew XX, 13; Mark XI, 17; Luke XIX, 46.

9 Bucher, 'Cistercian Architectural Purism' (1960), 93.

10 At Boyle, Baltinglass and Monasteranenagh, Gothic lancets replaced the original windows and at Jerpoint, a window with geometrical tracery was installed in the fourteenth century.

11 Stalley, 'Mellifont Abbey' (1980), 293–5.

12 Fergusson, *Architecture of Solitude* (1984), 37.

13 The English sources for Cormac's Chapel are discussed in Stalley, 'Three Irish Buildings' (1981), 62–5.

14 Petit, 'Architectural Notices of Buildwas Abbey' (1958), 335–44; Hamilton Thompson, *Buildwas Abbey, Shropshire* (London, HMSO, 1946). Buildwas does not provide a source for the alternation at Baltinglass, though the nave there begins with an isolated octagonal pier on each side as if an octagon/cylinder alternation was at one stage envisaged. At Furness there is emphatic alternation between circular piers and compound piers. Fergusson, *Architecture of Solitude* (1984), 93, assigns the first bays of the nave at Buildwas to a second building campaign of c1165, but the octagonal pier is more likely to belong to the first phase of building c1150–60. A break in building in the first or second bay of the nave was a common occurrence.

15 A similar procedure was adopted at Strata Florida and in the eastern chapels at Abbey Dore.

16 The distribution of the feature appears to follow no obvious geographical or historical pattern. English examples include the Anglo-Saxon churches at Brixworth and Lydd, as well as later churches at Overbury, Ripple, Bakewell, Bishops Cannings, Great Bedwyn, Northampton (St Peters), Llanaber, Workshop Priory, etc. In Scotland there is an important example in the Nuns' Church, Iona. Further Irish examples, probably influenced by the neighbouring Cistercian abbeys, include the thirteenth-century parish churches at Gowran and Thomastown.

17 C. A. Ralegh Radford, *Ewenny Priory, Glamorgan* (London, HMSO, 1952) and Stalley, 'Three Irish Buildings' (1981), 80. I am grateful to Dr Malcolm Thurlby for informing me of St Briavels.

18 Corbels in the nave of St David's Cathedral, likewise unvaulted, seem to have served a similar purpose.

19 Paul, 'The Church and Monastery of Abbey Dore' (1904), 117–26; *RCHM, Herefordshire*, I (1931), 1–11.

20 Other west of England features are the elongated western crossing piers, that on the south side projecting into the crossing space. This peculiarity can be paralleled at Tewkesbury, Hereford, Chester (St John's), Shrewsbury, Gloucester, Leominster and Llanthony, Carolyn Marino Malone, 'Abbey Dore: English versus French Design', *Studies in Cistercian Art and Architecture*, II, ed. M. D. Lillich (Kalamazoo, 1984), 65.

21 Gwynn, 'Origins of St Mary's' (1949), 116.

22 North and south arcades built in different styles or using different forms are not uncommon in early Gothic architecture, especially in England. It is a phenomenon discussed by Dr Lawrence Hoey in a forthcoming article entitled 'Pier Alternation in Early English Gothic Architecture'. Dr Hoey attributes such architectural contrasts to 'a mentality that saw vitue in experiment'. I am grateful to Dr Hoey for allowing me to read his paper prior to its publication.

23 Stalley, 'Medieval Sculpture of Christ Church' (1979), 109–16.

24 Fergusson, *Architecture of Solitude* (1984), 50. For literature on Furness and Holm Cultram see also chapter 3, notes 23 and 25.

25 This campaign took place between the raid on Boyle in 1202, *ALC*, I, 225 and the consecration of 1218/20, *ALC*, I, 261; *AFM*, III, 194–5.

26 The so-called English West Country 'school' was defined by Brakspear, 'A West Country School of Masons' (1931), 1–18.

27 In 1227 the abbot of Boyle was described as 'a principal conspirator' and deposed by the General Chapter, *Statuta*, 1227.29.

28 Fergusson, 'Roche Abbey' (1971), 31–42; Fergusson, 'The South Transept Elevation of Byland Abbey' (1975), 155–76.

29 McNeill, *Anglo-Norman Ulster* (1980), 46–7, suggests that building began at Inch in the 1180s, but when compared with Grey this is stylistically too early. Inch and Grey are described at length in *ASNI*, 275–83.

30 The development of this pier form is discussed by Fergusson, 'Byland Abbey' (1975), 161–4.

31 The flattened rolls with a single fillet ('squashed filleted rolls') that decorate the angles of the nave piers are also found on the late thirteenth-century niches on the east front of Downpatrick Cathedral. In England the flattened roll is common after the middle of the century, though it does occur earlier, as in the nave of Lincoln Cathedral.

32 *Ordnance Survey Letters*, Wexford, II, p. 61 (Royal Irish Academy). The best account of the ruins of Dunbrody is in the *78th Annual Report of the Commissioners of Public Works in Ireland* (1909–10), 6–12. See also Leask, *Irish Churches*, II, 83–4.

33 During the 1858 restorations the entrances to the chapels were repaired with ashlar blocks, in place of the thirteenth-century angle shafts, *78th Annual Report of the Commissioners of Public Works in Ireland* (1909–10), 8.

34 Banded masonry can be seen on the east

wall of the south transept at St David's Cathedral, in the east range at Margam Abbey and in the crossing at Strata Florida, Williams, *The Cistercian Abbey of Strata Florida* (1889), 198, 211. Among other examples in northern Europe are Worcester Cathedral (chapter house and parts of the church), Exeter Cathedral (twelfth-century fragments), Tournus, Vézelay, Le Mans Cathedral, etc. The Chronicle of the abbots of St Trond near Liège describes how the architect 'tastefully and artfully inserted distinct alternating courses of black and white stone', *Recueil de Textes*, ed. Mortet and Deschamps (1929), 12.

35 There are also examples at Ardmore, cf. Champneys, *Irish Ecclesiastical Architecture* (1910), 131.

36 Leask, Irish Churches, II, 83.

37 Champneys, *Irish Ecclesiastical Architecture* (1910), 234.

38 Harris, *Works of Sir James Ware* (1764), I, 456.

39 A number of stylistic details point to a date of c1230–60 for the nave. The design of the arcades recall those in the transept of St Patrick's Cathedral, and foliate capitals with an extra band around the stalks can be paralleled at Christ Church Cathedral (nave clerestory, c1216–34), Cashel Cathedral (choir, c1250) and Kilkenny Cathedral (north choir aisle, c1220–30).

40 The design of Waterford Cathedral, demolished in 1773, is discussed in Stalley, 'Three Irish Buildings' (1981), 66–71.

41 Grose, *Antiquities*, I, pl. 126.

42 Champneys, *Irish Ecclesiastical Architecture* (1910), 143.

43 The piers of the 'bridge' to the reredorter in the east range are comparable with Irish work, Butler, *Neath Abbey* (1976), 20.

44 Archdall, *Monasticon Hibernicum*, 740.

45 Grose, I, 39; Luckombe, *Tour Through Ireland* (1780), 41. O'Leary, 'Notes on Graiguenamanagh' (1892), 238, places the collapse in 1774, and this was followed by Leask, *Irish Churches*, II, 86.

46 Lexington's instruction to release lead for roofing the northern part of the church (1228) may possibly refer to Graiguenamanagh rather than Jerpoint, Lexington, 105.

47 Leask, *Irish Churches*, II, 87. The building history of Kilkenny Cathedral has been meticulously studied by Sioban Barry, *Kilkenny Cathedral, A Study of its Architecture* (unpublished M.Litt. thesis, Trinity College, Dublin, 1984). Miss Barry has pointed out that the similarities between the buildings are not as close as sometimes assumed. There are also analogies between the capitals at Graiguenamanagh and those in the chapter house at Mellifont, c1210, Stalley, 'Mellifont Abbey' (1980), 305.

48 *Annals of Ireland by Friar John Clyn*, ed. R. Butler (Dublin, 1849), 22.

49 Stalley, 'Mellifont Abbey' (1980), 280–8, 322–9, 350–1.

50 T. Dinely, *Observations in a Voyage through the Kingdom of Ireland* (N.L.I., Ms. 1972 TX), p. 114.

51 McNeill, *Anglo-Norman Ulster* (1980), 47–50.

52 Lexington, 82–3.

53 The principal accounts are Westropp, 'Monasteranenagh' (1889), 232–8; Champneys, *Irish Ecclesiastical Architecture* (1910), 151–2; Leask, *Irish Churches* II, 35–8; Power, Cistercian Abbeys of Munster (1930), 43–6.

54 Westropp, 'Monsteranenagh' (1889), 237.

55 *Ordnance Survey Letters, Limerick, I* (1840), 114–21 (Royal Irish Academy).

56 Leask, *Irish Churches* II, 53–76.

57 The style of the capitals in the hall at Athenry Castle, built by Meiler de Bermingham, betrays the influence of the school of the west, Leask, *Irish Castles* (1964), 36–9.

58 This technique was a feature of the English West Country school, Brakspear, 'West Country School' (1931), 6–7, and typical examples can be seen at St David's Cathedral (east windows, exterior) the Cistercian Abbey of Valle Crucis (lateral windows in the presbytery), and the priory at Ewenny (domestic building to the west of the church).

59 Leask, *Irish Churches*, II, 63; Stalley, *Architecture and Sculpture* (1971), 116–17.

60 For the architecture of Abbeyknockmoy see Blake, 'Knockmoy Abbey' (1900–1), 64–84; Cochrane, 'Knockmoy Abbey' (1904), 244–53; Champneys, *Irish Ecclesiastical Architecture* (1910), 147–9; Leask, *Irish Churches*, II, 38–9.

61 The architecture of Corcomroe is discussed at length in Stalley, 'Corcomroe Abbey' (1975), 24–46.

62 Leask, 'Bective Abbey' (1916), 49, incorrectly assigned this work to the twelfth century. The quatrefoil windows and carved chamfer stops leave no doubt as to the late thirteenth-century date.

63 *Statuta*, 1274.60. The archbishop had plans to move the entire monastery and the abbots of Mellifont and St Mary's, Dublin, were required to inspect the proposed site in 1274. Such a proposal would have been extraordinary if the monks of Bective had recently completed a new church.

64 D. H. Williams, *White Monks in Gwent and the Border* (Pontypool, 1976), 103; Hore, *Wexford*, III, 16. Lancaut is a hamlet just south of Tintern Major, so Henry was evidently a Welshman or Englishman. In 1413 the abbot of Tintern Major was so concerned about the safety of Tintern in Ireland that he sent a servant there to bring back for safe keeping a silver gilt cross, see chapter 10.

65 A number of details support this date. The bases of the east window can be compared with those on the sedilia in the friary at Kilmallock (founded 1291) and with those in the early fourteenth-century work at Mellifont. A capital in the south transept finds its closest analogies with capitals on the city gate at New Ross (post 1265) and in the nave at Ardfert Friary (post 1300 according to Leask, *Irish Churches*, II, 114). A base on the south-west crossing pier recalls those used in the cloister at Baltinglass. Links with Tintern Major and Neath also suggest the period 1270–1320.

66 Craster, *Tintern Abbey* (1956), 4–5; Blashill, 'Architectural History of Tintern Abbey' (1881–2), 88–106; Butler, *Neath Abbey* (1976), 8.

67 The curve of the original window is still visible in the masonry, both inside and outside.

68 The chancel was excavated in 1983 as part of a programme of archaeological work under the direction of Dr. Ann Lynch of the Office of Public Works.

69 Hore, *Wexford*, III, 98–101. The tower had already been heightened, probably after 1447, Archdall, *Monasticon Hibernicum*, 753.

70 The external length of the church is 162 feet 5 inches, a dimension which if subdivided marks the line of the west wall of the transept (see chapter 3).

71 The recent excavations failed to uncover any evidence of the north aisle wall or the north transept, yet the presence of nave arcades and a north crossing arch indicate that both must once have existed.

72 Archdall, *Monasticon Hibernicum*, 138; *CMA* I, XXXIX; II, 332.

73 de Paor, 'Excavations at Mellifont Abbey' (1969), 131.

74 Stalley, 'Mellifont Abbey' (1980), 289–298, 331–2, 351.

75 *Ibid.*, 351. I am grateful to Dr John Maddison for pointing out the possibility of connections with Vale Royal.

Chapter 5

1 *Irish Monastic and Episcopal Deeds*, 19, 23. For information about the life of James, the fourth earl of Ormond, see Otway-Ruthven, *A History of Medieval Ireland* (1968), Chapters XI and XII; Lydon, *Ireland in the later Middle Ages* (1973), 134–47; and Carte, *An History of the Life of James Duke of Ormonde* (1736), xxxvi–xl.

2 'Crow stepped' battlements form a prominent element of the church following the recent restoration, though Leask was of the opinion that it was not possible to say whether the battlements were 'of the stepped or plain type', Leask, *Irish Churches*, III, 62.

3 Quane, 'Tour in Ireland' by John Harden (1953), 30–2. Harden's views make an

interesting contrast with those of John O'Donovan in 1840: 'The ruins of this Abbey entirely disappointed my expectations; the architecture of the choir and side chapels is indeed truly beautiful but they are not lofty nor magnificent but the nave and side aisles are contemptible . . .', *Ordnance Survey Letters, Tipperary* I (1840), 171–8 (Royal Irish Academy).

4 Leask, *Irish Churches*, III, 60.

5 *CPL*, XL, 2–4.

6 *Rotulorum Patentium Calendarium* (1828), 189 (11).

7 Carte, *History of the Duke of Ormonde* (1736), xlii–xliii.

8 *Ormond Deeds*, III, no. 88.

9 *Ibid.*, II, no. 106.

10 *Irish Monastic and Episcopal Deeds*, 15–16.

11 *Ibid.*, 19–21.

12 *Ibid.*, 23–4.

13 The charter is published in MacNiocaill, *Na Manaigh Liatha*, 202–3.

14 *CPL*, XIV, 225, 256: 'Oblationibus que ad lignum sancte Crucis quod in ecclesia eiusdem monasterii existit per Christifideles offeruntur, et que per questores qui ad hoc deputantur colliguntur'.

15 The ambulatory of St Séverin in Paris comes to mind, R. Sanfacon, *L'architecture flamboyante en France* (Quebec, 1971), 93.

16 *Triumphalia*, lv.

17 *Ibid.*, lvii. In 1639 the relic was placed in 'the upper part of the church' over the high altar.

18 *Ibid.*, 156–7.

19 Champneys, *Irish Ecclesiastical Architecture* (1910), 175.

20 O'Halloran, *An Introduction to the Study of the History and Antiquities of Ireland* (1772), caption to pl. 1. Leask, with some hesitation, took the same view, Leask, *Irish Churches*, III, 67.

21 Coldstream, 'English Decorated Shrine Bases' (1976), 15–34. The shrine of St Alban is depicted in Trinity College, Dublin, Ms. 177, fol 54.

22 E. Fernie, 'The Spiral Piers of Durham Cathedral', *Medieval Art and Architecture at Durham Cathedral*, British Archaeological Association Conference Transactions (London, 1980), 49–58.

23 Coldstream, 'English Decorated Shrine Bases' (1976), 18.

24 *CMA*, II, xxiii.

25 *81st Report of the Commissioners of Public Works in Ireland* (1913), 40.

26 The stones are currently in store and it is to be regretted that no attempt has been made to restore the shrine in a permanent location.

27 According to Carville, *Heritage of Holycross* (1973), 121–2, there were two fragments, one of which is now at Mount Melleray, enshrined in a silver gilt cross. The other better-known fragment was for many years in the Ursuline Convent at Blackrock (County Cork), but it has

now been returned to Holycross. For a discussion of the shrine see chapter 10; also Comerford, 'Relic of the Holy Cross' (1874–9), 130–5 and Crawford, 'Descriptive List of Irish Shrines and Reliquaries' (1923), 89–90. The original acquisition of the relic by the Cistercians is discussed by Power, 'Cistercian Abbeys of Munster (1938), 3, as well as by Denis Murphy in *Triumphalia*, lx–lxii. The relic appears to have escaped damage in 1539 and the ensuing years, when Irish shrines were systematically destroyed. A sum of £24 was realised from the chattels of Holycross, Bradshaw, *Dissolution* (1974), 106.

28 This 'processional' doorway dates from c1190–1200. It has keeled mouldings and foliage capitals, one of which is reminiscent of a design used at Monasteranenagh.

29 The south arcade has been reconstructed with round arches. This, together with the bracing arches across the aisle, apparently dates from the repairs of Dr Charles William Wall in 1834–5. For Wall's activities at Holycross see Ireland, 'Holycross 1730–1840' (1982), 48–54. To judge from the quality of the masonry, the entire north aisle wall may have been rebuilt in the fifteenth century. The date of the solid walls which replace the two eastern bays of the nave is hard to determine. At the west end they have fifteenth century decorative details, but solid walls in this position were typical of twelfth-century practice.

30 During the restoration of 1970–5, a saddle roof was constructed, covering both nave and aisles in one sweep. The design aroused a certain amount of controversy at the time. It is interesting to note that the Cistercian church at Bonmont (Switzerland) has this type of roof, but, even in churches without a clerestory, it was not common. At Fontenay there is a break in the roof line above the arcades and this was the likely arrangement at Holycross.

31 There are no marks of a vault on adjacent walls, even before the recent restoration. Samuel Close was adamant that the south transept 'was without groining', Close, *Holy Cross Abbey, County Tipperary* (1868).

32 This window was wrongly attributed to the fifteenth century by Leask, *Irish Churches*, II, 131. For a discussion of Irish window tracery in this period see Stalley, 'Irish Gothic and English Fashion' (1984), 78–9. The reticulated window was derived from England, where such net patterns are common, e.g. Wells Cathedral (Lady Chapel and retro-choir), Higham Ferrars (Northamptonshire), St Mary Magdalene's, Oxford, Stoke Prior (Worcestershire), New Romney (Kent), etc.

33 The cuspless tracery of the Kilcooly

window appears to belong to the sixteenth century. This type of tracery can be found in a number of Irish churches (for example, the Dominican church at Cashel, Kilconnell Friary, the friary at Moyne, etc.), and it is especially common in Scotland after 1500. The handling of the Kilcooly tracery is reminiscent of that in the collegiate church at Mid-Calder (Lothian) of c1542, Fawcett, 'Scottish Medieval Window Tracery' (1984), 181–2; McWilliam, *Lothian* (1978), 322–4; *RCAHM Scotland: Midlothian and Westlothian* (1929), 135–8.

34 An improved version of this design was used in the Dominican Friary at Aghaboe (Leix), Leask, *Irish Churches*, III, 131.

35 Leask, *Irish Churches*, III, 168–9. Flamboyant tracery in England is analysed in E. A. Freeman, *An Essay on the Origin and Development of Window Tracery in England* (Oxford and London, 1851), 155–66.

36 It is disappointing that the excavations conducted at Holycross in 1969–70 have not yet been published, for they may throw considerable light on the way building proceeded.

37 The tracery of the southernmost chapel is surrounded on the exterior by thin mouldings. These were reduced in number on the window in the adjoining chapel and eliminated elsewhere in the building. Inside, the window in the more southerly of the north transept chapels was given an exceptionally lavish treatment, with engaged shafts supporting the moulded rear arch. Paradoxically, on the exterior of this same window the mouldings are plain and undistinguished. Even string courses vary in their profiles and decoration.

38 With its series of short vertical bars, the tracery of the west window has some perpendicular elements.

39 For analysis of the 'time-lag' see Stalley, 'Irish Gothic and English Fashion' (1984), 82–4.

40 Stalley, 'Medieval Sculpture of Christ Church Cathedral', (1979), 107–22; Stalley, 'William of Prene', (1978), 33.

41 This has a chamfered profile, with semicircular hollows cut out of the chamfers. It appears on both shrines, the ribs of the chancel vault and the west doorway.

42 Morris, 'Later Gothic mouldings', II (1979), 20.

43 Leask, *Irish Churches*, III, 74–5.

44 The national flavour of Irish late Gothic was analysed by Champneys, *Irish Ecclesiastical Architecture* (1910). For Scotland see MacGibbon and Ross, *The Ecclesiastical Architecture of Scotland* (1896–7), especially II, 331–4, and III, 6; also Fawcett, 'Scottish Medieval Window Tracery' (1984), 148–86.

45 Fawcett, 'Late Gothic Architecture in Scotland' (1982), 477–96.

46 There were however much closer links

between Ireland and the western Isles. One of the major families of late Gothic stone carvers, based at Iona, the O'Brolcháns, originated in the area around Derry and Donaldus O'Brolchán was responsible for part of the construction of the abbey church at Iona in the mid-fifteenth century. The canopied tomb at Dungiven (Derry) is almost certainly the work of craftsmen based in western Scotland. For these and other references to Scottish connections see K. A. Steer and J. W. M. Bannerman, *Late Medieval Sculpture in the West Highlands* (RCAHM Scotland, Edinburgh, 1977), 39–40, 43–4 and 106–7.

47 Irish examples of sixteenth-century uncusped loop tracery can be found at Clare Abbey near Ennis, St Nicholas' Galway, St Mary's Youghal, Kilconnell Friary etc.

48 There is a similar fireplace in the tower house at Burnchurch (Kilkenny), Leask, *Irish Castles* (1964), 94.

49 Woodward, *Measured Drawings, Holy Cross Abbey* (Royal Irish Academy).

50 *Ormond Deeds*, V, 226.

51 This tradition is discussed by Champneys, who cites a number of English parallels, *Irish Ecclesiastical Architecture* (1910), 230–3.

52 Leask, *Irish Churches*, I, 32–4, 39–40, 113–21.

53 Champneys, *Irish Ecclesiastical Architecture* (1910), 164–5.

54 Leask, *Irish Churches*, III, 20–1.

55 Westropp, 'Cliara Abbey' (1911–15), 29–37.

56 *CPL*, IX, 458; XI, 505. The abbey had already been burnt in 1418 (*AFM*), twenty-seven years before. Abbot Philip O'Molwanayn died in 1463 and his grave slab records that he had carried out 'many good works, both spiritual and temporal', Hunt, *Irish Figure Sculpture* (1974), I, 227.

57 Heraldic shields are sited above the abbot's stall and on the south wall of the south transept.

58 Hunt, *Irish Figure Sculpture* (1974), I, 228.

59 Chapter 3, pp. 66–7.

60 In the absence of laybrothers, the nave may have been left for the use of the laity.

61 The monastery was said to be in need of repair in 1442, *CPL*, IX, 248. See also chapter 10.

62 The barrel vault was erected at the same time as the crossing tower; it replaced an earlier pointed barrel.

63 A shield with the Ormond arms is carved under the western crossing arch, which may indicate Ormond patronage. Another Ormond shield, further blazoned with three spear heads, decorates the pier between the north transept chapels.

Chapter 6

1 Fergusson, 'Byland Abbey' (1975), 167.

2 Clapham, *English Romanesque Architecture*, II (1934), 55–7. In Norman architecture vaulting was generally restricted to the east end of the church and even at Durham Cathedral, famous for its early ribbed vaults, this was the original intention: J. Bony 'Le projet premier de Durham: voûtement partiel ou voûtement total?' *Urbanisme et architecture, études écrites et publiées en l'honneur de Pierre Lavedan* (Paris, 1954), 41–9.

3 The pointed barrel at Jerpoint was rebuilt with a circular profile in the fifteenth century, but marks of the original are still visible on the east wall.

4 At Monasteranenagh only the south transept chapels appear to have been vaulted in this way.

5 This favourite Irish constructional technique is explained by Leask, *Irish Castles* (1964), 86–7.

6 Hamilton Thompson, Clapham and Leask, 'Cistercian Order in Ireland' (1931), 33.

7 Leask, *Irish Churches*, I, 27–41. Barrel vaults were used in conjunction with stone roofs at Kells ('St Columba's House'), Glendalough ('Kevin's Kitchen'), Killaloe (St Flannan's), at Cashel (Cormac's Chapel), Louth ('St Mochta's House') and St Doulagh's (County Dublin). At Cashel, Louth and St Doulagh's the springing of the barrel vault is placed well below the start of the stone roof and the two elements are not structurally integrated. At Kells and Glendalough, however, the barrel vault plays an important role in countering the central sag of the roof.

8 Leask, *Irish Churches*, I, 33–4. Leask believed it was 'difficult to doubt' the 807–14 date, but apart possibly from Glendalough and Kells, the other buildings of the group are known to date from after 1100. The introduction of the barrel vault to Ireland deserves detailed study, so too does the relationship between Irish buildings and First Romanesque. In this context it is worth noting that many tenth- and eleventh-century churches in southern Europe had stone-slated roofs built directly on the vault, as for example at Banyoles (Catalonia) c957, see Puig I Cadafalch, *Premier Art Roman* (1928), 63.

9 Puig I Cadafalch, *Premier Art Roman* (1928), 60–83 and Puig I Cadafalch, *Géographie et Origines du Premier Art Roman* (1935); the author notes that 'Les faits semblent indiquer que le retour à la voûte en Occident s'est produit d'abord dans les pays où il y avait de nombreuses ruines romanes, sur la côte méditerranéene, en Italie, en Provence, en Languedoc, en Catalogne', *Premier Art Roman*, 61–2. As Ireland was not conquered by the Romans, the barrel vault must have been introduced from abroad, either from England or France.

10 Leask, *Irish Churches*, I, 39–40.

11 The use of wickerwork centering in Ireland may go back before the Romanesque era, since wickerwork was an essential element in secular building. Ann Hamlin informs me that it was used in the construction of the cap of the round tower at Antrim, a monument which almost certainly pre-dates the twelfth century. Wattle centering was also used by the Anglo-Saxons at Avebury (Wiltshire) and Hales (Norfolk) where it supported window arches, H. M. Taylor and J. Taylor, *Anglo-Saxon Architecture* (Cambridge, 1965/78), I, 33 and 279; III, 1062. The method was used occasionally in thirteenth-century England in preference to plank centering, as in a small chamber off the north transept at Lincoln Cathedral.

12 Stalley, 'Mellifont Abbey' (1980), 300–1.

13 Leask, 'Bective Abbey' (1916), 32. Both in the text and on the accompanying plan the vault is misleadingly dated to the twelfth century, but it rests on a pier with punch dressed masonry, which is late medieval in character.

14 Henry, *Irish Art in the Romanesque Period*, 172; Stalley, 'Three West Country Buildings' (1981), 63.

15 Leask, *Irish Churches*, II, 47. The profiles are not as close as Leask believed.

16 The chapter house at Mellifont is not a fourteenth-century work, as sometimes thought, Stalley, 'Mellifont Abbey' (1980), 300–8.

17 M. Aubert, 'Les plus anciennes croisée d'ogives', *Bulletin Monumental*, XCIII (1934), 7–24; A. K. Porter, *Lombard Architecture* (New Haven, 1915–17), I, 114–26. German vaults of this type can be found at Murbach, St Johann Alsbach, Speyer Cathedral (transepts), Worms Cathedral (east choir), Walderbach, Maulbronn (choir) and Bronnbach (choir); also at Heiligenkreuz, Zwettl and Klosterneuburg in Austria. Several of these vaults are constructed without the use of keystones, Hahn, *Die Frühe Kirchenbaukunst* (1957), 141–7 and Eydoux, *Architecture des Églises Cisterciennes d'Allemagne* (1952), 97–106. Vaults with square ribs appear in other contexts in Ireland, as in the thirteenth-century lighthouse at Hook Head (Wexford) and the round tower of the fifteenth-century castle at Fethard (Wexford).

18 For a technical analysis of the *tas de charge* see Viollet-le-Duc, *Dictionnaire Raisonné de l'Architecture Française* (Paris, 1854–68), IX, 7–12, and for its use in England, along with *formerets*, Bond, *Gothic Architecture in England* (1906), 300–3. The Lady Chapel at Glastonbury Abbey (1184–6) employs both techniques, one of the first buildings in England to do so.

19 Many of the late twelfth-century ribbed vaults in Germany do not employ keystones.

20 S. E. Rigold, *Lilleshall Abbey, Shropshire* (London, HMSO, 1969).

21 H. P. R. Finberg, 'St Patrick at Glastonbury' in H. P. R. Finberg, *West Country Studies* (Newton Abbot, 1969), 70–88. I am grateful to Marie-Thérèse Flanagan for bringing this reference to my attention.

22 For the architecture of the chapel, see Brakspear, 'West Country School' (1931), 1–18 and N. Pevsner, *North Somerset and Bristol* (Harmondsworth, 1958). The west gate at Gloucester also has a similar vault.

23 Stalley, 'Mellifont Abbey' (1980), 282.

24 The castle at Ferns is discussed by Leask, *Irish Castles* (1964), 49–50, Stalley, *Architecture and Sculpture* (1971), 26–7 and D. Sweetman, 'Archaeological Excavations at Ferns Castle, County Wexford', *PRIA* 79C (1979), 217–45.

25 General accounts of English vaulting in the Decorated era, including Bristol and Tewkesbury, are provided by Henning Bock, *Der Decorated Style* (Heidelburg, 1962), 44–70, and Bony, *English Decorated Style* (1979), 43–56.

26 There are parallels in the Beauchamp Chapel, Tewkesbury (c1432), the Fitzjames Gateway, Merton College, Oxford (c1500), the Proscholium Oxford (c1610–12), the south porch at Northleach, etc. The same pattern of ribs was used widely in the late Gothic architecture of Scotland.

27 A profile used two centuries before at Dunbrody (nave).

28 P. Harbison, 'Decorated Roof Boss found at Newpark Hotel', *Old Kilkenny Review*, New Series, volume I, no. 2 (1975), 120–3. Late medieval vault bosses can be found in a few non-Cistercian buildings, for example, in the towers of the Franciscan friaries at Kilkenny (decorated with a ram) and Drogheda, and in the south porch of Cashel Cathedral. A boss from the Dominican friary at Limerick can be seen in a neighbouring garden. In contrast to their scarcity in late Gothic vaults, bosses were common in the thirteenth century. A fine example, ornamented with stiff-leaf foliage, lies amidst the undergrowth south-east of the church at Graiguenamanagh. Carved bosses were also used in the vault at Ferns Castle.

29 Aubert, *Architecture Cistercienne*, I, 258–64.

30 Leask, *Irish Churches*, III, 174; J. Graves and J. G. A. Prim, *The History, Architecture and Antiquities of the Cathedral Church of St Canice, Kilkenny* (Dublin, 1857), 35–6, 89; Clapham, 'Some Minor Irish Cathedrals' (1949), 33–5.

31 The best account of how the stones of a rib vault were cut is still R. Willis, 'On the construction of the vaults of the Middle Ages', *Transactions of the Royal Institute of British Architects of London*, I,

part 2 (1842), reprinted in R. Willis, *Architectural History of Some English Cathedrals* II (Chicheley 1973).

32 There is no recent account of Leighlin Cathedral. Clapham, 'Some Minor Irish Cathedrals' (1949), 26–8, ascribes the tower and its vault to 1529–49, but on account of the links with other vaults in the Ormond area, a date in the later decades of the fifteenth century is equally plausible.

33 Another elaborate vault of this 'school' can be seen in the crossing of the Dominican Friary at Kilkenny, where seven ribs spring from each corner. This was erected in the early sixteenth century through the benefaction of James Schortall. About this time vaulting patterns became a popular decorative motif. At Old Leighlin a slab from a fifteenth-century tomb reproduces—or attempts to reproduce—the Kilkenny rib design and at Kilcooly there is a font ornamented in the same way. Many years later similar patterns were employed in the manor house at Carrick-on-Suir, as a decoration around the fireplace in the long gallery (c1565). Tomb chests at Fertagh and elsewhere furnish other examples of the practice, which illustrates the impact that complex vaulting made on the imagination of local craftsmen. Vault patterns were also used in England in the same way, as in a roof boss at St Mary Redcliffe, Bristol, C. P. J. Cave, *Roof Bosses in Medieval Churches* (Cambridge, 1948), 82, pl. 37.

34 Many pieces of vault rib survive amongst the stone debris from Mellifont and some may come from the tower. The latter provide an instructive opportunity to see how the ribs were prepared. The individual blocks are large (10 inches by 1 foot 4 inches; 0.266 by 0.406 metres) and they are cut with the wedge shaped profile characteristic of the time. The upper surface of the rib was rebated to receive the vaulting cells, a feature not all that common in early Gothic vaults. The length of the individual pieces of ribbing was also greater than those in earlier vaults. For an analysis of these fragments see Stalley, 'Mellifont Abbey' (1980), 332–4.

Chapter 7

1 *Statuta*, I, 61, no. 16.

2 Aubert, *L'Architecture Cistercienne* (1947), I, 369–78.

3 A tower existed at St Mary's, Dublin, by 1235, which may have preceded the tower at Grey, Archdall, *Monasticon Hibernicum*, 137.

4 Aubert, *L'Architecture Cistercienne* (1947), I, 142.

5 P. Fergusson, 'Early Cistercian Churches in Yorkshire and the Problem of the

Cistercian Crossing Tower' (1970), 211–21.

6 R. Wagner Rieger, *Die Italienische Baukunst zu Beginn der Gotik* (Rome 1956), I, 43. The upper parts of the tower at Chiaravalle Milanese are fourteenth-century.

7 Aubert, *L'Architecture Cistercienne* (1947), I, 372–3.

8 At Buildwas there is evidence that the western crossing arch was a later insertion and the tower may therefore have been an afterthought. But changes of design are far less evident at Fountains, Kirkstall and Roche. Fergusson's interpretation of the remains at Roche, 'Roche Abbey: the source and date of the Eastern Remains' (1971), 30–42, was rejected by D. Parsons, 'A Note on the East End of Roche Abbey Church', *JBAA*, XXXVII (1974), 123.

9 A change in the character of the quoin stones implies that the tower was heightened at a later stage, and the inserted barrel vault may have been associated with this remodelling, cf. *ASNI*, 275–6.

10 *Ibid.*, 279. There is no archaeological evidence to support Archdall's comment that there was a steeple 'on the south side', *Monasticon Hibernicum*, 122.

11 A mural staircase runs up the east wall of the north transept at Graiguenamanagh and its purpose must have been to provide access to a crossing tower. In 1330 Richard O'Nolan was besieged in a tower at Graiguenamanagh, *Annals of Ireland by Friar John Clyn*, 22. According to eighteenth-century writers this tower, which fell in 1744, was octagonal in plan, Seward, *Topographia Hibernica* (1795); Grose, *Antiquities*, I, 39. The tower at St Mary's, Dublin, is mentioned by Archdall, *Monasticon Hibernicum*, 137. Tintern had a regular crossing as part of the c1280–1300 reconstruction, probably to support a low tower. The tower was heightened in the fifteenth century, when inner arches were added on corbels to thicken the width of the walls. Abbeylara may also have had a crossing tower from the start though the ruins are difficult to interpret. The original church seems to have had a western crossing arch and the abaci which support it are consistent with an early thirteenth-century date. A regular crossing might imply a tower above. The masonry of the tower itself is of two periods: regular dressed quoins extend to a height level with the apex of the north transept roof; above this point the masonry is rougher. A barrel vault was erected over the crossing, but this rests on walls which block the transept arches. It thus appears that there were two phases of construction: (a) a low thirteenth-century tower, and (b) a fifteenth-century heightening, when the barrel vault and stair turret were inserted.

12 Leask, *Irish Churches*, II, 32. The transept arches at Boyle are unusually high, rising well above the level of the nave walls, and they could not have been covered by a continuation of the nave roof, as Leask points out. The way the crossing was roofed before the tower was erected thus remains a problem. It is possible that the transept arches were lifted when the western crossing arch was inserted, the twelfth-century capitals being reused.

13 The towers at Dunbrody, Holycross, Kilcooly, Hore, Jerpoint and Mellifont were built from ground level; those at Tintern, Grey and Abbeylara were heightened.

14 Stalley, 'Mellifont Abbey' (1980), 299–300, 352.

15 *CPL*, IX, 248.

16 Archdall, *Monasticon Hibernicum*, 753. Repairs to the monastery were also being undertaken in 1494 when the abbot referred to 'revenues which were to be expended in repairing the building of the said Convent', British Library, Additional Charter, 15426.

17 For Graiguenamanagh see note 11; the tower at Abington was illustrated by T. Dinely in 1681 (pl. 75), *Journal of the Kilkenny Archaeological Society*, V, (1856), 278–80; for Dublin see note 3. A tower over the crossing at Baltinglass is known from the engraving published by Grose, *Antiquities of Ireland*, II, 7; it was supported on solid walls constructed under the transept arches and it was almost certainly post-dissolution, like that over the south transept at Monasteranenagh. A tower over the crossing at Assaroe is illustrated on a map of the battle of Ballyshannon (1593), British Library, Ms. Augustus I (ii), 38. A belfry is mentioned at Inislounaght in 1540; according to the Ordnance Survey Letters the last abbot was 'seized of a Church and belfry; a cemetery, hall, dormitory, 4 chambers, a kitchen, store and barn . . .', *Ordnance Survey Letters*, Kilkenny I, fol. 105–37, RIA. The narrow fifteenth-century arch of the south transept at Bective suggests it had a tower like those at Holycross and Kilcooly.

18 Archdall, *Monasticon Hibernicum*, 753.

19 Morrin, 'Historical Notes on the Abbey of Dunbrody' (1874–9), 409.

20 O'Sullivan, 'The Cistercian Abbey of Fermoy' (1946), 177, (quoting *CPL*).

21 O'Conbhuidhe, *Story of Mellifont* (1959), 157.

22 *Extents*, 157.

23 The Irish looking 'crow stepped' battlements on the tower at Ewenny (Glamorgan) are furnished with arrow loops. This priory has a fortified precinct like many an Irish monastery, Ralegh Radford, *Ewenny Priory* (1952).

24 At Kinloss in Scotland, the crossing tower erected in 1470–80 collapsed in 1574, MacGibbon and Ross, *Ecclesiastical Architecture of Scotland* (1896–7), I, 416–21.

25 *Extents*, 198.

26 Aubert, *L'Architecture Cistercienne* (1947), I, 378; *Statuta*, 1157.21. One large and one small bell were allowed in the church and they were not to exceed 500 pounds in weight.

27 *Extents*, 25, 270, 357, 363. O'Conbhuidhe, *Story of Mellifont* (1959), 208.

28 It has been suggested that as many as seven bells were hung in the tower at Dunbrody, *78th Annual Report of the Commissioners of Public Works in Ireland* (1909–10), 18. At Holycross five holes were provided for bell ropes in the vault under the crossing tower.

29 *Ormond Deeds*, V, 226.

30 At Dunbrody the lower chamber was fitted out as a columbarium, a not uncommon procedure in the upper parts of medieval churches, cf. Elkstone (Gloucestershire), where a room above the chancel was so used.

31 If a crossing tower existed at Bective, it probably had a similar plan.

32 On the east and south sides of the tower at Kilcooly there are just single ogee-headed lights. The windows at Hore are small and flat-headed.

33 *Ordnance Survey Letters*, 1840, Tipperary, I, fol. 296–7, pp. 110–11.

34 The windows are displaced in the low twelfth-century tower at Buildwas (Shropshire). The north window at Dunbrody was also moved off axis to accommodate a mural staircase in the wall below.

35 Leask, *Irish Castles* (1964), 77, 88–9.

36 *Extents*, 213.

37 Leask, *Irish Castles* (1964), 118–21.

38 R. A. Stalley, 'Monastery on the Defensive, Kells Priory, Co. Kilkenny', *Country Life*, CLVII, 4064, 22 May 1975, 1344–6.

39 *Extents*, 126–33.

Chapter 8

1 Cochrane, 'Note' (1892), 247.

2 de Paor, 'Excavations at Mellifont' (1969), 158–9. When re-erected the Mellifont arcade was given an even sequence of arches, but it is possible that they were originally interrupted by piers as was common in cloister design. Such piers broke up the monotony of a continuous sequence of colonettes and provided extra lateral stability against any thrust from the roof.

3 Cloister arcades with coupled colonettes are known from Rievaulx, Kirkstall, Newminster, Forde, Stanley, Whitland, Fountains, Furness, Byland and Jervaulx. French examples are discussed by Aubert, *Architecture Cistercienne* (1947), II, 4–14.

4 Fragments of what appears to be a twelfth-century cloister are built into a nineteenth-century mausoleum at Monasteranenagh. Recent excavations at Boyle disappointingly produced no evidence for the cloister design.

5 Cochrane, 'Note' (1892), 247. The cloister at Stanley, the mother house of Graiguenamanagh, had coupled columns with moulded capitals and bases of blue lias. These were thought to belong to the fourteenth century, Brakspear, 'Stanley Abbey' (1908), 562.

6 Three hundred years later, trefoiled arches were used by the Augustinian canons at Inistioge, six miles from Graiguenamanagh, C. Manning, 'The Inistioge Priory Cloister Arcade', *Old Kilkenny Review* (1976), 190–200. This late Gothic cloister was embellished with carved figures and it was in effect a synthesis of the designs at Jerpoint and Graiguenamanagh, the two neighbouring Cistercian monasteries. Another cloister with trefoiled arcading may have existed at Abbeyshrule, to judge from a drawing of 1864 by Du Noyer which shows an arch of this form, Antiquarian Sketches, Volume IX, p. 68 (R.I.A.).

7 John Blair, Philip Lankester and Jeffrey West, 'A Transitional Cloister Arcade at Haughmond Abbey, Shropshire', *Medieval Archaeology*, XXIV (1980), 210–12. A fine trefoiled headed cloister also existed in the Augustinian abbey of Kells (Kilkenny), soon to be published by Thomas Fanning. In Scotland there was a similar cloister arcade at Dundrennan (Kirkcudbright), MacGibbon and Ross, *Ecclesiastical Architecture of Scotland* (1896–7), I, 392.

8 Aubert, *Architecture Cistercienne* (1947), II, 15–20. A few cloisters were also glazed, Jane Hayward, 'Glazed Cloisters and their Development in the Houses of the Cistercian Order', *Gesta*, XII (1973), 93–109. A Cistercian cloister with Perpendicular tracery has recently come to light at Bordesley in England, Walsh, 'A Rebuilt Cloister at Bordesley Abbey' (1979), 42–9.

9 A cloister with 'dumb-bell' piers was erected at Valle Crucis in the fifteenth century, H. Hughes, 'Valle Crucis Abbey', *Archaeologia Cambrensis*, 5th series, XI (1894), 274, and XII (1895), 6–7. This type of cloister may have been more widespread in the British Isles than now appears.

10 The cloister at Cong (Mayo) is sometimes regarded as the first example, but this is a reconstruction carried out in 1860 by a local stone carver at the behest of Sir Benjamin Lee Guinness and it cannot be trusted as evidence, *Shell Guide to Ireland* (London, 1967), 179. There is no trace of the cloister in Grose's illustration of Cong in *Antiquities of Ireland* (1791–5). The date of the Jerpoint cloister is discussed at length in chapter 9, pp. 191–3.

11 Leask, *Irish Churches*, III, 137–8.

12 I am grateful to David Sweetman, who

13 Leask, *Irish Churches*, III, 148–9; D. Mooney, 'De Provincia Hiberniae S. Francisci,' ed. B. Jennings, *Analecta Hibernica*, VI (1934), 63.

14 Two completely different arcades survive at Holycross. Six arches in the west range, rebuilt in concrete in 1928, have simple round heads and plain octagonal supports. Their original location and date is far from clear.

15 This decorated pier was not used in the recent restoration. It is now apparently in store. One of the pier forms is a type C 'dumb-bell'.

16 This information is taken from an unpublished preliminary report by Mr Patrick Healy, who has generously given me access to his notes and drawings. In addition to the cloister fragment, pieces of window jamb, mullions and Gothic door heads were found.

17 Leask, 'St Mary's Abbey', *Archaeological Journal*, LXXXVIII (1931), 348.

18 Mr Healy has drawn up a table of all the Dublin religious houses with their respective distances from Cook street.

19 J. Harvey, *The Perpendicular Style* (London, 1978), 167.

20 Leask, 'Bective Abbey' (1916), 53–4. Leask's plan shows the west range without intermediate piers, but these were restored soon after he wrote.

21 According to Wakeman, one arch was decorated with a 'hawk-like bird', but this is no longer to be seen, W. Wakeman, *Archaeologia Hibernica* (Dublin, 1848), 117.

22 Gilyard-Beer, *Cleeve Abbey* (1960), 14–15, 42. In Ireland the earliest surviving example of the integrated cloister, with arcades reinforced by embracing arches, is to be found in the fourteenth-century cloisters in the Dominican friary at Kilmallock.

23 Leask, *Irish Churches*, III, 147–8.

24 *Ibid.*, 145–7.

25 *Ibid.*, 140–2.

26 See note 13.

27 None of this cloister remains *in situ*, but many fragments are in store at the site. Before 1922 the Dublin Board of Works surveyed this material and prepared reconstruction drawings.

28 Leask, *Irish Churches*, III, 143–5.

29 *CPL*, XII, 271.

30 The importance of timber architecture for the early Cistercians has recently been examined by P. Fergusson, 'The First Architecture of the Cistercians in England and the Work of Abbot Adam of Meaux,' *J.B.A.A.*, CXXXVI (1983), 74–86.

31 According to Ralegh Radford it was not until the fifteenth century that the timber supports at Strata Florida in Wales were rebuilt in stone, Ralegh Radford, *Strata Florida Abbey* (1949), 3, 7.

32 Gilyard-Beer, 'Boxley Abbey and the Pulpitum Collationis' (1981), 123–31. Where the cloister was constructed to the north of the church as at Hore, the collation was of course held in the south alley.

33 *Lexington*, 102.

34 Gilyard-Beer has identified three examples of the reader's bay in Britain, at Tintern, Strata Florida and Byland, Gilyard-Beer, *op. cit.*, 130.

35 Salzman, *Building in England* (1967), 448–50.

36 Hamlin, 'Collation Seats in Irish Cistercian Houses' (1983), 156–8. Gilyard-Beer cites examples of collation seats at Cleeve, Melrose and Tintern, Gilyard-Beer, *op. cit.*, 130. The most ornate Cistercian collation seat, built in 1468, is to be found in the French monastery at Cadouin, Aubert, *L'Architecture Cistercienne* (1947), II, 22.

37 The western half of the sacristy was apparently used as the book cupboard at Boyle, Abbeyknockmoy, Hore and Grey. Aubert, *L'Architecture Cistercienne*, II, 40–2 cites French examples of this arrangement.

38 A spacious cupboard was designed under the fifteenth-century night stair at Holycross, but it was not accessible from the cloister walk and was unlikely to have been used for books.

39 The best impression of a Cistercian library in the British Isles is provided by the fifteenth-century library inventory at Meaux, which lists over three hundred items, *Chronica Monasterii de Melsa*, III, lxxxiii–c.

40 There is also a piscina in the sacristy at Nydala (Sweden), Swartling, *Nydala Abbey* (1967), 103. Aubert suggests that the sacristy was sometimes used as a supplementary chapel, Aubert, *Architecture Cistercienne*, II (1947), 50.

41 Mentioned in several annals, e.g. *ALC* (1235), 320–3. The room is described as a crypt, but clearly the sacristy is meant.

42 Aubert, *L'Architecture Cistercienne* (1947), II, 61.

43 T. Wright, *Louthiana* (Dublin, 1748), 19. The bases of this door remain *in situ* and the design is discussed in detail in Stalley, 'Mellifont Abbey' (1980), 303–4.

44 There are a few parallels in English chapter houses for this arrangement, at Durham, Rochester, Westminster Abbey and St Albans. For the latter see D. Kahn, 'Recent Discoveries of Romanesque Sculpture at St Albans', in *Studies in Medieval Sculpture*, ed. F. H. Thompson (London, 1983), 73.

45 Gilyard-Beer, *Cleeve Abbey* (1960) 23–4.

46 Aubert, *L'Architecture Cistercienne*, II, 52–8.

47 At this time the chapter house was divided into three sections and revaulted. The small 'chapter house' at Bective, covered by four bays of groin vaulting, is the result of fifteenth-century reconstruction, as shown by the punch-dressed masonry of the centre pier.

48 Described in detail in *ASNI*, 277.

49 National Library of Ireland, TX 1975, vol. XII, Frazer Sketchbook.

50 Leask incorrectly states that the rib mouldings have the same section as those in the chapter house at Buildwas, Leask, *Irish Churches*, II, 47. Although both have twin rolls divided by a fillet, those at St. Mary's are fronted by large keeled mouldings.

51 Waterman, 'Somersetshire and other Foreign Building Stone in Medieval Ireland' (1970), 72.

52 The second Mellifont chapter house is analysed at length in Stalley, 'Mellifont Abbey' (1980), 301–6.

53 The dimensions are similar to those of the thirteenth century chapter house at Stanley, the mother house of Graiguenamanagh. This was an aisled building, 60 × 30 feet, Brakspear, 'Stanley Abbey' (1908), 563.

54 O'Leary, 'Notes on Graiguenamanagh' (1892), 243. Both O'Leary and Cochrane failed to identify the chapter house, suggesting it was a scriptorium.

55 Butler, *Neath Abbey* (1976), 19.

56 Swartling, *Alvastra Abbey* (1969), 107–8. Aubert believes it was used by the novices in the twelfth century, but by the thirteenth century they had a separate building and it thus became 'la salle de travail', Aubert, *L'Architecture Cistercienne*, II, 74.

57 Gilyard-Beer, *Cleeve Abbey*, 29–30; Aubert, *L'Architecture Cistercienne*, II, 85.

58 Doorways leading from the dormitory to the space over the south transept chapels are found in several English houses, Cleeve, Valle Crucis, Buildwas (in this case leading to north transept), etc.

59 *AFM*, VI, p. 1273.

60 This is the origin of the tales about secret passages which are current among the local population at many a Cistercian site in Ireland.

61 Parts of the main drain also survive at Graiguenamanagh.

62 I am grateful to Dr Ann Lynch for discussing the excavations at Tintern with me prior to publication of her report.

63 Aubert, *L'Architecture Cistercienne*, II, 114.

64 *ALC*, I, 275.

65 Aubert, *L'Architecture Cistercienne* (1947), II, 98–104; Bilson and St John Hope, 'The Architecture of Kirkstall Abbey Church' (1907), 52–3; Gilyard-Beer, *Abbeys* (1959), 41; Butler, 'Valle Crucis Abbey: An Excavation in 1970' (1976), 94.

66 The arguments for the change of axis at Mellifont are set out in Stalley, 'Mellifont Abbey' (1980), 309.

67 Aubert, *L'Architecture Cistercienne* (1947), I, 39.

68 *Rites of Durham*, Surtees Society, 107 (1903), 82, 261.

69 Aubert, *L'Architecture Cistercienne* (1947), II, 26; Eydoux, *Églises Cisterciennes d'Allemagne* (1952), 12, 160.

70 Godfrey, 'English Cloister Lavatories' (1952), 91–7.

71 N. Stratford, 'Notes on the Norman Chapterhouse at Worcester', *Medieval Art and Architecture at Worcester Cathedral*, ed. A. Borg, British Archaeological Association Conference Transactions (London, 1978), 51–70. D. H. S. Cranage, 'The Monastery of St Milburge at Much Wenlock, Shropshire', *Archaeologia*, LXXII (1922), 115–16; *English Romanesque Art 1066–1200*, exhibition catalogue (London 1984), 200–1. The main arches at Wenlock were supported by slender columns, not substantial piers as at Mellifont.

72 Stalley, 'Mellifont Abbey' (1980), 321–2.

73 *Archaeological Journal*, 131 (1974), 280; *Journal of Roman Studies*, 46 (1956), 32; 'The Life and Miracles of St Cuthbert' in *Bede's Ecclesiastical History of the English Nation* (Everyman edition, London, 1963), 323.

74 Duby, *Saint Bernard—L'art Cistercien* (1976), 146.

75 *78th Report of the Commissioners of Public Works in Ireland* (1910), 18.

76 C. A. Ralegh Radford, *Cymmer Abbey, Gwynedd*, 4.

77 Lexington, 101.

78 During the recent 'restoration', the wall between two of the cellars has been removed, one of a number of regrettable alterations to the medieval fabric.

79 The architectural context of this range deserves more research. The background is provided by M. Wood, *The English Medieval House* (London, 1965) and P. A. Faulkner, 'Domestic Planning from the Twelfth to the Fourteenth Centuries', *Archaeological Journal*, CXV (1958), 150–84.

80 *Lexington*, 99–106.

81 *ALC*, I, 225.

82 Luckombe, *Tour Through Ireland* (1780), 300.

83 Hutchinson Papers, Trinity College Dublin, Ms. 8856, nos 6, 13, 20.

84 *Extents*, 1–2.

85 *Ibid.*, 126.

86 FitzGerald, 'Baltinglass Abbey' (1906–8), 379–414. According to a note on a drawing in the Office of Public Works, a bull of Alexander III and a canon ball were found embedded in the walls.

87 *Ibid.*, 407.

88 *Statuta*, 1206.4, 1229.6.

89 Hore, *Wexford*, II, 105–8.

90 *CMA*, I, 6–7.

91 *Ibid.*, I, XXX.

92 The abbot's lodgings and the so-called guest house have not been examined in detail. There have clearly been additions and alterations to both buildings, but none so disgraceful as the concrete shed that has recently been erected between them.

93 *Extents*, 213. Columbaria were a standard component of medieval monasteries, Aubert, *L'Architecture Cistercienne* (1947), II, 170. Medieval columbaria also survive at Ballybeg (Cork) and Shanagolden (Limerick).

94 Leask, *Irish Churches*, III, 71, described it as an infirmary, but Healy in 1890 was closer to the truth when he referred to it as 'a quadrangular building called the stables, but which is in reality nothing less than a very strong keep', Healy, 'The Cistercian Abbey of Kilcooley' (1890), 221. Like the Desmond hall at Askeaton, it has battered walls and a vaulted basement.

95 *Extents*, 126.

96 R. Stalley, 'Monastery on the Defensive: Kells Priory, Co Kilkenny', *Country Life*, CLVII, 4064, 22 May 1975, 1344–6. The site will soon be fully published by Mr T. Fanning, following his excavation there.

97 *Extents*, 213; Stalley, 'Mellifont Abbey' (1980), 314.

98 Hamlin, 'A Recently Discovered Enclosure at Inch Abbey' (1977), 85–8.

99 *Extents*, 10.

100 *Ibid.*, 126–32.

101 T. J. Westropp, 'Proceedings', *JRSAI*, XXX (1900), 302.

102 *Lexington*, 103.

103 *Statuta*, 1217.78.

104 *Ordnance Survey Letters* (1840), I, fol. 436–44 (Royal Irish Academy). The graveyard to the north of the abbey at Inch marks the site of an ancient chapel, the history of which goes back to pre-Cistercian times. After 1180 it may have functioned as a *capella ante portas*, Hamlin, 'A Recently Discovered Enclosure at Inch Abbey' (1977), 85–8. Without citing evidence, Power claimed that chapels also existed at Tracton, Midleton, Abbeyknockmoy, Corcomroe, Assaroe, Monasteranenagh and Grey, Power, 'Irish Cistercian Abbeys' (1926), 29.

105 Ten abbey churches were described as parish churches: Baltinglass, Tracton, Fermoy, Middleton, Abbeymahon, Jerpoint, Mellifont, Kilcooly, Hore and Tintern, *Extents*, passim.

Chapter 9

1 These are currently accepted dates for the statutes on painting and sculpture, but when considering Cistercian promulgations about artistic matters caution is necessary in view of the controversies and uncertainties surrounding the history of the early statutes. For an introduction to the problems see Knowles, 'Primitive Cistercian Documents' (1962), 198–224, though there have been many developments since Knowles wrote this summary. There is a useful note on the artistic implications of the controversies by Neil Stratford, 'A Romanesque Marble altarfrontal in Beaune and Some Cistercian Manuscripts' in *The Vanishing Past*, ed. A. Borg and A. Martindale (Oxford, BAR, 1981), 227–8. The text of the 1151 statute in Ljubljana Ms.51, statute XX (as cited by Stratford) is: 'Sculpture vel picture in ecclesiis nostris seu in officinis aliquibus monasterii ne fiant interdicimus, quia dum talibus intenditur, utilitas bone meditationis vel discipline religiose gravitatis sepe negligitur. Cruces tamen pictas que sunt lignee habemus'. For a full discussion of the problems associated with early legislation on art and architecture see Holdsworth, 'Chronology and Character of early Cistercian legislation' (1986).

2 Lexington, 104.

3 For the full text of the *Apologia*, see J. Leclercq and H. Rochais (ed.), *S. Bernardi Opera*, III, *Tractatus et Opuscula* (Rome, 1963), 61–108. There are many translations of relevant excerpts, for example Braunfels, *Monasteries of Western Europe* (1972), 241–2. For a complete translation see Bernard of Clairvaux, *Treatises*, I: *Apologia to Abbot William* (translated), M. Casey (Kalamazoo, 1970). The *Apologia* is now thought to date from 1125 at the latest.

4 This argument is discussed, and rejected, by Esser, 'Über den Kirchenbau' (1953), 205–6. Esser argues that St Bernard's sermons at consecration ceremonies reveal a sensitivity to architectural design. An excellent analysis of St Bernard's artistic views is provided by Melczer and Soldwedel, 'Monastic Goals in the Aesthetics of Saint Bernard' (1982), 31–44.

5 Bernard of Clairvaux, *On the Song of Songs III* (translated), K. Walsh and I. Edwards (Kalamazoo, 1970), 53–4.

6 The influence of Cormac's Chapel is discussed by de Paor, 'Cormac's Chapel' (1967), 133–45. See also Leask, *Irish Churches*, I (1955), 113–20 and Stalley, 'Three Irish Buildings' (1981), 62–5. The sculpture of the chapel still awaits a full analysis, so too does the interior painting, for which see M. McGrath, 'The Wall Paintings in Cormac's Chapel at Cashel', *Studies*, LXIV (1975), 327–32.

7 The bulbous base above the carvings has a prominent spur, which some authorities have interpreted as a frog. The sculpture of Baltinglass is discussed at length by Beuer-Szlechter, 'Les débuts de l'art cistercienne en Irlande' (1970), 208–18.

8 Leask, *Irish Churches*, I, 96–100; also Leask, *Glendalough Co. Wicklow Official Historical and Descriptive Guide* (Dublin, nd.), 33–8. Beside the east window of St Saviour's is a lion almost identical to that at Baltinglass. Other motifs at Glendalough also relate to the Cistercian abbey: a

fret design fitted above a scalloped capital and a stepped pattern used on one of the bases. The stylistic links fit the documentary evidence which shows that St Saviour's was founded by St Laurence O'Toole, abbot of Glendalough, 1154–62, C. Plummer, 'Vie et Miracles de St Laurent, archevêque de Dublin', *Analecta Bollandiana*, XXXIII (1914), 135. Comparisons have also been made between the ornament at St Saviour's and Saddell abbey in Argyll, another daughter house of Mellifont. One stone from the Scottish abbey is decorated with an eight petalled flower, cut in shallow relief, a motif which appears on the window jamb at Glendalough, and it is possible that Irish masons were employed at Saddell, *Royal Commission on Ancient and Historical Monuments of Scotland, Argyll*, I. Kintyre (HMSO, 1971), 21–2, 140–5.

9 Leask, *Irish Churches*, I, 101–6; Henry, *Irish Art*, III, 177–9. There is some slight evidence in the form of a very worn inscription that the patron was Dermot MacMurrough, King of Leinster, who also founded Baltinglass. For a 'reading' of the inscription see R. A. S. Macalister, *Corpus Inscriptionum Insularum Celticarum*, II, 26–8.

10 Henry, *Irish Art*, III, pls 76, 78; Leask, *Irish Churches*, I, pl. XIVb.

11 Stalley, 'Romanesque Sculpture of Tuam' (1981), 179–95.

12 At Jerpoint the height of the capitals varies from $8\frac{1}{2}$ to $12\frac{1}{2}$ inches (21.5 to 31.5 cm).

13 The designs are well known through the drawings of Leask, first published in 'The Architecture of the Cistercian Order in Ireland' (1939), 140, and reproduced many times since.

14 If Jerpoint was not begun until 1180, as some authorities suppose, the activities of this workshop would stretch from c1155 to c1190–5.

15 Here I disagree with Mlle Henry, who argued that these capitals are within the traditions of Irish art, Henry, 'Irish Cistercian Monasteries and their carved decoration' (1966), 264–5. Irish details are rare, but they do include a triquetra knot on one of the capitals at Jerpoint (north-west crossing pier, west face). Beaded straps can also be found on capitals at Cormac's Chapel (1127–34), a building where the English affiliations are strong.

16 The rings appear on the north impost of the west doorway at Leominster, *RCHM, Herefordshire*, III, *North-West* (London, 1934), pl. 139.

17 Williams, *Strata Florida* (1889), 220.

18 For Cistercian grisaille glass see H. Zakin, *French Cistercian Grisaille Glass* (New York, 1979).

19 Before Mellifont, scalloped capitals had already been used in Cormac's Chapel, Cashel, by 1134. Among developments of the scalloped capital was the fluting of the cones (Mellifont chapter house). At Boyle the cones of a trumpet scalloped capital were turned into a series of hollow tubes. At Graiguenamanagh and Mellifont (chapter house) there are several capitals in which the cones are transformed into narrow bending stems, terminating in an outgrowth of foliage—a compromise between stiff-leaf and the trumpet scallop.

20 Bilson, 'Architecture of the Cistercians' (1909), 254–5.

21 *Ibid.*, 256–7.

22 It was used on the portals at Devenish (Fermanagh), Donaghmore (Tipperary), Killeshin (Carlow) and Dysert O'Dea (Clare), cf. Henry, *Irish Art*, III, 177. There are parallels in the Book of Kells (fol. 8r), F. Henry, *The Book of Kells* (London, 1974), 11, and in Canterbury manuscripts of the twelfth century.

23 The Mellifont fragments are published in Stalley, 'Mellifont Abbey' (1980), 315 and Pl. VIIIa. The fragment at Boyle is built into the north wall of the refectory.

24 This type of chevron became common in the 'school of the west' and it was employed for example at Ballintober (east windows) and Cong. The chevron at Corcomroe and Abbeyknockmoy is distinctive, since the zigzags are placed in a parallel sequence, and not arranged point to point. This form was copied in the doorway of the small church at Noughaval (Clare), and a fragmentary piece can be seen on the east window of Killaloe Cathedral.

25 *AFM*, 1124–5.

26 E. C. Gardner, *The Book of St Bernard on the Love of God* (London, 1915), 57.

27 His work is discussed by the author in *Architecture and Sculpture* (1971), 110–16, and in 'A Romanesque Sculptor in Connaught', *Country Life* (1973), 1826–30. Peter Harbison suggested that he should be called the Ballintober Master, 'The Ballintober Master and a date for the Clonfert Cathedral Chancel' (1976), 96–9.

28 The abbey was founded in 1216, R. Dodsworth and W. Dugdale, *Monasticon Anglicanum*, II (London, 1673), 1037. When recording the death of the first abbot, Maelbrighde O'Maicin, the Annals of Loch Cé state 'it was by him the church of Tobur-Patraic (Ballintober) was begun, and its sanctuary and crosses were diligently finished', *ALC*, 1225.

29 *AFM* gives 1218, *ALC* gives 1220 (261), and *AU* gives 1219 (*AU*, II, 265).

30 Stalley, 'The Medieval Sculpture of Christ Church Cathedral, Dublin' (1979), 109–13.

31 *RCHM, Oxford* (London, 1934), p. 35, pl. 101.

32 Similar foliage was also used on the capitals in the west bays of Worcester Cathedral, dated c1175, Christopher Wilson, 'The Sources of the Late Twelfth Century Work at Worcester Cathedral', *Medieval Art and Architecture at Worcester Cathedral* (British Archaeological Association, London, 1978), 89–90. I am grateful to Dr Wilson for sending me a photograph of one such capital.

33 The Annaghdown window is discussed and illustrated by Garton, 'A Romanesque Doorway at Killaloe' (1981), 31–57.

34 Stalley, 'The Romanesque Sculpture of Tuam' (1981), pls 13.4, 13.6.

35 British Library, Add. Ms. 36, 929; Henry, *Irish Art in the Romanesque Period* (1970), 72–3 and Henry and Marsh-Micheli, 'A Century of Irish Manuscript Illumination' (1962), 161–4. In her article 'Irish Cistercian Monasteries and their carved decoration' (1966), 265, Mlle Henry suggests a Baltinglass provenance for Cormac's Psalter, but Boyle has an equally good claim. Figures holding branches of foliage also appear on the twelfth-century shrine known as the Breac Maodhóg, Henry, *Irish Art in the Romanesque Period* (1970), 117–19 and pls 35–7.

36 Peter Harbison, 'The Ballintober Master' (1976), 96–9, suggests that he carved a base in the chancel of Clonfert Cathedral c1210–20. Despite the similarities in the animals depicted, the carving lacks the energy, the depth of cutting and involved composition, which was a feature of the Master's style. Rather than a tentative early work, it is more likely to be a later imitation, a view adopted by Garton, 'A Romanesque Doorway at Killaloe' (1981), 45. Dr Garton has also pointed out (p. 45) the similarity of one of the beasts at Killaloe to those at Ballintober. It has the same rounded body and spiralling cuts on the neck. The carving at Killaloe (c1200) is almost two decades earlier, however.

37 Stalley, 'A Romanesque Sculptor in Connaught' (1973), 1830.

38 Stalley, 'Mellifont Abbey' (1980), pp. 320–1, pls VII, VIII. The palmette foliage at Mellifont provides a possible link between English versions of this ornament and those in the west of Ireland. Moreover, one of the capitals in the lavabo has tiny flutes arranged below the foliage, a device which appears at Boyle (south arcade, pier 7, corbel).

39 Garton, 'Romanesque Doorway at Killaloe' (1981), 39–40.

40 Among the plants, Dr Nelson has tentatively identified Atropa belladona (deadly nightshade), Papaver somniferum (opium poppy) and Convallaria majalis (lily of the valley). I am very grateful to Dr Nelson for telling me about his discoveries, prior to his own publication on the subject. The only other instance of the archway into a chapel being decorated with carved ornament is at Monasteranenagh (north transept). Here the ornament consisted of a series of circular motifs, the remnants of which are now very worn.

41 Stalley, 'Mellifont Abbey' (1980), p. 321, pl. IXb. The cutting of the eyes and mouth have some similarities with the work of the Ballintober Master.

42 *Ibid.*, 310.

43 *Ibid.*, 320–3. One other building at Mellifont contained a large capital with three half-length figures linking hands against a background of foliage. The few sculptures that survive probably represent a fraction of the total, suggesting that the architecture of the abbey had become richly ornamental by the early thirteenth century.

44 Aubert, *Architecture Cistercienne* (1947), I, 146.

45 Bilson, 'Architecture of the Cistercians' (1909), 253–4.

46 There is a brief discussion of the corbels in A. Weir, *Early Ireland, A Field Guide* (Belfast, 1980), 136. I cannot accept the author's suggestion that these are reused Romanesque corbels. Some subjects favoured by Romanesque sculptors remained popular throughout the middle ages and anal exhibitionists appear on a fifteenth-century misericord at All Souls College, Oxford, and on a sixteenth-century misericord at Tréguier Cathedral in France, D. and H. Kraus, *The Hidden World of Misericords* (London, 1976), pl. 78.

47 Rae, 'The Sculpture of the Cloister of Jerpoint Abbey' (1966), 59–91. An important fragment of dumb-bell pier, carved with a woman on one side, is in private hands at Newtown Jerpoint. Further pieces were used as gravestones at Thomastown, but their present location is not known. Also lost is the carving of the 'Walsh' knight, formerly in the Protestant Church at Piltown: cf. Peter Harbison, 'An Illustration of the Lost Walsh Knight from the Jerpoint Cloister Arcade', *Old Kilkenny Review*, 25 (1973), 13–15. Con Manning has discovered capitals from Jerpoint in the garden of Colonel D. Price at Great Island (Wexford) and he also found a pier fragment at Sheepstown, Manning, 'Jerpoint Cloister Fragment at Sheepstown' (1975), 118–19. A list of all the pieces with carving is given by Hourihane, *Iconography of Religious Art* (1984), 172–81.

48 Aubert, *Architecture Cistercienne* (1947), II, 20–2.

49 Leask, *Irish Churches*, III, 138, Hunt, *Irish Medieval Figure Sculpture* (1978), I, 177–8.

50 For the identifications, see Rae, 'Sculpture of the Cloister of Jerpoint Abbey' (1966), 66–79.

51 As the patron saint of wayfarers, large paintings of St Christopher were common on the walls of parish churches in the later middle ages. If the relief was fitted to the corner piers, its position would be analogous to the Romanesque apostle reliefs at Moissac (Tarn et Garonne) and the biblical reliefs at Santo Domingo de Silos (Burgos).

52 Hunt's suggestion that this figure represents St Dominic is misleading. No reasons are given for the attribution and St Dominic would be out of place in a

53 Cistercian environment, Hunt, *Irish Figure Sculpture* (1974), I, 179.

Rae believes there may have been as many as nine knights in the original cloister, 'Sculpture of the Cloister of Jerpoint Abbey' (1966), 90.

54 Parts of the double-bodied beast are now at Sheepstown, Manning, 'Jerpoint Cloister Fragment' (1975), 118–19; Manning shows that Rae's identification of this panel as a cherub was incorrect.

55 Rae, 'Sculpture of the Cloister of Jerpoint Abbey' (1966), 91.

56 M. Schapiro, *Romanesque Art* (London, 1977), 131–200.

57 S. Pressouyre, *Images d'un Cloître Disparu: le cloître de Notre Dame-en-Vaux à Chalons sur Marne* (Paris, 1976). In some respects Jerpoint is an Irish equivalent of Notre Dame-en-Vaux—a destroyed cloister with a varied range of figures, the order and arrangement of which are unknown.

58 L. Stone, *Sculpture in Britain, the Middle Ages* (Harmondsworth, 1972, 2nd edition), 188, 193.

59 Hunt, *Irish Medieval Figure Sculpture* (1974), 177–8.

60 *An Inventory of the Historical Monuments in London, I, Westminster Abbey* (RCHM, London, 1924) p. 30b and pl. 55.

61 *Buckinghamshire* (North) (RCHM, London, 1913), 92.

62 M. D. Anderson, *The Choir Stalls of Lincoln Minster* (Lincoln, 1967), 34; Smith, *Guide to Church Woodcarvings* (1974), 33; L. M. C. Randall, *Images in the Margins of Gothic Manuscripts* (Berkeley and London, 1966), fig. 452 (Christ Church, Oxford, Ms. E II fol. 36).

63 These parallels were pointed out to me by Dr Hourihane. For the two shrines see A. Mahr and J. Raftery, *Christian Art in Ancient Ireland*, 2 vols (Dublin, 1932/41).

64 Roe, *Medieval Fonts of Meath* (1968), 37–45.

65 *CPR*, IX, 248.

66 It is worth summarising the reasons for this conclusion:

1 The design is not like other documented cloisters of the fifteenth century. The mouldings of both bases and capitals can be paralleled in the fourteenth century, for example at Baltinglass cloister and at Athassel.

2 Capitals with heads peering out between leaves are not found in fifteenth-century work. They were a fashion introduced at Christ Church Cathedral, Dublin, c1215 and employed extensively in the area of Cashel and Kilkenny over the next hundred years.

3 The dragon with foliate tail found on one of the webs can be closely paralleled on the Domnach Airgid c1353, and the shrine of St Patrick's Tooth c1376, both in the National Museum, Dublin.

4 The best parallels for the figure style

are to be found in English sculpture c1370–80. The carving is significantly different from Irish work in the second half of the fifteenth century.

5 The armour of the knights belongs to the late fourteenth century as John Hunt showed. The dress of the ladies is consistent with this date.

6 The 1442 indulgence should not be interpreted too literally. It states that the bell tower, universally accepted as a fifteenth-century insertion, was in bad repair, a puzzling statement since in 1442 it was either new or not yet built!

67 Conleth Manning, 'The Inistioge Priory Cloister Arcade', *Old Kilkenny Review* (1976), 190–200. The cloister at Inistioge has long since been demolished, but fragments show that the arcades rested on dumb-bell piers with relief carvings on the webs (a Trinity, the Apostles and grotesques). The work was carried out under prior Milo Baron, 1510–28, in a late Gothic style which is quite different from that at Jerpoint. This stylistic gap helps to confirm the early date for the Jerpoint cloister.

68 Leask, *Irish Churches*, III, 144, suggests the arms indicate a member of the de Caunteton or Condon family, but his reasons for thinking so are not explicit. The arms are charged with three fleurs-de-lis and a bend sinister (not bend dexter as Leask suggests).

69 The lively pose of the abbot and the strong tubular drapery are reminiscent of the delightful angels on the Plunkett tomb at Killeen, Hunt, *Irish Medieval Figure Sculpture* (1974), I, 207–8. Further analogies can be seen on the cross at Killeen and the font at Rathmore, Roe, *Medieval Fonts of Meath* (1968), 92–9.

70 It is tempting to believe that the panels were carved for an exterior facade or portal, but the shaping of the individual blocks precludes this. The crucifixion and the St Christopher are dovetailed together and St John is moved over slightly to allow for this. If the sculptures were moved, almost the whole wall must have been moved too. The Kilcooly carvings are all described by Hourihane, *Iconography of Religious Art* (1984), 187–8.

71 Smith, *Guide to Church Carvings* (1974), 89–90. The mermaid was also carved on the chancel arch at Clonfert, the west doorway at Clontuskert and on one of the cloister piers at Inistioge.

72 B. Rowland, *Animals with Human Faces* (Knoxville Tennessee, 1973), 139–41; White, *Bestiary* (1960), 134.

73 G. Benwell and A. Waugh, *Sea Enchantress. The Tale of the Mermaid and her Kin* (London, 1961). I am grateful to Dr Colum Hourihane who told me of this reference.

74 G. L. Remnant, *A Catalogue of Misericords*

in Great Britain (Oxford, 1969), cites thirty-five examples on misericords. Dr Hourihane has identified fourteen examples in Ireland which he will discuss in a forthcoming article. These include stone carvings at Holycross and Clontuskert.

75 F. Bond, *Wood Carvings in English Churches, I, Misericords* (Oxford, 1910), 45–6. According to St Augustine, 'the males of these birds are wont to kill their young by blows of their beaks, and then to bewail their death for the space of three days. At length however the female inflicts a severe wound on herself, and letting her blood flow over the dead young ones, brings them to life again.' The presence of a chalice as a nest is rare, but one interesting precedent can be seen on the shrine of St Elizabeth at Marburg (c1236–49), G. Schiller, *Iconography of Christian Art*, II (London, 1972), 137.

76 E. W. Tristram, *English Wall Painting of the Fourteenth Century* (London, 1955), 115.

77 A. M. Hind, *An Introduction to a History of Woodcut* (New York, 1963), 104–6; F. J. Bigger, 'St Christopher in Irish Art', *JRSAI*, XL (1910), 166–9, drew attention to the Buxheim St Christopher in connection with Jerpoint but failed to point out the analogies with Kilcooly. A good English parallel for the 'striding' type of St Christopher exists at Bradfield Combust (Norfolk), H. C. Whaite, *St Christopher in English Medieval Wall Painting* (London 1929), 15.

78 Quane, 'Tour in Ireland by John Harden' (1953), 30–2. A list of carvings at Holycross is given in Hourihane, *Iconography of Religious Art* (1984), 164–7.

79 It is reminiscent of the lion mask on tiles from Swords Castle, Fanning, 'An Irish Medieval Tile Pavement' (1975), 54.

80 An angel holding a shield is amongst the most common of all late Gothic motifs, especially in tomb sculpture. Irish examples, which include an angel on a fifteenth-century niche at Mellifont, have been listed by Hourihane, *Iconography of Religious Art* (1984), 595–633. A further example on a window head was recently discovered on Inishkeen (Fermanagh) and this is now in the Museum at Enniskillen. (I am grateful to Ann Hamlin for telling me about this find.)

81 White, *Bestiary* (1960), 133–4.

82 E. Male, *L'art religieux du XIIᵉ siècle en France* (Paris, 1922), 33; 'The Parliament of Fowls', line 343, *The Complete Works of Geoffrey Chaucer*, ed., F. N. Robinson (2nd edition, London 1957).

83 W. S. Gibson, *Hieronymous Bosch* (London, 1973), 103. An owl carved high up under the crossing tower at Kilconnell Friary may be the work of a Holycross sculptor, as suggested to me by Colum Hourihane.

84 Harbison 'Animals in Irish Art' (1974), pp. 59–60; John Hunt, 'The Limerick Cathedral Misericords', *Ireland of the Welcomes,*

Volume XX, no. 3 (1971), p. 15. The unicorns with necks entwined also appear under a holy water stoup at Oughtmama (Clare), at Clontuskert and at Athenry on the base of the market cross.

85 For the Ormond school of carvers, Rae, 'Irish Sepulchral Monuments of the Later Middle Ages' (1970), 1–38.

86 The two figures are set under ogee arches, formed of straggling tendrils and foliage, and they are now situated high up on the interior jambs of the east window.

87 J. Bradley, 'A Medieval Figure Sculpture from near the Black Abbey, Kilkenny', *Old Kilkenny Review*, 2nd series, volume II, no 5 (1983), 542–5.

88 Hourihane, *Iconography of Religious Art* (1984), 296–8, 376, 433, 615–16.

89 Hunt, *Irish Medieval Figure Sculpture* (1974), II, pl. 277. The Cashel tomb is not illustrated by Hunt, but it is shown in Harbison, 'Animals in Irish Art' (1974), 61.

90 Found in the cloister at Bective, on a decorated niche at Mellifont and among fragments at Abbeyknockmoy.

Chapter 10

1 Medieval altars in whole or part survive at Dunbrody, Kilcooly, Holycross and Corcomroe, as well as Clare Island. There are no Irish altars with an arcade at the front like that at Preuilly, Aubert, *Architecture Cistercienne* (1947), I, 319. Outside the order an elaborate altar can be found in the friary at Sligo.

2 For Cistercian legislation on altars see Aubert, *Architecture Cistercienne* (1947), I, 318.

3 The Boyle type of sedilia, with a single enclosing arch, was also employed at Grey, Kilcooly and Clare Island.

4 At Hore enough remains to show that the sedilia, embellished with dog tooth, had three trefoiled arches which rested on detached shafts. The sedilia at Inch had three trefoiled arches under a relieving arch.

5 The fourth shield is charged with a cross, the fifth is plain. The coats of arms have been much discussed: Leask, *Irish Churches*, III, 65; Long, 'Old Cistercian Abbeys' (1896), 256. The leopards on the English coat of arms have been defaced.

6 Leask, *Irish Churches*, III, 164. The Callan sedilia also has a sloping 'roof', but despite this and other similarities it does not appear to be by the same workshop.

7 The projecting canopy, with a vault below, has affinities with that on the wooden screen at Attleborough (Norfolk), A. Clifton Taylor, *English Parish Churches as Works of Art* (London, 1974), Pl. 172. Compare also many of the screens illustrated by F. Bond, *Screens and Galleries in English Churches* (London, 1908).

8 Sedilia in other cathedrals were, however, more exotic and flamboyant, with several storeys of delicate traceried arches and canopies. Those at Exeter and Gloucester are especially memorable.

9 Aubert, *Architecture Cistercienne* (1947), I, 316–17.

10 J. S. Richardson and M. Wood, *Melrose Abbey* (Edinburgh, HMSO, 1949), 8–9.

11 de Paor, 'Excavations at Mellifont' (1969), 128; Aubert, *Architecture Cistercienne* (1947), I, 317.

12 *CMA*, I, 6–7.

13 When the tower was added at Dunbrody in the fifteenth century, a new screen was apparently erected under the west crossing arch, as indicated by projecting stones in the enlarged crossing piers.

14 Freezing conditions in the choir were a hazard of monastic life and abbot Suger of St Denis was proud of giving his monks comfortable seats in place of stone ones, E. Panofsky, *Abbot Suger on the Abbey Church of St Denis and its Art Treasures* (Princeton, 1979, 2nd edition), 73.

15 Joist holes for a timber rood or screen can also be seen at the entrance to the chancel on Clare Island, Westropp, 'Cliara Abbey' (1911–15), 30. At Abbeyshrule there are the remains of what may have been a stone rood screen in the nave, so enveloped by vegetation that it is hard to disentangle its history. It was erected at a late date in the building's history, since it was fitted into an earlier archway. A central entrance passage is barrel-vaulted and flanked by vaulted chambers each side. These were open to the nave and might have contained altars. The general arrangement recalls the vaulted rood screens of the fifteenth century in the friaries at Sligo, Clontuskert and Ballindoon. However, the wall above these vaulted compartments reaches to the full height of the building forming a gable, and as it is surmounted by a bellcot, at some stage it functioned as the exterior wall of a shortened church.

16 Vaulting and tracery patterns were frequently used to decorate tombs, as at Kilcooly, Fertagh and Leighlin. One of the patterns at Kilcooly, showing a vault with five tiercerons, is identical to that erected in the crossing at Leighlin Cathedral. Another relates to the vault under the tower at Hore. Tomb chests decorated in this way can also be seen in England and there is an outstanding example at Loversall (Yorkshire).

17 A font of c1200 in the church at Fethard-on-Sea (County Wexford) is traditionally said to have come from Dunbrody. This seems unlikely unless it was originally made for the capella ante portas. It consists of a fine square basin, shaped like a massive scalloped capital, and decorated with zigzag and beaded foliage. A font at Monasterevin, with a round basin, is

18 *Extents*, 198.

19 A. Robertson and D. Stevens, *The Pelican History of Music* (Harmondsworth, 1960), 195. The quotation comes from St Bernard's letter to the abbot of Montiéramey.

20 Lexington, 105.

21 There is, however, some musical notation in Cormac's Psalter (British Library, Additional Ms. 36, 929) and the Monasterevin Ordinal (Oxford, Bodleian Library, Rawlinson Ms. C32).

22 The practice of burial in medieval ruins still continues. A few years ago I watched a grave being dug on the site of the west range at Corcomroe. Sizeable pieces of rotten timber were unearthed, not part of the monastery's fabric but remnants of a coffin buried only eighteen years before. In 1969, over a hundred graves were cleared from the interior of Holycross, almost all dating from after 1750, W. J. Hayes, *Burials in Holycross Abbey* (Holycross, 1970).

23 Aubert, *Architecture Cistercienne*, I, 329; MacNiocaill, *Na Manaigh Liatha*, (1959) 22–4; Bucher, *Bonmont* (1957), 49. Each monk was allowed to ask for the burial of two of his relatives or friends in the cemetery. From 1157 founders of the monastery were permitted to be buried within the precincts (*Statuta*, 1157.63). The General Chapter tried to enforce the ban on interments inside the church and in 1205 the abbot of Val-Notre-Dame in France was punished for illegally burying a nobleman (*Statuta*, 1205).

24 Gwynn, 'Origins of St Mary's' (1949), 124.

25 There are particularly full lists in the annals for Boyle and Abbeyknockmoy.

26 MacNiocaill, *Na Manaigh Liatha* (1959), 23–4. The bishop of Ferns issued several complaints against Dunbrody, including the accusation that the monastery was burying excommunicants.

27 *Charters of Duiske*, 37–8.

28 *ALC*, 1224. Hore states that Hervé de Montmorency, the founder of Dunbrody, was buried in the abbey, Hore, *Wexford*, II (1900–11), 19.

29 Orpen, *Ireland under the Normans* (1911), II, 70.

30 Archdall, *Monasticon Hibernicum*, 137. Felix gave the abbey a substantial grant of land in 1231, *CMA*, II, 26.

31 de Paor, 'Excavations at Mellifont' (1969), 126.

32 Lexington, 105.

33 Aubert, *Architecture Cistercienne* (1947), I, 348–9. At Vaux-de-Cernay an abbot's grave is carved in this manner. Lawrence Butler has informed me of a slab at the Cistercian abbey of Flaxley in England, where there is a sleeved arm holding a crosier. According to Dr Butler, similar designs were employed outside the order at Welbeck, Romsey, Eccleston Priory and Dorchester (brass indent). At Boyle another very worn slab with an inscription may belong to this type.

34 Hunt, *Irish Medieval Sculpture* (1974), I, 174.

35 *Ibid.*, 227–8.

36 *Ibid.*, 173; Leask, *Jerpoint Abbey*, 9. The line of single leaves along the edge of the slab can be paralleled on the tomb of Longespée (d. 1226) in Salisbury Cathedral.

37 Leask, *Jerpoint*, 10. Hunt, *Irish Medieval Figure Sculpture*, I (1974), 173.

38 Aubert, *Architecture Cistercienne* (1947), I, 348–9. Aubert notes that graves along the walls of the sanctuary were usually reserved for founder bishops or protectors of the abbey. Tomb recesses in the north wall are found in some English and Welsh houses, for example Kirkstall and Valle Crucis.

39 Stalley, 'Mellifont Abbey' (1980), 282. A line of three tomb recesses was installed at Jerpoint in the middle of the thirteenth century. They are decorated with stiff-leaf capitals and dog-tooth. There were two such recesses in the mid-thirteenth-century presbytery at Mellifont.

40 Until its destruction by soldiers in 1798, there was a tomb of 'black marble' in the chancel at Dunbrody, said to be erected to the memory of Hervé de Montmorency. However a drawing suggests it was erected in the fourteenth century at the earliest, for it was surmounted by an ogee arch and pointed gable. These were supported on twin shafts. The effigy was that of a priest, not a lay lord, Hore, *Wexford*, II, (1900–11), 16–20.

41 F. Bond, *Wood Carvings in English Churches*, II, *Stalls and Tabernacle Work* (London, 1910), 39–44.

The tomb chest at Clare Island is placed slightly off centre, as if it was not designed as part of the tomb canopy. The chest was buried below ground level until a few years ago when the interior was cleared by the Office of Public Works.

42 Hunt, *Irish Medieval Figure Sculpture* (1974), I, 119; Orpen, *Ireland under the Normans* (1911–20), IV, 64. Hunt's argument that the effigies at Corcomroe and Roscommon both date from c1300 (or later) is not convincing.

43 Ledwich, *Antiquities of Ireland* (1790), pl. XIX.

44 Several such alabasters exist in Irish collections, J. Hunt and P. Harbison, 'Medieval English Alabasters in Ireland', *Studies*, LXV (1976), 310–14. Dr Colum Hourihane pointed out that the Abbeyknockmoy carving was derived from a 'St John's head'.

45 Such crosses are not uncommon in the Gothic era. The Abbeyknockmoy example is related to the free-standing medieval cross at Devenish as well as to the floriated crosses often depicted on grave slabs.

46 Crawford, 'Mural Paintings at Knockmoy' (1919), 29–31.

47 Hunt, *Irish Medieval Figure Sculpture* (1974), I, 134, 171–2. The comparable effigies in England have been studied by H. A. Tummers, *Early Secular Effigies in England. The Thirteenth Century* (Leiden, 1980). Comments about the effigy at Graiguenamanagh by Carville, *Duiske* (1979), 81–2, are without historical foundation.

48 Hunt, *Irish Medieval Figure Sculpture* (1974), I, 133–4. On account of the double cushion a date in the early fourteenth century is preferable to Hunt's late thirteenth-century date.

49 Orpen, *Ireland under the Normans* (1911–20), I, 57–8; *AC*, 108–9.

50 Hunt, *Irish Medieval Figure Sculpture* (1974), I, 173–7; Rae, 'Irish Sepulchral Monuments, II' (1971), 1–39.

51 The tombs at Kilcooly and Abbeyleix are discussed at length by Hunt, *Irish Medieval Figure Sculpture* (1974), I, 198–9, 228–9; and Rae, 'Irish Sepulchral Monuments II' (1971), 22–4, 29. There is no evidence to prove that the so-called monks' bridge at Abbeyleix was built before the dissolution of the abbey.

52 Among grave slabs not mentioned in the text is one with a floriated cross built into a wall at Inislounaght. A fragment of a thirteenth-century slab is set upside-down in the graveyard at Comber (information from Ann Hamlin). The slab of the last abbot of Dunbrody, Alexander Devereux, is reputed to lie in the graveyard at Fethard (Hore, *Wexford* (1900–11), IV, 318). A thirteenth-century slab from Grey, engraved with a sword, is in the Ulster Museum (*ASNI*, 278) and at Holycross there is a fine floriated cross in memory of James Purcell, Baron of Loughmore, who died in 1505. Several fragmentary slabs of great interest have recently come to light at Boyle.

53 At Bordesley (Worcestershire), a tiled floor was installed in the south transept in the early thirteenth century; before this the floor was of beaten earth, Rahtz and Hirst, *Bordesley Abbey* (1976), 108–11.

At Mellifont the chapter house surprisingly had a clay floor, 'Excavations at Mellifont' (1969), 137; Stalley, 'Mellifont Abbey' (1980), 307–8. Stone flags were an improvement over this, and they were much used in the monasteries of the west where hard limestone slabs were readily available. The interior of Holycross abbey, following excavation in 1969–70, should have provided information about Irish medieval flooring methods but a report is yet to be published.

54 Norton, 'Early Cistercian Tile Pavements' (1986), 231–6; Bucher, *Bonmont* (1957), 109–11, 213 n. 6.

55 The translation is from Braunfels, *Monasteries of Western Europe* (1972), 241.

56 *Statuta*, 1205, 1210.

57 Norton, 'Early Cistercian Tile Pavements' (1986), 228.

58 St John Hope, 'Fountains Abbey' (1899), 278.

59 An excellent account of the techniques of tile making is provided by Eames, *Catalogue* (1980), I, 17–52.

60 Bradley and Manning, 'Excavations at Duiske' (1981), 404.

61 Even Marcel Aubert in his comprehensive study of French Cistercian monasteries reflected this lack of interest. Only two of his six hundred pages were devoted to tiles.

62 Fanning, 'An Irish Medieval Tile Pavement' (1975), 47–82.

63 The north transept may have been nearing completion in 1228 (Lexington, 105) and the church was probably finished about 1240. It is likely that the tiles were laid as part of the main building programme.

64 Stalley, 'Mellifont Abbey' (1980), 336.

65 Eames, *Catalogue* (1980), 186–99.

66 *Ibid.*, 92–4.

67 The sites are Mellifont, St Mary's, Dublin, Graiguenamanagh, Bective, Baltinglass, Jerpoint, Dunbrody and Tintern. One of the tiles from St Mary's Abbey, Dublin, is frequently supposed to depict the facade of the church, *Remains of St Mary's Abbey* (1886), but it was in fact a standard design, appearing for example at Titchfield (Hampshire); cf. Eames, *Catalogue* (1980), II, design no.2004/5.

68 W. S. Parker, 'A Decorated Tile from Baltinglass Abbey', *JRSAI*, LXXI (1941), 148; Henry, *Irish Art in the Romanesque Period* (1970), 82–3, pl. 48; Eames, *Catalogue* (1980), I, 158–9.

69 Eames, *Catalogue* (1980), I, 279.

70 Parallels for the Graiguenamanagh tiles can be found in the two Dublin cathedrals, Bradley and Manning, 'Excavations at Duiske' (1981), 409–16, 422.

71 E. S. Eames, 'A thirteenth-century tile kiln site at North Grange, Meaux, Beverley, Yorkshire', *Medieval Archaeology*, 5 (1961), 137–68.

72 Eames, *Medieval Tiles* (1968), 13.

73 Tiles made in Flanders were exported to England in substantial quantities (Salzman, *Building in England* (1967), 145; Eames, *Catalogue* (1980), I, 215, so there is no reason why English tiles might not have been exported to Ireland. Thomas Fanning has pointed out that the distribution of tiles in Ireland is remarkably similar to the distribution of imported limestone from Dundry, Fanning, 'B.M. Catalogue—a Review' (1981), 16.

74 Eames, *Catalogue* (1981), I, 91.

75 This is based on the assumption that the whole church was tiled, though the evidence for this is not conclusive. The church at Graiguenamanagh appears to have been tiled throughout.

76 In 1395/6 Richard Porteur of Farnham was paid 18/6 by Winchester College for digging clay and transporting it to the kilns at Otterbourne, Eames, *Catalogue*, (1980), I, 215–16.

77 In 1397/8 John Davy and his assistants were paid 11/- by Winchester College for laying 5,500 tiles in the buttery and granary at a rate of two shillings per thousand, *Ibid.*, 216.

78 Fanning, 'B.M. Catalogue—Review' (1981), 14–16.

79 Aubert, *Architecture Cistercienne* (1947), I, 144, 268; Park, 'Cistercian wall and panel painting' (1986), 189–90. Red masonry jointing is particularly well preserved in the thirteenth-century sacristy at Cleeve.

80 False ashlar painted in red on white plaster survives in the chancel at Grey, high up near the south window, as pointed out to me by Ann Hamlin.

81 Westropp, 'Cliara Abbey' (1911–15), 31; Stalley, 'Mellifont Abbey' (1980), 274, 320.

82 Westropp, 'Corcumroe Abbey' (1900), 302. Red paint is also visible on the bases of the east window of the chapter house at Abbeyknockmoy and there are remnants of painted plaster on the north wall of the presbytery at Hore.

83 *81st Report of the Commissioners of Public Works* (1913), 41–2; Crawford, 'Mural Paintings in Holy Cross' (1915), 149–51; Carville, *Heritage of Holy Cross* (1973), 128–33.

84 Park, 'Cistercian wall and panel painting' (1986), 204; J. M. Lewis, *Welsh Medieval Paving Tiles* (Cardiff, National Museum of Wales, 1976), 18; a similar episode was used to illustrate a *Novum Digestum* from Neath, J. M. Lewis and D. H. Williams, *The White Monks in Wales* (Cardiff, National Museum of Wales, 1976), 15–16. See also D. F. Gleeson, 'Drawing of a hunting scene at Urlan Castle, Co. Clare', *JRSAI*, LXVI (1936), 193. Deer hunts were a relatively common theme on medieval tiles, Eames, *Catalogue* (1980), I, 195.

85 Oxford, Bodleian Library, Rawlinson Ms. C32, fol. 58r.

86 *CMA*, I, 4; *CPR*, XII, 89.

87 Ledwich, *Antiquities of Ireland* (1790), pl. XIX; Du Noyer, *Antiquarian Sketches*, VII, no. 55; Cochrane, 'Abbeyknockmoy' (1904), 248–53; Cochrane, 'Notes' (1905), 419–21; Crawford, 'Mural Paintings at Knockmoy' (1919), 25–34; Roe, 'Holy Trinity in Ireland' (1979), 143–4.

88 David Park has suggested that this might represent the death of St Edmund, though an English royal saint is unlikely to have received much veneration in the west of Ireland in the fifteenth century.

89 Roe, 'Holy Trinity in Ireland' (1979), 144. The 1541 date suggested by Crawford, 'Mural Paintings at Knockmoy' (1919), 31–2, is unlikely since, with the dissolution of the monasteries well advanced, this was not an auspicious moment for the monks to embark on new schemes of decoration.

90 Westropp, 'Cliara Abbey' (1911–15), 31–6.

91 Leask, *Irish Churches*, III, 175, suggests a date in the seventeenth century.

92 Few Irish Cistercian manuscripts appear to survive. They include a book of devotional treatises in Irish from Hore (British Library, Add. Ms. 11809, c1465–1500) and various books from St Mary's, Dublin: a thirteenth-century compilation of theological and devotional treatises, some by St Bernard (Bodleian Library, Ms. Rawlinson C60); a fourteenth-century text with various apocryphal works relating to the Virgin Mary and the life of Christ (Bodleian Library, Ms. Rawlinson D1236); a fifteenth-century copy of St Augustine's *In Genesim ad Litteram* (TCD. Ms. 123) and a thirteenth-century copy of Giraldus Cambrensis' *Expugnatio Hibernica*, decorated with red and blue initials (Cambridge University Library, Additional Ms. 3392). There are also the chartularies and annals from St Mary's, Dublin, and Dunbrody (*CMA*). From Graiguenamanagh, as well as its charters, comes an early thirteenth-century copy of the *Epistles of St Gregory* (British Library, Ms. Royal 6 B III), the text ornamented with initials coloured in red, green and purple.

93 Lexington, 106.

94 The fullest discussion of the manuscript is provided by Henry and Marsh-Micheli, 'A Century of Irish Illumination' (1962), 161–4; see also Henry, *Irish Art in the Romanesque Period* (1970), 72–3.

95 'Litterae unius coloris fiant, et non depictae. Vitreae albae fiant, et sine crucibus et picturis', *Statuta*, 1134, LXXX.

96 Following the reassessments of the history of early Cistercian legislation, 1145/51 is the date suggested by Holdsworth, 'Chronology and Character of early Cistercian legislation' (1986), 54.

97 C. Oursel, *Miniatures Cisterciennes* (Macon, 1960); J. Porcher, 'Enluminure Cistercienne' in *L'Art Cistercien* (Zodiaque, 1974), 334–5; N. Stratford, 'A Romanesque Marble Altar-Frontal in Beaune and Some Citeaux Manuscripts', in *The Vanishing Past*, ed. A. Borg and A. Martindale (Oxford, B.A.R., 1981), 226–30.

98 There are a number of Irish illuminated books for which no provenance has been established, and in two cases the possibility of a Cistercian origin ought not to be excluded. One is a Gospel book (Corpus Christi College, Oxford, Ms. 122) in

which the general appearance and layout of the script imitates continental writing. The canon tables have been compared with those in the Great Bible of Clairvaux by Henry and Marsh-Micheli. These authors nonetheless argue for a non-Cistercian origin on account of the inclusion of the 'Alea Evangelii', which has Bangor associations. The second manuscript is the Coupar Angus Psalter (Rome, Vatican Library, Ms. Pal. Lat. 65), which although of Irish origin, found its way to the Scottish Cistercian monastery, probably in the thirteenth century. Its ornament has similarities with that in the Corpus Gospels. For both manuscripts see Henry and Marsh-Micheli, 'Century of Irish Illumination' (1962), 152–5, 157–9. The authors have a tendency to adopt the year 1170 as a *terminus ante quem* for ornament in a traditional manner, but there is every likelihood that such styles continued for many decades after the Anglo-Norman invasion, especially west of the Shannon.

99 *ALC*, 122; *AFM*, 1244.
100 The manuscript has not been adequately published. There is a brief discussion of it in a survey of Irish medieval manuscript illumination prepared by Françoise Henry and Genevieve Marsh-Micheli for a forthcoming volume of the *New History of Ireland*.
101 TCD. Ms. 653; W. O'Sullivan, Medieval Meath Manuscripts', *Ríocht na Míde*, vii (4) (1985–6), 8–9.
102 'Omnia monasterii ornamenta, vasa, utensilia, sine auro et argento et gemmis, praeter calicem et fistulam: quae quidem duo sola argentea et deaurata, sed aurea nequaquam habere permittitur, *Statuta*, 1134, X.
103 *AFM*, 1157, 1124–5.
104 'Annales Monasterii de Duiske', in *Miscellanea de Rebus Hibernicis ab Usserio Collecta, TCD*, Ms. 579, fol. 16. Kilcooly and Inislounaght both had gilded silver crosses, *Extents*, 339.
105 D. H. Williams, 'The Welsh Cistercians and Ireland', *Cistercian Studies*, XV (1980), 20–3, quoting Early Chancery Proceedings (Rec. Com.), II (1830), p. viii; PRO C 1/2 6.
106 *AC*, 228–99; *ALC*, 561. Several entries in the annals indicate that Boyle became a centre of pilgrimage.
107 *Letters and Papers, Domestic and Foreign*, XIV (ii), p. 237.
108 *Chronica de Melsa*, lxxvii–lxxxii.
109 *ALC*, 320–3; Lexington, 105–6.
110 McNeill, 'Accounts of Sums Realised by Sales of Chattels' (1922), 11–17.
111 *Triumphalia*, 83.
112 *Extents*, passim.
113 Now in the National Museum of Ireland.
114 O'Conbhuidhe, *Story of Mellifont* (1958), 242.
115 de Paor, 'Excavations at Mellifont' (1969), 138–9. The chalice and paten are

now on display in the National Museum of Ireland.
116 Armstrong, 'Processional Cross, Pricket-Candlestick' etc. (1915), 27–31.
117 O'Conbhuidhe, 'Seven Documents from the Old Abbey of Mellifont' (1953), 55–61.
118 Two further examples are preserved in the National Museum of Ireland, one from Sligo, the other from Kilkenny. In England there are examples in the Victoria and Albert Museum and the Society of Antiquaries. For the latter see J. C. Cox and A. Harvey, *English Church Furniture* (London, 1907), 54.
119 Comerford, 'Relic of the Holy Cross' (1874–9), 130–5; Coleman, 'Relic and Reliquary of the Holy Cross' (1894), 45–8; Crawford, 'Descriptive List of Irish Shrines' (1923), 89–90.
120 There is a brief account of it in C. MacLeod, 'Late Medieval Wood Sculptures in Ireland', *JRSAI*, LXXVII (1947), 55–7. See also K. MacGowan, 'Our Lady of Dublin' (Dublin, Carmelite Publications, nd). The attribution to St Mary's rests on a tradition which is documented in 1749. See also Archdall (1786), 147, who mentions a beautiful image of the Virgin Mary. The figure has been restored and the outstretched hand of the Christ child is modern. It is now the focal point of an elaborate shrine, described in the Shell Guide as 'a vulgar and utterly incongruous setting', *Shell Guide*, 226. Placed ten to fifteen feet above the floor, it is impossible to examine at close quarters.
121 M. Baxandall, *The Limewood Sculptors of Renaissance Germany* (New Haven and London, 1980), 255–8, pls 11, 18. The parallels with Michael Erhart's Blaubeuren altar c1493–4 are especially striking. I am grateful to Dr Malcolm Baker of the Victoria and Albert Museum for discussing the stylistic affinities of the Dublin figure with me.
122 *RCHM, London, I, Westminster* (London, 1924), 59, pl. 205.
123 The Exeter figures at the top of the west front 'image screen' were added c1500, as John Allan demonstrated during the British Archaeological Association's conference at Exeter in April 1985.
124 J. L. Robinson, 'Church Wardens' Accounts 1484–1600', *JRSAI*, XLIV (1914), 136.
125 In 1250–3 William Yxeworth was paid 53/4 for two figures at Westminster; in 1449 John Massingham was paid the enormous sum of £9.6.8 for an image of the Madonna for the high altar at Eton. In 1385 Thomas Canon carved two kings in Westminster Hall for 66/8 each and a further thirteen kings at 46/8. All these works were executed in masonry. L. Stone, *Sculpture in Britain, The Middle Ages* (Harmondsworth, 1972), 120, 206; Salzman, *Building in England* (1967), 130.

126 MacGowan, *Our Lady of Dublin*, 4.
127 Aubert, *Architecture Cistercienne*, I (1947), 307.
128 Lexington, 35, 48.
129 The following paragraphs on seals could not have been written without the guidance of Mr T. A. Heslop, who kindly sent me a copy of his paper 'Cistercian Seals in England and Wales' prior to its publication in *Cistercian Art and Architecture in the British Isles* (1986), 266–85.
130 Irish seals have been little studied. The only general account is Armstrong, *Irish Seal-Matrices and Seals* (1913), but it is far from comprehensive. The last serious discussion of seals was Curtis, 'Some Medieval Seals out of the Ormond archives' (1937), but this article is marred by errors and confusions in the plates. The thirteenth-century seal of Citeaux is mistakenly described as that of the prior of Holycross (p. 73) and the seal of Jerpoint discussed on page 74 and illustrated in pl. vii (4) is not in fact the seal of Jerpoint, nor is it attached to the document cited (N.L.I. Ms. D.1896). The publication of calendars and editions has meant that fewer historians now consult the original documents, which has led to a decline of interest in seal design.
131 Armstrong, *Irish Seal Matrices* (1913), 90. The matrix carries the inscription s. COVETN DE BNDCONE DI (De Benedictione Dei), but Armstrong was at a loss to identify the monastery concerned. The Latin name of Kilbeggan was De Benedictio Dei. The diameter of the seal is 34 mm. There is also a surviving matrix of a counter seal from Dunbrody, discussed below.
132 *Statuta*, 1200.15.
133 Caulfield, 'Note on a Seal of the Abbot of Albus Tractus' (1864), 170.
134 Graiguenamanagh: N.L.I., Ms. D.359 (1288); Jerpoint: N.L.I., Ms. D.382 (1290); Hore: N.L.I., Mss. D.360, D.361 (1289); a cast of the thirteenth-century seal of Tintern is preserved in the Society of Antiquaries of London. The measurements are as follows: Graiguenamanagh: 34 × 45 mm; Jerpoint: 35 × 55 mm; Hore: 30 × 50 mm; Tintern: 25 × 39 mm.
135 It is unlikely that the two Irish foundations, Jerpoint and Hore, would go outside the country for the manufacture of their seals.
136 Heslop, 'Cistercian Seals' (1986), 270–1.
137 Heslop, 'Cistercian Seals' (1986), 278. *Statuta*, 1335.2.
138 Kingsford, *Seals* (1920), 29. In Ireland Lombard lettering sometimes remained in use in the second half of the fourteenth century, as on the shrine of St Patrick's Tooth, c1370.
139 N.L.I., Ms. D.2250 (1533). The seal is slightly oval in shape, measuring 55 × 60 mm.
140 Cast in the National Museum of Dublin, affixed to a copy of the Down Petition of

1500; diameter 36 mm. See also a note by W. Reeves in *PRIA*, V (1850–3), 133–5.

141 N.L.I. Mss: D.1070 (1362); D.1896 (1501–2); D.2005 (1513); D. 2259 (1536). Diameter 40 mm.

142 Cast in Society of Antiquaries of London. The seal is 45 mm in diameter.

143 National Library of Ireland, Ms. D.1695 (1440).

144 British Library Additional Ms. 15,426. Walter de G. Birch, *Catalogue of Seals in the Department of Manuscripts in the British Museum*, IV (London, 1895), p. 716 and pl. XII, no. 17,388. Diameter 45 mm. The inscription includes the words De Voto (not De Tyto as printed by Birch).

145 N.L.I. Mss. D.1629 (1429); D.2250 (1533); D.2255 (1534).

146 *Treasures of Early Irish Art*, ed. G. F. Mitchell, (New York, 1977), no. 65, p. 216; *Trésors d'Irlande*, ed. M. Ryan, (Paris, 1982), 230; R. O'Floinn, 'The Shrine of the Book of Dimma', *Éile*, No. 1 (1982), 25–38.

147 Graiguenamanagh: N.L.I. Ms. D. 2245 (1530); the seal measures 27×45 mm; Monasteranenagh: N.L.I. Ms. D.1886 (1499); the seal measures 35×50 mm; Tracton: cast in Society of Antiquaries of London; R. Caulfield, *Archaeological Journal*, XXI (1864), 170. An effigial seal with the abbot under a floriated canopy also survives from Grey, Armstrong, *Irish Seal Matrices* (1913), 121 (cast in Society of Antiquaries).

148 N.L.I. Ms. D. 1737. The seal measures 27×44 mm.

149 Armstrong, *Irish Seal Matrices* (1913), 116. Armstrong claims it was found at Ballyhack, but a different account is given by John H. Glascott, *A Genealogical History of the Baronial Family styled formerly Etchingham subsequently Etchingham of Dunbrody Abbey* (1868), manuscript at Dunbrody Park, 163–6.

150 T. A. Heslop, 'The Conventual Seals of Canterbury Cathedral 1066–1232', *Medieval Art and Architecture at Canterbury*, ed. N. Coldstream and P. Draper (British Archaeological Association, London, 1982), 94–6.

Chapter 11

1 *Extents*, 181, 267.

2 Gwynn and Hadcock, *Medieval Religious Houses* (1970), 134; *CPR, Ireland*, I, 525; Westropp, 'Monasteranenagh' (1889), 235–6. The story of forty monks being executed at Monasteranenagh is now thought to be highly exaggerated.

3 *Ormond Deeds*, V, 220–1, 271.

4 *Triumphalia*, 219. According to Hartry, during the early seventeenth century the church had seven altars. A 'beautiful altar' with paintings was erected by Luke Archer in 1628 and placed above it, in a painted tabernacle, was a Spanish statue 'in cedar wood' of the Virgin Mary, *ibid.*, 149, 171, 175–7.

5 As early as 1829, a reuse of the ruins was proposed, to judge from the comments of Bell: '. . . but the renovators of our ancient ruins are, it is said, meditating its overthrow, by converting it into a Catholic chapel. By such a change all the minor beauties which now combine to give effect to the whole, will disappear. . . .' Bell, *Essay* (1829), 232.

6 O'Leary, *Graignamanagh Abbey* (1924), 15 n. 1.

7 *CPR, Henry VIII to Elizabeth*, I, 75.

8 *Extents*, I; *Letters and Papers, Domestic and Foreign*, XIV (i), no. 1025.

9 *CPR, Henry VIII to Elizabeth*, I, 103.

10 Hutchinson Papers, TCD Ms. 8856/10, 13, 20.

11 Bradshaw's remark that 'Despite the alteration in use in these cases, there is little evidence of reconstruction in the "Henrician" period' is misleading, Bradshaw, *Dissolution* (1974), 130.

12 *Letters and Papers, Domestic and Foreign*, XII (ii), 90, 91; *Extents*, 270.

13 *Ibid.*, XIII (i), no. 677, p. 257.

14 In 1545 Agard's existing lease was extended by a further ten years, *Letters and Papers*, XX (ii), p. 217, though this is contradicted by a statement that John Alen, Lord Deputy and Lord Chancellor held the farm of Bective in that year, *CPR, Henry VIII to Elizabeth*, I, 113. It appears that Agard continued to live there for some years. In 1552 it was purchased by Andrew Wyse for £1380.16.7, *ibid.*, I, 265, 280. For the complex history of subsequent ownership see Leask, 'Bective Abbey' (1916), 48.

15 Bradshaw, *Dissolution* (1974), 231–2.

16 *Letters and Papers, Domestic and Foreign*, XX(i), no. 274; Hore, *Wexford*, II, 118, 131–4.

17 *Calendar of State Papers, Ireland, 1509–73*, 79, 101, 103, 315; *CPR, Henry VIII to Elizabeth*, I, 497, 517. An informative memorial tablet in the chapel at Tintern States:

HEER LIETH THE BODY OF SYR ANTHONY COLCLOUGHE KNIGHT ELDEST SUNE OF RICHARD COLCLOUGHE OF WOLSTANTON IN STAFORD SHIRE ESQUIER WHO CAME FIRST UNTO THIS LAND THE 34 YEER OF HENRY THE

8 AND THEN WAS CAPTAYN A MOST FAYTHFUL SURVITER DURING THE LIFE OF EDWARD THE VI AND QUEEN MARY AND UNTIL THE XXVI YER OF OUR MOST NOBLE QUEEN ELIZABUTH AND THEN DIED THE IX OF DECEMBER 1584.

18 The abbey was given to the state by Miss Lucy Colclough in 1958.

19 This wing is shown incorrectly as twelfth century in Leask's plan, 'Bective Abbey' (1916), 46–7.

20 The most recent study of the manor house at Carrick-on-Suir is by F. Nowlan, *The Castle and Manor House at Carrick-on-Suir, Co. Tipperary*, unpublished B.A. thesis, Trinity College, Dublin (1982).

21 Apartments once existed over the north transept chapels and it has been suggested that at some stage a floor was inserted across the whole of the north transept, *78th Annual Report of the Commissioners of Public Works* (1909–10), 11.

22 Hore, *Wexford*, II, 187.

23 *Ibid.*, III, 98–9; *CPR, Henry VIII to Elizabeth*, I, 497, 517.

24 Hore, *Wexford*, III, 147–8.

25 Grose, *Antiquities*, I, 51.

26 Since writing this passage, one of the towers has collapsed.

27 Platt, *Abbeys and Priories* (1984), 238, 241.

28 John Windele, *Notes on Excursions*, Royal Irish Academy (12.i.3), 522–3.

29 de Paor, 'Excavations at Mellifont' (1969), 133; Stalley, 'Mellifont Abbey' (1980), 273, 308–9.

30 Stevens, *Journal* (1912), 110.

31 *Ibid.*, 136–7.

32 *Ormond Deeds*, IV, 281.

Appendix 3

1 R. B. McDowell and D. A. Webb, *Trinity College, Dublin 1592–1952* (Cambridge, 1982), 98.

2 *Transactions of the Kilkenny Archaeological Society*, II (1852–3), 206.

3 *Ibid.*, 206, 209–10.

4 *Ibid.*, 385.

5 An excellent account of the National Monuments Branch of the Office of Public Works is provided by H. Wheeler, 'State's Participation', in *Architectural Conservation, An Irish Viewpoint*, The Architectural Association of Ireland (Dublin, 1974), 79–94.

6 *76th Report of the Commissioners of Public Works* (1908), 18–19.

7 *77th Report of the Commissioners of Public Works* (1909), 71.

Select Bibliography

This bibliography is a list of books consulted or cited in the notes and it makes no claim to be comprehensive. The first section deals with general works relating to Cistercian art and architecture, the second section is specifically related to Ireland.

General Works

Atkinson, J.C., and Brownhill, J. (eds.), *The Coucher Book of Furness Abbey*, 6 volumes, (Manchester, 1886–1919).

Aubert, M., *L'Architecture Cistercienne en France* (Paris, 1947).

Aubert, M., 'Existe-t-il une architecture cistercienne?', *Cahiers de Civilisation Médiévale Xᵉ–XIIᵉ siècles*, I (1958), 153–8.

Bégule, L., *L'Abbaye de Fontenay et l'architecture cistercienne* (Paris, 1928).

Bernard of Clairvaux's Life and Death of Saint Malachy the Irishman, translated by R. T. Meyer (Kalamazoo, 1978).

Beuer-Szlechter, H.V., 'Evolution du Plan des Églises Cisterciennes en France, dans les Pays Germaniques et en Grande-Bretagne', *Citeaux in de Nederlanden*, VIII (1957), 269–89.

Beuer-Szlechter, H.V., 'Vicissitudes de l'Ordre Cistercien en Pays de Galles', *CCC*, XXI (1980), 273–97.

Bilson, J. and St John Hope, W. H., 'The Architecture of Kirkstall Abbey Church', *Thoresby Society*, XVI (1907), 1–149.

Bilson, J., 'The Architecture of the Cistercians with special reference to some of their earlier churches in England', *Archaeological Journal*, LXVI (1909), 185–280.

Birch, W. De G., *A History of Margam Abbey* (London, 1897).

Birch, W. de G., *A History of Neath Abbey* (London, 1902).

Blashill, T., 'The Architectural history of Tintern Abbey', *Transactions of the Bristol and Gloucestershire Archaeological Society*, VI (1881–2), 88–106.

Blashill, T., 'The architectural history of Dore Abbey', *JBAA*, XLI (1885), 363–71.

Bond, F., *Gothic Architecture in England* (London, 1906).

Bony, J., *The English Decorated Style* (Oxford, 1979).

Brakspear, H., 'Stanley Abbey', *The Wiltshire Archaeological and Natural History Magazine*, XXXV (1908), 541–81.

Brakspear, H., 'A West Country School of Masons', *Archaeologia*, LXXXI (1931), 1–18.

Branner, R., 'Villard de Honnecourt, Reims and the Origin of Gothic Architectural Drawing', *Gazette des Beaux Arts*, VIe 61 (1963), 129–46.

Braunfels, W., *Monasteries of Western Europe* (London, 1972).

Brown, A.L., 'The Cistercian Abbey of Saddell, Kintyre', *Innes Review*, XX–2 (1969), 130–7.

Bucher, F., *Notre Dame de Bonmont und die ersten Zisterzienser Abteien der Schweiz* (Bern, 1957).

Bucher, F., 'Cistercian Architectural Purism', *Comparative Studies in Society and History*, III (1960), 98–105.

Butler, L.A.S., 'Valle Crucis Abbey: An Excavation in 1970', *Archaeologia Cambrensis*, CXXV (1976), 80–126.

Butler, L.A.S., *Neath Abbey, West Glamorgan* (London, HMSO, 1976).

Butler, L.A.S., 'The Cistercians in England and Wales. A Survey of Recent Archaeological Work 1960–1980', *Studies in Cistercian Art and Architecture*, I, ed. M. P. Lillich (Kalamazoo, 1982).

Chabeuf, H., 'Voyage d'un Délégue au Chapitre Général de Citeaux en MDCLXVII; Étude sur l'Iter Cisterciense de Joseph Meglinger', *Memoires de l'Académie de Dijon* (1883–4), 1–405.

Chronica Monasterii de Melsa ab anno 1150 usque ad annum 1506, ed. E. A. Bond (London, 1866–8, Rolls Series).

Clapham, A.W., 'Three Monastic Houses of South Wales', *Archaeologia Cambrensis*, LXXVI (1921), 205–14.

Clapham, A.W., *English Romanesque Architecture after the Conquest* (Oxford, 1934).

Coldstream, N., 'English Decorated Shrine Bases', *JBAA*, CXXIX (1976), 15–34.

Cowan, I.B., and Easson, D.E., *Medieval Religious Houses, Scotland* (London, 1976).

Cowley, F.G. *The Monastic Order in South Wales, 1066–1349* (Cardiff, 1977).

Craster, O.E., *Tintern Abbey, Monmouthshire* (London, HMSO, 1956).

Dickinson, J.C., *Furness Abbey* (London, HMSO, 1965).

Dickinson, J.C., 'Furness Abbey—an archaeological reconsideration', *Transactions of the Cumberland and Westmoreland Antiquarian and Archaeological Society*, LXVII (1967), 51–80.

Dimier, A., *Recueil de Plans d'églises cisterciennes* (Paris 1949; Supplement, Paris 1967).

Dimier, A., 'Églises cisterciennes sur plan bernardin et sur plan benedictin', *Mélanges offerts à René Crozet*, ed. P. Gallais and Y.-J. Riou (Poitiers, 1966), II, 697–704.

Dimier, A., and Porcher, J., *L'Art cistercien en France* (Zodiaque series, 1962).

Dimier, A., *L'Art cistercien hors de France* (Zodiaque Series, 1971).

Donkin, R.A. 'The Growth and Distribution of the Cistercian Order in Medieval Europe', *Studia Monastica*, IX (1967), 275–86.

Donkin, R.A., *A Check List of Printed Works relating to the Cistercian Order as a whole and to the houses of the British Isles in particular* (Rochefort, Belgium, 1969).

Donkin, R.A., *The Cistercians: Studies in the Geography of Medieval England and Wales* (Toronto, 1978).

Duby, G., *St Bernard, L'Art Cistercien* (Paris, 1976).

Eames, E.S., *Medieval Tiles, A Handbook* (London, 1968).

Eames, E.S., *Catalogue of Medieval Lead-Glazed Earthenware Tiles in the Department of Medieval and Later Antiquities, British Museum* (London, 1980).

Ecclesiastical History of Orderic Vitalis, edited and translated by M. Chibnall, volume IV (Oxford, 1973).

Esser, K.H. 'Über den Kirchenbau des Hl. Bernhard von Clairvaux', *Archiv für Mittelrheinische Kirchengeschichte*, V (1953), 195–222.

Esser, K.H., 'Les Fouilles à Himmerod et le Plan Bernardin', *Mélanges St Bernard*, XXIV Congrès de l'Association Bourguignonne des Sociétés Savantes (Dijon, 1953), 311–15.

Eydoux, H.-P., *L'Architecture des Églises Cisterciennes d'Allemagne* (Paris, 1952).

Fawcett, R., 'Late Gothic Architecture in Scotland: Considerations on the influence of the Low Countries', *Proceedings of the Society of Antiquaries of Scotland*, 112 (1982), 477–96.

Fawcett, R., 'Scottish Medieval Window Tracery', in *Studies in Scottish Antiquity*, ed. D. J. Breeze and N. Reynolds (Edinburgh, 1984), 148–86.

Ferguson, C.J., 'St Mary's Abbey, Holme Cultram', *Transactions of the Cumberland and*

Westmoreland Antiquarian and Archaeological Society, I (1872), 263–75.

Fergusson, P., 'Early Cistercian Churches in Yorkshire and the Problem of the Cistercian Crossing Tower', *Journal of the Society of Architectural Historians*, XXIX (1970), 211–21.

Fergusson, P., 'Roche Abbey: the Source and Date of the Eastern Remains', *JBAA*, XXXIV (1971), 30–42.

Fergusson, P., 'The Late Twelfth-Century Rebuilding at Dundrennan Abbey', *Antiquaries Journal*, LIII (1973), 232–43.

Fergusson, P., 'The South Transept Elevation of Byland Abbey', *JBAA*, XXXVIII (1975), 155–76.

Fergusson, P., 'Notes on Two Cistercian Engraved Designs', *Speculum*, LIV (1979), 1–17.

Fergusson, P., *Architecture of Solitude. Cistercian Abbeys in Twelfth Century England* (Princeton, 1984).

Ferguson, R., 'Holm Cultrum, Remains lately brought to light', *Archaeological Journal*, XXIV (1867), 269–73.

Fernie, E., 'Historical Metrology and Architectural History', *Art History*, I (1978), 383–99.

Gilbert, P., 'Un chef-d'oeuvre d'art cistercien peut-être influencé par Cluny, l'Abbatiale de Fontenay', *Académie royale de Belgique, Bulletin de la Classe des Beaux-Arts*, LII (1970), 1–3, 20–45.

Gilyard-Beer, R., *Abbeys* (London, 1959).

Gilyard-Beer, R., *Cleeve Abbey* (London, HMSO, 1960).

Gilyard-Beer, R. *Fountains Abbey* (London, HMSO, 1970).

Gilyard-Beer, R., 'Boxley Abbey and the Pulpitum Collationis', *Collectanea Historica: Essays in Memory of Stuart Rigold*, edited by A. Detsices (Maidstone, 1981) 123–31.

Godfrey, W.H., 'English Cloister Lavatories as Independent Structures', *Archaeological Journal*, CVI, supplement for the year 1949 (1952), 91–7.

Grainger, F., and Collingwood, W. D., *The Register and Records of Holm Cultram* (Cumberland and Westmoreland Antiquarian and Archaeological Society Record Series, VII, Kendal, 1929).

Graves, C.V., 'The Economic Activities of the Cistercians in Medieval England (1128–1307)', *Analecta Sacri Ordinis Cisterciensis*, XIII (1957), 3–60.

Hahn, H., *Die frühe Kirchenbaukunst der Zisterzienser* (Berlin, 1957).

Hamilton Thompson, A., *Buildwas Abbey, Shropshire* (London, HMSO, 1946).

Heslop, T.A., 'Cistercian Seals in England and Wales' in *Cistercian Art and Architecture in the British Isles*, ed. E. C. Norton and W. D. Park (Cambridge, 1986), 266–83.

Hill, B.D., *English Cistercian Monasteries and their Patrons in the Twelfth Century* (Urbana, 1968).

Hirst, S.M., Walsh, D. A., and Wright, S. M., *Bordesley Abbey* II, B.A.R. (British Series), 111 (Oxford, 1983).

Holdsworth, C., 'The chronology and character of early Cistercian legislation on art and architecture', in *Cistercian Art and Architecture in the British Isles*, ed. E. C. Norton and W. D. Park (Cambridge, 1986), 40–55.

Horn, W., 'On the Origins of the Medieval Cloister', *Gesta*, XII (1973), 13–52.

Horn, W., and Born, E., *The Plan of St Gall* (Berkeley, Los Angeles, London, 1980).

Janauschek, P., *Origines Cisterciensium* (Vienna, 1877).

Kingsford, H.S., *Seals* (London, 1920).

Knowles, D., *The Monastic Order in England* (Cambridge, 1940).

Knowles, D., *The Religious Orders in England*, 3 volumes (Cambridge, 1948–59).

Knowles, D., and Hadcock, R.N. *Medieval Religious Houses, England and Wales* (London, 1953).

Knowles, D., 'The Primitive Cistercian Documents', *Great Historical Enterprises* (London, 1962), 198–224.

Le Clerq, J., *Bernard of Clairvaux and the Cistercian Spirit* (Kalamazoo, 1976).

The Letters of St Bernard of Clairvaux, translated by Bruno Scott James (London, 1953).

Lewis, J.M., and Williams, D. H., *The White Monks in Wales* (Cardiff, 1976).

Lewis, J.M., *Welsh Medieval Paving Tiles* (Cardiff, 1976).

MacGibbon, D., and Ross, T., *The ecclesiastical architecture of Scotland* (Edinburgh, 1896–7).

Martindale, J.H., 'The Abbey of St Mary, Holm Cultram', *Transactions of the Cumberland and Westmoreland Antiquarian and Archaeological Society*, XIII (1913), 244–51.

Melczer, E., and Soldwedel, E., 'Monastic Goals in the Aesthetics of St Bernard' *Studies in Cistercian Art and Design*, I, edited by M. P. Lillich (Kalamazoo, 1982), 31–44.

Morris, R., 'The development of later Gothic mouldings in England c1250–1400', *Architectural History*, XXI (1978), 18–57; and XXII (1979), 1–48.

Mortet, V., and Deschamps, P., *Recueil de Textes Relatifs à l'histoire de l'architecture et à la condition des architects en France au moyen age* (Paris, 1911/1929).

Norton, E.C., 'Early Cistercian tile pavements', in *Cistercian Art and Architecture in the British Isles*, ed. E. C. Norton and W. D. Park (Cambridge, 1986), 228–55.

Oursel, C., *Miniatures Cisterciennes* (Dijon, 1960).

Park, W.D., 'Cistercian wall and panel Painting' in *Cistercian Art and Architecture in the British Isles*, ed. E. C. Norton and W. D. Park (Cambridge 1986), 181–210.

Paul, R.W., 'The church and monastery of Abbey Dore, Herefordshire', *Transactions of the Bristol and Gloucestershire Archaeological Society*, XXVII (1904), 117–26.

Paul, R.W., 'Abbey Dore Church, Herefordshire', *Archaeologia Cambrensis*, LXXXII (1927), 269–75.

Petit, J.L., 'Architectural Notices of the Conventual Church of Buildwas Abbey, Shropshire', *Archaeological Journal*, XV (1858), 335–44.

Platt, C., *The Abbeys and Priories of Medieval England* (London, 1984).

Powicke, F.M. (ed.), *Walter Daniel's Life of St Aelred of Rievaulx* (London, 1950).

Puig I Cadafalch, J., *Le Premier Art Roman* (Paris, 1928).

Puig I Cadafalch, J., *La Géographie et les Origines du Premier Art Roman* (Paris, 1935).

Rahtz, P.A., and Hirst, S.M., *Bordesley Abbey, Redditch: First Report on excavations 1969–1973*, British Archaeological Reports, 23 (Oxford, 1976).

Ralegh Radford, C.A., *Strata Florida Abbey, Cardiganshire* (London, HMSO, 1949).

Ralegh Radford, C. A., *Ewenny Priory* (London, HMSO, 1952).

Rose, H., *Die Baukunst der Zisterzienser* (Munich, 1916).

St John Hope, W.H., 'Fountains Abbey', *Yorkshire Archaeological Journal*, XV (1899), 269–402.

St John Hope, W.H., *The Abbey of St Mary in Furness, Lancashire* (Kendal, 1902).

Salzman, L.F., *Building in England down to 1540* (Oxford, 1967).

Schmoll gen Eisenwerth, J.A., 'Zisterzienser-Romanik, Kritische Gedanken zur jüngsten Literatur', *Formositas Romanica: Joseph Gantner Zugeeignet* (Frauenfeld, 1958), 153–80.

Schneider, A., Bickel, W., and Wienaud, A., *Die Cistercienser: Geschichte, Geist, Kunst* (Cologne, 1974).

Smith, J.D.C., *A Guide to Church Woodcarvings* (Newton Abbot, 1974).

Southern, R.W., *Western Society and the Church in the Middle Ages* (Harmondsworth, 1970).

Statuta Capitulorum Generalium Ordinis Cisterciensis ab anno 1116 ad annum 1786, ed. J. M. Canivez, 8 volumes, (Louvain, 1933–41).

Swartling, I., 'Did the Cistercians introduce a new unit of measurement into Swedish architecture?', *Konsthistoriska Studier tillägnade Sten Karling* (Stockholm, 1966), 25–30.

Swartling, I., *Nydala Abbey* (Stockholm, 1967).

Swartling, I., 'Cistercian Abbey Churches in Sweden and the "Bernardine Plan"', *Nordisk Medeltid Konsthistoriska Shidier Tillägnade Armin Tuulse* (Stockholm, 1967), 193–8.

Swartling, I., *Alvastra Abbey. The first Cistercian settlement in Sweden* (Stockholm, 1969).

Talbot, C.H., *The Cistercian Abbeys of Scotland* (London, 1939).

Tummers, H.A., *Early Secular Effigies in England: The Thirteenth Century* (Leiden, 1980).

Van der Meer, F., *Atlas de l'Ordre Cistercien* (Paris, 1965).

Walsh, D.A., 'A Rebuilt Cloister at Bordesley Abbey', *JBAA*, CXXXII (1979), 42–9.

Walsh, D.A., 'Measurement and Proportion at Bordesley Abbey', *Gesta*, *XIX* (1980), 109–13.

White, T.H., *The Bestiary* (New York, 1960).

Williams, D.H., 'The Welsh Cistercians and Ireland', *Cistercian Studies*, XV (1980), 17–23.

Williams, D.H., *The Welsh Cistercians* (Caldey Island, Tenby, 1984), 2 volumes.

Williams, S.W., *The Cistercian Abbey of Strata Florida* (London, 1889).

Williams, W., *St Bernard of Clairvaux* (Manchester, 1935).

Works Relating to Ireland

Abbot, T.C., 'The Birth of Fermoy', *JCHAS*, XXXIII (1928), 16–19.

Annals of Ireland by Friar John Clyn, ed. R. Butler (Dublin, 1849).

Alemand, L.A., *Monasticon Hibernicum* (translated J. Stevens, London 1722).

Archdall, M., *Monasticon Hibernicum* (Dublin, 1786).

Armstrong, E.C.R., *Irish Seal Matrices and Seals* (Dublin, 1913).

Armstrong, E.C.R., 'Processional Cross, Pricket Candlestick and Bell, found together at Sheephouse, near Oldbridge, Co. Meath', *JRSAI*, XLV (1915), 2–31.

Bagwell, R., 'Innislonagh Abbey', *JRSAI*, XXXIX (1909), 267–8.

Barrow, G.L., *The Round Towers of Ireland* (Dublin, 1979).

Barry, J.G., 'Monasternenagh or Nenay de Magio, Co. Limerick', *JRSAI*, L (1920), 178–9.

Bell, T., *An Essay on the Origins and Progress of Gothic Architecture with reference to the ancient history and present state of the remains of such architecture in Ireland* (Dublin, 1829).

Bence-Jones, M., *Burke's Guide to Country Houses*, I, *Ireland* (London, 1978).

Bernard, J.H., 'The Foundation of Tintern Abbey, Co. Wexford', *PRIA*, 33C (1917), 527–9.

Bernard of Clairvaux, *The Life and Death of Saint Malachy the Irishman*, translated and annotated by Robert T. Meyer (Kalamazoo, 1978).

Beuer-Szlechter, H. V., 'Les Débuts de l'Art Cistercien en Irlande d'Apres les Vestiges des Abbayes de Mellifont (Louth) et de Baltinglass (Wicklow)', *CCC*, XXI (1970), 201–18.

Beuer-Szlechter, H.V., 'Contributions à l'Iconographie de Saint-Bernard', *CCC*, XXVI (1975), 241–54.

Beuer-Szlechter, H.V., 'L'Abbaye de Dunbrody, Comté de Wexford, en Irlande', *CCC*, XXVIII (1977), 208–23.

Beuer-Szlechter, H.V., 'L'Église de l'Abbaye de Holy Cross', *Mélanges à la memoire du Père Anselme Dimier*, ed. B. Chauvin (Arbois, 1982), volume VI, 423–46.

Blake, M.J., 'Knockmoy Abbey (with some hitherto unpublished ancient charters)', *Journal of the Galway Archaeological and Historical Society*, I (1900–1), 64–84.

Bolster, E., *A History of the Diocese of Cork* (Shannon, 1972).

'Boyle Abbey', *72nd Report of the Commissioners of Public Works in Ireland* (1904), 14–16.

Bradley, J., and Manning C., 'Excavations at Duiske Abbey, Graiguenamanagh, Co. Kilkenny', *PRIA*, 81C (1981), 397–426.

Bradshaw, B., *The Dissolution of the Religious Orders in Ireland under Henry VIII* (Cambridge, 1974).

Brannon, N.F., 'Rescue Excavations in Macosquin, County Londonderry', *UJA*, 46 (1983), 93–9.

Brash, R.R., *Ecclesiastical Architecture of Ireland* (Dublin, 1875).

de Breffny, B., and Mott G., *The Churches and Abbeys of Ireland* (London, 1976).

Brenan, J., 'A note on Abbey Knockmoy, Co. Galway', *JRSAI*, XXV (1905), 420–1.

Burke, J.M., 'The Abbey of Sancta Mauro or De Fonte Vivo', *JCHAS*, X (1904), 251–3.

Burke, W.P., 'Our Lady of Ynislaunagh, being an account of the Abbey of Inislounaght, Co. Tipperary', *Journal of the Waterford and South-East of Ireland Archaeological Society*, I (1895), 85–93.

Calendar of the Patent Rolls, Ireland, Henry VIII to Queen Elizabeth, ed. J. Morrin (1862).

Carrigan, W., *The History and Antiquities of the Diocese of Ossory*, 4 volumes (Dublin, 1905).

Carte, T., *An History of the Life of James, Duke of Ormonde* (London, 1736).

Carville, G., *The Heritage of Holycross* (Belfast, 1973).

Carville, G., 'The Cistercian Settlement of Ireland (1142–1541)', *Studia Monastica*, XV (1973), 23–41.

Carville, G., *Norman Splendour, Duiske Abbey, Graignamanagh* (Belfast, 1979).

Carville, G., A Historical, Geographical and Archaeological Study of the Relative Importance of Cistercian Abbeys in Medieval Ireland, *Mélanges à la Memoire du Père Anselme Dimier*, ed. B. Chauvin (Arbois, 1982), volume V, 39–64.

Carville, G., *The Occupation of Celtic Sites in Ireland by the Canons Regular of St Augustine and the Cistercians* (Kalamazoo, 1982).

Caulfield, R., 'Note on a Seal of the Abbot of Albus Tractus or Tracton Abbey, Co. Cork', *Archaeological Journal*, XXI (1864), 170.

Champneys, A.C., *Irish Ecclesiastical Architecture* (London, 1910).

Charters of Duiske: 'Charters of the Cistercian Abbey of Duiske', ed. C. M. Butler and J. H. Bernard, *PRIA*, 35C (1918), 1–188.

'Church and Monastic Buildings of Grey Abbey, Co. Down', *The Irish Builder*, XII (1 April 1870), 72–9.

Clapham, A.W., 'Some Minor Irish Cathedrals', *Archaeological Journal*, CVI (1949), supplement, 16–39.

Close, S.P., *Holy Cross Abbey, County Tipperary: A series of Measured Drawings of the Church with Descriptive Letterpress* (Belfast, 1868).

Cochrane, R., 'Note by Hon. General Secretary' (on Graiguenamanagh), *JRSAI*, XXII (1892), 247.

Cochrane R., 'Knockmoy Abbey, Co. Galway, Notes on the Building and "Frescoes"', *JRSAI*, XXXIV (1904), 244–53.

Cochrane, R., 'The frescoes, Abbey Knockmoy, Co. Galway', *JRSAI*, XXXV (1905), 419–20.

Coleman, J., 'The Relic and Reliquary of the Holy Cross in the Ursuline Convent, Blackrock', *JCHAS*, III (1894), 45–8.

Comerford, M. 'Relic of the Holy Cross and Silver Case in which it is placed; now deposited in the Ursuline Convent Blackrock, Cork', *Transactions of the Ossory Archaeological Society*, I (1874–9), 130–5.

Comerford, M., 'Monasterevan—Abbey and Parish', *Transactions of the Ossory Archaeological Society*, I (1874–9), 115–30.

Cooke, T.L., 'Observations on Holy Cross Abbey and its celebrated monument', *Transactions of the Kilkenny Archaeological Society*, I (1849), 59–75, 112.

Craig, M., *The Architecture of Ireland, From the earliest times to 1880* (London and Dublin, 1982).

Crawford, H.S., 'Mural Paintings in Holy Cross Abbey', *JRSAI*, XLV (1915), 149–51.

Crawford, H.S., 'The Mural Paintings and Inscriptions at Knockmoy Abbey', *JRSAI*, LXIX (1919), 25–34.

Crawford, H.S., 'A Descriptive List of Irish Shrines and Reliquaries', *JRSAI*, CIII (1923), 74–93.

Curtis, E., 'Some Medieval Seals out of the Ormond archives', *JRSAI*, LXVII (1937), 72–6.

Curtis, E., *A History of Medieval Ireland* (London, 1938).

de Paor, L., 'Cormac's Chapel: The Beginnings of Irish Romanesque', *Munster Studies, Essays in Commemoration of Monsignor Michael Moloney*, ed. E. Rynne (Limerick, 1967), 133–45.

de Paor, L., 'Excavations at Mellifont Abbey, Co. Louth', *PRIA*, 68C (1969), 109–64.

'Drawings of Corcomroe Abbey', *The Irish Builder*, XXI (15 August 1879), 250.

Dudley Edwards, R., *Church and State in Tudor Ireland* (Dublin, 1935).

'Dunbrody Abbey', *78th Report of the Commissioners of Public Works in Ireland* (1909–10), 6–12, 22–9.

Du Noyer, G., *Antiquarian Sketches* (Royal Irish Academy).

Extents of Irish Monastic Possessions, 1540–1541, ed. Newport B. White (Dublin, 1943).

Fanning, T., 'An Irish Medieval Tile Pavement. Recent Excavations at Swords Castle, County Dublin', *JRSAI*, CV (1975), 47–82.

Fanning, T., 'The British Museum Catalogue of Medieval Tiles—a Review, incorporating the Irish evidence', *North Munster Antiquarian Journal*, XXIII (1981), 9–16.

Ffrench, J.F.M., 'Dunbrody and its History', *JRSAI*, XXVI (1896), 336–48.

FitzGerald, W., 'Baltinglass Abbey, its possessions and their post-Reformation properties', *Journal of the Kildare Archaeological Society*, V (1906–8), 379–414.

Frazer, 'Early Pavement Tiles in Ireland', *JRSAI*, XXIII (1893), 357–66; XXIV (1894), 136–8; XXV (1895), 171–5.

Garton, T., 'A Romanesque Doorway at Killaloe', *JBAA*, CXXXIV (1981), 31–57.

Glynn, J.A., 'Knockmoy Abbey, County Galway', *JRSAI*, XXXIV (1904), 239–42.

'Grey Abbey', *76th Report of the Commissioners of Public Works in Ireland* (1908), 16–21.

Grose, F., *Antiquities of Ireland*, 2 volumes, (London, 1791–5).

Gwynn, A., 'The Origins of St Mary's Abbey, Dublin', *JRSAI*, LXXIX (1949), 110–25.

Gwynn, A., and Hadcock, R.N., *Medieval Religious Houses, Ireland* (London, 1970).

Hall, S.C., *Ireland, Its Scenery and Character* (Dublin, 1842).

Hamilton Thompson, A., Clapham, A.W., and Leask, H.G., 'The Cistercian Order in Ireland', *Archaeological Journal*, LXXXVIII (1931), 1–36.

Hamlin, A., 'A recently discovered enclosure at Inch Abbey, County Down', *UJA*, XL (1977), 85–8.

Hamlin, A., 'Collation Seats in Irish Cistercian Houses: Grey Abbey, County Down and Graiguenamanagh, County Kilkenny', *Medieval Archaeology*, XVII (1983), 156–8.

Hamlin, A., 'The Study of early Irish churches', *Ireland und Europa, Ireland and Europe, Die Kirche im Frühmittelalter, The Early Church*, ed. Próinséas Ní Chatháin and Michael Richter (Stuttgart, 1984), 117–26.

Hand, G.J., 'The Dating of the early fourteenth-century ecclesiastical valuations of Ireland', *Irish Theological Quarterly*, XXIV (1957), 271–4.

Harbison, P., 'Animals in Irish Art—2, *The Arts in Ireland*, II, No. 4 (1974), 54–63.

Harbison, P., 'Twelfth- and Thirteenth-Century Irish Stonemasons in 'Regensburg (Bavaria) and the end of the "School of the West" in Connacht', *Studies* (1975), 333–46.

Harbison, P., 'The Ballintober Master and a date for the Clonfert Cathedral Chancel', *Journal of the Galway Archaeological and Historical Society*, XXXV (1976), 96–9.

Harris, W., *The Antient and Present State of the County of Down* (Dublin, 1744).

Harris, W., (ed.), *The Whole Works of Sir James Ware* (Dublin, 1764).

Healy, J., 'The Cistercians in Ireland', *Irish Ecclesiastical Record*, IX (1901), 481–98.

Healy, J., 'Our Irish Romanesque Architecture', *Galway Archaeological Society Journal*, III (1903–4), 167–79.

Healy, R.W., 'The Cistercian Abbey of Kilcooly, Co. Tipperary', *JRSAI*, XX (1890), 216–27.

Hennig, J., 'Medieval Ireland in Cistercian Records', *Irish Ecclesiastical Record*, LXXIII (1950), 226–42.

Henry, F., and Marsh-Micheli, G.L., 'A Century of Irish Illumination (1070–1170)', *PRIA* 62 (1962), 101–64.

Henry, F., 'Irish Cistercian Monasteries and their carved decoration', *Apollo*, LXXXIV, No. 56 (October 1966), 260–7.

Henry, F., *Irish Art During the Viking Invasions* (London, 1967).

Henry, F., *Irish Art in the Romanesque Period, 1020–1170 AD* (London, 1970).

Herity, M., 'The Buildings and Layout of Early Irish Monasteries before the year 1000', *Monastic Studies*, XIV (1983), 247–84.

Herity, M., 'The layout of Irish early Christian monasteries' in *Irland und Europa, Ireland and Europe, Die Kirche im Frühmittelalter, The Early Church*, ed. Próinséas Ní Chatháin and Michael Richter (Stuttgart, 1984), 105–16.

'Holy Cross Abbey', *74th Report of the Commissioners of Public Works in Ireland* (1906), 11–14.

Hore, P.H., *A History of the Town and County of Wexford*, 6 volumes, (London, 1900–11).

Hourihane, C., *The Iconography of Religious Art in Ireland, 1250–1550*, unpublished PhD. thesis, University of London (1984).

Hughes, K., and Hamlin, A., *The Modern Traveller to the Early Irish Church* (London, 1977).

Hunt, J., *Irish Medieval Figure Sculpture* (Dublin and London, 1974).

Hunt, J., 'The Abbey of Corcomroe', *North Munster Antiquarian Journal*, XX (1978), 74–5.

Ireland, A., 'Holycross 1730–1840', *North Munster Antiquarian Journal*, XXIV (1982), 48–54.

Irish Monastic and Episcopal Deeds, AD. 1200–1600, ed. Newport B. White (Dublin, 1936).

'Jerpoint Abbey', *Architectural and Topographical Record*, I (1908), 53–64.

The Journal of John Stevens, ed. R. H. Murray (Oxford, 1912).

Langan, T., 'Abbeyshrule, Co. Longford', *Irish Ecclesiastical Record*, V (1884), 652–6.

Langrishe, R., 'Notes on Jerpoint Abbey, Co. Kilkenny', *JRSAI*, XXXVI (1906), 179–87.

Leask, H.G., 'Bective Abbey, County Meath', *JRSAI*, XLVI (1916), 46–57.

Leask, H.G., 'The Architecture of the Cistercian Order in Ireland in the XIIth and Early XIIIth centuries', *North Munster Antiquarian Journal*, I (1939), 132–41.

Leask, H.G., *Jerpoint Abbey, Co. Kilkenny* (Dublin, 1939).

Leask, H.G., 'Mellifont Abbey', *County Louth Archaeological Journal*, XI (1945), 29–33.

Leask, H.G., 'Irish Cistercian Monasteries: A Pedigree and Distribution Map', *JRSAI*, LXXVIII (1948), 63–4.

Leask, H.G., *Irish Churches and Monastic Buildings*, 3 volumes (Dundalk, 1955–60).

Leask, H.G., *Irish Castles and Castellated Houses* (Dundalk, 1964).

Le Clercq, J., 'Deux Épitres de Saint Bernard et de son Secrétaire', in *Recueil d'Études sur Saint Bernard et ses Écrits*, II (Rome, 1966).

Ledwich, R., *The Antiquities of Ireland* (Dublin, 1790).

Lexington: Registrum Epistolarum Stephani de Lexington, ed. P. B. Greisser, *Analecta Sacri Ordinis Cisterciensis*, II (1946), 1–118.

Lexington: *Stephen of Lexington, Letters from Ireland 1228–1229*, translated with an introduction by Barry W. O'Dwyer (Kalamazoo, 1982).

Life of St Malachy: St Bernard's Life of St Malachy of Armagh, edited and translated by H. C. Lawlor (London 1920). [See also St Bernard of Clairvaux, *The Life and Death of Saint Malachy the Irishman*].

Long, R.H., 'The Old Cistercian Abbeys in the Diocese of Cashel and Emly', *JCHAS*, II (1896), 250–6.

Luckombe, P., *A Tour Through Ireland* (London, 1780).

Lydon, J.F., *The Lordship of Ireland in the Middle Ages* (Dublin, 1972).

Lydon, J.F., *Ireland in the later Middle Ages* (Dublin, 1973).

McNeill, C., 'Accounts of Sums Realized by Sales of Chattels of Some Suppressed Irish Monasteries', *JRSAI*, CII (1922), 11–17.

McNeill, T.E., *Anglo-Norman Ulster, The History and Archaeology of an Irish Barony, 1177–1400* (Edinburgh, 1980).

MacNiocaill, G., *Na Manaigh Liatha in Éirinn 1142–c1600* (Dublin, 1959).

Manning, C., 'Jerpoint Cloister Fragment at Sheepstown', *Old Kilkenny Review*, N.S. volume I, no. 2 (1975), 118–19.

'Mellifont Abbey', *52nd Report of the Commissioners of Public Works in Ireland* (1883–4), 30.

'Mellifont Abbey', *71st Report of the Commissioners of Public Works in Ireland* (1903), 10–11.

Moloney, M., 'Kilcooley: foundation and restoration', *JRSAI*, LXXIV (1944), 219–23.

Moody, T.W., Martin, F.X., and Byrne, F.J., *A New History of Ireland*, volume III, *Early Modern Ireland, 1534–1691* (Oxford, 1976).

Morrin, J., 'Historical Notes on the Abbey of Dunbrody', *Transactions of the Ossory Archaeological Society*, I (1874–9), 407–31.

Nichols, K., *Gaelic and Gaelicised Ireland in the Middle Ages* (Dublin, 1972).

O'Conbhuidhe, Colmcille, 'Seven Documents from the Old Abbey of Mellifont', *County Louth Archaeological Journal*, XIII (1953), 55–61.

O'Conbhuidhe, Colmcille, 'The Irish Cistercian Documents in Octavian's Register, Armagh', *Seanchas Ardmhacha*, II (1954–7), 269–94.

O'Conbhuidhe, Colmcille, 'The Cistercian Abbey of Inislounaght', *Clonmel Historical and Archaeological Society*, I (1955–6), 3–52.

O'Conbhuidhe, Colmcille, 'Decline and attempted reform of the Irish Cistercians, 1445–1531', *Collectanea Ordinis Cisterciensium Reformatorum*, XVIII (1956), 290–305; XIX (1957), 146–62, 371–84.

O'Conbhuidhe, Colmcille, *The Story of Mellifont* (Dublin, 1958).

O'Conbhuidhe, Colmcille, 'The Suppression of the Irish Cistercian Abbeys', *CCC*, X (1959), 44–61, 107–24, 199–211.

O'Conbhuidhe, Colmcille, 'The Abbey of the Rock of Cashel', *CCC*, XII (1961), 307–20.

O'Conbhuidhe, Colmcille, 'The Lands of St Mary's Abbey, Dublin', *PRIA*, 62C (1962), 21–84.

O'Conbhuide, Colmcille, 'The Origins of Jerpoint Abbey, Co. Kilkenny', *CCC*, XIV (1963), 293–306.

O'Conbhuidhe, Colmcille, 'Taxation of the Irish Cistercian Houses, c1329–1479', *CCC*, XV (1964), 144–60.

O'Conbhuidhe, Colmcille, 'Studies in Irish Cistercian History, I, The Irish Cistercians under the Tudors, 1539–1603', *CCC*, XVI (1965), 5–28.

O'Conbhuidhe, Colmcille, 'Studies in Irish Cistercian History, II, The Irish Cistercians under the Stuarts', *CCC*, XVI (1965), 177–87, 257–77; XVII (1966), 5–24; XVIII (1967), 38–50, 152–63.

O'Conbhuidhe, Colmcille, 'Studies in Irish Cistercian History, III, The Controversy with the Bishops', *CCC*, XIX (1968), 325–50; XX (1969), 170–96.

O'Dwyer, B.W. 'The Impact of the native Irish on the Cistercians in the XIIIth Century', *Journal of Religious History*, IV (1966–7), 287–301.

O'Dwyer, B.W., 'Gaelic Monasticism and the

Irish Cistercians, c1228', *Irish Ecclesiastical Record*, CVIII (1967), 19–28.

O'Dwyer, B.W., *The Conspiracy of Mellifont 1216–31* (Dublin Historical Association, 1970).

O'Halloran, S., *An Introduction to the Study of the History and Antiquities of Ireland* (Dublin, 1772).

O'Laverty, J., *An Historical Account of the Diocese of Down and Connor, Ancient and Modern* (Dublin, 1880).

O'Leary, P., 'Notes on the Cistercian Abbey of Graignamanagh', *JRSAI*, XXII (1892), 237–47.

O'Leary, P.W., and J. *Graignamanagh Abbey* (Graig-na-Managh, 1924).

O'Riordain, S.P., 'Sculptured Stone at Tracton Abbey, Co. Cork', *JCHAS*, XLIX (1944), 56–7.

Ormond Deeds: Calendar of Ormond Deeds, ed. E. Curtis (Dublin, 1932–43).

Orpen, G.H., *Ireland Under the Normans 1169–1333* (Oxford 1911–20).

O'Sullivan, D., 'The Cistercian Abbey of Tracton, Co. Cork', *JCHAS*, XLIV (1939), 1–15.

O'Sullivan, D., 'The Cistercian Abbey of St Mary de Fonte Vivo, Diocese of Ross, Co. Cork', *JCHAS*, XLIX (1944), 1–9.

O'Sullivan, D., 'Some medieval religious houses in the Barony of Imokilly', *JCHAS*, L (1945), 104–11.

O'Sullivan, D., 'The Cistercian Abbey of St Mary de Castro Dei, Fermoy, Co. Cork', *JCHAS*, LI (1946), 170–81.

Otway-Ruthven, J., *A History of Medieval Ireland* (London, 1968).

Parker, W.S., 'A decorated tile from Baltinglass Abbey', *JRSAI*, LXXI (1941), 148.

Petit, J.L., 'On the Abbeys of Ireland', *Royal Institute of British Architects: Sessional Papers* (1862–3), 191–208.

Petrie, G., *The Ecclesiastical Architecture of Ireland anterior to the Anglo-Norman Invasion, comprising an Essay on the Origin and Uses of the Round Towers of Ireland* (Dublin, 1845).

Phillips, J.J., St Mary's of Grey Abbey, County Down, Ireland, as existing in the year AD 1874 (Belfast, 1874).

Phillips, J.J., 'Grey Abbey Illustrated', *The Irish Builder*, XVI (1874), 196, 383, 385.

Phillips, J.J., 'Grey Abbey, Co. Down', *The Irish Builder*, XVII (1875), 225, 287.

Power, P., 'Dunbrody Abbey, Waterford', *Journal of the Waterford and South-East of Ireland Archaeological Society*, I (1895), 67–82.

Power, P., 'Repairs to Dunbrody Abbey', *Journal of the Waterford and South-East of Ireland Archaeological Society*, II (1896), 123–9.

Power, P., 'The Irish Cistercian Abbeys', *Irish Ecclesiastical Record*, XXVII (1926), 23–35.

Power, P., 'The Cistercian Abbeys of Down and Connor', *Down and Connor Historical Society Journal*, I (1928), 9–25.

Power, P., 'The Cistercian Abbeys of Munster', *JCHAS*, XXXIII (1928), 75–82; XXXIV (1929), 22–9, 91–7; XXXV (1930), 43–46; XLIII (1938), 1–11, 96–100.

Quane, M., 'Tour in Ireland by John Harden in 1797', *JCHAS* LVIII (1953), 26–32, 81–90; LIX (1954), 34–41, 69–77; LX (1955), 15–21, 80–7.

Rae, E.C., 'The Sculpture of the cloister at Jerpoint Abbey', *JRSAI*, XCVI (1966), 59–91.

Rae, E.C., 'Irish Sepulchral Monuments of the Later Middle Ages, Part I, The Ormond Group', *JRSAI*, C (1970), 1–38.

Rae, E.C., 'Irish Sepulchral Monuments of the Later Middle Ages, Part II, The O'Tunney Atelier', *JRSAI*, CI (1971), 1–39.

Ralegh Radford, C.A., 'The Earliest Irish Churches', *UJA*, 40 (1977), 1–11.

'Records and Remains of St Mary's Abbey, Dublin', *The Irish Builder*, XXIV (1882), 129.

Reeves, W., *Ecclesiastical Antiquities of Down, Connor and Dromore* (Dublin, 1847).

Remains of St Mary's Abbey, Dublin: Their Explorations and Researches, compiled by P. J. Donnelly (Dublin, 1886).

Roe, H.M., *The Medieval Fonts of Meath* (1968).

Roe, H.M., 'Illustrations of the Holy Trinity in Ireland, 13th to 17th Centuries', *JRSAI*, CIX (1979), 101–50.

Rotulorum Patentium et Clausorum Cancellariae Hiberniae Calendarium, ed. W. Ball and E. Tresham (Dublin, 1828).

Rowan, A.B., 'Monument at the Abbey of Holycross', *Transactions of the Kilkenny Archaeological Society*, II (1853), 358–61, 369–74, 380–2.

Rynne, E., 'The Corcomroe Wooden Graveslab', *North Munster Antiquarian Journal*, XIII (1970), 37–9.

Scott, B., *Malachy* (Dublin, 1976).

Seward, W.W., *Topographia Hibernica* (Dublin, 1795).

Seymour, St. J., 'Abbey Owney, County Limerick', *JRSAI*, XXXVII (1907), 174.

Stalley, R.A., *Architecture and Sculpture in Ireland, 1150–1350* (Dublin and New York, 1971).

Stalley, R.A., 'A Romanesque Sculptor in Connaught', *Country Life* (21 June 1973), 1826–30.

Stalley, R.A., 'Corcomroe Abbey, Some Observations on its Architectural History', *JRSAI*, CV (1975), 21–46.

Stalley, R.A., 'Mellifont Abbey: Some Observations on its Architectural History', *Studies* (1975), 347–67.

Stalley, R.A., 'Contradictions in medieval

style; the Cistercian Abbey at Boyle, Co. Roscommon', *Country Life* (6 May 1976), 1176–7.

Stalley, R.A., 'William of Prene and the Royal Works in Ireland', *JBAA*, CXXXI (1978), 30–49.

Stalley, R.A., 'The Medieval Sculpture of Christ Church Cathedral, Dublin', *Archaeologia*, CVI (1979), 107–22.

Stalley, R.A., 'Mellifont Abbey: A Study of its Architectural History', *PRIA*, 80C (1980), 263–354.

Stalley, R.A., 'Three Irish Buildings with West Country Origins', *Medieval Art and Architecture at Wells and Glastonbury*, ed. N. Coldstream and P. Draper (London, 1981, British Archaeological Association), 62–80.

Stalley, R.A., 'The Romanesque Sculpture of Tuam', *The Vanishing Past, Studies of Medieval Art, Liturgy and Metrology presented to Christopher Hohler*, ed. A. Borg and A. Martindale (Oxford, 1981, B.A.R. International Series 111), 179–95.

Stalley, R.A., 'Irish Gothic and English Fashion', *The English in Medieval Ireland*, ed. J. F. Lydon (Dublin, Royal Irish Academy, 1984), 65–86.

Todd, J.H., 'Remarks on the fresco painting in the Abbey of Knockmoy', *PRIA*, VI (1853), 3–16.

Topographia Hiberniae: Giraldus Cambrensis, *Topographia Hiberniae*, translated by J. J. O'Meara (Dundalk, 1951).

Triumphalia Chronologica Monasterii Sanctae Crucis in Hibernia (1640), ed. D. Murphy (Dublin, 1891).

Vendryes, J., 'Mellifont, fille de Clairvaux', *Medieval Studies in Memory of Gertrude Schoepperle Loomis* (New York, 1927), 277–83.

Waterman, D., 'Somersetshire and Other Foreign Building Stone in Medieval Ireland, c1175–1400', *UJA*, XXXIII (1970), 63–75.

Watt, J., *The Church in Medieval Ireland* (Dublin, 1972).

Westropp, T.J., 'History of the Abbey and Battles of Monasteranenagh, Croom, Co. Limerick: 1148–1603', *JRSAI*, IX (1889), 232–8.

Westropp, T.J., 'Corcumroe Abbey', *JRSAI*, XXX (1900), 299–304.

Westropp, T.J., 'Cliara Abbey', *PRIA* 31 C (1911–15), 29–37.

Wilkinson, G., *Practical Geology and Ancient Architecture of Ireland* (London, 1845).

Williams, D.H., 'The Welsh Cistercians and Ireland', *Cistercian Studies* XV (1980), 17–23.

Wilson, J.M., 'The Abbey of Shrule, Co. Longford', *JRSAI*, XXVII (1897), 433–4.

Woodward, B., *Measured Drawings, Holy Cross Abbey* (Royal Irish Academy).

Glossary

ABACUS	The flat stone placed on top of a capital at the springing of an arch.
ASHLAR	Stones cut in squared blocks with well-dressed surfaces.
AUMBRY	A small cupboard or niche used for storing vessels needed for the conduct of Mass.
BARBUT	A helmet with an open front, originating in fourteenth-century Italy.
BARREL VAULT	A simple form of stone vault with a continuous semi-circular profile. A 'pointed barrel vault' is a term used when the top of the vault is brought to a point, as in many twelfth-century Cistercian churches.
BAWN	A walled courtyard beside a fortified house or castle.
BOWTELL	A roll moulding, usually with a section of about three-quarters of a circle. A 'pointed bowtell' is when the moulding is brought to a point, a form commonly used around 1200.
CAPELLA ANTE PORTAS	A chapel for the laity, usually placed beside the precinct wall of a monastery near the main gate.
CENTERING	The temporary wooden framework used to support an arch or vault while it is under construction.
CINQUEFOIL	An arch or circle which has five foils or lobes on its inner face.
COLLATION	A ceremony performed at the end of the day in the north walk of the cloister which took its name from a reading from the *Collationes* of St John Cassian.
COLUMBARIUM	A dovecote, often an independent building, circular in form.
CORBEL	A stone, often carved or moulded, which projects from a wall in order to support wall shafts, roof timbers or arches.
CUIRASS	A piece of body armour, consisting of a breast and back plate linked together.
CUSP	A projecting point formed by the meeting of two foils or lobes on a Gothic arch.
DECORATED STYLE	A phase of English architecture, lasting from c1290 until the mid-fourteenth century, distinguished by elaborate tracery patterns, complex vaulting and exotic decorative forms.
'DUMB-BELL' PIER	A cloister pier which gives the impression of being formed of two separate colonettes, the latter in fact linked by a thin web or plate (see Fig. 44).
EARLY ENGLISH STYLE	A term applied to the first phase of English Gothic architecture, lasting from c1170 to c1290, characterised by lancet windows, detached shafting, stiff-leaf capitals, etc.
EN FUSEAU	A term used to describe the merging of ribs in a fine tapering point at the place from which they spring from the wall.
FALCHION	A motif used in curvilinear tracery, shaped like a broad curving sword.
FILLET	A flat, narrow band projecting from a roll moulding or shaft.
FORMERET	A rib marking the point at which the cells of a vault meet the wall, sometimes known as a wall arch.
GARDEROBE	A medieval lavatory.

GREAVES	Metal plates used to defend the lower part of the legs below the knee.
GROIN VAULT	A stone vault, without ribs, produced by the intersection of two barrel vaults, so named on account of the sharp angles which are formed on the diagonals.
HOOD MOULDING	The projecting moulding placed around the top of a window, door or arch, sometimes known as a 'label'.
JAMB	The side of an arch, doorway or window.
JOGGLED LINTEL	A lintel made of several stones held together by notched joints which prevent individual stones sliding out; commonly found in late medieval fireplaces in Ireland.
KEELED MOULDING	A roll moulding with a pointed rather than circular profile, as in the keel of a ship.
LANCET	A narrow window with a pointed head, commonly found in early Gothic architecture.
LAVABO	The water basin or washing place in a medieval monastery.
LIERNE	An intermediate rib in a vault which is not linked directly to the wall or the centrepoint of the vault.
MACHICOULIS	A projecting parapet or gallery, usually found on a castle or defensive wall, through which missiles can be dropped on attackers below.
MANIPLE	Part of the vestments of a priest, consisting of an embroidered band hanging from the left arm.
MONSTRANCE	A liturgical vessel used to display the consecrated host.
MULLION	The vertical post which divides a window into two or more lights.
OGEE	An arch formed of reverse curves (concave below, convex above), giving an onion-shaped profile; much used in the Decorated Style.
PERPENDICULAR STYLE	The term applied to the last phase of English Gothic architecture from the mid-fourteenth century onwards; characterised by panel motifs, straight verticals and horizontals, consistency, uniformity, etc.
PISCINA	A stone basin with a drain hole contained in a recess to the south of an altar, used for washing the eucharist vessels after Mass.
POLEYN	A small piece of armour used to protect the knee.
PYX	A liturgical vessel, usually of gold or silver, designed to contain the eucharist host.
QUADRIPARTITE VAULT	The simplest form of ribbed vault in which two diagonal ribs cross each other in the centre, forming four separate compartments or cells.
QUOINS	The dressed stones at the angle of a building.
RETICULATED WINDOW	A tracery window with a uniform net-like pattern made up of rows of 'soufflets' or dagger shaped motifs.
ROMANESQUE	The style which precedes Gothic and is particularly associated with the eleventh and twelfth centuries; characterised by the round arch, thick masonry walls, chevron decoration, etc.
SCALLOPED CAPITAL	A decorated capital, much favoured in Romanesque architecture, in which convex cone-like motifs rise to form a series of upturned semi-circles at the top.
SCROLL MOULDING	A roll-moulding associated with Gothic capitals in which the top half of the roll projects slightly forward over the bottom section.
SEDILIA	The seats for the priest, deacon, and subdeacon officiating at Mass, usually built into the south wall of the chancel.
SHINGLES	Roof tiles made of wood.
SLYPE	A passageway through the east range of the claustral buildings in a monastery.
SOFFIT	The underside of an arch or lintel.
SOUFFLET	A tracery motif, in the shape of a broad dagger, pointed at both top and bottom.
STIFF-LEAF	Stylised foliage designs, particularly associated with Early English Gothic.

STOLE	Part of the vestments of a priest, consisting of a strip of material hanging from the neck over the shoulders and down to the knees.
TAS DE CHARGE	A term applied to a particular form of vault construction, in which the lower stones of the ribs are laid horizontally (as opposed to radially) and bonded back into the wall.
TRACERY	The decorative pattern work in the upper part of a Gothic window.
TREFOIL	An arch head with three foils or lobes on its inner face.
TIERCERON	An extra rib which starts at the main springers and rises (usually) to the ridge rib.
TRIQUETRA	A simple piece of interlace formed of three intersecting arcs.
TRISKELE	A Celtic design in which three trumpet-like motifs are linked together in a circle.
URNES	A Scandinavian style of animal ornament of the eleventh and twelfth centuries, so named after the decoration of the stave church at Urnes in Norway, and characterised by highly attenuated beasts and thin, circular coils.
VESICA	A pointed oval set upright, often used in European art to enclose a figure of Christ in Majesty.
WICKERWORK CENTERING	A form of centering for a vault in which the stones are temporarily supported on a framework of timber and plaited wooden mats, the latter often leaving an impression in the mortar.

Index

Figures in **bold** indicate substantial discussion of the subject.

Abbey Dore (Herefordshire) 25, 63, 89–90, 141, 243
Abbeydorney (Kerry) 25, 29, 53, 239, **240**
  cloister arches 153, 156
  design of church **127–8**
  foundation 13
  mouldings 255
  origin of name 40
  plan of church 59, 128
  site 31
  tomb canopy 207–8
  tower 144
Abbeyknockmoy (Galway) 28, 29, 45, 53, 64, 65, 239, **240,** 243
  carved decoration 122, 164, 183, 188
  chapter house 164, 240
  cloister arcades 153, 156, 160
  cloister garth 54
  design of church 77, 81, 87, 93, 103–9, 123, 236
  lavabo 171
  masons' marks 42
  missal 219
  mouldings 257
  mural painting 214–6
  plan of church 57, **59–60**, 63
  private apartments 167
  progresss of building 44
  proportions 71, 75
  refectory 48, 169, 240
  remodelling of church 68
  rere-dorter 168
  site 16–17, 31, 37–8
  stonework 48
  tombs and burials 205, 208–9
  valuation 25
  vaulting 129, 132–5
  west range 172
Abbeylara (Longford) 23, 28, 103, 239, **240–1**
  crossing tower 144–5, 150
  foundation 22, 39
  income 25
Abbeyleix (Laois) 25, 210, 237, 239, **241**
Abbeymahon (Cork) 1, 25, 35, 239, **241**
Abbeyshrule (Longford) 25, 40, 53, 59, 239, **241**
Abington (Limerick) 24, 25, 26, 28, 35, **103**, 144, 239, **241–2**
Achard, monk at Himmerod (Germany) 41
Adare (Limerick)
  Austin friary 158, 160
  Franciscan friary 156, 160

Aelred of Rievaulx 2, 31
Affreca, wife of John de Courcy 16, 209–10, 245
Agard, Thomas 228, 230–2, 242
Aghamanister (Cork) 35, 241
Alan, laybrother of Buildwas 10, 35–6, 38
altars 199
Alvastra Abbey (Sweden) 59, 71, 79
Anderson, John 245
Annaghdown (Galway) 186–7
Annamult (Kilkenny) 34, 262 n57
Archdall, Mervyn 4, 99, 241, 244–5
Archer, Luke 29
Ardfert Cathedral (Kerry) 242
Armagh, 9
Askeaton (Limerick)
  castle 175
  Franciscan friary 156
Assaroe Abbey (Donegal) 1, 25, 29, 40, 48, 144, 239, **242**
Athboy (Meath) 168
Athenry (Galway) 22

Bagnal, Sir Nicholas 249
Ballintober Abbey (Mayo) 42, 107, 134, 184–7, 240
Ballintober Master 184–7, 243
Ballymascanlon (Louth) 20, 37
Ballymore (Westmeath), nunnery 6
Baltinglass Abbey (Wicklow) 2, 18, 20, 53, 239, **242**
  abbot's castle 174
  abbots: see Galboly and Malachy
  capitals and sculpture 41, **179–82**, 235
  castles on estates 152, 176
  cloister 54, 153–4
  crucifix figure 221
  design of church 64, 79–80, **83–7**, 89, 98, 235
  floor tiles 213
  foundation 13
  plan of church **58–9**, 103
  post-dissolution history 227
  precinct wall 175
  progress of building 44, 45
  seal 18, 223
  sedilia 199
  suppression 27
  valuation 25
Baltinglass Master 181, 242, 247
Bangor (Down) 7, 9
Barker, Sir William 247

Barralet, John 233
barrel vaults 78–80, 94, 104, 123, 128, **129–30**, 235, 286
  use in conventual buildings 130, 162, 165, 166, 172
  use in late medieval church design 105, 126, 128, 139, 148, 216
Barry, John de, abbot of Tracton 249
Barry, Odo de 249
Barry, Philip FitzDavid, abbot of Midleton 248
Battle Abbey (Sussex) 171
bay division 236
Beaubec Abbey (France) 20, 211, 213
Bective Abbey (Meath) 5, 35, 45, 205, 239, **242–3**
  bells 146
  book of hours 219–20
  carved decoration 192–4
  chattels 221
  cloister arcades 153, 156, **158–60**, 258
  cloister garth 54–5, 152, 158–9, 160
  crossing tower 144
  design of church 83, **109–12**
  foundation 13
  latin name 40
  masons' marks 42
  mouldings 258
  plan of church 57, 66–7
  plan of monastery **230**
  post-dissolution history **227–33**
  rere-dorter 168
  roofs 48
  site 31
  south-west tower 150–2, 231
  vaulting 130
  valuation 25
bells 146, 221
Benedictine Rule 2, 15, 26–7, 54, 162, 216
Beranger, Gabriel 233
Berteaucourt-les-Dames, nunnery (France) 91
Beverley Minster (Yorkshire) 121
Bilson, John 188
Bindon Abbey (Dorset) 59
Black Death 21
Bohéries Abbey (France) 46, 141
Bolton Priory (Yorkshire) 121
Bonmont Abbey (Switzerland) 78–9, 82
book cupboard 162
Boquen Abbey (France) 59
Bordesley Abbey (Worcestershire) 237
Bosch, Hieronymous 198

bosses 138
Boyle Abbey (Roscommon) 2, 14, 15, 25, 29,
    30, 107, 122, 236, 239, **244,** 242
  abbot's grave slab 205, 210, 224
  abbots: see O'Culleanain and
    O'Maelbhrenauin
  carved capitals and sculpture 122, 179–89,
    198, 218–9
  chapter house 162, 164
  choir stalls 202
  cloister garth 54
  consecration of church 43
  cross 220
  crossing tower 143–4
  design of church 41–2, 64–5, 77, **80–2,**
    87–92, 104, 107, 235–6
  dimensions 70–1
  dormitory 167
  excavations 5, 263 n 7
  foundation at Boyle 13, 34–5
  gatehouse 172
  guest house 47, 173
  latin name 40
  masons' marks 42
  mouldings 252–3, 259
  plan of church 49, 57–8, 63
  plan of monastery 87
  progress of building 47
  refectory 169
  robberies and raids 44, 92, 162, 220
  sacristy 162
  seals 224–5
  sedilia 180–1, 199
  site 32, 39
  stone 34, 48, 91
  vaults 79, 129
Boxley Abbey (Kent) 15, 162
Brabazon, William 228
Bradshaw, Brendan 26, 27
Branner, Robert 50
Bristol, St Augustine's Abbey 137
Bruce, Edward, 1315 invasion 18, 21
Bucher, Francois 79
Buckland Abbey (Devon), 233
Buildwas Abbey (Shropshire) 19, 25, 35–6,
    47, 85–6, 90, 141–2, 183
  see Alan, laybrother of
Bullock harbour (Dublin) 176
Burnchurch (Kilkenny), tower house 147–8
Butlers, earls of Ormond 126
    James, 2nd earl 115
    James, 4th earl 24, 113, 116, 117
    James, 9th earl 246, 247
    Thomas, 10th earl 29, 123, 245, 246
Butler, Piers Fitzjames Oge 210, 247
Butler, Thomas, son of 4th earl of Ormond
    114
Byland Abbey (Yorkshire) 23, 50, 62, 92, 95,
    211

Cadouin Abbey (France) 189
Calder Abbey (Cumberland) 162
calefactories 169–170, 217
Callan (Kilkenny), Augustinian friary 200
Camus Iuxta Bann (Derry) 248
Canterbury, Christ Church Cathedral 225
Cantwell, John 29, 227
Cantwell, William 210
capella ante portas 176–7, 286

Carlisle 172
Carrickfergus (Antrim), parish church 103
Carrick on Suir (Tipperary), manor house
    231–3
Carta Caritatis 1
Cashel (Tipperary) 224, 246
  cathedral 59, 99, 103, 198, 246
    Cormac's chapel 9, 84, 123, 129, 130, 180
    Rock of 40
Castledermot (Kildare) 22
cellarer 26, 41, 46
cemeteries 205
Chalons-sur-Marne, Notre Dame en Vaux
    (France) 191
Champfleur, Walter, abbot of St Mary's,
    Dublin 29
Champmol, Carthusian monastery (France)
    172
Champneys, Arthur 4, 96, 98, 116
Chapaize (France) 77
chapter houses 20, 24, 45, 46, 51, 153, **162–6**
Chaucer, Geoffrey 196
chevron ornament 134, 135, 157, 164, **183,**
    199, 200
Chiaravalle della Columba (Italy) 188
Chiaravalle Milanese (Italy) 141
Chipping Norton (Oxfordshire) 121
choir stalls 59–62, 86, 199, 202, 237
Christian, abbot of Mellifont 16, 29, 128, 240
Cirencester (Gloucestershire), parish church
    158
Citeaux Abbey (France) 1, 15, 18, 30, 38, 61,
    63, 171, 218
Clairvaux Abbey (France) 1, 40, 54, 57, 63,
    77, 78, 176, 179, 218, 235
  architectural influence 41, 77, 79, 235
  Irish monks trained at 13, 248
  life at 11
  mother house of Irish monasteries 19, 239
  mother house of Mellifont 15, 56–7, 71, 77
  visited by St Malachy 11, 13
Clare Island (Mayo), Cistercian cell 6, **124–5,**
    139, **243**
  altar 199
  painting 214–16, 219
  tomb canopy 208–9
Clarendon (Wiltshire), Henry III's palace 213
Cleeve Abbey (Somerset) 160, 162, 164, 165,
    211
Clermont Abbey (France) 83
Clifton Reynes (Buckinghamshire) 191–3
cloisters 9, 18, 19, 22–3, 25, 47
  arcades 113, 153–161, 236
  planning 51–6
Clonfert Cathedral (Galway) 183
Clonmacnois (Offaly) 9, 51, 180, 196
Clonmines (Wexford) 48
Clontuskert (Galway) 122, 196
Cluny Abbey (France) 2, 77
Cochrane, Robert 154
Cokaygne, Land of (poem) 22–3
Colclough, Sir Anthony 177, 230, 233, 249
Colclough, Sir Vesey 233
Colclough, Sir Caesar 233
collation ceremony 160–1, 286
collation pulpit 161–2
collation seats 154, 160–2
Collon (Louth) 21
columbaria 175, 286

Comber Abbey (Down) 25, 37, 38, 39, 40,
    103, 227, 237, 239, **243**
Combermere Abbey (Cheshire) 244
Cong (Mayo), Augustinian abbey 164, 187
Cong, cross of 10, 237
Contour, Richard, abbot of Mellifont 28
Conyngham, Colonel William Burton 4
Corcomroe Abbey (Clare) ii, 15, 25, 28, 29,
    53, 239, **243–4**
  carved capitals and sculpture 179, 184,
    187–8
  chapter house 164
  chevron ornament 134, 183
  choir stalls 202
  cloister garth 54
  design of church 44, 64, 65, 80, 83, **103–9,**
    236
  gatehouse 176
  incised drawings 49–50
  latin name 40
  mouldings 252, 259
  painting 214
  plan of church 49, 59, **72**
  progress of building 45
  proportions 71
  remodelling of church 68
  sedilia 199–200
  site 16, 31, 33, 37–8
  stonework 34, 48, 235
  tomb of Conor O'Brien 208–9
  valuation and income 25
  vaulting 129, **133–5,** 259
  west range 172
Cormac's Psalter 187, 217–19
Crickstown (Meath) 193
Cromwell, Thomas 220, 228
crosses 199, 220
Crowle (Worcestershire) 186
Croxden Abbey (Staffordshire) 25
Cusack, Patrick of Gerardstown 243
Cymmer Abbey (Wales) 172

Daniel, Walter 29, 34
Daunt, Thomas 249
day stairs 168
debts of Irish houses 20, 44, 46, 245, 248
Derry, nunnery 6
Devenish monastery (Fermanagh) 51
Devorgilla, wife of Tiernan O'Rourke 13,
    210
Dinely, Thomas 103, 242
dissolution of monasteries 27–9, 227–8, 237
Donkin, R.A. 34
Donnsleibhe O hInmhainén, monk of Boyle
    41
dormitories 9, 18, 26–7, 39, 43, 44, 45, 153,
    164, 166–7
dorter undercroft 166, 217
Downpatrick Cathedral (Down) 246
drains 168, 237
drawings (incised) 49–50
Drogheda (Louth) 29
Dublin 21, 26, 29
Dublin, Christ Church Cathedral 41, 42, 90,
    92, 98, 157, 186, 213, 237
Dublin, St Mary's Abbey 13, 24, 25–6, 27,
    37, 90, 117, 133, 239, **244**
  abbot's lodging 174, 228

abbots 37, 215; see also Chamfleur and
   Ross
bells 146, 221
carpenters 43
chapter house 38, 130–1, 153, **165**, 228,
   257, 259
chattels 221
cloister arcades 153, 157–9, 258
cloisters 228
excavations 4; potential for, 237, 244
fire of 1304 22
floor tiles 211–12
granges 6, 175–6
masons 43
mouldings 257–9
post-dissolution history 228
precinct wall 176
pyx 220
roofs 48, 205
site 38
size of community 23
statue of Virgin Mary **222–3**, 236, 244
stone 34
suppression 28
tower 143–5
valuation and income 24
Dublin, St Patrick's Cathedral 61, 98
Dublin, St Werburgh's 223
Dublin, cloister arcades discovered (1975)
   157–9, 258
Duby, Georges 172
Ducklington (Oxfordshire) 120
Dunbrody Abbey (Wexford) 3, 20, 29, 53,
   107, 110, 129, 239, 244
   abbot of 144
   bells 146
   book cupboard 162
   capella ante portas 176
   capitals and corbels 122, 188–9
   chapter house 164, 211
   choir stalls 202
   cloister arcades 153, 156
   cloister garth 53–4, 233
   collapse of 1852 251
   crossing tower 144–6, 148–50, 232
   design of church 64, 65, 66, 80, 87, 94,
      96–103
   dormitory 167, 232–3
   dorter undercroft 166
   entrance to cloister 172–3
   estates 16
   floor tiles 211
   foundation of abbey 35–6
   gatehouse 176
   laments for 238
   latin name 40
   mouldings 256–7, 259
   plan of church and monastery **62**
   possible lavabo 172
   post-dissolution history 29, 228–30, 232–3
   prison 174
   progress of buildings 45
   proportions 72, 75
   refectory 169–70
   seal 225
   site 38
   slype 166
   stone 34
   valuation and income 21, 25

vaults 135, 164, 259
Dundry (Somerset) quarry 34, 48, 101, 165
Du Noyer, George 4, 5, 19
Dunsoghly (Dublin), castle 152
Durham Cathedral 171
Dysert O'Dea (Clare) 188

Eames, Elizabeth 213
Eberbach Abbey (Germany) 68–9, 79
Edward II, king of England 22
Elizabeth I, queen of England 233, 242
Ely, St Etheldreda's 220
   sacrist's rolls 213
Ennis (Clare), Franciscan friary 198
Erenagh Abbey (Down) 13, 239, 242
Erhart, Michael 223
Etchingham, Sir Osborne 228–9, 244
Etchingham, Edward 230, 232
Etchingham, John 233
Ewenny Priory (Glamorgan) 87
Exeter
   cathedral 223
   St Nicholas 171
Exordium Parvum 1

Fanning, Thomas 214
Fergusson, Dr Peter 141–2
Fermoy Abbey (Cork) 14, 38, 40, 239, **244–5**
   abbots of 20, 144, 160
   cloister 144, 160
   foundation 13
   valuation 25
Ferns (Wexford) 137, 205
Fertagh (Kilkenny) 198
Fethard (Tipperary) 198
feudal rights 20–1
Finglas, Sir Patrick 28, 230
FitzEustace, Thomas 242
FitzGerald, Gerald, earl of Kildare 115, 245,
   246
FitzGerald, James, earl of Desmond 115
FitzGerald, John FitzEdmond 248
Fontenay Abbey (France) 44, 81
   capitals 179, 188
   cloister 53
   design of church **76–9**, 81
   lavabo 171
   plan of church **57–9**, 63, 69, 80, 235
Fontfroide Abbey (France) 46, 188
fonts 204, 237, 249
Fore (Westmeath), Augustinian abbey 152,
   158, 160, 258
Fountains Abbey (Yorkshire) 1, 6, 15, 19, 24,
   38, 41, 45, 211, 217, 235
   church 59, 63, 65, 86, 141, 146
      cloister and conventual buildings 53,
      162, 166, 171, 172
Furness Abbey (Lancashire) 6, 23, 24, 200,
   235
   architecture of church 62–3, 90, 146
   architecture of conventual buildings 162,
      166, 176
   mother house of Irish monasteries 16, 19,
      35, 45, 95, 239, 242, 246

Galboly, John, abbot of Baltinglass 174
Galway, church of St Nicholas 115, 121, 209
garderobe: see rere-dorter
gates (of monasteries) 17, 172, 176

General Chapter of the order 22, 38, 44, 46,
   53, 144, 211
   poor attendance by Irish abbots 15, 18,
      209, 262 n41;
   criticism of Boxley 15
   conspiracy of Mellifont 17–20
   statutes 235, 261 n2
   statutes concerning burial 205; floor tiles
      211; painting and sculpture 179, 188,
      218; prisons 174; seals 224; towers 53,
      141–2
Geoffrey d'Ainai, monk at Fountains Abbey
   41
Gerald of Wales (Giraldus Cambrensis) 7, 10
Glanawydan Abbey (Waterford) 16, 239
Glastonbury Abbey (Somerset) 15, 134–5,
   174
Glendalough (Wicklow) 9, 41, 48, 51, 129,
   180
Gloucester Abbey, west gate 183
golden section 75
Gowran (Kilkenny) 65, 110
Graiguenamanagh (Kilkenny) 2, 34, 35, 45,
   48, 53, 107, 108, 176, 239, **245**
   abbots: see Kavanagh
   bells 146
   book cupboard 162
   capitals 188–9
   chapter house 162–3, 166
   cloister arcades 153–4
   cloister garth 53–4
   collation seat 154, 162
   crtiticised by Lexington 45–7
   cross of silver 220
   crossing tower 142, 144
   debts 20
   design of church 64, 65, 66, 87, 92, 93, 96,
      98, **99–103**, 236
   dormitory 167
   excavations 5
   floor tiles 211–14
   foundation 16
   mason of 43
   masons' marks 42
   monk of 215
   mouldings 254, 256, 259
   paint 214
   parlour 166
   plan of church and monastery 62–3, 68, **73**
   post-dissolution history 227
   proportions 72–3, 75
   refectory 169–70
   seals 224–5
   site 31–2
   size of community 23
   stone used 34
   suppression 27
   tombs and burials 205, 208–9
   valuation and income 16, 21, 25
Granard (Longford) 22, 240
granges 6, 20, 46, 48, 173
   defences 152, 176
Great Connell Abbey (Kildare) 145
Gregorian reform 11
Grellachdinach 13
Grey, Leonard 174, 228
Grey Abbey (Down) 2, 4, **8**, 20, 25, 45, 53,
   107, 122, 129, 239, 241, **245**
   abbot of 37

attacked by Scots 21
capitals 188–9
chapter house 162, 164
cloister garth 54
collation seat 162
conservation of ruins 251
corbel table 189
crossing tower 140–2, 144
design of church 64–5, 66, **93–5,** 96, 103
day stairs 168
dorter undercroft 166
drain 168
masons' marks 42
mouldings 254
paint 214
plan of church and monastery **55,** 63
post-dissolution history 227, 228
proportions 72, 75
refectory 54, 153, 169–70
tombs and tomb recesses 207, 209–10
groin vaulting 130, 231
Grose, Francis 3, 4, 98, 170, 173, 226, 227, 228
guest houses 39, 44–5, 46, 47, 172–3
Gylford, Henry 249

Hahn, Hanno 68–75
Hailes Abbey (Gloucestershire) 21, 24, 215
Halesowen Abbey (Worcestershire) 213
Hamilton, Sir James, Viscount Clandeboye 243
Harbison, Dr Peter 198
Harden, John 113
Harding, Stephen 1, 23
Hartry, Malachy 115–16, 221
Haughmond Abbey (Shropshire) 154
Healy, Archbishop John 6
Heffernan, Edward, clerk of Hore 234
Henry II, king of England 7
Henry VIII, king of England 27, 28
Henry of Lancaut, abbot of Tintern (Wexford) 110
Hereford Cathedral 181–2
Herlewin, bishop of Leighlin 96
Hildemar of Corbie 54
Himmerod Abbey (Germany) 41
Holm Cultram Abbey (Cumberland) 16, 63, 90, 93, 95, 239, 245
Holycross Abbey (Tipperary) 1, 2, 4, 14, 27, 40, 50, 226, 239, **245–6**
abbot's lodging 174–5
abbots: see O'Congail, O'Heffernan, Purcell and William
chapter house 162–4
chattels, loss of 221
chronology of building 113–15
cloister arcades 113, 153, 156–7, 258
cloister garth 52, 54
conservation of ruins 251
corbels 122
crossing tower 144, 146, 148
decorative carving 196–8
design of church 83, **113–27,** 236
dormitory 168
dorter undercroft 166
early history 16
excavation and restoration 5
masons' marks 43
mouldings 253, 255, 257–9

mural painting 214–15, 219
night stairs 65–6
piscinae 199
plan of church and monastery 57–9, 68, **121,** 235
post-dissolution history 29, 227
private apartments 167, 172
relics of true cross 26, 45, 115–17, 123, 221–3
sacristy 162
seals 224–5
sedilia 114, 116, 126, 137–8, 197–8, **200–2**
shrines 115–17, 137, 196–9
site 31
stonework 48, 235
suppression 29
turned into secular college 28
valuation and income 25, 45
vaulting 119, 121, 129–30, 135–9, 148
visitation of 1536 26
west range 130, 153, **172**
window tracery 120–1
Hore Abbey (Tipperary) 4, 5, 28, 45, 64, 239, **246**
carving, absence of 189
chapter house 166, 234
cloister arcades 153, 156, 258
cloister garth, 52, 54, 56
crossing tower 144–5, 146–50
design of church 83, 87, 94, **109–112,** 237
foundation 22, 40
latin name 40
masons' marks 42–3
mouldings 257–8
piscinae 162, 199
plan of church and monastery **57–9,** 68
post dissolution history 233
proportions 71
refectory 169
remodelling of church 128
rere-dorter 168
sacristy 162
seals 224–5
site 31
size of community 23
slype 166
steps in church 199
stonework 48
valuation and income 25
vaults 129, 137, 139, 148, 235, 259
west range 172
Hourihane, Dr Colum 198
Hunt, John 190–1, 209

Iconography
abbots 155, 192–4, 195, 219, 224–5
angels 116, 163, 189, 195, 196–7, 216
animals and beasts 10–11, 184–5, 188, 190–1, 193, 196, 198, 216, 217–18
Annunciation 219
apostles 190–3, 210
arms of the Passion 206–7
beast heads 180–1
birds 185–6, 188, 196
crucifixions 196, 208, 215–16, 221, 223, 225
David 185
dragons 186, 187, 190, 193, 216
ecclesiastics 155, 190, 192, 194, 198

entombment 219
evangelist symbols 221
exhibitionist 189
foxes 213
griffon 212–13
human figures 185–7, 190
human heads 186, 187–8, 189, 219
human masks 180, 186
hunting 214–15
ladies 190–2
Last Judgement 189
lions 117, 180, 196, 198, 212–13
memento mori 215–16
mermaids 194–5
owl 197–8
pelicans 117, 195, 216
St Catherine 190–1, 193
St Christopher 190–1, 195–6
St Edmund 223
St Eustace 215
St John the Evangelist 196, 208–9, 221
St John the Baptist 223
St Margaret of Antioch 138, 190, 193
St Martin 223
St Michael 193
St Sebastian 216
Trinity 193
unicorn 198
Virgin Mary 196, 220, 221, 222–3, 224–5, 236
warrior 213
Inch Abbey (Down) 2, 20, 22, 25, 45, 107, 108, 129, 239, **246**
abbot 37
capitals 188–9
chapter house 164
cloister arcades 153, 156, **160–1,** 258
cloister garth 54
crossing tower 142
design of church 65, 66, **92–6,** 98, 236
foundation 16
masons' marks 42
mouldings 254, 258
piscina 199
plan of church and monastery 62–3, **94**
precinct wall 176
proportions 72
refectory 169
remodelling of church 27, 67–8, 113
seal 224
site 38–9
vaults 135
tomb recess 207
income of Irish Cistercian houses 24–5, 44, 45
infirmaries 173
Iniscealtra (Clare) 9, 51, 52
Inis Cumhscraigh (Down) 39, 45, 242
Inislounaght Abbey (Tipperary) 18, 20, 27, 237, 239, **246–7**
foundation 13
name 40
nunnery 6
plan 58
silver cross 221
site 31
size of community 23
target of satire 23
tower 144

valuation 25
Inistioge (Kilkenny), Augustinian abbey 193,
198

James, earl of Desmond 228
Jerpoint Abbey (Kilkenny) 2, 14, 17, 27, 34,
35, 40, 45, 53, 123, 125, 170, 176, 239,
247
carved capitals in church **180–3**, 235
chapter house 165
cloister arcades 153, 155–6, 160, 178, 179,
189–93, 198, 207, 214, 236, 258
cloister garth 54–5
collation pulpit 161–2
criticised by Lexington 19, 45–7
crossing tower 144, 146, 148–9
debts 20
design of church 64, 65, 66, 77, **80–7,** 89,
98, 235
disputed foundation date 13, 261 n25
dormitory 166–7
drain 168
gateway 172
laments for 238
mouldings 252–3, 258
name 40
neglect of ruins 251
nunnery 6
paint 214
parlour 166
plan of church and monastery **55,** 57, 59,
67–8
poverty 21–2
progress of building 43
proportions 69–71, 75
refectory 169
remodelling of church 127–8
roofs 48
sacristy 162
seals 224
sedilia 199–200
size of community 23
slype 166
stone 34
suppression 28, 227
tombs and burials 207, 210, 237
valuation and income 25, 45
vault boss at 138
vaulting 79, 129–30, 137–9, 148
Jervaulx Abbey (Yorkshire) 6
Jervis, Sir Humphrey 228, 244
Jocelyn, abbot of Mellifont 20
John, abbot of Newry 26–7
John, abbot of Tracton 224–5
John, monk of Holycross 29, 227
John de Courcy, lord of Ulster 16, 38–9, 242
Johnstown (Meath) 193–4

Kavanagh, Charles, abbot of
Graiguenamanagh 245
Kedenor, William, monk of St Mary's,
Dublin 174, 202
Kells (Kilkenny) 103, 152, 175
Kells (Meath) 10, 13, 123, 129
Kilbeggan Abbey (Westmeath) 13, 25, 38,
39, 40, 224, 237, 239, 247
Kilclief (Down), tower house 148
Kilconnell (Galway), Franciscan friary 198

Kilcooly Abbey (Tipperary) 14, 18, 27, 29,
40, 239, **247**
abbots: see Philip and O'Molwanayn
abbot's stall 202–3
capella ante portas 176
cloister arcades 153, 156, 160
cloister garth 54–5
columbarium 175
cross of silver 221
crossing tower 144–5, 148–50
decorated screen **194–6,** 198, 200, 236
design of church 83, 113, **120–8**
font 204
'hall' 175
latin name 40
masons' marks 43, 127
mouldings 255, 257
plan of church and monastery 57, 59, **66–7**
post-dissolution history 29, 233–4
private apartments 167
proportions 71
sacristy 162, 196
site 31, 39
size of community 23
stonework 48
tombs and burials 206, 210, 237
valuation 25
vaults 129, 137–9, 148
Kildare
cathedral 98
gospel book 10
Franciscan friary 22
Kilkenny 22, 29
Kilkenny, St Canice's Cathedral 65, 96, 100,
103, 110
vaulting 137–9
Kilkenny, Dominican friary 145, 148, 198
Kilkenny Archaeological Society 251
Killaloe Cathedral 106, 183, 187
Killenny Abbey (Kilkenny) 14, 16, 35, 40,
239, 247
Killeshin (Carlow) 9, 41, 180
Kilmallock (Limerick), Dominican friary 22,
120
Kilteel (Kildare) 185
Kilmore Cathedral (Cavan) 180
King's Lynn (Norfolk) 214
Kirkstall Abbey (Yorkshire) 24, 122, 141
Kirkstead Abbey (Lincolnshire) 176
kitchens 170, 172–3
Knowles, David 6, 15

Lacy, Hugh de, earl of Ulster 37, 205
la Ferté Abbey (France) 1
Lancaster 207
language problems 7, 10, 15, 16, 19, 262 n57
Lanercost Abbey (Cumberland) 95
lavabos 170–2
laybrothers 42, 45, 54, 63, 64, 89
accommodation 24, 52, 172
choir of 59, 68, 98, 108
decline of 16, 21, 23–4, 66
numbers 13, 44
responsibilities and routine of life 2, 21, 39,
41
see Alan, laybrother of Buildwas
lead, use in building 48
Leask, Harold 5, 96, 106, 113–14, 143, 160,
190

le Blunde, Margeret 22
Ledwich, Rev. Edward 4, 208, 209
Lehnin Abbey (Germany) 47
Leighlin Cathedral (Carlow) 137, 139
Leominster Priory (Herefordshire) 182
Leonard, abbot of St Mary's, Dublin 205
Le Thoronet Abbey (France) 164
Lewes Priory (Sussex) 171
Lexington, Stephen of 22, 24, 38, 41, 176,
188, 223
account of monastic buildings 173
criticism of abbot of Tracton 249
criticism of Jerpoint or Graiguenamanagh
19, 20, 45–7, 53, 175, 205, 235
poor opinion of Irish building 7–9
reform of Irish houses 15, 18–20, 160–1
siege of Monasteranenagh 14, 18, 104, 145
Lilleshall Abbey (Shropshire) 133, 183
Limerick Cathedral
architecture 237
misericords 198
Lincoln Cathedral 172, 193
Llandaff Cathedral (Glamorgan) 91
Llanthony Priory (Monmouthshire) 92
Loc-Dieu Abbey (France) 141–2
Loftus, Adam Viscount Ely 249
Longpont Abbey (France) 170, 235
Louth Park Abbey (Lincolnshire) 171
Lynch, Dr Ann 249, 263 n7

MacCarthy, Dermot, king of Desmond 241
MacCarville, David, archbishop of Cashel 22,
40, 110, 111, 246
MacCostelloe, Thomas, abbot of
Monasterevin 219
MacDermot, Conor, king of Moylurg 14
MacDermots of Moylurg 14
MacGillapatrick, Donal, king of Ossory 247
MacLoughlin, Murtagh, high king 13, 249
MacMurrough, Dermot, king of Leinster 86,
205, 242
MacNiocaill, Dr Gearóid 5
Macosquin Abbey (Londonderry) 25, 103,
237, 239, **247–8**
Malachy, abbot of Baltinglass 242
Malachy, archbishop of Armagh 37, 220, 248
church at Bangor 7, 9
chooses site of Mellifont 8–9
reform of Irish church 11–13
visits to Clairvaux 11, 13
Malby, Sir Nicholas 227, 248
manuscripts 20, 162, 216–20
Cormac's Psalter (British Library) 187,
217–19
Monasterevin Ordinal (Bodleian Library)
219
Bective Hours (Trinity College Dublin)
219–20
Abbeyknockmoy missal 219
Margam (Glamorgan) 19, 83, 92, 96
Marlfield (Tipperary) 247
Marshal, William, earl of Pembroke and lord
of Leinster 205
founder of Graiguenamanagh 16, 19, 48,
245
founder of Tintern 15, 16, 37, 40, 249
Marshal, William, the younger earl of
Pembroke 46
masons' marks 41–3, 127

masons, recorded names 43
Matthew Paris 116
Maulbronn (Germany) 64, 171
Meaux (Yorkshire) 160, 211, 220
Mellifont Abbey (Louth) 22, 24, 25, 27, 80,
   133, **177**, 237, **248**
  abbot's stall 202
  abbots: 37; see Christian, Contour,
    Jocelyn, Waring
  affiliation of 12, 16, 17, 19
  book cupboard 162
  capella ante portas 176–7
  capitals 180–3, 187–8
  castles and towers 150, 233
  chapter house 130, 131, 153, 162–5, 214
  cloister arcades 153–4
  cloister garth 54, 233
  columbaria 175
  conspiracy of 5, **17–20**, 92, 184, 246, 247,
    248
  consecration of 1157 13, 183
  crossing tower 143–4, 146
  crypt 57
  design of first church 41, 64, 65, 66, 77,
    79, **81–2**, 235
  donations 13, 183, 220
  early history 13–15
  estates 6, 16
  excavations 4–5, 53, 205, 251
  floor tiles 211–14
  foundation 1, 7, 10, 11–14, 37
  gatehouse 176
  latin name 1, 2, 40
  lavabo 48, 131, 153–4, **171–2**, 188, 214,
    233, 256, 258
  masons' marks 42
  metalwork 220–1
  monk Robert, see Robert
  mouldings 252–4, 256–7, 259
  nunnery 6
  plan of church and monastery 49, **56–63**,
    70
  post dissolution history 29, 223, 228
  precinct wall 175
  private apartments 167
  progress of building 39, 44, 45
  proportions 71, 74–5
  refectory 169–70
  remodelling of church 20, **61–2**, 74, 92,
    98, **102–3**, 112
  site 8, 32, 38, 39, 71
  size of community 13, 20, 23
  stone 34, 48
  suppression 28
  tombs and burials 205–6
  valuation and income 21, 24
  vaulting 135, 148, 258
  west range 172
Melrose Abbey (Roxburgh) 171, 202
Midleton Abbey (Cork) 25, 28, 40, 237, 239,
  248
Moissac (France) 190–1
Monasteranenagh (Limerick) 4, 20, 25, 45,
  239, **248–9**
  battle at 227
  chapter house 166
  cloister garth 54
  collapse of vaults 251
  design of church 77, 83, 87, **103–6**, 235

foundation 13, 18
  name 40
  plan 59, 68
  proportions 71
  refectory 169
  remodelling of church 27, 113
  seal 225
  siege of 1228 14, **18–19**, 145
  site 31, 33
  tower 105
  vaulting 79, 129–30, 251
Monasterboice (Louth) 14
Monasterevin (Kildare) 25, 39, 40, 239, 249
  ordinal 215, 219
  abbot: see MacCostelloe
Monkstown (Dublin) 176
Montmorency Hervé de 16, 17, 35, 244
Moore, Edward 233, 248
Moore Abbey (Kildare) 249
Morienval (France) 133
Morimond Abbey (France) 1, 57, 239, 247
mouldings 252–9
Mount Melleray (Waterford) 6
Much Wenlock (Shropshire) 171
Muckross (Kerry), Franciscan friary 156, 160

names of abbeys 40
Naumburg Cathedral (Germany) 190
Neath Abbey (Glamorgan) 98, 111, 166,
  172–3
New Ross (Wexford), St Mary's 59
Newry Abbey (Down) 27, 38, 40, 239, **249**
  abbot: see John
  abbot's lodging 174
  foundation 13
  secular college 28
  size of community 23
  valuation 25
Newtown Jerpoint (Kilkenny) 191–2
  Nicholas of Verdun 16
night stairs 65–6, 168
Noirlac Abbey (France) 81, 101, 164
  cloister arcades 154
  refectory 170
Norton Priory (Cheshire) 213
nunneries (Cistercian) 6, 22, 46, 246
Nydala Abbey (Sweden) 47

O'Anly, Matthew 209
Obazine Abbey (France) 182
O'Briens, kings (later earls) of Thomond
  Turlough 248
  Donal Mór 14, 205, 244, 245, 246, 247
  Donnchadh Cairbrech 18, 244
  Conor 208, 244
  Murrough 28, 244
O'Carroll, Donough king of Uriel 37, 39, 44
  achievements as a reformer 14
  burial at Mellifont 205
  founder and benefactor of Mellifont 10,
    13, 248
  achievements as a reformer 14
O'Conbhuidhe, Father Colmcille 5, 26, 261
  n25
O'Congail, Dionysius, abbot of Holycross
  113–5, 156
O'Conors, kings of Connacht
  Turlough 14
  Rory 14

Cathal Crovderg 17, 44, 188, 205, 240
O'Culleanain, Glaisne, abbot of Boyle 29
O'Dea, John titular, abbot of Corcomroe 29
O'Dempsey, Dermot, king of Offaly 249
O'Dullany, Felix, bishop of Ossory 207
O'Dwyer, Dr Barry 5
O'Kelly, Donatus, monk of Monasterevin
  215, 219
O'Kelly, Hugh, abbot of Abbeyknockmoy
  28
O'Kelly, Malachy 208–9, 215, 240
O'Heffernans, abbots of Holycross
  Dermot 26
  Fergal 26
Old Sarum Cathedral (Wiltshire) 48
O'Maelbhrenauin, abbot of Boyle 169
O'Melaghlin, Murchad king of Meath 242
O'Molwanayn, Philip abbot of Kilcooly 195
  tomb 206–7, 247
O'More, Malachy 210, 241
O'Mulreyan, Cornelius 24
O'Mulreyan, John 242
O'Neill, Sir Brian 245
O'Nolan, Richard 100
O'Phelan, Malachy 246
Ordericus Vitalis 40, 41
organs 204–5, 220
O'Ruadan, Felix archbishop of Tuam 48, 205
O'Sullivan, William 220
O'Tunneys, stone carvers 210, 241, 247
Oxford, St Frideswide 186
  Merton College 158

parlour 166
Philip, abbot of Kilcooly 125, 127
piscinae 61, 126, 162, **199**, 287
plaster 48, 49–50, 83, 199, 214
Poblet Abbey (Spain) 171
Pontigny Abbey (France) 1, 64, 101, 179,
  182, 188, 211
porte des morts 65
precinct walls 21, 175–6, 237
Preuilly Abbey (France) 101
prisons 174–5
proportional formulae 68–75
Purcell, James Fitzwilliam 123, 146
Purcell, Philip abbot of Holycross 245

Rae, Dr Edwin 189–90
refectories 9, 18, 39, 43, 52, 54, **169–70**, 172
Reims Cathedral (France) 50
rere-dorters 168
Reynell, Sir Richard 228, 244
ribbed vaults 92, 95, 96, 100, 108, 111, 121–
  2, 126, **130–9**
  introduction into Ireland 50, 106, 130
  late medieval examples 121, 122, 126, 148
  in conventual buildings 164–6, 170–1
  miniature examples 200, 202
  painted ribs 216
Rievaulx Abbey (Yorkshire) 1, 23, 24, 34, 38,
  83
  cloister arcades 153
  floor tiles 211
  tower 141
Robert, monk from Clairvaux 41, 56, 57, 71,
  81, 179, 235, 248
Robert of Molesme 1
Roche Abbey (Yorkshire) 62, 92, 95, 141

Rochester Cathedral (Kent) 200
roofing 41, 44, 46–8, 235
Roscrea (Tipperary) 225
Ross, Stephen abbot of Mellifont 25–6
Royaumont Abbey (France) 235
ruelle des convers 54–5

sacristy 162
Saddell Abbey (Argyll) 13, 262 n26
St Albans Abbey (Hertfordshire), shrine 116
St Bernard of Clairvaux 1–2, 9, 15
    Apologia 180, 182, 188, 189, 218
    as abbot of Clairvaux 1, 11, 13
    belief in uniform observance 53
    criticism of Cluniac monks 191
    life of Malachy 7
    role in foundation of Mellifont 15, 37, 41
    views on architecture 57, 69, 77, 79
    views on art 179–80, 183–4
    views on singing 204–5
    views on tiled pavements 211
St Briavel's (Gloucestershire) 87
St David's Cathedral (Pembroke) 96
St Doulagh's Church (Dublin) 123
St Gall Plan 52, 54, 69, 169
St Patrick's bell 10
St Vincent des Prés (France) 77
Savigny Abbey (France) 13, 141, 239
scalloped capitals 182–3
'school of the west' 91–2, 106–7, 244
Scottish architecture 123, 139
screens 61, 86, 111
scribes 217, 219
scriptoria 46, 173, 217
seals 18, 223–5
secular colleges 28
sedilia 199–202, 287
Seton collegiate church (Lothian) 123
Seymour, Richard, abbot of Abington 26
Sheephouse (Louth) 221
shrine of the book of Dimma 225
Sligo, Dominican friary 160
slype 166, 168, 287
Soissons Cathedral (France) 50
Southwark Cathedral (London) 200
staircases 65–6
Stanley Abbey (Wilstshire) 16, 63, 166, 213, 239
Stapleton, John 247
statutes of Cistercian order: see General Chapter
Stepney, Joseph 242
Stevens, John 234
stone 4, 45, 235
    first use in Irish churches 9
    types used by cistercians 32–4, 47–8
    native carboniferous limestone 34, 48, 101, 109, 113, 196, 198, 200, 235
    banded stonework 96

see also Dundry
Strade (Mayo) 121, 209
Strata Florida (Cardiganshire) 86, 96, 182
Strongbow, Richard de Clare earl of Pembroke 16, 244
Swartling, Ingrid 71
Swords Castle (Dublin), tiled pavement 213

Taghmon (Westmeath), fortified church 124–5
Tewkesbury Abbey (Gloucestershire) 138
Thomastown (Kilkenny) parish church 98
Thurstan, abbot of Glastonbury 15
tiles (floor) 211–14, 236
Tintern Abbey (Monmouthshire) 1, 63, 110–11, 162, 189, 220, 249
Tintern Abbey (Wexford) 1, 45, 53, 129, 239, **249**
    bells 146
    capella ante portas 177
    corbel table 189
    crossing tower 143–5, 148, 150, 233
    design of church 83, 94, **109–12**
    drain 168–9
    estates 16
    excavations 5, 168–9
    foundation 15, 16, 37, 40
    latin name 40
    mouldings 253, 257
    plan of church 59, 62–3, **74**
    post dissolution history 230, 233–4
    proportions 74
    sculpture 198
    seals 224–5, 249
    silver cross 220
    site 36, 38
    stone 34
    suppression 27
    valuation 25
    vaults 135
tombs 205–10
tomb recesses 49, 207–9
Tournus (France) 77, 78
towers: Irish round towers 10, 14, 34, 51, 53, 261 n7
    Cistercian 22, 25, 53, 67, 94, 96, 102, 105, 111, 113, 127, 128, **141–52**, 236
tower houses 139, 145–8, 152, 174, 233, 241
tracery 49, 50, 99, 111, 112, 115, **120–1**, **123**, 126, 128, 177, 209
tracing floors 50
Tracton Abbey (Cork) 103, 237, 239, 249–50
    abbot: see Barry
    abbot criticised 19
    latin name 40
    seal 224–5
    valuation 24, 25
Travers, John 228
Trim (Meath) 227, 241

Tristernagh (Westmeath) 28
Tristram, E.W. 196
Troy, John, abbot of Mellifont 23, 24, 26, 27, 28, 29
    description of Irish monasteries (1498) 144–5, 219
Tuam (Galway)
    cathedral 10, 11, 180, 186
    market cross 187, 188
Tuit, Richard, lord of Granard 22, 240
Turvey (Bedfordshire) 215

Urnes ornament 188, 288

Vale Royal Abbey (Cheshire) 112
Villard de Honnecourt 69

Wales, Cistercian houses in 3, 15, 18, 21, 48
Wall, Dr Charles 251
Walter de Lacy 16, 20
Walter, master mason of St Mary's Abbey, Dublin 43
Walter, Theobald 35, 242
Ware, Sir James 4, 96, 243
Waring, John, abbot of Mellifont 24
Waterford Cathedral 98, 103, 237
water supply 31–2, 56
wattle building 7, 9, 43
Weir Anthony 189
Wells Cathedral (Somerset) 50, 139
Westminster Abbey 116
    sculpture in Henry VII's chapel 223
    tomb of Edward III 191–3
Westropp, Thomas 214, 216
Whalley Abbey (Lancashire) 193
Whitland Abbey (Carmarthen) 18, 19, 40, 239, 249
wickerwork centering 129–30, 132, 288
Wilde, Sir William 188
Wilkinson, George 4
William, abbot of Holycross 225
William, bishop of Cork 207
William de Burgh 44–5
William of Malmesbury 48
Winchester Cathedral 116
Windele, John 233
wine press 45, 173
wood, use in building 9, 32, 41, 45, 48, 65, 237
    cloisters 160, 227, 236
    stalls and screens 202, 237
    west range 172
Wood Eaton (Oxfordshire) 195
wool trade 20
Worcester Cathedral 171

York
    minster 50
    St Mary's Abbey 15